# Study Guide and Casebook

for use with

# Auditing & Assurance Services
## A Systematic Approach

Sixth Edition

William F. Messier, Jr.
*University of Nevada, Las Vegas*

Steven M. Glover
*Brigham Young University*

Douglas F. Prawitt
*Brigham Young University*

Prepared by
Helen M. Roybark
*Radford University*

 **McGraw-Hill**
**Irwin**

Boston   Burr Ridge, IL   Dubuque, IA   New York   San Francisco   St. Louis
Bangkok   Bogotá   Caracas   Kuala Lumpur   Lisbon   London   Madrid   Mexico City
Milan   Montreal   New Delhi   Santiago   Seoul   Singapore   Sydney   Taipei   Toronto

Study Guide and Casebook for use with
AUDITING & ASSURANCE SERVICES: A SYSTEMATIC APPROACH
William F. Messier, Jr., Steven M. Glover, and Douglas F. Prawitt

Published by McGraw-Hill/Irwin, an imprint of The McGraw-Hill Companies, Inc., 1221 Avenue of the Americas, New York, NY 10020. Copyright © 2008, 2006 by The McGraw-Hill Companies, Inc. All rights reserved.

1 2 3 4 5 6 7 8 9 0 BKM/BKM 0 9 8

ISBN: 978-0-07-335958-8
MHID: 0-07-335958-0

www.mhhe.com

# About the Author

Professor **Helen M. Roybark** is an Assistant Professor of Accounting at Radford University, where she teaches auditing and accounting information systems. Professor Roybark holds a PhD from Virginia Commonwealth University, an EdS from Wright State University, an MS from Old Dominion University, and a BA from Saint Leo University. Professor Roybark is a coauthor of published research relating to the history of the Office of the Chief Accountant of the U.S. Securities and Exchange Commission (Abacus). Professor Roybark has also published research in the *Journal of Accounting Education, Journal of Accounting, Ethics & Public Policy*, and *Journal of Government Financial Management*. She is currently conducting research in accounting and auditing regulation and auditor independence. Professor Roybark is a Certified Public Accountant in the Commonwealth of Virginia and a Certified Fraud Examiner. She previously worked in the accounting profession for twenty-five years and owned and operated a public accounting firm for fifteen years.

# Table of Contents

To the Student ............................................................................................................. vii

**Section I: Townsend Office Supplies and Equipment** ..................................... xi

**Section II: Chapter Summaries** ........................................................................ xxi

1   An Introduction to Assurance and Financial Statement Auditing ...................... 1

2   The Financial Statement Auditing Environment ................................................ 17

3   Risk Assessment and Materiality ...................................................................... 37

4   Audit Evidence and Audit Documentation ........................................................ 65

5   Audit Planning and Types of Audit Tests ......................................................... 89

6   Internal Control in a Financial Statement Audit ............................................... 113

7   Auditing Internal Control Over Financial Reporting ......................................... 141

8   Audit Sampling: An Overview and Application to Tests of Controls .................. 167

9   Audit Sampling: An Application to Substantive Tests of Account Balances ....... 189

10   Auditing the Revenue Process ......................................................................... 213

11   Auditing the Purchasing Process ...................................................................... 237

12   Auditing the Human Resource Management Process ....................................... 259

13   Auditing the Inventory Management Process .................................................... 279

14   Auditing the Financing/Investing Process:
Prepaid Expenses and Property, Plant and Equipment ..................................... 301

15   Auditing the Financing/Investing Process: Long-Term Liabilities,
Stockholders' Equity, and Income Statement Accounts .................................... 317

16   Auditing the Financing/Investing Process: Cash and Investments .................... 337

17   Completing the Engagement ........................................................................... 359

18   Reports on Audited Financial Statements ......................................................... 385

19   Professional Conduct, Independence, and Quality Control ............................... 403

20   Legal Liability .................................................................................................. 435

21   Assurance, Attestation, and Internal Auditing Services .................................... 457

**Section III: Extra Crossword Puzzles and Solutions** ..................................... 487

# To the Student

Welcome to the exciting world of auditing and assurance services. This study guide has been designed as a companion resource to your study of *Auditing and Assurance Service: A Systematic Approach* (Sixth Edition) by William F. Messier, Steven M. Glover and Douglas F. Prawitt, published by McGraw-Hill/Irwin, Inc. This is a supplemental resource, and as such, it does not take the place of reading your textbook. This is particularly important because you will be introduced to a completely new vocabulary and language that is significantly different from other accounting courses you have taken. An example of the unique word usage in auditing is provided to illustrate this point. The term "observation" refers to an audit procedure used to gather audit evidence. Some individuals may use this term to describe a procedure such as the inspection of a tangible asset or a document, but, in an auditing context, the term is defined as "looking at a process or procedure being performed by others," thus, observation is limited to the point in time at which the observation takes place. Examples include observation of the counting of inventories by the entity's personnel and observation of the performance of control activities. In short, an auditor would not use the terms "observation" and inspection" interchangeably. Technical terms serve an important role in professional communication and you will want to develop the proper vocabulary.

## How to Use This Companion Resource

This companion resource includes three major sections. To acquire you with this resource, each section is discussed below.

**Section I** includes a case study entitled "Townsend Office Supplies and Equipment." The following information is provided for the case study: a brief introduction (Part 1), general instructions (Part 2), history and background information (Part 3) an organizational chart (Part 4), accounting polices and related information (Part 5), and selected financial information for 2006 and 2007 (Part 6).

**Section II** includes a unit for each chapter of material presented in the textbook. Each unit provides a summary of the chapter with self-assessment materials and solutions (**shown in bold**). Review the chapter summary before completing the self-assessment materials. There are five types of self-assessment materials, which are designed to test your understanding of the materials introduced in the chapter. The self-assessment activities and solutions include:

**Part I: True and False Questions.** Ten true and false questions are provided, which are designed to test key terms and concepts introduced in the chapter.

**Part II: Multiple Choice Questions.** Ten multiple choice questions are provided, which are designed to test key terms and concepts introduced in the chapter.

**Part III: Short Essay Questions.** Three short essay questions are provided, which are designed to test key terms and concepts introduced in the chapter.

**Part IV: Crossword Puzzle.** Learning the vocabulary and language used by accountants and auditors is important to your academic and professional success. As a fun way to learn the vocabulary used by accountants and auditors, a crossword puzzle is provided for each chapter. The puzzle includes key terms and concepts introduced in the chapter.

**Part V: Case Activity for Townsend Office Supplies and Equipment.** While it is difficult to duplicate an actual audit environment, experiential learning activities provide you with an opportunity to develop a practical hands-on understanding of the materials. An activity for the Townsend Office Supplies and Equipment case study is provided in each chapter to afford you the opportunity to apply what you have learned.

**Section III** includes 46 additional crossword puzzles. The puzzles cover key terms and concepts by topic and are arranged by chapter. There are two crossword puzzles for each topic. A solution for each crossword puzzle is provided.

A matrix summarizing the learning objective for each self-assessment question is provided on the following page.

# Learning Objectives for Self-Assessment Questions

| Section/Question | | Chapter | | | | | | | | | | | | | | | | | | | | |
|---|---|---|---|---|---|---|---|---|---|---|---|---|---|---|---|---|---|---|---|---|---|---|
| | | 1 | 2 | 3 | 4 | 5 | 6 | 7 | 8 | 9 | 10 | 11 | 12 | 13 | 14 | 15 | 16 | 17 | 18 | 19 | 20 | 21 |
| **True and False Questions** | 1 | 1 | 1 | 1 | 1 | 1 | 1 | 1 | 1 | 1 | 1 | 1 | 1 | 1 | 1 | 1 | 1 | 1 | 2 | 1 | 2 | 1 |
| | 2 | 2 | 2 | 1 | 1 | 1 | 1 | 1 | 2 | 1 | 1 | 4 | 3 | 2 | 1 | 3 | 2 | 1 | 2 | 1 | 2 | 2 |
| | 3 | 2 | 3 | 2 | 1 | 1 | 4 | 1 | 2 | 1 | 1 | 4 | 4 | 3 | 2 | 3 | 2 | 2 | 2 | 5 | 2 | 3 |
| | 4 | 2 | 4 | 2 | 2 | 1 | 4 | 2 | 2 | 1 | 3 | 4 | 4 | 6 | 3 | 5 | 3 | 3 | 2 | 6 | 2 | 4 |
| | 5 | 3 | 4 | 2 | 2 | 4 | 5 | 3 | 2 | 1 | 3 | 5 | 5 | 7 | 4 | 5 | 4 | 5 | 2 | 6 | 3 | 4 |
| | 6 | 3 | 5 | 2 | 2 | 5 | 5 | 3 | 2 | 2 | 4 | 5 | 6 | 7 | 6 | 5 | 5 | 5 | 2 | 6 | 3 | 5 |
| | 7 | 4 | 6 | 2 | 2 | 5 | 6 | 4 | 2 | 2 | 5 | 8 | 6 | 9 | 7 | 6 | 6 | 5 | 3 | 6 | 3 | 5 |
| | 8 | 4 | 7 | 2 | 4 | 5 | 6 | 4 | 2 | 4 | 5 | 9 | 6 | 11 | 8 | 6 | 8 | 6 | 3 | 7 | 3 | 6 |
| | 9 | 6 | 7 | 2 | 4 | 6 | 10 | 5 | 4 | 4 | 14 | 11 | 9 | 12 | 8 | 11 | 9 | 8 | 4 | 8 | 4 | 6 |
| | 10 | 6 | 7 | 11 | 4 | 8 | 10 | 8 | 4 | 4 | 14 | 14 | 11 | 13 | 9 | 12 | 10 | 9 | 4 | 9 | 4 | 7 |
| **Multiple Choice Questions** | 1 | 1 | 1 | 2 | 5 | 1 | 6 | 4 | 2 | 1 | 9 | 9 | 11 | 1 | 1 | 1 | 1 | 1 | 6 | 9 | 2 | 7 |
| | 2 | 2 | 3 | 2 | 5 | 1 | 6 | 5 | 2 | 2 | 9 | 9 | 11 | 3 | 1 | 3 | 1 | 1 | 6 | 9 | 2 | 7 |
| | 3 | 4 | 5 | 2 | 5 | 1 | 6 | 10 | 2 | 2 | 11 | 9 | 11 | 7 | 2 | 4 | 3 | 1 | 8 | 10 | 3 | 7 |
| | 4 | 5 | 5 | 2 | 6 | 5 | 7 | 11 | 2 | 2 | 11 | 9 | 11 | 7 | 4 | 4 | 3 | 5 | 8 | 10 | 4 | 8 |
| | 5 | 5 | 5 | 3 | 6 | 5 | 7 | 11 | 2 | 2 | 12 | 9 | 12 | 7 | 5 | 6 | 3 | 5 | 9 | 10 | 4 | 8 |
| | 6 | 5 | 7 | 5 | 7 | 7 | 7 | 18 | 2 | 4 | 12 | 9 | 12 | 8 | 7 | 9 | 6 | 9 | 9 | 10 | 5 | 8 |
| | 7 | 5 | 7 | 6 | 8 | 8 | 7 | 18 | 2 | 5 | 12 | 10 | 12 | 12 | 9 | 9 | 8 | 9 | 9 | 11 | 5 | 8 |
| | 8 | 5 | 7 | 6 | 8 | 8 | 7 | 18 | 4 | 5 | 12 | 10 | 12 | 13 | 9 | 9 | 10 | 10 | 9 | 12 | 6 | 9 |
| | 9 | 7 | 7 | 12 | 8 | 8 | 8 | 18 | 4 | 5 | 12 | 12 | 12 | 13 | 9 | 9 | 10 | 10 | 9 | 12 | 6 | 10 |
| | 10 | 7 | 11 | 12 | 8 | 9 | 15 | 14 | 4 | 5 | 14 | 12 | 12 | 13 | 9 | 9 | 10 | 10 | 10 | 13 | 6 | 10 |
| **Essays** | 1 | 4 | 4 | 2 | 1 | 7 | 4 | 5 | 2 | 1 | 5 | 5 | 4 | 1 | 4 | 4 | 6 | 1 | 2 | 10 | 7 | 4 |
| | 2 | 5 | 6 | 4 | 2 | 8 | 7 | 11 | 3 | 1 | 6 | 6 | 5 | 4 | 8 | 5 | 8 | 5 | 3 | 12 | 8 | 5 |
| | 3 | 6 | 11 | 9 | 6 | 9 | 8 | 17 | 4 | 2 | 10 | 10 | 11 | 5 | 9 | 12 | 10 | 9 | 8 | 16 | 9 | 8 |
| **CWP** | 1 | All | All | All | All | All | All | All | All | All | All | All | All | All | All | All | All | All | All | All | All | All |
| **Case** | 1 | All | All | All | All | All | All | All | All | All | All | All | All | All | All | All | All | All | All | All | All | All |
| **Extra CWPs** | 1 | All | All | All | All | All | All | All | All | All | All | All | All | All | All | All | All | All | All | All | All | All |
| | 2 | All | All | All | All | All | All | All | All | All | All | All | All | All | All | All | All | All | All | All | All | All |

# Townsend Office Supplies and Equipment

## Part 1: Introduction

Townsend Office Supplies and Equipment is an audit case study that will be used throughout this study guide. It was conceived as a running case as a means of providing you with a practical activity for each chapter. In other words, these activities will afford you an opportunity to apply what you have learned.

You will find that the study of auditing is different from any of the other accounting courses you have taken in college. The activities are designed to further develop the types of analytical and critical thinking skills necessary to evaluate accounting information systems and business processes. Some activities are designed to develop your skills for assessing business risks, while other activities will introduce you to various businesses processes. The activities require two specific investments on your part – the willingness to think and the ability to question.

## Part 2: General Instructions

The Townsend Office Supplies and Equipment case is provided to demonstrate and apply important auditing concepts presented throughout the textbook. Townsend's history and background information is provided in Part 3. The company's organizational chart is provided in Part 4 and accounting polices and related information is provided in Part 5. Selected financial information for 2005 and 2006 is provided in Part 6. You will use this information to complete a number of the case activities.

## Part 3: History and Background Information

**Company History and Operations**
Sharon Townsend started Townsend Office Supplies and Equipment, as a sole proprietorship, in 1980. Paul Green joined the company in 1984, at which time, the business was reorganized as a partnership with Sharon and Paul owning 60% and 40% of the partnership, respectively. Emily Watson joined the company in 1988 as the director of sales and marketing. On January 1, 1990, Townsend was incorporated in the Commonwealth of Virginia. The company's privately-held stock is owned by Sharon Townsend (60%), Paul Green (30%) and Emily Watson (10%).

## Executive Officers of the Company

Executive officers include Sharon Townsend , Paul Green and Emily Watson. Sharon Townsend is president and chief executive officer and also serves as the company's chief financial officer. Paul Green is executive vice-president and chief operating officer. Emily Watson is senior vice-president of sales and marketing. The three officers have a good working relationship. Sharon and Paul first met at Old Dominion University, where they were both business students. Sharon holds a BA in accounting and a MBA and Paul holds a BA degree in management. Emily Watson holds a BA degree in marketing from the University of Virginia.

## Board of Directors

Sharon Townsend is the chairman of the board. Other directors include: Paul Green, Emily Watson, Thomas Elliott (an executive from Old Dominion University), Brenda Allen (the Director of the local United Way Agency) and William Miller (the CFO of Unicorp, a local engineering firm).

## Managerial Philosophy

Accordingly to its mission statement, Townsend has four organizational goals: (1) to provide quality products to its customers at a reasonable price, (2) to provide timely delivery and high quality service to its customers, (3) to value its human assets, and (4) to make a positive contribution to the community as a corporate citizen. Management believes that a strong control environment will facilitate meeting the company's goals. For example, training sessions that emphasize these goals are held twice a year. All employees are required to attend at least one of the three-day training sessions each year. The cost of the training and lunch is provided by Townsend, as is the employee's regular compensation while attending the training session. In addition, the company has a reimbursement program for college courses taken by its employees.

## Integrity and Ethical Values

From all accounts, Townsend's officers, managers and personnel exhibit the highest level personal and professional standards, integrity and ethical values. The executive officers are active in a number of civil groups and activities in the Greater Hampton Roads area.

## Control Environment

In all previous engagements, Townsend's control environment has been assessed as good or better for a company of its size. No material control weaknesses or deficiencies were detected during the past two audits (2005 and 2006).

## Strategic and Short-Term Goals and Initiatives

The officers want to utilize technology to expand sales and its commercial customer base by January 1, 2009. Planning for this project is scheduled to begin in March 2008. The officers hope to sell Townsend's stock on the New York Stock Exchange by 2010. The company plans on hiring an internal auditor by the end of 2009. In addition, the officers plan to establish an audit committee by the end of 2009. The officers have agreed to hire an individual to assume the CFO responsibilities by the end of 2008. The company's legal counsel is working on developing a brand-name "trademark" partnership with four of Townsend's primary vendors. The brand-name trademark will include 50 of Townsend's most popular products. This will allow the company to significantly reduce the selling price for these products while increasing its profit margin. The trademark project will be completed by June 2008 in time to update the 2009 product catalog.

## Headquarters and Branch Locations

The company is headquartered in Norfolk, Virginia. The Norfolk location includes administrative facilities, a general warehouse and a large retail storeroom. The company has smaller retail and warehouse facilities in Hampton, Williamsburg, Richmond, Roanoke, Fairfax and eastern Maryland. Each branch location has a sales manager and one or two support personnel.

## Townsend's Growth Strategy

Sharon Townsend started the business as a small retail provider of office supplies and equipment. She believed that technology and office equipment sales would expand during the 1980s, so her early strategy was to increase commercial sales (office supplies and equipment) by serving local businesses.

The second phase of growth was to increase commercial sales by establishing relationships with government and military organizations. The greater Hampton Roads area has a high concentration of government and military bases.

The third phase of growth occurred in 2001 when Townsend expanded its operations by opening locations in the Washington, D.C. area (Fairfax) and eastern Maryland (Bethesda). Again, these areas have a high concentration of governmental and military organizations.

A three-year contract was executed between Townsend and a military installation located in Norfolk, Virginia. The contract was executed on November 1, 2007 (effective February 1, 2008). The contract includes sales of office equipment and furniture. Annual sales from this contract are estimated at $1.6 million. The contract guarantees Townsend a 55 percent profit margin on all orders. A customer purchase order for $1.2 million (dated December 5, 2007) was received by Townsend for the first order. This order is for office equipment and furniture and will be delivered on February 1, 2008. This order will yield a 58 percent profit margin due to volume and cash discounts offered by the vendor for purchasing the merchandise by December 31, 2007.

In the spring of 2008, the company plans on launching a website that will facilitate a commercial inventory availability and order-entry format.

## Sales and Catalog Operations

Currently, the company has 20 outside sales representatives. Each sales representative visits his or her commercial customers on a weekly basis. The company has seven outside sales territories. They include: (1) Norfolk and Virginia Beach, (2) Hampton and Newport News, (3) Williamsburg and surrounding areas, (4) Richmond and surrounding areas, (5) Roanoke and surrounding areas (6) Fairfax and surrounding areas and (7) Bethesda, Maryland and surrounding areas.

The company publishes a product catalog which includes all of its regular office supplies, technology and equipment products. The catalog is updated annually (pricing, products, etc.) and mailed to all of Townsend's regular customers in mid-December of each year.

The company has an electronic toll-free telephone service that customers can use to place orders 24-hours a day, seven days a week. Generally, these orders are shipped within 48 hours of when the orders are placed.

Retail cash sales are significant at the Norfolk store, due to its close proximity to Old Dominion University. Townsend offers special discounts to all ODU students, staff and faculty members.

## Customer Database

Townsend's customer base includes general retail customers (students from Old Dominion University), approximately 147 local businesses, 27 governmental agencies and multiple customers from all military bases located in the Greater Hampton Roads and Washington, D.C. areas.

## Townsend's Competition

Townsend's competition includes Office Depot and Office Max for general retail customers. An organization located in Virginia Beach, Supplies and More, sells to some of the local businesses (about 15% of the market). More recently, Office Depot has been bidding on some of Townsend's government contracts. Townsend views Office Depot as a potentially serious threat to its commercial sales base at its Norfolk, Hampton and Richmond locations. While Dell Computers is a strategic concern, Townsend's "quality service" continues to thwart this threat.

## Inventory Vendors

While Townsend's vendors list includes 210 suppliers, the company routinely purchases its inventory from 45 vendors. Townsend has established strong partnerships with 30 of its largest suppliers.

## Human Resources

The company has 40 employees, which includes 15 full-time and 5 part-time employees and 20 outside sales representatives. Townsend pays above average wages and salaries and provides a competitive benefits package to all of its full-time employees. Employee turnover is low. For example, 31 of the employees have been with the company for five years or more. Annual employee evaluations are conducted in March of each year. The executive management has chosen a participatory process for annual evaluations. Managers and subordinates prepare a summary of the employee's accomplishments and contributions for the previous year, which are evaluated. Managers are responsible for the identification of areas of weakness that need corrective action. The process is complete when the manager and employee agree to the employee's final written evaluation, which is signed by both parties and placed in the employee's personnel file.

Hiring, promotion and dismissal are carried out by the various department managers after consultation with and approval by the human resources executive officer (Paul Green).

The company has a retirement plan that covers full-time employees and provides for annual contributions at the discretion of the board of directors. Included in the plan is a 401(k) feature that allows each employee to make additional contributions to his or her retirement plan.

# Part 4: Organizational Chart

## Departments

The company is divided into thirteen departments or functions. Sharon Townsend, Paul Green and Emily Watson are responsible for these departments. Sharon Townsend is responsible for administration and facilities. She also serves as the company's chief financial officer. Paul Green is responsible for general operations, which includes human resources, internal control, purchasing, inventory and warehousing. Emily Watson is responsible for all sales and marketing for the seven branches. Townsend's organizational chart is shown on the following page.

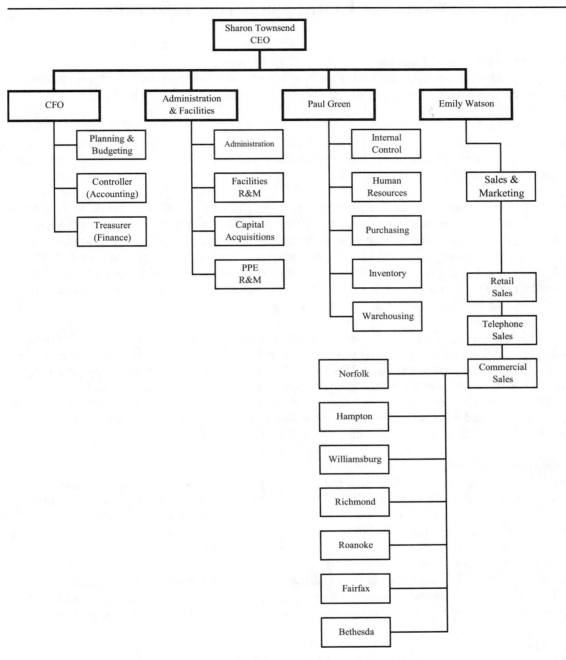

Townsend Office Supplies and Equipment, Inc.
Organizational Chart
(Not all functions and positions are shown)

# Part 5: Accounting Policies and Related Information

**Advertising and Promotional Expense**

The company expenses the costs of advertising the first time the advertising takes place. Promotional expenses are recognized when consumed.

**Banking and Credit**

Townsend has four accounts with Eastern Fidelity Bank – a general operating account, an interest bearing account, a high-yield savings account and a $600,000 unsecured line of credit account. Eastern Fidelity has branches throughout Virginia and Maryland.

All surplus cash in the general operating account is swept every 24 hours into the interest bearing account. Surplus funds which are not needed for at least a one-year period are transferred into the high-yield account. In 1992, the company established an unsecured $200,000 line of credit to primarily facilitate its inventory and/or capital asset purchases. The line of credit was subsequent changed to $300,000 in 1995, $500,000 in 1999, and $600,000 in 2002. The line of credit contract was renewed last on April 1, 2007 (Section 5 and 6). At December 31, 2007, $100,000 was outstanding, which was for the purchase of inventory. The average interest rate for 2007 was 5 percent.

While inventory is not pledged against the line of credit, Eastern Fidelity requires Townsend to have an annual audit completed by March 1 of each year in order to maintain the company's line of credit. The company must maintain a current ratio of 1.75:1, an acid ratio of 1:1, a total debt to equity ratio that cannot exceed 110%, and a short-term debt to equity ratio that cannot exceed 55 percent. Should any two or more of the ratio benchmarks not be met, any unpaid balance will be callable and immediately due and the account will be closed for a period of not less than one year. In addition, no dividends can be distributed should the total debt to equity ratio exceed 1.10:1.

**Building Operating Leases**

The company leases storefront and office space under lease arrangements [(1) Fairfax, Virginia, (2) Roanoke, Virginia, (3) Williamsburg, Virginia and (4) Bethesda, Maryland]. The leases are accounted for as operating leases. All monthly lease payments are due on the first day of the month. Townsend owns its facilities in Norfolk, Hampton and Richmond.

**Capital and Operating Budgets**

A ten-year budget is updated each year. Annual and five-year operating budgets are prepared in early October. Department managers are responsible for preparing their budgets, which are submitted to the executive officers by November 1. Budget compliance is a part of the managers' annual evaluation.

**Capital Assets**

The company has no capital leases. On June 30, 2007, 15 new vehicles were purchased for $254,000. Due to low interest yields, money market funds were used to purchase the vehicles. At the same time, 9 vehicles with the zero book value as of January 1, 2007 were sold for $3,000.

**Depreciation Expense**

Depreciation expense is calculated using the straight-line method over the estimated useful lives, which includes 20-30 years for buildings and land improvements and 5-10 years for leasehold improvements and furniture, fixtures and equipment. Vehicles are depreciated for 5 years.

**Independent Auditors – Armstrong, Batten and Collins LLP**

From 1992 through 2004, the company was audited by Mark Fletcher, CPA. The company received unqualified (clean) opinions and reports on all audits. Mr. Fletcher, a sole practitioner, was scheduled to retire at the end of 2007, so Townsend elected to change auditors before Mr. Fletcher retired. The firm of Armstrong, Batten & Collins LLP (ABC) was engaged to conduct the 2005 and 2006 audits. ABC is a member of the AICPA and Virginia Society of CPAs. The firm annually conducts approximately 90 audit and review engagements. The firm's most recent peer review was conducted in November 2006.

As the predecessor auditor, Mark Fletcher provided the appropriate background information to ABC. The audit team has found Townsend's management to be cooperative and there were no unresolved issues or problems during either engagement. One material adjustment to the 2005 financial statements was required. This adjustment related to the valuation of inventory based on the application of the lower of cost or market rule; management agreed to the adjustment. ABC issued a standard unqualified opinion for the 2005 and 2006 financial statement audits.

**Information systems**

All information systems (management, estimation, order-entry, inventory, accounting and budgeting) are automated and fully integrated, with real-time accessibility. Financial statements are prepared each month and compared to the month-to-date and year-to-date budgets.

**Inventory**

A perpetual inventory system is used to account for all inventory purchases. Inventory reductions and the cost of goods sold are recorded at the point of sale. Inventory is accounted for using a first-in-first-out flow assumption, with ending inventory valued using the lower of cost (FIFO) or market rule.
The company is closed from December 24 to December 28 and December 31. A complete inventory is taken on December 29-30. Based on an every other year rotation, one half of the employees participate in the annual inventory each year. A purchase order is issued for all inventory purchases. All purchases are recorded in the purchases journal (debit inventory and credit accounts payable).

On December 15, $505,000 of inventory was purchased for two reasons: (1) to satisfy upcoming sales requirements for the new government contract (February 1, 2008) and (2) to take advantage of significant volume and cash discounts for purchasing this inventory before December 31, 2007.

**Petty Cash Accounts**

A $100 petty cash account is maintained at each of Townsend's locations.

**Payroll**

Employee records and payroll are processed by the human resource personnel in the accounting department and approved by the controller. Payroll is processed and paid on a bimonthly basis (5th and 20th). Townsend's largest operating cost is salaries and related fringe benefits expense.

**Profitability**

Townsend's fixed costs are higher than its competitors, primarily due to Townsend's higher than average salary scale. Nevertheless, the company has been profitable for 14 of its 17 corporate years. The three unprofitable years included periods of major expansion of sales territories.

**Purchases and Cash Disbursements**

Purchases and other expenses are recognized when incurred, using the gross method. All expenses are recorded when incurred or consumed. When possible, all cash discounts offered by vendors are taken. All vendor invoices (only original invoices are processed) are processed through accounts payable.

## Sales and Cash Receipts

Sales are recognized at delivery (when earned and realizable), using the gross method. Customer credit is approved by the finance department before a commercial account is opened. Terms for commercial accounts are 2%-15/Net 30. Prices are reduced for a special sales campaign during the month of December. Customer payments on account are mailed to a lockbox at Eastern Fidelity. Cash sales represent 15 percent of total sales (11% from Norfolk and 4% from all other locations). Cash and credit card transactions are deposited on a daily basis by 1:00 p.m.

## Retail Office Supplies and Equipment Industry Financial Information

### Liquidity and Solvency Information

| | |
|---|---|
| Current Ratio | 1.57:1 |
| Quick Ratio | 0.98:1 |
| Accounts Receivables Turnover (in Days) | 32 |
| Inventory on Hand (in Days) | 45 |
| Working Capital to Total Assets | $2.11 |
| Inventory to Total Assets | 22% |
| Total debt to equity | 115% |
| Short-term debt to equity | 51% |

### Earnings Per Share Information

| | |
|---|---|
| Basic EPS from Continuing Operations | $0.98 |
| Diluted EPS from Continuing Operations | $0.96 |
| Basic Net Earnings Per Share | $0.89 |
| Diluted Net earnings Per share | $0.88 |

### Sales Growth and Profitability Information

| | |
|---|---|
| Average Sales Growth | 9% |
| Average Cost of Goods Sold & Occupancy Costs | 69% |
| Average Cost of Goods Sold | 48% |
| Average Gross Profit Margin (COGS & Occupancy) | 31% |
| Average Gross Profit Margin (COGS only) | 52% |
| Average Selling Expenses | 32% |
| Average General and Administrative Expenses | 6% |
| Average Interest Income | .4% |
| Average Interest Expense | 2% |
| Times Interest Earned | 5 |
| Average Profit Margin | 4% |
| Return on Assets | 9% |
| Return on Equity | 14% |

Townsend's financial information for 2006 and 2007 is presented on the following pages.

# Part 6: Selected Financial Information

Townsend Office Supplies and Equipment, Inc.
Statements of Operations
(in thousands, except per share data)

| | For the period ended December 31 | |
|---|---|---|
| | 2007 | 2006 |
| Net sales | $ 5,231 | $ 4,891 |
| Cost of sales | 2,511 | 2,201 |
| Gross profit | 2,720 | 2,690 |
| Selling expenses | 1,004 | 1,027 |
| General and administrative expenses | 1,109 | 936 |
| Depreciation expense | 172 | 146 |
| Total operating expenses | 2,285 | 2,109 |
| Income from operations | 435 | 581 |
| | | |
| Other income (expenses) | | |
| Interest expense | (117) | (115) |
| Interest income | 23 | 33 |
| Gain (loss) on sale of retired equipment | 3 | (1) |
| | | |
| Total other income (expense), net | (91) | (83) |
| | | |
| Income before taxes | 344 | 498 |
| | | |
| Income tax provision | 103 | 154 |
| | | |
| Net income | $ 241 | $ 344 |
| | | |
| Earnings per share | $24.10 | $34.40 |

Townsend Office Supplies and Equipment, Inc.
Statement of Retained Earnings
(in thousands)

| | For the period ended December 31 | |
|---|---|---|
| | 2007 | 2006 |
| Retained earnings at beginning of year | $ 1,728 | $ 1,484 |
| Net income for the year | 241 | 344 |
| Less dividends | (100) | (100) |
| Retained earnings at end of year | $ 1,869 | $ 1,728 |

## Townsend Office Supplies and Equipment, Inc.
## Balance Sheets
### (in thousands)

|  | December 31 | |
|---|---|---|
|  | 2007 | 2006 |

### Assets

| Current Assets: | | |
|---|---|---|
| Checking account - Eastern Fidelity | $ 210 | $ 213 |
| Money market accounts - Eastern Fidelity | 274 | 670 |
| Leasehold deposits | 19 | 19 |
| Receivables, net | 310 | 432 |
| Inventory | 672 | 124 |
| Prepaid advertising | 84 | 39 |
| Other prepaid expenses | 23 | 14 |
| Total current assets | 1,592 | 1,511 |
| Property, plant and equipment, at cost | | |
| Land and buildings | 2,100 | 2,100 |
| Fixtures and equipment | 1,009 | 1,009 |
| Vehicles | 610 | 438 |
| Total property, plant and equipment | 3,719 | 3,547 |
| Less accumulated depreciation | 1,210 | 1,120 |
| Property, plant and equipment, net | 2,509 | 2,427 |
| Total Assets | $ 4,101 | $ 3,938 |

### Liabilities and Stockholders' Equity

| Current liabilities: | | |
|---|---|---|
| Line of credit - Eastern Fidelity | $ 100 | $ 35 |
| Accounts payable | 483 | 279 |
| Accrued taxes payable | 64 | 83 |
| Accrued interest payable | 4 | 1 |
| Mortgages payable (current portion) | 247 | 298 |
| Total current liabilities | 898 | 699 |
| Mortgages payable | 1,202 | 1,388 |
| Total liabilities | 2,100 | 2,087 |
| Deferred income taxes | 12 | 3 |
| Shareholders' Equity: | | |
| Common stock, 10,000 shares issued | 10 | 10 |
| Additional paid-in capital | 110 | 110 |
| Retained earnings | 1,869 | 1,728 |
| Total shareholders' equity | 1,989 | 1,848 |
| Total liabilities & Stockholders' Equity | $ 4,101 | $ 3,938 |

# Chapter Summaries

# An Introduction to Assurance and Financial Statement Auditing

## KEY THOUGHT

Auditing is a systematic process of objectively obtaining and evaluating evidence regarding assertions about economic actions and events to ascertain the degree of correspondence between those assertions and established criteria and communicating the results to interested users (American Accounting Association, Committee on Basic Auditing Concepts 1973, 2).

## CHAPTER SUMMARY

**[LO1] Understand why studying auditing can be valuable to you and why it is different from studying accounting.** *Auditing helps ensure that information is reliable, credible, relevant, and timely.*

A. Auditing is different from any of the other accounting courses you have taken in college.

B. The vocabulary and language used in auditing is unique.

C. Auditing focuses on learning the analytical and logical skills necessary to evaluate the relevance and reliability of the systems and processes responsible for recording and summarizing information.

D. Auditing is more conceptual in nature than your other accounting courses.

E. Learning auditing essentially helps you understand how to gather and assess evidence so you can evaluate assertions made by others.
*Auditing can improve the reliability of information for decision makers of all kinds.*

**[LO2] Understand why there is a demand for auditing and assurance.**

A. Legal and contractual requirements.

B. The modern corporation led to the prevalence of absentee stockholders and the use of professional managers who run the day-to-day operations.
*managers are as agents for the owners/stockholders (Principal)*

C. Principal-agent relationships often result in information asymmetry.

D. Conflicts of interest between management and absentee shareholders.
*Conflicts of interest of maximizing their self-interest.*

E. An audit is a cost-effective monitoring device.
*- a set of criteria is needed to govern the form and content of the manager's reports.*

F. Restrictive covenants in debt agreements.
*- make sure the manager use the borrowed funds appropriately.*

**[LO3] Understand intuitively the demand for auditing and the desired characteristics of auditors and audit services through an analogy to a house inspector and a house inspection service.**

    A. Review the "Case of the House Inspector" presented in the textbook.

**[LO4] Understand the relationships among auditing, attestation, and assurance services.**

    A. At a general level, auditing, attestation, and assurance services encompass the same process: the evaluation of evidence to determine the correspondence of some information to a set of given criteria, and the issuance of a report to indicate the degree of correspondence.

    B. Auditing services are a subset of attest services, which, in turn, are a subset of assurance services. As defined by the Committee on Basic Auditing Concepts (AAA 1973), auditing is a systematic process of objectively obtaining and evaluating evidence regarding assertions about economic actions and events to ascertain the degree of correspondence between those assertions and established criteria and communicating the results to interested users.

    C. The phrase "systematic process" implies that there should be a well-planned and thorough approach for conducting an audit. This plan involves "objectively obtaining and evaluating evidence." The auditor must objectively search for and evaluate the relevance and validity of evidence. While the type, quantity, and reliability of evidence may vary between audits, this process of obtaining and evaluating evidence makes up most of the auditor's activities on an audit. *— communicate the results to interested users with some type of reports*

    D. Attestation services occur when a practitioner is engaged to issue a report on subject matter, or an assertion about subject matter, that is the responsibility of another party. Attestation services are not limited to economic events or actions.

    E. Assurance services are independent professional services that improve the quality of information, or its context, for decision makers (a cost-effective monitoring device).

**[LO5] Understand the basic definition and three fundamental concepts of a financial statement audit.**

    A. Figure 1-3 presents a simplified overview of the audit function for a financial statement audit. Three concepts must be considered in a financial statement audit: (1) audit risk, (2) materiality, and (3) evidence relating to management assertions. The auditor's assessment of audit risk and materiality influence the type and amount of work to be performed (referred to as the scope of the audit). In establishing the scope of the audit, the auditor must make decisions about the nature, timing, and extent of evidence to be gathered in order to evaluate management's assertions.

    B. **Audit risk** is defined as the risk that the auditor may unknowingly fail to appropriately modify his or her opinion on financial statements that are materially misstated. An audit does not guarantee or provide absolute assurance that all misstatements will be detected; instead, the auditor provides reasonable assurance, which implies some risk that a material misstatement could be present in the financial statements and the auditor will fail to detect it.

    C. **Materiality** is the magnitude of an omission or misstatement of accounting information that, in the light of surrounding circumstances, makes it probable that the judgment of a reasonable person relying on the information would have been changed or influenced by the omission or misstatement (AU 312). The focus of this definition is on the users of the financial statements.

*— is a matter of professional judgment and perceives as the view of a reasonable person who is relying on the financial statement*

In planning the engagement, the auditor assesses the magnitude of a misstatement that may affect the users' decisions. This assessment helps the auditor determine the nature, timing and extent of audit procedures. A common rule of thumb is that total (aggregated) misstatements of more than about 3 to 5 percent of net income before tax would cause financial statements to be materially misstated.

Note that the auditor's consideration of materiality is a matter of professional judgment and is affected by what the auditor perceives as the view of a reasonable person who is relying on the financial statements. There are no formal standards or guidelines for making this judgment.

D. **Evidence regarding management's assertions** is the third major concept involved in auditing. Most of the auditor's work in arriving at an opinion on the financial statements consists of obtaining and evaluating evidence regarding management's assertions. These assertions, made by management, in conjunction with the assessment of materiality and audit risk, are used by the auditor to determine the nature, timing and extent of evidence to be gathered.

In obtaining and evaluating evidence, the auditor is concerned with the relevance and reliability of the evidence. Relevance refers to whether the evidence relates to the specific management assertion being tested, whereas, reliability refers to whether a specific type of evidence can be relied upon to signal the true state of the management assertion being examined.

Once the auditor has obtained sufficient competent evidence that the management assertions can be relied upon for each significant account, reasonable assurance is provided that the financial statements are fairly presented.

**[LO6] Understand why on most audit engagements an auditor tests only a sample of transactions that occurred.**

A. Testing all transactions that occurred during the period is cost prohibitive. To deal with this problem, the auditor uses (1) his or her knowledge about the transactions and/or (2) a sampling approach to examine the transactions. Examples of auditor knowledge include previous audits of the client and knowledge of the client's industry.

B. When the auditor has no special knowledge about which particular transactions or items may be misstated, he or she uses sampling procedures that increase the likelihood of obtaining a sample representative of the population of transactions or account items. In other words, the auditor uses the laws of probability to make inferences about potential misstatements in total based on examining a sample of transactions or items.

C. The sample size is a function of materiality and acceptable audit risk. There is an inverse relationship between sample size and materiality and between sample size and acceptable audit risk. For example, if an auditor assesses materiality for an account to be a small amount, a larger sample will be needed than if materiality were a larger amount. Similarly, as the amount of audit risk the auditor is willing to accept decreases for a given materiality amount, the sample size necessary to test the management assertion under examination becomes greater. This occurs because the auditor must gather more evidence in order to further reduce the amount of uncertainty or risk associated with the test.

**[LO7] Understand the basic financial statement auditing process and the phases in which an audit is carried out.**

A. The goal of a financial statement audit is to express an opinion on whether or not the financial statements are fairly presented. The audit process can be broken down into eight steps or phases (see Figure 1-4). While Figure 1-4 suggests that these phases are sequential, the eight phases are cumulative and interrelated in nature:

*P.19*

**Phase 1 Client Acceptance/Continuance and Establishing Engagement Terms.** Standards require that public accounting firms establish policies and procedures for deciding whether to accept new clients or retain current clients. The purpose of these policies is to minimize the likelihood that an auditor will be associated with clients who lack integrity. The knowledge that the auditor gathers during this phase may provide valuable understanding about the entity and its environment, which can be used subsequently to assess risk and plan the audit. Once the acceptance/continuance decision has been made, the auditor establishes an understanding with the client regarding the services to be performed and the terms of the engagement.

*Preliminary Engagement Activities*

**Phase 2 Preplan the Audit.** Preplanning the audit requires: (1) understanding of an existing client or gaining a deeper understanding of a new client and its environment beyond that obtained during the acceptance/continuance process, (2) determining audit engagement team requirements, and (3) ensuring the independence of the audit team and audit firm. In order to understand the client and its environment, the auditor should evaluate the following:

1. Industry, regulatory and other external factors.
2. Nature of entity, including accounting policies.
3. Objectives and strategies and the related business risks.
4. Measurement and review of the entity's financial performance.
5. Client's internal control system.

**Phase 3 Assess Risk and Establish Materiality.** To plan the audit, the audit team must make a preliminary assessment of the client's business risks and determine materiality.

**Phase 4 Plan the Audit.** In developing the audit plan, the auditor should be guided by: (1) the audit procedures performed to gain and document an understanding of the entity and (2) the results of the risk assessment process. The auditor should prepare a written audit plan that sets forth, in reasonable detail, the nature, extent, and timing of the audit work.

**Phase 5 Consider and Audit Internal Control.** The auditor should gain an understanding of internal control. Internal control is designed to provide reasonable assurance regarding the achievement of objectives in the following categories: (1) reliability of financial reporting, (2) effectiveness and efficiency of operations, and (3) compliance with applicable laws and regulations (AU 319).

**Phase 6 Audit Business Processes and Related Accounts.** The auditor assesses the risk of material misstatement by examining the entity's business processes (also known as accounting cycles). The auditor then determines the audit procedures that are necessary to reduce the risk of material misstatement to a low level for the financial statement accounts affected by a particular business process or cycle. The individual audit procedures are directed toward specific assertions in the account balance that are likely to be misstated. On most engagements, conducting the planned audit tests comprises most of the time spent on a financial statement audit or an audit of internal control over financial reporting.

**Phase 7 Complete the Audit**. The auditor must evaluate the sufficiency of the evidence gathered. The auditor also assesses the possibility of contingent liabilities, such as lawsuits, and searches for any events subsequent to the balance sheet date that may impact the financial statements.

**[LO8] Understand what an audit report is and the nature of an unqualified report.**

**Phase 8 Evaluate Results and Issue the Audit Report**. The final phase in the audit process is choosing the appropriate audit report to issue. If the audit client is a public company, the auditor is also required to report on the design and effectiveness of the company's system of internal controls over financial reporting. *unquality means the financial statements are free of material misstatement; the auditor does not find it necessary to qualify his opinion.*

**The Unqualified Audit Report**. The unqualified (i.e., clean) audit report is the most common type of report issued. Exhibit 1-1 presents an audit report issued on EarthWear Clothier's financial statements. For an audit report to be unqualified, the audit must be conducted in accordance with applicable standards, the auditor must be independent, there must be no significant limitations imposed on the auditor's procedures, and the client's financial statements must be free of material departures from GAAP.

**Other Types of Audit Reports**. If any one of the conditions as described above is not met, the auditor issues a report that appropriately conveys to the reader the nature of the report and the reasons why the report is not unqualified. An audit report may be qualified or if the misstatement *so material* is considered so material that it pervasively affects the interpretation of the financial statements, the auditor will issue an adverse opinion. Other types of reports may be issued, depending on the circumstances (see Chapter 18). *Qualified when there is a misstatement identified by auditor and clients refuse to change. and it is material.*

**[LO9] Understand why auditing demands logic, reasoning, and resourcefulness.**

A. A financial statement auditor needs to understand not only accounting, but also the concepts and techniques of gathering and evaluating evidence to assess management's financial statement assertions. An auditor needs a significant understanding of business in general as well as of the specific industries of his or her clients. Auditing is a logical process of thinking and reasoning. Lastly, being a good auditor sometimes requires imagination and innovation (refer to the example in the text about cattle inventory).

# CHAPTER 1: SELF-ASSESSMENT

## Part I: True or False Questions

[LO1] _F_ 1. Independence standards are required for audits of public companies, but not for audits of private companies.

[LO2] _F_ 2. Decision makers demand reliable information that is provided by accountants.

[LO2] _T_ 3. Information asymmetry seldom occurs.

[LO2] _T_ 4. Conflicts of interest often occur between absentee owners and managers.

[LO4] _F_ 5. Auditing services and attestation services are the same.

[LO4] _T_ 6. Auditing is a type of attest service.

[LO5] _T_ 7. An auditor provides reasonable assurance that a material misstatement is not present in the financial statements.

[LO5] _T_ 8. Audit risk is defined as the risk that the auditor may unknowingly fail to appropriately modify his or her opinion on financial statements that are materially misstated.

[LO6] _F_ 9. Assessing the possibility of contingent liabilities should be performed during the planning phase of the audit.

[LO6] _T_ 10. Testing all transactions that occurred during the period is cost prohibitive.

## Part II: Multiple Choice Questions

[LO1] 1. Auditing is different from most other accounting courses because:
   a. Auditing is closely related to systems and processes.
   b. Auditing is more conceptual in nature.
   c. Auditing vocabulary and language is unique.
   d. All of the above.

[LO2] 2. There is a demand for auditing and assurance services because:
   a. Information asymmetry exists between principals and agents.
   b. An audit is a cost-effective monitoring device.
   c. It keeps auditors in business.
   d. Both a and b are explanations for the demand.

[LO4] 3. The fundamental purpose of the attest function is to:
   a. Assure the application of generally accepted accounting principles.
   b. Examine transactions so that the auditor may certify the account balance.
   c. Detect fraud.
   d. Determine whether the client's assertions are fairly stated.

[LO5]  4.  The auditor's judgment concerning the overall fairness of the financial statements is applied within the framework of:
    a.  Generally accepted accounting principles.
    b.  Generally accepted auditing standards.
    c.  The auditor's assessment of the internal control system.
    d.  Management's assertions.

[LO5]  5.  The concepts that must be considered in a financial statement audit include:
    a.  Audit risk, internal control and materiality.
    b.  Audit risk, materiality and evidence.
    c.  Audit risk, materiality and management assertions.
    d.  All of the above.

[LO5]  6.  Which statement below is incorrect?
    a.  An auditor must use his or her professional judgment when determining materiality.
    b.  There are no formal standards or guidelines for determining materiality.
    c.  Audit evidence collected must be relevant but not reliable.
    d.  Audit evidence collected must be both relevant and reliable.

[LO5]  7.  The purpose of a financial audit is:
    a.  To determine whether the overall financial statements are fairly presented.
    b.  To determine whether fraud is present.
    c.  To determine whether management is effective.
    d.  To determine whether management is efficient.

[LO5]  8.  The relevance of audit evidence is based on:
    a.  The cost to collect the evidence.
    b.  The availability of the evidence.
    c.  The specific assertions being tested.
    d.  The reliability of the evidence.

[LO7]  9.  In correct order, the basic financial statement auditing process includes:
    a.  Accept client, consider internal control, and plan the audit.
    b.  Plan the audit, assess risk/materiality, and consider internal control.
    c.  Plan the audit, consider internal control, and audit processes and accounts.
    d.  Accept client, assess risk/materiality, and preplan the audit.

[LO7]  10. Preplanning the audit includes:
    a.  Understanding client and industry.
    b.  Determining audit engagement team requirements.
    c.  Ensuring the independence of audit team and audit firm.
    d.  All of the above.

## Part III: Short Essay Questions

[LO4] What the phrase "systematic process" imply and how does such a process relate to audit evidence?

[LO5] Discuss the level of assurance provided in a financial audit?

[LO6] Who is responsible for the internal control system? How does the auditor's work concerning the internal control system change when auditing a public company versus a private company?

# Part IV: Crossword Puzzle – Chapter 1 [LO ALL]

## Across

1  Financial accounting and reporting guidelines are called _____ (abbreviation).
3  An auditor must study the client's _____ control system during an audit.
6  An abbreviation for the title of a company's head accountant.
8  These independent services improve the overall quality of information for decision makers.
9  Another name for an unqualified audit opinion.
11  A CPA must maintain this professional standard at all times.

## Down

2  This type of enterprise is required to have an annual audit.
4  The audit failure of this engagement led to the demise of Arthur Andersen.
5  A service to issue a report on the assertions of another party.
7  A representation of the population of transactions.
10  A public company is required to obtain this attestation service before publishing its annual report.
12  A person with this professional designation (abbreviation) can conduct a financial statement audit.

**Part IV: Townsend Office Supplies and Equipment [LO ALL]**

<table>
<tr><td align="center">

**Chapter 1**
**Townsend Office Supplies and Equipment**

</td></tr>
<tr><td>

You are the audit manager for the Townsend 2007 audit. You have completed Phase 1 (Client Acceptance/Continuance) of the engagement. Based on what you have learned thus far about a financial statement audit and what you now know about this client, explain what you need to do to successfully complete Phase 2 (Preplanning) of the 2007 financial statement audit for Townsend.

</td></tr>
</table>

# CHAPTER 1: SELF-ASSESSMENT SOLUTIONS

## Part I: True or False Questions

[LO1] **False** 1.  Independence standards are required for audits of public companies, but not for audits of private companies.

[LO2] **True** 2.  Decision makers demand reliable information that is provided by accountants.

[LO2] **False** 3.  Information asymmetry seldom occurs.

[LO2] **True** 4.  Conflicts of interest often occur between absentee owners and managers.

[LO4] **False** 5.  Auditing services and attestation services are the same.

[LO4] **True** 6.  Auditing is a type of attest service.

[LO5] **True** 7.  An auditor provides reasonable assurance that a material misstatement is not present in the financial statements.

[LO5] **True** 8.  Audit risk is defined as the risk that the auditor may unknowingly fail to appropriately modify his or her opinion on financial statements that are materially misstated.

[LO6] **False** 9.  Assessing the possibility of contingent liabilities should be performed during the planning phase of the audit.

[LO6] **True** 10.  Testing all transactions that occurred during the period is cost prohibitive.

## Part II: Multiple Choice Questions

[LO1]  1.  Auditing is different from most other accounting courses because:
   a.  Auditing is closely related to systems and processes.
   b.  Auditing is more conceptual in nature.
   c.  Auditing vocabulary and language is unique.
   **d.  All of the above.**

[LO2]  2.  There is a demand for auditing and assurance services because:
   a.  Information asymmetry exists between principals and agents.
   b.  An audit is a cost-effective monitoring device.
   c.  It keeps auditors in business.
   **d.  Both a and b are explanations for the demand.**

[LO4]  3.  The fundamental purpose of the attest function is to:
   a.  Assure the application of generally accepted accounting principles.
   b.  Examine transactions so that the auditor may certify the account balance.
   c.  Detect fraud.
   **d.  Determine whether the client's assertions are fairly stated.**

[LO5]  4.  The auditor's judgment concerning the overall fairness of the financial statements is applied within the framework of:
   **a.  Generally accepted accounting principles.**
   b.  Generally accepted auditing standards.
   c.  The auditor's assessment of the internal control system.
   d.  Management's assertions.

[LO5]  5.  The concepts that must be considered in a financial statement audit include:
   a.  Audit risk, internal control and materiality.
   **b.  Audit risk, materiality and evidence.**
   c.  Audit risk, materiality and management assertions.
   d.  All of the above.

[LO5]  6.  Which statement below is incorrect?
   a.  An auditor must use his or her professional judgment when determining materiality.
   b.  There are no formal standards or guidelines for determining materiality.
   **c.  Audit evidence collected must be relevant but not reliable.**
   d.  Audit evidence collected must be both relevant and reliable.

[LO5]  7.  The purpose of a financial audit is:
   **a.  To determine whether the overall financial statements are fairly presented.**
   b.  To determine whether fraud is present.
   c.  To determine whether management is effective.
   d.  To determine whether management is efficient.

[LO5]  8.  The relevance of audit evidence is based on:
   a.  The cost to collect the evidence.
   b.  The availability of the evidence.
   **c.  The specific assertions being tested.**
   d.  The reliability of the evidence.

[LO7]  9.  In correct order, the basic financial statement auditing process includes:
   a.  Accept client, consider internal control, and plan the audit.
   b.  Plan the audit, assess risk/materiality, and consider internal control.
   **c.  Plan the audit, consider internal control, and audit processes and accounts.**
   d.  Accept client, assess risk/materiality, and preplan the audit.

[LO7] 10.  Preplanning the audit includes:
   a.  Understanding client and industry.
   b.  Determining audit engagement team requirements.
   c.  Ensuring the independence of audit team and audit firm.
   **d.  All of the above.**

## Part III: Short Essays

[LO4] What the phrase "systematic process" imply and how does such a process relate to audit evidence?

**The phrase "systematic process" implies that there should be a well-planned and thorough approach for conducting an audit. This plan involves "objectively obtaining and evaluating evidence." The auditor must objectively search for and evaluate the relevance and validity of evidence. While the type, quantity, and reliability of evidence may vary between audits, this process of obtaining and evaluating evidence makes up most of the auditor's activities on an audit.**

[LO5] Discuss the level of assurance provided in a financial audit?

**An audit does not guarantee or provide absolute assurance that all misstatements will be detected. Instead, the auditor provides "reasonable assurance," which implies some risk that a material misstatement could be present but the auditor will fail to detect it.**

[LO6] Who is responsible for the internal control system? How does the auditor's work concerning the internal control system change when auditing a public company versus a private company?

**Management is responsible for the internal control system. For financial statement audits, the auditor must gain an understanding of the internal control system sufficient to assess misstatement risk and plan the audit. When performing a financial statement audit of a public company, the auditor is also required to audit the company's internal controls, which goes well beyond the understanding and testing of internal control to plan a financial audit.**

## Part IV: Crossword Puzzle – Chapter 1 Solution [LO ALL]

Crossword grid solution:

- 1 Across / 1 Down: G A A P
- 3 Across: I N T E R N A L
- 6 Across: C F O
- 8 Across: A S S U R A N C E
- 9 Across: C L E A N
- 11 Across: I N D E P E N D E N C E
- 2 Down: P U B L I C
- 4 Down: E N R O N
- 5 Down: A T T E S T
- 7 Down: S A M P L E
- 10 Down: A U D I T
- 12 Down: C P A

**Across**

1    Financial accounting and reporting guidelines are called _____ (abbreviation).
3    An auditor must study the client's _____ control system during an audit.
6    An abbreviation for the title of a company's head accountant.
8    These independent services improve the overall quality of information for decision makers.
9    Another name for an unqualified audit opinion.
11   A CPA must maintain this professional standard at all times.

**Down**

2    This type of enterprise is required to have an annual audit.
4    The audit failure of this engagement led to the demise of Arthur Andersen.
5    A service to issue a report on the assertions of another party.
7    A representation of the population of transactions.
10   A public company is required to obtain this attestation service before publishing its annual report.
12   A person with this professional designation (abbreviation) can conduct a financial statement audit.

## Part IV: Townsend Office Supplies and Equipment [LO ALL]

| **Chapter 1** |
| :---: |
| **Townsend Office Supplies and Equipment** |

You are the audit manager for the Townsend 2007 audit. You have completed Phase 1 (Client Acceptance/Continuance). Based on what you have learned thus far about a financial statement audit and what you now know about this client, explain what you need to do to successfully complete Phase 2 (Preplanning) of the 2007 financial statement audit for Townsend.

**During the "preplanning" phase, three specific objectives must be accomplished. First, the lead auditor needs to understand the client and its environment (client and industry specific). To accomplish the first step, the following information will be gathered about Townsend:**

1. **Industry, regulatory and other external factors.**
2. **Expand my understanding of Townsend and its accounting policies.**
3. **Review Townsend's objectives and strategies and related business risks.**
4. **Evaluate the financial statements for the year ending December 31, 2004.**
5. **Evaluate Townsend's current internal control system.**

**Second, the audit team requirements for this engagement need to be identified. This includes choosing the audit team members that have experience in the retail office supplies and equipment industry. In order to complete the third activity, the firm's policy on "independence" should be reviewed. Finally, independence of the audit team members and the firm itself must be evaluated to ensure that the parties associated with the engagement are independent of Townsend, as specified in the firm's independence policy.**

# The Financial Statement Auditing Environment

## KEY THOUGHT

The objective of the ordinary examination of financial statements by the independent auditor is the expression of an opinion on the fairness with which they present, in all material respects, financial position, results of operations, and cash flows in conformity with generally accepted accounting principles [Auditing Standards Board (AU 110.01)].

## CHAPTER SUMMARY

**[LO1] Understand the recent changes in the auditing profession.**

A. During the past few years, the auditing profession has been dramatically reshaped by events taking place in the business community. The Sarbanes-Oxley Act of 2002 established the Public Company Accounting Oversight Board (PCAOB) as the auditing standards-setting body for public companies.

B. Accounting firms aggressively sought opportunities to market a variety of high-margin nonaudit services to their audit clients. Independence standards in force at the time allowed auditors to perform many of these services, including information systems design and implementation and internal audit services, even for public company audit clients. Exhibit 2-1 provides a sample of audit and nonaudit fees reported in 2000.

C. In October 2001, Enron, one of the largest public companies in the United States, reported its first quarterly loss. The SEC launched an investigation, which uncovered a massive financial deception that had been going on for several years. Enron was forced to restate billions of dollars in overstated earnings and previously undisclosed debt obligations. Shortly after the Enron scandal, numerous other scandals involving corporate giants, brokerage firms, stock exchanges, the Arthur Andersen accounting firm, and managers of mutual funds (Piper Jaffray) were uncovered. The Enron scandal alone weakened investor confidence in the stock market, but the subsequent series of scandals caused many investors to doubt the integrity of the entire system of public ownership and accountability in the United States.

D. Under pressure to restore public confidence, Congress passed the Sarbanes-Oxley Public Company Accounting Reform and Investor Protection Act in July 2002. The Act mandated broad reform in corporate governance practices that would affect the duties and practices of public companies, financial analysts, external auditors, and securities exchange markets.

E.  The Act transferred authority to set and enforce auditing standards for public company audits to the Public Company Accounting Oversight Board (PCAOB). The Act mandated that the SEC impose strict independence rules, prohibiting the provision of most types of nonaudit services to public company audit clients. The Act imposed several other important mandates, including that audit firms rotate audit partners off audit engagements every five years, and that public companies obtain an integrated audit, which includes audits of both financial statements and internal control over financial reporting. The Act is extremely important in its implications for boards and managements of public companies, for the accounting profession, and for the U.S. capital markets system..

F.  The impact of the events of the past decade, culminating in the Sarbanes-Oxley Act of 2002 and the formation of the PCAOB, cannot be overemphasized. The public accounting profession has been through a revolutionary shift from an era of self-regulation toward governmental regulation and oversight. Most of the large firms, prohibited from providing many nonaudit services for public company audit clients, sold their consulting divisions and began to refocus their efforts once again on their core service: financial statement audits. These changes have been painful, but they highlight the essential importance of auditing in our economic system and have created new opportunities for auditors. While the profession has undergone revolutionary changes, the events of the last few years have served to solidify the crucial role of accounting and auditing.

**[LO2] Recognize that auditing takes place in a context that is shaped largely by the audit client's business.**

A.  How an auditor approaches a given engagement will depend on the nature of the client's business. In other words, the context of the client's business impacts the auditor and the audit. While every business is different, business organizations can be conceptualized or modeled in common ways.

**[LO3] Understand a high-level model of a business entity, including the elements of corporate governance, objectives, strategies, processes, controls, transactions, and financial statements.**

A.  Due to the way resources are invested and managed in the modern business world, a system of corporate governance is necessary, through which managers are overseen and supervised. **Corporate governance** consists of all of the people, processes and activities in place to help ensure the proper stewardship over an entity's assets. Corporate governance is the implementation and execution of processes to ensure that those managing a company properly utilize their time, talents, and available resources in the best interest of absentee owners. The body primarily responsible for management oversight in U.S. corporations is the **board of directors**. The **audit committee**, consisting of members of the board, oversees the internal and external auditing work done for the organization. Through this link, and through the audit of financial statements (a form of stewardship), auditors play an important role in facilitating effective corporate governance.

B.  Management, with guidance and direction from the board of directors, decides on a set of objectives, along with strategies designed to achieve those objectives. The organization must then undertake certain processes in order to implement management's strategies. The business also must assess and manage risks that may threaten achievement of the entity's objectives. Most organizations establish processes that fit in five broad process categories, sometimes referred to as cycles. Each process involves a variety of economic transactions. The company must design and implement systems to capture its economic events. In addition, a system of internal controls must be implemented to ensure that the transactions are recorded appropriately and that its resources are protected.

**[LO4] Be familiar with a five-component model of business processes (or cycles) that auditors often use in organizing the audit into manageable components.**

A.  Auditors rely on the process model to divide the audit of a business's financial statements into manageable pieces. Figure 2-1 illustrates the five cycles, in context with the overall business model including the concepts of corporate governance, objectives, strategies, information systems, and internal control. The five cycles include:

**Financing Process**. Businesses typically invest in assets such as land, buildings, and equipment in accordance with their strategies. Capital is generated through borrowing or soliciting investments from owners. As part of this process, businesses also need to repay lenders and provide a return on owner investments. These types of transactions are all part of the financing process (the financing cycle). Accounts involved in the financing process include the following income statement accounts: depreciation, gains and losses on sales of long-term assets, interest income, and interest expense. The following balance sheet accounts are included in the financing process: long-term debt and long-term asset accounts, and owners' equity accounts. Management establishes internal controls to ensure the appropriate handling and recording of financing transactions.

**Purchasing Process**. Businesses acquire goods and services to support the sales of its products or services. The company must also purchase office supplies, needed services, and other items to support its activities. Accounts involved in the purchasing process (also known as the acquisition and payment cycle) include the following income statement accounts: cost of goods sold or purchases, purchase returns and allowances, and various expense accounts. Balance sheet accounts in the purchasing process include: accounts payable, inventory, cash and various asset accounts. Management establishes internal controls to ensure that transactions involving the purchase of raw materials, supplies, and other items are conducted and recorded appropriately.

**Human Resource Management Process**. Business organizations hire personnel to perform various functions in accordance with the enterprise's mission and strategy. The human resource management process (also known as the payroll cycle) includes all of the payroll-related activities. Accounts involved in the human resource management process include the following income statement accounts: direct and indirect labor expense, period (selling and general and administrative) wages and salaries expense, and various payroll-related expense accounts. The following balance sheet accounts included in the human resource management process: wages and salaries payable, inventory, cash, and various other payroll-related liability accounts. Management establishes internal controls to ensure that payroll transactions are handled and recorded appropriately.

**Inventory Management Process**. This process (also known as the inventory and warehousing cycle) varies widely between different types of businesses. Service providers (such as auditors) rarely have significant inventories to manage, since their primary resources typically consist of information, knowledge, and the time and effort of people. For these businesses, the human resource management process is of correspondingly greater importance. Manufacturers, wholesalers and retailers all typically have significant, numerous, and often complex transactions falling in the inventory management process category. While the actual purchasing of finished goods or raw materials inventories is included in the purchasing process, the inventory management process for a manufacturer includes the cost accounting transactions to accumulate and allocate costs to inventory. Accounts involved in the inventory management process include: cost of goods sold, raw materials inventory, in-process inventory, finished goods inventory, and various accounts in the product costing system (overhead accounts). Management establishes internal controls to ensure that transactions relating to cost accounting and inventory are appropriately conducted and recorded.

**Revenue Process**. Businesses generate revenue through sales of goods or services to customers, and collect the proceeds of those sales in cash, either immediately or through collections on receivables. Accounts involved in the revenue process (also known as the sales and collection cycle) include the following income statement accounts: sales, sales returns and allowances, and bad debt expense. Balance sheet accounts in the revenue process include: accounts receivable, allowance for uncollectible accounts, and cash. Management establishes internal controls to ensure that sales and collection transactions are appropriately handled and recorded.

**[LO5] Recognize the sets of management assertions that are implicit in a business entity's financial statements.**

A. Management makes explicit and implicit assertions that can be evaluated within three categories: transactions, account balances, and presentation and disclosure. Specific assertions by category are summarized below (Table 2-1):

   1. Assertions about classes of transactions and events for the period include: (a) occurrence, (b) completeness, (c) authorization, (d) accuracy and (e) cutoff and classification.

   2. Assertions about account balances at period end include: (a) existence, (b) rights and obligations, (c) completeness and (d) valuation and allocation.

   3. Assertions about presentation and disclosure include: (a) occurrence, (b) rights and obligations, (c) completeness, (d) classification and understandability and (e) accuracy and valuation.

**[LO6] Understand that auditing standards are established by the AICPA's Auditing Standards Board (ASB) for private entities, and by the Public Company Accounting Oversight Board (PCAOB) for public companies.**

A. Prior to the passage of the Sarbanes-Oxley Act (2002), establishing auditing standards for all financial statements audits was the responsibility of the Auditing Standards Board (ASB), a committee of the American Institute of CPAs (AICPA). The Act legally transferred responsibility and authority to set auditing standards for public company audits to the PCAOB, which is overseen by the SEC. Thus, auditors of public companies are regulated. Public accounting firms that audit public companies are required to perform these audits in accordance with the auditing standards established by the PCAOB. Firms that audit non-public companies are required to comply with the standards established by the ASB. AICPA's ASB

ASB- Auditing Standard Board

**[LO7] Be familiar with the 10 "generally accepted auditing standards" (GAAS).**

A. The ASB first issued what are known as the ten generally accepted auditing standards (GAAS) in 1947. Because the PCAOB adopted these standards as of April 2003, the PCAOB now also refers to them as "the standards of the PCAOB." The GAAS are composed of three categories of standards: (1) three general standards, (2) three standards of fieldwork and (3) four standards of reporting (Table 2-2).

B. **The general standards** are concerned with the auditor's qualifications and quality of work. The three general standards include:

   1. The audit is to be performed by a person or persons having adequate technical training and proficiency as an auditor.

2. In all matters relating to the assignment, independence in mental attitude is to be maintained by the auditor or auditors.

3. Due professional care is to be exercised in the planning and performance of the audit and the preparation of the report.

C. **The standards of fieldwork** relate to the actual conduct of the audit. These standards provide the conceptual background for the audit process. The three standards of fieldwork include:

1. The work is to be adequately planned and assistants, if any, are to be properly supervised.

2. A sufficient understanding of internal control is to be obtained to plan the audit and to determine the nature, timing, and extent of tests to be performed.

3. Sufficient, competent evidential matter is to be obtained through inspection, observation, inquiries, and confirmations to afford a reasonable basis for an opinion regarding the financial statements under audit.

D. **The standards of reporting** relate to the issues that must be considered before rendering the audit report. They include:

1. The report shall state whether the financial statements are presented in accordance with generally accepted accounting principles.

2. The report shall identify those circumstances in which such principles have not been consistently observed in the current period in relation to the preceding period.

3. Informative disclosures in the financial statements are to be regarded as reasonably adequate unless otherwise stated in the report.

4. The report shall contain either an expression of opinion regarding the financial statements, taken as a whole, or an assertion to the effect that an opinion cannot be expressed. When an overall opinion cannot be expressed, the reasons therefore should be stated. In all cases where an auditor's name is associated with financial statements, the report should contain a clear-cut indication of the character of the auditor's work, if any, and the degree of responsibility the auditor is taking.

**[LO8] Understand the nature of the Statements on Auditing Standards (SAS) as interpretations of the 10 GAAS.**

A. Statements on Auditing Standards (SAS) are issued by the Auditing Standards Board and are considered interpretations of GAAS. The SAS receive their authority from Rule 202 of the AICPA's Code of Professional Conduct. SAS are classified by two numbering categories: SAS and AU numbers ("AU" for Auditing Standards). The SAS numbering applies to the order in which the standards were issued by the ASB and are thus chronological. The SAS are then reorganized by topical content. The AU numbering follows a codification scheme organized by the ten GAAS. Note that the GAAS and the SAS are considered to be minimum standards of performance for auditors.

**[LO9] Be aware that the PCAOB adopted the ASB's SAS on an interim basis and is now issuing its own Auditing Standards (AS) that apply to the audits of public companies.**

A. The PCAOB has adopted, on an interim basis, the ASB's Statements on Auditing Standards as constituted as of April 2003. Standards issued by the PCAOB are called "Auditing Standards" (AS). Remember that the standards issued by the PCAOB must be used when auditing public companies. A major complication for auditors in the future will be the development of two different sets of auditing standards as the PCAOB standards diverge from those it adopted from the ASB.

**[LO10] Understand that auditing is a profession that places a premium on ethical behavior and that is governed by a Code of Professional Conduct.**

A. **Ethics** refers to a system or code of conduct based on moral duties and obligations that indicates how we should behave. Ethical behavior and independence on the part of the auditor are vital to the audit function. The demand for auditing arose from the need for a competent, independent person to monitor the contractual arrangements between the principal and agent. If an auditor is either incompetent or lacks independence, the parties to the contract will place little or no value on the service provided.

B. **Professionalism** refers to the conduct, aims, or qualities that characterize or mark a profession or professional person. All professions (medicine, law and accounting) operate under some type of code of ethics or code of conduct. The 10 GAAS and the AICPA Code of Professional Conduct establish acceptable behavior for auditors. The Code of Professional Conduct applies to all auditors, including those auditing public companies. The Code of Professional Conduct was adopted by the PCAOB on an interim basis.

**[LO11] Know that management is primarily responsible for the entity's financial statements and understand the auditor's responsibility for detecting errors, material fraud, and illegal acts.**

A. Many readers of financial statements believe that auditors are ultimately responsible for the financial statements or that auditors have a responsibility to detect all errors, fraud, and illegal acts. This is simply not true. The financial statements are the responsibility of management and the auditor's responsibility is to express an opinion on the financial statements. The auditor is responsible to plan and perform the audit in order to obtain reasonable assurance about whether the financial statements are free of material misstatement, whether caused by error, fraud and/or illegal acts. It is possible that an auditor could conduct an audit in accordance with GAAS, and issue an unqualified opinion, and the financial statement might still contain material misstatements. Professional skepticism requires that the auditor objectively evaluate audit evidence. The auditor must exercise due professional care, or he or she can be held liable for civil damages and even criminal penalties. *Auditor exercise professional skepticism which is an attitude includes a questioning mind and a critical assessment of audit evidence.*

B. The Sarbanes-Oxley Act (2002) requires that CEOs and CFOs assume explicit responsibility for their company's financial statements by "certifying" among other things, that they are responsible for establishing and maintaining internal controls, and that the financial statements are fairly presented.

**[LO12] Understand the organization and composition of public accounting firms.**

A. Public accounting firms range in size from firms with a single proprietor to firms with thousands of owners (or partners) and thousands of professional and administrative staff employees. Public accounting firms are categorized by size. Public accounting firms are organized as proprietorships, general or limited liability partnerships, or corporations.

B. The largest firms are the "Big 4" public accounting firms: Deloitte, Ernst & Young, KPMG, and PricewaterhouseCoopers. These large international organizations have annual global revenues ranging from $16 billion to over $20 billion. As a group, the Big 4 audit about 80 percent of all publicly traded companies in the U.S. and over 90 percent of publicly traded companies with annual sales greater than $1 million. There are several national firms with international affiliations. These include such firms as Grant Thorton, RSM McGladrey and BDO Seidman. These firms provide audit, tax, and accounting services, generally to smaller organizations (Figure 2-2).

C. Audits are usually conducted by teams of auditors. The typical audit team is composed of, in order of authority, a partner, a manager, one or two seniors, and several staff members. Large international company audit teams are made up of several partners and managers and many seniors and staff. A summary of selected duties of audit team members is presented in Table 2-3.

D. Accounting firms offer audit, attest and assurance services. In addition, public accounting firms perform three other broad categories of service: (1) tax services, (2) management advisory services and (3) accounting and review services.

## [LO13] Be familiar with the various services offered by assurance providers.

A. Opportunities where auditors can provide auditing, attest, or assurance services arise from the need for management to be accountable to employees, shareholders, customers, and communities.

B. In additional to the financial statement audit, there are four major types of audits. These types of audits can be performed by public accounting firms or by other types of auditors such as internal or governmental auditors. They are: (1) internal control audits, (2) compliance audits, (3) operational audits and (4) forensic audits.

C. Auditors can provide numerous types of attest services. Two examples include: (1) reporting on internal control and (2) financial forecasts and projections.

D. Auditors can provide three general types of assurance services. They are: (1) risk assessment, (2) performance measurement and (3) information system reliability and e-commerce.

In addition to the audit, attest, and assurance services discussed in this chapter, public accounting firms perform three other broad categories of services – (1) tax preparation and planning services; (2) management advisory services; and (3) accounting and review services. Note that the Sarbanes-Oxley Act prohibited external auditors from providing most forms of nonaudit assurance and consulting work to a public company that is also a financial statement audit client. Assurance services provided by CPAs are governed by either the attest or consulting standards.

## [LO14] Be familiar with the different types of auditors.

A. A number of different types of auditors can be identified, but they can all be classified under four headings: external auditors, internal auditors, government auditors, and forensic auditors. One important requirement for each type of auditor is independence, in some form, from the entity being audited. A discussion about each type of auditor is presented in the textbook.

**[LO15] Identify and be familiar with the major organizations that affect the public accounting profession's environment.**

    A.  A number of organizations affect the practice of auditing by independent auditors. Figure 2-3 presents a summary of five organizations that affect the financial statement audit. They include:

          1.  American Institute of Certified Public Accountants (AICPA).
          2.  Securities and Exchange Commission (SEC).
          3.  Public Company Accounting Oversight Board (PCAOB).
          4.  Financial Accounting Standards Board (FASB).
          5.  Governmental Accounting Standards Board (GASB).

# CHAPTER 2: SELF-ASSESSMENT

## Part I: True or False Questions

[LO1] __T__ 1. Auditing failures led to the passage of the Sarbanes-Oxley Act (2002).

[LO2] __T__ 2. The primary context with which an auditor is concerned with is the client's industry or business.

[LO3] __F__ 3. The audit committee includes senior executives of the organization.

[LO4] __T__ 4. A financial statement audit is based on the five basic processes or cycles.

[LO4] __F__ 5. One of the five basic processes includes the warehousing cycle.

[LO5] __T__ 6. Audit procedures are chosen based on the assertions being tested.

[LO6] __F__ 7. PCAOB auditing standards must be followed on all financial audits.

[LO7] __T__ 8. A financial statement audit must be conducted based on GAAP.

[LO7] __T__ 9. Generally, the financial statements must be prepared based on GAAP.

[LO7] __T__ 10. PCAOB auditing standards must be followed on all financial audits of public companies.

## Part II: Multiple Choice Questions

[LO1] 1. An "integrated audit" includes:
   a. A special audit related to management fraud.
   b. A financial statement audit and a special audit related to management fraud.
   c. A financial statement audit and an audit of internal control over financial reporting.
   d. A special audit related to management fraud and an audit of internal control over financial reporting.

[LO3] 2. Which of the following best describes the levels of responsibility between management and the board of directors?
   a. Management reports to the board of directors.
   b. Both groups hold the same level of responsibility.
   c. The board of directors reports to management.
   d. Both groups report directly to the shareholders.

[LO5] 3. Which assertions may be tested for the "account balances at period end" category?
   a. Existence, accuracy, rights and obligations, completeness.
   b. Existence, rights and obligations, completeness, valuation and allocation.
   c. Occurrence, rights and obligations, completeness, valuation and allocation.
   d. Existence, rights and obligation, completeness, accuracy and valuation.

[LO5]  4.  Which assertions may be tested for the "transactions and events for the period" category?
   a.  Existence, completeness, rights and obligations, accuracy.
   b.  Occurrence, completeness, rights and obligations, accuracy.
   c.  Occurrence, completeness, authorization, accuracy, cutoff and classification.
   d.  Existence, completeness, accuracy, cutoff and classification.

[LO5]  5.  Which assertions may be tested for the "presentation and disclosure" category?
   a.  Occurrence, rights and obligations, cutoff and classification, completeness.
   b.  Occurrence, rights and obligations, existence, accuracy, cutoff and classification.
   c.  Occurrence, completeness, classification and understandability, cutoff and classification.
   d.  Occurrence, rights and obligations, completeness, accuracy and valuation.

[LO7]  6.  The auditor must be independent of the audit client unless:
   a.  The lack of independence does not influence his or her professional judgment.
   b.  Both parties agree that the independence issue is not a problem.
   c.  The lack of independence is insignificant.
   d.  None of the above because the auditor cannot lack independence.

[LO7]  7.  The three general standards are concerned with:
   a.  Adequate training and proficiency of the auditor, proper planning and supervision, and due professional care.
   b.  Adequate training and independence.
   c.  Due professional care.
   d.  Both b and c.

[LO7]  8.  The three standards of fieldwork are concerned with:
   a.  Planning and supervision and understanding the client's internal control system.
   b.  Obtaining sufficient, competent evidence to render an opinion.
   c.  Adequate training to understand the client's internal controls system.
   d.  Both a and b.

[LO7]  9.  The four standards of reporting are concerned with:
   a.  The presentation of the financial statements based on GAAS.
   b.  The presentation of the financial statements based on GAAP.
   c.  Whether principles are consistently applied, whether all informative disclosures have been made and the degree of responsibility the auditor is taking.
   d.  Both b and c.

[LO11] 10.  Who bears ultimate responsibility for the financial statements?
   a.  Management of the organization and the external auditor that audits the statements.
   b.  Management and the shareholders of the organization.
   c.  The external auditor that audits the statements.
   d.  Management of the organization.

## Part III: Short Essay Questions

[LO4] The audit function is broken down into five processes or cycles. Identify these processes and the accounts used to record transactions for each of the cycles.

[LO6] What auditing standards are used to conduct an audit for a privately-held corporation? What auditing standards are used to conduct an audit for a publicly held-and-traded corporation?

[LO11] Who is primarily responsible for the entity's financial statements and what is the auditor's responsibility for detecting errors, material fraud, and illegal acts.

## Part IV: Crossword Puzzle – Chapter 2 [LO ALL]

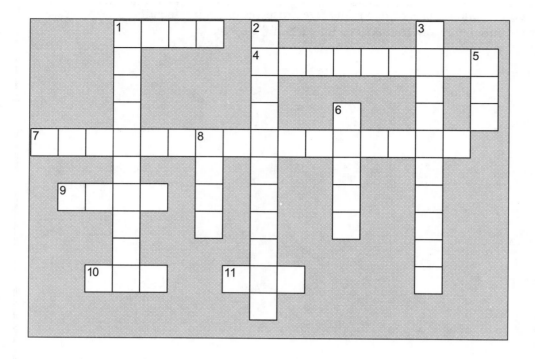

### Across

1     An abbreviation for the broad statements for conducting a financial statement audit.
4     These are established and implemented by management.
7     Individuals elected by shareholders to oversee the executive management of an entity (three words).
9     An abbreviation for financial reporting standards.
10    The number of general statements which relate to the conduct of a financial statement audit for a nonpublic company.
11    The federal agency responsible for overseeing the PCAOB.

### Down

1     One part of the oversight mechanism to safeguard assets.
2     Auditors are _____ !
3     Expressed or implied representations made by management about the financial statements.
5     An abbreviation for the interpretations of GAAS that are issued by the AICPA Auditing Standards Board.
6     An abbreviation for the organization that sets auditing standards for public entities.
8     The body that promulgates financial accounting and reporting guidelines.

**Part V: Townsend Office Supplies and Equipment [LO ALL]**

| Chapter 2 |
| --- |
| **Chapter 2** <br> **Townsend Office Supplies and Equipment** |
| As audit manager for the Townsend engagement, which standards should you use to conduct the company's financial statement audit for 2007? Provide a detailed explanation to support your response. <br><br> As audit manager, you have determined that Townsend's inventory is a material account. Using the information provided to you about Townsend and what you have learned thus far about a financial statement audit, discuss the issues that are relevant as you preplan this engagement. Identify the specific assertions that should be considered for each of the three categories. |

# CHAPTER 2: SELF-ASSESSMENT SOLUTIONS

## Part I: True or False Questions

[LO1] **True** 1.  Auditing failures led to the passage of the Sarbanes-Oxley Act (2002).

[LO2] **True** 2.  The primary context with which an auditor is concerned with is the client's industry or business.

[LO3] **False** 3.  The audit committee includes senior executives of the organization.

[LO4] **True** 4.  A financial statement audit is based on the five basic processes or cycles.

[LO4] **False** 5.  One of the five basic processes includes the warehousing cycle.

[LO5] **True** 6.  Audit procedures are chosen based on the assertions being tested.

[LO6] **False** 7.  PCAOB auditing standards must be followed on all financial audits.

[LO7] **False** 8.  A financial statement audit must be conducted based on GAAP.

[LO7] **True** 9.  Generally, the financial statements must be prepared based on GAAP.

[LO7] **True** 10.  PCAOB auditing standards must be followed on all financial audits of public companies.

## Part II: Multiple Choice Questions

[LO1]  1.  An "integrated audit" includes:
   a.  A special audit related to management fraud.
   b.  A financial statement audit and a special audit related to management fraud.
   **c.  A financial statement audit and an audit of internal control over financial reporting.**
   d.  A special audit related to management fraud and an audit of internal control over financial reporting.

[LO3]  2.  Which of the following best describes the levels of responsibility between management and the board of directors?
   **a.  Management reports to the board of directors.**
   b.  Both groups hold the same level of responsibility.
   c.  The board of directors reports to management.
   d.  Both groups report directly to the shareholders.

[LO5]  3.  Which assertions may be tested for the "account balances at period end" category?
   a.  Existence, accuracy, rights and obligations, completeness.
   **b.  Existence, rights and obligations, completeness, valuation and allocation.**
   c.  Occurrence, rights and obligations, completeness, valuation and allocation.
   d.  Existence, rights and obligation, completeness, accuracy and valuation.

[LO5]  4.  Which assertions may be tested for the "transactions and events for the period" category?
   a.  Existence, completeness, rights and obligations, accuracy.
   b.  Occurrence, completeness, rights and obligations, accuracy.
   **c.  Occurrence, completeness, authorization, accuracy, cutoff and classification.**
   d.  Existence, completeness, accuracy, cutoff and classification.

[LO5]  5.  Which assertions may be tested for the "presentation and disclosure" category?
   a.  Occurrence, rights and obligations, cutoff and classification, completeness.
   b.  Occurrence, rights and obligations, existence, accuracy, cutoff and classification.
   c.  Occurrence, completeness, classification and understandability, cutoff and classification.
   **d.  Occurrence, rights and obligations, completeness, accuracy and valuation.**

[LO7]  6.  The auditor must be independent of the audit client unless:
   a.  The lack of independence does not influence his or her professional judgment.
   b.  Both parties agree that the independence issue is not a problem.
   c.  The lack of independence is insignificant.
   **d.  None of the above because the auditor cannot lack independence.**

[LO7]  7.  The three general standards are concerned with:
   a.  Adequate training and proficiency of the auditor, proper planning and supervision, and due professional care.
   b.  Adequate training and independence.
   c.  Due professional care.
   **d.  Both b and c.**

[LO7]  8.  The three standards of fieldwork are concerned with:
   a.  Planning and supervision and understanding the client's internal control system.
   b.  Obtaining sufficient, competent evidence to render an opinion.
   c.  Adequate training to understand the client's internal controls system.
   **d.  Both a and b.**

[LO7]  9.  The four standards of reporting are concerned with:
   a.  The presentation of the financial statements based on GAAS.
   b.  The presentation of the financial statements based on GAAP.
   c.  Whether principles are consistently applied, whether all informative disclosures have been made and the degree of responsibility the auditor is taking.
   **d.  Both b and c.**

[LO11] 10.  Who bears ultimate responsibility for the financial statements?
   a.  Management of the organization and the external auditor that audits the statements.
   b.  Management and the shareholders of the organization.
   c.  The external auditor that audits the statements.
   **d.  Management of the organization.**

## Part III: Short Essay Questions

[LO4] The audit function is broken down into five processes or cycles. Identify these processes and the accounts used to record transactions for each of the cycles.

**The audit function includes: (1) financing cycle, (2) the purchasing cycle, (3) the human resources cycle, (4) the inventory cycle and (5) the revenue cycle. The accounts used to record transactions for each of the cycles include:**

**Financing Cycle – The income statement accounts include: depreciation expense, gains and losses on sales of long-term assets, interest income and interest expense. Balance sheet accounts include: long-term debt and long-term assets accounts, and owners' equity accounts.**

**Purchasing Cycle – Income statement accounts include: cost of goods sold or purchases, purchase returns and allowances and various expense accounts. Balance sheet accounts include: accounts payable, inventory, cash and various asset accounts.**

**Human Resources Cycle – Income statement accounts include: direct and indirect labor expense and various payroll-related expense accounts. Balance sheet accounts include: wages and salaries payable, inventory, cash and various other payroll-related liability accounts.**

**Inventory Cycle – The income statement account is the cost of goods sold. Balance sheet accounts include: raw materials inventory, in-process inventory, finished goods inventory, and various accounts involved in product costing systems (overhead accounts).**

**Revenue Cycle – Income statement accounts include sales, sales returns and allowances, and bad-debt expense. Balance sheet accounts include accounts receivable, allowance for uncollectible accounts and cash.**

[LO6] What auditing standards are used to conduct an audit for a privately-held corporation? What auditing standards are used to conduct an audit for a publicly held-and-traded corporation?

**Auditing standards developed by the Auditing Standards Board are used to conduct an audit for a privately-held corporation. This includes the ten generally accepted auditing standards (GAAS) and the Statements on Auditing Standards (SAS). Auditing standards developed by the Public Company Accounting Oversight Board (PCAOB) must be used to conduct an audit for a publicly held-and-traded corporation.**

[LO11] Who is primarily responsible for the entity's financial statements and what is the auditor's responsibility for detecting errors, material fraud, and illegal acts.

**The financial statements are the responsibility of management and the auditor's responsibility is to express an opinion on the financial statements. The auditor is responsible to plan and perform the audit in order to obtain reasonable assurance about whether the financial statements are free of material misstatement, whether caused by error, fraud and/or illegal acts. It is possible that an auditor could conduct an audit in accordance with GAAS, and issue an unqualified opinion, and the financial statement might still contain material misstatements. Professional skepticism requires that the auditor objectively evaluate audit evidence. The auditor must exercise due professional care, or he or she can be held liable for civil damages and even criminal penalties. The Sarbanes-Oxley Act (2002) requires that CEOs and CFOs assume explicit responsibility for their company's financial statements by "certifying" among other things, that they are responsible for establishing and maintaining internal controls, and that the financial statements are fairly presented.**

## Part IV: Crossword Puzzle – Chapter 2 Solution [LO ALL]

```
 1                        2                                  3
 G  A  A  S              O                                  A
 O                    4  P  R  O  C  E  S  S  E          5  S
 V                       I                     S            A
 E                       N           6  P      S            S
 7                    8                                     
 B  O  A  R  D  O  F  D  I  R  E  C  T  O  R  S
    N                 A  O           A         T
 9  G  A  A  P        S  N           O         I
    N                 B  A           B         O
    C                    T                     N
10  T  E  N         11  S  E  C                S
                        D
```

### Across

| | |
|---|---|
| 1 | An abbreviation for the broad statements for conducting a financial statement audit. |
| 4 | These are established and implemented by management. |
| 7 | Individuals elected by shareholders to oversee the executive management of an entity (three words). |
| 9 | An abbreviation for financial reporting standards. |
| 10 | The number of general statements which relate to the conduct of a financial statement audit for a nonpublic company. |
| 11 | The federal agency responsible for overseeing the PCAOB. |

### Down

| | |
|---|---|
| 1 | One part of the oversight mechanism to safeguard assets. |
| 2 | Auditors are _____ ! |
| 3 | Expressed or implied representations made by management about the financial statements. |
| 5 | An abbreviation for the interpretations of GAAS that are issued by the AICPA Auditing Standards Board. |
| 6 | An abbreviation for the organization that sets auditing standards for public entities. |
| 8 | The body that promulgates financial accounting and reporting guidelines. |

| **Chapter 2** |
| :---: |
| **Townsend Office Supplies and Equipment** |

As audit manager for the Townsend engagement, which standards should you use to conduct the company's financial statement audit for 2007? Provide a detailed explanation to support your response.

As the audit manager, you have determined that Townsend's inventory is a material account. Using the information provided to you about Townsend and what you have learned thus far about a financial statement audit, discuss the issues that are relevant as you preplan this engagement. Identify the specific assertions that should be considered for each of the three categories.

**Because the client, Townsend Office Supplies and Equipment, is a privately-held corporation, the Auditing Standards Board's guidelines will be used to conduct the audit. These guidelines include the ten generally accepted auditing standards (GAAS) and the Statements on Auditing Standards (SAS). Barbara Townsend has indicated that she hopes to sell Townsend's stock on the New York Stock Exchange by 2010, at which time, the PCAOB Auditing Standards would be required for the audit.**

**The fact that Townsend's inventory is a material account increases the risk associated with any assertions being made about inventory. As a retail business, Townsend processes its inventory transactions using the purchasing cycle. The gross method is used to record inventory purchases and purchase returns and allowances. During past engagements, you determined that the inventory and accounting personnel have been with the company for several years and that these employees are highly skilled and perform their responsibilities appropriately. There have been no changes in the personnel, so these facts support a lower overall risk.**

**The assertions about the "classes of transactions and events for the period" include: (1) occurrence, (2) completeness, (3) authorization, (4) accuracy and (5) cutoff and classification.**

**The assertions about the "account balances at period end" include: (1) existence, (2) rights and obligations, (3) completeness and (4) valuation and allocation.**

**The assertions about "presentation and disclosure" include: (1) occurrence, (2) rights and obligations, (3) completeness, (4) classification and understandability and (5) accuracy and valuation.**

# Risk Assessment and Materiality

## KEY THOUGHT

The auditor has a responsibility to plan and perform the audit to obtain reasonable assurance about whether the financial statements are free of material misstatement, whether caused by error or fraud. Because of the nature of audit evidence and the characteristics of fraud, the auditor is able to obtain reasonable, but not absolute, assurance that material misstatements are detected [Auditing Standards Board (AU 110.02)].

## CHAPTER SUMMARY          *Audit risk ↓ is good*

**[LO1] Understand the concept of audit risk.**

A.  Risk is the first concept that underlies the audit process. An auditor engaged to perform a financial statement audit faces two types of risk: audit risk and engagement risk. Audit risk is the risk that the auditor may unknowingly fail to appropriately modify the opinion on financial statements that are materially misstated. Engagement risk is the auditor's exposure to loss or injury to professional practice from litigation, adverse publicity, or other events arising in connection with financial statements audited and reported on.

B.  The auditor should perform the audit to reduce audit risk to a level appropriate for expressing an opinion on the financial statements. In doing so, the auditor needs to consider audit risk at the financial statement level (pervasively) and at the account balance or class of transactions level.

C.  In considering audit risk at the overall financial statement level, the auditor considers risks of material misstatement that relate pervasively to the financial statements and potentially affect many assertions. Such risks often relate to the entity's control environment and may be relevant to the auditor's consideration of the risks of material misstatement arising from fraud (management override of internal control).

D.  The auditor also considers audit risk at the individual account balance or class of transactions level because such consideration directly assists the auditor to plan the appropriate audit procedures.

E.  Like audit risk, the auditor must consider engagement risk. Engagement risk relates to an auditor's exposure to financial loss and damage to his or her professional reputation. For example, an auditor may conduct an audit in accordance with GAAS (or PCAOB auditing standards for public companies) and still be sued by the client or a third party. Even if the auditor wins the lawsuit, his or her professional reputation may be damaged in the process by the negative publicity.

F.  While engagement risk cannot be directly controlled by the auditor, some control can be exercised through the careful acceptance and continuance of clients. Audit risk, on the other hand, can be directly controlled by the scope (nature, timing and extent of audit procedures) of the auditor's work.

**[LO2] Learn the form and components of the audit risk model.**

A.  Auditing standards do not provide specific guidance on what is an acceptable level of audit risk, but auditors use the audit risk model as a framework for assessing risks.

B.  The determination of audit risk and the use of the audit risk model involve professional judgment on the part of the auditor. Auditors use the audit risk model to determine the scope of auditing procedures for a particular account balance or class of transactions level. The model can be specified as:

*Client risk — no control*

$$AR = IR \times CR \times DR$$

where

AR = Audit risk (the risk that the auditor may fail to modify the opinion on materially misstated financial statements)

IR = Inherent risk (the susceptibility of an assertion to material misstatements, assuming no related controls)

CR = Control risk (the risk that material misstatements that could occur in an assertion will not be prevented or detected on a timely basis by the internal controls)

DR = Detection risk (the risk that the auditor will not detect a material misstatement that exists in an assertion)

Note that detection risk can be divided further into analytical procedures risk and substantive tests of details risk. Analytical procedures risk is the risk that substantive analytical procedures and other relevant substantive procedures will fail to detect material misstatements, while tests of details risk is the allowable risk for failing to detect a material misstatement that is not detected by internal controls or analytical procedures and other relevant substantive procedures. In discussion of the audit risk model, detection risk will not be divided for ease of presentation.

C.  Detection risk results from two uncertainties that are a function of the effectiveness of an audit procedure and of its application by the auditor. The first uncertainty is called sampling risk. Because the auditor examines only a subset of the population, the sample may not represent the population, and the auditor may draw the wrong conclusion on the fairness of the account balance. The second uncertainty is called nonsampling risk and can occur because the auditor used an inappropriate audit procedure, failed to detect a misstatement when applying an appropriate audit procedures, or misinterpreted the audit results. Nonsampling risk can be reduced to a negligible level through adequate planning, proper assignment of audit staff, supervision and review of the audit work performed, and supervision and conduct of a firm's audit practice in accordance with appropriate quality control standards.

D. At the account balance or class of transaction level, audit risk consists of:

1. The risk that the balance or class and related assertions contain misstatements that could be material to the financial statements when aggregated with misstatements in other balances or classes (inherent risk and control risk).

2. The risk that the auditor will not detect such misstatements (detection risk).

E. Inherent risk and control risk differ from detection risk. Inherent risk and control risk are functions of the entity and its environment, so the auditor has little or no control over these risks. Sometimes the combination of these two risks is referred to as auditee risk.

F. Detection risk can be controlled by the auditor through the scope of the audit procedures performed. Detection risk has an inverse relationship to inherent risk and control risk. For example, if inherent risk and control risk are judged to be high, the auditor sets a lower level of detection risk in order to meet the planned level of audit risk.

G. The auditor's assessment of audit risk and its component risks (IR, CR and DR) is a matter of professional judgment. At the completion of the audit, the actual level of audit risk is not known with certainty by the auditor. If the auditor assesses the achieved audit risk as being less than or equal to the planned level of audit risk, an unqualified report can be issued. If the assessment of the achieved level of audit risk is greater than the planned level, the auditor should either conduct additional audit work or qualify the audit report.

**[LO3] Understand how to use the audit risk model.**

A. The audit risk model expresses the general relationship of audit risk and the components of the model. The model is not intended to be a mathematical formula including all factors that may influence the assessment of audit risk, but auditors find the model useful when planning appropriate risk levels for audit procedures to reduce the desired audit risk to an appropriate level (Figure 3-1).

B. The discussion that follows concerning the model is limited to its use as an audit planning tool. Three steps are involved in the use of the model at the account balance or class of transaction level:

1. Setting a planned level of audit risk.
2. Assessing inherent risk and control risk.
3. Solving the audit risk equation for the appropriate level of detection risk.

After the planned level of audit risk has been established (Step 1) and the inherent risk and control risk has been assessed (Step 2), the auditor determines the appropriate level of detection risk by solving the audit risk model as shown below (Step 3):

$$DR = \frac{AR}{IR \times CR}$$

The auditor uses this level of detection risk to design the audit procedures that will reduce audit risk to an acceptable level. However, the auditor should not rely completely on his or her assessments of inherent risk and control risk to the exclusion of performing substantive tests of account balances, where material misstatement could exist. Consider the example of the computation of detection risk that was provided in your textbook:

Suppose that the auditor has determined that the planned audit risk for the accounts receivable balance can be set at 0.05 based on the significance of the account to the financial statements. By establishing such a low level of audit risk, the auditor is reducing the possibility that the account may contain a material misstatement. Assume further that the auditor assesses inherent risk for accounts receivable to be 0.80. After evaluating the internal control over the revenue process, the auditor assesses control risk to be 0.60. Substituting the values for AR, IR and CR into the equation indicates that the auditor should set detection risk at approximately 0.10 [DR = 0.05/(0.80 × 0.60)] for testing the accounts receivable balance. Thus, the auditor establishes the scope of the audit for accounts receivable so that there is only a 10 percent chance that a material misstatement, if present, is not detected.

An auditor may find it more appropriate to substitute qualitative terms to utilize the risk model. For example, audit risk might be classified into three categories, very low, low and moderate. It is unlikely that an audit planned in accordance with GAAS (or PCAOB standards for public company audits) would consider a high level of audit risk. The remaining component of the model may be classified into categories such as low, moderate or high. This method of using the model is identical to that followed when using numerical values. Audit risk would be set using one of the category choices. Similarly, the auditor would assess the appropriate category for inherent and control risk.

## [LO4] Learn the limitations of the audit risk model.

A. Auditing standards provide for the use of the audit risk model as a way of ensuring that the risk of issuing materially misstated financial statements is kept to an acceptably low level. However, this model has a number of limitations that must be considered by auditors and their firms.

B. The audit risk model is a planning tool. If an auditor uses the model to revise an audit plan or to evaluate audit results, the actual level of audit risk may be greater than the audit risk indicated by the formula. This may occur because the model assumes that the components (IR, CR and DR) are independent of one another as indicated by the multiplicative form of the model. However, in practice, the risk of a material misstatement (IR) occurring may be a function of the client's internal controls (CR). Thus, inherent risk may depend on control risk. In practice, some public accounting firms make a combined risk assessment for IR and CR (auditee risk).

C. Other limitations may also be present. For example, because the auditor assesses inherent risk and control risk, such assessments may be higher or lower than the actual inherent risk and control risk that exist for the client. Such differences can affect the determination of detection risk and the achieved audit risk. The audit risk model also does not specifically consider the possibility of auditor error.

**[LO5] Understand the auditor's risk assessment process.**

A. Strategies are operational approaches used to achieve objectives. Business risks are threats to management's ability to execute its strategies and to achieve its objectives. Business activities, strategies, objectives and the business environment are ever changing and the dynamic and complex nature of business cause business risks. Management is responsible for identifying these risks and responding to them.

B. Business risk is broader than the risk of materially misstated financial statements, but most business risks have the potential to affect the financial statements either immediately or in the long run. Auditors need to identify business risks and understand the potential misstatements that may result.

C. The audit process starts by obtaining and supporting an understanding of the entity and its environment, including internal control. Obtaining an understanding of the entity and its environment is a continuous, dynamic process of gathering, updating and analyzing information throughout the audit. The goal of this step is to assess the business risks faced by the entity. Based on the auditor's understanding of the entity's business risks and how those risks are controlled or not controlled, the auditor assess the risk of material misstatement at the assertion level. The auditor's assessment of business risk and the risk of material misstatement (i.e., the auditor's risk assessment process) includes the following steps (Figure 3-2):

   1. Perform risk assessment procedures to obtain an understanding of the entity and its environment, including internal control.

   2. Identify business risks that may result in material misstatements in the financial statements.

   3. Evaluate the entity's responses to those business risks and obtain evidence of their implementation.

   4. Assess the risk of material misstatement at the assertion level and determine the audit procedures that are necessary based on that risk assessment.

D. Business risks include any external and internal factors, pressures, and forces that bear on the entity's ability to survive and be profitable. The auditors understanding of the entity and its environment includes knowledge about:

   1. Industry, regulatory and other external factors.
   2. Nature of the entity.
   3. Objectives and strategies and related business risks
   4. Measurement and review of the entity's financial performance.
   5. Internal control.

E. The auditor obtains an understanding of the entity and its environment by performing the following risk assessment procedures:

   1. Inquires of management and others.
   2. Analytical procedures.
   3. Observation and inspection.

F.  Sources where the auditor can obtain information for developing an understanding of the entity and its environment include (Table 3-5):

1. Cumulative knowledge and experience obtained from prior audits, including the nature and cause of misstatements and accounts affected.

2. Procedures performed in client acceptance and continuance process.

3. Knowledge obtained from performing interim procedures.

4. Consulting, tax and other engagements performed for the entity.

5. Communications with predecessor auditors including review of predecessor auditor working papers.

6. Published annual reports and interim reports to shareholders, if applicable.

7. Discussions with management.

8. Minutes of board of directors and/or audit committee meetings.

9. Entity's business and/or strategic plans, budgets or other documentation.

10. Reports prepared by analysts, banks, underwriters, rating agencies, etc.

11. Individuals knowledgeable about the industry, such as the engagement team members for clients in a similar business or industry.

12. Audit firm-generated industry guidance, databases, and practice aids, where applicable.

13. Government statistics.

14. Economic and financial journals.

15. Industry or trade journals.

16. Client press releases, publications, and brochures.

17. Internal audit reports.

Note that information obtained or derived from sources external to the entity generally can be deemed reliable in the absence of evidence to the contrary. Information obtained from sources within the entity may require a more in-depth assessment of the reliability. Inquiries are an important source of evidence, but they generally provide stronger evidence when integrated with other procedures or similar inquiries made of multiple people.

G.  Entities generally face a broad array of business risks that may affect their operations, compliance with laws and regulations and financial reporting. Examples of conditions and events that may indicate the existence of business risks are:

1. Significant changes in the entity such as large acquisitions, reorganizations or other unusual events.

2.  Significant changes in the industry in which the entity operates.

3.  Significant new products or services or significant new lines of business.

4.  New locations.

5.  Significant changes in the IT environment.

6.  Operations in areas with unstable economies.

7.  High degree of complex regulation.

The auditor should evaluate management's response to identified risks. If the response is adequate, the risk of material misstatement may be reduced, but if the response to the risk is inadequate, the auditor may increase the risk of material misstatement.

**[LO6] Identify the factors that determine the auditor's assessment of the risk of material misstatement.**

A.  To assess the risk of material misstatement, the auditor:

1.  Identify risks by considering the entity and its environment, including controls that relate to the risks, and by considering the classes of transactions and account balances in the financial statements.

2.  Relates the identified risks to what can go wrong at the assertion level.

3.  Considers whether the risks are of a magnitude that could result in a material misstatement of the financial statements.

4.  Considers the likelihood that the risks will result in a material misstatement of the financial statements.

The auditor must determine whether the identified risks of material misstatement relate to specific classes of transactions or account balances and related assertions, or whether they relate more pervasively to the financial statements as a whole and potentially affect many assertions.

B.  A misstatement of the financial statements may consist of any of the following:

1.  The difference between the amount, classification or presentation of a reported financial statement element, account, or item and the amount, classification or presentation that would have been reported under GAAP.

2.  The omission of a financial statement element, account or item.

3.  A financial statement disclosure that is not presented in accordance with GAAP.

4.  The omission of information required to be disclosed in accordance with GAAP.

C. Misstatements can result from error or fraud. The primary distinction between errors and fraud is whether the misstatement was intentional or unintentional. However, it is often difficult to determine intent.

D. Errors are unintentional misstatements or omissions of amounts or disclosures and may involve:

1. Mistakes in gathering or processing data from which statements are prepared.

2. Unreasonable accounting estimates arising from oversight or misinterpretation of facts.

3. Mistakes in the application of accounting principles relating to amount, classification, manner of presentation, or disclosure.

E. Fraud, from the auditor's perspective involves intentional misstatements that can be classified into two types: (1) misstatements arising from fraudulent financial reporting and (2) misstatements arising from misappropriation of assets. Fraudulent financial reporting may involve acts such as:

1. Manipulation, falsification or alteration of accounting records or supporting documents from which financial statements are prepared.

2. Misrepresentation in, or intentional omission from, the financial statements of events, transactions, or other significant information.

3. Intentional misapplication of accounting principles relating to amounts, classification, manner of presentation, or disclosure.

Misstatements arising from misappropriation of assets (sometimes referred to as defalcation) involve the theft of an entity's assets where the defalcation causes the financial statements to be misstated. Examples of misappropriation include:

1. Embezzling cash received.
2. Stealing assets.
3. Causing the entity to pay for goods or services not received.

Note that misappropriation of assets may be accompanied by false or misleading records or documents, possibly created by circumventing controls, and may involve one or more individuals among management, employees, or third parties.

F. Three conditions are generally present when material misstatements due to fraud occur (incentives and pressures, opportunities and attitudes and rationalization):

1. Management or other employees have an incentive or are under pressure that provides a reason to commit fraud.

2. Circumstances exist that provide opportunity for fraud to be carried out.

3. Those involved are able to rationalize committing a fraudulent act. Some individuals possess an attitude, character, or other set of ethical values that allow them to knowingly and intentionally commit a dishonest act. Even honest individuals can commit fraud in an environment where sufficient pressure is being exerted on them. The greater the incentive or pressure, the more likely an individual will be able to rationalize the acceptability of committing fraud.

G. Management has the ability to perpetrate fraud because it is in a position to directly or indirectly manipulate the accounting records and prepare fraudulent financial reports. In most cases, fraudulent financial reporting also involves some management override of controls. Because of the characteristics of fraud, particularly those involving concealment through collusion (withheld, misrepresented or falsified documentation) and the ability of management to override or instruct others to override controls, an auditor may unknowingly rely on fraudulent audit evidence.

H. The fraud risk identification process includes (Figure 3-3):

    1. Sources of information used to identify risks.

        a. Communications among the audit team.
        b. Inquiries of management and others.
        c. Fraud risk factors.
        d. Analytical procedures.
        e. Other information.

    2. Conditions for fraud.

        a. Incentives and pressures.
        b. Opportunities.
        c. Attitudes and rationalization.

    3. Identify risks of material misstatement due to fraud.

**[LO7] Learn how to respond to the results of the risk assessments.**

A. Based on the assessment of the entity's business risks and the risk of material misstatement due to error or fraud, the auditor should decide what responses to take given the risk assessment. The main consideration for the auditor based on the assessed level of the risks of material misstatement is the nature, timing and extent of audit procedures.

B. The auditor should first determine overall responses to address the risks of material misstatement at the financial statement level. The assessment of the risks of material misstatement at the financial statement level is generally affected by the auditor's assessment of the control environment. If the environment is effective, the auditor can have more confidence in internal control and the reliability of audit evidence generated internally within the entity. If the risks of material misstatements are high, the auditor might include assigning more experienced staff or those with special skills or using specialist, providing more supervision, or incorporating additional elements of unpredictability in the selection of further audit procedures to be performed. Additionally, the auditor may decide to perform substantive procedures at period end instead of at an interim date.

C. The auditor has to consider how to respond to the risks of misstatement at the assertion level (Figure 3-4). A distinction is made between high-risk and low-risk assertions. For high-risk assertions, the auditor should consider how material misstatements may occur and design and perform extended audit procedures to specifically address the potential misstatements. Examples of the types of items that may require specific audit procedures include:

    1. Assertions identified with fraud risk factors.
    2. Nonroutine or unsystematically processed transactions.

3. Significant accounting estimates and judgments.
4. Highly complex transactions.
5. Application of new accounting standards.
6. Revenue recognition in certain industries or for certain types of transactions.
7. Industry specific issues.

For low-risk assertions, the auditor may not require procedures of a specific nature. Usually, low-risk assertions relate to routine processing of significant transactions whose characteristics often allow highly automated processing with little or no manual intervention. Such transactions are likely to be: (1) recurring, (2) objectively measurable and (3) processed in a similar way.

D. If the risk factor assessment indicates that fraud might be present, the auditor might respond as follows:

1. Increase professional skepticism by questioning and critically assessing evidence.

2. Assign more experienced auditors who have the knowledge, skill and ability commensurate with the increased risk of the engagement.

3. Consider management's selection and application of significant accounting policies, particularly those related to recognizing revenue, valuing assets or capitalizing versus expensing.

4. Modify the nature, timing, and extent of audit procedures to obtain more reliable evidence and use increased sample sizes or more extensive analytical procedures.

**[LO8] Learn how to evaluate the results of the audit tests.**

A. At the completion of the audit, the auditor should consider whether the accumulated results of audit procedures affect the assessments of the entity's business risks and the risk of material misstatements due to error or fraud. The auditor should aggregate the total uncorrected misstatements that were detected and determine if they cause the financial statements to be materially misstated.

B. If the auditor concludes that the total misstatements cause the financial statements to be materially misstated, the auditor should request management to eliminate the material misstatement. If management does not eliminate the material misstatement, the auditor should issue a qualified (not pervasive) or adverse opinion (pervasive across the financial statements). If, however, the uncorrected total misstatements do not cause the financial statements to be materially misstated, the auditor should issue an unqualified report.

C. If the auditor has determined that the misstatement is or may be the result of fraud, and either has determined that the effect could be material to the financial statements or has been unable to evaluate whether the effect is material, the auditor should:

1. Attempt to obtain audit evidence to determine whether, in fact, material fraud has occurred, and, if so, its effect.

2. Consider the implications for other aspects of the audit.

3. Discuss the matter and the approach to further investigation with an appropriate level of management that is at least one level above those involved in committing the fraud, and with senior management.

4. If appropriate, suggest that the client consult with legal counsel.

If the results of the audit test indicate a significant risk of fraud, the auditor should consider withdrawing from the engagement and communicating the reasons for withdrawal to the audit committee or others with equivalent authority and responsibility.

## [LO9] Understand the documentation requirements for risk assessments and responses.

A. The auditor has extensive documentation requirements for understanding the entity and its environment, the consideration of fraud, and responding to assessed risks. The auditor should document the risk of material misstatement for all material accounts and classes of transactions in terms of the related assertions. The level of risk may be described quantitatively or nonquantitatively (high, medium or low). Exhibit 3-3 illustrates the use of a questionnaire to document the nature of the entity. Other areas that require documentation include the following:

1. The nature and results of the communication among engagement personnel that occurred in planning the audit regarding the risks of material misstatement due to fraud.

2. The steps performed in obtaining knowledge about the entity's business and its environment. The documentation should include:

   a. The risks identified.

   b. An evaluation of management's response to such risks.

   c. The auditor's assessment of the risk of error or fraud after considering the entity's response.

3. The nature, timing, and extent of the procedures performed in response to the risks of material misstatement due to fraud and the results of that work.

4. Fraud risks or other conditions that caused the auditor to believe that additional audit procedures or other responses were required to address such risks or other conditions.

5. The nature of the communications about fraud made to management, the audit committee, and others.

## [LO10] Learn the auditor's communication requirements to management and the audit committee.

A. When the auditor has found evidence that a fraud may exist, that matter should be brought to the attention of an appropriate level of management. Fraud involving senior management and fraud that causes a material misstatement of the financial statements should be reported directly to the audit committee of the board of directors. In addition, the auditor should reach an understanding with the audit committee regarding the expected nature and extent of communications about misappropriations perpetrated by lower-level employees.

B. The disclosure of fraud to parties other than the client's senior management and its audit committee is not part of the auditor's responsibility and ordinarily would be precluded by the auditor's ethical or legal obligations of confidentiality. The auditor should recognize that in the following circumstances a duty to disclose outside the entity may exist:

1. To comply with certain legal and regulatory requirements.

2. To a successor auditor when the successor makes inquires in accordance with AU 315 (Communications between Predecessor and Successor Auditors).

3. In response to a subpoena.

4. To a funding agency or other specified agency in accordance with requirements for the audits of entities that receive governmental financial assistance.

## [LO11] Understand the concept of materiality.

A. The auditor's consideration of materiality on an audit is a matter of professional judgment. Materiality is assessed in terms of the potential effect of a misstatement on decisions made by a reasonable user of the financial statements. This focus arises from the FASB's Statement of Financial Accounting Concepts No. 2, which states:

> **Materiality** is the magnitude of an omission or misstatement of accounting information that, in the light of surrounding circumstances, makes it probable that the judgment of a reasonable person relying on the information would have been changed or influenced by the omission or misstatement.

B. Professional standards do not provide specific guidance on how to assess what is material to a reasonable user. The AICPA and auditing firms have developed policies and procedures to assist auditors in establishing materiality. Note that the auditor will consider both quantitative and qualitative aspects of the engagement.

## [LO12] Identify the steps to applying materiality in an audit.

A. While the policies and procedures of individual auditing firms may differ in some respects, a three-step approach is presented below to provide the reader with a basic framework for understanding the consideration of materiality in an audit (Figure 3-5). Steps 1 and 2 are normally performed early in the engagement as part of planning the audit. Step 3 is performed usually just prior to, or when the auditor evaluates the evidence at the completion of the audit to determine if it supports the fair presentation of the financial statements.

**Step 1 Determine a Materiality Level for the Overall Financial Statement (Planning Materiality).** The first step is to establish a materiality level for the financial statements taken as a whole (planning materiality). Planning materiality is the maximum amount by which the auditor believes the financial statements could be misstated and still not affect the decisions of reasonable users. Materiality, however, is a relative, not an absolute concept. Thus, the relative size of the company being audited affects the preliminary judgment about materiality. In specifying materiality, an auditor should establish a base (or bases) that, when multiplied by a percentage factor, determines the initial quantitative judgment about materiality. The following quantitative bases are used for establishing materiality:

1. Total assets.
2. Total revenues.

3. Net income before taxes.
4. Net income from continuing operations.
5. Gross profit.
6. Average of three years' net income before taxes.

The resulting materiality amount can then be adjusted for any qualitative factors that may be relevant to the engagement (Table 3-12).

Total assets, total revenues, or some form of net income are frequently used by auditors when establishing materiality. When net income before taxes is relatively stable, predictable and representative of the entity's size, a rule of thumb to determine overall financial statement materiality that is commonly used in practice is three to five percent of net income before taxes. In determining where in the range to establish materiality, the auditor would generally use a percentage at the lower end of the range if any of the following factors are present:

1. First-year engagement.
2. Known material weaknesses in controls.
3. Significant management turnover.
4. Unusually high market pressures.
5. Higher than normal fraud risk.
6. Higher than normal risk of bankruptcy in the near future.

This amount is often referred to as planning materiality. Auditors may also decide to use a lower amount because of qualitative factors such as those listed above and to allow for some aggregation of potential misstatements across accounts. The auditor might use an average of the previous year's income or another base if the current year pretax income is not stable, predictable or representative of an entity's size.

**Step 2 Determine tolerable misstatement.** The second step involves determining tolerable misstatement based on planning materiality. Tolerable misstatement is the amount of planning materiality that is allocated to an account or class of transactions. An account balance represents an individual line item on the financial statements, such as accounts receivable or inventory. A class of transactions refers to a type of transaction processed by the client's accounting system, such as revenue or purchase transactions. The purpose of allocating a portion of planning materiality is to plan the scope of audit procedures for the individual account balance or class of transactions. Because of the many factors involved, there is no required or optimal method for allocating materiality to an account balance or class of transactions.

As with overall materiality, there are qualitative factors that must be considered in determining tolerable misstatement. Examples of qualitative factors that the auditor would consider for a given account include: the size and complexity of the account, the importance of changes in the account to key performance indicators, debt covenants, and meeting published forecasts or estimates (see Table 3-12). In conjunction with qualitative factors, common computational benchmarks used in practice to determine tolerable misstatement for an account are up to 50 to 75 percent of planning materiality. These approaches result in an allocation of combined tolerable misstatement that is greater than materiality. Some firms cap the size of combined or aggregated tolerable misstatement to a multiple of materiality. For example, combined tolerable misstatement allocated to accounts can be up to a multiple of 4 times planning materiality. There are a number of reasons why allocating combined tolerable misstatement greater than materiality makes sense from an audit planning perspective, including:

1. Not all accounts will be misstated by the full amount of their tolerable misstatement allocation.

2. Audits of individual accounts are conducted simultaneously. In other words, for all but the smallest of audit clients, the audit team will be made up of several auditors who are testing different accounts at the same time. If accounts were audited sequentially, unadjusted misstatements observed during testing would count against materiality, and theoretically, the auditor could carry the unused portion of materiality to the next account, and so forth.

3. Materiality as a percentage of large accounts such as inventory, accounts receivable, revenues, or plant, property and equipment, is often a very small fraction of the account (often less than 2 percent). By using a tolerable misstatement percentage that is considerably less than materiality, the scope of planned auditor procedures will be sufficiently precise to identify significant misstatements.

4. When deviations or misstatements are identified, the auditors typically perform additional procedures. The actual testing will often achieve a much smaller margin for misstatement than planned tolerable misstatement.

5. Overall financial statement materiality serves as a "safety net." If individual unadjusted misstatements are less than tolerable misstatement, but aggregate to an amount greater than materiality, the auditor cannot accept the financial statements as presented fairly in accordance with GAAP. When this occurs, the client would need to (1) make adjustments to lower the unadjusted misstatements below materiality, (2) the auditor would need to perform more testing, and/or (3) the auditor would issue a qualified or adverse opinion.

Taken together, these points suggest that it would be inefficient for the auditor to simply subdivide materiality proportionally to each account because this would result in unnecessarily low tolerable misstatement levels. The lower the tolerable misstatement is, the more extensive the required audit testing. In the extreme, if tolerable misstatement were very small or zero, the auditor would have to test every transaction in an account.

**Step 3 Evaluate Auditing Findings.** The third step is completed near the end of the audit, when the auditor evaluates all the evidence that has been gathered. Based on the results of the audit procedures conducted, the auditor aggregates misstatements from each account or class of transactions. The aggregate amount includes known and likely misstatements. In evaluating likely misstatements, the auditor should consider the risk of material misstatements in accounts that are subject to estimation (such as inventory obsolescence).

In evaluating the aggregate misstatement, the auditor should consider the effect of misstatements not adjusted in the prior period because they were judged to be immaterial. The auditor compares this aggregate misstatement to the planning materiality.

If the auditor's judgment about materiality at the planning stage (Step 1) was based on the same information available at the evaluation stage (Step 3), materiality for planning and evaluation would be the same. However, the auditor may identify factors or items during the course of the audit that cause a revision to the planning materiality. Thus, planning materiality may differ from the materiality used in evaluating the audit findings. When this occurs, the auditor should carefully document the reasons for revising planning materiality.

When the aggregated misstatements are less than the planning materiality, the auditor can conclude that the financial statements are fairly presented. Conversely, when the aggregated misstatements are greater than the planning materiality, the auditor should request that the client adjust the financial statements. If the client refuses to adjust the financial statements for the likely misstatements, the auditor should issue a qualified or adverse opinion because the financial statements do not present fairly in conformity with GAAP.

**[LO13] Apply the materiality steps to an example (EarthWear).**

A. The three steps for applying materiality are presented using financial information for EarthWear Clothiers (see this example in the textbook).

# CHAPTER 3: SELF-ASSESSMENT

## Part I: True or False Questions

[LO1] _____ 1. Audit risk is the auditor's exposure to loss or injury of his or her reputation from events arising in connection with financial statements audited.

[LO1] _____ 2. Engagement risk is the auditor's exposure to loss or injury of his or her reputation from events arising in connection with financial statements audited.

[LO2] _____ 3. The components of the audit risk model include inherent risk, control risk and detection risk.

[LO2] _____ 4. Inherent risk is the susceptibility of an assertion to material misstatement, assuming no related controls.

[LO2] _____ 5. Professional judgment must be used when evaluating business risk.

[LO2] _____ 6. Audit risk and materiality significantly impact the auditor's evidence decisions.

[LO2] _____ 7. The risk of a material misstatement includes inherent risk and sampling risk.

[LO2] _____ 8. The combination of inherent risk and control risk is referred to as auditee risk.

[LO2] _____ 9. Inherent risk includes sampling risk and nonsampling risk.

[LO11] _____ 10. Materiality is the value of an omission in the financial statements that must be adjusted.

## Part II: Multiple Choice Questions

[LO2] 1. If internal control over sales and cash receipts is excellent, detection risk would be:
    a. Decreased.
    b. Unaffected.
    c. Increased.
    d. Cannot be determined from the information provided.

[LO2] 2. The audit risk model includes all but the following components:
    a. Detection risk.
    b. Engagement risk.
    c. Inherent risk.
    d. Control risk.

[LO2] 3. Inherent risk and control risk are:
    a. Functions of the engagement risk.
    b. Functions of uncertainty.
    c. Functions of the entity and its environment.
    d. Functions of sampling and nonsampling risks.

[LO2]  4.  The audit risk model is used at the account balance or class of transaction level to:
a.  Assess inherent risk and control risk so that detection risk can be determined.
b.  Establish the preliminary judgment about materiality (tolerable misstatement).
c.  Set a planned level of audit risk.
d.  Both a and c.

[LO3]  5.  Planned audit risk for inventory has been set at 0.05. Inherent risk has been set at 0.70 and control risk was assessed to be 0.60. The detection risk will be set at (rounded):
a.  0.15.
b.  0.14.
c.  0.12.
d.  Cannot be computed based on the information provided.

[LO4]  6.  The auditor obtains an understanding of the entity and its environment by performing all of the following assessment procedures except:
a.  Inquires of management and others.
b.  Compute the level of detection risk.
c.  Analytical procedures.
d.  Observation and inspections.

[LO5]  7.  An example of an error is:
a.  Stealing inventory.
b.  An intentional omission of a significant transaction.
c.  A mistake in the application of an accounting principle.
d.  Embezzling cash receipts.

[LO5]  8.  Certain conditions are generally present when fraud occurs, including:
a.  Incentives and pressures.
b.  Opportunities.
c.  Attitudes and rationalization.
d.  All of the above.

[LO12] 9.  The three-step approach for evaluating materiality includes (in correct order):
a.  Determine tolerable misstatement, establish preliminary judgment about materiality and estimate likely misstatements, and compare totals to the preliminary judgment about materiality.
b.  Determine tolerable misstatement, estimate likely misstatements and compare totals to the preliminary judgment about materiality, and establish preliminary judgment about materiality.
c.  Establish a preliminary judgment about materiality, determine tolerable misstatement and estimate likely misstatements, and compare totals to the preliminary judgment about materiality.
d.  Establish a preliminary judgment about materiality, estimate likely misstatements and compare totals to the preliminary judgment about materiality, and determine tolerable misstatements.

[LO12] 10.  When likely misstatements are greater than planned materiality, the auditor should:
a.  Request that the client adjust the financial statements.
b.  Issue unqualified opinion.
c.  Issue a qualified or adverse opinion if client refuses to adjust the statements.
d.  Both a and c.

## Part III: Short Essay Questions

[LO2] Why does an auditor use the audit risk model? Discuss the specifications of the audit risk model and identify the components of the model.

[LO4] Discuss the auditor's basic process for assessing business risk and the risk of material misstatements.

[LO9] Discuss the auditor's responsibilities for communicating with management and the audit committee regarding issues of fraud.

# Part IV: Crossword Puzzle – Chapter 3 [LO ALL]

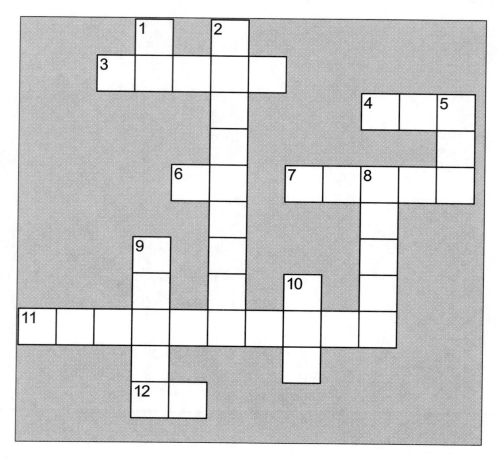

**Across**

| | |
|---|---|
| 3 | An unintentional misstatement or omission of an amount or a disclosure. |
| 4 | An auditor holds this professional designation. |
| 6 | A two-letter abbreviation for the component of the audit risk model that assumes no related controls. |
| 7 | An abbreviation for the body that promulgates auditing standards used for audits of publicly-held companies. |
| 11 | _____ risk is the exposure that an auditor assumes in a financial statement audit. |
| 12 | A two-letter abbreviation for the component of the audit risk model that the auditor will not detect a material misstatement. |

**Down**

| | |
|---|---|
| 1 | A two-letter abbreviation for the component of the audit risk model that a misstatement will not be prevented or detected by controls. |
| 2 | _____ misstatement is the amount of the preliminary judgment about account materiality. |
| 5 | An abbreviation for the AICPA body that promulgates auditing standards used for audits of privately-held companies. |
| 8 | The type of risk that an auditor faces because he or she may fail to modify the opinion on materially misstated financial statements. |
| 9 | An intentional misstatement or omission of an amount or a disclosure. |
| 10 | ____ Performance Indicators. |

**Part V: Townsend Office Supplies and Equipment [LO ALL]**

| Chapter 3 |
| :---: |
| **Townsend Office Supplies and Equipment** |

For audit engagements with less than four years experience, the firm's audit risk policy for a material account is .03. Inventory is considered a material account. The inherent risk has been set at .80 and control risk was assessed at .50. Complete the following: (1) compute detection risk; (2) discuss what detection risk means; (3) identify at least two factors that may help explain the assessed level of inherent risk; and (4) using qualitative terms, classify audit risk (use very low, low, or moderate) and each of the risk components (use low, moderate or high).

# CHAPTER 3: SELF-ASSESSMENT SOLUTIONS

## Part I: True or False Questions

[LO1] **False** 1.   Audit risk is the auditor's exposure to loss or injury of his or her reputation from events arising in connection with financial statements audited.

[LO1] **True** 2.   Engagement risk is the auditor's exposure to loss or injury of his or her reputation from events arising in connection with financial statements audited.

[LO2] **True** 3.   The components of the audit risk model include inherent risk, control risk and detection risk.

[LO2] **True** 4.   Inherent risk is the susceptibility of an assertion to material misstatement, assuming no related controls.

[LO2] **True** 5.   Professional judgment must be used when evaluating business risk.

[LO2] **True** 6.   Audit risk and materiality significantly impact the auditor's evidence decisions.

[LO2] **False** 7.   The risk of a material misstatement includes inherent risk and sampling risk.

[LO2] **True** 8.   The combination of inherent risk and control risk is referred to an auditee risk.

[LO2] **False** 9.   Inherent risk includes sampling risk and nonsampling risk.

[LO11]**False** 10.   Materiality is the value of an omission in the financial statements that must be adjusted.

## Part II: Multiple Choice Questions

[LO2]   1.   If internal control over sales and cash receipts is excellent, detection risk would be:
   a.   Decreased.
   b.   Unaffected.
   **c.   Increased.**
   d.   Cannot be determined from the information provided.

[LO2]   2.   The audit risk model includes all but the following components:
   a.   Detection risk.
   **b.   Engagement risk.**
   c.   Inherent risk.
   d.   Control risk.

[LO2]   3.   Inherent risk and control risk are:
   a.   Functions of the engagement risk.
   b.   Functions of uncertainty.
   **c.   Functions of the entity and its environment.**
   d.   Functions of sampling and nonsampling risks.

[LO2]  4.  The audit risk model is used at the account balance or class of transaction level to:
    a.  Assess inherent risk and control risk so that detection risk can be determined.
    b.  Establish the preliminary judgment about materiality (tolerable misstatement).
    c.  Set a planned level of audit risk.
    **d.  Both a and c.**

[LO3]  5.  Planned audit risk for inventory has been set at 0.05. Inherent risk has been set at 0.70 and control risk was assessed to be 0.60. The detection risk will be set at (rounded):
    a.  0.15.
    b.  0.14.
    **c.  0.12.**
    d.  Cannot be computed based on the information provided.

[LO4]  6.  The auditor obtains an understanding of the entity and its environment by performing all of the following assessment procedures except:
    a.  Inquires of management and others.
    **b.  Compute the level of detection risk.**
    c.  Analytical procedures.
    d.  Observation and inspections.

[LO5]  7.  An example of an error is:
    a.  Stealing inventory.
    b.  An intentional omission of a significant transaction.
    **c.  A mistake in the application of an accounting principle.**
    d.  Embezzling cash receipts.

[LO5]  8.  Certain conditions are generally present when fraud occurs, including:
    a.  Incentives and pressures.
    b.  Opportunities.
    c.  Attitudes and rationalization.
    **d.  All of the above.**

[LO12]  9.  The three-step approach for evaluating materiality includes (in correct order):
    a.  Determine tolerable misstatement, establish preliminary judgment about materiality and estimate likely misstatements, and compare totals to the preliminary judgment about materiality.
    b.  Determine tolerable misstatement, estimate likely misstatements and compare totals to the preliminary judgment about materiality, and establish preliminary judgment about materiality.
    **c.  Establish a preliminary judgment about materiality, determine tolerable misstatement and estimate likely misstatements, and compare totals to the preliminary judgment about materiality.**
    d.  Establish a preliminary judgment about materiality, estimate likely misstatements and compare totals to the preliminary judgment about materiality, and determine tolerable misstatements.

[LO12]10.  When likely misstatements are greater than planned materiality, the auditor should:
    a.  Request that the client adjust the financial statements.
    b.  Issue unqualified opinion.
    c.  Issue a qualified or adverse opinion if client refuses to adjust the statements.
    **d.  Both a and c.**

**Part III: Short Essay Questions**

[LO2] Why does an auditor use the audit risk model? Discuss the specifications of the audit risk model and identify the components of the model.

**The auditor uses the audit risk model as a planning tool to determine the scope of auditing procedures for a particular account balance or class of transactions level. The model is specified as:**

$$AR = IR \times CR \times DR$$

**where**

**$AR$ = Audit risk (the risk that the auditor may fail to modify the opinion on materially misstated financial statements)**

**$IR$ = Inherent risk (the susceptibility of an assertion to material misstatements, assuming no related controls)**

**$CR$ = Control risk (the risk that material misstatements that could occur in an assertion will not be prevented or detected on a timely basis by the internal controls)**

**$DR$ = Detection risk (the risk that the auditor will not detect a material misstatement that exists in an assertion)**

[LO4] Discuss the auditor's basic process for assessing business risk and the risk of material misstatements.

**The auditor's assessment of business risk and the risk of materials misstatement (i.e., the auditor's risk assessment process) includes the following steps:**

**Perform risk assessment procedures to obtain an understanding of the entity and its environment, including internal control.**

**Identify business risks that may result in material misstatements in the financial statements.**

**Evaluate the entity's responses to those business risks and obtain evidence of their implementation.**

**Assess the risk of material misstatement at the assertion level and determine the audit procedures that are necessary based on the risk assessment.**

[LO9] Discuss the auditor's responsibilities for communicating with management and the audit committee regarding issues of fraud.

**When the auditor has found evidence that a fraud may exist, that matter should be brought to the attention of an appropriate level of management. Fraud involving senior management and fraud that causes a material misstatement of the financial statements should be reported directly to the audit committee and the board of directors. In addition, the auditor should reach an understanding with the audit committee regarding the expected nature and extent of communications about misappropriations perpetrated by lower-level employees.**

**The disclosure of fraud to parties other than the client's senior management and its audit committee ordinarily is not part of the auditor's responsibility and ordinarily would be precluded by the auditor's ethical or legal obligations of confidentiality. The auditor should recognize, however, that in the following circumstances a duty to disclose outside the entity may exist:**

1. **To comply with certain legal and regulatory requirements.**

2. **To a successor auditor when the successor makes inquires in accordance with AU 315 (Communications between Predecessor and Successor Auditors).**

3. **In response to a subpoena.**

4. **To a funding agency or other specified agency in accordance with requirements for the audits of entities that receive governmental financial assistance.**

## Part IV: Crossword Puzzle – Chapter 3 Solution [LO ALL]

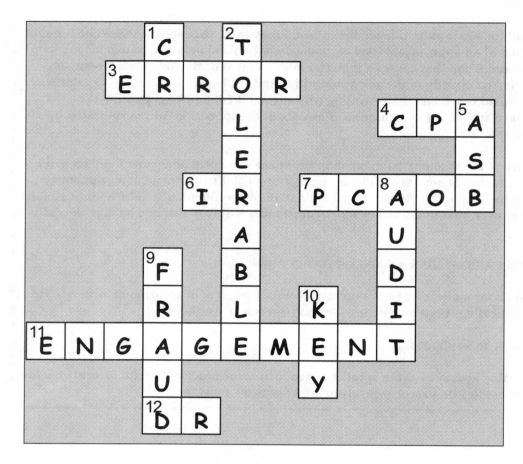

### Across

3     An unintentional misstatement or omission of an amount or a disclosure.
4     An auditor holds this professional designation.
6     A two-letter abbreviation for the component of the audit risk model that assumes no related controls.
7     An abbreviation for the body that promulgates auditing standards used for audits of publicly-held companies.
11    _____ risk is the exposure that an auditor assumes in a financial statement audit.
12    A two-letter abbreviation for the component of the audit risk model that the auditor will not detect a material misstatement.

### Down

1     A two-letter abbreviation for the component of the audit risk model that a misstatement will not be prevented or detected by controls.
2     _____ misstatement is the amount of the preliminary judgment about account materiality.
5     An abbreviation for the AICPA body that promulgates auditing standards used for audits of privately-held companies.
8     The type of risk that an auditor faces because he or she may fail to modify the opinion on materially misstated financial statements.
9     An intentional misstatement or omission of an amount or a disclosure.
10    ___ Performance Indicators.

## Chapter 3
## Townsend Office Supplies and Equipment

For audit engagements with less than four years experience, the firm's audit risk policy for a material account is .03. Inventory is considered a material account. The inherent risk has been set at .80 and control risk was assessed at .50. Complete the following: (1) compute detection risk; (2) discuss what detection risk means; (3) identify at least two factors that may help explain the assessed level of inherent risk; and (4) using qualitative terms, classify audit risk (use very low, low, or moderate) and each of the risk components (use low, moderate or high).

1. **DR = AR/(IR × CR)**
   **DR = .03/(.80 × .50)**
   **DR = .08**

2. **A detection risk of .08 means that the auditor will establish the scope of the audit for inventory so that there is only an 8 percent chance that a material misstatement, if present, is not detected. A low assessment for detection risk implies that the auditor will conduct a more detailed investigation of this account than if the assessment of detection risk were high.**

3. **Factors that may help explain why inherent risk was set high include:**

   - **A few individuals dominate management and operations.**
   - **Covenant restrictions associated with line of credit.**
   - **Townsend is engaged in a highly competitive industry.**
   - **Office Depot is considered a competitive threat in key regions.**
   - **Gross margin may need to be reduced for competitive government environment.**
   - **Townsend cannot increase its market share without additional investment.**
   - **Concerns about current year inventory obsolescence.**
   - **Significant LCM inventory adjustment was required for previous year audit.**
   - **Significant increase in ending inventory to facilitate new customer.**

4. **Audit Risk (AR) = Very Low.**

   **Inherent Risk (IR) = High; Control Risk (CR) = Moderate; and Detection Risk (DR) = Low.**

# Audit Evidence and Audit Documentation

## KEY THOUGHT

Sufficient competent evidential matter is to be obtained through inspection, observation, inquiries, and confirmations to afford a reasonable basis for an opinion regarding the financial statements under audit [Auditing Standards Board (AU 150.02)].

## CHAPTER SUMMARY

**[LO1] Understand the relationship between audit evidence and the auditor's report.**

A.  This chapter covers audit evidence, which is the third concept underlying the audit process. Audit evidence can be defined as all of the information used by the auditor in arriving at the conclusions on which the audit opinion is based, and includes the information contained in the accounting records underlying the financial statements and other information.

B.  The standard on audit evidence provides the basic framework for understanding audit evidence and its relationship to the auditor's opinion on the financial statements. There is a top-down relationship from the financial statements to the audit procedures. These relationships are shown below (Figure 4-1):

> **Financial statements → Management assertions about components of financial statements → Audit procedures → Evidence on the fairness of the financial statements → Audit report → Financial statements.**

C.  The auditor conducts audit procedures to gather evidence to test whether each relevant management assertion is being supported. Auditors typically divide financial statements into components or segments in order to manage the audit. A component can be a financial statement account or a business process.

D.  As discussed in Chapter 2, the basic processes of most businesses include the revenue process, the purchasing process, the human resource management process, the inventory management process, and the financing process (also called transaction cycles).

**[LO2] Know management assertions about classes of transactions and events for the period under audit, assertions about account balances at the period end, and assertions about presentation and disclosure.**

A. Management is responsible for the fair presentation of the financial statements. Assertions are expressed or implied representations by management that are reflected in the financial statement components. Management assertions fall into the following categories (Table 4-1 & Table 4-2):

    1. Assertions about classes of transactions and events for the period under audit include:

        a. **Occurrence.** Transactions and events that have been recorded have occurred and pertain to the entity.

        b. **Completeness.** All transactions and events that should have been recorded have been recorded.

        c. **Authorization.** All transactions and events have been properly authorized.

        d. **Accuracy.** Amounts and other data relating to recorded transactions and events have been recorded appropriately.

        e. **Cutoff.** Transactions and events have been recorded in the correct accounting period.

        f. **Classification.** Transactions and events have been recorded in the proper accounts.

    2. Assertions about account balances at the period end include:

        a. **Existence.** Assets, liabilities and equity interests exist.

        b. **Rights and Obligations.** The entity holds or controls the rights to assets, and liabilities are the obligations of the entity.

        c. **Completeness.** All assets, liabilities and equity interests that should have been recorded have been recorded.

        d. **Valuation and Allocation.** Assets, liabilities and equity interests are included in the financial statements at appropriate amounts and any resulting valuation or allocation adjustments are appropriately recorded.

    3. Assertions about presentation and disclosure include:

        a. **Occurrence and rights and obligations.** Disclosed events, transactions and other matters have occurred and pertain to the entity.

        b. **Completeness.** All disclosures that should have been included in the financial statements have been included.

        c. **Classification and understandability.** Financial information is appropriately presented and described, and disclosures are clearly expressed.

        d. **Accuracy and valuation.** Financial and other information are disclosed fairly and at appropriate amounts.

**[LO3] Define audit procedures and understand their relationship to assertions.**

A. Audit procedures are specific acts performed by the auditor to gather evidence to determine if specific assertions are being met. Audit procedures are performed to (Table 4-3):

   1. Obtain an understanding of the entity and its environment, including its internal control, to assess the risks of material misstatement at the financial statement level and assertion levels (Chapter 3).

   2. Test the operating effectiveness of controls in presenting, or detecting and correcting material misstatements at the assertion level. Audit procedures performed for this purpose are referred to as tests of controls (Chapters 5 and 6).

   3. Detect material misstatements at the assertion level. These audit procedures are referred to as substantive procedures. Substantive procedures include tests of details of transactions, account balances, and disclosures; and substantive analytical procedures (Chapter 5 and each business process chapter).

**[LO4] Learn the basic concepts of audit evidence.**

A. Understanding the nature, competence, sufficiency and evaluation of audit evidence is important to understanding the conduct of the audit.

B. **Nature of audit evidence.** Audit evidence includes accounting records and other forms of information (manual and electronic forms):

   1. Accounting records include the records of initial entries and supporting records, such as checks and records of electronic fund transfers.

   2. Invoices and contracts.

   3. General and subsidiary ledgers, journal entries and other adjustments to the financial statements that are not reflected in formal journal entries.

   4. Records such as work sheets and spreadsheets supporting cost allocations, computations, reconciliations and disclosures.

   5. Minutes of meetings.

   6. Confirmations from third parties.

   7. Analysts' reports.

   8. Benchmarking data about competitors, controls manuals and information obtained by the auditor from such audit procedures as inquiry, observation and inspection and other information developed by, or available to, the auditor.

C. **The competence of evidence.** Competence is a measure of the quality of audit evidence. Audit evidence, regardless of its form, is considered competent when it provides information that is both relevant and reliable.

1. The competence of evidence depends on its relevance to the assertion being tested.

2. The reliability of evidence refers to whether a particular type of evidence can be relied upon to signal the true state of an assertion. Reliability of evidence is influenced by its source and by its nature and is dependent on the individual circumstances under which it is obtained, therefore, the auditor should consider:

   a. Independent source of the evidence.
   b. Effectiveness of internal control.
   c. Auditor's direct personal knowledge.

   Note that audit evidence is more reliable when it exists in documentary form, whether paper, electronic or other medium and original documents are more reliable than audit evidence provided by photocopies or facsimiles.

D. **The sufficiency of evidence.** Sufficiency is the measure of the quantity of audit evidence. The quantity of audit evidence needed is affected by the risk of misstatement and by the quality of the audit evidence gathered. The greater the risk of misstatement, the more audit evidence is likely to be required to meet the audit test. In short, there is an inverse relationship between the sufficiency and competence of audit evidence.

In most instances, the auditor must rely on evidence that is persuasive rather than convincing in forming an opinion on a set of financial statements. This occurs for two reasons. First, because the audit must be completed in a reasonable amount of time and at a reasonable cost, the auditor examines only a sample of the transactions that make up the account balance or class of transactions; hence, the auditor uses a subset of available evidence to reach a conclusion. Second, due to the nature of evidence, auditors must often rely on evidence that is not perfectly reliable. The types of audit evidence have different degrees of reliability, and even highly reliable evidence has weaknesses. For example, an auditor can physically examine inventory, but such evidence will not ensure that obsolescence is not a problem. In other words, the nature of the evidence obtained by the auditor seldom provides absolute assurance about an audit assertion. The amount of audit evidence is determined by the auditor's professional judgment, which is affected by the risk of material misstatement.

E. **The evaluation of audit evidence.** The ability to evaluate evidence appropriately is another important skill an auditor must develop. Proper evaluation of evidence requires that the auditor understand the types of evidence that are available and their relative reliability. In other words, the auditor must be capable of assessing when a sufficient amount of competent evidence has been obtained in order to determine whether the fairness of management's assertions can be supported.

**[LO5] Identify and define the audit procedures used for obtaining audit evidence.**

A. In conducting audit procedures, the auditor examines various types of audit evidence. Evidence is categorized into the following types:

   1. **Inspection of records or documents** consists of examining internal or external records or documents that are in paper form, electronic form or other media. On most audit engagements, inspection of records or documents makes up the bulk of the evidence gathered by the auditor. Two issues are important in discussing the reliability of such evidence and its relationship to specific audit assertions.

**Reliability of records or documents.** Evidence obtained from a source outside he entity is generally considered more reliable than evidence obtained solely from within the entity. Typically a distinction is made between internal and external documents. Internal documents are generated and maintained within the entity, that is, these documents have not been seen by any party outside the client's organization. Examples include duplicate copies of sales invoices, shipping documents and materials requisition forms. External documents are of two forms: documents originating within the entity but circulated to independent sources outside the entity (e.g., remittance advices returned with cash receipts from customers and payroll checks) and documents generated outside the entity but included in the client's accountings records (e.g., bank statements and vendors' invoices). In general, such external documentary evidence is viewed as more reliable than internal evidence because a third party either initiated or reviewed it. This difference in reliability between internal and external documents is, however, relative. Internal documents generated by good internal controls are likely to be highly reliable. Conversely, external documents may be manipulated or withheld by client personnel. If this is likely on an engagement, the auditor would discount the reliability of the external documents in the client's possession. In such a situation, the auditor would also discount the reliability of the internal documents. In short, the auditor must use his or her professional judgment to assess the reliability of documentary evidence.

**Documentary evidence related to assertions.** The second issue concerning records or documents relates directly to the occurrence and completeness assertions and to the direction of testing taken when documentary evidence is examined. The direction of testing between the accounting records and source documents (such as sales invoices or shipping documents) is important when testing the occurrence and completeness objectives. **Vouching** refers to first selecting an item for testing from the accounting journals or ledgers and then examining the underlying source document. Thus, the direction of testing is from the journals or ledgers back to the source documents. This provides evidence that items included in the accounting records occurred (are valid transactions). For example, an auditor may want to examine a sample of sales transactions from the sales journal to ensure that sales are not fictitious. If adequate source documents exist for each sales transaction selected from the sales journal, the auditor can conclude that each sale was valid. **Tracing** refers to first selecting an accounting transaction (source document) and then following it into the journal or ledger. The direction of testing in this case is from the source documents to the journals or ledgers. Testing in this direction ensures that transactions that occurred are recorded (completeness) in the accounting records. For example, if the auditor selects a sample of shipping documents and traces them to the related sales invoices and then to the sales journal, he or she would have evidence on the completeness of sales. These relationships are shown in the diagram below (Figure 4-2):

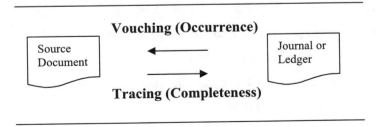

2. **Inspection of tangible assets** consists of physical examination of the assets. This type of evidence is a relatively reliable form of evidence that involves the auditor inspecting or counting tangible assets, but it provides little or no assurance on the rights and obligations assertions.

3. **Reperformance** is the auditor's independent execution of procedures or controls that were originally performed as part of the entity's internal control, either manually or through the use of computer-assisted audit techniques (CAATs). For example, the auditor may reperform the aging of accounts receivable. Because the auditor creates this type of evidence it is normally viewed as highly reliable.

4. **Recalculation** consists of checking the mathematical accuracy of documents or records. Examples of this type of procedure include recalculation of depreciation expense on fixed assets and recalculation of accrued interest. Recalculation can be performed through the use of information technology (obtaining an electronic file from the entity and using CAATs to check the accuracy of the summarization of the file). Recalculation also includes footing, crossfooting, reconciling subsidiary ledgers to account balances, and testing postings from journals to ledgers. Again, because the auditor creates this type of evidence, it is normally viewed as highly reliable.

5. **Scanning** is the review of accounting data to identify significant or unusual items. This includes the identification of anomalous individual items within account balances or other client data through the scanning or analysis of entries in transaction listings, subsidiary ledgers, general ledger control accounts, adjusting entries, suspense accounts, reconciliations and other detailed reports. Scanning includes searching for large and unusual items in the accounting records (nonstandard journal entries), as well as reviewing transaction data (suspense accounting, adjusting journal entries) for indications of errors that have occurred. It might be used in conjunction with analytical procedures, but scanning can be used as a stand-alone procedure.

6. **Inquiry** consists of seeking information of knowledgeable persons, both financial and nonfinancial, throughout the entity or outside the entity. Inquiry is an audit procedure that is used extensively throughout the audit and often is complementary to performing other audit procedures. For example much of the audit work conducted to understanding the entity and its environment including internal control involves inquiry. Inquires may range from formal written inquiries to informal oral inquiries. Evaluating responses to inquiries is an integral part of the inquiry process. In conducting inquiry, the auditor should (Table 4-4):

    a. Consider the knowledge, objectivity, experience, responsibility and qualifications of the individual to be questioned.

    b. Ask clear, concise and relevant questions.

    c. Use open or closed questions appropriately.

    d. Listen actively and effectively.

    e. Consider the reactions and responses and ask follow-up questions.

    f. Evaluate the response.

Responses to inquiries may provide the auditor with information not previously possessed or with corroborative audit evidence. Alternatively, responses might provide information that differs significantly from other information that the auditor has obtained (information regarding the possibility of management override of controls).

The reliability of audit evidence obtained from responses to inquiries is also affected by the training, knowledge and experience of the auditor performing the inquiry, because the auditor analyzes and assesses the responses while performing the inquiry and refines subsequent inquiries according to the circumstances. In some cases, the nature of the response may be so significant that the auditor requests a written representation from the source. Inquiry alone ordinarily does not provide sufficient audit evidence and the auditor will gather additional corroborative evidence to support the response. For example, inquiry will not provide sufficient competent audit evidence for testing the operating effectiveness of controls. Additionally, when inquiring about management intent, the information available to support management's intent may be limited. In this case, understanding management's past history of carrying out its stated intentions may provide relevant information about management's intent.

7. **Observation** consists of looking at a process or procedure being performed by others. The actions being observed typically do not leave an audit trail that can be tested by examining records or documents. Examples include observation of the counting of inventories by the entity's personnel and observation of the performance of control activities. Observation provides audit evidence about the performance of a process or procedure, but is limited to the point in time at which the observation takes place. It is also limited by the fact that the client personnel may act differently when the auditor is not observing them. Observation is generally not considered very reliable and generally requires additional corroboration by the auditor. Corroborating evidence includes data or documents from the accounting records and other documentary information (contracts and written confirmations).

8. **Confirmation** is a specific type of inquiry (Table 4-5). It is the process of obtaining a representation of information or of an existing condition directly from a third party. Confirmations also are used to obtain audit evidence about the absence of certain conditions (e.g., the absence of a "side agreement" that may influence revenue recognition). The reliability of evidence obtained through confirmations is directly affected by factors such as:

   a. The form of the confirmation.
   b. Prior experience with the entity.
   c. The nature of information being confirmed.
   d. The intended respondent.

Confirmations are used extensively on audits; they generally provide reliable evidence for the existence assertion (such as accounts receivable) and, in testing certain financial statement components, can provide evidence about the completeness assertion (such as accounts payable). Evidence about other assertions can also be obtained through the use of confirmations. For example, an auditor can send a confirmation to a consignee to verify that a client's inventory has been consigned. The returned confirmation provides evidence that the client owns the inventory (rights and obligations assertion). Information frequently confirmed by auditors include: cash balance, accounts receivable, inventory on consignment, accounts payable, bonds payable, common stock outstanding, insurance coverage and collateral for a loan.

9. **Analytical procedures** are an important type of audit evidence. They consist of evaluations of financial information made by a study of plausible relationships among both financial and nonfinancial data. For example, the current-year accounts receivable balance can be compared to the prior-year balance after adjusting for any increase or decrease in sales and other economic factors. The auditor makes the comparison either to identify accounts that may contain material misstatements and require more investigation or as a reasonable test of the account balance. Analytical procedures are an effective and efficient type of audit evidence. The reliability of analytical procedures is a function of:

   a. The availability and reliability of the data used in the calculations.
   b. The plausibility and predictability of the relationship being test.
   c. The precision of the expectation and the rigor of the investigation.

**[LO6] Understand the reliability of the types of evidence.**

A. Inspection of the tangible assets, reperformance and recalculation are generally considered of high reliability because the auditor has direct knowledge about them. Inspection of records and documents, scanning, confirmation and analytical procedures are generally considered to be of medium reliability. The reliability of inspection of records and documents depends primarily on whether a document is internal or external, and the reliability of confirmation is affected by the four factors listed previously. The reliability of analytical procedures may be affected by the availability and reliability of the data. Finally, observation and inquiry (other than confirmations) are generally low-reliability types of evidence because both require further corroboration by the auditor. The reliabilities of the types of evidence are summarized below (Table 4-6):

| Hierarchy of the Reliability of Types of Evidence | |
|---|---|
| Reliability Level | Type of Evidence |
| High | Inspection of tangible assets, reperformance and Recalculation |
| Medium | Inspection of records and documents, scanning, confirmation and analytical procedures |
| Low | Observation and inquiry |

**[LO7] Understand the objectives of audit documentation.**

A. **Audit documentation** is the auditor's principal record of the work performed and the basis for the conclusions in the auditor's report. Audit documentation also facilitates the planning, performance, and supervision of the engagement and provides the basis for the review of the quality of the work by providing the reviewer with written documentation of the evidence supporting the auditor's significant conclusions. You can think of audit documentation as the "story" of the audit. It should allow the reader to easily understand the issues and risks, the assertions tested, the audit procedures performed to gather evidence, the findings, and the conclusion.

B. Auditing documentation is also referred to as working papers or the audit file. Auditing standards stipulate that working papers have two functions: (1) to provide support for the auditor's report and (2) to aid in the conduct and supervision of the audit. The form and content of the working papers are a function of the circumstances of the specific engagement. While some working papers may be prepared in hard-copy format, audit software is normally used to prepare them. At the completion of the audit, the auditor should consider whether the accumulated results of audit procedures affect the assessments of the entity's business risks and the risk of material misstatements due to error or fraud. The auditor should aggregate the total uncorrected misstatements that were detected and determine if they cause the financial statements to be materially misstated.

C. When the engagement is complete, the auditor must decide on the appropriate type of report to issue. The basis for this decision rests in the audit evidence gathered and the conclusions reached and documented in the working papers. The working papers also document that the scope of the audit was adequate for the report issued and information on the correspondence of the financial statements with GAAP is also included.

D. The working papers contain the audit evidence that documents the auditor's compliance with GAAS. Working papers document the auditor's compliance with the standards of fieldwork. The planning of the engagement, along with the execution of the audit plan, is contained in the working papers. The working papers are also the focal point for reviewing the work of subordinates and quality control reviewers.

**[LO8] Develop an understanding of the content, types, organization, and ownership of audit documentation.**

A. Audit documentation is the principal record of auditing procedures applied, evidence obtained, and conclusions reached by the auditor in the engagement. Because audit documentation provides the principal support for the representations in the auditor's report, it should:

1. Demonstrate how the audit complied with auditing and related professional practice standards.

2. Support the basis for the auditor's conclusions concerning every material financial statement assertion.

3. Demonstrate that the underlying accounting records agreed or reconciled with the financial statements.

Audit documentation should include a written audit program for the engagement. The audit program should set forth in reasonable detail the auditing procedures that the auditor believed necessary to accomplish the objectives of the audit. Audit documentation should be sufficient to show that standards of fieldwork have been followed. Audit documentation should enable a reviewer with relevant knowledge and experience to:

1. Understand the nature, timing, extent and results of the procedures performed, evidence obtained, and conclusions reached.

2. Determine who performed the work and the date such work was completed, as well as the person who reviewed the work and the date of such review.

The auditor should consider the following factors when determining the nature and extent of the documentation for a particular audit area or auditing procedure:

1. Risk of material misstatements associated with the assertion, account or class of transactions.

2. Extent of judgment involved in performing the work and evaluating the results.

3. Significance of the evidence obtained to the assertion being tested.

4. Nature and extent of exceptions identified.

5. The need to document a conclusion or the basis for a conclusion not readily determinable from the documentation of the work performed.

PCAOB's Auditing Standard No. 3 for audit documentation is more stringent than the standard issued by the ASB (AU 339) for nonpublic companies. Examples of significant findings or issues that require documentation under AS No. 3 include (Table 4-7):

1. Significant matters involving the selection, application and consistency of accounting principles, including related disclosures.

2. Results of auditing procedures that indicate a need for significant modification of planned auditing procedures or the existence of material misstatements or omissions in the financial statements or the existence of significant deficiencies in internal control over financial reporting.

3. Audit adjustments and the ultimate resolution of these items.

4. Disagreements among members of the engagement team or with others consulted on the engagement about conclusions reached on significant accounting or auditing matters.

5. Significant findings or issues identified during the review of quarterly financial information.

6. Circumstances that cause significant difficulty in applying auditing procedures.

7. Significant changes in the assessed level of audit risk for particular audit areas and the auditor's response to those changes.

8. Any other matters that could result in modification of the audit report.

When documenting the quantity of evidence gathered through inspection of documents or confirmation of balances, the auditor should identify the items tested. Where appropriate, the audit files should contain abstracts or copies of significant documents (Table 4-8).

Public accounting firms maintain audit documentation in two types of files: permanent and current. **Permanent files** contain historical data about the client that are of continuing relevance to the audit. Examples of information in the permanent file include (Table 4-9):

1. Copies of or excerpts from the corporate charter.
2. Chart of accounts.

3. Organizational chart.
4. Accounting manual.
5. Copies of important contracts (pension and union contracts, leases).
6. Documentation of internal control (flowcharts).
7. Terms of stock and bond issues.
8. Prior years' analytical procedure results.

**Current files** include information and data related specifically to the current year's engagement. Examples of information in the current file include (Table 4-9):

1. Copy of financial statements and auditor's report.
2. Audit plan and audit programs.
3. Copies of, or excerpts from, minutes of important committee meetings.
4. Working trial balance.
5. Adjusting and reclassification journal entries.
6. Working papers supporting financial statement accounts.

B. The more common audit documentation includes the audit plan and programs, working trial balance, account analysis and listings, audit memoranda, and adjusting and reclassification entries.

1. The **audit plan** contains the strategy to be followed by the auditor in conducting the audit. Risks must be identified and a basic framework for how the audit resources (budgeted audit hours) are to be allocated to various parts of the engagement must be included. The **audit programs** contain the audit procedures that will be conducted by the auditor.

2. The **working trial balance** links the amounts in the financial statements to the audit working papers. A lead schedule is used to show the detailed general ledger accounts that make up a financial statement category.

3. **Account analysis** working papers generally include the activity in a particular account for the period. A **listing** is a schedule of items remaining in the ending balance of an account (trial balances).

4. Much of the auditor's work is documented in **written memoranda**. These include discussions of items such as internal controls, inventory observation, errors identified and problems encountered during the audit.

5. The audit documentation should include the **adjusting and reclassification entries** identified by the auditor or client. Adjusting entries are made to correct errors in the clients' records. Adjusting entries are posted in both the client's records and the working trial balance. Reclassification entries are made to properly present information on the financial statements. A reclassification entry affects income statement accounts or balance sheet accounts, but not both. Reclassification entries are not posted to the client's records.

C. Audit documentation is usually formatted based on three general characteristics:

1. All audit documentation should have a proper heading, which includes the name of the client, the title of the working paper and the client's year-end date.

2. Audit documents must be organized so that members of the audit team or firm can find relevant audit evidence (see Figure 4-3 for organization from general to detail). Some firms

use a lettering system, while other firms use some type of numbering system. When the auditor performs audit work on one working paper and supporting information is obtained from another working paper, the auditor cross-references the information on each working paper. This process of indexing and cross-referencing provides a trail from the financial statements to the individual audit documents that a reviewer can follow.

3. Tick marks are used to document work performed. They are notations made by the auditor near an item or amount on an audit document. The tick mark symbol is typically explained or defined at the bottom of the audit document. Many firms use a standard set of tick marks.

D. Audit documentation is the property of the auditor. This includes the audit documents prepared by the auditor and audit documents prepared by the client at the request of the auditor. The audit documentation should be retained for a reasonable period of time in order to meet the needs of practice and legal record retention requirements.

# CHAPTER 4: SELF-ASSESSMENT

## Part I: True or False Questions

[LO1] _____ 1. Audit evidence includes only written information used by the auditor in arriving at an opinion about the fairness of financial statements.

[LO1] _____ 2. The auditor gathers audit evidence to test management's assertions.

[LO1] _____ 3. There is a top-down relationship from the financial statements to the audit procedures.

[LO2] _____ 4. Management assertions fall into four categories.

[LO2] _____ 5. Classification means that transactions and events have been recorded in the correct accounting period.

[LO2] _____ 6. Completeness means that transactions and events that should have been recorded have been recorded.

[LO2] _____ 7. Cutoff relates to whether transactions and events have been recorded in the correct accounting period.

[LO4] _____ 8. The relevance of audit evidence depends on the assertion being tested.

[LO4] _____ 9. The auditor must use his or her professional judgment to determine the amount of audit evidence.

[LO4] _____ 10. The sufficiency of evidence refers to the quality of audit evidence.

## Part II: Multiple Choice Questions

[LO5] 1. An example of audit evidence with a medium level of reliability is:
    a. Scanning.
    b. Recalculation.
    c. Observation.
    d. All of the above.

[LO5] 2. When conducting an inquiry, the auditor should:
    a. Listen actively and effectively.
    b. Consider the qualifications of the individual being questioned.
    c. Rely on closed questions because they are more objective and reliable.
    d. Both a and b.

[LO5] 3. A confirmation is used to:
    a. Verify the inventory count is correct.
    b. Verify that a control is being observed.
    c. Verify a representation from a third party.
    d. Verify that a specific trend is correct.

[LO6]  4.  An example of audit evidence with a low level of reliability is:
a.  Scanning.
b.  Inspection.
c.  Observation.
d.  Analytical procedures.

[LO6]  5.  An example of audit evidence with a high level of reliability is:
a.  Scanning.
b.  Recalculation.
c.  Observation.
d.  Confirmation.

[LO7]  6.  Audit documentation provides the principal support for which of the following:
a.  Demonstrate how the audit complied with auditing and related professional practice standards.
b.  Support the basis for the auditor's conclusions concerning every material financial statements assertion.
c.  Demonstrate that the underlying accounting records agreed or reconciled with the financial statements.
d.  All of the above.

[LO8]  7.  The permanent audit file usually includes:
a.  Working trial balance.
b.  Organizational chart.
c.  Audit plan.
d.  Audit programs.

[LO8]  8.  The current audit file usually includes:
a.  Working trial balance.
b.  Organizational chart.
c.  Accounting manual.
d.  Copies of important contracts.

[LO8]  9.  All audit documentation should have a heading, which includes:
a.  Name of the client.
b.  Title of the working paper.
c.  Client's year-end date.
d.  All of the above.

[LO8] 10.  The audit working papers belong to the:
a.  The client.
b.  The auditor.
c.  The audit firm.
d.  Both the client and the audit firm.

## Part III: Short Essay Questions

[LO1] Discuss the relationship between audit evidence and the auditor's opinion on the financial statements and the top-down relationship from the financial statements to the audit procedures.

[LO2] Who is responsible for the financial statements? What does the term "assertions" mean? Identify the assertion categories and the specific assertions for each category.

[LO6] Discuss the reliability of the types of audit evidence and identify the level of reliability for each type of evidence.

# Part IV: Crossword Puzzle – Chapter 4 [LO ALL]

## Across

4   Auditors use this notation in the working papers to document work performed (two words).
7   To _____ means to express or imply.
8   The auditor's independent execution of procedures or controls originally performed as part of the entity's internal control.
9   An assertion that addresses whether financial or other information is disclosed at the appropriate amounts.
10  Every publicly held and traded enterprise must have this service performed annually.
12  The abbreviation for a type of technology used by an auditor to evaluate client data.

## Down

1   An audit procedure used to obtain information directly from third parties.
2   An assertion relating to whether all disclosures that should have been included in the financial statements have been included.
3   Examining internal or external records or documents or physical examination of assets.
5   The purpose of this audit assertion is to determine that transactions have been recorded in the correct period.
6   Refers to whether a particular type of evidence can be replied upon to signal the true state of an assertion.
11  Reviewing accounting data to identify significant or unusual items.

## Part V: Townsend Office Supplies and Equipment [LO ALL]

| Chapter 4 |
| :---: |
| **Townsend Office Supplies and Equipment** |

1. Based on the inventory account, discuss management's assertions, by category.

2. Given that inventory is a material account (detection risk of 0.08), identify some of the audit procedures that should be used for obtaining audit evidence to test the inventory assertions?

3. You want to establish that the inventory purchases recorded in the accounting records are valid transactions. What assertions should be tested and what audit procedures should you use to test these assertions?

4. You want to establish that ending inventory as shown on the balance sheet is correct. What assertions should be tested and what audit procedures should you use to test these assertions?

# CHAPTER 4: SELF-ASSESSMENT SOLUTIONS

## Part I: True or False Questions

[LO1] **False** 1. Audit evidence includes only written information used by the auditor in arriving at an opinion about the fairness of financial statements.

[LO1] **True** 2. The auditor gathers audit evidence to test management's assertions.

[LO1] **True** 3. There is a top-down relationship from the financial statements to the audit procedures.

[LO2] **False** 4. Management assertions fall into four categories.

[LO2] **False** 5. Classification means that transactions and events have been recorded in the correct accounting period.

[LO2] **True** 6. Completeness means that transactions and events that should have been recorded have been recorded.

[LO2] **True** 7. Cutoff relates to whether transactions and events have been recorded in the correct accounting period.

[LO4] **True** 8. The relevance of audit evidence depends on the assertion being tested.

[LO4] **True** 9. The auditor must use his or her professional judgment to determine the amount of audit evidence.

[LO4] **False** 10. The sufficiency of evidence refers to the quality of audit evidence.

## Part II: Multiple Choice Questions

[LO5] 1. An example of audit evidence with a medium level of reliability is:
    **a. Scanning.**
    b. Recalculation.
    c. Observation.
    d. All of the above.

[LO5] 2. When conducting an inquiry, the auditor should:
    a. Listen actively and effectively.
    b. Consider the qualifications of the individual being questioned.
    c. Rely on closed questions because they are more objective and reliable.
    **d. Both a and b.**

[LO5] 3. A confirmation is used to:
    a. Verify the inventory count is correct.
    b. Verify that a control is being observed.
    **c. Verify a representation from a third party.**
    d. Verify that a specific trend is correct.

[LO6] 4. An example of audit evidence with a low level of reliability is:
a. Scanning.
b. Inspection.
c. **Observation.**
d. Analytical procedures.

[LO6] 5. An example of audit evidence with a high level of reliability is:
a. Scanning.
b. **Recalculation.**
c. Observation.
d. Confirmation.

[LO7] 6. Audit documentation provides the principal support for which of the following:
a. Demonstrate how the audit complied with auditing and related professional practice standards.
b. Support the basis for the auditor's conclusions concerning every material financial statements assertion.
c. Demonstrate that the underlying accounting records agreed or reconciled with the financial statements.
d. **All of the above.**

[LO8] 7. The permanent audit file usually includes:
a. Working trial balance.
b. **Organizational chart.**
c. Audit plan.
d. Audit programs.

[LO8] 8. The current audit file usually includes:
a. **Working trial balance.**
b. Organizational chart.
c. Accounting manual.
d. Copies of important contracts.

[LO8] 9. All audit documentation should have a heading, which includes:
a. Name of the client.
b. Title of the working paper.
c. Client's year-end date.
d. **All of the above.**

[LO8] 10. The audit working papers belong to the:
a. The client.
b. The auditor.
c. **The audit firm.**
d. Both the client and the audit firm.

## Part III: Short Essay Questions

[LO1] Discuss the relationship between audit evidence and the auditor's opinion on the financial statements and the top-down relationship from the financial statements to the audit procedures.

**The standard on audit evidence provides the basic framework for understanding audit evidence and its relationship to the auditor's opinion on the financial statements. There is a top-down relationship from the financial statements to the audit procedures. These relationships are shown below (see Figure 4-1):**

**Financial statements → Management assertions about components of financial statements → Audit procedures → Evidence on the fairness of the financial statements → Audit report → Financial statements.**

[LO2] Who is responsible for the financial statements? What does the term "assertions" mean? Identify the assertion categories and the specific assertions for each category.

**Management is responsible for the fair presentation of the financial statements. Assertions are expressed or implied representations by management that are reflected in the financial statement components. Management assertions fall into the following categories:**

**Assertions about classes of transactions and events for the period under audit. Assertions about classes of transactions and events for the period under audit include: (1) occurrence, (2) completeness, (3) authorization, (4) accuracy, (5) cutoff and (6) classification.**

**Assertions about account balances at the period end. Assertions about account balances at the period end include: (1) existence, (2) rights and obligations, (3) completeness and (4) valuation and allocation.**

**Assertions about presentation and disclosure. Assertions about presentation and disclosure include: (1) occurrence and rights and obligations, (2) completeness, (3) classification and understandability and (4) accuracy and valuation.**

[LO6] Discuss the reliability of the types of audit evidence and identify the level of reliability for each type of evidence.

**Inspection of the tangible assets, reperformance and recalculation are generally considered of high reliability because the auditor has direct knowledge about them. Inspection of records and documents, scanning, confirmation and analytical procedures are generally considered to be of medium reliability. The reliability of inspection of records and documents depends primarily on whether a document is internal or external, and the reliability of confirmation is affected by (1) the form of the confirmation, (2) prior experience with the entity, (3) the nature of the information being confirmed and (4) the intended respondent.**

**The reliability of analytical procedures may be affected by the availability and reliability of the data. Finally, observation and inquiry (other than confirmation) are generally low-reliability types of evidence because both require further corroboration by the auditor. The reliabilities of the types of evidence are summarized in below:**

**High Reliability**
1. **Inspection of tangible assets**
2. **Reperformance**
3. **Recalculation**

**Medium Reliability**
1. **Inspection of records and documents**
2. **Scanning**
3. **Confirmation**
4. **Analytical procedures**

**Low Reliability**
1. **Observation**
2. **Inquiry**

# Part IV: Crossword Puzzle – Chapter 4 Solutions [LO ALL]

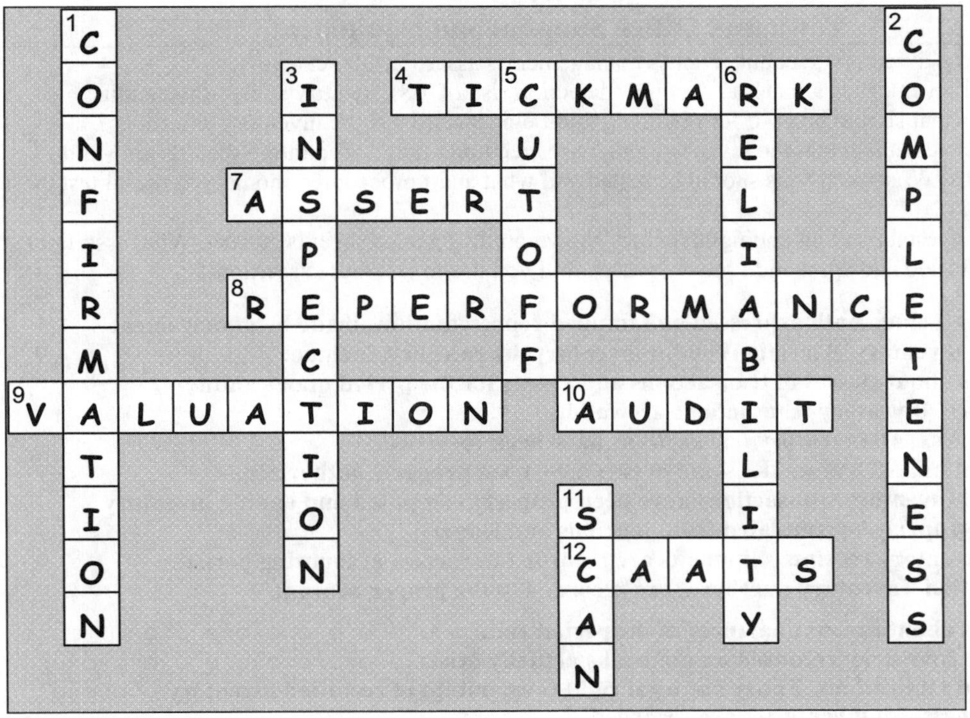

The crossword puzzle grid contains the following filled-in answers:

- 1 Down: CONFIRMATION
- 2 Down: COMPLETENESS
- 3 Down: INSPECTION
- 4 Across: TICKMARK
- 5 Down: CUTOFF
- 6 Down: RELIABILITY
- 7 Across: ASSERT
- 8 Across: REPERFORMANCE
- 9 Across: VALUATION
- 10 Across: AUDIT
- 11 Down: SCAN
- 12 Across: CAATS

## Across

4  Auditors use this notation in the working papers to document work performed (two words).
7  To _____ means to express or imply.
8  The auditor's independent execution of procedures or controls originally performed as part of the entity's internal control.
9  An assertion that addresses whether financial or other information is disclosed at the appropriate amounts.
10 Every publicly held and traded enterprise must have this service performed annually.
12 The abbreviation for a type of technology used by an auditor to evaluate client data.

## Down

1  An audit procedure used to obtain information directly from third parties.
2  An assertion relating to whether all disclosures that should have been included in the financial statements have been included.
3  Examining internal or external records or documents or physical examination of assets.
5  The purpose of this audit assertion is to determine that transactions have been recorded in the correct period.
6  Refers to whether a particular type of evidence can be replied upon to signal the true state of an assertion.
11 Reviewing accounting data to identify significant or unusual items.

## Part V: Townsend Office Supplies and Equipment [LO ALL]

---

### Chapter 4
### Townsend Office Supplies and Equipment

1. Based on the inventory account, discuss management's assertions, by category.
2. Given that inventory is a material account (detection risk of .08), identify some of the audit procedures that should be used for obtaining audit evidence to test the inventory assertions?
3. You want to establish that the inventory purchases recorded in the accounting records are valid transactions. What assertions should be tested and what audit procedures should you use to test these assertions?
4. You want to establish that ending inventory shown on the balance sheet is correct. What assertions should be tested and what audit procedures should you use to test these assertions?

---

1. **Assertions include both expressed and implied representations made by management about the inventory. Assertions about inventory, by category, include:**
   **Assertions about classes of transactions and events for the period under audit.**
   **Occurrence. Inventory transactions are valid.**
   **Completeness. All inventory transactions have been recorded.**
   **Authorization. All transactions and events have been properly authorized.**
   **Accuracy. Inventory transactions have been properly computed and ending inventory has been properly accumulated from journals and ledgers.**
   **Cutoff. Inventory receipts/shipments are recorded in correct accounting period.**
   **Classification. Inventory purchases are recorded in the proper account.**

   **Assertions about account balances at the period end.**
   **Existence. Inventory recorded on the books actually exists.**
   **Rights and Obligations. Entity has legal right (ownership) of recorded inventory.**
   **Completeness. All inventories are recorded.**
   **Valuation and Allocation. Inventory is properly recorded (GAAP).**

   **Assertions about presentation and disclosure.**
   **Occurrence and Rights and Obligations. All disclosed events and transactions relating to inventory have occurred and pertain to the entity.**
   **Completeness. All disclosures relating to inventory that should have been included in the financial statements have been included.**
   **Classification and Understandability. Financial information relating to inventory is appropriately presented and the disclosures are clearly expressed.**
   **Accuracy and Valuation. Financial and other information relating to inventory are disclosed fairly and at appropriate amounts.**

2. **Because inventory is a material account, the auditor would want to rely on audit evidence that is highly reliable, which would include inspection of inventory, reperformance and recalculation. In addition, inventory records and documents would be inspected.**

3. **The validity of recorded transactions relates to the occurrence assertion. The auditor should select a sample of transactions from the inventory account and examine the underlying source documentation, including vendor invoices (external), bills of lading (external) and receiving reports (internal). The process of inspecting the records and documents is known as vouching, which provides evidence that items included in the accounting records occurred and are valid transactions.**

4. **A number of assertions relate to the valuation of ending inventory. For example, the application of the LCM rule and inventory obsolescence must be considered. The valuation assertion can be tested by tracing costs to the vendors' invoices. The auditor can perform a lower-of-cost-or-market test on inventory product lines. The auditor should ask management about obsolete or slow-moving inventory concerns.**

# Audit Planning and Types of Audit Tests

## KEY THOUGHT

Audit planning involves developing an overall strategy for the expected conduct and scope of the audit. The nature, extent, and timing of planning vary with the size and complexity of the entity, experience with the entity, and knowledge of the entity's business [Auditing Standards Board (AU 311.03)].

## CHAPTER SUMMARY

**[LO1] Understand the auditor's requirements for client acceptance and continuance.**

A.  The first standard of fieldwork requires that the audit be properly planned. If the audit is not properly planned, the auditor may issue an incorrect audit report or conduct an inefficient audit. Analytical procedures are required to be performed as part of the planning of the audit and as part of wrapping up the audit. They also are useful for providing substantive audit evidence during the conduct of the audit of business processes and related accounts.

B.  Table 5-1 lists procedures that a firm might conduct to evaluate a prospective client. These procedures would normally be documented in a memo or by completion of a client acceptance questionnaire or checklist.

C.  When the prospective client has previously been audited, auditing standards require that the successor auditor make certain inquires of the predecessor auditor before accepting the engagement. Because of confidentiality, the successor auditor should request permission of the prospective client before contacting the predecessor auditor. If the prospective client refuses to permit the predecessor to respond, the successor auditor should have reservations about accepting the client. Such a situation should raise serious questions about management's motivations and integrity.

D.  The auditor's communications with the predecessor auditor should include questions related to:

   1.  The integrity of management.

   2.  Disagreements with management over accounting and auditing issues.

   3.  Communication with the audit committee or an equivalent group regarding fraud, illegal acts, and internal-control-related matters.

   4.  The predecessor's understanding of the reason for the change in auditors.

   Note that if the predecessor's response is limited, the successor auditor must be informed that the response is limited.

E.  If the client has not previously been audited, the public accounting firm should complete all the procedures listed in Table 5-1, except for the communication with the predecessor auditor.

F.  Public accounting firms need to evaluate periodically whether to retain their current clients. This evaluation may take place at or near the completion of an audit or when some significant event occurs. Conflicts over accounting and auditing issues or disputes over fees may lead the firm to disassociate itself from a client. The additional work required for public company audits brought on by the Sarbanes-Oxley Act resulted in many smaller public clients shifting from the Big 4 firms to national and regional public accounting firms.

## [LO2] Know what is required to establish an understanding with the client.

A.  The auditor and the client must agree on the terms of the engagement, including the type, scope and timing of the engagement. This understanding reduces the risk that either party may misinterpret what is expected or required of the other party. The terms of the engagement, which are documented in the engagement letter, should include the objectives of the engagement, management's responsibilities, the auditor's responsibilities and the limitations of the engagement. In establishing the terms of the engagement, three topics must be discussed: (1) the engagement letter, (2) the internal auditors and (3) the audit committee.

## [LO3] Know the types of information that are included in an engagement letter.

A.  An engagement letter formalizes the arrangement reached between the auditor and the client. It serves as a contract, outlining the responsibilities of both parties and preventing misunderstandings between the two parties. While such a letter is not required by auditing standards, good audit practice dictates that firms use such letters with their clients in order to avoid misunderstandings. Exhibit 5-1 shows a sample engagement letter for EarthWear. In addition to the items mentioned in the sample engagement letter (Exhibit 5-1), the engagement letter may include:

   1.  Arrangements involving the use of specialist or internal auditors.

   2.  Any limitation of the liability of the auditor or client, such as indemnification to the auditor for liability arising from knowing misrepresentations to the auditor by management (regulatory bodies, such as the SEC may restrict or prohibit such liability-limiting arrangements).

   3.  Additional services to be provided relating to regulatory requirements.

   4.  Arrangements regarding other services (assurance, tax or consulting services).

## [LO4] Understand how the work of the internal auditors can assist in the performance of the audit.

A.  When the client has internal auditors, the auditor may request their assistance in conducting the audit (Figure 5-2). The major issue for the independent auditor is assessing the competence and objectivity of the internal auditors and the effect of their work on the audit. Table 5-2 presents factors that the auditor should consider when assessing the competence and objectivity of the internal auditors.

B. The internal auditors' work may affect the nature, timing and extent of the audit procedures performed by the independent auditor. For example, as part of their regular work, internal auditors may review, assess and monitor the entity's controls that are included in the accounting system. Similarly, part of their work may include confirming receivables or observing physical inventories. If the internal auditors are competent and objective, the independent auditor may use the internal auditors' work in these areas to reduce the scope of audit work. The materiality of the account balance or class of transactions and its related audit risk also may determine how much the independent auditor can rely on the internal auditors' work. When internal auditors provide direct assistance, the external auditor should supervise, review, evaluate, and test their work.

**[LO5] Know the responsibilities of the audit committee and how it relates to the external auditors.**

A. An audit committee is a subcommittee of the board of directors that is responsible for the financial reporting and disclosure process. For privately-held companies, there are no specific requirements for the composition of the audit committee, but under Section 301 of the Sarbanes-Oxley Act, the audit committee of a public company has the following requirements:

    1. Each member of the audit committee must be a member of the board of directors and shall be independent. "Independent" is defined as not receiving, other than for service on the audit committee, any consulting, advisory, or other compensatory fee, and not being affiliated with the company.

    2. The audit committee is directly responsible for the appointment, compensation and oversight of the work of any registered public accounting firm employed by the company.

    3. The audit committee must preapprove all audit and non-audit services provided by its auditor.

    4. The audit committee must establish procedures for the receipt, retention and treatment of complaints received by the company regarding accounting, internal control and auditing.

    5. Audit committee members must have the authority to engage independent counsel or other advisors, as they determine necessary to carry out their duties.

B. The audit committee also should interact with the internal audit function. An ideal arrangement for establishing the independence of the internal audit function is for the internal auditors to report either directly or indirectly to the audit committee.

C. The audit committee should meet with the external auditor before the engagement starts to discuss the auditor's responsibilities and significant accounting policies. The audit committee may also engage the external or internal auditors to conduct special investigations. The external auditor is required to make a number of important communications to the audit committee during or at the end of the engagement (AU 380). Most of the required communications are made at the completion of the engagement (see Chapter 17).

**[LO6] Understand the steps that are involved in the preliminary engagement activities.**

A. There are generally two preplanning activities: (1) determining the audit engagement team requirements and (2) ensuring the independence of the audit team and audit firm.

B.  Public accounting firms need to ensure that their engagements are completed by auditors having the proper degree of technical training and proficiency given the circumstances of the clients. Factors that should be considered in determining staffing requirements include:

1.  Engagement size and complexity.
2.  Level of risk.
3.  Any special expertise.
4.  Personnel availability
5.  Timing of the work to be performed.

A time budget is prepared in order to assist with the staffing requirements and to schedule the fieldwork.

In some instances, the audit may require consulting with a specialist. Auditing standards (AU 336) define a specialist as a person or firm possessing special skill or knowledge in a field other than accounting or auditing (actuaries, appraisers, attorneys, engineers, and geologists). Specialist may assist the auditor with valuation issues, determination of physical quantities, amounts derived from specialized techniques, or interpretations of regulations or agreements.

C.  The second general standard requires that the auditor be independent of the client in order to issue an opinion; hence, a disclaimer of opinion must be issued when the auditor is not independent. A public accounting firm should establish policies and procedures to ensure that individuals at all organizational levels within the firm maintain independence in accordance with Rule 101 of the Code of Professional Conduct (AICPA Statements on Quality Control Standards). A firm should document compliance with this policy by having all personnel complete an annual independence questionnaire or report. At the engagement level, the partner-in-charge should ensure that all individuals assigned to the engagement are independent of the client. This can be accomplished by reviewing the annual independence reports for each member of the audit team. Another area of concern related to independence is unpaid client fees, which can impair the auditor's independence. Many public accounting firms adopt a policy of not completing the current audit until all of the prior year's fees have been paid. The CPA firm must be concerned when it also provides consulting services for an audit client. While the performance of consulting services does not, in and of itself, impair independence, the audit team must remain objective when evaluating client activities that were developed by their firm's consultants. For entities subject to the Sarbanes-Oxley Act (public companies), the auditor is not permitted to provide certain types of consulting services for audit clients (see Chapter 19 for a list of these prohibited services).

**[LO7] Identify the steps that are performed in planning an audit engagement.**

A.  Engagement planning involves all the issues the auditor should consider in developing an overall strategy for conducting the audit. The objective of the audit plan is to conduct an effective and efficient audit. This means that the audit is to be conducted in accordance with auditing standards and that the risk of material misstatements is reduced to an acceptably low level. The audit plan should also consider how to conduct the engagement in a cost-effective manner. When preparing the audit plan, the auditor should be guided by the results of the risk assessment procedures performed to gain understanding of the entity. Additional steps that should be performed include:

1.  Assess a preliminary level for control risk by account and assertion.
2.  Assess the possibility of illegal acts.
3.  Identify related parties.
4.  Conduct preliminary analytical procedures.

5. Develop an overall audit strategy and prepare audit programs.
6. Consider additional value-added services.

Note that Table 5-3 provides information or circumstances that may indicate an illegal act. See the textbook for the definition of "related parties" as defined by FAS No. 57.

**[LO8] Know the types of audit tests.**

A. There are three general types of audit tests. They include: (1) risk assessment procedures, (2) tests of controls and (3) substantive procedures.

B. **Risk assessment procedures** are used to obtain an understanding of the entity and its environment, including its internal control. Risk assessment procedures are used to assess the risks of material misstatement at the financial statement and assertion levels. These procedures include:

1. Inquires of management and others.
2. Analytical procedures.
3. Observation and inspection.

C. **Tests of controls** consist of procedures directed toward the evaluation of the effectiveness of the design and implementation of internal controls. When tests of controls look at design issues, the auditor evaluates whether the control has been properly designed to prevent or detect material misstatements. Tests of controls directed toward the implementation of a control are concerned with whether the control is operating effectively at a point in time. The following audit procedures are examples of tests of controls (Table 5-4):

1. Inquires of appropriate management, supervisory and staff personnel.

2. Inspection of documents, reports, and electronic files.

3. Observation of the application of specific controls.

4. Walkthroughs, which involve tracing a transaction from its origination to its inclusion in the financial statements through a combination of audit procedures including inquiry, observation and inspection.

5. Reperformance of the application of the control by the auditor.

D. **Substantive procedures** detect material misstatements (monetary errors) in a transaction class, account balance and disclosure component of the financial statements. There are two categories of substantive procedures:

1. **Tests of details of classes of transactions, account balances and disclosures.** These substantive procedures test for errors or fraud in individual transactions. These tests establish whether any material misstatements are included in the accounts or disclosures included in the financial statements. These tests provide the auditor evidence about the occurrence, completeness and accuracy assertions. Tests of controls look for errors in the design and implementation of controls, while substantive tests of transactions are concerned with monetary misstatements. For some audit tests, it is difficult to determine whether the audit procedure is a test of controls or a substantive test of transactions. In most audit situations substantive tests of transactions are conducted at the same time as tests of controls, which is referred to as "dual purpose tests."

2. **Substantive analytical procedures** will be discussed in the next section.

**[LO9] Learn the purposes and types of analytical procedures.**

A. Auditing standards (AU 329) define **analytical procedures** as consisting of evaluations of financial information made by a study of plausible relationships among both financial and nonfinancial data. An important aspect of the definition of analytical procedures is that they involve a comparison of recorded values with expectations developed by the auditor. Analytical procedures can facilitate an effective audit by helping the auditor understand the client's business, directing attention to high-risk areas, identifying audit issues that might not be otherwise apparent, providing audit evidence and assisting in the evaluation of audit results.

B. Analytical procedures are used for three purposes:

   1. **Preliminary analytical procedures** are used to assist the auditor to better understand the business and to plan the nature, timing and extent of audit procedures.

   2. **Substantive analytical procedures** are used as a substantive procedure to obtain evidential matter about particular assertions related to account balances or classes of transactions.

   3. **Final analytical procedures** are used as an overall review of the financial information in the final review stage of the audit.

Auditing standards require the use of analytical procedures for the first and third purposes, but these tests also are commonly used to gather substantive evidence because they are effective at detecting misstatements. In addition, analytical procedures are also relatively inexpensive tests to perform.

C. The purpose of the analytical procedures and the facts and circumstances will dictate the type of procedure used to form an expectation and the techniques involved in investigating a significant difference. Analytical procedures may range from the use of simple trend analysis to the use of complex regression models. Three types of analytical procedures are used to form expectations (Table 5-5):

   1. **Trend analysis** is the examination of changes in an account over time.

   2. **Ratio analysis** is the comparison, across time or to a benchmark, of relationships between financial statement accounts or between an account and nonfinancial data.

   3. **Reasonableness analysis** is the development of a model to form an expectation using financial data, nonfinancial data, or both, to test account balances, or changes in account balances between accounting periods.

D. Figure 5-3 presents an overview of the auditor's decision process when using substantive analytical procedures to collect audit evidence. This process includes the following steps (see the comprehensive example for EarthWear):

   1. **Develop an expectation**. An expectation can be developed using information from a variety of sources such as:

      a. Financial and operating data.
      b. Budgets and forecasts.

    c. Industry publications.
    d. Competitor information.
    e. Management's analyses.
    f. Analyst's reports.

Examples of expectations formed by analytical procedures include:

    a. Comparison of current-year financial information with comparable prior periods(s) after consideration of known changes.

    b. Comparison of current-year financial information with budgets, projections and forecasts.

    c. Relationships among elements of financial information within the current period.

    d. Comparison of the client's financial information with industry data.

    e. Relationships of financial information to nonfinancial information.

    f. Plotting trends over multiple periods.

The precision of the expectation must be determined. The quality of an expectation is referred to as the precision of the expectation. Factors that may affect the precision of analytical procedures include:

    a. Disaggregation of the data.
    b. Plausibility and predictability of the relationship being studied.
    c. Data reliability.
    d. Type of analytical procedure used to form an expectation.

2. **Define a tolerable difference.** The second step in the substantive analytical procedures decision process is to define a tolerable difference that would require further investigation. The amount of difference that can be tolerated will always be lower than planning materiality, and when testing an entire account will usually be equal to the account's tolerable misstatement. Auditors often use rules of thumb such as "tolerable difference is 10% of the predicted amount and/or a difference less than $75,000."

3. **Compare the expectation to the recorded amount.** If the observed difference is less than the tolerable difference, the auditor accepts the account, but if not, the auditor must investigate the difference using other audit procedures.

4. **Investigate the differences greater than the tolerable difference.** There are four possible causes of significant differences - accounting changes, economic conditions or events, error and fraud. Auditors typically reexamine and understand the various relationships in the financial and nonfinancial data, and based on their previous experience with the client, other audit work performed, and discussions with other members of the audit team, they develop potential explanations for the observed difference. Explanations for significant differences observed for substantive analytical procedures must be followed up and resolved through quantification, corroboration and evaluation.

The way in which differences are investigated diverges in important ways for preliminary and final analytical procedures. At planning, the auditor is not required to obtain corroborative evidence because analytical procedures performed at the planning phase are not intended to provide substantive audit evidence regarding specific assertions. When conducting final analytical procedures, the auditor investigates unexpected differences by first going to the working papers to determine if sufficient competent evidence has already been gathered to explain the difference. If the auditor cannot find sufficient evidence within the working papers, then the auditor would formulate possible explanations, conduct additional testing and seek an explanation from the client.

5. **Documentation requirements for decision process.** When an analytical procedure is used as the principal substantive procedure for a significant financial statement assertion, the auditor should document all of the following:

   a. The expectation and how it was developed.

   b. Results of the comparison of the expectation to the recorded amounts or ratios developed from recorded amounts.

   c. Any additional auditing procedures performed in response to significant unexpected differences arising from the analytical procedure and the results of the additional procedures.

## [LO10] Understand the audit testing hierarchy.

A. The risk-driven audit approach is referred to as a "top-down" approach, where the auditor obtains an understanding of the client's business objectives and strategies, identifies business and audit risks, documents an understanding of internal control and then gathers sufficient, competent audit evidence using a combination of tests of controls, substantive analytical procedures, and tests of details to support the audit opinion (or audit opinions for public companies – auditor performs an integrated audit and opines on both internal control and the financial statements).

B. The overall decision approach used to gather evidence is depicted in Figure 5-5 and is referred to in the textbook as the audit testing hierarchy. This hierarchy starts with tests of controls and substantive analytical procedures because it is more effective and more efficient than starting with tests of details.

C. Applying the audit testing hierarchy is more effective. For example, understanding and testing of controls will influence the nature, timing and extent of substantive procedures and will enhance the auditor's ability to hone in on areas where misstatements are more likely to be found. If controls are highly effective, less extensive substantive procedures (substantive analytical procedures and tests of details) will need to be performed. Similarly, substantive analytical procedures can direct attention to higher-risk areas where the auditor can design and conduct focused tests of details.

D. Applying the audit testing hierarchy is more efficient. For example, tests of controls and analytical procedures are less costly to perform than are tests of details. This is usually because tests of controls and substantive analytical procedures provide assurance on multiple transactions. In other words, by testing controls and related processes, the auditor generally gains a degree of assurance over thousands or even millions of transactions. Substantive analytical procedures often provide evidence related to more than one assertion and often more than one balance or class of transactions. On the other hand, tests of details often only provide assurance related to one or two specific assertions pertaining to the specific transaction(s) or balance tested.

E.  Auditing standards require that auditors perform substantive procedures for significant account balances and classes of transactions, regardless of the assessed level of control risk. In other words, assurance obtained solely from testing controls is not sufficient for significant balances and classes of transactions. For this reason, Figure 5-5 depicts that either substantive analytical procedures, tests of details, or both, will always be conducted for significant accounts or classes of transactions. For high-risk areas or highly material accounts, the auditor will always perform some tests of details in additional to tests of controls and substantive analytical procedures. The decision process depicted in Figure 5-5 recognizes that for some assertions, tests of details may be the only form of testing used, because in some cases it is more efficient and effective to move directly to tests of details (low volume of large transactions or poor controls resulting in unreliable client data).

F.  An "Assurance Bucket" Analogy is used to explain audit evidence. Figure 5-6 illustrates the "assurance bucket," which must be filled with sufficient evidence to obtain the level of assurance necessary to support the auditor's opinion. Following the top-down hierarchy means that auditors first begin to fill the bucket with evidence from the risk assessment procedures (about 20 percent full). The auditor would next conduct tests of controls (which might add another 30 percent to the bucket). The auditor next performs substantive analytical procedures and adds the assurance gained from these procedures to the bucket (now the bucket is about 70 percent full). In this illustration, the auditor would need to top off the assurance bucket with evidence obtained through tests of details. For lower-risk, well-controlled accounts, the assurance bucket may be entirely filled with tests of controls and substantive analytical procedures. For other accounts or assertions, the bucket may be filled primarily with tests of details.

G.  The size of the assurance bucket can vary, depending on the auditor's risk assessment and the assertion being tested. Certain assertions will be more important or present bigger risks for some accounts than for others (Figure 5-7). After the auditor has determined the risks associated with the assertions for an account balance, he or she can determine the size of the assurance buckets (how much assurance is needed) and then begin filling the buckets by applying the audit testing hierarchy. The auditor's decisions are subjective and require considerable professional judgment.

# ADVANCED MODULE
## SELECTED FINANCIAL RATIOS

**[LO11] Identify financial ratios that are useful as analytical procedures.**

A. A number of financial ratios are used by auditors as analytical procedures. The auditor may compare the client's ratios with industry averages (see Exhibit 5-4). While the industry averages serve as useful benchmarks, certain limitations should be recognized. For example, industry ratios are averages, and as such, they may not capture operating or geographical factors that may be specific to the client. The use of different accounting principles for valuing inventory or calculating depreciation may also result in differences from industry averages for certain ratios. The industry data may not be available in sufficient detail for a particular client. In addition, audit research has shown that material misstatements may not significantly affect certain ratios. This is particularly true for activity ratios. The auditor must be careful not to evaluate a financial ratio in isolation. For example, a ratio may be favorable because its components are unfavorable, so if related ratios are not examined, the auditor may draw an incorrect conclusion. Ratios are broken down into four categories: short-term liquidity, activity, profitability and coverage ratios.

B. **Short-term liquidity ratios** indicate the entity's ability to meet its current obligations. Three ratios commonly used for this purpose are the current ratio, quick (or acid test) ratio and the operating cash flow ratio. The formula for these ratios are shown below:

$$\text{Current Ratio} = \frac{\text{Current Assets}}{\text{Current Liabilities}}$$

$$\text{Quick Ratio} = \frac{\text{Liquid Assets}}{\text{Current Liabilities}}$$

$$\text{Operating Cash Flow Ratio} = \frac{\text{Cash Flow from Operations}}{\text{Current Liabilities}}$$

C. **Activity ratios** indicate how effectively the entity's assets are managed. Only ratios related to accounts receivable and inventory are discussed here because for most wholesale, retail or manufacturing companies these two accounts represent the assets that have high activity. Activity ratios also may be effective in helping the auditor determine if these accounts contain material misstatements.

$$\text{Receivables Turnover} = \frac{\text{Credit Sales}}{\text{Receivables}}$$

$$\text{Days Outstanding in Accounts Receivable} = \frac{365 \text{ days}}{\text{Receivables Turnover}}$$

$$\text{Inventory Turnover} = \frac{\text{Cost of Goods Sold}}{\text{Inventory}}$$

$$\text{Days of Inventory on Hand} = \frac{365 \text{ days}}{\text{Inventory Turnover}}$$

D. **Profitability ratios** indicate the entity's success or failure for a given period. A number of ratios measure the profitability of an entity and each ratio should be interpreted by comparison to industry data. They include: (1) gross profit percentage, (2) profit margin, (3) return on assets and (4) return on equity.

$$\text{Gross Profit Percentage} = \frac{\text{Gross Profit}}{\text{Net Sales}}$$

$$\text{Profit Margin} = \frac{\text{Net Income}}{\text{Net Sales}}$$

$$\text{Return on Assets} = \frac{\text{Net Income}}{\text{Total Assets}}$$

$$\text{Return on Equity} = \frac{\text{Net income}}{\text{Stockholders' Equity}}$$

E. **Coverage ratios** provide information on the long-term solvency of the entity. These ratios provide the auditor important information on the entity's ability to continue as a going concern. They include: (1) debt to equity ratio and (2) times interest earned ratio.

$$\text{Debt to Equity} = \frac{\text{Short-term Debt} + \text{Long-term Debt}}{\text{Stockholders' Equity}}$$

$$\text{Times Interest Earned} = \frac{\text{Net income} + \text{Interest Expense}}{\text{Interest Expense}}$$

# CHAPTER 5: SELF-ASSESSMENT

## Part I: True or False Questions

[LO1] _____ 1.  The first phase of audit planning is risk assessment.

[LO1] _____ 2.  When the prospective client has previously been audited, auditing standards require that the successor auditor make certain inquires of the predecessor auditor before accepting the engagement.

[LO1] _____ 3.  The Code of Professional Conduct does not allow an auditor to disclose confidential client information without the client's consent.

[LO1] _____ 4.  If the prospective client refuses to allow the predecessor auditor to communicate with the successor auditor, the successor auditor should have reservations about accepting the client.

[LO4] _____ 5.  Generally, the auditor may rely on the work of an internal auditor if the internal auditor is competent and objective.

[LO5] _____ 6.  All companies must have an audit committee.

[LO5] _____ 7.  The audit committee is directly responsible for the appointment, compensation and oversight of the work of any accounting firm employed by a public company.

[LO5] _____ 8.  The external auditor is required to make a number of important communications to the audit committee during or at the end of the audit engagement.

[LO6] _____ 9.  In order to properly preplan the audit, the auditor must determine the engagement team requirements and ensure the independence of the audit team and audit firm.

[LO8] _____ 10.  There are four general types of audit tests.

## Part II: Multiple Choice Questions

[LO1]  1.  Evaluating a prospective client requires the following step(s):
   a.  Communicate with the predecessor auditor.
   b.  Preplan the audit.
   c.  Establish the terms of the engagement.
   d.  None of the above.

[LO1]  2.  Evaluating a prospective client requires the following steps(s):
   a.  Communicate with the SEC.
   b.  Preplan the audit.
   c.  Determine if the firm is independent of the client.
   d.  All of the above.

[LO1]  3.  An engagement letter may include:
   a.  Additional services to be provided relating to regulatory requirements.
   b.  Inquires about the competence and objectivity of the internal auditors.
   c.  Any limitation of the liability of the auditor.
   d.  Both a and c.

[LO5]  4.  Under Section 301 of the Sarbanes-Oxley Act, the audit committee of a privately-held company has the following requirement(s):
   a.  Each member of the committee must be a board member and shall be independent.
   b.  The audit committee must preapprove all audit and non-audit services.
   c.  The audit committee must establish and maintain procedures to handle all issues which relate to accounting, internal control, and auditing.
   d.  None of the above.

[LO5]  5.  Under Section 301 of the Sarbanes-Oxley Act, the audit committee of a public company has the following requirement(s):
   a.  Each member of the committee must be a board member and shall be independent.
   b.  The audit committee must preapprove all audit and non-audit services.
   c.  The audit committee must establish and maintain procedures to handle all issues which relate to accounting, internal control, and auditing.
   d.  All of the above.

[LO7]  6.  When preparing the audit plan, the auditor should perform the following step(s):
   a.  Determine the control risk.
   b.  Make certain that no related parties are involved with the company.
   c.  Develop an overall audit strategy and prepare audit programs.
   d.  All of the above.

[LO8]  7.  A general audit test may include:
   a.  Fee assessment procedures.
   b.  Tests of controls.
   c.  Preparation of corporate tax returns.
   d.  None of the above.

[LO8]  8.  The auditor's risk assessment procedures may include the following procedure(s):
   a.  Observation and final analytical procedures.
   b.  Observation and substantive analytical procedures.
   c.  Inquiries of management and others.
   d.  None of the above.

[LO8]  9.  In correct order, general types of audit tests include:
   a.  Substantive procedures, tests of controls and risk assessment procedures.
   b.  Substantive procedures, risk assessment procedures and tests of controls.
   c.  Risk assessment procedures, tests of controls and substantive procedures.
   d.  Risk assessment procedures, substantive procedures and tests of controls.

[LO9]  10.  An expectation about an amount or an account balance may be formulated using:
   a.  Budgets and forecasts.
   b.  Analyst's reports.
   c.  Financial and operating data.
   d.  All of the above.

## Part III: Short Essay Questions

[LO7] Discuss the purposes for planning the audit and identify the steps that are performed during this phase of the engagement.

[LO8] Identify and discuss the types of audit tests.

[LO9] What are analytical procedures and what are the purposes for using these procedures?

# Part IV: Crossword Puzzle – Chapter 5 [LO ALL]

## Across

4  An abbreviation for a component used to fill the "Assurance Bucket" (account balances/classes of transactions).
7  The SEC uses this system as a means of providing financial and other information about public companies.
8  The auditor's communications with the predecessor auditor should include questions related to the _____ of management.
10 Change in an account over time.
11 The organization that develops auditing standards for public companies.
12 An abbreviation for the AICPA organization which develops auditing standards for nonpublic companies.

## Down

1  _____ analytical procedures are used as an overall review of the financial information.
2  A risk-driven audit approach (two words).
3  These parties are associated and transactions between them may not be at an arm's length.
5  An audit procedure for evaluating or comparing plausible relationships.
6  Analytical procedures broken down into four categories: liquidity, activity, profitability, and coverage.
9  The auditor must assess inherent, control, and detection _____ .

**Part V: Townsend Office Supplies and Equipment [LO ALL]**

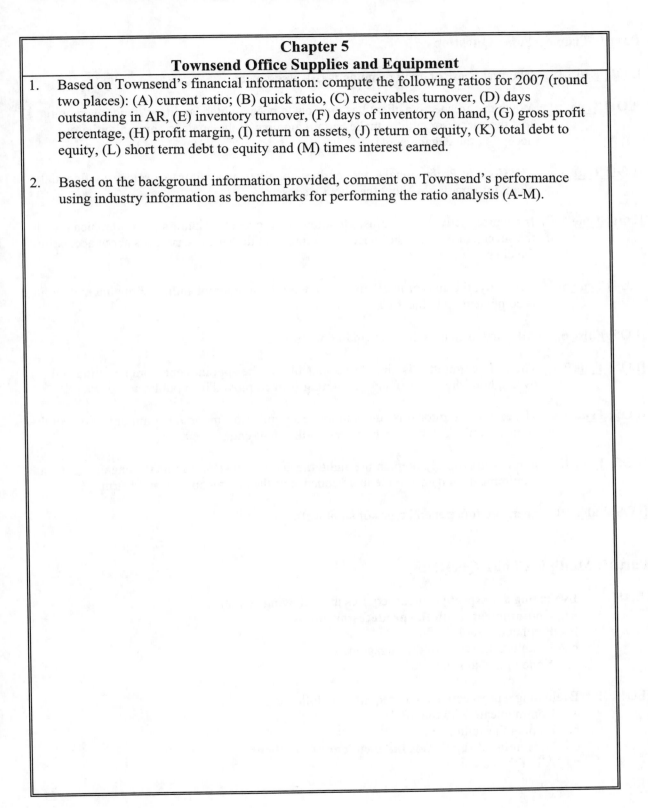

**Chapter 5**
**Townsend Office Supplies and Equipment**

1. Based on Townsend's financial information: compute the following ratios for 2007 (round two places): (A) current ratio; (B) quick ratio, (C) receivables turnover, (D) days outstanding in AR, (E) inventory turnover, (F) days of inventory on hand, (G) gross profit percentage, (H) profit margin, (I) return on assets, (J) return on equity, (K) total debt to equity, (L) short term debt to equity and (M) times interest earned.

2. Based on the background information provided, comment on Townsend's performance using industry information as benchmarks for performing the ratio analysis (A-M).

# CHAPTER 5: SELF-ASSESSMENT SOLUTIONS

## Part I: True or False Questions

[LO1] **False** 1.     The first phase of audit planning is risk assessment.

[LO1] **True** 2.     When the prospective client has previously been audited, auditing standards require that the successor auditor make certain inquires of the predecessor auditor before accepting the engagement.

[LO1] **True** 3.     The Code of Professional Conduct does not allow an auditor to disclose confidential client information without the client's consent.

[LO1] **True** 4.     If the prospective client refuses to allow the predecessor auditor to communicate with the successor auditor, the successor auditor should have reservations about accepting the client.

[LO4] **True** 5.     Generally, the auditor may rely on the work of an internal auditor if the internal auditor is competent and objective.

[LO5] **False** 6.     All companies must have an audit committee.

[LO5] **True** 7.     The audit committee is directly responsible for the appointment, compensation and oversight of the work of any accounting firm employed by a public company.

[LO5] **True** 8.     The external auditor is required to make a number of important communications to the audit committee during or at the end of the audit engagement.

[LO6] **True** 9.     In order to properly preplan the audit, the auditor must determine the engagement team requirements and ensure the independence of the audit team and audit firm.

[LO8] **False** 10.     There are four general types of audit tests.

## Part II: Multiple Choice Questions

[LO1]   1.   Evaluating a prospective client requires the following step(s):
   a.   **Communicate with the predecessor auditor.**
   b.   Preplan the audit.
   c.   Establish the terms of the engagement.
   d.   None of the above.

[LO1]   2.   Evaluating a prospective client requires the following steps(s):
   a.   Communicate with the SEC.
   b.   Preplan the audit.
   c.   **Determine if the firm is independent of the client.**
   d.   All of the above.

[LO1]  3.  An engagement letter may include:
    a.  Additional services to be provided relating to regulatory requirements.
    b.  Inquires about the competence and objectivity of the internal auditors.
    c.  Any limitation of the liability of the auditor.
    **d.  Both a and c.**

[LO5]  4.  Under Section 301 of the Sarbanes-Oxley Act, the audit committee of a privately-held company has the following requirement(s):
    a.  Each member of the committee must be a board member and shall be independent.
    b.  The audit committee must preapprove all audit and non-audit services.
    c.  The audit committee must establish and maintain procedures to handle all issues which relate to accounting, internal control, and auditing.
    **d.  None of the above.**

[LO5]  5.  Under Section 301 of the Sarbanes-Oxley Act, the audit committee of a public company has the following requirement(s):
    a.  Each member of the committee must be a board member and shall be independent.
    b.  The audit committee must preapprove all audit and non-audit services.
    c.  The audit committee must establish and maintain procedures to handle all issues which relate to accounting, internal control, and auditing.
    **d.  All of the above.**

[LO7]  6.  When preparing the audit plan, the auditor should perform the following step(s):
    a.  Determine the control risk.
    b.  Make certain that no related parties are involved with the company.
    **c.  Develop an overall audit strategy and prepare audit programs.**
    d.  All of the above.

[LO8]  7.  A general audit test may include:
    a.  Fee assessment procedures.
    **b.  Tests of controls.**
    c.  Preparation of corporate tax returns.
    d.  None of the above.

[LO8]  8.  The auditor's risk assessment procedures may include the following procedure(s):
    a.  Observation and final analytical procedures.
    b.  Observation and substantive analytical procedures.
    **c.  Inquiries of management and others.**
    d.  None of the above.

[LO8]  9.  In correct order, general types of audit tests include:
    a.  Substantive procedures, tests of controls and risk assessment procedures.
    b.  Substantive procedures, risk assessment procedures and tests of controls.
    **c.  Risk assessment procedures, tests of controls and substantive procedures.**
    d.  Risk assessment procedures, substantive procedures and tests of controls.

[LO9] 10.  An expectation about an amount or an account balance may be formulated using:
    a.  Budgets and forecasts.
    b.  Analyst's reports.
    c.  Financial and operating data.
    **d.  All of the above.**

## Part III: Short Essay Questions

[LO7] Discuss the purposes for planning the audit and identify the steps that are performed during this phase of the engagement.

**Engagement planning involves all the issues the auditor should consider in developing an overall strategy for conducting the audit. The objective of the audit plan is to conduct an effective and efficient audit. This means that the audit is to be conducted in accordance with auditing standards and that the risk of material misstatements is reduced to an acceptably low level. The audit plan should also consider how to conduct the engagement in a cost-effective manner. When preparing the audit plan, the auditor should be guided by the results of the risk assessment and procedures performed to gain and support the understanding of the entity. Additional steps that should be performed include:**

1. **Assess a preliminary level for control risk by account and assertion.**

2. **Assess the possibility of illegal acts.**

3. **Identify related parties.**

4. **Conduct preliminary analytical procedures.**

5. **Develop an overall audit strategy and prepare audit programs.**

6. **Consider additional value-added services.**

---

[LO8] Identify and discuss the types of audit tests.

**There are three general types of audit tests. They include: (1) risk assessment procedures, (2) tests of controls and (3) substantive procedures.**

**Risk assessment procedures are used to obtain an understanding of the entity and its environment, including its internal control. Risk assessment procedures are used to assess the risks of material misstatement at the financial statement and assertion levels.**

**Tests of controls consist of procedures directed toward the evaluation of the effectiveness of the design and implementation of internal controls. When tests of controls look at design issues, the auditor evaluates whether the control has been properly designed to prevent or detect material misstatements. Tests of controls directed toward the implementation of a control are concerned with whether that control is operating effectively at a point in time.**

**Substantive procedures detect material misstatements (monetary errors) in a transaction class, account balance and disclosure component of the financial statements.**

[LO9] What are analytical procedures and what are the purposes for using these procedures?

**Auditing standards (AU 329) define analytical procedures as consisting of evaluations of financial information made by a study of plausible relationships among both financial and nonfinancial data. An important aspect of the definition of analytical procedures is that they involve a comparison of recorded values with expectations developed by the auditor. Analytical procedures can facilitate an effective audit by helping the auditor understand the client's business, directing attention to high-risk areas, identifying audit issues that might not be otherwise apparent, providing audit evidence and assisting in the evaluation of audit results. Analytical procedures are used for three purposes:**

**Preliminary analytical procedures are used to assist the auditor to better understand the business and to plan the nature, timing and extent of audit procedures.**

**Substantive analytical procedures are used as a substantive procedure to obtain evidential matter about particular assertions related to account balances or classes of transactions.**

**Final analytical procedures are used as an overall review of the financial information in the final review stage of the audit.**

**Auditing standards require the use of analytical procedures for the first and third purposes, but these tests are also commonly used to gather substantive evidence because they are effective at detecting misstatements and relatively inexpensive tests to perform.**

## Part IV: Crossword Puzzle – Chapter 5 Solution [LO ALL]

```
                    1F
                     I                    4S  5A  P        2T
              3R     N              S   A  P              O
      6R   7E  D  G  A  R              N                  P
       A    L              A          A                  D
       T    A                         L                  O
      8I  N  T  E  G  9R  I  T  Y                         W
       O    E          I          10T  R  E  N  D
       S    D          S           I
                       K        11P  C  A  O  B
                  12A  S  B        A
                                   L
```

### Across

4  An abbreviation for a component used to fill the "Assurance Bucket" (account balances/classes of transactions).
7  The SEC uses this system as a means of providing financial and other information about public companies.
8  The auditor's communications with the predecessor auditor should include questions related to the _____ of management.
10  Change in an account over time.
11  The organization that develops auditing standards for public companies.
12  An abbreviation for the AICPA organization which develops auditing standards for nonpublic companies.

### Down

1  _____ analytical procedures are used as an overall review of the financial information.
2  A risk-driven audit approach (two words).
3  These parties are associated and transactions between them may not be at an arm's length.
5  An audit procedure for evaluating or comparing plausible relationships.
6  Analytical procedures broken down into four categories: liquidity, activity, profitability, and coverage.
9  The auditor must assess inherent, control, and detection _____ .

---

**Chapter 5**
**Townsend Office Supplies and Equipment**

1. Based on Townsend's financial information: compute the following ratios for 2007 (round two places): (A) current ratio; (B) quick ratio, (C) receivables turnover, (D) days outstanding in AR, (E) inventory turnover, (F) days of inventory on hand, (G) gross profit percentage, (H) profit margin, (I) return on assets, (J) return on equity, (K) total debt to equity, (L) short term debt to equity and (M) times interest earned.

2. Based on the background information provided, comment on Townsend's performance using industry information as benchmarks for performing the ratio analysis (A-M).

1. **Townsend's 2007 ratios are:**
   **Current ratio = 1592/898 = 1.77:1.00**
   **Quick ratio = 210 + 274 + 310/898 = 794/898 = 0.88:1.00**
   **Receivables turnover = 5231 − 785/(310 + 432)/2 = 4446/371 = 11.98 times**
   **Days outstanding in AR = 365/11.98 = 31 days**
   **Inventory turnover = 2511/(672 + 124)/2 = 2511/398 = 6.31 times**
   **Days of inventory on hand = 365/6.31 = 58 days**
   **Gross profit percentage = 2720/5231 = 52%**
   **Profit margin = 241/5231 = 4.61%**
   **Return on assets = 241/(4101 + 3938)/2 = 241/4019.5 = 6%**
   **Return on equity = 241/(1989 + 1848)/2 = 241/1918.5 = 12.56%**
   **Total debt to equity = 2100/1989 = 106%**
   **Short-term debt to equity = 898/1989 = 45.15%**
   **Times interest earned = (241 + 117/117 = 358/117 = 3.06 times**

2. **Townsend's performance using industry financial information as benchmarks:**
   **(F) Above industry standard (Current ratio = 1.77:1.00 to industry 1.57:1:00)**
   **(U) Below industry standard (Quick ratio = 0.88:1.00 to industry 0.98:1.00)**
   **(I) Receivables turnover – industry benchmark not provided**
   **(F) In line with industry standard (Days outstanding in AR = 31 days to 32 days)**
   **(I) Inventory turnover – industry benchmark not provided**
   **(U) Above industry standard (Inventory on hand = 58 days to industry to 45)**
   **(F) Below industry standard (Gross profit percentage = 52% to industry 55%)**
   **(F) Above industry standard (Profit margin = 4.61% to industry 4%)**
   **(U) Below industry standard (Return on assets = 6% to industry 9%)**
   **(U) Below industry standard (Return on equity = 12.56% to 14%)**
   **(F) Below industry standard (Total debt to equity = 106% to industry 115%)**
   **(F) Below industry standard (Short-term debt to equity = 45.15% to industry 51%)**
   **(F) Below industry standard (TIE = 3.06 times to industry to industry 5.1 times)**

**Note: F = Favorable, I = Industry benchmark not available, and U = Unfavorable (comparison of Townsend to industry).**

**While most of Townsend's ratios meet the industry benchmarks, all differences greater than the established tolerable differences should be investigated.**

# Internal Control in a Financial Statement Audit

## KEY THOUGHT

In all audits, the auditor should obtain an understanding of internal control sufficient to plan the audit by performing procedures to understand the design of controls relevant to an audit of financial statements, and whether they have been placed in operation [Auditing Standards Board (AU 319.02)].

## CHAPTER SUMMARY

**[LO1] Understand the importance of internal control to management and auditors.**

A. Management has the responsibility to maintain controls that provide reasonable assurance that adequate control exists over the entity's assets and records. Proper internal control not only ensures that assets and records are safeguarded but also creates an environment in which efficiency and effectiveness are encouraged and monitored. Management also needs a control system that generates reliable information for decision making.

B. The auditor needs assurance about the reliability of the data generated by the information system in terms of how it affects the fairness of the financial statements and how well the assets and records of the entity are safeguarded. The auditor uses risk assessment procedures to obtain an understanding of the entity's internal control. The auditor uses this understanding of internal control to identify the types of potential misstatements; consider factors that affect the risk of material misstatement; and design the nature, timing, and extent of further audit procedures. There is an inverse relationship between the reliability of internal control (achieved control risk) and the amount of substantive procedures required of the auditor. In short, when the auditor is filling the assurance bucket for an assertion, obtaining more controls evidence means he or she needs to obtain less substantive evidence to top the bucket off.

C. The auditor's understanding of internal control is a major factor in determining the overall audit strategy. The auditor's responsibilities for internal control include: (1) obtaining an understanding of internal control and (2) assessing control risk.

**[LO2] Know the definition of internal control.**

A. **Internal control** is designed and affected by an entity's board of directors, management and other personnel to provide reasonable assurance about the achievement of the entity's objectives in the following categories: (1) reliability of financial reporting, (2) effectiveness and efficiency of operations, and (3) compliance with applicable laws and regulations. Internal control over the safeguarding of assets against unauthorized acquisition, use, or disposition is also important and it may include controls relating to financial reporting and operations objectives.

**[LO3] Know what controls are relevant to the audit.**

A. Not all of the entity's internal controls are relevant to a financial statement audit. Internal controls pertaining to the preparation of financial statements for external purposes are relevant to an audit. Controls relating to operations and compliance objectives may be relevant when they relate to data the auditor uses to apply auditing procedures. On the other hand, some controls that relate to management's planning or operating decisions may not be relevant for audit purposes.

**[LO4] Be able to identify the components of internal control.**

A. Internal control consists of five components. They include (Table 6-1):

1. **Control Environment.** The control environment sets the tone of an organization, influencing the control consciousness of its people. It is the foundation for effective internal control, providing discipline and structure. The control environment includes the attitudes, awareness, policies and actions of management and the board of directors concerning the entity's internal control and its importance in the entity.

2. **The Entity's Risk Assessment Process.** For financial reporting purposes, the entity's risk assessment process includes how management identifies risks relevant to the preparation of financial statements that are fairly presented in conformity with GAAP, estimates their significance, assesses the likelihood of their occurrence, and decides upon actions to manage them.

3. **The Entity's Information System and Related Business Processes Relevant to Financial Reporting and Communication.** The information system relevant to financial reporting objectives includes the accounting system, which consists of the procedures, whether automated or manual, and records established to initiate, record, process, and report entity transactions and to maintain accountability for the related assets, liabilities and equity. Communication involves providing an understanding of individual roles and responsibilities pertaining to internal control over financial reporting.

4. **Control Activities.** Control activities are the policies and procedures that help ensure that management directives are carried out, for example, that necessary actions are taken to address risks to achievement of the entity's objectives. Control activities, whether automated or manual, have various objectives and are applied at various organizational and functional levels.

5. **Monitoring of Controls.** Monitoring of control is a process to assess the quality of internal control performance over time. It involves assessing the design and operation of controls on a timely basis and taking necessary corrective actions.

**[LO5] Understand the effect of information technology on internal control.**

A. The extent of an entity's use of information technology (IT) can affect any of the five components of internal control. The use of IT affects the way that transactions are initiated, recorded, processed and reported. Controls in most IT systems consist of a combination of manual controls and automated controls. In such situations, manual controls may be independent of the IT environment.

B. There are benefits associated with using IT for an entity's internal control. They include (Table 6-2):

1. Consistent application of predefined business rules and performance of complex calculations in processing large volumes of transactions or data.

2. Enhancement of the timeliness, availability and accuracy of information.

3. Facilitation of additional analysis of information.

4. Enhancement of the ability to monitor the performance of the entity's activities and its policies and procedures.

5. Reduction in the risk that controls will be circumvented.

6. Enhancement of the ability to achieve effective segregation of duties by implementing security controls in applications, databases and operating systems.

C. There are risks associated with using IT for an entity's internal control. They include (Table 6-2):

1. Reliance on systems or programs that inaccurately process data, process inaccurate data, or both.

2. Unauthorized access to data that may result in destruction of data or improper changes to data, including the recording of unauthorized or nonexistent transactions or inaccurate recording of transactions.

3. Unauthorized changes to data in master files.

4. Unauthorized changes to systems or programs.

5. Failure to make necessary changes to systems or programs.

6. Inappropriate manual intervention.

7. Potential loss of data.

Another common challenge that increases controls risk is the fact that many clients have a large variety of technological platforms, software and hardware. Companies that have grown through merger and acquisition frequently band the legacy systems together rather than replace one or both systems. The resulting montage of servers, computers, off-the-shelf and custom-programmed software creates a complex and potentially risk-prone IT environment.

**[LO6] Understand how to plan an audit strategy.**

A. In applying the audit risk model (AR = IR × CR × DR), the auditor must assess control risk. The auditor's initial step is obtaining a preliminary understanding of internal control. This understanding will be developed as part of the auditor's risk assessment process using risk assessment procedures.

B. With a recurring engagement, the auditor is likely to possess substantial knowledge about the client's internal control; hence, the auditor may be able to choose an audit strategy that includes little updating of the understanding of the entity's internal control. For a new client, the auditor may delay making a judgment about an audit strategy until a more detailed understanding of internal control is obtained.

C. The auditor must assess the risk of material misstatement. The information gathered by performing risk assessment procedures is used to evaluate the design of controls and to determine whether they have been implemented. The auditor uses the understanding and assessment of internal control to determine the nature, timing and extent of audit procedures. There are two audit strategies: a substantive strategy and a reliance strategy. There is no one strategy for the entire audit; instead, the auditor establishes a strategy for individual business processes or by a specific assertion within a business process.

D. **Substantive Strategy.** When the auditor's risk-assessment procedures indicate that the controls are not properly designed or not operating effectively, the auditor is not likely to test controls because control risk will be set at maximum (Figure 6-2):

   1. The auditor will use substantive procedures to reduce the risk of material misstatement to an acceptably low level. In other words, the assurance bucket is filled almost entirely with substantive evidence.

   2. Even when a substantive strategy is followed, the auditor is still required by auditing standards to have an understanding of the five components of internal control. A substantive audit approach means that the auditor has decided not to rely on the entity's controls and to directly audit the related financial statement accounts. The auditor may decide to follow a substantive strategy and set control risk at the maximum for some or all assertions because of one or all of the following factors:

      a. The controls do not pertain to an assertion.
      b. The controls are assessed as ineffective.
      c. Testing the effectiveness of controls is inefficient.

   3. Substantive tests are designed and performed based on the assessment of a maximum level of control risk. In other words, the assurance bucket is filled with evidence from the risk assessment procedures and an extensive amount from substantive procedures (substantive analytical procedures and tests of details).

E. **Reliance Strategy.** When the auditor's risk-assessment procedures suggest that the controls are operating effectively and the auditor intends to set control risk in the audit risk model at less than maximum, the auditor is required to perform tests of controls to obtain audit evidence that the controls are, in fact, operating effectively (Figure 6-2).

---

It's reasonable to assume that more reliable audit evidence is generated from a system where the internal control is operating correctly, and normally, less audit evidence is required when the internal control system is effective. For the moment, here's a simple way to remember how an auditor's reliance on a client's internal control will affect control risk, detection risk, and audit evidence (based on audit risk model):

where M = The Model Rule. When the auditor's reliance on the internal control system goes up, control risk goes down, detection risk goes up, and audit evidence goes down.

---

116

1. Even when an auditor is following a reliance strategy, the amount of assurance obtained by controls testing will vary from assertion to assertion from low to high. In short, a reliance strategy means that the auditor intends to begin filling the assurance bucket with controls evidence, but the percentage of the bucket filled with controls evidence will differ between assertions. It is important to understand that auditing standards require some substantive evidence for all significant accounts and assertions; thus, a reliance strategy reduces, but does not eliminate the need to gather some substantive evidence.

2. Situations where the auditor may find it necessary to follow a reliance strategy include the following:

   a. An entity that initiates orders using electronic data interchange (EDI) for goods based on predetermined decision rules and pays the related payables based on system-generated information regarding receipt of goods. No other documentation is produced or maintained.

   b. An entity that provides electronic services to customers, such as an Internet service provider or a telephone company, and uses IT to log services provided to users, initiate bills for the services, process the billing transactions, and automatically record such amounts in electronic accounting records.

3. The auditor obtains an understanding of internal control as the basis for assessing a lower level of control risk. The reliance strategy requires a more detailed understanding of internal control than the substantive strategy because the auditor intends to rely on the controls. The auditor documents his or her understanding of internal control and plans and performs tests of controls. Control risk is then assessed based on the results of the tests. If the achieved level of control risk does not support the planned level of control risk, the auditor normally increases the planned substantive procedures and documents the revised control risk assessment. If the planned level of control risk is supported, no revisions of the planned substantive procedures are required. The level of control risk is documented, and substantive procedures are performed.

Note that the Sarbanes-Oxley Act (2002) requires public company auditors to test and report on the design and effectiveness of public company internal controls (PCAOB Auditing Standard No. 5). Thus, it is expected that every public company audit will follow a reliance strategy to some degree.

F.  The level of control risk is normally set in terms of the assertions about classes of transactions and events for the period under audit. These assertions and control procedures are summarized in the table below (Table 6-4):

Assertions about Classes of Transactions and Related Control Procedures

| Assertion | Control Procedures |
|-----------|--------------------|
| Occurrence | Segregation of duties.<br>Prenumbered documents that are accounted for.<br>Daily/monthly reconciliation of subsidiary records with independent review. |
| Completeness | Prenumbered documents that are accounted for.<br>Segregation of duties.<br>Daily/monthly reconciliation of subsidiary records with independent review. |
| Cutoff | Procedures for prompt recording of transactions.<br>Internal review and verification. |
| Authorizations | General and specific authorization at import control points. |
| Accuracy | Internal verification of amounts and calculations.<br>Monthly reconciliation of subsidiary records by an independent person. |
| Classification | Chart of accounts.<br>Internal review and verification. |

## [LO7] Know how to develop an understanding of an entity's internal control.

A.  The auditor should obtain an understanding of each of the five components of internal control, including the design of relevant controls to plan the audit. This knowledge is used to:

1.  Identify the types of potential misstatement.
2.  Consider factors that affect the risk of material misstatement.
3.  Design tests of controls.
4.  Design substantive procedures.

In deciding on the nature and extent of the understanding of internal control needed for the audit, the auditor should consider the complexity and sophistication of the entity's operations and systems, including the extent to which the entity relies on manual controls or on automated controls. More attention should be devoted to understanding internal control as the complexity and sophistication of the operations and systems increase.

To understand a client's internal control, an auditor must understand the five components of internal control. The main difference between the reliance and substantive audit strategies, in terms of understanding internal control, is the extent of required knowledge about each of the components; a greater understanding is normally required if a reliance strategy is followed. In addition to previous experience with a client, an auditor may use the following audit procedures to learn about internal control:

1.  Inquiry of appropriate management, supervisory and staff personnel.
2.  Inspection of entity documents and reports.
3.  Observation of entity activities and operations.

118

B. The **control environment** sets the tone of an organization, influencing the control consciousness of its people. It is the foundation for all other components of internal control, providing discipline and structure. Factors that affect the control environment include (Table 6-5):

1. Communication and enforcement of integrity and ethical values.
2. A commitment to competence.
3. Participation of the board of directors or audit committee.
4. Management's philosophy and operating style.
5. Organizational structure.
6. Assignment of authority and responsibility.
7. Human resource polices and practices.

The importance of control to an entity is reflected in the overall attitude to, awareness of, and actions of the board of directors, management and owners regarding control. The control environment can be thought of as an umbrella that covers the entire entity and establishes the framework for implementing the entity's accounting systems and internal controls. To that end, the auditor should gain sufficient knowledge about the control environment to understand management's and the board of directors' attitudes, awareness and actions concerning the control environment, considering both the substance of controls and their collective effect.

C. An entity's **risk assessment process** is its process for identifying and responding to business risks. This process includes how management identifies risks relevant to the preparation of financial statements. For example, the entity's risk assessment process may address how the entity identifies and analyzes significant estimates recorded in the financial statements. The risk assessment process should consider external and internal events and circumstances that may arise and adversely affect the entity's ability to initiate record, process and report financial data consistent with the assertions of management in the financial statements. When risks are identified by management, they should initiate plans, programs or actions to address the specific risks. Client business risks can arise or change due to the following circumstances:

1. Changes in the operating environment.
2. New personnel.
3. New or revamped information systems.
4. Rapid growth.
5. New technology.
6. New business models, products or activities.
7. Corporate restructurings.
8. Expanded international operations.
9. New accounting pronouncements.

The auditor should obtain sufficient information about the entity's risk assessment process to understand how management considers and responds to risks relevant to financial reporting objectives.

D. The auditor must understand **information systems and communication**. The information system consists of infrastructure (physical and hardware components), software, people, procedures (manual and automated), and data. The information system relevant to financial reporting includes the accounting system and its procedures, whether automated or manual, and records established to initiate, record, process and report an entity's transactions and to maintain accountability for the related assets and liabilities. An effective accounting system gives appropriate consideration to establishing methods and records that will:

1. Identify and record all valid transactions.

2. Describe on a timely basis the transactions in sufficient detail to permit proper classification of transactions for financial reporting.

3. Measure the value of transactions in a manner that permits recording their proper monetary value in the financial statements.

4. Determine the time period in which transactions occurred to permit recording of transactions in the proper accounting period.

5. Properly present the transactions and related disclosures in the financial statements.

**Communication** involves providing an understanding of the individual roles and responsibilities pertaining to internal control over financial reporting. It includes the extent to which personnel understand how their activities in the financial reporting information system relate to the work of others and the means of reporting exceptions to an appropriate higher level within the entity. Policy manuals, accounting and reporting manuals and memoranda communicate policies and procedures to the entity's personnel.

E. **Control procedures** are the policies and procedures that help ensure that management's directives are carried out. Control procedures may be either automated or manual. Those control procedures that are relevant to the audit include: (1) performance reviews, (2) information processing, (3) physical controls, and (4) segregation of duties.

The extent of the auditor's understanding of control procedures is a function of the audit strategy adopted. When a substantive strategy approach is taken, little work is done on understanding control procedures. When a reliance strategy is followed, the auditor has to understand the control procedures that relate to assertions for which a lower level of control risk is expected. Auditors normally use walkthroughs to develop an understanding of control procedures.

F. **Monitoring of controls** is a process that assesses the quality of internal control performance over time. Monitoring can be done through ongoing activities or separate evaluations. Ongoing procedures are usually built into the normal, recurring activities of the entity. In many entities, the information system produces much of the information used in monitoring.

G. The size of an entity may affect how the various components of internal control are implemented. While the basic concepts of the five components should be present in all entities, they are likely to be less formal in a small or midsize entity than in a large entity.

H. An internal control system should be designed and operated to provide reasonable assurance that an entity's objectives are being achieved. The concept of reasonable assurance should be based on a cost-benefit expectation. The necessity of balancing the cost of controls with the related benefits requires considerable estimation and judgment on the part of management.

I. The effectiveness of any internal control system is subject to certain inherent limitations, including:

1. **Management Override of Internal Controls.** An entity's controls may be overridden by management. The auditor is particularly concerned when senior management is involved in such activities because it raises serious questions about management's integrity. Violations of control procedures by senior management may be difficult to detect with normal audit procedures.

2. **Human Errors or Mistakes.** The internal control system is only as effective as the personnel who implement and perform the controls. Breakdowns in internal control can occur because of human failures, such as simple errors or mistakes.

3. **Collusion.** The effectiveness of segregation of duties lies in individuals' performing only their assigned tasks or in the performance of one person being checked by another. There is always a risk that collusion between individuals will destroy the effectiveness of segregation of duties.

## [LO8] Identify the tools available for documenting the understanding of internal control.

A. Auditing standards require that the auditor document the understanding of the entity's internal control components. An auditor should also document his or her understanding of an entity's internal control to provide evidence that the auditor conducted the audit in conformity with GAAS. A number of tools are available to the auditor for documenting his or her understanding of internal control. They include:

1. Copies of the entity's procedures manuals and organizational charts.
2. Narrative description.
3. Internal control questionnaires.
4. Flowcharts.

On many engagements, auditors combine these tools to document their understanding of the components of internal control. The combination depends on the complexity of the entity's internal control system.

## [LO9] Know how to assess the level of control risk.

A. Assessing control risk is the process of evaluating the effectiveness of an entity's internal control in preventing or detecting material misstatements in the financial statements (maximum for a substantive strategy and lower level for a reliance strategy).

B. When the auditor assesses control risk at the maximum (a substantive strategy), the control risk assessment is documented and planned substantive procedures are performed.

C. When the auditor plans to set control risk below the maximum, the auditor must:

1. Identify specific controls that will be relied upon.
2. Perform tests of controls.
3. Conclude on the achieved level of control risk.

The auditor's understanding of internal control is used to identify the controls that are likely to prevent or detect material misstatement in specific assertions. In identifying controls to be relied upon, the auditor should consider that the controls could have a pervasive effect on many assertions. Alternatively, some controls only affect an individual assertion contained in the financial statements. General controls are pervasive to all information systems, while application controls relate to a specific business process (such as sales or purchasing).

**[LO10] Know the types of tests of controls.**

A. Audit procedures directed toward evaluating the effectiveness of either the design or the operation of an internal control are referred to as tests of controls. Tests of controls are performed in order to provide evidence to support the lower level of control risk. Tests of controls directed toward the effectiveness of the design of a control are concerned with evaluating whether that control is suitably designed to prevent material misstatements. Tests of controls directed toward operating effectiveness are concerned with assessing how the control was applied, the consistency with which it was applied during the audit period, and by whom it was applied. Procedures used as tests of controls include:

1. Inquiry of appropriate entity personnel.

2. Inspection of documents, reports or electronic files indicating the performance of the control.

3. Observation of the application of the control.

4. Walkthroughs, which involve tracing a transaction from its origination to its inclusion in the financial statements through a combination of audit procedures including inquiry, observation and inspection.

5. Reperformance of the application of the control by the auditor.

A combination of these procedures may be necessary to evaluate the effectiveness of the design or operation of a control. The operating effectiveness of the control can be affected by whether the control is performed manually or is automated. If the control is performed manually it may be subject to personnel errors or mistakes. If properly designed, automated controls should operate more effectively. Because of the inherent consistency of IT processing, the auditor may be able to reduce the extent of testing of an automated control. To test automated controls, the auditor may need to use techniques that are different from those used to test manual controls. For example, computer-assisted audit techniques (CAATs) may be used to test automated controls.

B. The conclusion that results from the tests of controls is referred to as the achieved level of control risk. The auditor uses the achieved level of control risk and the assessed level of inherent risk to determine the acceptable level of detection risk. The level of detection risk is used to determine the substantive tests. If the tests of controls are consistent with the auditor's planned assessment of control risk, no revision in the nature, timing or extent of substantive procedures is necessary. On the other hand, if the tests of controls achieved indicate that the controls are not operating as preliminarily assessed, the level of control risk will have to be increased, and the nature, timing and extent of planned substantive procedures will have to be modified.

C. Auditing standards require the auditor to document the basis of his or her conclusions about the assessed level of control risk. For those assertions where the achieved level of control risk is below the maximum level, the auditor should document the basis for his or her conclusion that the effectiveness of the design and operation of controls supports that assessed level. The auditor's assessment of control risk and the basis for the achieved level of control risk can be documented using a structured working paper, an internal control questionnaire or a memorandum.

**[LO11] Understand audit strategies for the nature, timing, and extent of substantive procedures based on different levels of detection risk.**

A. The last step in the decision process under either strategy is performing substantive procedures. Substantive procedures include substantive analytical procedures and tests of details. The nature, timing and extent of substantive procedures may vary as a function of the detection risk. For example, assume that audit risk is set low for two clients, but that Client 1 has a high level of inherent risk and control risk, while Client 2 has a low level of inherent risk and control risk. Remembering that detection risk and audit evidence is inversely related, the use of the audit risk model yields the following generalizations:

**Client 1 (Low Detection Risk)** high level of control risk

1. More reliable types of audit evidence, such as confirmation and reperformance, must be obtained (the nature of evidence).

2. Most of the audit work can be conducted at year-end (the timing of evidence).

3. A larger sample size should be used (the extent of the evidence).

**Client 2 (High Detection Risk)**

1. Less reliable types of audit evidence, such as analytical procedures, can be obtained (the nature of evidence).

2. Most of the audit work can be conducted at an interim date (the timing of evidence).

3. A smaller sample size can be used (the extent of the evidence).

**[LO12] Understand the considerations for the timing of audit procedures.**

A. Audit procedures may be conducted at an interim date or at year-end. An auditor might test controls at an interim date because the assertion being tested may not be significant, the control has been effective in prior audits, or it may be more efficient to conduct the tests at that time (i.e., less busy time and overtime can be reduced). Additionally, if the controls are found not to be operating effectively, testing them at an interim date gives the auditor more time to reassess the control risk and modify the audit plan. It also gives the auditor time to inform management so that likely misstatements can be located and corrected before the rest of the audit is performed. An important question that the auditor must address is the need for additional audit work in the period following the interim testing period. The auditor must consider factors such as the significance of the assertion, the evaluation of the design and operation of the control, the results of tests of controls, the length of the remaining period, and the planned substantive procedures in determining the nature and extent of audit work for the remaining period. At a minimum, the auditor would inquire about the nature and extent of changes in policies, procedures, or personnel that occurred subsequent to the interim period. If significant changes have occurred, or if the results of tests of controls are unfavorable, the auditor may need to conduct additional audit procedures for the period not included in the interim testing.

B. Conducting substantive procedures at an interim date may increase the risk that material misstatements are present in the financial statements. The auditor can control for this potential problem by considering when it is appropriate to examine an account at an interim date and by performing selected audit procedures for the period between the interim date and year-end. The auditor should consider the following factors when substantive tests are to be completed at an interim date:

1. The control environment.

2. The relevant controls.

3. The objective of the substantive procedure.

4. The assessed risk of material misstatement.

5. The nature of the class of transactions or account balances and related assertions.

6. The ability of the auditor to reduce the risk that misstatements which exist at the end of the period are not detected by performing appropriate substantive procedures or substantive procedures combined with tests of controls to cover the remaining period.

Note that if the entity's accounting system has control weaknesses that result in a high level of assessed control risk, it is unlikely that the auditor would conduct substantive procedures at an interim date.

When the auditor conducts substantive procedures of an account at an interim date, some additional substantive procedures are ordinarily conducted in the remaining period. This may include comparing the year-end account balance with the interim account balance. It might also involve conducting some analytical procedures or reviewing related journals and ledgers for large or unusual transactions. If misstatements are detected during interim testing, the auditor will have to revise the planned substantive procedures for the remaining period or reperform some substantive procedures at year-end.

**[LO13] Understand how to assess control risk when an entity's accounting transactions are processed by a service organization.**

A. In some instances, a client may have some or all of its accounting transactions processed by an outside service organization. Examples of such service organizations include mortgage bankers that service mortgages for others and trust departments that invest or hold assets for employee benefit plans. More frequently, service organizations are IT service centers that process transactions such as payroll and the related accounting reports. Auditing standards provide guidance to the auditor when a client uses a service organization to process certain transactions. When a client obtains services from a service organization, those services are part of an entity's information system if they affect any of the following:

1. How the client's transactions are initiated.

2. The accounting records, supporting information, and specific accounts in the financial statements involved in the processing and reporting of the client's transactions.

3. The accounting processing involved from the initiation of the transactions to their inclusion in the financial statements, including electronic means (such as computers and electronic data interchange) used to transmit, process, maintain and access information.

4. The financial reporting process used to prepare the client's financial statements, including significant accounting estimates and disclosures.

B. The significance of the controls of the service organization to those of the client depends on the nature of the services provided by the service organization, primarily the nature and materiality of the transactions it processes for the user organization and the degree of interaction between its activities and those of the user organization. For example, if the client initiates transactions and the service organization executes and does the accounting processing of those transactions, there is a high degree of interaction.

C. Because the client's transactions are subjected to the controls of the service organization, one of the auditor's concerns is the internal control system in place at the service organization. The auditor's understanding of the client's internal control components may include controls placed in operation by the client and the service organization whose services are part of the entity's information system. After obtaining an understanding of the internal control, the auditor identifies controls that are applied by the client or the service organization that will allow an assessment of reduced control risk. The auditor may obtain evidence to support the lower assessment of control risk by testing the client's controls over the activities performed by the service organization or by tests of controls at the service organization.

D. Because service organizations process data for many customers, it is not uncommon for them to have an auditor issue a report on their operations. Such reports can be distributed to the auditors of a service organization's customers. There are two types of reports by a service organization's auditor on its internal control. One type of report is a description of the service organization's controls and an assessment of whether they are suitably designed to achieve specified internal control objectives. The other type of report goes further by testing whether the controls provide reasonable assurance that the related control objectives were achieved during the period. An auditor may reduce control risk below the maximum only on the basis of a service auditor's report that includes tests of controls.

**[LO14] Understand about the auditor's communication of internal control-related matters.**

A. Standards for reporting internal control deficiencies differ for public versus private (referred to as nonissuers) companies. Under the Sarbanes-Oxley Act (2002), management of public companies must prepare an assertion on internal control effectiveness and its registered auditors must issue an opinion on management's assertion and the effectiveness of internal control. These requirements are covered in Chapter 7.

B. For private companies, auditing standards (AU 325) require that the auditor report to the audit committee, or to a similar level of authority when the entity does not have an audit committee, matters that are serious enough to be considered a significant deficiency or a material weakness.

C. A significant deficiency is a control, or combination of control deficiencies, that adversely affects the entity's ability to initiate, authorize, record, process, or report financial data reliably in accordance with generally accepted accounting principles such that there is more than a remote likelihood that a misstatement of the entity's financial statements that is more than inconsequential will not be prevented or detected.

D.  A material weakness is a significant deficiency, or combination of significant deficiencies, that results in more than a remote likelihood that a material misstatement of the financial statements will not be prevented or detected.

E.  Significant deficiencies and material weaknesses may be identified as part of the auditor's consideration of the five components of internal control or through substantive procedures. Table 6-8 presents examples of circumstances that might indicate a control deficiency, significant deficiency, or material weakness.

F.  The auditor must communicate, in writing, any discovered significant deficiencies and material weaknesses to management and those charged with governance. The following items should be included in the report:

   1.  A statement that the purpose of the audit was to report on the financial statements and not to provide assurance on internal control.

   2.  A definition of the terms significant deficiency and, where relevant, material weakness.

   3.  A description of the matters that are considered to be significant deficiencies and material weaknesses.

   4.  A statement of restrictions on the distribution of the report.

# ADVANCED MODULE 1
## TYPES OF CONTROLS IN AN IT ENVIRONMENT

**[LO15] Identify and understand general and application controls.**

A. There are two broad categories of information systems control activities: general controls and application controls.

B. **General controls** relate to the overall information processing environment and have a pervasive effect on the entity's computer operations. General controls are sometimes referred to as supervisory, management or information technology controls. General controls include controls over:

1. Data center and network operations.
2. System software acquisition, changes and maintenance controls.
3. Access security.
4. Application system acquisition, development and maintenance.

C. **Application controls** apply to the processing of specific computer applications and are part of the computer programs used in the accounting system (for example, revenues or purchasing). Application controls can be grouped into the following categories:

1. Data capture controls.
2. Data validation controls.
3. Processing controls.
4. Output controls.
5. Error controls.

# ADVANCED MODULE 2
# FLOWCHARTING TECHNIQUES

**[LO16] Understand how to flowchart an accounting cycle.**

A. From the auditor's perspective, a flowchart is a diagrammatic representation of the entity's accounting system. The information systems literature typically discusses three types of flowcharts: document flowcharts, systems flowcharts and program flowcharts.

   1. A **document flowchart** represents the flow of documents among departments in the entity.

   2. A **systems flowchart** extends this approach by including the processing steps, including computer processing, in the flowchart.

   3. A **program flowchart** illustrates the operations performed by the computer in executing a program.

B. Flowcharts that are typically used by public accounting firms combine document and systems flowcharting techniques. Such flowcharts show the path from the origination of the transactions to their recording in the accounting journals and ledgers. While there are some general guidelines on preparing flowcharts for documenting accounting systems, the reader should understand that a public accounting firm often modifies these techniques to correspond with their firm's audit technologies.

C. See Figure 6-6 in the textbook for examples of the more commonly used symbols. Note that the symbols are divided into three groups: input/output symbols, processing symbols and data flow and storage symbols.

D. A well-designed flowchart should start in the upper left part of the page and proceed to the lower right part of the page. When it is necessary to show the movement of a document or report back to a previous function, an on-page connector should be used. When the flowchart continues to a subsequent page, the movement of documents or reports can be handled by using an off-page connector. Flow arrows should show the movement of documents, records or information. When processes or activities cannot be fully represented by flowchart symbols, the auditor should supplement the flowchart with written comments. This can be accomplished by using the annotation symbol or just writing the comment directly on the flowchart. A flowchart is typically designed along the lines of departments or functions. It is thus important to indicate the delineation of activities between the departments or functions, which can be accomplished by using a vertical dashed line.

# CHAPTER 6: SELF-ASSESSMENT

## Part I: True or False Questions

[LO1] _____ 1. The concept of internal control includes IT systems and manual systems.

[LO1] _____ 2. The auditor must understand internal control before assessing inherent risk.

[LO4] _____ 3. Internal control consists of six components.

[LO4] _____ 4. Internal control includes monitoring of controls.

[LO5] _____ 5. The extent of an entity's use of IT can affect any of the components of internal control.

[LO5] _____ 6. One of the risks associated with internal control from IT is potential loss of data.

[LO6] _____ 7. A reliance strategy is used when control risk has been set at the maximum level.

[LO6] _____ 8. A substantive strategy is used when control risk has been set at the maximum level.

[LO10] _____ 9. Once a level of control risk has been established, it cannot be changed.

[LO10] _____ 10. Tests of controls must be performed if control risk is set below the maximum level.

## Part II: Multiple Choice Questions

[LO6] 1. A reliance strategy is chosen when the auditor:
- a. Plans on conducting tests of controls.
- b. Has set the control risk at the maximum level.
- c. Has set the control risk below the maximum level.
- d. Both a and c.

[LO6] 2. A substantive strategy is chosen when the auditor:
- a. Plans on conducting tests of controls.
- b. Has set the control risk at the maximum level.
- c. Has set the control risk below the maximum level.
- d. Both a and b.

[LO6] 3. An auditor may decide to follow a substantive strategy because:
- a. One of the controls that pertain to the assertion being tested is effective.
- b. The controls that pertain to the assertion being tested are effective.
- c. The controls that pertain to the assertion being tested are ineffective.
- d. None of the above.

[LO7] 4. Understanding each of the components of internal control provides knowledge about:
- a. The design of tests of controls.
- b. The assessment of inherent risks.
- c. Factors that affect the risk of material misstatement.
- d. Both a and c.

[LO7] 5. Factors that affect the control environment include:
a. Management's commitment to competence.
b. Management's commitment to integrity and ethical values.
c. Management's philosophy and operating style.
d. All of the above.

[LO7] 6. Client business risks can arise or change due to:
a. New personnel.
b. Corporate restructurings.
c. Rapid growth.
d. All of the above.

[LO7] 7. Control procedures that are relevant to the audit include:
a. New personnel.
b. Corporate restructurings.
c. Segregation of duties.
d. Both a and c.

[LO7] 8. The effectiveness of internal control is reduced by:
a. Management override of internal control.
b. Human errors or mistakes.
c. Collusion.
d. All of the above.

[LO8] 9. Tools used to document the internal control include:
a. Narrative description.
b. Flowcharts.
c. CAATs.
d. Both a and b.

[LO15] 10. General controls may include:
a. System software acquisition.
b. Accounting software.
c. Access security.
d. Both a and c.

## Part III: Short Essay Questions

[LO4] Identify and discuss the five components of internal control.

[LO7] Identify and discuss the inherent limitations of an entity's internal control.

[LO8] Auditing standards require the auditor to document his or her understanding of the entity's internal control components. Discuss the documentation requirements and identify the tools used by the auditor to document his or her understanding of internal control.

# Part IV: Crossword Puzzle – Chapter 6 [LO ALL]

## Across

4  An auditor is concerned that senior management may _____ internal controls.
6  A computer program that allows the auditor to test a client's computer files and databases.
8  Controls that relate to the processing and the computer programs used in the accounting system.
10  The auditor must ____ the controls when a reliance strategy is chosen.
11  An audit strategy where the auditor relies on the entity's controls, tests those controls, and reduces the substantive tests of accounts, if appropriate.
12  Controls that relate to the overall information processing environment.

## Down

1  An abbreviation for the federal law that established the PCAOB.
2  A condition that represents a significant deficiency in the design or operation of internal control.
3  An audit strategy where the controls will not be relied on.
5  Financial statements are prepared using these criteria.
7  Detection risk determines the nature, extent, and _____ of the substantive procedures.
9  Policies and procedures which help ensure that management directives are carried out.

**Part V: Townsend Office Supplies and Equipment [LO ALL]**

| Chapter 6 |
| Townsend Office Supplies and Equipment |

1.  The sales account is considered material, so audit risk was set at 0.03. If inherent risk were set at .80, compute detection risk given control risk is assessed at the maximum level [no reliance on internal control (1.00)].

2.  Based on the actual risk-assessment procedures, the auditor has assessed control risk for sales assertions at less than the maximum level (0.25). Recompute detection risk based on this level of control risk.

3.  What control strategy has the auditor chosen and what does this mean (#2)?

4.  Identify what types of audit procedures will be used as tests of controls.

5.  The tests of controls for sales assertions revealed an achieved level of control risk which supports the reduced planned level of control risk (#2). What does this mean?

# CHAPTER 6: SELF-ASSESSMENT SOLUTIONS

## Part I: True or False Questions

[LO1] **True** 1. The concept of internal control includes IT systems and manual systems.

[LO1] **False** 2. The auditor must understand internal control before assessing inherent risk.

[LO4] **False** 3. Internal control consists of six components.

[LO4] **True** 4. Internal control includes monitoring of controls.

[LO5] **True** 5. The extent of an entity's use of IT can affect any of the components of internal control.

[LO5] **True** 6. One of the risks associated with internal control from IT is potential loss of data.

[LO6] **False** 7. A reliance strategy is used when control risk has been set at the maximum level.

[LO6] **True** 8. A substantive strategy is used when control risk has been set at the maximum level.

[LO10] **False** 9. Once a level of control risk has been established, it cannot be changed.

[LO10] **True** 10. Tests of controls must be performed if control risk is set below the maximum level.

## Part II: Multiple Choice Questions

[LO6] 1. A reliance strategy is chosen when the auditor:
    a. Plans on conducting tests of controls.
    b. Has set the control risk at the maximum level.
    c. Has set the control risk below the maximum level.
    **d. Both a and c.**

[LO6] 2. A substantive strategy is chosen when the auditor:
    a. Plans on conducting tests of controls.
    **b. Has set the control risk at the maximum level.**
    c. Has set the control risk below the maximum level.
    d. Both a and b.

[LO6] 3. An auditor may decide to follow a substantive strategy because:
    a. One of the controls that pertain to the assertion being tested is effective.
    b. The controls that pertain to the assertion being tested are effective.
    **c. The controls that pertain to the assertion being tested are ineffective.**
    d. None of the above.

[LO7] 4. Understanding each of the components of internal control provides knowledge about:
    a. The design of tests of controls.
    b. The assessment of inherent risks.
    c. Factors that affect the risk of material misstatement.
    **d. Both a and c.**

[LO7]  5.  Factors that affect the control environment include:
   a.  Management's commitment to competence.
   b.  Management's commitment to integrity and ethical values.
   c.  Management's philosophy and operating style.
   **d.  All of the above.**

[LO7]  6.  Client business risks can arise or change due to:
   a.  New personnel.
   b.  Corporate restructurings.
   c.  Rapid growth.
   **d.  All of the above.**

[LO7]  7.  Control procedures that are relevant to the audit include:
   a.  New personnel.
   b.  Corporate restructurings.
   **c.  Segregation of duties.**
   d.  Both a and c.

[LO7]  8.  The effectiveness of internal control is reduced by:
   a.  Management override of internal control.
   b.  Human errors or mistakes.
   c.  Collusion.
   **d.  All of the above.**

[LO8]  9.  Tools used to document the internal control include:
   a.  Narrative description.
   b.  Flowcharts.
   c.  CAATs.
   **d.  Both a and b.**

[LO15] 10. General controls may include:
   a.  System software acquisition.
   b.  Accounting software.
   c.  Access security.
   **d.  Both a and c.**

## Part III: Short Essay Questions

> [LO4] Identify and discuss the five components of internal control.
>
> **Internal control consists of five components. They include:**
>
> 1. **Control Environment. The control environment sets the tone of an organization, influencing the control consciousness of its people. It is the foundation for effective internal control, providing discipline and structure. The control environment includes the attitudes, awareness, policies and actions of management and the board of directors concerning the entity's internal control and its importance in the entity.**
>
> 2. **The Entity's Risk Assessment Process. For financial reporting purposes, the entity's risk assessment process includes how management identifies risks relevant to the preparation of financial statements that are fairly presented in conformity with GAAP, estimates their significance, assesses the likelihood of their occurrence, and decides upon actions to manage them.**
>
> 3. **The Entity's Information System and Related Business Processes Relevant to Financial Reporting and Communication. The information system relevant to financial reporting objectives includes the accounting system, which consists of the procedures, whether automated or manual, and records established to initiate, record, process, and report entity transactions and to maintain accountability for the related assets, liabilities and equity. Communication involves providing an understanding of individual roles and responsibilities pertaining to internal control over financial reporting.**
>
> 4. **Control Procedures. Control procedures are the policies and procedures that help ensure that management directives are carried out, for example, that necessary actions are taken to address risks to achievement of the entity's objectives. Control procedures, whether automated or manual, have various objectives and are applied at various organizational and functional levels.**
>
> 5. **Monitoring of Controls. Monitoring of controls is a process to assess the quality of internal control performance over time. It involves assessing the design and operation of controls on a timely basis and taking necessary corrective actions.**

[LO7] Identify and discuss the inherent limitations of an entity's internal control.

**The effectiveness of any internal control system is subject to certain inherent limitations, including management override of internal control, personnel errors or mistakes and collusion.**

1. **Management Override of Internal Controls.** An entity's controls may be overridden by management. The auditor is particularly concerned when senior management is involved in such activities because it raises serious questions about management's integrity. Violations of control procedures by senior management may be difficult to detect with normal audit procedures.

2. **Human Errors or Mistakes.** The internal control system is only as effective as the personnel who implement and perform the controls. Breakdowns in internal control can occur because of human failures, such as simple errors or mistakes.

3. **Collusion.** The effectiveness of segregation of duties lies in individuals' performing only their assigned tasks or in the performance of one person being checked by another. There is always a risk that collusion between individuals will destroy the effectiveness of segregation of duties.

---

[LO8] Auditing standards require the auditor to document his or her understanding of the entity's internal control components. Discuss the documentation requirements and identify the tools used by the auditor to document his or her understanding of internal control.

**Auditing standards require that the auditor document the understanding of the entity's internal control components. An auditor should also document his or her understanding of an entity's internal control to provide evidence that the auditor conducted the audit in conformity with GAAS. A number of tools are available to the auditor for documenting his or her understanding of internal control. They include:**

1. **Copies of the entity's procedures manuals and organizational charts.**

2. **Narrative description.**

3. **Internal control questionnaires.**

4. **Flowcharts.**

**On many engagements, the auditor combines these tools to document his or her understanding of the components of internal control. The combination depends on the complexity of the entity's internal control system.**

**Part IV: Crossword Puzzle – Chapter 6 Solution [LO ALL]**

```
 1        2                                            3
 S        R                                            S
 4
 O  V  E  R  R  I  D  E                                U
    X     P                                            B
          O     5        6        7                    S
          R     G        C  A  A  T  S                 T
          R     A                 I                    A
          T     A                 M                    N
          8                       9                    T
          A  P  P  L  I  C  A  T  I  O  N              I
          B                 O     N                    V
          L                 N     G                    I
          E    10          T                           V
               T  E  S  T
                        11
                         R  E  L  I  A  N  C  E
                         O
       12
        G  E  N  E  R  A  L
```

**Across**

4    An auditor is concerned that senior management may _____ internal controls.
6    A computer program that allows the auditor to test a client's computer files and databases.
8    Controls that relate to the processing and the computer programs used in the accounting system.
10   The auditor must _____ the controls when a reliance strategy is chosen.
11   An audit strategy where the auditor relies on the entity's controls, tests those controls, and reduces the substantive tests of accounts, if appropriate.
12   Controls that relate to the overall information processing environment.

**Down**

1    An abbreviation for the federal law that established the PCAOB.
2    A condition that represents a significant deficiency in the design or operation of internal control.
3    An audit strategy where the controls will not be relied on.
5    Financial statements are prepared using these criteria.
7    Detection risk determines the nature, extent, and _____ of the substantive procedures.
9    Policies and procedures which help ensure that management directives are carried out.

<table>
<tr><td colspan="2" align="center">**Chapter 6**<br>**Townsend Office Supplies and Equipment**</td></tr>
</table>

| | |
|---|---|
| 1. | The sales account is considered material, so audit risk was set at 0.03. If inherent risk were set at .80, compute detection risk given control risk is assessed at the maximum level [no reliance on internal control (1.00)]. |
| 2. | Based on the actual risk-assessment procedures, the auditor has assessed control risk for sales assertions at less than the maximum level (0.25). Recompute detection risk based on this level of control risk. |
| 3. | What control strategy has the auditor chosen and what does this mean (#2)? |
| 4. | Identify what types of audit procedures will be used as tests of controls. |
| 5. | The tests of controls for sales assertions revealed an achieved level of control risk which supports the reduced planned level of control risk (#2). What does this mean? |

1. **DR = 0.03/0.80 × 1**
   **DR = <u>0.04</u>**

2. **DR = 0.03/0.80 × .25**
   **DR = <u>0.15</u>**

3. **The auditor has chosen a reliance strategy for testing sales assertions. This means that tests of controls will be conducted to obtain audit evidence to support the lower level of control risk (0.25 because the controls are expected to be operating effectively). In short, a reliance strategy means that the auditor will begin filling the accounts receivable assurance bucket with controls evidence.**

4. **Audit procedures routinely used as tests of controls include:**

   a. **Inquiry of appropriate entity personnel.**
   b. **Inspection of documents, reports or electronic files indicating performance of control.**
   c. **Observation of the application of the control.**
   d. **Walkthroughs, which involve tracing a transaction from its origination to its inclusion in the financial statements through a combination of audit procedures including inquiry, observation and inspection.**
   e. **Reperformance of the application of the control by the auditor.**

5. **When the tests of control are consistent with the auditor's planned assessment of control risk, no revision in the substantive procedures is necessary. The auditor uses the achieved level of control risk and the assessed level of inherent risk to determine the acceptable level of detection risk, which is used to determine the nature, timing and extent of substantive tests. Since the tests of controls are consistent with the auditor's planned assessment of control risk, no revision in the nature, timing or extent of substantive procedures is necessary; hence, detection risk remains at 0.15 (#2).**

# Auditing Internal Control Over Financial Reporting

**KEY THOUGHT**

Effective internal control over financial reporting provides reasonable assurance regarding the reliability of financial reporting and the preparation of financial statements for external purposes. If one or more material weaknesses exist, the company's internal control over financial reporting cannot be considered effective [PCAOB (AS 5 ¶2)].

**CHAPTER SUMMARY**

**[LO1] Be familiar with management's responsibilities for reporting on internal control under Section 404 of the Sarbanes-Oxley Act.**

A. The Sarbanes-Oxley Act (2002) was passed in response to a series of business scandals and auditing failures. Section 404 of the Act requires management of a publicly traded company to issue an internal control report that explicitly accepts responsibility for establishing and maintaining "adequate" internal control over financial reporting (ICFR). Management must also issue an assertion as to whether internal control over financial reporting is effective as the end of the fiscal year. The Act provides no guidance on what constitutes adequate internal control; thus the SEC PCAOB was left to address the issue of adequacy.

B. Management's assessment is to be made as of a specific point in time – that is, as of the end of the accounting period; hence, the assessment does not cover the entire year. This has implications for the timing of both management's and the auditor's work and the handling of any control deficiencies discovered during the year. The as-of nature of the assessment in many cases allows management to remediate deficiencies discovered prior to year-end and still receive an unqualified opinion on ICFR. This also has implications for the use of the auditor's internal control work for financial statement audit purposes.

C. Management must comply with the following requirements in order for their registered public accounting firm (external auditor) to complete an audit of internal control over financial reporting:

1. Accept responsibility for the effectiveness of the entity's ICFR.

2. Evaluate the effectiveness of the entity's ICFR using suitable control criteria.

3. Support the evaluation with sufficient evidence, including documentation.

4. Present a written assessment regarding the effectiveness of the entity's ICFR as of the end of the entity's most recent fiscal year.

While each of the steps will be discussed, note that the second and third requirements entail a substantial investment of time, energy and money on the part of management.

**[LO2] Understand the auditor's responsibilities for reporting on internal control under Section 404 of the Sarbanes-Oxley Act.**

A.  Section 404 requires the entity's auditor to audit management's assertion about the effectiveness of ICFR. AS5 states that the auditor must conduct an "integrated audit" of the entity's ICFR and its financial statements. AS5 makes it clear that while the two audits are to be integrated, they have different objectives. The auditor's objective in an audit of ICFR is "to express an opinion on the effectiveness of the company's internal control over financial reporting," (AS5, ¶3) while the objective in a financial statement audit is to express an opinion on whether the financial statements are fairly stated in accordance with generally accepted accounting principles (GAAP).

B.  To form a basis for expressing an opinion on management's assertion regarding the effectiveness of internal control over financial reporting, the auditor must plan and perform the audit to obtain reasonable assurance about whether the entity maintained, in all material respects, effective internal control as of the date specified in management's assessment. Reasonable assurance in this context recognizes that no system of internal control is perfect, and that there will be a remote likelihood that material misstatements will not be prevented or detected on a timely basis, even if controls are, in fact, effective (AS5, ¶3). While reasonable assurance is not absolute assurance, in this context it indicates a high level of assurance.

**[LO3] Know the definition of internal control over financial reporting (ICFR).**

A.  The PCAOB utilizes the COSO (presented in Chapter 6) integrated framework when defining internal control. In addition to the reliability of the financial reporting objective, it also included objectives in two other categories: (1) effectiveness and efficiency of operations and (2) compliance with laws and regulations. For purposes of both management's assessment and the audit of internal control, ICFR is defined as

> A process designed by, or under the supervision of, the company's principal executive and principal financial officers, or persons performing similar functions, and effected by the company's board of directors, management, and other personnel, to provide reasonable assurance regarding the reliability of financial reporting and the preparation of financial statements for external purposes in accordance with generally accepted accounting principles and includes those policies and procedures that:
>
> 1.  Pertain to the maintenance of records that, in reasonable detail, accurately and fairly reflect the transactions and dispositions of the assets of the company.
>
> 2.  Provides reasonable assurance that transactions are recorded as necessary to permit preparation of financial statements in accordance with generally accepted accounting principles, and that receipts and expenditures of the company are being made only in accordance with authorizations of management and directors of the company.
>
> 3.  Provides reasonable assurance regarding prevention or timely detection of unauthorized acquisition, use or disposition of the company's assets that could have a material effect on the financial statements (AS5, ¶A5).

B.  The above definition makes it clear that the CEO and CFO are responsible for the reliability of internal control over financial reporting and the preparation of the financial statements. It is the responsibility of the board of directors and management to implement an effective internal control system. Note that the objectives of internal control in the Carob's definition are much more specific than the objectives listed in the COSO definition. Items 1 and 2 relate directly to controls for initiating, authorizing, recording, processing, and reporting significant accounts and disclosures and related assertions embodied in the financial statements. Item 3 is concerned with controls over safeguarding of assets.

**[LO4] Understand the difference between a control deficiency, a significant deficiency, and a material weakness.**

A.  A **control deficiency** exists when the design or operation of a control does not allow management or employees, in the normal course of performing their assigned functions, to prevent or detect misstatements on a timely basis. A **design deficiency** exists when (1) a control necessary to meet the relevant control objective is missing or (2) an existing control is not properly designed so that, even if the control operates as designed, the control objective is not always met. A deficiency in **operation** exists when a properly designed control does not operate as designed or when the person performing the control does not possess the necessary authority or qualifications to perform the control effectively (AS5, ¶3),

B.  The PCAOB defines a **material weakness** as a deficiency, or combination of deficiencies, in ICFR, such that there is a reasonable possibility that a material misstatement of the annual or interim financial statements will not be prevented or detected on a timely basis (AS5, ¶A7).

C.  A **significant deficiency** is a control deficiency, or combination of control deficiencies, in ICFR that is less severe than a material weakness, yet important enough to merit attention by those responsible for oversight of the company's financial reporting (AS5, ¶A11).

D.  **Likelihood and Magnitude.** Management and the auditor must consider two dimensions of the control deficiency: likelihood and magnitude of misstatements that could result from the control deficiency. The definition of material weakness includes the phrase "reasonable possibility." The term "reasonable possibility" is to be interpreted using the guidance in FAS 5 (Accounting for Contingencies). The likelihood that an event is a "reasonable possibility" if it is either "reasonably possible" or "probable." While this guidance is helpful, these concepts are clearly subjective and require the application of considerable professional judgment. Determining the magnitude of a financial statement misstatement that might result from a control deficiency also requires a great deal of professional judgment. In making such judgments, the auditor should also be satisfied that a "prudent official" would be likely to concur. Figure 1 represents how likelihood and magnitude relate to each other in the determination of whether a control deficiency rises to the level of a significant deficiency or a material weakness.

**[LO5] Understand management's assessment process.**

A.  In order to issue a report on the effectiveness of internal control, management needs to first design and implement an effective system of internal control over financial reporting, and then develop an ongoing assessment process.

B.  The SEC issued guidance for evaluating and assessing ICFR. This guidance provides a top-down, risk-based approach for management to follow in evaluating and assessing ICFR. The purpose of the evaluation of ICFR is to provide management with a reasonable basis for its assessment as to whether any material weaknesses in ICFR exist as of the end of the period. The evaluation process has three steps:

1. Identify financial reporting risks and related controls.
2. Evaluate evidence about the operating effectiveness of ICFR.
3. Consider which locations to include in the evaluation.

C.  In determining its reporting responsibilities, management first evaluates the severity of the control deficiencies identified. Management considers the likelihood of and degree to which the financial statements could be misstated by the control failure. If a control deficiency is determined to be a material weakness, management must disclose the material weakness in its assessment of the effectiveness of ICFR on an annual basis. The disclosure about the material weakness(es) should include the following:

1. The nature of the material weakness(es).

2. Its impact on the company's financial reporting and its ICFR.

3. Management's current plans, if any, for remediating the material weakness.

4. Determining which controls should be tested, including controls over all relevant assertions related to all significant accounts and disclosures in the financial statements.

D.  Note that any control deficiency that is considered a significant deficiency or material weakness should be reported to the audit committee and the external auditor.

E.  Management's assessment process involves special consideration of two topics. These topics must also be considered by the auditor during the audit of ICFR. The two topics are: (1) service organizations and (2) safeguarding assets (see Advanced Module 1).

## [LO6] Understand the extent of management's documentation of internal control.

A.  The SEC's guidance allows flexibility to management in how it documents reasonable support for its assessment. Reasonable support would include the basis for management's assessment, such as documentation of the methods and procedures it utilizes to gather and evaluate evidence. This includes the design of the controls management has placed in operation to adequately address identified financial reporting risks, including the entity-level and other pervasive elements necessary for effective ICFR. Documentation of how management formed its conclusion about the effectiveness of the company's entity-level controls and other pervasive elements of ICFR is needed.

B.  Documentation of ICFR may take many forms, such as paper, electronic files or other media. It will also include a variety of information, such as policy manuals, process models, flowcharts, job descriptions, documents and forms. Such documentation provides the foundation for appropriate communication concerning responsibilities for performing controls and for the entity's evaluation and monitoring of the effective operation of controls.

## [LO7] Know the framework used by management to assess internal control.

A.  Management is required to base its assessment of the effectiveness of the entity's internal control over financial reporting on a suitable, recognized control framework established by a body of experts that follow due-process procedures. In the United States, most entities use the framework

144

developed by COSO in the early 1990s (COGS Internal Control – Integrated Framework). Some may use the new COSO Enterprise Risk Management framework (Enterprise Risk Management – Integrated Framework), which subsumes and builds on the COSO internal control framework.

B. The COSO framework identifies three primary objectives of internal control: reliable financial reporting, efficiency and effectiveness of operations, and compliance with laws and regulations. While the PCAOB focuses on the financial reporting objective, the controls that management designs and implements in the other two areas may help achieve objectives relating to financial reporting. Additionally, not all controls relevant to financial reporting are accounting controls, therefore, all controls that could materially affect financial reporting are considered a part of ICFR.

**[LO8] Be familiar with how auditors conduct an audit of ICFR reporting.**

A. The auditor's goal of an audit of internal control over financial reporting is to obtain sufficient competent evidence about the design and operating effectiveness of controls. The auditor does this by planning and performing the audit of ICFR to obtain reasonable assurance that deficiencies rising to the level of material weakness are identified.

**[LO9] Understand how the audits of internal control and financial statements are integrated.**

A. The purpose of tests of controls in an audit of ICFR is to provide evidence on the effectiveness of the entity's control over financial reporting as of the end of the reporting period. The purpose of tests of controls in an audit of financial statements is to assist the auditor in assessing control risk, which in turn affects the nature, timing, and extent of the auditor's substantive tests.

B. The auditor should incorporate the results of tests of controls in the audit of ICFR into the tests of controls for the audit of the financial statements and should use those results for determining the nature, timing, and extent of substantive procedures. Similarly, the auditor should consider the results of substantive procedures on the conclusions about the effectiveness of ICFR.

C. **The steps** involved in performing an audit of ICFR include (see Figure 7-2):

    1. Plan the engagement.
    2. Identify controls to test using a top-down, risk-based approach.
    3. Test the design and operating effectiveness of selected controls.
    4. Evaluate identified control deficiencies.
    5. Form an opinion on the effectiveness of ICFR.

D. While Figure 7-2 suggests a sequential process, the audit of ICFR involves an iterative process of gathering, updating and analyzing information. The auditor may perform some of the procedures and evaluations described in Figure 7-2 while performing the internal control phase of the financial statement audit.

**[LO10] Understand how the auditor plans the audit of ICFR.**

A. The process for planning an audit of ICFR is similar to planning a financial audit. In fact, because results from the two audits interrelate, the planning process should be integrated. Table 7-2 provides examples of some of the factors that may affect planning an audit of ICFR. In planning the engagement, the auditor considers the following activities.

    1. Plan the engagement.
    2. The role of risk assessment and the risk of fraud.

3. Scaling the audit.
4. Using the work of others.
5. Materiality.

**[LO11] Know how the auditor utilizes a top-down, risk-based approach for an audit of ICFR.**

A. Obtaining an understanding of ICFR as part of an audit of internal control is similar to the process for understanding internal control described in Chapter 6, except that the understanding needed for an audit of internal control is more extensive. The procedures the auditor can perform to obtain an understanding of specific controls include inquiring of appropriate management, supervisory, and staff personnel; inspecting company documents; observing the application of specific control; and tracing transactions through the information system. Figure 7-3 outlines the top-down approach the auditor should follow in obtaining an understanding of ICFR.

B. Entity-level controls can have a pervasive effect on the entity's ability to meet the COSO control criteria. Table 7-3 provides examples of entity-level controls. Two categories of entity-level controls require evaluation by the auditor: (1) the control environment and (2) the period-end financial reporting process.

C. The auditor should identify significant accounts and disclosures and their relevant assertions. To do so, the auditor should evaluate risk factors related to the financial statements accounts and disclosures.

D. In order to understand the likely sources of potential misstatements, and to assist in selecting controls to test, the auditor needs to do the following:

   1. Understand the follow of transactions related to the relevant assertions, including how these transactions are initiated, authorized, processed, and recorded;

   2. Identify the points within the entity's processes at which a misstatement (including a misstatement due to fraud) could arise that, individually or in combination with other misstatements, would be material;

   3. Identify the controls that management has implemented to address these potential misstatements; and

   4. Identify the controls that management has implemented over the prevention or timely detection of unauthorized acquisition, use, or disposition of the company's assets that could result in a material misstatement of the financial statements (AS5, ¶34).

E. Performing walkthroughs is often the best way to achieve these objectives. To perform a walkthrough, the auditor traces a transaction from origination through the entity's processes and information system until it is reflected in the entity's financial reports. It should encompass the entire information flow through the subprocesses of initiating, authorizing, recording, processing, and reporting individual transactions for each of the significant processes identified. Walkthroughs help the auditor in confirming his or her understanding of control design and transaction process flow, as well as in determining whether all points at which misstatements could occur have been identified, evaluating the effectiveness of the design of controls, and confirming whether controls have been placed in operation.

In performing the walkthrough, the auditor should make inquiries of relevant personnel involved in significant aspects of the process or controls. The auditor should use probing questions to determine client personnel's understanding of what is required by the controls and determine whether the processing procedures are performed as understood and on a timely basis.

F.  The auditor needs to test only those control that are important to the auditor's conclusion about whether the entity's controls sufficiently address the assessed risk of misstatement to each relevant assertions including preventive, detection, or a combination of both). Identifying the controls to be tested is a subjective task that requires professional judgment. Table 7-4 provides a list of factors that the auditor should consider in deciding which controls to test.

**[LO12] Understand how to test the design and operating effectiveness of controls.**

A.  Controls are effectively designed when they prevent or detect errors or fraud that could result in material misstatements in the financial statements. The auditor should determine whether the entity has controls to meet the objectives of the control criteria selected by management (e.g., COSO). The auditor evaluates design effectiveness through inquiry, observation, walkthroughs, inspection of relevant documentation, and subjective evaluations of whether the controls are likely to prevent or detect errors or fraud that could result in misstatements assuming they are operated as prescribed by qualified persons. The procedures performed by the auditor to test and evaluate design effectiveness might in some cases also provide some evidence about operating effectiveness.

B.  In testing the operating effectiveness of a controls, the auditor needs to consider the scope (nature, timing, and extent) of testing. The evidence must persuade the auditor that the control is effective based on the risk that the control might not be effective and, if not effective, the risk that a material weakness would result. Table 7-5 presents the factors that affect the risk associated with a control.

**[LO13] Understand how to evaluate identified control deficiencies.**

A.  The auditor is required to evaluate the severity of each control deficiency (AS5, ¶62). The assessment of the significance of a control deficiency in ICFR depends on the potential for a misstatement, not on whether a misstatement actually has occurred. The severity of a control deficiency depends on the likelihood (reasonable possibility) and magnitude of the potential misstatement resulting from the deficiency or deficiencies. Table 7-6 presents the risk factors that affect whether there is a reasonable possibility that a control deficiency (or combination of control deficiencies) will result in a misstatement of an account balance or disclosure. Table 7-7 presents indicators of material weaknesses in ICFR. Exhibit 7-1 presents a detailed example of an application control and IT-dependent manual control.

**[LO14] Understand how an auditor forms an opinion on the effectiveness of ICFR.**

A.  The auditor should evaluate all evidence obtained before forming an opinion on ICFR, including:

1.  The presentation of the elements that management is required by the SEC's rules to present in its report on ICFR;

2.  The results of the auditor's evaluation of the design and tests of operating effectiveness of controls;

3. Any negative results of substantive procedures performed during the financial statement audit; and

4. Any identified control deficiencies.

B. Exhibit 7-2 presents two scenarios illustrating the process of assessing a control deficiency as either a significant deficiency or material weakness.

**[LO15] Know the written representations that the auditor must obtain from management.**

A. In addition to the management representations obtained as part of a financial statement audit, the auditor must also obtain written representations from management related to the audit of ICFR. Table 7-8 presents the typical management representations made to the auditor related to the audit of internal control. Failure to obtain written representations from management, including management's refusal to furnish them, constitutes a limitation on the scope of the audit sufficient to preclude an unqualified opinion. While the required representations are typically drafted by the auditor, they are addressed to the auditor and are signed (and worded as if written) by the CEO and CFO.

**[LO16] Be familiar with the auditor's documentation requirements.**

A. The auditor should document the processes, procedures, judgments and results relating to the audit of internal control. Documentation includes the auditor's understanding and evaluation of the design of each of the components of the entity's ICFR. The auditor must document the process used to determine and the points at which misstatements could occur within, significant accounts, disclosures and major classes of transactions. The auditor must justify and document the extent to which he or she relied upon work performed by others. The auditor must describe the evaluation of any deficiencies discovered as well as any other findings that could result in a modification to the auditor's reports.

**[LO17] Know what information must be included in management's report on ICFR.**

A. The Sarbanes-Oxley Act requires managements of public companies to report on the effectiveness of ICFR in the company's annual report. Management's description must include the following (AS2, ¶162):

1. A statement of management's responsibility for establishing and maintaining adequate internal control over financial reporting for the entity.

2. A statement identifying the framework used by management to conduct the required assessment of the effectiveness of the company's ICFR (e.g., the COSO internal control framework).

3. An assessment of the effectiveness of the company's ICFR as of the end of the company's most recent fiscal year, including an explicit statement as to whether ICFR is effective.

See Exhibit 7-3 for EarthWear's management report on the financial statements and its ICFR.

**[LO18] Understand the unqualified and adverse reports for the audit of ICFR.**

A. Once the auditor has completed the audit of ICFR, he or she must issue an opinion to accompany management's assessment, and both are included in the company's annual report.

B. The auditor's report contains an opinion on the effectiveness of ICFR based on the auditor's independent audit work. The basic options for the opinion on ICFR are unqualified or adverse.

C. The auditor issues an unqualified opinion if the client's internal control is designed and operating effectively in all material respects. Significant deficiencies do not require a departure from an unqualified opinion because they relate to possible financial statements misstatements that are less than material. If the scope of the auditor's work is limited, a disclaimer of opinion is issued on the effectiveness of ICFR. If a material weakness is identified, the auditor issues an adverse opinion.

D. Figure 7-4 gives an overview of the types of audit reports relating to the effectiveness of ICFR. Exhibit 7-4 presents an example of an auditor's unqualified report that is presented separately from the auditor's report on the financial statements. Note that the report includes an explanatory paragraph referring to the financial statements audit report. Exhibit 7-5 presents an example of a combined report for EarthWear that gives an unqualified opinion on both the financial statement audit and the audit of ICFR. See Exhibit 7-6 for an example of an adverse report.

E. Note that it is possible for the auditor to issue an adverse opinion on internal control while at the same time issuing an unqualified opinion on the financial statements.

**[LO19] Know when the auditor issues a disclaimer for a scope limitation.**

A. The auditor can express an unqualified opinion on the effectiveness of ICFR only if the auditor has been able to supply all the procedures necessary in the circumstances. If the scope of the auditor's work is limited because of circumstances beyond the control of management or the auditor, the auditor should disclaim an opinion or withdraw from the engagement. The auditor's decision depends on an assessment of the importance of the omitted procedure(s) to his or her ability to form an opinion.

B. Other reporting issues include:

   1. Management's report is incomplete or improperly presented.
   2. The auditor decides to refer to the report of other auditors.
   3. Subsequent events.
   4. Management's report contains additional information.
   5. Reporting on a remediated material weakness at an interim date.

**[LO20] Know the auditor's communication responsibilities on an audit of ICFR.**

A. The auditor has a number of communication responsibilities under AS5 including (in writing):

   1. To management and the audit committee all significant deficiencies and material weaknesses identified during the audit.

   2. To management all control deficiencies (deficiencies in internal control that are of a lesser magnitude than significant deficiencies) identified during the audit and inform the audit committee when such a communication has been made.

3. When the auditor becomes aware of fraud or other possible illegal acts.

   If the matter involves fraud, it must be brought to the attention of the appropriate level of management. If the fraud involves senior management, the auditor must communicate the matter directly to the audit committee.

   If the matter involves other possible illegal acts, the auditor must be assured that the audit committee is adequately informed, unless the matter is clearly inconsequential.

   Note that when timely communication is important, the auditor communicates such matters during the course of the audit rather than at the end of the engagement.

# ADVANCED MODULE 1
## SPECIAL CONSIDERATIONS FOR AN AUDIT OF INTERNAL CONTROL

The PCAOB specifies two areas that require special consideration by management and the auditor during an audit of ICFR: service organizations and safeguarding assets.

**[LO21] Understand how to obtain assurance on controls at a service organization that processes transactions for the entity.**

    A.  Many companies use service organizations to process transactions. If the service organization's services comprise part of a company's information system, then they are part of the information and communication component of the company's ICFR. Thus, both management and the auditor must consider the activities of the service organization. Management and the auditor should perform the following procedures with respect to the activities performed by the service organization:

        1.  Obtain an understanding of the controls at the service organization that are relevant to the entity's internal control and the controls at the user organization over the activities of the service organization.

        2.  Obtain evidence that the controls that are relevant to management's assessment and the auditor's opinion are operating effectively.

        3.  Evidence about the operating effectiveness of controls that are relevant to management's assessment and the auditor's opinion may be obtained by: (1) are operating effectively.

           a.  Performing tests of the user organization's controls over the activities of the service organization.

           b.  Performing tests of controls at the service organization.

           c.  Obtaining a service auditor's report on the design and operating effectiveness of controls placed in operation at the service organization.

        4.  If a significant period of time has elapsed between the time period covered by the tests of controls in the service auditor's report and the date of management's assessment, additional procedures should be performed.

**[LO22] Know management's and the auditor's responsibilities for controls that provide reasonable assurance for safeguarding company assets.**

    A.  **Safeguarding of assets** is defined in AS2 as policies and procedures that "provide reasonable assurance regarding prevention or timely detection of unauthorized acquisition, use or disposition of the company's assets that could have a material effect on the financial statement."
This definition is consistent with the definition in the Addendum to the COSO report.

    B.  An example of safeguarding of assets is provided to illustrate this definition. A company could have safeguarding controls over inventory tags (preventive controls) and also perform timely periodic physical inventory counts (detective control) for its quarterly and annual financial reporting dates. Given that the definitions of material weakness and significant deficiency relate to the likelihood of misstatement of the financial statements, the failure of the inventory tag control will not result in a significant deficiency or material weakness if the physical inventory prevents a misstatement of the financial statements. Therefore, the COSO definition indicates that although losses might occur, controls over financial reporting are effective if they provide reasonable assurance that those losses are properly reflected in the financial statements.

# ADVANCED MODULE 2
# COMPUTER-ASSISTED AUDIT TECHNIQUES

**[LO23] Be familiar with computer-assisted audit techniques.**

A.  Auditors use computer-assisted audit techniques (CAATs) to assist in testing application controls. Many of these controls are embedded into the client's computer program. Additionally, the auditor may need to use CAATs to execute substantive procedures when the information is maintained in machine-readable form. Three types of CAATs will be discussed including: (1) generalized audit software (GAS), (2) custom audit software and (3) test data (other techniques are discussed in advanced IT auditing books).

B.  **Generalized audit software** (GAS). Generalized audit software includes programs that allow the auditor to perform tests on computer files and databases. ACL is an example of a GAS program. GAS was developed so that auditors would be able to conduct similar computer-assisted audit techniques in different IT environments. For example, GAS permits an auditor to select and prepare accounts receivable confirmations from a variety of computer systems. This type of software provides a high-level computer language that allows the auditor to easily perform various functions on a client's computer files and databases. See Table 7-9 for examples of functions performed by GAS.

GAS offers several advantages including:

1.  It is easy to use.
2.  Limited IT expertise or programming skills are required.
3.  The time required to develop the application is usually short.
4.  An entire population can be examined.

GAS has some disadvantages including:

1.  It involves auditing after the client has processed the data rather than while the data are being processed.

2.  It provides a limited ability to verify programming logic because its application is usually directed to testing client files or databases.

3.  It is limited to audit procedures that can be conducted on data available in electronic form.

C.  **Custom Audit Software.** Custom audit software is generally written by auditors for specific audit tasks. Such programs are necessary when the entity's computer system is not compatible with the auditor's GAS or when the auditor wants to conduct some testing that may not be possible with GAS. It may also be more efficient to prepare custom programs if they will be used in future audits of the entity or if they may be used on similar engagements. The major disadvantages of custom software are that: (1) it is expensive to develop, (2) it may require a long development time and (3) it may require extensive modification if the client changes its accounting application programs. Inventory observation and testing provide a good example of where such a program might be useful.

153

D. **Test Data.** The auditor uses test data for testing the application controls in the client's computer programs. In using this method, the auditor first creates a set of simulated data (test data) for processing. The data should include both valid and invalid data. After calculating the expected results of processing the test data, the auditor uses the client's computer and application programs to process the data. The valid data should be properly processed, while the invalid data should be identified as errors. The results of this processing are compared to the auditor's predetermined results. This technique can be used to check:

1. Data validation controls and error detection routines.
2. Processing logic controls.
3. Arithmetic calculations.
4. The inclusion of transactions in records, files and reports.

The objective of using the test data method is to ensure the accuracy of the computer processing of transactions. The main advantage of the test data method is that it provides direct evidence on the effectiveness of the controls included in the client's application programs. However, the test data method has a number of potential disadvantages. First, it can be very time-consuming to create the test data. Second, the auditor may not be certain that all relevant conditions or controls are tested. The use of special computer programs called "test data generators" may help alleviate these potential disadvantages. Third, the auditor must be certain that the test data are processed using the client's regular production programs. This concern can be alleviated if the client's general controls for program changes, access and library functions are reliable. Last, the auditor must be sure to remove the valid test data from the client's files.

# CHAPTER 7: SELF-ASSESSMENT

## Part I: True or False Questions

[LO1] _____ 1.    All companies must follow the guidelines of AS5.

[LO1] _____ 2.    All public companies must follow the guidelines of AS5.

[LO1] _____ 3.    Management must assess and report on internal control over financial reporting.

[LO2] _____ 4.    Based on PCAOB guidelines, the internal control and financial statements audits should be conduced as an "integrated audit."

[LO3] _____ 5.    Management's report on internal control must be signed by the audit committee.

[LO3] _____ 6.    The PCAOB makes it clear that the CEO and CFO are responsible for the internal control over financial reporting and the preparation of the statements.

[LO4] _____ 7.    A control deficiency includes the design and operation of the control.

[LO4] _____ 8.    The likelihood of an event is a "reasonable possibility" if it is either reasonably possible or probable.

[LO5] _____ 9.    AS 5 allows for the idea that a small, less-complex entity might achieve its control objectives differently from a large, complex entity.

[LO8] _____ 10.   The auditor must form an opinion on the effectiveness of internal control over financial reporting.

## Part II: Multiple Choice Questions

[LO4] 1.  In judging the significance of a control deficiency, management and the auditor must consider which dimensions of the control deficiency?
   a.  Likelihood only.
   b.  Magnitude of misstatements only.
   c.  Likelihood and magnitude of misstatements.
   d.  None of the above.

[LO5] 2.  Management's assessment process includes the following item(s):
   a.  Identify financial reporting risks and related controls.
   b.  Evaluate evidence about the operating effectiveness of ICFR.
   c.  Consider which locations to include in the evaluation.
   d.  All of the above.

[LO10] 3.  The five step process in the audit of ICFR includes:
   a.  Test the design and operating effectiveness of selected controls.
   b.  Form an opinion on the safeguarding of the entity's assets.
   c.  Form an opinion on the fairness of the presentation of the financial statements.
   d.  All of the above.

[LO11] 4. Examples of entity-level controls include:
   a. The entity's risk assessment process.
   b. Controls to monitor results of operations.
   c. Policies that address significant business control and risk management practices.
   d. All of the above.

[LO11] 5. When evaluating the control environment, the auditor must assess whether:
   a. Management's philosophy and operating style promote effective ICFR.
   b. Sound integrity and ethical values, particularly of top management, are developed and understood.
   c. The Board or audit committee understands and exercises oversight responsibility over financial reporting and internal control.
   d. All of the above.

[LO18] 6. The basic options for the audit opinion on ICFR are:
   a. unqualified.
   b. qualified.
   c. adverse.
   d. Both a and c.

[LO18] 7. If management's report states that internal control over financial reporting was effective and the auditor disagrees because of a material weakness, the auditor must:
   a. Issue a qualified opinion.
   b. Issue a disclaimer.
   c. Issue an adverse opinion.
   d. None of the above.

[LO18] 8. If the auditor issues an adverse opinion on the internal control, the auditor must:
   a. Issue an adverse opinion on the financial statement audit.
   b. Issue a qualified opinion on the financial statement audit.
   c. Issue a disclaimer.
   d. Issue an unqualified opinion on the financial statement audit if the audit evidence from substantive procedures supports such an opinion.

[LO18] 9. The auditor can issue the audit opinion on ICFR using:
   a. a separate report only.
   b. a separate report or a combined report.
   c. a combined report only.
   d. None of the above.

[LO14] 10. The PCAOB requires special consideration by management and the auditor during an audit of ICFR for which of the following:
   a. Subsidiary units only.
   b. Service organizations.
   c. Safeguarding assets.
   d. Both b and c.

**Part III: Short Essay Questions**

[LO5] Discuss management's assessment process.

LO11] Discuss entity-level controls and provide examples of these types of controls.

[LO17] Discuss the criteria for management's report on ICFR as required by the Sarbanes-Oxley Act.

# Part IV: Crossword Puzzle – Chapter 7 [LO ALL]

## Across

1. A deficiency that results in more than a remote likelihood of a misstatement.
3. This exists when the design or operation of a control does not prevent or detect a misstatement.
5. Tracing a transaction from origination through the information system.
8. An effective audit committee helps set a positive ____ __ ___ ___ (four words).
10. The organization that establishes auditing standards for audits of public companies.
12. The first person that must sign the written representations about the effectiveness of internal control.

## Down

2. The group that is overseen and evaluated by the board of directors (two words).
4. The second person that must sign the written representations about the effectiveness of internal control.
6. The PCAOB issued these internal control guidelines for audits of public companies in June 2007.
7. An abbreviation for the group that developed "Internal Control - Integrated Framework."
9. The period over which the auditor performs tests of controls varies with nature and frequency.
11. An abbreviation for audit tools used by the auditor to test application controls and to conduct substantive procedures.

**Part V: Townsend Office Supplies and Equipment [LO ALL]**

| Chapter 7 |
| :---: |
| **Townsend Office Supplies and Equipment** |
| Townsend's management hopes to meet initial public offering (IPO) requirements for selling its stock on the New York Stock Exchange by 2010. Recently, Paul Green asked you to identify the major audit implications and responsibilities of being a public company. Based on what you have learned about the auditing issues presented in this chapter, prepare a memo in response to Paul Green's request. |

# CHAPTER 7: SELF-ASSESSMENT SOLUTIONS

## Part I: True or False Questions

[LO1] **False** 1.   All companies must follow the guidelines of AS5.

[LO1] **True** 2.   All public companies must follow the guidelines of AS5.

[LO1] **True** 3.   Management must assess and report on internal control over financial reporting.

[LO2] **True** 4.   Based on PCAOB guidelines, the internal control and financial statements audits should be conduced as an "integrated audit."

[LO3] **False** 5.   Management's report on internal control must be signed by the members of the audit committee.

[LO3] **True** 6.   The PCAOB makes it clear that the CEO and CFO are responsible for the internal control over financial reporting and the preparation of the statements.

[LO4] **True** 7.   A control deficiency includes the design and operation of the control.

[LO4] **True** 8.   The likelihood of an event is a "reasonable possibility" if it is either reasonably possible or probable.

[LO5] **True** 9.   AS 5 allows for the idea that a small, less-complex entity might achieve its control objectives differently from a large, complex entity.

[LO8] **True** 10.   The auditor must form an opinion on the effectiveness of internal control over financial reporting.

## Part II: Multiple Choice Questions

[LO4]   1.   In judging the significance of a control deficiency, management and the auditor must consider which dimensions of the control deficiency?
   a.   Likelihood only.
   b.   Magnitude of misstatements only.
   **c.   Likelihood and magnitude of misstatements.**
   d.   None of the above.

[LO5]   2.   Management's assessment process includes the following item(s):
   a.   Identify financial reporting risks and related controls.
   b.   Evaluate evidence about the operating effectiveness of ICFR.
   c.   Consider which locations to include in the evaluation.
   **d.   All of the above.**

[LO10]   3.   The five step process in the audit of ICFR includes:
   **a.   Test the design and operating effectiveness of selected controls.**
   b.   Form an opinion on the safeguarding of the entity's assets.
   c.   Form an opinion on the fairness of the presentation of the financial statements.
   d.   All of the above.

[LO11] 4. Examples of entity-level controls include:
    a. The entity's risk assessment process.
    b. Controls to monitor results of operations.
    c. Policies that address significant business control and risk management practices.
    **d. All of the above.**

[LO11] 5. When evaluating the control environment, the auditor must assess whether:
    a. Management's philosophy and operating style promote effective ICFR.
    b. Sound integrity and ethical values, particularly of top management, are developed and understood.
    c. The Board or audit committee understands and exercises oversight responsibility over financial reporting and internal control.
    **d. All of the above.**

[LO18] 6. The basic options for the audit opinion on ICFR are:
    a. unqualified.
    b. qualified.
    c. adverse.
    **d. Both a and c.**

[LO18] 7. If management's report states that internal control over financial reporting was effective and the auditor disagrees because of a material weakness, the auditor must:
    a. Issue a qualified opinion.
    b. Issue a disclaimer.
    **c. Issue an adverse opinion.**
    d. None of the above.

[LO18] 8. If the auditor issues an adverse opinion on the internal control, the auditor must:
    a. Issue an adverse opinion on the financial statement audit.
    b. Issue a qualified opinion on the financial statement audit.
    c. Issue a disclaimer.
    **d. Issue an unqualified opinion on the financial statement audit if the audit evidence from substantive procedures supports such an opinion.**

[LO18] 9. The auditor can issue the audit opinion on ICFR using:
    a. a separate report only.
    **b. a separate report or a combined report.**
    c. a combined report only.
    d. None of the above.

[LO14]10. The PCAOB requires special consideration by management and the auditor during an audit of ICFR for which of the following:
    a. Subsidiary units only.
    b. Service organizations.
    c. Safeguarding assets.
    **d. Both b and c.**

## Part III: Short Essay Questions

[LO5] Discuss management's assessment process.

In order to issue a report on the effectiveness of internal control, management needs to first design and implement an effective system of ICFR and then develop an ongoing assessment process. To assist management, the SEC issued guidance for evaluating and assessing ICFR. The SEC's guidance provides a top-down, risk-based approach for management to follow in evaluating and assessing ICFR. The purpose of the evaluation of ICFR is to provide management with a reasonable basis for its assessment as to whether any material weaknesses in ICFR exist as of the end of the period. The evaluation process has three steps. It includes:

1. Identify financial reporting risks and related controls.

2. Evaluate evidence about the operating effectiveness of ICFR.

3. Consider which locations to include in the evaluation.

---

[LO11] Discuss entity-level controls and provide examples of these types of controls.

Entity-level controls can have a pervasive effect on the entity's ability to meet the COSO control criteria. Because of the pervasive effect of entity-level controls, the auditor must test the effectiveness of entity-level controls. The auditor's evaluation of the entity-level controls can result in increasing or decreasing the testing performed on other controls. Two categories of entity-level controls require evaluation by the auditor: (1) the control environment and (2) the period-end financial reporting process. Examples of entity-level controls include (see Table 7-3):

1. Controls within the control environment (e.g., tone at the top, assignment of authority and responsibility, consistent policies and procedures, and companywide programs, such as codes of conduct and fraud prevention, that apply to all locations and business units);

2. Control over management override;

3. The entity's risk assessment process;

4. Centralized processing and controls, including shared service environments;

5. Controls to monitor results of operations;

6. Controls to monitor other controls, including activities of the internal audit function, the audit committee, and self-assessment programs;

7. Controls over period-end financial reporting process; and

8. Policies that address significant business control and risk management practices.

[LO17] Discuss the criteria for management's report on ICFR as required by the Sarbanes-Oxley Act.

The Sarbanes-Oxley Act requires managements of public companies to report on the effectiveness of ICFR in the company's annual report. Management's description should include the following:

1. A statement of management's responsibilities for establishing and maintaining adequate ICFR for the entity.

2. A statement identifying the framework used by management to conduct the required assessment of the effectiveness of the company's ICFR (e.g., the COSO internal control framework).

3. An assessment of the effectiveness of the company's ICFR as of the end of the company's most recent fiscal year, including an explicit statement as to whether ICFR is effective.

# Part IV: Crossword Puzzle – Chapter 7 Solution [LO ALL]

```
 1 M  2 A  T  E  R  I  A  L
       U
     3 D  E  F  I  C  I  E  N  4 C  Y
       I                       F
 5 W 6 A  L  K  T  H  R  O  U  G  H  O
    S                            7 C
    5  8 T  O  N  E  A 9 T  T  H  E  T  O  P
       M              I          S
       M              M    10 P 11 C  A  O  B
       I              I          A
       T              N          A
       T              G          T
12 C  E  O                       S
       E
```

## Across

1   A deficiency that results in more than a remote likelihood of a misstatement.
3   This exists when the design or operation of a control does not prevent or detect a misstatement.
5   Tracing a transaction from origination through the information system.
8   An effective audit committee helps set a positive ____ __ ___ ___ (four words).
10  The organization that establishes auditing standards for audits of public companies.
12  The first person that must sign the written representations about the effectiveness of internal control.

## Down

2   The group that is overseen and evaluated by the board of directors (two words).
4   The second person that must sign the written representations about the effectiveness of internal control.
6   The PCAOB issued these internal control guidelines for audits of public companies in June 2007.
7   An abbreviation for the group that developed "Internal Control - Integrated Framework."
9   The period over which the auditor performs tests of controls varies with nature and frequency.
11  An abbreviation for audit tools used by the auditor to test application controls and to conduct substantive procedures.

# Part V: Townsend Office Supplies and Equipment [LO ALL]

---

## Chapter 7
## Townsend Office Supplies and Equipment

Townsend's management hopes to meet initial public offering (IPO) requirements for selling its stock on the New York Stock Exchange by 2010. Recently, Paul Green asked you to identify the major audit implications and responsibilities of being a public company. Based on what you have learned about the auditing issues presented in this chapter, prepare a memo in response to Paul Green's request.

Date:       **February 2, 2008**
To:         **Paul Green - Vice-President, Townsend Office Supplies and Equipment**
From:       **Your Name – Audit Manager, Armstrong, Batten & Collins, LLP**
Subject:    **Implications and Responsibilities Associated with 2010 IPO**

There are three significant responsibilities associated with a "public" company that you should consider. They include:

### Annual Financial Audit

An annual audit must be conducted by a registered public accounting firm, even if the specific covenants associated with the company's line of credit were to be eliminated.

### Management's Assessment of Internal Control over Financial Reporting

The management of a publicly traded company must issue an internal control report that explicitly accepts responsibility for establishing and maintaining adequate internal control over financial reporting. Specifically, management must comply with the following requirements:

1.  Accept responsibility for the effectiveness of the entity's internal control.
2.  Evaluate the effectiveness of internal control using suitable control criteria.
3.  Support its evaluation with sufficient evidence, including documentation.
4.  Present a written assessment on the effectiveness of the entity's internal control over financial reporting as of the end of the entity's most recent fiscal year.

Management cannot conclude that the company's internal control over financial reporting is effective, if any material weaknesses are identified. In addition, management must provide sufficient documentation to support its conclusions about the internal control. You should know that the external auditor cannot participate in management's assessment process. It is the responsibility of the board of directors and management to implement an effective internal control system. For most companies, management's assessment is a difficult and costly process involving a substantial amount of work by the entities' personnel. Specifically, the CEO and CFO are responsible for the reliability of internal control over financial reporting and the preparation of the financial statements. These officers must sign the internal control report. After reviewing the company's ten-year strategic plan, I noted that management plans to hire a CFO and an internal auditor and to establish an audit committee before 2010. These actions would significantly support the company's overall requirements associated with a public company status.

### Audit of Management's Assessment of Internal Control and the Auditor's Assessment of Effectiveness of Internal Control over Financial Reporting

In addition to the requirements associated with the company's audit of its financial statements, the external auditor must issue an appropriate report to accompany management's assessment of internal control over financial reporting, which must be published in the company's annual report. The auditor's report must include an opinion on the effectiveness of internal control based on the auditor's independent audit work.

You should know that the expanded engagement will significantly increase the company's costs associated with satisfying its audit requirements.

I trust you will find this information helpful when reviewing Townsend's strategic plan.

# Audit Sampling: An Overview and Application to Tests of Controls

## KEY THOUGHT

To determine the number of items to be selected for a particular sample for a test of controls, the auditor should consider the tolerable rate of deviation from the controls being tested, the likely rate of deviations, and the allowable risk of assessing control risk too low. An auditor applies professional judgment to relate these factors in determining the appropriate sample size [Auditing Standards Board (AU 350.38)].

## CHAPTER SUMMARY

**[LO1] Learn the definition of audit sampling.**

A. Auditing standards define audit sampling as the application of an audit procedure to less than 100 percent of the items within an account balance or class of transactions for the purpose of evaluating some characteristic of the balance or class (AU 350.01).

**[LO2] Understand basic sampling terminology.**

A. When sampling is used by an auditor, an element of uncertainty enters into the auditor's conclusions. This element of uncertainty is referred to as sampling risk. Sampling risk refers to the possibility that the sample drawn is not representative of the population and that, as a result, the auditor will reach an incorrect conclusion about the account balance or class of transactions based on the sample.

B. Due to sampling risk, the auditor faces the chance that sampling may lead to one of two possible types of decision errors: (1) deciding that the population tested is not acceptable when in reality it is (a Type I error) and (2) deciding that the population tested is acceptable when in reality it is not (a Type II error).

1. **Risk of incorrect rejection (Type I).** In testing an internal control, this is the risk that the sample supports a conclusion that the control is not operating effectively when the control is operating effectively. When evaluating the level of reliance that can be placed on a control in the context of a financial statement audit, this risk is also commonly referred to as the risk of underreliance or the risk of assessing control risk too high. In substantive testing, this is the risk that the sample supports the conclusion that the recorded account balance is materially misstated when it is actually not materially misstated.

2. **Risk of incorrect acceptance (Type II).** In testing a control, this is the risk that the sample supports a conclusion that the control is operating effectively when the control is not operating effectively. When evaluating the level of reliance that can be placed on a control in the context of a financial statement audit, this risk is also commonly referred to as the risk of overreliance or the risk of assessing control risk too low. In substantive testing, this is the risk that the sample supports the conclusion that the recorded account balance is not materially misstated when it is actually materially misstated.

C. The risk of incorrect rejection (a Type I decision error) relates to the efficiency of the audit. This type of decision error can result in the auditor conducting more audit work than necessary in order to reach the correct conclusion. The risk of incorrect acceptance (a Type II decision error) relates to the effectiveness of the audit. This type of decision error can result in the auditor failing to detect a material misstatement in the financial statements. This can lead to litigation against the auditor by parties that rely on the financial statements. Because of the potentially severe consequences of a Type II decision error, auditors design their sampling applications to keep this risk to an acceptably low level. Auditors typical focus only on Type II decision errors in determining their sample sizes because Type I decision errors affect efficiency and not effectiveness, and because by controlling for the risk of Type II errors they also obtain relatively good coverage for the risk of Type I errors.

D. Audit sampling can also involve nonsampling risk, which is defined as the risk of auditor error arising from the possibility that the auditor may sample the wrong population to test an assertion, fail to detect a misstatement when applying an audit procedure, or misinterpret an audit result. While statistical sampling allows the auditor to quantify and control sampling risk, no sampling method allows the auditor to measure nonsampling risk. The uncertainty related to nonsampling risk can be controlled by adequate training, proper planning, and effective supervision.

E. Three important inputs to determine sample sizes for all of the types of audit sampling include: (1) desired level of assurance in the results (or confidence level), (2) acceptable defect rate (or tolerable error) and (3) historical defect rate (or estimated error).

1. Confidence level is the complement of sampling risk. The auditor determines his or her acceptable level of sampling risk by considering the amount of reliance to be placed on the tests and the consequences of a decision error. The more the reliance placed on your inspection and the more severe the consequences of a Type II decision error, the less risk you will want to accept (the more confident you will want to be in your testing). Because risk is the complement of confidence level, auditors can either set confidence level or sampling risk. For example, the auditor may set sampling risk for a particular sampling application at 5 percent, which results in a confidence level of 95 percent. Confidence level and sampling risk are related to sample size: The larger the sample, the higher the confidence level and the lower the sampling risk.

2. Once the desired confidence level is established, the appropriate sample size is determined largely by how much tolerable error exceeds expected error. The smaller the difference between these two variables, the more precise the sampling results must be and therefore the larger the sample size needed.

3. The term precision relates to how close a sample estimate is to the population characteristic being estimated, given a specified sampling risk. Thus, precision at the planning stage of an audit-sampling application is the difference between the expected and the tolerable deviation rate or misstatement. Auditing standards use the term allowance for sampling risk to reflect the concept of precision in a sampling application.

For example, if an auditor expected that a control would have a 2 percent deviation (failure) rate and he or she was willing to tolerate a deviation rate of 5 percent; the allowance for sampling risk would be 3 percent. Remember that in order to successfully apply audit sampling to gather audit evidence, auditors must be able to "tolerate" some amount of deviations (for controls testing) or misstatement (for substantive testing) to provide an allowance for sampling risk. The only way to completely remove this risk is to test all of the items in a population.

## [LO3] Learn the types of audit procedures that do and do not involve sampling.

A. In assessing inherent risk or control risk, or in auditing an account balance or a class of transactions, the auditor seldom relies on a single test. Generally, the auditor applies a number of audit procedures in order to reach a conclusion. Some audit procedures involve sampling, while others do not. The relationships between the types of audit evidence and audit sampling are shown below (Table 8-1):

### Relationships Between Evidence Types and Audit Sampling

| Types of Evidence | Audit Sampling Commonly Used |
|---|---|
| Inspection of tangible assets | Yes |
| Inspection of records or documents | Yes |
| Reperformance | Yes |
| Recalculation | Yes |
| Confirmation | Yes |
| Analytical procedures | No |
| Scanning | No |
| Inquiry | No |
| Observation | No |

B. It is common for auditors to use other testing approaches instead of sampling or in combination with sampling to gather evidence. For example, when an account or class of transactions is made up of a few large items, the auditor may examine all the items in the account or class of transactions. Because the entire class or balance is subjected to a 100 percent examination, such an audit procedure does not involve sampling. More common than testing 100 percent of the items in an account balance or class of transactions is a technique in which the auditor tests all items with a particular characteristic of interest based on risk or monetary value. For example, if the auditor is aware of certain transactions that look unusual or present greater risk, the auditor should examine all of these items rather than applying audit sampling. Similarly, if a relatively small number of large transactions make up a relatively large percentage of an account or class of transactions, auditors will typically test all of the transactions greater than a particular dollar amount.

## [LO4] Learn the types of audit sampling.

A. There are two general approaches to audit sampling: nonstatistical and statistical. In nonstatistical sampling the auditor considers sampling risk when evaluating the results of an audit sample without using statistical theory to measure sampling risk. On the other hand, statistical sampling uses the laws of probability to select and evaluate the results of an audit sample, thereby permitting the auditor to quantify the sampling risk for the purpose of reaching a conclusion about the population. Both approaches require the use of the auditor's professional judgment to plan, perform and evaluate the sample evidence.

The major advantages of statistical sampling are that it helps the auditor:

1. Design an efficient sample.
2. Measure the sufficiency of evidence obtained.
3. Quantify sampling risk.

The major disadvantages of statistical sampling include:

1. Training auditors in the proper use of sampling techniques.

2. Designing and conducting the sampling application.

3. Lack of consistent application across audit teams due to the complexity of the underlying concepts.

B. Auditors use three major types of statistical sampling techniques: attribute sampling, monetary-unit sampling and classical variables sampling.

1. **Attribute sampling** is used to estimate the proportion of a population that possesses a specified characteristic. The most common use of attribute sampling is for tests of controls. In this case, the auditor wants to determine the deviation rate for a control implemented within the client's accounting system. Attribute sampling may also be used with a substantive test of transactions when such a test is conducted with a test of controls as a dual-purpose test.

2. **Monetary-unit sampling** uses attribute sampling theory and techniques to estimate the dollar amount of misstatement for a class of transactions or an account balance. Variations of monetary-unit sampling are known as probability-proportional-to-size sampling and cumulative monetary amount sampling. Auditors use this sampling technique extensively because it has a number of advantages over classical variables sampling. Monetary-unit sampling builds upon attribute sampling to express a conclusion in dollar amounts.

3. **Classical variables sampling** includes the sampling techniques typically taught in an undergraduate statistics class. While auditors sometimes use variables sampling to estimate the dollar value of a class of transactions or account balance, it is more frequently used to determine whether an account is materially misstated.

**[LO5] Learn the sampling requirements in auditing standards.**

A. Regardless of the approach or type of sampling, auditing standards contain requirements that auditors must follow when planning, selecting a sample for, and performing and evaluating the audit sampling applications (see LO6 for continuation of requirements).

**[LO6] Learn how to apply attribute sampling to tests of controls.**

A. **Attribute sampling** is a statistical sampling method used to estimate the proportion of a characteristic in a population. In applying this technique to tests of controls, the auditor normally attempts to determine the operating effectiveness of a control in terms of deviations from a prescribed internal control. In conducting a statistical sample for a test of controls, auditing standards (AU 350) require the auditor to properly plan, perform and evaluate the sampling application and adequately document each phase of the sampling application in the working papers.

B. Attribute sampling includes three important phases – planning, performance and evaluation. Each of these phases requires the use of professional judgment on the part of the auditor (Table 8-2 Steps 1-7).

**Phase 1.** Planning of an attribute sampling application includes:

1.  Determine the test objectives.

2.  Define the population characteristics.

    a.  Define the sampling population.
    b.  Define the sampling unit.
    c.  Define the control deviation conditions.

3.  Determine the sample size, using the following inputs (see sample size below):

    a.  Desired confidence level or risk of incorrect acceptance.
    b.  Tolerable deviation rate.
    c.  Expected population deviation rate.

**Phase 2.** After the sampling application has been planned, the auditor performs each of the following steps:

4.  Select sample items.

    a.  Random-number selection.
    b.  Systematic selection.

5.  Perform the auditing procedures.

**Phase 3.** The evaluation phase includes the following steps:

6.  Calculate the sample deviation and the computed upper deviation rates.

7.  Draw final conclusions.

C. **Sample size.** There is a direct relationship between the confidence level and sample size. The tolerable deviation rate is inversely related to the sample size. The lower the tolerable deviation rate, the larger the sample size. Suggested tolerable deviation rates for assessed levels of control risk include (Table 8-3):

Tolerable Deviation Rates

| Assessed importance of a control | Tolerable Deviation Rate |
|---|---|
| Highly important | 3–5% |
| Moderately important | 6–10% |

The expected population deviation rate has a direct relationship to sample size. The larger the expected population deviation rate, the larger the sample size must be, all else equal. The population size has little or no effect on the sample size, unless the population is relatively small (e.g., 500 or less). These relationships on the size of the sample are summarized below (Table 8-7):

The Effect of Sample Selection Factors on Sample Size

| Factor | Relationship to Sample Size | Change in Factor | Effect on Sample |
|---|---|---|---|
| Desire confidence level | Direct | Lower / Higher | Decrease / Increase |
| Tolerable deviation rate | Inverse | Lower / Higher | Increase / Decrease |
| Expected population deviation rate | Direct | Lower / Higher | Decrease / Increase |
| Population size | Samples size is decreased only when population size is small (e.g., ≤ 500 items). | | |

**[LO7] Work through an example of attribute sampling.**

A. See Calabro Wireless, Inc. for an example of an attribute-sampling plan.

**[LO8] Learn how to apply nonstatistical sampling to tests of controls.**

A. When conducting a nonstatistical sampling application for tests of controls, the auditor considers each of the steps shown in Table 8-2. The only differences between nonstatistical and statistical sampling occur in the following steps: (1) determining the sample size, (2) selecting the sample items and (3) calculating the computed upper deviation rate.

B. **Determining the sample size.** When a nonstatistical sampling application is used, the auditor should consider the desired confidence, the tolerable deviation rate and the expected population deviation rate when determining sample size. The auditor is not required to use a statistical formula or table to determine sample size. Instead, guidance in audit firm policy and professional judgment are used to relate these factors and determine the appropriate sample size for the application. A number of public accounting firms establish guidelines for nonstatistical sample sizes for tests of controls. Typically, accounting firms' nonstatistical guidelines are consistent with sampling theory and are designed to provide two primary benefits: (1) to simplify the judgments required by field auditors by having experts at firm headquarters make firm-wide judgments and (2) to improve consistency in sampling applications within and across engagement teams. For example, a firm might establish a sample size of 15-20 for a low desired level of controls reliance, a sample of 25-35 for a moderate desired level of controls reliance and a sample of 40-60 for a high desired level of controls reliance. In developing nonstatistical sampling guidelines like these, the firm's experts have decided what confidence levels achieve low, moderate and high assurance (say 70-75%, 80-85% and 90-95% confidence). The experts have decided reasonable levels of tolerable deviation rates (say 5-10%) and they have decided to base an initial sample on zero expected deviations. Following this guidance, if one or more deviations are found in the sample, the auditor needs to expand the sample or increase the assessed level of control risk.

C. **Selecting the sample items.** While random-sample or systematic sample with a random start selection is required for statistical sampling, nonstatistical sampling allows the use of those selection methods as well as other selection methods such as haphazard sampling. When a haphazard selection approach is used, sampling units are selected without any conscious bias – that is, without a special reason for including or omitting items from the sample. This does not imply that the items are selected in a careless manner; rather, the sampling units are selected to represent the population. Haphazard selection may be useful for nonstatistical sampling, but it should not be used for statistical sampling because the auditor cannot measure the probability of an item being selected. When using audit sampling of any kind, the auditor should avoid distorting the sample by selecting only items that are unusual or large, or items that are the first or last items in the frame, because the auditor needs a sample that represents the population in order to draw inferences about the population from the sample. This is not to say that selection of unusual, large or risky events, transactions or balances should be avoided in nonsampling audit procedures. To the contrary, the auditor should focus specific audit procedures on all such items and not turn the selection of these items over to chance (i.e., random or haphazard selection) which is required for audit sampling.

D. **Calculating the computed upper deviation rate.** With a nonstatistical sample, the auditor can calculate the sample deviation rate but cannot quantify the computed upper deviation rate and the sampling risk associated with the test. The AICPA Audit Guide *Audit Sampling* provides guidance for considering sampling risk in a nonstatistical test of controls.

> [I]t is generally appropriate for the auditor to assume that the sample results do not support the planned assessed level of control risk if the rate of deviation identified in the sample exceeds the expected population deviation rate used in designing the sample. In that case, there is likely to be an unacceptably high risk that the true deviation rate in the population exceeds the tolerable rate. If the auditor concludes that there is an unacceptably high risk that the true population deviation rate could exceed the tolerable rate, it might be practical to expand the test to sufficient additional items to reduce the risk to an acceptable level. Rather than testing additional items, however, it is generally more efficient to increase the auditor's assessed level of control risk to the level supported by the results of the original sample.

Suppose an auditor planned a nonstatistical sampling application by setting the desired confidence level at high (i.e., 90-95 percent), the expected population deviation rate at 1.5 percent and the tolerable deviation rate at 8 percent. Assume the auditor judgmentally determines to select a sample size of 50 items and makes the selections haphazardly. If the auditor detects one control deviation, the sample deviation rate is 9 percent. Because the sample deviation rate is greater than the expected population deviation rate (1.5 percent), there is an unacceptably high risk that the true population deviation rate exceeds the tolerable deviation rate. Referring to the statistical evaluation table illustrates why the results of the nonstatistical sample are not likely to support the effectiveness of the control. Table 8-8 shows that if one deviation is found in a sample of 50 items, the computed upper deviation rate is 9.2 percent. This greatly exceeds the tolerable deviation rate of 8 percent.

Students and auditors are sometimes confused by what causes a sampling approach to be "nonstatistical." An approach is nonstatistical if (1) judgment is used to determine the sample size, (2) a haphazard sample selection technique is used, and/or (3) the sample results are evaluated judgmentally. A nonstatistical approach can involve random selection and a judgmental evaluation. While haphazardly selected samples cannot be statistically evaluated, any randomly drawn sample can be statistically evaluated – even if the auditor labels the approach nonstatistical and even if the sample size was not statistically derived. This is an important point because it highlights the need for auditors to understand the key concepts of sampling theory even if they are using a nonstatistical approach. Remember, if an auditor randomly selects a sample and then evaluates the results judgmentally, the quality of his or her judgment can be evaluated against statistical theory by outside experts.

# ADVANCED MODULE
## CONSIDERING THE EFFECT OF THE POPULATION SIZE

A.  The population size generally has little or no effect on the sample size. If the population contains more than 500 units, the effect on the sample size is negligible. The following examples assume a desired confidence of 90 percent, a tolerable deviation rate of 10 percent, and an expected population deviation rate of 1 percent (see page 310 in text).

Examples

| Population Size | Sample Size |
|:---:|:---:|
| 100 | 31 |
| 500 | 38 |
| 1,000 | 39 |
| 5,000 | 39 |

B.  The attribute sampling tables presented earlier assume a large population. When the population size is smaller than 500, the sample size taken from the tables can be adjusted by using the finite population correction factor as follows:

$$\text{Finite Population Correction Factor} = \sqrt{(1 - n/N)}$$

where

$n$ = the sample size from the tables
$N$ = the number of units in the population

For example, the sample size shown in the above table is 39 when population size is 1,000. If the population size were 100, the sample size of 39 could be adjusted as follows:

$$\text{Sample Size} = n\sqrt{(1 - n/N)}$$

$$31 = 39\sqrt{(1 - 39/100)}$$

## CHAPTER 8: SELF-ASSESSMENT

### Part I: True or False Questions

[LO1] _____ 1. Auditing standards permit both statistical and nonstatistical methods of audit sampling.

[LO2] _____ 2. A Type I error is the risk of incorrect acceptance.

[LO2] _____ 3. A Type II error is the risk of incorrect acceptance.

[LO2] _____ 4. Confidence level is the complement of sampling risk.

[LO2] _____ 5. Confidence level and sampling risk are related to sample size.

[LO2] _____ 6. The larger the sample, the lower the confidence level and the lower the sampling risk.

[LO2] _____ 7. Audit sampling is commonly used to gather confirmation audit evidence.

[LO2] _____ 8. Audit sampling is commonly used to gather scanning audit evidence.

[LO4] _____ 9. Attribute sampling is used to estimate the proportion of a population that possesses a specified characteristic.

[LO4] _____ 10. With a nonstatistical sampling application, the auditor relies on professional judgment rather than the laws of probability to reach a conclusion about the audit test.

### Part II: Multiple Choice Questions

[LO2] 1. A Type I error is associated with:
    a. Inherent risk.
    b. Sampling risk.
    c. Nonsampling risk.
    d. Auditor risk.

[LO2] 2. A Type II error is:
    a. The risk of incorrect rejection.
    b. The risk of nonsampling.
    c. The risk of incorrect acceptance.
    d. None of the above.

[LO2] 3. A Type I error is:
    a. The risk of incorrect rejection.
    b. The risk of nonsampling.
    c. The risk of incorrect acceptance.
    d. None of the above.

[LO2] 4. Sample size is determined by:
    a. Confidence level.
    b. Tolerable error.
    c. Estimated error.
    d. All of the above.

[LO2]  5.  The term precision relates to:
a.  The difference between confidence level and estimated error.
b.  The difference between confidence level and tolerable error.
c.  The difference between expected and tolerable deviation rate.
d.  None of the above.

[LO2]  6.  Audit sampling is commonly used for which type of audit evidence:
a.  Inquiry.
b.  Analytical procedures.
c.  Reperformance.
d.  Observation.

[LO2]  7.  Audit sampling is not used for which type of audit evidence:
a.  Inquiry.
b.  Inspection of tangible assets.
c.  Reperformance.
d.  Recalculation.

[LO4]  8.  To properly plan an attribute sampling application, the auditor must:
a.  Select sample items.
b.  Determine the sample size.
c.  Calculate the sample deviation.
d.  All of the above.

[LO4]  9.  Attribute sampling application requires:
a.  A planning phase.
b.  A performance phase.
c.  An evaluation phase.
d.  All of the above.

[LO4]  10. A major advantage of statistical sampling is that it helps the auditor:
a.  Reduce the confidence level.
b.  Quantify sampling risk.
c.  Measure the sufficiency of evidence obtained.
d.  Both b and c.

**Part III: Short Essay Questions**

[LO2] Discuss sampling risk and Type I and Type II decision errors.

[LO3] Identify the types of audit evidence that are tested using audit sampling techniques.

[LO4] Discuss the two general approaches to audit sampling.

# Part IV: Crossword Puzzle – Chapter 8 [LO ALL]

## Across

2 Some _____ procedures involve sampling.
3 When an item has an equal chance of being selected from the population.
6 Software used by an auditor to test the client's data.
8 The compliment of sampling risk (two words).
9 Sampling used to estimate the proportion of a population that possesses a specified characteristic.
12 The auditor must determine that the physical representation of the population is complete.

## Down

1 The possibility that the sample is not representative of the population, thereby causing an incorrect conclusion about the population (two words).
4 Population size typically has a limited effect on this, except when the population is relatively small (two words).
5 An abbreviation for the effect of the population size.
7 The individual member of the population being sampled.
10 The risk of incorrect acceptance.
11 The risk of incorrect rejection.

---

**Chapter 8**
**Townsend Office Supplies and Equipment**

You will use an attribute-sampling plan to test Townsend's revenue process. You have decided to rely on selected controls to reduce control risk below the maximum. The objective of the test is to determine if Townsend's revenue process is functioning as documented (controls are operating effectively). One of the control procedures that you have decided to rely on is that sales are properly authorized for credit approval. You have decided to test the entire year and the population of sales for the year contains 210,000 items (1-210,000). The planned assessed level of control risk is low. The desired confidence level is 95% and the risk of incorrect acceptance is 5%. The expected population deviation rate is 1%.

1.    Define the deviation for this test of control.

2.    Based on the planned assessed level of control risk, what should the tolerable deviation rate be (at the mid point for a low control risk)?

3.    Using the appropriate table (8-5 or 8-6), compute the sample size.

4.    What would the risk of incorrect acceptance be if the confidence level was set at 90%?

5.    Recompute the sample size if the desired confidence level is 90%?

---

# CHAPTER 8: SELF-ASSESSMENT SOLUTIONS

## Part I: True or False Questions

[LO1] **True** 1.   Auditing standards permit both statistical and nonstatistical methods of audit sampling.

[LO2] **False** 2.   A Type I error is the risk of incorrect acceptance.

[LO2] **True** 3.   A Type II error is the risk of incorrect acceptance.

[LO2] **True** 4.   Confidence level is the complement of sampling risk.

[LO2] **True** 5.   Confidence level and sampling risk are related to sample size.

[LO2] **False** 6.   The larger the sample, the lower the confidence level and the lower the sampling risk.

[LO2] **True** 7.   Audit sampling is commonly used to gather confirmation audit evidence.

[LO2] **False** 8.   Audit sampling is commonly used to gather scanning audit evidence.

[LO4] **True** 9.   Attribute sampling is used to estimate the proportion of a population that possesses a specified characteristic.

[LO4] **False** 10.   With a nonstatistical sampling application, the auditor relies on professional judgment rather than the laws of probability to reach a conclusion about the audit test.

## Part II: Multiple Choice Questions

[LO2]   1.   A Type I error is associated with:
   a.   Inherent risk.
   **b.   Sampling risk.**
   c.   Nonsampling risk.
   d.   Auditor risk.

[LO2]   2.   A Type II error is:
   a.   The risk of incorrect rejection.
   b.   The risk of nonsampling.
   **c.   The risk of incorrect acceptance.**
   d.   None of the above.

[LO2]   3.   A Type I error is:
   **a.   The risk of incorrect rejection.**
   b.   The risk of nonsampling.
   c.   The risk of incorrect acceptance.
   d.   None of the above.

[LO2]   4.   Sample size is determined by:
   a.   Confidence level.
   b.   Tolerable error.
   c.   Estimated error.
   **d.   All of the above.**

[LO2]  5.  The term precision relates to:
- a.  The difference between confidence level and estimated error.
- b.  The difference between confidence level and tolerable error.
- **c.  The difference between expected and tolerable deviation rate.**
- d.  None of the above.

[LO2]  6.  Audit sampling is commonly used for which type of audit evidence:
- a.  Inquiry.
- b.  Analytical procedures.
- **c.  Reperformance.**
- d.  Observation.

[LO2]  7.  Audit sampling is not used for which type of audit evidence:
- **a.  Inquiry.**
- b.  Inspection of tangible assets.
- c.  Reperformance.
- d.  Recalculation.

[LO4]  8.  To properly plan an attribute sampling application, the auditor must:
- a.  Select sample items.
- **b.  Determine the sample size.**
- c.  Calculate the sample deviation.
- d.  All of the above.

[LO4]  9.  Attribute sampling application requires:
- a.  A planning phase.
- b.  A performance phase.
- c.  An evaluation phase.
- **d.  All of the above.**

[LO4]  10.  A major advantage of statistical sampling is that it helps the auditor:
- a.  Reduce the confidence level.
- b.  Quantify sampling risk.
- c.  Measure the sufficiency of evidence obtained.
- **d.  Both b and c.**

## Part III: Short Essay Questions

[LO2] Discuss sampling risk and Type I and Type II decision errors.

When sampling is used by an auditor, an element of uncertainty enters into the auditor's conclusions. This element of uncertainty is referred to as sampling risk. Sampling risk refers to the possibility that the sample drawn is not representative of the population and that, as a result, the auditor will reach an incorrect conclusion about the account balance or class of transactions based on the sample.

Due to sampling risk, the auditor faces the chance that sampling may lead to one of two possible types of decision errors: (1) deciding that the population tested is not acceptable when in reality it is (a Type I error) and (2) deciding that the population tested is acceptable when in reality it is not (a Type II error).

Risk of incorrect rejection (Type I). In testing an internal control, this is the risk that the sample supports a conclusion that the control is not operating effectively when the control is operating effectively. When evaluating the level of reliance that can be placed on a control in the context of a financial statement audit, this risk is also commonly referred to as the risk of underreliance or the risk of assessing control risk too high. In substantive testing, this is the risk that the sample supports the conclusion that the recorded account balance is materially misstated when it is actually not materially misstated.

Risk of incorrect acceptance (Type II). In testing a control, this is the risk that the sample supports a conclusion that the control is operating effectively when the control is not operating effectively. When evaluating the level of reliance that can be placed on a control in the context of a financial statement audit, this risk is also commonly referred to as the risk of overreliance or the risk of assessing control risk too low. In substantive testing, this is the risk that the sample supports the conclusion that the recorded account balance is not materially misstated when it is actually materially misstated.

The risk of incorrect rejection (a Type I decision error) relates to the efficiency of the audit. This type of decision error can result in the auditor conducting more audit work than necessary in order to reach the correct conclusion. The risk of incorrect acceptance (a Type II decision error) relates to the effectiveness of the audit. This type of decision error can result in the auditor failing to detect a material misstatement in the financial statements. This can lead to litigation against the auditor by parties that rely on the financial statements. Because of the potentially severe consequences of a Type II decision error, auditors design their sampling applications to keep this risk to an acceptably low level. Auditors typical focus only on Type II decision errors in determining their sample sizes because Type I decision errors affect efficiency and not effectiveness, and because by controlling for the risk of Type II errors they also obtain relatively good coverage for the risk of Type I errors.

[LO3] Identify the types of audit evidence that are tested using audit sampling techniques.

In assessing inherent risk or control risk, or in auditing an account balance or a class of transactions, the auditor seldom relies on a single test. Generally, the auditor applies a number of audit procedures in order to reach a conclusion. Some audit procedures involve sampling, while others do not. The following types of audit evidence can be tested using audit sampling techniques:

1. Inspection of tangible assets
2. Inspection of records or documents
3. Reperformance
4. Recalculation
5. Confirmation

Audit sampling is not used to test the following types of audit evidence:
1. Analytical procedures
2. Scanning
3. Inquiry
4. Observation

---

[LO4] Discuss the two general approaches to audit sampling.

There are two general approaches to audit sampling: nonstatistical and statistical. In nonstatistical sampling the auditor considers sampling risk when evaluating the results of an audit sample without using statistical theory to measure sampling risk. On the other hand, statistical sampling uses the laws of probability to select and evaluate the results of an audit sample, thereby permitting the auditor to quantify the sampling risk for the purpose of reaching a conclusion about the population. Both approaches require the use of the auditor's professional judgment to plan, perform and evaluate the sample evidence. The major advantages of statistical sampling are that it helps the auditor:

- Design an efficient sample.
- Measure the sufficiency of evidence obtained.
- Quantify sampling risk.

The major disadvantages of statistical sampling include:

- Training auditors in the proper use of sampling techniques.
- Designing and conducting the sampling application.
- Lack of consistent application across audit teams due to the complexity of the underlying concepts.

**Part IV: Crossword Puzzle – Chapter 8 Solution [LO ALL]**

|   |   |   |   |   | ¹S |   |   |   |   |   |   | ⁴S |
|---|---|---|---|---|---|---|---|---|---|---|---|---|
|   |   |   |   | ²A | U | D | I | T |   |   |   | A |
| ³R | A | N | D | O | M |   |   |   |   |   |   | M |
|   |   |   |   | P |   |   |   |   |   |   |   | P |
| ⁵F |   | ⁶A | C | L |   |   |   |   |   |   |   | L |
| P |   | ⁷U |   | I |   |   |   |   |   |   |   | I |
| ⁸C | O | N | F | I | D | E | N | C | E | L | E | V | E | L | I |
| F |   | I |   | G |   |   |   |   |   |   |   | N |
|   | T | ⁹A | ¹⁰T | T | R | I | B | U | ¹¹T | E |   | G |
|   |   | Y | I |   |   |   | Y |   | S |   |
|   |   | P | S |   |   |   | P |   | I |
| ¹²F | R | A | M | E | K |   |   | E | Z |
|   |   | I | I |   |   |   | I | E |
|   |   | I |   |   |   |   |

**Across**

2   Some _____ procedures involve sampling.
3   When an item has an equal chance of being selected from the population.
6   Software used by an auditor to test the client's data.
8   The compliment of sampling risk (two words).
9   Sampling used to estimate the proportion of a population that possesses a specified characteristic.
12  The auditor must determine that the physical representation of the population is complete.

**Down**

1   The possibility that the sample is not representative of the population, thereby causing an incorrect conclusion about the population (two words).
4   Population size typically has a limited effect on this, except when the population is relatively small (two words).
5   An abbreviation for the effect of the population size.
7   The individual member of the population being sampled.
10  The risk of incorrect acceptance.
11  The risk of incorrect rejection.

| Chapter 8 |
| :---: |
| **Townsend Office Supplies and Equipment** |

You will use an attribute-sampling plan to test Townsend's revenue process. You have decided to rely on selected controls to reduce control risk below the maximum. The objective of the test is to determine if Townsend's revenue process is functioning as documented (controls are operating effectively). One of the control procedures that you have decided to rely on is that sales are properly authorized for credit approval. You have decided to test the entire year and the population of sales for the year contains 210,000 items (1-210,000). The planned assessed level of control risk is low. The desired confidence level is 95% and the risk of incorrect acceptance is 5%. The expected population deviation rate is 1%.

1.    Define the deviation for this test of control.

2.    Based on the planned assessed level of control risk, what should the tolerable deviation rate be (at the mid point for a low control risk)?

3.    Using the appropriate table (8-5 or 8-6), compute the sample size.

4.    What would the risk of incorrect acceptance be if the confidence level was set at 90%?

5.    Recompute the sample size if the desired confidence level is 90%?

1.    **The deviation in this test could be defined as the failure of Townsend's credit department personnel to follow proper credit approval procedures for new and existing customers.**

2.    **Using Table 8-3, the mid-point tolerable deviation rate is <u>4%</u>.**

3.    **Desired confidence level = 95%**
       **Tolerable deviation rate = 4%**
       **Expected population deviation rate 1%**
       **Based on Table 8-5, the sample size is <u>156</u>.**

4.    **The risk of incorrect acceptance is the inverse of the confidence level; hence, the risk of incorrect acceptance for a 90 % confidence level is <u>10%</u> (1 – 0.90).**

5.    **Desired confidence level = 90%**
       **Tolerable deviation rate = 4%**
       **Expected population deviation rate 1%**
       **Based on Table 8-6, the sample size is <u>96</u>.**

# Audit Sampling: An Application to Substantive Tests of Account Balances

## KEY THOUGHT

Evaluation in monetary terms of the results of a sample for a substantive test of details contributes directly to the auditor's purpose, since such an evaluation can be related to his judgment of the monetary amount of misstatements that would be material. When planning a sample for a substantive test of details, the auditor should consider how much monetary misstatement in the related account balance or class of transactions may exist without causing the financial statements to be materially misstated. This maximum monetary misstatement for the balance or class is called tolerable misstatement for the sample. Tolerable misstatement is a planning concept and is related to the auditor's preliminary judgments about materiality levels in such a way that tolerable misstatement, combined for the entire audit plan, does not exceed those estimates [Auditing Standards Board (AU 350.18)].

## CHAPTER SUMMARY

**[LO1] Understand the similarities and differences between audit sampling for tests of controls and substantive tests of details of account balances.**

A. This chapter demonstrates the application of audit sampling to substantive tests of details of account balances. Attribute sampling is used to determine whether controls are operating effectively and can be relied on by the auditor to generate accurate accounting information. Thus, the objective of attribute sampling is to determine the reliability of the client's controls. The purpose of sampling application is to determine if a financial statement account is fairly stated. Two statistical sampling techniques, monetary-unit sampling and classical variables sampling, and nonstatistical sampling can be used for substantive tests of account balances. Both statistical sampling methods can provide sufficient, competent evidential matter, but monetary-unit sampling may be more practical for most audit applications. The basic statistical concepts discussed in Chapter 8 are also applicable for sampling approaches used to test account balances.

B. The three determinants of sample size include: (1) desired confidence level, (2) tolerable misstatement, and (3) estimated misstatement. As in Chapter 8, changes in these relationships must be considered in determining sample size. These relationships are summarized below (Table 9-2):

| Factor | Relationship To Sample Size | Change in Factor | Effect on Sample |
|---|---|---|---|
| Desired confidence level | Direct | Lower<br>Higher | Decrease<br>Increase |
| Tolerable misstatement | Inverse | Lower<br>Higher | Increase<br>Decrease |
| Expected misstatement | Direct | Lower<br>Higher | Decrease<br>Increase |
| Population size | Direct | Lower<br>Higher | Decrease<br>Increase |

The Effect of Sample Selection Factors on Sample Size

C. Misstatements discovered in the audit sample must be projected to the population and there must be an allowance for sampling risk. The purpose of audit sampling is to draw inferences about a given population. The example below is provided to illustrate sampling results related to a test of the inventory balance:

| | |
|---|---|
| Book Value of Inventory Account Balance | $ 3,000,000 |
| | |
| Book Value of Items Sampled | $ 100,000 |
| Audited Value of Items Sampled | $ 98,000 |
| Overstatement Observed in Audit Sample | $ 2,000 |

What is your best estimate of the misstatement in the inventory account balance? In Chapter 8 the best estimate of the population deviation rate for control testing was the sample deviation rate. Similarly, when using audit sampling to test account balances, the auditor wants to project the misstatement observed in the sample to the population. One method of misstatement projection is to compute the ratio of misstatement to the total dollars sampled (2% = $2,000/$100,000). Applying this ratio to the entire account balance produces a best estimate or projected misstatement in the inventory account of $60,000 (2% × $3,000,000). If the best estimate is that the account is overstated by $60,000, do you believe the account is fairly stated? The answer to this question, like many questions in auditing is, "it depends." It depends in part on the amount of misstatement that can be tolerated for the inventory account. If the amount of misstatement that can be tolerated for this account is $50,000, then the auditor cannot conclude that the account is fairly stated because the best estimate (or projected misstatement) is higher than the amount we can be tolerated. What if tolerable misstatement was $110,000; would you conclude that the account is fairly stated? The answer is again, "it depends." Whenever sampling is used, the evaluation must include an allowance for sampling risk. When sampling is used to estimate monetary misstatement, an upper and lower confidence bound or misstatement limit must be established as an allowance for sampling risk. In the above example, the misstatement in the population could be $60,000, but it also might be higher or lower because the estimate is based on a sample. If tolerable misstatement is $110,000, and the upper limit on the account's possible misstatement is less than $110,000, then the account is considered fairly stated. The size of the upper limit on misstatement is largely dependent on sample size, which is also directly related to the desired confidence level. The more confident the auditor wants to be that the interval between the computed upper and lower limits contain the actual misstatement in the population, the wider the computed limits would need to be.

D. You may remember from your statistics courses using concepts such as "standard deviation" and a "normal distribution" (i.e., Z scores) to compute confidence limits (which produce a confidence interval). This traditional statistical approach is used for classical variables sampling, which is covered in the advanced module. Before personal computers were commonly available, the mathematical complexity of classical variable sampling was problematic for auditors. In response, auditors developed an audit sampling approach that is based on attribute sampling concepts. While the computations involved in classical variables sampling can now easily be performed with a personal computer or hand-held calculator, auditors have found that monetary-unit sampling provides other important advantages. For this reason, popular audit sampling software, such as ACL, include monetary-unit sampling but not classical variables sampling. However, monetary-unit sampling is not the best approach to use for all substantive testing, therefore, nonstatistical sampling and classical variables sampling will also be discussed.

**[LO2] Learn to apply monetary-unit sampling.**

A. **Monetary-unit sampling** (MUS) uses attribute-sampling theory to express a conclusion in dollar amounts rather than as a rate of occurrence. MUS is commonly used by auditors to test accounts such as accounts receivable, loans receivable, investment securities and inventory. MUS is designed to test monetary amounts rather than internal control effectiveness; hence, there are important differences in these techniques. The differences are driven by the characteristics of control deviations and monetary misstatements. In attribute sampling the control either works or it does not. Thus, all items sampled are either correct or a deviation. Attribute sampling provides an estimate and upper limit on the percentage of the time that a control is failing. With MUS, the sampling item tested may be valid and posted to the correct account in the correct period, but the dollar amount may not be accurately recorded. The basic underlying concepts of MUS are straightforward. MUS uses attribute sampling concepts to estimate the percentage of monetary units in a population that might be misstated, and then multiplies this percentage by an estimate of how much the dollars are misstated.

B. MUS is designed primarily to test for overstatement errors, but it can accommodate understatement errors if special considerations are made during the evaluation of the sample results. MUS is most appropriate for low-error-rate populations because it provides as effective a test as classical variables sampling does but has a more efficient sample size.

The major advantages of MUS include:

1. When the auditor expects no misstatements, monetary-unit sampling usually results in a smaller sample size than classical variables sampling.

2. The calculation of the sample size and the evaluation of the sample results are not based on the variation (standard deviation) between items in the population. The standard deviation is required to compute the sample size for a classical variables sampling application because it relies on the central limit theorem.

3. When applied using a probability-proportional-to-size sample selection procedure, monetary-unit sampling automatically results in a stratified sample because sampled items are selected in proportion to their dollar amounts. Thus, larger dollar items have a higher probability of being selected. With classical variables sampling, the population must be stratified in order to get an efficient sample size.

The major disadvantages of MUS include:

1. The selection of zero or negative balances generally requires special design consideration. For example, if examining zero balances (for example, searching for unrecorded liabilities in accounts payable) is important, the auditor must test those items separately because such items will not be selected using a probability-proportional-to-size selection method. Alternatively, if an account such as accounts receivable contains credit balances, the auditor should segregate those items and test them separately.

2. The general approach to monetary-unit sampling assumes that the audited amount of the sample item is not in error by more than 100 percent. If the auditor detects items that are in error by more than 100 percent, special adjustments will be necessary when calculating sample results. For example, suppose an accounts receivable account contains a debit balance book value of $1,500. If the auditor determines that the correct value for the account should be a credit balance of $3,000, the account will be in error by 300 percent. Such an item would require special consideration when the auditor projects the amount of misstatement.

3. When more than one or two misstatements are detected using a monetary-unit sampling approach, the sample results calculations as shown in the textbook may overstate the allowance for sampling risk. This occurs because the methods used to determine the amount of misstatement are very conservative. Thus, an auditor is more likely to reject an acceptable recorded book value and overaudit.

C. Monetary-unit sampling includes three important phases – planning, performance and evaluation. Each of these phases requires the use of professional judgment on the part of the auditor (Table 9-1 Steps 1-7).

**Phase 1.** Planning of a MUS application includes several important steps:

1. Determine the test objectives.

2. Define the population characteristics.

   a. Define the population.
   b. Define the sampling unit.
   c. Define a misstatement.

3. Determine sample size, using the following inputs (see sample size below):

   a. Desired confidence level or risk of incorrect acceptance.
   b. Tolerable misstatement.
   c. Expected population misstatement.
   d. Population size.

**Phase 2.** After the sampling application has been planned, the auditor performs each of the following steps:

4. Select sample items (Figure 9-1).

5. Perform the auditing procedures.

   a. Understand and analyze any misstatements observed.

**Phase 3.** The evaluation phase includes the following steps:

    6.   Calculate the projected misstatement and the upper limit on misstatement.

    7.   Draw final conclusions.

D.  **Computing sample sizes using the attributes sampling tables.** A monetary-unit sample size can be determined by using the attribute sample size tables shown in Chapter 8 (Table 8-5 for 95% confidence level and Table 8-6 for 90% confidence level). The auditor first determines the desired confidence level and then converts the tolerable misstatement and the expected misstatement to percentages of the book value of the balance tested. For example, suppose the auditor has established a tolerable misstatement of $125,000 and an expected misstatement of $25,000 for an accounts receivable account with a book value of $2,500,000. The tolerable misstatement would be 5 percent ($125,000/$2,500,000), and the expected misstatement would be 1 percent ($25,000/$2,500,000). If the desired confidence level is 95 percent (for a risk of incorrect acceptance of 5 percent), the sample size is 93 (using Table 8-5).

E.  **Computing sample sizes using ACL.** Software program likes ACL can also be used to determine sample size. Exhibit 9-1 shows the computation of sample size for the previous example using ACL software. Note that with ACL the auditor enters tolerable and expected misstatement in dollars rather than in percentage terms, like attribute sampling in Chapter 8. The result is a sample size of 92, which is slightly smaller than the size determined using the tables. ACL produces an exact sample size calculation, while the tables contain approximate sample sizes. While the underlying concepts and sample sizes produced by the attribute sampling tables in Chapter 8 and ACL are similar, ACL uses a different approach to compute sample sizes. Rather than first solve for sample size and then compute the sampling interval, ACL first computes the sampling interval (i.e., the interval in Exhibit 9-1 is defined as every 27,083[rd] dollar) using factors based on the proportion of expected misstatement to tolerable misstatement. ACL then divides the population by the sampling interval to determine the sample size.

**[LO3] Work through an extended example of monetary-unit sampling.**

A.  See the extended sample provided in the textbook which demonstrates the computation and evaluation of projected and upper misstatement limit (UML).

B.  Table 9-3 shows the auditor's risk when evaluating an account balance based on sample evidence.

Auditor's Risk When Evaluating a Financial Statement Account Based on Sample Evidence

| | True State of Financial Statement Account | |
|---|---|---|
| Auditor's Decision Based on Sample Evidence | Not Materially Misstated | Materially Misstated |
| **Supports** the fairness of the account balance | Correct decision | Incorrect acceptance (Type II error) |
| **Does not support** the fairness of the account balance | Incorrect rejection (Type I error) | Correct decision |

**[LO4] Learn to apply nonstatistical sampling techniques.**

A. When conducting a nonstatistical sampling application for testing an account balance, the auditor considers each of the steps shown in Table 9-1. The sampling unit for nonstatistical sampling is normally a customer account, an individual transaction, or a line item on a transaction. When a nonstatistical sampling application is used, the following items need further explanation: (1) identifying individually significant items, (2) determining the sample size, (3) selecting sample items and (4) calculating the sample results.

**Identifying individually significant items.** In many nonstatistical sampling applications, the auditor determines which items should be tested individually and which items should be subjected to sampling. The items that will be tested individually are items that may contain potential misstatements that individually exceed the tolerable misstatement. These items are tested 100 percent because the auditor is not willing to accept any sampling risk. For example, an auditor using nonstatistical sampling may be examining a client's accounts receivable balance in which 10 customer accounts are greater than tolerable misstatement. The auditor would test all 10 large accounts and, supposing that those 10 made up 40 percent of the account balance, the auditor would apply audit sampling to the remaining customer accounts making up the other 60 percent of the balance. Testing all individually significant items proxies for the probability-proportionate-to-size selection used with MUS, which guarantees that all items greater than the sampling interval will be included in the sample.

**Determining the sample size.** When determining the sample size, the auditor should consider the variation in the population, the risk of incorrect acceptance, the tolerable and expected misstatements, and the population size. While an auditor may determine a nonstatistical sample size by using professional judgment, the following formula, based on the AICPA Audit Guide *Audit Sampling*, can be used (this formula is based on the statistical theory underlying monetary-unit sampling):

$$\text{Sample size} = \left( \frac{\text{Population book value}}{\text{Tolerable misstatement}} \right) \text{Assurance factor}$$

where, "population book value" excludes the amount of items to be individually audited and "tolerable misstatement" represents the amount of materiality allocated to the account being audited. The assurance factor is determined by assessing inherent and control risk and the risk that other relevant substantive auditing procedures will fail to detect material misstatements.

Assurance factors for various combinations of assessments are shown below (Table 9-4):

## Assurance Factors for Nonstatistical Sampling

| Combined Assessment of IR and CR | Risk That Other Substantive Procedures Will Fail to Detect Material Misstatements | | | |
| | Maximum | Slightly below Maximum | Moderate | Low |
| --- | --- | --- | --- | --- |
| Maximum | 3.0 | 2.7 | 2.3 | 2.0 |
| Slightly below maximum | 2.7 | 2.4 | 2.0 | 1.6 |
| Moderate | 2.3 | 2.1 | 1.6 | 1.2 |
| Low | 2.0 | 1.6 | 1.2 | 1.0 |

**Risk that other substantive procedures will fail to detect a material misstatement:**

**Maximum:** No other substantive procedures are performed to test the same assertion(s).

**Slightly below maximum:** Other substantive procedures that are performed to test the assertion(s) are expected to be slightly effective in detecting material misstatements in those assertion(s).

**Moderate:** Other substantive procedures that are performed to test the assertion(s) are expected to be moderately effective in detecting material misstatements in those assertions(s).

**Low:** Other substantive procedures that are performed to test the assertion(s) are expected to be highly effective in detecting material misstatements in those assertion(s).

When any form of audit sampling is used to gather evidence, auditing standards require that the sample items be selected in such a way that the sample can be expected to represent the population. While some form of random-sample or systematic selection (e.g., probability-proportionate-to-size) is required for statistical sampling, auditing standards allow the use of these selection methods as well as other selection methods including haphazard sampling (auditor randomly selects items judgmentally with no conscious biases or reasons for including or omitting items from the sample) when using nonstatistical sampling.

**Selecting sample items.** Auditing standards require that the sample items be selected in such a way that the sample can be expected to represent the population. While some form of random-sample or systematic selection is required for statistical sampling, auditing standards allow the use of these selections methods, as well as other selection methods including haphazard sampling when using nonstatistical sample.

**Calculating the sample results.** Auditing standards require that the auditor project the amount of misstatement found in the sample to the population. The AICPA Guide *Audit Sampling* describes two acceptable methods of projecting the amount of misstatement found in a nonstatistical sample. The first method of projecting the same results to the population is to apply the misstatement ratio observed in the sample to the population. This method of projection is often referred to as ratio estimation, and it is used with both nonstatistical sampling and classical variables statistical sampling. The second method projects the average misstatement of each item in the sample to all items in the population. This method of projection is referred to as difference estimation. These two methods of projecting misstatements yield identical results if the sample includes the same proportion of items in the population as the proportion of the population's recorded amount included in the sample. If the proportions are different, the auditor chooses between the two methods on the basis of his or her understanding of the magnitude and distribution of misstatements in the population. If the auditor expects the amount of misstatement to relate closely to the size of the item, ratio estimation should be used. If the auditor expects the misstatements to be relatively constant for all items in the population, difference estimation should be used.

In evaluating the results of a nonstatistical sample, the auditor uses professional judgment and experience to draw a conclusion. If the sample is drawn haphazardly (versus randomly), the allowance for sampling risk cannot be statistically quantified within a specified level of confidence. If the projected misstatement is close to or exceeds the tolerable misstatement, the auditor should conclude that there is an unacceptably high risk that the account is misstated. If the projected misstatement is considerably less than the tolerable misstatement, the auditor should compare the projected misstatement to the expected misstatement. If the projected misstatement is less than the expected misstatement, the auditor can conclude that there is an acceptably low sampling risk that the projected misstatement exceeds the tolerable misstatement. Conversely, if the projected misstatement significantly exceeds the expected misstatement, the auditor would generally conclude that there is an unacceptably high risk that the true misstatement exceeds the tolerable misstatement.

As noted in Chapter 8, students and auditors sometimes are unclear as to the factors that cause a sampling approach to be nonstatistical. An approach is nonstatistical if: (1) judgment is used to determine the sample size, (2) a haphazard sample selection technique is used, and/or (3) because the sample results are evaluated judgmentally. A nonstatistical approach can involve random selection and a judgmental evaluation. While haphazardly selected samples cannot be statistically evaluated, any randomly drawn sample can be statistically evaluated – even if the auditor labels the approach nonstatistical and even if the sample size was not statistically derived. This is an important point because it highlights the need for auditors to understand the key concepts of sampling theory even if they are using a nonstatistical approach. If an auditor selects a sample and evaluates the results judgmentally, the quality of his or her judgment can be compared to statistical theory by an outside expert.

B. **Calabro Wireless Services, Inc.** This example extends the example presented in Chapter 8 of the textbook. The audit senior, Andrew Judd, has decided to design a nonstatistical sampling application to examine the accounts receivable balance of Calabro Wireless Services, Inc. at December 31, 2007. As of December 31, there were 11,800 accounts receivable accounts with a balance of $3,717,900 ($3,582,600 + $135,300 for the allowance for doubtful accounts), and the population is composed of the following strata:

| Number and Size of Accounts | Book Value of Stratum |
| --- | --- |
| 15 accounts > $25,000 | $ 550,000 |
| 250 accounts > $3,000 | $ 850,500 |
| 11,535 accounts < $3,000 | $ 2,317,400 |

Judd has made the following decisions:

1. Based on the results of the tests of controls, a low assessment is made for inherent and control risk.

2. The tolerable misstatement allocated to accounts receivable is $40,000 and the expected misstatement is $15,000.

3. There is a moderate risk that other auditing procedures will fail to detect material misstatements.

4. Customer accounts with balances greater than $25,000 are to be audited.

Based on these decisions, the sample size is determined as follows: First, individually significant items are deducted from the account balance, leaving a balance of $3,167,900 ($3,717,900 − $550,000) to be sampled. Second, the sample size for the remaining balance is determined using the AICPA's sample size formula:

$$\text{Sample size} = (\$3,167,900/\$40,000)1.2 = \underline{95}$$

The assurance factor of 1.2 is determined by using Table 9-4 and a low assessment for inherent and control risk and a moderate risk that other auditing procedures will fail to detect material misstatements. The sample items are divided between the two strata based on the recorded amount for each stratum; hence, 26 of the 95 [95($950,500/$3,167,900)] are allocated to the stratum of accounts greater than $3,000 and 69 to the stratum of accounts less than $3,000. The total number of items tested is 110, which is composed of 15 individually significant accounts tested 100 percent and a sample of 95 items.

Judd mailed positive confirmations to each of the 110 accounts selected for testing. Four customers indicated that their accounts were overstated, and Judd determined that the misstatements had resulted from unintentional errors by client personnel. The results of the sample are summarized as follows:

| Stratum | Book Value of Stratum | Book Value of Sample | Audit Value of Sample | Amount of Overstatement |
|---|---|---|---|---|
| > $25,000 | $550,000 | $550,000 | $549,500 | $500 |
| > $ 3,000 | $850,500 | $425,000 | $423,000 | $2,000 |
| < $ 3,000 | $2,317,400 | $92,000 | $91,750 | $250 |

Based on analysis of the misstatements found, Judd concluded that the amount of misstatement in the population was likely to correlate to the total dollar amount of the items in the population and not to the number of items in the population. Thus, he decided to use ratio estimation to compute the misstatement in the sampling strata to project his results. His projection of the misstatements follows:

| Stratum | Amount of Misstatement | Ratio of Misstatement in Stratum Tested | Projected Misstatement |
|---|---|---|---|
| > $25,000 | $ 500 | 100% | $500 |
| > $ 3,000 | $2,000 | $2,000/($425,000 × $850,500) | $4,002 |
| < $ 3,000 | $250 | $250/($92,000 × $2,317,400) | $6,298 |
| Total projected misstatement | | | $10,800 |

The total projected misstatement is $10,800. Judd should conclude that there is an acceptably low risk that the true misstatement exceeds the tolerable misstatement because the projected misstatement of $10,800 is less than the expected misstatement of $15,000. Before reaching a final conclusion on the fair presentation of Calabro's accounts receivable balance, Judd would consider the qualitative characteristics of the misstatements detected and the results of other auditing procedures. If these steps are successfully completed, Judd can conclude that the accounts receivable is fairly presented in conformity with GAAP.

# ADVANCED MODULE
## CLASSICAL VARIABLES SAMPLING

**[LO5] Learn to apply classical variables difference estimation.**

A. **Classical variables sampling** uses normal distribution theory to evaluate the characteristics of a population based on sample data. In Figure 9-2 you will see two normally distributed, bell-shaped curves that depict sampling distributions. The mean or average of the distributions is $10,000. Auditors most commonly use classical variables sampling to estimate the size of misstatement, so in our example let's say the $10,000 represents the size of the total misstatement in an account or population. The flatter, wider distribution in Figure 9-2 is based on a sample size of 50, and the taller, thinner distribution is based on a sample size of 200. Both sampling distributions are taken from the same underlying population. The sampling distributions are formed by plotting the projected misstatements yielded by an infinite number of audit samples of the same size taken from the same underlying population. For example, the height of the flatter distribution at $9,000 represents the number (or percent) of times a sample of size 50 would return a projected misstatement of $9,000. Rather than actually take an infinite number of samples of the same size to form a picture of the distribution, the distribution is modeled using the mathematical properties of the normal distribution. Thus, a sampling distribution is really a theoretical distribution that models how the means of an infinite number of hypothetical samples of a given sample size would be distributed. A sampling distribution is useful because it allows the auditor to estimate the probability of observing any single sample result. Two important features of sampling distributions are very useful to auditors:

   1. The mean of the sampling distribution will be equal to the true mean of the underlying population. Thus, Figure 9-2 tells us that the true misstatement in the population is $10,000.

   2. The area under the curve can be used to quantify likelihoods. For example, the standard error for the flatter curve is $1,000. If we look at the area covered by 2 standard errors above and 2 standard errors below the mean (i.e., the area under the curve between $8,000 and $12,000) we know that the area captures about 95% of all observed sample results. This is simply a mathematical property of the bell-shaped, normal distribution.

B. **Distribution theory** can be very useful, even when the auditor is only drawing one sample, because the theory allows for an uncertain, but informed, prediction to be made about the underlying population. As sample size increases the results from the sample are increasingly likely to approximate the true population mean. In the extreme, if the sample size equaled the size of the population, the sample mean would exactly equal the true population mean. Distribution theory allows auditors to quantify sampling risk through the use of confidence bounds, which are used to form what is commonly called a confidence interval. A number of classical variables sampling estimators are available to the auditor for projecting the sample results to the population. These estimators differ basically on the assumed relationship between the book value and the audit value.

C. Classical variables sampling can easily handle both overstatement and understatement errors. It is most appropriate for populations that contain a moderate to high rate of misstatement. Some applications of this sampling approach include auditing accounts receivable in which unapplied credits exist or a large amount of misstatement is expected, and inventory in which significant audit differences are expected between test counts and pricing tests.

Classical variables sampling has several advantages including:

1.  When the auditor expects a large number of differences between book and audited values, classical variables sampling will normally result in a smaller sample size than monetary-unit sampling.

2.  Classical variables sampling techniques are effective for both overstatements and understatements. No special evaluation considerations are necessary if the sample data include both types of misstatements.

3.  The selection of zero balances generally does not require special sample design considerations because the sampling unit will not be an individual dollar but rather an account or a transaction.

Disadvantages associated with classical variables sampling include:

1.  In order to determine the sample size, the auditor must estimate the standard deviation of the audited value or differences. However, the auditor may be able to develop a reasonably good estimate of the standard deviation by measuring the standard deviation of the book values using computer software, calculating the standard deviation from a pilot sample, or basing the estimate on prior years' audit results.

2.  If few misstatements are detected in the sample data, the true variance tends to be underestimated, and the resulting projection of the misstatements to the population is likely not to be reliable.

**[LO6] Work through an example of classical variables difference estimation.**

A.  When the auditor uses classical variables sampling techniques, the sampling unit can be a customer account, an individual transaction or a line item. For example, in auditing accounts receivable, the auditor can define the sampling unit to be a customer's account balance or an individual sales invoice included in the account balance.

B.  The following formula can be used to determine the sample size for a classical variables sample:

$$\text{Sample size} = \frac{N(Z_{IA} \times SD)}{TM - EM}$$

where

$N$ = Population size; $Z_{IA}$ = One-tailed Z value for the specified level of the risk of incorrect acceptance; $SD$ = Estimated standard deviation; $TM$ = Tolerable misstatement; $EM$ = Estimated misstatement.

The risk of incorrect acceptance is the risk that the auditor will mistakenly accept a population as fairly stated when the true population misstatement is greater than tolerable misstatement. This risk is represented in one tail of the distribution, because the only time the auditor would incorrectly accept a population is if the sample projected misstatement came from the far left tail of the sampling distribution (i.e., the sample is nonrepresentative and yields a low misstatement). For the auditor to incorrectly accept a misstated account or group of transactions, the sample results would have to fall far enough to the left that even when the allowance for sampling risk (i.e., confidence bounds) is added, the upper limit is still below tolerable misstatement. If the audit sample yields a result anywhere on the distribution other than the extreme left tail, the auditor will add an allowance for sampling risk and appropriately reject the population.

C. Sample selection for classical variables sampling normally relies on random-selection techniques. If the sampling unit is defined to be a customer account, the accounts to be examined can be selected randomly from the aged trial balance of accounts receivable.

D. See the accounts receivable example provided in the textbook for calculating the sample results.

# CHAPTER 9: SELF-ASSESSMENT

## Part I: True or False Questions

[LO1] _____ 1. The purpose of audit sampling is to draw inferences about the entire population from the results of a sample.

[LO1] _____ 2. The size of the upper limit on misstatement is largely dependent on the sample size, which is inversely related to the desired confidence level.

[LO1] _____ 3. Monetary-unit sampling is based on attribute sampling concepts.

[LO1] _____ 4. Confidence level is inversely related to sample size.

[LO1] _____ 5. Expected misstatement is directly related to sample size.

[LO2] _____ 6. Monetary-unit sampling is commonly used by auditors to test controls.

[LO2] _____ 7. The objective of monetary-unit sampling is to test the assertion that no material misstatements exist in an account balance, a class of transactions, or a disclosure component of the financial statements.

[LO4] _____ 8. Haphazard selection allows the auditor to randomly select items judgmentally.

[LO4] _____ 9. After a sample is drawn haphazardly (versus randomly), the allowance for sampling risk must be statistically quantified within a specified level of confidence.

[LO5] _____ 10. Classical variables sampling uses normal distribution theory to evaluate the characteristics of a population based on sample data.

## Part II: Multiple Choice Questions

[LO1] 1. The following relationship(s) are correct:
    a. Desired confidence level and sample size are inversely related.
    b. Tolerable misstatement and sample size are inversely related.
    c. Expected misstatement and sample size are directed related.
    d. Both b and c.

[LO2] 2. Advantages of monetary-unit sampling include:
    a. When no misstatements are expected, MUS usually results in a smaller sample size than classical variables sampling.
    b. The selection of zero balances can be easily tested.
    c. The selection of negative balances can be easily tested.
    d. All of the above.

[LO2] 3. Disadvantages of monetary-unit sampling include:
    a. When no misstatements are expected, MUS usually results in a larger sample size than classical variables sampling.
    b. The selection of zero balances generally requires special design consideration.
    c. The selection of negative balances can be easily tested.
    d. All of the above.

[LO2] 4. In conducting MUS for substantive testing of account balances, the auditor must:
  a. Determine the test objectives.
  b. Define the population characteristics.
  c. Determine the haphazard criteria for selecting the sample.
  d. Both a and b.

[LO2] 5. When determining the sample size for MUS application, the auditor must determine:
  a. The desired confidence level or risk of incorrect acceptance.
  b. The tolerable misstatement.
  c. the expected population misstatement.
  d. All of the above.

[LO4] 6. When a nonstatistical application is used to test an account balance, the auditor must:
  a. Compute the mean of the sampling distribution.
  b. Identify individually significant items.
  c. Compute the standard errors.
  d. None of the above.

[LO5] 7. When determining a nonstatistical sample size, the auditor should consider:
  a. The variation in the population.
  b. The risk of incorrect acceptance.
  c. The tolerable and expected misstatements.
  d. All of the above.

[LO5] 8. Distribution theory allows auditors to quantify sampling risk through the use of:
  a. Actual sampling distribution.
  b. Confidence bounds.
  c. Confidence interval.
  d. Both b and c.

[LO5] 9. Classical variables sampling can easily handle:
  a. Overstatement errors.
  b. Understatement errors.
  c. Overstatement errors but not understatement errors.
  d. Both a and b.

[LO5] 10. Advantages associated with classical variables sampling include:
  a. When the auditor expects a large number of differences between book and audited values, classical variables sampling will normally result in a smaller sample size than monetary-unit sampling.
  b. Standard deviation values or differences do not have to be computed in order to determine sample size.
  c. The projected misstatements are always highly reliable.
  d. None of the above.

## Part III: Short Essay Questions

[LO1] Discuss the similarities and differences between audit sampling for tests of controls and substantive tests of account balances and identify the types of techniques used to conduct substantive tests of account balances.

[LO1] Identify the three determinants of sample size and the types of audit evidence that is tested using audit sampling techniques.

[LO2] Discuss how a sample size is computed for a monetary-unit sample application using: (1) Attribute sample size tables and (2) ACL software.

# Part IV: Crossword Puzzle – Chapter 9 [LO ALL]

**Across**

3     Probability that a true but unknown measure is within specified limits.
4     The risk of incorrect acceptance.
7     An _____ misstatement limit is the total of projected misstatement plus the allowance for sampling risk.
9     A bell-shaped curve used to compute interval of values likely to contain the true population value (two words).
11    Confidence bounds are used to form a confidence _____ .
12    An abbreviation for attribute sampling techniques used to estimate the dollar amount of misstatement.

**Down**

1     The amount of the preliminary judgment about materiality that is allocated to a financial statement account.
2     A population audit sampling software used for monetary-unit sampling but not for classical variables sampling.
5     The risk of incorrect rejection.
6     ACL refers to total projected misstatement + allowance for sampling risk as the upper error _____ .
8     Standard deviation and normal distribution for computing confidence limits (two words).
10    _____ estimation is used to project the sample results to the population.

**Part V: Townsend Office Supplies and Equipment [LO ALL]**

---

### Chapter 9
### Townsend Office Supplies and Equipment

You have decided to use a nonstatistical sampling application to examine the accounts receivable balance of Townsend at December 31, 2007. There are 187 accounts with a balance of $342,000 ($310,000 + $32,000 for the allowance for doubtful accounts), and the population is composed of the following strata:

| Number of Size of Accounts | Book Value of Stratum |
|---|---|
| Stratum 1: 12 accounts > $11,000 | $145,000 |
| Stratum 2: 54 accounts > $2,000 | 135,000 |
| Stratum 3: 121 accounts < $1,000 | 62,000 |
| 187 accounts | $342,000 |

You have made the following decisions: Based on the results of the tests of controls, a moderate assessment is made for IR and CR. The tolerable misstatement allocated to accounts receivable is $5,000 and the expected misstatement is $3,000. There is a moderate risk that other auditing procedures will fail to detect material misstatements. All customer account balances greater than $11,000 will be audited.

1. Using the AICPA's formula, compute the sample size.
2. What should you do next given that you want to test the existence assertion for accounts receivable?

---

# CHAPTER 9: SELF-ASSESSMENT SOLUTIONS

## Part I: True or False Questions

[LO1] **True** 1. The purpose of audit sampling is to draw inferences about the entire population from the results of a sample.

[LO1] **False** 2. The size of the upper limit on misstatement is largely dependent on the sample size, which is inversely related to the desired confidence level.

[LO1] **True** 3. Monetary-unit sampling is based on attribute sampling concepts.

[LO1] **False** 4. Confidence level is inversely related to sample size.

[LO1] **True** 5. Expected misstatement is directly related to sample size.

[LO2] **False** 6. Monetary-unit sampling is commonly used by auditors to test controls.

[LO2] **True** 7. The objective of monetary-unit sampling is to test the assertion that no material misstatements exist in an account balance, a class of transactions, or a disclosure component of the financial statements.

[LO4] **False** 8. Haphazard selection allows the auditor to randomly select items judgmentally.

[LO4] **False** 9. After a sample is drawn haphazardly (versus randomly), the allowance for sampling risk must be statistically quantified within a specified level of confidence.

[LO5] **True** 10. Classical variables sampling uses normal distribution theory to evaluate the characteristics of a population based on sample data.


## Part II: Multiple Choice Questions

[LO1]  1. The following relationship(s) are correct:
   a. Desired confidence level and sample size are inversely related.
   b. Tolerable misstatement and sample size are inversely related.
   c. Expected misstatement and sample size are directed related.
   d. **Both b and c.**

[LO2]  2. Advantages of monetary-unit sampling include:
   a. **When no misstatements are expected, MUS usually results in a smaller sample size than classical variables sampling.**
   b. The selection of zero balances can be easily tested.
   c. The selection of negative balances can be easily tested.
   d. All of the above.

[LO2] 3. Disadvantages of monetary-unit sampling include:
   a. When no misstatements are expected, MUS usually results in a larger sample size than classical variables sampling.
   b. **The selection of zero balances generally requires special design consideration.**
   c. The selection of negative balances can be easily tested.
   d. All of the above.

[LO2] 4. In conducting MUS for substantive testing of account balances, the auditor must:
   a. Determine the test objectives.
   b. Define the population characteristics.
   c. Determine the haphazard criteria for selecting the sample.
   d. **Both a and b.**

[LO2] 5. When determining the sample size for MUS application, the auditor must determine:
   a. The desired confidence level or risk of incorrect acceptance.
   b. The tolerable misstatement.
   c. the expected population misstatement.
   d. **All of the above.**

[LO4] 6. When a nonstatistical application is used to test an account balance, the auditor must:
   a. Compute the mean of the sampling distribution.
   b. **Identify individually significant items.**
   c. Compute the standard errors.
   d. None of the above.

[LO5] 7. When determining a nonstatistical sample size, the auditor should consider:
   a. The variation in the population.
   b. The risk of incorrect acceptance.
   c. The tolerable and expected misstatements.
   d. **All of the above.**

[LO5] 8. Distribution theory allows auditors to quantify sampling risk through the use of:
   a. Actual sampling distribution.
   b. Confidence bounds.
   c. Confidence interval.
   d. **Both b and c.**

[LO5] 9. Classical variables sampling can easily handle:
   a. Overstatement errors.
   b. Understatement errors.
   c. Overstatement errors but not understatement errors.
   d. **Both a and b.**

[LO5] 10. Advantages associated with classical variables sampling include:
   a. **When the auditor expects a large number of differences between book and audited values, classical variables sampling will normally result in a smaller sample size than monetary-unit sampling.**
   b. Standard deviation values or differences do not have to be computed in order to determine sample size.
   c. The projected misstatements are always highly reliable.
   d. None of the above.

# Part III: Short Essay Questions

[LO1] Discuss the similarities and differences between audit sampling for tests of controls and substantive tests of account balances and identify the types of techniques used to conduct substantive tests of account balances.

**Attribute sampling is used to determine whether controls are operating effectively and can be relied on by the auditor to generate accurate accounting information. Thus, the objective of attribute sampling is to determine the reliability of the client's controls. The purpose of sampling application is to determine if a financial statement account is fairly stated. Two statistical sampling techniques, monetary-unit sampling and classical variables sampling and nonstatistical sampling can be used for substantive tests of account balances. Both statistical sampling methods can provide sufficient, competent evidential matter, but monetary-unit sampling may be more practical for most audit applications. The basic statistical concepts discussed in Chapter 8 are also applicable for sampling approaches used to test account balances. Like attribute sampling, there are three determinants of sample size for substantive tests of account balance. They include: (1) desired confidence level, (2) tolerable misstatement, and (3) estimated misstatement. Changes in these relationships must be considered in determining sample size.**

[LO1] Identify the three determinants of sample size and the types of audit evidence that is tested using audit sampling techniques.

**The three determinants of sample size include: (1) desired confidence level, (2) tolerable misstatement, and (3) estimated misstatement. Changes in these relationships must be considered in determining sample size. These relationships are summarized below (Table 9-2):**

### The Effect of Sample Selection Factors on Sample Size

| Factor | Relationship To Sample Size | Change in Factor | Effect on Sample |
|---|---|---|---|
| Desired confidence level | Direct | Lower<br>Higher | Decrease<br>Increase |
| Tolerable deviation rate | Inverse | Lower<br>Higher | Increase<br>Decrease |
| Expected population deviation rate | Direct | Lower<br>Higher | Decrease<br>Increase |
| Population size | Direct | Lower<br>Higher | Decrease<br>Increase |

[LO2] Discuss how a sample size is computed for a monetary-unit sample application using: (1) Attribute sample size tables and (2) ACL software.

**Computing sample sizes using the attributes sampling tables.** A monetary-unit sample size ca n be determined by using the attribute sample size tables shown in Chapter 8 (Table 8-5 for 95% confidence level and Table 8-6 for 90% confidence level). The auditor first determines the desired confidence level and then converts the tolerable misstatement and the expected misstatement to percentages of the book value of the balance tested.

For example, suppose the auditor has established a tolerable misstatement of $125,000 and an expected misstatement of $25,000 for an accounts receivable account with a book value of $2,500,000. The tolerable misstatement would be 5 percent ($125,000/$2,500,000), and the expected misstatement would be 1 percent ($25,000/$2,500,000). If the desired confidence level is 95 percent (for a risk of incorrect acceptance of 5 percent), the sample size is 93 (using Table 8-5).

**Computing sample sizes using ACL.** Software program likes ACL can also be used to determine sample size. Exhibit 9-1 shows the computation of sample size for the previous example using ACL software. Note that with ACL the auditor enters tolerable and expected misstatement in dollars rather than in percentage terms, like attribute sampling in Chapter 8. The result is a sample size of 92, which is slightly smaller than the size determined using the tables. ACL produces an exact sample size calculation, while the tables contain approximate sample sizes. While the underlying concepts and sample sizes produced by the attribute sampling tables in Chapter 8 and ACL are similar, ACL uses a different approach to compute sample sizes. Rather than first solve for sample size and then compute the sampling interval, ACL first computes the sampling interval (i.e., the interval is defined as every 27,083$^{rd}$ dollar) using factors based on the proportion of expected misstatement to tolerable misstatement. ACL then divides the population by the sampling interval to determine the sample size.

# Part IV: Crossword Puzzle – Chapter 9 Solution [LO ALL]

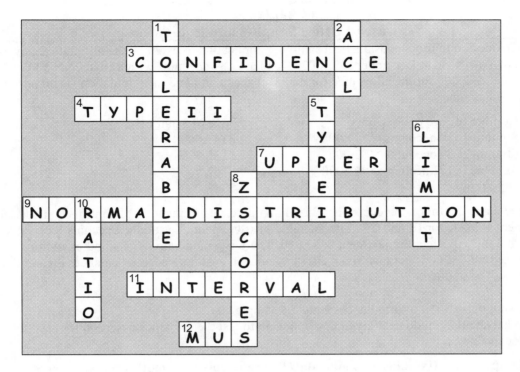

## Across

3  Probability that a true but unknown measure is within specified limits.
4  The risk of incorrect acceptance.
7  An _____ misstatement limit is the total of projected misstatement plus the allowance for sampling risk.
9  A bell-shaped curve used to compute interval of values likely to contain the true population value (two words).
11  Confidence bounds are used to form a confidence _____ .
12  An abbreviation for attribute sampling techniques used to estimate the dollar amount of misstatement.

## Down

1  The amount of the preliminary judgment about materiality that is allocated to a financial statement account.
2  A population audit sampling software used for monetary-unit sampling but not for classical variables sampling.
5  The risk of incorrect rejection.
6  ACL refers to total projected misstatement + allowance for sampling risk as the upper error _____ .
8  Standard deviation and normal distribution for computing confidence limits (two words).
10  _____ estimation is used to project the sample results to the population.

| Chapter 9 |
|---|
| **Townsend Office Supplies and Equipment** |

You have decided to use a nonstatistical sampling application to examine the accounts receivable balance of Townsend at December 31, 2007. There are 187 accounts with a balance of $342,000 ($310,000 + $32,000 for the allowance for doubtful accounts), and the population is composed of the following strata:

| Number of Size of Accounts | Book Value of Stratum |
|---|---|
| Stratum 1: 12 accounts > $11,000 | $145,000 |
| Stratum 2: 54 accounts > $2,000 | 135,000 |
| Stratum 3: 121 accounts < $1,000 | 62,000 |
| 187 accounts | $342,000 |

You have made the following decisions: Based on the results of the tests of controls, a moderate assessment is made for IR and CR. The tolerable misstatement allocated to accounts receivable is $5,000 and the expected misstatement is $3,000. There is a moderate risk that other auditing procedures will fail to detect material misstatements. All customer account balances greater than $11,000 will be audited.

1.  Using the AICPA's formula, compute the sample size.
2.  What should you do next given that you want to test the existence assertion for accounts receivable?

**1.      Sample size = (Population book value/Tolerable misstatement)/Assurance factor**

**Stratum 1 will be tested 100 percent.**

**Accounts receivable balance for sample = $342,000 – $145,000 = 197,000.**

**Sample size = ($197,000/$5,000)1.6 = 63.**

**The assurance factor is based on moderate IR/CR and moderate risk that other substantive procedures will fail to detect material misstatements (Table 9-4).**

**The 63 sample items will be divided between Stratum 2 and Stratum 3.**

**Stratum 1: Accounts to be tested 100% = 12.**

**Stratum 2: Sample size = 43 [63($135,000/$197,000)].**

**Stratum 3: Sample size = 20 [63 – 43].**

**Total accounts to be tested = 75 [12 + 63].**

**2.      After the sample items have been selected, positive confirmations should be mailed to the 75 accounts selected for testing.**

# Auditing the Revenue Process

## KEY THOUGHT

Revenues are defined as "inflows or other enhancements of assets of an entity or settlements of its liabilities (or a combination of both) from delivery or producing goods, rendering services, or other activities that constitute the entity's major or central operations" [FASB Statement of Financial Accounting Concepts No. 6, paragraph 78].

## CHAPTER SUMMARY

**[LO1] Understand why knowledge of an entity's revenue recognition policies is important to the audit.**

A. Auditors generally divide an entity's information system into business processes or transaction cycles. Using this approach, the auditor is able to gather evidence by examining the processing of related transactions from their origin to their ultimate disposition in accounting journals and ledgers. The concept of viewing a business from a process perspective was introduced in Chapter 2.
As shown in Figure 10-1, the five basic processes are: (1) the revenue process, (2) the purchasing process, (3) the human resource management process, (4) the inventory management process, and (5) the financing process. Auditors divide the financial statement components into business processes or cycles in order to better manage the audit. This chapter introduces the basic concepts related to revenue recognition. An overview of the revenue process is presented along with the specific factors that affect the assessment of inherent risk for the revenue process and the auditor's assessment of control risk (for private and public companies). Substantive procedures used will be covered.

B. Revenue must be recognized in conformity with GAAP in order for an auditor to issue an unqualified opinion. A revenue-producing transaction generally consists of the sale of a product or the rendering of a service. Revenue is recognized (recorded) when realized and earned. Revenue is realized when a product or service is exchanged for cash, a promise to pay cash, or other assets than can be converted into cash. The SEC provides the following criteria for revenue recognition (SAB 101):

1. Persuasive evidence of an arrangement exists.
2. Delivery has occurred or services have been rendered.
3. The seller's price to the buyer is fixed or determinable.
4. Collectibility is reasonably assured.

Revenue recognition continues to pose a significant audit risk to auditors and has resulted in questions about the integrity of the financial reporting process. Note that the auditing standard on fraud states that the auditor should ordinarily presume that there is a risk of material misstatement due to fraud relating to revenue recognition (AU 316.41). The auditor should be alert for the following issues related to revenue recognition:

1. **Side agreements** are arrangements that are used to alter the terms and conditions of recorded sales in order to entice customers to accept delivery of goods and services.

2. **Channel stuffing** (also known as trade loading) is a marketing practice that suppliers sometimes use to boost sales by inducing distributors to buy substantially more inventory than they can promptly resell (Exhibit 10-1).

## [LO2] Understand the revenue process.

A. Figure 10-2 presents a flowchart of the revenue process (EarthWear). The accounting system must be tailored to meet the specific needs of an entity. Notice that the revenue process interacts with the inventory management process. Many accounting systems integrate the revenue, purchasing, human resources and inventory processes. Figure 10-2 shows the points where the processes interact with one another. As entities use more advanced IT technology, it is becoming easier to integrate the information flow among the various accounting processes. Four topics related to the revenue process must be evaluated:

1. Types of transactions and financial statement accounts affected.
2. Types of documents and records.
3. The major functions.
4. The key segregation of duties.

## [LO3] Identify the types of transactions in the revenue process and the financial statement accounts affected.

A. Three types of transactions are typically processed within the revenue process:

1. The sale of goods or rendering of a service for cash or credit.
2. The receipt of cash from the customer in payment for the goods or services.
3. The return of goods by the customer for credit or cash.

For some entities, other types of transactions that may occur as part of the revenue process include scrap sales, intercompany sales, and related-party sales.

B. The revenue process affects numerous accounts in the financial statements. The most significant accounts affected by each type of transaction are as follows:

---

### The Revenue Process

| Type of Transaction | Account Affected |
|---|---|
| Sales transactions | Trade accounts receivable<br>Sales<br>Allowance for uncollectible accounts<br>Bad-debt expense |
| Cash receipts transactions | Cash<br>Trade accounts receivable<br>Cash discounts |
| Sales return and allowance transactions | Sales returns<br>Sales allowances<br>Trade accounts receivable |

---

**[LO4] Identify and describe the types of documents and records used in the revenue process.**

A. The textbook provides a brief discussion on each of the more important documents and records that are normally contained in the revenue cycle. They include (Table 10-1):

1. Customer sales order.
2. Credit approval form.
3. Open-order report.
4. Shipping document.
5. Sales invoice.
6. Sales journal.
7. Customer statement.
8. Accounts receivable subsidiary ledger.
9. Aged trial balance of accounts receivable.
10. Remittance advice.
11. Cash receipts journal.
12. Credit memorandum.
13. Write-off authorization.

The reader should keep in mind that in advanced IT systems some of these documents and records may exist for only a short period of time or may be maintained only in machine-readable form.

215

**[LO5] Understand the functions in the revenue process.**

A. The principal objective of the revenue process is selling the entity's goods or services at prices and terms that are consistent with management's policies. The functions that normally take place in a typical revenue process include (Table 10-2):

---

Functions in the Revenue Process

| Function | Description of Function |
|---|---|
| Order entry | Acceptance of customer orders for goods and services into the system in accordance with management criteria. |
| Credit authorization | Appropriate approval of customer orders for creditworthiness. |
| Shipping | Shipping of goods that have been authorized. |
| Billing | Issuance of sales invoices to customers for goods shipped or services provided: also, processing of billing adjustments for allowances, discounts, and returns. |
| Cash receipts | Processing of the receipt of cash from customers. |
| Accounts receivable | Recording of all sales invoices, collections, and credit memoranda in individual customer accounts. |
| General ledger | Proper accumulation, classification and summarization of revenues, collections, and receivables in the financial statement accounts. |

---

**[LO6] Know the appropriate segregation of duties for the revenue process.**

A. One of the most important controls in any accounting system is proper segregation of duties. This is particularly important in the revenue process because of the potential for theft and fraud. Some of the key segregation of duties for the revenue process, as well as examples of possible errors or fraud that can result from conflicts in duties include (Table 10-3):

---

Key Segregation of Duties in the Revenue Process and Possible Errors or Fraud

| Segregation of Duties | Possible Errors/Fraud Resulting from Conflicts of Duties |
|---|---|
| Credit function should be segregated from billing function | If one individual has the ability to grant credit to a customer and also has responsibility for billing that customer, it is possible for sales to be made to customers who are not creditworthy. This can result in bad debts. |
| Shipping function should be segregated from billing function | If one individual who is responsible for shipping goods is also involved in the billing function, it is possible for unauthorized shipments to be made and for the usual billing procedures to be circumvented. This can result in unrecorded sales transaction and theft of goods. |
| Accounts receivable function should be segregated from general ledger function | If one individual is responsible for the accounts receivable records and also for the general ledger, it is possible for that individual to conceal unauthorized shipments. This can result in unrecorded sales transactions and theft of goods. |
| Cash receipts function should be segregated from accounts receivable function | If one individual has access to both the cash receipts and the accounts receivable records, it is possible for cash to be diverted and the shortage of cash in the accounting records to be covered. This can result in theft of the entity's cash. |

---

B. Table 10-4 in the textbook shows the proper segregation of duties for individual revenue functions across the various departments that process revenue transactions.

**[LO7] Identify and evaluate inherent risks relevant to the revenue process and related accounts.**

A. In examining the revenue process, the auditor should consider the inherent risk factors that may affect both the revenue and cash receipts transactions and the financial statement accounts affected by those transactions. The assessment of the potential effects of inherent risk factors is one of the inputs for the risk of material misstatements. Remember that three conditions – incentive-pressure, opportunity, and attitude – are generally present when fraud occurs. Four specific inherent risk factors that may affect the revenue process are:

1. Industry-related factors.
2. The complexity and contentiousness of revenue recognition issues.

3. The difficulty of auditing transactions and account balances.
4. Misstatements detected in prior audits.

## [LO8] Assess control risk for a revenue process.

A. The concepts involved in control risk assessment were discussed in Chapter 6. This approach is applied to the revenue process. For discussion purposes, it is assumed that the auditor has decided to follow a reliance strategy. Three major steps in setting control risk for the revenue process must be followed when a reliance strategy is being followed (Figure 10-3):

   1. Understand and document the revenue process based on a reliance approach.
   2. Plan and perform tests of controls on revenue transactions.
   3. Set and document the control risk for the revenue process.

**Step 1**. In order to assess the control risk for the revenue process, the auditor must understand the five components of an entity's internal control including:

   1. Control environment.
   2. The entity's risk assessment process.
   3. Control procedures.
   4. Information systems and communication.
   5. Monitoring of controls.

**Step 2**. To evaluate the entity's risk assessment process, the auditor systematically examines the client's revenue process to identify relevant controls that help to prevent, or detect and correct, material misstatements. Because these controls are relied upon in order to set control risk below the maximum, the auditor conducts tests of controls to ensure that the controls in the revenue process operate effectively. Audit procedures used to test controls in the revenue process include:

   1. Inquiry of client personnel.
   2. Inspection of documents and records.
   3. Observation of the operation of the control (walkthroughs).
   4. Reperformance by the auditor of the control procedures.

**Step 3**. Once the tests of controls in the revenue process have been completed, the auditor sets the level of control risk. If the results of the tests of controls support the planned level of control risk, the auditor conducts the planned level of substantive procedures for the related account balances. If the results of the tests of controls do not support the planned level of control risk, the auditor should set control risk at a level higher than planned. Additional substantive procedures in the accounts affected by the revenue process must then be conducted. The auditor should document both the achieved level of control risk and the basis for his or her conclusion. The level of control risk for the revenue process can be set using either quantitative amounts or qualitative terms (such as low, medium and high). The documentation of the achieved level of control risk for the revenue process would include documentation of the accounting system such as the flowchart included in Figure 10-2, the results of the tests of controls, and a memorandum indicating the overall conclusions about control risk.

**[LO9] Identify key internal controls and develop relevant tests of controls for revenue, cash receipts, and sales returns transactions.**

A. The assertions for the revenue process about classes of transactions and events for the period under audit include (Table 10-5):

  1. **Occurrence**. Transactions and events that have been recorded have occurred and pertain to the entity.

  2. **Completeness**. All transactions and events that should have been recorded have been recorded.

  3. **Authorization**. All transactions and events are properly authorized.

  4. **Accuracy**. Amounts and other data relating to recorded transactions and events have been recorded appropriately.

  5. **Cutoff**. Transactions and events have been recorded in the correct accounting period.

  6. **Classification**. Transactions and events have been recorded in the proper accounts.

The auditor's decision process on planning and performing tests of controls involves considering the assertions and the possible misstatements that can occur if internal control does not operate effectively. The auditor evaluates the client's accounting system to determine the controls that will prevent or detect such misstatements. When controls are present and the auditor decides to rely on them, they must be tested to evaluate their effectiveness. The choice of which type of test of controls is appropriate for a particular assertion will be a function of the following:

  1. The volume of transactions or data.

  2. The nature and complexity of the systems by which the entity processes and controls information.

  3. The nature of the available evidential matter, including audit evidence that is available only in electronic form.

B. **Revenue transactions**. See Table 10-6 in the textbook for a summary of the assertions, possible misstatements, internal control procedures, and tests of controls for revenue transactions.

C. **Cash receipts transactions**. See Table 10-7 in the textbook for a summary of the assertions, possible misstatements, internal control procedures and tests of control for cash receipt transactions.

D. **Sales returns and allowances transactions**. For most entities, sales returns and allowances transactions are few and do not represent a material amount in the financial statements. As a result, this text does not cover them in as much detail as revenue or cash receipts transactions. However, credit memoranda that are used to process sales returns and allowances transaction can also be used to cover an unauthorized shipment of goods or conceal a misappropriation of cash. Two important controls should be present regarding the processing of credit memoranda. They are:

  1. Each credit memorandum should be approved by someone other than the individual who initiated it. This provides proper segregation of duties between access to the customer's record and authorization for issuing a credit memorandum.

2. A credit for returned goods should be supported by a receiving document indicating that the goods have been returned. The auditor can perform tests of controls on credit memorandum by examining a sample of credit memoranda for proper approval and the presence of the respective receiving documents. For a credit memorandum issued for a reason other than a return of goods, approval by an appropriate individual is the critical control.

For entities with few or immaterial sales returns and allowances transactions, the auditor may decide only to gain an understanding of how such transactions are processed and not to conduct tests of control. Analytical procedures can then be used to provide sufficient evidence on the fairness of the sales returns and allowances account.

**[LO10] Relate the assessment of control risk to substantive testing.**

A. The results of the auditor's testing of internal control for the revenue process directly impact detection risk and therefore the level of substantive procedures that will be required for the accounts affected by this process. This includes balance sheet accounts (accounts receivable, allowance for uncollectible accounts and cash) as well as income statement accounts (bad-debt expense, sales, and sales returns and allowances).

B. When the results of testing controls support the planned level of control risk, the auditor can conduct substantive procedures. If the results of testing controls indicate that the control risk can be further reduced, the auditor can increase the detection risk. This might lead to a reduction in the amount or the mix of the substantive procedures. If the results of the tests of control do not support the planned level of control risk, the detection risk will have to be set lower. This normally leads to an increase in the amount of substantive procedures.

C. The auditor uses substantive procedures to detect material misstatements in accounts receivable and related accounts. As discussed in Chapter 5, there are two categories of substantive procedures: (1) substantive analytical procedures and (2) tests of details of classes of transactions, account balances and disclosures.

    1. **Substantive analytical procedures** are used to examine plausible relationships among accounts receivable and related accounts.

    2. **Tests of details** focus on transactions, account balances or disclosures.

    In the revenue process, **tests of details of transactions** (also called substantive tests of transactions) focus mainly on the sales and cash receipts transactions.

    **Tests of details of account balances** concentrate on the detailed amounts or estimates that make up the ending balance for accounts receivable and related accounts.

    **Tests of details of disclosures** are concerned with the presentation and disclosures related to accounts receivable and related accounts.

D. Assertions about account balances for accounts receivable and related accounts at the period end include (Table 10-8):

    1. **Existence**. Recorded accounts receivable and related accounts exists.

2. **Rights and obligations**. The entity holds or controls the rights to account receivable and related accounts, and any liabilities related to those accounts are the obligations of the entity.

3. **Completeness**. All accounts receivable and related accounts that should have been recorded have been recorded.

4. **Valuation and allocation**. Accounts receivable and related accounts are included in the financial statements at appropriate amounts and any resulting valuation or allocation adjustments are appropriately recorded.

Assertions about presentation and disclosure for accounts receivable and related accounts include (Table 10-8):

1. **Occurrence and rights and obligations**. All disclosed events, transactions, and other matters relating to accounts receivable and related accounts have occurred and pertain to the entity.

2. **Completeness**. All disclosures relating to accounts receivable and related accounts that should have been included in the financial statements have been included.

3. **Classification and understandability**. Financial information relating to accounts receivable and related accounts is appropriately presented and described, and disclosures are clearly expressed.

4. **Accuracy and valuation**. Financial and other information relating to accounts receivable and related accounts are disclosed fairly and at appropriate amounts.

Note that the auditor may test assertions related to transactions (substantive tests of transactions) in conjunction with testing the account balance. If the tests of controls indicate that the controls are not operating effectively, the auditor may need to test transactions at the date the account balance is tested.

**[LO11] Identify substantive analytical procedures used to audit accounts receivable and revenue-related accounts.**

A. **Analytical procedures** are useful audit tests for examining the fairness of accounts such as sales, accounts receivable, allowance for uncollectible accounts, bad-debt expense, and sales returns and allowances because such tests provide sufficient evidence at low cost. When performed as part of audit planning, analytical procedures can effectively identify accounts that may contain material misstatements. Analytical procedures are also useful as an overall review for the revenue-related accounts. Table 10-9 lists analytical procedures that are useful in auditing accounts receivable and related accounts either at the planning stage or as an overall review.

**[LO12] Identify substantive tests of transactions used to audit accounts receivable and revenue-related accounts.**

A. **Tests of details of transactions** are tests conducted to detect monetary misstatements in the individual transactions processed through all accounting applications. The auditor conducts substantive tests of transactions at the same time as tests of controls. Additionally, it is often difficult to distinguish a substantive test of transactions from a test of controls because the specific audit procedure may both test the operation of a control procedure and a test for monetary misstatement.

B. **Substantive tests of transactions**. Table 10-10 presents a substantive test of transactions for each assertion for revenue transactions. They include: (1) occurrence, (2) completeness, (3) authorization and accuracy, (4) cutoff and (5) classification. Each of these substantive tests of transactions could be conducted as a test of controls or a dual-purpose test. Of these six assertions, the cutoff assertion is the one that is mostly conducted as a substantive procedure. However, if the controls are not operating effectively or if the auditor did not rely on those controls, substantive tests of transactions may be necessary for the auditor to reach an appropriate level of evidence.

**[LO13] Identify tests of details of account balances and disclosures used to audit accounts receivable and revenue-related accounts.**

A. **Tests of details of account balances and tests of details of disclosures**. Table 10-10 presents the assertions for accounts receivable, allowance for uncollectible accounts and bad-debt expense along with related tests of transactions, account balances, and disclosures. Assertions about account balances (tests of details of account balances) include: (1) existence, (2) rights and obligations, (3) completeness, and (4) valuation and allocation. Assertions about presentation and disclosure (tests of details of disclosures) include: (1) occurrence, (2) rights and obligations, (3) completeness, (4) classification and understandability and (5) accuracy and valuation.

See Table 10-11 for examples of disclosure items for the revenue process and related accounts. See Exhibit 10-6 for sample disclosures for revenue recognition and related-party transactions.

**[LO14] Describe the confirmation process and how confirmations are used to obtain evidence about accounts receivable.**

A. **Confirmation** is the process of obtaining and evaluating a direct communication provided by a third party in response to an auditor's request for information about a particular item affecting financial statement assertions (AU 330). Confirmation of accounts receivable is considered a generally accepted auditing procedure (AU 330.34), and therefore, auditors normally request confirmation of accounts receivable during an audit. However, auditing standards allow the auditor to omit confirming accounts receivable in the following circumstances:

1. The accounts receivable are immaterial to the financial statements.

2. The use of confirmations would not be effective as an audit procedure. This might occur if, based on prior experience, the auditor determines that the response rate might be low or the responses might not be reliable.

3. The auditor's assessment of inherent risk and control risk is low, and evidence gathered from other substantive procedures is sufficient to reduce audit risk to an acceptably low level.

Note that the auditor should document completely the decision not to gather such evidence.

B. Confirmations can address more than one assertion. However, confirmations normally provide different levels of assurance for different assertions.

C. A number of factors affect the reliability of accounts receivable confirmations. The auditor should consider each of the following factors when using confirmations to test accounts receivable:

1. The type of confirmation request.

2. Prior experience with the client or similar engagements.
3. The intended respondent.

D. There are two types of confirmations: positive and negative.

    1. **Positive confirmations.** A positive accounts receivable confirmation requests that customers indicate whether they agree with the amount due to the client stated in the conformation. Thus, a response is required regardless of whether the customer believes the amount is correct or incorrect. Sometimes an auditor will use a "blank" form of positive confirmation, in which the request requires the customer to provide the amount owed to the client. Positive confirmations are generally used when an account's individual balances are large or if errors are anticipated because the control risk has been judged to be high. Exhibit 10-7 presents an example of a positive confirmation request.

    Because positive accounts receivable confirmations require that customers respond to the auditor, any amounts for which responses are not received must be verified by the auditor using alternative procedures.

    2. **Negative confirmations.** A negative confirmation requests that customers respond only when they disagree with the amount due to the client. An example of a negative confirmation request is shown in Exhibit 10-8. Negative confirmation requests are used when there are many accounts with small balances, control risk is assessed to be low, and the auditor believes that the customers will devote adequate attention to the confirmation.

    Negative accounts receivable confirmations require a response only when the information about the customer's balance is incorrect. Therefore, a non-response to a negative confirmation request is generally assumed to represent a valid accounts receivable. This can be a major drawback to the use of negative confirmations.

On many audit engagements, a combination of positive and negative confirmations is used to test accounts receivable because of materiality considerations and a mix of customers. For example, positive confirmation may be sent to selected large-dollar customer accounts and negative confirmations sent to a sample of small-dollar customer accounts.

Note that the accuracy of the accounts receivable confirmation request can generally be improved if a copy of the customer's monthly statement is enclosed with the confirmation request.

E. Accounts receivable may be confirmed at an interim date or at year-end. The auditor must maintain control over the accounts receivable confirmations so as to minimize the possibility that direct communication between the customers and the auditor is biased by interception or alteration of the receivable confirmation by the client. For control purposes, the auditor should mail the confirmations outside the client's facilities. Direct mailing from the CPA's office generally provides the best control. The CPA firm's address should be used as the return address and the envelopes for returning the confirmations should be addressed to the CPA firm.

F. When positive confirmations are used, the auditor generally follows up with second, and possibly third, requests to customers who do not reply. Each confirmation exception (difference between recorded balance and balance confirmed by customer) should be examined by the auditor to determine the reason for the difference. In many cases, exceptions result from what are referred to as timing differences. See Table 10-12 for examples of exceptions to confirmation requests.

G. When the auditor does not receive responses to positive confirmations, an alternative procedure is used to determine the existence and valuation of the accounts receivable. The following alternative audit procedures may be used:

1. Examination of subsequent cash receipts.

2. Examination of customer orders, shipping documents, and duplicate sales invoices.

3. Examination of other client documentation.

## [LO15] Learn how to audit other types of receivables.

A. Other types of receivables may be reported on the balance sheet. They include:

1. Receivables from officers and employees.
2. Receivables from related parties.
3. Notes receivable.

B. The auditor's concern with satisfying the assertions for these receivables is similar to that for trade accounts receivable. Typically, each of these types of receivables is confirmed and evaluated for collectibility. The transactions that result in receivables from related parties are examined to determine if they were at "arms length." Notes receivable would also be confirmed and examined for repayment terms and whether interest income has been properly recognized.

## [LO16] Evaluate the audit findings and reach a final conclusion on accounts receivable and revenue-related accounts.

A. After the planned substantive procedures have been completed, the likely misstatement (projected misstatement plus an allowance for sampling risk) for accounts receivable is determined using either statistical or nonstatistical sampling techniques. The likely misstatement is then compared to the tolerable misstatement. If the likely misstatement is less than the tolerable misstatement, the auditor may accept the account as fairly presented. Conversely, if the likely misstatement exceeds the tolerable misstatement, the auditor may conclude that the account is not fairly presented. The auditor should also analyze the misstatements discovered through substantive procedures. In some instances, these misstatements may provide additional evidence on control risk. By identifying the causes of the misstatements, the auditor may determine that the original assessment of control risk was too low. If the auditor concludes that audit risk is unacceptably high, additional audit procedures should be performed, the client should adjust the related financial statement accounts to an acceptable level, or a qualified report should be issued. The final decision about accounts receivable and the related accounts is based on whether sufficient competent evidence has been obtained from the substantive procedures conducted.

# CHAPTER 10: SELF-ASSESSMENT

## Part I: True or False Questions

[LO1] _____ 1. Revenue is realized when a product or service is exchanged for cash or a promise to pay cash or other assets that can be converted into cash.

[LO1] _____ 2. Revenue must be realized and earned to be recognized.

[LO1] _____ 3. Trade loading is a marketing practice used to boost sales by inducing distributors to buy more inventory than they can promptly resell.

[LO3] _____ 4. The return of vendor purchases is a part of the revenue process.

[LO3] _____ 5. The revenue process affects numerous accounts in the financial statements.

[LO4] _____ 6. A remittance advice is used to track purchases.

[LO5] _____ 7. Order entry is the initial function in the revenue cycle.

[LO5] _____ 8. Credit authorization is used to determine if a customer is able to pay for goods.

[LO14] _____ 9. A negative confirmation requests that customers respond whether they agree or not with the amount due to the client stated in the confirmation.

[LO14] _____ 10. A positive confirmation requests that customers respond whether they agree or not with the amount due to the client stated in the confirmation.

## Part II: Multiple Choice Questions

[LO9] 1. The existence assertion is used to test:
    a. Whether the entity controls the rights to accounts receivable.
    b. Whether the accounts receivable that should have been recorded have been recorded.
    c. Whether disclosures relating to accounts receivable are complete.
    d. Whether recorded accounts receivable exist.

[LO9] 2. The completeness assertion is used to test:
    a. Whether the entity controls the rights to accounts receivable.
    b. Whether the accounts receivable that should have been recorded have been recorded.
    c. Whether disclosures relating to accounts receivable are complete.
    d. Whether recorded accounts receivable exist.

[LO11] 3. When comparing gross profit percentage by product line with previous years and industry data (an analytical procedure), the auditor is attempting to detect the following possible misstatement(s):
    a. Under/overstatement of allowance for uncollectible accounts and bad debt expense.
    b. Fictitious revenues (overstated).
    c. Changes in pricing policies.
    d. Both b and c.

[LO11] 4.  When comparing receivables turnover and days outstanding in accounts receivable to previous years' and/or industry data (an analytical procedure), the auditor is attempting to detect the following possible misstatement(s):
   a. Under/overstatement of allowance for uncollectible accounts and bad debt expense.
   b. Fictitious revenues (overstated).
   c. Changes in pricing policies.
   d. Both b and c.

[LO12] 5.  When comparing prices and terms on a sample of sales invoices with authorized price list and terms of trade, the auditor is testing the _____ assertion:
   a. Cutoff.
   b. Occurrence.
   c. Authorization and accuracy.
   d. None of the above.

[LO12] 6.  When a sample of sales transactions recorded in the sales journal is traced back to the customer orders and shipping documents, the auditor is testing the _____ assertion:
   a. Cutoff.
   b. Occurrence.
   c. Authorization and accuracy.
   d. None of the above.

[LO12] 7.  When tracing a sample of shipping documents to the details of the sales invoices and to the sales journal and customers' accounts receivable subsidiary ledger, the auditor is testing the _____ assertion:
   a. Classification.
   b. Completeness.
   c. Cutoff.
   d. Both a and b.

[LO12] 8.  When reviewing bank confirmation for any liens on receivables, the auditor is testing the _____ assertion:
   a. Valuation and allocation.
   b. Existence.
   c. Rights and obligations.
   d. Both a and b.

[LO12] 9.  When reading the footnotes to ensure that required disclosures are understandable, the auditor is testing the _____ assertion:
   a. Completeness.
   b. Accuracy and valuation.
   c. Classification and understandability.
   d. Both a and c.

[LO14] 10.  When confirmations are sent, the auditor is testing the _____ assertion:
   a. Completeness.
   b. Existence.
   c. Rights and obligations.
   d. None of the above.

## Part III: Short Essay Questions

[LO5] Identify the primary functions in the revenue cycle and describe each function.

[LO6] Discuss the key segregation of duties in the revenue process and possible errors or fraud.

[LO10] Identify the types of substantive procedures used by the auditor to test accounts receivable and revenue-related accounts. Provide an example of how the auditor may use each substantive procedure. Identify if any of the substantive procedures can be used as a test of controls or a dual-purpose test.

# Part IV: Crossword Puzzle – Chapter 10 [LO ALL]

## Across

3    This type of risk is affected by industry-related factors.

6    A _____ confirmation is a request that requires the recipient to respond to whether or not the customer agrees.

7    A two-letter abbreviation for the journal used to record the receipt of cash from customers.

10   An inappropriate market practice used to boost sales by inducing distributors to buy more inventory than can be resold (two words).

11   A _____ confirmation is a request that requires the recipient to respond only if the amount is incorrect.

12   An ____ trial balance is a report that summarizes customer balances in categories (< 30 days, 30-60 days, 60-90 days, etc.).

## Down

1    Another name for trade loading (two words).

2    A process of covering a cash shortage by applying cash from one customer's A/R balance against another customer's A/R balance.

4    A document prepared when goods are shipped (three words).

5    The _____ cycle includes sales, cash receipts, and sales return and allowances.

8    An audit strategy where the auditor decides to reply on the entity's controls, test those controls, and reduce the substantive procedures, if appropriate.

9    The result of estimated accounts that will not be collected (two words).

## Part V: Townsend Office Supplies and Equipment [LO ALL]

---

### Chapter 10
### Townsend Office Supplies and Equipment

The existence of accounts receivable is an important assertion because the auditor wants assurance that this account balance is not overstated due to fictitious customer accounts or amounts. The major audit procedure for testing the existence assertion is confirmation of customers' account balances and you have decided to use positive confirmations. In Chapter 9, you computed a sample size of 75 for accounts receivable confirmations (total accounts to be confirmed). The tolerable misstatement allocated to accounts receivable is $5,000 and the expected misstatement is $3,000. There are 187 accounts with a balance of $342,000 ($310,000 + $32,000 for the allowance for doubtful accounts). The population is composed of the following strata:

| Number of Size of Accounts | Book Value of Stratum |
|---|---|
| Stratum 1: 12 accounts > $11,000 | $145,000 |
| Stratum 2: 54 accounts > $2,000 | 135,000 |
| Stratum 3: 121 accounts < $1,000 | 62,000 |
| 187 accounts | $342,000 |

A moderate assessment is made for IR and CR. The tolerable misstatement allocated to accounts receivable is $5,000 and the expected misstatement is $3,000. There is a moderate risk that other auditing procedures will fail to detect material misstatements. All customer account balances greater than $11,000 will be confirmed. Three customers have indicated that their accounts were overstated and you determined that these misstatements resulted from unintentional errors by client personnel (Stratum 1 $400, Stratum 2 $600 and Stratum 3 $200). You have concluded that the amount of misstatement in the population was likely to correlate to the total dollar amount of the items in the population and not to the number of items in the population; hence, the ratio estimation method should be used to compute misstatement in the sampling strata. For informational purposes, the computation of the sample size is shown below [Sample size = (Population book value/Tolerable misstatement)(Assurance factor)]:

Stratum 1 will be tested 100 percent.
Accounts receivable balance for sample = $342,000 – $145,000 = 197,000.
Sample size = ($197,000/$5,000)1.6 = 63.
The assurance factor is based on moderate IR/CR and moderate risk that other substantive procedures will fail to detect material misstatements (Table 9-4).
The 63 sample items will be divided between Stratum 2 and Stratum 3.
Stratum 1: Accounts to be tested 100% = 12
Stratum 2: Sample = 43 [63($135,000/$197,000)] + Stratum 3: Sample size = 20 [63 – 43]
Total accounts to be tested = 75 [12 + 63]

1. Compute the projected misstatement.
2. Assuming no qualitative considerations need to be considered, what is your conclusion about whether the accounts receivable balance is fairly presented.

# CHAPTER 10: SELF-ASSESSMENT SOLUTIONS

## Part I: True or False Questions

[LO1] **True** 1. Revenue is realized when a product or service is exchanged for cash or a promise to pay cash or other assets that can be converted into cash.

[LO1] **True** 2. Revenue must be realized and earned to be recognized.

[LO1] **True** 3. Trade loading is a marketing practice used to boost sales by inducing distributors to buy more inventory than they can promptly resell.

[LO3] **False** 4. The return of vendor purchases is a part of the revenue process.

[LO3] **True** 5. The revenue process affects numerous accounts in the financial statements.

[LO4] **False** 6. A remittance advice is used to track purchases.

[LO5] **True** 7. Order entry is the initial function in the revenue cycle.

[LO5] **True** 8. Credit authorization is used to determine if a customer is able to pay for goods.

[LO14] **False** 9. A negative confirmation requests that customers respond whether they agree or not with the amount due to the client stated in the confirmation.

[LO14] **True** 10. A positive confirmation requests that customers respond whether they agree or not with the amount due to the client stated in the confirmation.

## Part II: Multiple Choice Questions

[LO9] 1. The existence assertion is used to test:
   a. Whether the entity controls the rights to accounts receivable.
   b. Whether the accounts receivable that should have been recorded have been recorded.
   c. Whether disclosures relating to accounts receivable are complete.
   **d. Whether recorded accounts receivable exist.**

[LO9] 2. The completeness assertion is used to test:
   a. Whether the entity controls the rights to accounts receivable.
   **b. Whether the accounts receivable that should have been recorded have been recorded.**
   c. Whether disclosures relating to accounts receivable are complete.
   d. Whether recorded accounts receivable exist.

[LO11] 3. When comparing gross profit percentage by product line with previous years and industry data (an analytical procedure), the auditor is attempting to detect the following possible misstatement(s):
   a. Under/overstatement of allowance for uncollectible accounts and bad debt expense.
   b. Fictitious revenues (overstated).
   c. Changes in pricing policies.
   **d. Both b and c.**

[LO11] 4. When comparing receivables turnover and days outstanding in accounts receivable to previous years' and/or industry data (an analytical procedure), the auditor is attempting to detect the following possible misstatement(s):

   **a. Under/overstatement of allowance for uncollectible accounts and bad debt expense.**
   b. Fictitious revenues (overstated).
   c. Changes in pricing policies.
   d. Both b and c.

[LO12] 5. When comparing prices and terms on a sample of sales invoices with authorized pricelist and terms of trade, the auditor is testing the _____ assertion:

   a. Cutoff.
   b. Occurrence.
   **c. Authorization and accuracy.**
   d. None of the above.

[LO12] 6. When a sample of sales transactions recorded in the sales journal is traced back to the customer orders and shipping documents, the auditor is testing the _____ assertion:

   a. Cutoff.
   **b. Occurrence.**
   c. Authorization and accuracy.
   d. None of the above.

[LO12] 7. When tracing a sample of shipping documents to the details of the sales invoices and to the sales journal and customers' accounts receivable subsidiary ledger, the auditor is testing the _____ assertion:

   a. Classification.
   **b. Completeness.**
   c. Cutoff.
   d. Both a and b.

[LO12] 8. When reviewing bank confirmation for any liens on receivables, the auditor is testing the _____ assertion:

   a. Valuation and allocation.
   b. Existence.
   **c. Rights and obligations.**
   d. Both a and b.

[LO12] 9. When reading the footnotes to ensure that required disclosures are understandable, the auditor is testing the _____ assertion:

   a. Completeness.
   b. Accuracy and valuation.
   **c. Classification and understandability.**
   d. Both a and c.

[LO14]10. When confirmations are sent, the auditor is testing the _____ assertion:

   a. Completeness.
   **b. Existence.**
   c. Rights and obligations.
   d. None of the above.

# Part III: Short Essay Questions

[LO5] Identify the primary functions in the revenue cycle and describe each function.

**There are seven basic functions in the revenue process. They include:**

| | |
|---|---|
| **Order entry** | Acceptance of customer orders for goods and services into the system in accordance with management criteria. |
| **Credit authorization** | Appropriate approval of customer orders for creditworthiness. |
| **Shipping** | Shipping of goods that have been authorized. |
| **Billing** | Issuance of sales invoices to customers for goods shipped or serviced provided: also, processing of billing adjustments for allowances, discounts, and returns. |
| **Cash receipts** | Processing of the receipt of cash from customers. |
| **Accounts receivable** | Recording of all sales invoices, collections, and credit memoranda in individual customer accounts. |
| **General ledger** | Proper accumulation, classification and summarization of revenues, collections, and receivables in the accounts. |

[LO6] Discuss the key segregation of duties in the revenue process and possible errors or fraud.

| Segregation of Duties | Possible Errors/Fraud Resulting from Conflicts of Duties |
|---|---|
| **Credit function should be segregated from billing function** | If one individual has the ability to grant credit to a customer and also has responsibility for billing that customer, it is possible for sales to be made to customers who are not creditworthy. This can result in bad debts. |
| **Shipping function should be segregated from billing function** | If one individual who is responsible for shipping goods is also involved in the billing function, it is possible for unauthorized shipments to be made and for the usual billing procedures to be circumvented. This can result in unrecorded sales transaction and theft of goods. |
| **Accounts receivable function should be segregated from general ledger function** | If one individual is responsible for the accounts receivable records and also for the general ledger, it is possible for that individual to conceal unauthorized shipments. This can result in unrecorded sales transactions and theft of goods. |
| **Cash receipts function should be segregated from accounts receivable function** | If one individual has access to both the cash receipts and the accounts receivable records, it is possible for cash to be diverted and the shortage of cash in the accounting records to be covered. This can result in theft of the entity's cash. |

233

[LO10] Identify the types of substantive procedures used by the auditor to test accounts receivable and revenue-related accounts. Provide an example of how the auditor may use each substantive procedure. Identify if any of the substantive procedures can be used as a test of controls or a dual-purpose test.

**The auditor uses substantive procedures to detect material misstatements in accounts receivable and related accounts. There are two categories of substantive procedures: (1) substantive analytical procedures and (2) tests of details of classes of transactions, account balances and disclosures.**

1. **Substantive analytical procedures are used to examine plausible relationships among accounts receivable and related accounts.**
   **Example: The auditor might compare the gross profit percentage to previous years' or industry data which may provide valuable evidence on unrecorded revenue (an understatement) or fictitious revenue (an overstatement) and related accounts receivable when this ratio is significantly higher or lower than previous years' or industry data.**

2. **Tests of details focus on transactions, account balances or disclosures.**
   **In the revenue process, tests of details of transactions (also called substantive tests of transactions) focus mainly on the sales and cash receipts transactions. Example: To test the occurrence assertion about sales, the auditor can test a sample of sales transactions recorded in the sales journal, by tracing the sales invoices back to customer orders and shipping documents.**

   **Tests of details of account balances concentrate on the detailed amounts or estimates that make up the ending balance for accounts receivable and related accounts. Example: To test the existence assertion about an account receivable, the auditor can send confirmations to selected accounts receivable customers.**

   **Tests of details of disclosures are concerned with the presentation and disclosures related to accounts receivable and related accounts. Example: To test the completeness assertions about accounts receivable, the auditor can complete a financial reporting checklist to ensure that all financial statement disclosures related to accounts receivable and related accounts have been appropriately disclosed.**

**A test of details of transactions (the occurrence assertion about sales) can be used as a test of controls or a dual-purpose test. However, if the tests of controls indicate that the controls are not operating effectively, the auditor may need to test transactions at the date the account balance is tested.**

# Part IV: Crossword Puzzle – Chapter 10 Solution [LO ALL]

The crossword grid solution contains the following answers:

- 1 Down: CHANNELSTUFFIN (CHANNEL STUFFING)
- 2 Down: LAPPING
- 3 Across: INHERENT
- 4 Down: BILLOFLADIN (BILL OF LADING)
- 5 Down: REVENUE
- 6 Across: POSITIVE
- 7 Across / 8 Down: CR / RELIANCE
- 9 Down: BADDEBTS (BAD DEBTS)
- 10 Across: TRADELOADING (TRADE LOADING)
- 11 Across: NEGATIVE
- 12 Across: AGED

**Across**

3  This type of risk is affected by industry-related factors.
6  A _____ confirmation is a request that requires the recipient to respond to whether or not the customer agrees.
7  A two-letter abbreviation for the journal used to record the receipt of cash from customers.
10  An inappropriate market practice used to boost sales by inducing distributors to buy more inventory than can be resold (two words).
11  A _____ confirmation is a request that requires the recipient to respond only if the amount is incorrect.
12  An ____ trial balance is a report that summarizes customer balances in categories (< 30 days, 30-60 days, 60-90 days, etc.).

**Down**

1  Another name for trade loading (two words).
2  A process of covering a cash shortage by applying cash from one customer's A/R balance against another customer's A/R balance.
4  A document prepared when goods are shipped (three words).
5  The _____ cycle includes sales, cash receipts, and sales return and allowances.
8  An audit strategy where the auditor decides to reply on the entity's controls, test those controls, and reduce the substantive procedures, if appropriate.
9  The result of estimated accounts that will not be collected (two words).

## Part V: Townsend Office Supplies and Equipment [LO ALL]

---

### Chapter 10
### Townsend Office Supplies and Equipment

The existence of accounts receivable is an important assertion because the auditor wants assurance that this account balance is not overstated due to fictitious customer accounts or amounts. The major audit procedure for testing the existence assertion is confirmation of customers' account balances and you have decided to use positive confirmations. In Chapter 9, you computed a sample size of 75 for accounts receivable confirmations (total accounts to be confirmed). The tolerable misstatement allocated to accounts receivable is $5,000 and the expected misstatement is $3,000. There are 187 accounts with a balance of $342,000 ($310,000 + $32,000 for the allowance for doubtful accounts). The population is composed of the following strata:

| Number of Size of Accounts | Book Value of Stratum |
|---|---|
| Stratum 1: 12 accounts > $11,000 | $145,000 |
| Stratum 2: 54 accounts > $2,000 | 135,000 |
| Stratum 3: 121 accounts < $1,000 | 62,000 |
| 187 accounts | $342,000 |

A moderate assessment is made for IR and CR. The tolerable misstatement allocated to accounts receivable is $5,000 and the expected misstatement is $3,000. There is a moderate risk that other auditing procedures will fail to detect material misstatements. All customer account balances greater than $11,000 will be confirmed. Three customers have indicated that their accounts were overstated and you determined that these misstatements resulted from unintentional errors by client personnel (Stratum 1 $400, Stratum 2 $600 and Stratum 3 $200). You have concluded that the amount of misstatement in the population was likely to correlate to the total dollar amount of the items in the population and not to the number of items in the population; hence, the ratio estimation method should be used to compute misstatement in the sampling strata. For informational purposes, the computation of the sample size is shown below [Sample size = (Population book value/Tolerable misstatement)(Assurance factor)]:

Stratum 1 will be tested 100 percent.
Accounts receivable balance for sample = $342,000 - $145,000 = 197,000.
Sample size = ($197,000/$5,000)1.6 = 63.
The assurance factor is based on moderate IR/CR and moderate risk that other substantive procedures will fail to detect material misstatements (Table 9-4).
The 63 sample items will be divided between Stratum 2 and Stratum 3.
Stratum 1: Accounts to be tested 100% = 12
Stratum 2: Sample = 43 [63($135,000/$197,000)] + Stratum 3: Sample size = 20 [63 – 43]
Total accounts to be tested = 75 [12 + 63]

1. Compute the projected misstatement.
2. Assuming no qualitative considerations need to be considered, what is your conclusion about whether the accounts receivable balance is fairly presented.

**1.**

| Stratum | Book Value of Stratum | Book Value of Sample | Audit Value of Sample | Amount of Overstatement |
|---|---|---|---|---|
| 1 > $11,000 | $145,000 | $145,000 | $144,600 | $ 400 |
| 2 > $ 2,000 | $135,000 | $ 94,000 | $ 93,400 | $ 600 |
| 3 < $ 1,000 | $ 62,000 | 13,000 | $ 12,800 | $ 200 |

| Stratum | Amount of Misstatement | Ratio of Misstatement Tested | Projected Misstatement |
|---|---|---|---|
| 1 > $11,000 | $ 400 | 100 % | $ 400 |
| 2 > $ 2,000 | $ 600 | $600/($94,000 × $135,000) | $ 862 |
| 3 < $ 1,000 | $ 200 | $200/($13,000 × $62,000) | $ 954 |
| **Total projected misstatement** | | | **$2,216** |

# Auditing the Purchasing Process

**KEY THOUGHT**

Expenses are defined as "outflows or other using up of assets or incurrences of liabilities (or a combination of both) from delivering or producing goods, rendering services, or carrying out other activities that constitute the entity's ongoing major or central operations" [FASB Statement of Financial Account Concepts No. 6, paragraph 85]. Liabilities are defined as "probable future sacrifices of economic benefits arising from present obligations of a particular entity to transfer assets or provide services to other entities in the future as a result of past transactions or events [FASB Statement of Financial Accounting Concepts No. 6, paragraph 35].

**CHAPTER SUMMARY**

**[LO1] Understand why knowledge of an entity's expense and liability recognition policies is important to the audit.**

A. This chapter introduces the basic concepts related to the purchase of and payment for goods and services from outside vendors. The acquisition of goods and services includes the purchase of raw materials, supplies, manufacturing equipment, furniture, and fixtures, and payment for repairs and maintenance, utilities, and professional services.

B. An entity's expense recognition policies and the type of expenses involved affect how the transactions are recorded and accounted for in the financial statements. FASB Statement of Financial Accounting Concepts No. 5 (Recognition and Measurement in Financial Statements of Business Enterprises) indicates that expenses can be classified into three categories:

   1. Certain expense can be matched directly with specific transactions or events and are recognized upon recognition of revenue. These types of expenses are referred to as product costs and include expenses such as cost of goods sold.

   2. Many expenses are recognized during the period in which cash is spent or liabilities incurred for goods and services that are used up at that time or shortly thereafter. Such expenses cannot be directly related to specific transactions and are assumed to provide no future benefit. These expenses are referred to as period costs. Examples of such expenses include administrative salaries and rent expense.

   3. Some expenses are allocated by systematic and rational procedures to the periods during which the related assets are expected to provide benefits. Depreciation of plant and equipment is an example of such an expense.

C. In general, the liabilities normally incurred as part of the purchasing process are trade accounts payable. Other incurred expenses are accrued as liabilities at the end of each accounting period. Most expenses recognized are product or period costs.

**[LO2] Develop an understanding of the purchasing process.**

A. A purchase transaction usually begins with a purchase requisition being generated by a department or support function. When the goods are received or the services have been rendered, the entity records a liability to the vendor. Finally, the entity pays the vendor. Figure 11-1 present the flowchart for EarthWear's purchasing system.

B. Four topics related to the purchasing process must be evaluated:

   1. Types of transactions and financial statement accounts affected.
   2. Types of documents and records.
   3. The major functions.
   4. The key segregation of duties.

**[LO3] Identify the types of transactions in the purchasing process and the financial statement accounts affected.**

A. Three types of transactions are typically processed within the purchasing process:

   1. The purchase of goods and services for cash or credit.
   2. The payment of the liabilities arising from such purchases.
   3. Return of goods to supplies for cash or credit.

B. The purchasing process affects numerous accounts in the financial statements. The most significant accounts affected by each type of transaction are as follows:

The Purchasing Process

| Type of Transaction | Account Affected |
| --- | --- |
| Purchase transactions | Accounts payable<br>Inventory<br>Purchases or cost of goods sold<br>Various asset and expense accounts |
| Cash disbursement transactions | Cash<br>Accounts payable<br>Cash discounts<br>Various asset and expense accounts |
| Purchase return transactions | Purchase returns<br>Purchase returns<br>Accounts payable<br>Various asset and expense accounts |

**[LO4] Identify and describe the types of documents and records used in the purchasing process.**

A. The textbook provides a brief discussion on each of the more important documents and records that are normally contained in the purchasing cycle. They include (Table 11-1):

1. Purchase requisition.
2. Purchase order.
3. Receiving report.
4. Vendor invoice.
5. Voucher.
6. Voucher register/purchases journal.
7. Accounts payable subsidiary ledger.
8. Vendor statement.
9. Check.
10. Cash disbursements journal/check register.

The reader should keep in mind that in advanced IT systems some of these documents and records may exist for only a short period of time or may be maintained only in machine-readable form.

**[LO5] Understand the functions in the purchasing process.**

A. The principal objective of the purchasing process are acquiring goods and services at the lowest cost consistent with quality and service requirements and effectively using cash resources to pay for those goods and services. The functions that normally take place in a typical purchasing process include (Table 11-2):

Functions in the Purchasing Process

| Function | Description of Function |
|---|---|
| Requisitioning | Initiation and approval of request for goods and services by authorized individuals consistent with management criteria. |
| Purchasing | Approval of purchase orders and proper execution as to price, quantity, quality and vendor. |
| Receiving | Receipt of properly authorized goods or services. |
| Invoice Processing | Processing of vendor invoices for goods and services received; also, processing of adjustments for allowances, discounts and returns. |
| Disbursements | Processing of payment to vendors. |
| Accounts payable | Recording of all vendor invoices, cash disbursements, and adjustments in individual vendor accounts. |
| General ledger | Proper accumulation, classification and summarization of purchases, cash disbursements and payables in the general ledger. |

**[LO6] Know the appropriate segregation of duties for the purchasing process.**

A. Proper segregation of duties is one of the most important control procedures in any accounting system. Duties should be assigned so that no one individual can control all phases of processing a transaction in a way that permits errors or fraud to go undetected. Because of the potential for theft and fraud in the purchasing process, individuals responsible for requisitioning, purchasing and receiving should be segregated from the invoice-processing, accounts payable and general ledger functions.

B. Some of the key segregation of duties for the purchasing process, as well as examples of possible errors or fraud that can result from conflicts in duties include (Table 11-3):

Key Segregation of Duties in the Purchasing Process and Possible Errors or Fraud

| Segregation of Duties | Possible Errors/Fraud Resulting from Conflicts of Duties |
|---|---|
| Purchasing function should be segregated from requisition and receiving functions | If one individual is responsible for the requisition, purchasing and receiving functions, fictitious or unauthorized purchases can be made. This can result in the theft of goods and possibly payment for unauthorized purchases. |
| Invoice processing function should be segregated from accounts payable function | If one individual is responsible for invoice processing and the accounts payable functions, purchase transactions can be processed at the wrong price or terms, or a cash disbursement can be processed for goods or services not received. This can result in overpayment for goods and services or the theft of cash. |
| Disbursement function should be segregated from accounts payable function | If one individual is responsible for the disbursement function and also has access to the accounts payable records, unauthorized checks supported by fictitious documents can be issued, and unauthorized transactions can be recorded. This can result in theft of the entity's cash. |
| Accounts payable function should be segregated from general ledger function | If one individual is responsible for the accounts payable records and also for the general ledge, that individual can conceal any defalcation that would normally be detected by reconciling subsidiary records with the general ledger control account. |

C. Table 11-4 in the textbook shows the proper segregation of duties for purchasing and accounts payable functions across the various departments that process purchase transactions.

**[LO7] Identify and evaluate inherent risks relevant to the purchasing process and related accounts.**

A. In examining the purchasing process and its related accounts, the auditor should consider the relevant inherent risk factors that may impact the transactions processed and the financial statement accounts. Two specific inherent risk factors that may affect the purchasing process are:

    1. **Industry-related factors.** When auditing the purchasing process, the auditor must consider two important industry-related factors in assessing inherent risk: whether the supply of raw materials is adequate and how volatile raw material prices are. If the entity deals with many vendors and prices tend to be relatively stable, there is less risk that the entity's operations will be affected by raw material shortages or that production costs will be difficult to control.

    2. **Misstatements detected in prior audits.** Auditing research has shown that the purchasing process and its related accounts are likely to contain materials misstatements. The auditor's previous experience with the entity's purchasing process should be reviewed as a starting point for determining the inherent risk.

**[LO8] Assess control risk for a purchasing process.**

A. The concepts involved in control risk assessment were discussed in Chapter 6. This approach is applied to the purchasing process. For discussion purposes, it is assumed that the auditor has decided to follow a reliance strategy. Three major steps in setting control risk for the purchasing process must be followed when a reliance strategy is being followed (Figure 11-2):

    1. Understand and document the purchasing process based on a reliance approach.
    2. Plan and perform tests of controls on purchase transactions.
    3. Set and document the control risk for the purchasing process.

**Step 1**. In order to assess the control risk for the purchasing process, the auditor must understand the five components of an entity's internal control including:

    1. Control environment.
    2. The entity's risk assessment process.
    3. Control procedures.
    4. Information systems and communication.
    5. Monitoring of controls.

**Step 2**. To evaluate the entity's risk assessment process, the auditor systematically examines the client's purchasing process to identify relevant controls that help to prevent, or detect and correct, material misstatements. Because these controls are relied upon in order to set control risk below the maximum, the auditor conducts tests of controls to ensure that the controls in the purchasing process operate effectively. For example, the auditor may examine a sample of purchase transactions to determine if the acquisition of the goods or services is consistent with the entity's authorization policy.

**Step 3**. After the controls are tested, the auditor sets the level of control risk. When tests of controls results support the planned level of control risk, the auditor conducts the planned level of substantive procedures for the related account balances. If the results of the tests of controls do not support the planned level of control risk, the auditor should set control risk at a level higher than planned. Additional substantive procedures in the accounts affected by the purchasing process must then be conducted. The auditor should document both the achieved level of control risk and the basis for his or her conclusion. The level of control risk for the purchasing process can be set using either quantitative amounts or qualitative terms (such as low, medium and high). The documentation of the achieved level of control risk for the purchasing process would include documentation of the accounting system such as the flowchart included in Figure 11-1, the results of the tests of controls, and a memorandum indicating the overall conclusions about control risk.

**[LO9] Identify key internal controls and develop relevant tests of controls for purchasing, cash disbursements, and purchase return transactions.**

A. The assertions for the purchasing process about transactions and events for the period under audit include (Table 11-5):

1. **Occurrence**. All purchase and cash disbursement transactions and events that have been recorded have occurred and pertain to the entity.

2. **Completeness**. All purchase and cash disbursement transactions and events that should have been recorded have been recorded.

3. **Authorization.** All purchase and cash disbursement transactions and events are properly authorized.

4. **Accuracy**. Amounts and other data relating to recorded purchase and cash disbursement transactions and events have been recorded appropriately.

5. **Cutoff**. Purchase and cash disbursement transactions and events have been recorded in the correct accounting period.

6. **Classification**. Purchase and cash disbursement transactions and events have been recorded in the proper accounts.

The auditor's decision process on planning and performing tests of controls involves considering the assertions and the possible misstatements that can occur if internal control does not operate effectively. The auditor evaluates the client's accounting system to determine the controls that will prevent or detect such misstatements. When controls are present and the auditor decides to rely on them, they must be tested to evaluate their effectiveness.

Note that the choice of which type of test of controls is appropriate for a particular assertion will be a function of the following:

1. The volume of transactions or data.

2. The nature and complexity of the systems by which the entity processes and controls information.

3. The nature of the available evidential matter, including audit evidence that is available only in electronic form.

B. **Purchase transactions**. See Table 11-6 in the textbook for a summary of the assertions, possible misstatements, internal control procedures, and tests of controls for purchase transactions.

C. **Cash disbursement transactions**. See Table 11-7 in the textbook for a summary of the assertions, possible misstatements, internal control procedures and tests of control for cash disbursement transactions.

D. **Purchase returns and allowances transactions**. For most entities, purchase returns and allowances transactions are few and do not represent a material amount in the financial statements. As a result, this text does not cover them in as much detail as revenue or cash receipts transactions. However, because of the possibility of manipulation the auditor should, at a minimum, inquire about how the client controls purchase returns transactions. When goods are returned to a vendor, the client usually prepares a document (sometimes called a debit memo) that reduces the amount of the vendor's accounts payable. This document is processed through the purchasing process in a manner similar to the processing of a vendor invoice. The auditor normally does not test controls of these transactions, but substantive analytical procedures are usually performed to test the reasonableness of purchase returns. For example, comparison of purchase returns as a percentage of revenue to prior years' and industry data may disclose any material misstatement in this account.

**[LO10] Relate the assessment of control risk to substantive testing.**

A. The decision process followed by the auditor is similar to that discussed in Chapter 10 for the revenue process. If the results of the tests of controls support the achieved level of control risk, the auditor conducts substantive procedures at the planned level. If the results indicate that the control risk can be reduced further, the auditor can increase the detection risk, which will reduce the nature, extent and timing of substantive procedures needed. However, if the results of the tests of controls do not support the planned level of control risk, the detection risk to has be set lower and the substantive procedures will be increased. The main accounts affected by the auditor's achieved control risk for the purchasing process include accounts payable, accrued expenses and most of the expense accounts in the income statement. Additionally, the tests of controls over purchase transactions affect the assessment of detection risk for other business processes. For example, purchase transactions for the acquisition of inventory and property, plant and equipment are subject to the controls included in the purchasing process. If those controls are reliable, the auditor may be able to increase the detection risk for the affected financial statement accounts and therefore reduce the number of substantive procedures needed.

B. The assessments of inherent risk and control risk for the purchasing process are used to determine the level of detection risk for conducting substantive procedures of accounts payable and accrued expenses. Accounts payable generally represent normal recurring trade obligations. Accrued expenses represent expenses that have been incurred during the period but that have not been billed or paid for as of the end of the period; these include accruals for taxes, interest, royalties, and professional fees.

C. The auditor uses substantive procedures to detect material misstatements in accounts payable and accrued expenses. As discussed in Chapter 5, there are two categories of substantive procedures: (1) substantive analytical procedures and (2) tests of details of classes of transactions, account balances and disclosures.

   1. **Substantive analytical procedures** are used to examine plausible relationships among accounts payable and accrued expenses.

   2. **Tests of details** focus on transactions, account balances or disclosures.

**Tests of details of transactions** (also called substantive tests of transactions) in the purchasing process focus mainly on purchases and cash disbursements transactions.

**Tests of details of account balances** concentrate on the detailed amounts or estimates that make up the ending balance for accounts payable and accrued expenses.

**Tests of details of disclosures** are concerned with the presentation and disclosures related to accounts payable and accrued expenses.

D. Assertions about account balances at the period end for accounts payable and accrued expenses include (Table 11-8):

1. **Existence**. Accounts payable and accrued expenses are valid liabilities.

2. **Rights and obligations**. Accounts payable and accrued expenses are the obligations of the entity.

3. **Completeness**. All accounts payable and accrued expenses have been recorded.

4. **Valuation and allocation**. Accounts payable and accrued expenses are included in the financial statements at appropriate amounts and any resulting valuation or allocation adjustments are appropriately recorded.

Assertions about presentation and disclosure for accounts payable and accrued expenses include (Table 11-8):

1. **Occurrence and rights and obligations**. All disclosed events, transactions, and other matters relating to accounts payable and accrued expenses have occurred and pertain to the entity.

2. **Completeness**. All disclosures relating to accounts payable and accrued expenses that should have been included in the financial statements have been included.

3. **Classification and understandability**. Financial information relating to accounts payable and accrued expenses is appropriately presented and described, and disclosures are clearly expressed.

4. **Accuracy and valuation**. Financial and other information relating to accounts payable and accrued expenses are disclosed fairly and at appropriate amounts.

Note that the auditor may test assertions related to transactions (substantive tests of transactions) in conjunction with testing the account balance. If the tests of controls indicate that the controls are not operating effectively, the auditor may need to test transactions at the date the account balance is tested.

**[LO11] Identify substantive analytical procedures used to audit accounts payable and accrued expenses.**

A. **Analytical procedures** are useful audit tests for examining the reasonableness of accounts payable and accrued expenses. Analytical procedures can effectively identify accounts payable and accrual accounts that are misstated as well as provide evidence regarding the fairness of the recorded amounts. Table 11-9 lists analytical procedures that are useful in auditing accounts payable and accrued expenses.

**[LO12] Identify tests of details of transactions used to audit accounts payable and accrued expenses.**

A. **Substantive tests of transactions**. The intended purpose of tests of details of transactions is to detect monetary misstatements in the individual transactions processed through the purchasing application. As previously mentioned, tests of details of transactions are often conducted in conjunction with tests of controls. Table 11-10 presents the assertions for classes of transactions (substantive tests of transactions) and examples of the procedures used to test the assertions for the tests of details of transactions. They include: (1) occurrence, (2) completeness, (3) authorization, (4) accuracy, (5) cutoff and (6) classification.

**[LO13] Identify tests of details of account balances and disclosures used to audit accounts payable and accrued expenses.**

A. **Tests of details of account balances and tests of details of disclosures**. Table 11-10 presents the assertions for account balances and examples of the procedures used to test the assertions for account balances (tests of details of account balances). Assertions for account balances for accounts payable and accrued expenses include: (1) existence, (2) rights and obligations, (3) completeness, and (4) valuation and allocation. Table 11-10 presents the assertions for presentation and disclosure and examples of the procedures used to test the assertions for presentation and disclosure. Assertions for presentation and disclosure (tests of details of disclosures) include: (1) occurrence, (2) rights and obligations, (3) completeness, (4) classification and understandability and (5) accuracy and valuation.

**[LO14] Describe how confirmations are used to obtain evidence about accounts payable.**

A. Accounts payable confirmations are used less frequently by auditors than accounts receivable confirmations because the auditor can test accounts payable by examining vendor invoices and monthly vendor statements. These documents originate from sources external to the client, so this evidence is viewed as reliable. However, if the client has weak internal control, vendor statements may not be available to examine. In such a case, confirmations may be used as a main source of evidence.

B. While accounts payable confirmations provide evidence on a number of assertions, they primarily test the completeness assertion. If the client has strong control procedures for ensuring that liabilities are recorded, the auditor focuses on confirmation of large-dollar accounts. However, if the auditor has concerns about liabilities not being recorded, regular vendors with small or zero balances and a sample of other accounts may be confirmed in addition to large-dollar accounts. Small and zero balance accounts are confirmed because the client may owe such vendors for purchases but the amounts may not be recorded in the client's accounting records.

C. When confirming accounts payable, auditors generally use a form of positive confirmation referred to as a blank or zero-balance confirmation. This type of positive confirmation does not state the balance owed. Instead, the confirmation requests that the recipient fill in the amount or furnish other information. Exhibit 11-5 presents an example of an accounts payable confirmation request. Note that the confirmation requests the balance owed and a detailed statement of the account. The confirmation also requests additional information on notes payable and consigned inventory.

D.  Generally, accounts payable confirmations are mailed at year-end rather than at an interim date because of the auditor's concerns about unrecorded liabilities. The selection and mailing of accounts payable confirmations should be controlled using the procedures outlined in Chapter 10. When accounts payable confirmations are received, the amounts provided by the vendors must be reconciled with the client's records. Differences are often due to the same types of timing differences noted in Chapter 10 for accounts receivable confirmations. The two major timing differences are due to inventory in transit to the client and cash paid by the client but not yet received by the vendor: any inconsistencies not due to timing differences normally result in adjustments to the client's records.

### [LO15] Evaluate the audit findings and reach a final conclusion on accounts payable and accrued expenses.

A.  When the auditor has completed the planned substantive procedures, all identified misstatements should be aggregated, including known misstatements detected by the auditor and projected misstatements plus an allowance for sampling risk. The likely misstatement is then compared to tolerable misstatement. If the likely misstatement is less than the tolerable misstatement, the auditor has evidence that the account is fairly presented. Conversely, if the likely misstatement exceeds the tolerable misstatement, the auditor should conclude that the account is not fairly presented. In this case, the auditor would have two choices: adjust the accounts to reduce the misstatement to an amount less than the tolerable misstatement or qualify the audit report.

B.  The auditor should again analyze the misstatements discovered through the application of substantive procedures because these misstatements may provide additional evidence as to the control risk. For example, if most misstatements identified indicate that accounts payable are not properly valued, the auditor may reassess the control procedures used by the client for ensuring proper valuation. If the auditor concludes that the audit risk is unacceptably high, additional audit procedures should be performed, or the auditor must be satisfied that the client has adjusted the related financial statement accounts to an acceptable level. If the client does not adjust the accounts, the auditor should qualify the audit report.

# CHAPTER 11: SELF-ASSESSMENT

## Part I: True or False Questions

[LO1] _____ 1. Expenses should be matched directly with specific transactions and are recognized upon recognition of revenue.

[LO4] _____ 2. A purchase transaction usually begins with the preparation of a purchase order.

[LO4] _____ 3. A receiving report is used to document the ordering of goods.

[LO4] _____ 4. The purchase journal is referred to as a check register.

[LO5] _____ 5. The principal business objectives of the purchasing process are acquiring goods and services and paying for those goods and services.

[LO5] _____ 6. The accounts payable department is responsible for ensuring that all vendor invoices, cash disbursements and adjustments are recorded in the accounts payable records.

[LO8] _____ 7. After the controls are tested, the auditor sets the level of control risk.

[LO9] _____ 8. Because of the low volume of purchase return transactions, the auditor normally does not test the controls associated with these transactions.

[LO11] _____ 9. Analytical procedures can be used to examine the reasonableness of accounts payable and accrued expenses.

[LO14] _____ 10. Account payable confirmations are used less frequently by auditors than accounts receivable confirmations.

## Part II: Multiple Choice Questions

[LO9] 1. When comparing the dates on receiving reports with the dates on the relevant vouchers, the auditor is testing the _____ assertion:
   a. Authorization.
   b. Occurrence.
   c. Cutoff.
   d. None of the above.

[LO9] 2. When examining paid vouchers and supporting documents for indication of cancellation, the auditor is testing the _____ assertion:
   a. Occurrence.
   b. Existence.
   c. Rights and obligations.
   d. None of the above.

[LO9] 3. When reviewing the client's dollar limits authorization for acquisitions, the auditor is testing the _____ assertion:
   a. Cutoff.
   b. Occurrence.

c. Authorization.
d. None of the above.

[LO9]  4. When reviewing client's procedures for reconciling vendor statements, the auditor is testing the _____ assertion:
a. Occurrence.
b. Existence.
c. Cutoff.
d. Both a and b.

[LO9]  5. When reviewing daily cash reconciliations, the auditor is testing the _____ assertion:
a. Cutoff.
b. Completeness.
c. Rights and obligations.
d. None of the above.

[LO9]  6. When reviewing cash disbursements journal for reasonableness of account distribution, the auditor is testing the _____ assertion:
a. Completeness.
b. Accuracy and valuation.
c. Classification.
d. Both a and c.

[LO10]  7. Assertions about classes of transactions and events for the period under audit include:
a. Existence, completeness, and accuracy.
b. Existence, completeness, and classification.
c. Occurrence, completeness, and cutoff.
d. Occurrence, completeness, and valuation and allocation.

[LO10]  8. Assertions about account balances at the period end include:
a. Existence, completeness, and accuracy.
b. Existence, completeness, and classification.
c. Existence, rights and obligations, and completeness.
d. Existence, rights and obligations, and classification.

[LO12]  9. The following test(s) of details of transactions can be used as a dual-purpose test in conjunction with tests of controls:
a. Test a sample of purchase requisitions for proper authorization.
b. Obtain selected vendors' statements and reconcile to vendor accounts.
c. Obtain listing of accounts payable and compare total to general ledger.
d. Review results of confirmations of selected accounts payable.

[LO12]  10. The cutoff assertion can be tested by:
a. Obtaining a listing of accounts payable and compare total to general ledger.
b. Comparing voucher date with date transaction recorded in purchases journal.
c. Testing transactions around year-end to determine if recorded in the proper period.
d. Both b and c.

## Part III: Short Essay Questions

[LO5] Identify the primary functions in the purchases cycle and describe each function.

[LO6] Discuss the key segregation of duties in the purchases process and possible errors or fraud.

[LO10] Identify the types of substantive procedures used by the auditor to test accounts payable and accrued expenses. Provide an example of how the auditor may use each substantive procedure. Identify if any of the substantive procedures can be used as a test of controls or a dual-purpose test.

# Part IV: Crossword Puzzle – Chapter 11 [LO ALL]

## Across

1    This assertion means that amounts and other data relating to recorded transactions and events have been recorded appropriately.
3    A two-letter abbreviation used for short-term liabilities resulting from trade obligations.
7    This document is used to record the receipt of goods (two words).
8    A two-letter abbreviation for the journal used to record the outflow of cash.
9    An abbreviation for auditing technology used to test client data.
12   This document is the bill from a supplier (two words).

## Down

2    _____ transactions represent expenses which have been incurred during the period, but that have not been paid.
4    The _____ cycle includes purchases, cash disbursements, and purchase returns and allowances.
5    A ____ balance confirmation requests that the recipient fill in the amount or furnish the information requested.
6    The _____ principle requires that expenses be accrued as incurred.
10   A negotiable document that is signed by an authorized individual to pay for goods or services.
11   A two-letter abbreviation used for a document that includes a description, quality, and quantity of, and other information on goods/services purchased.

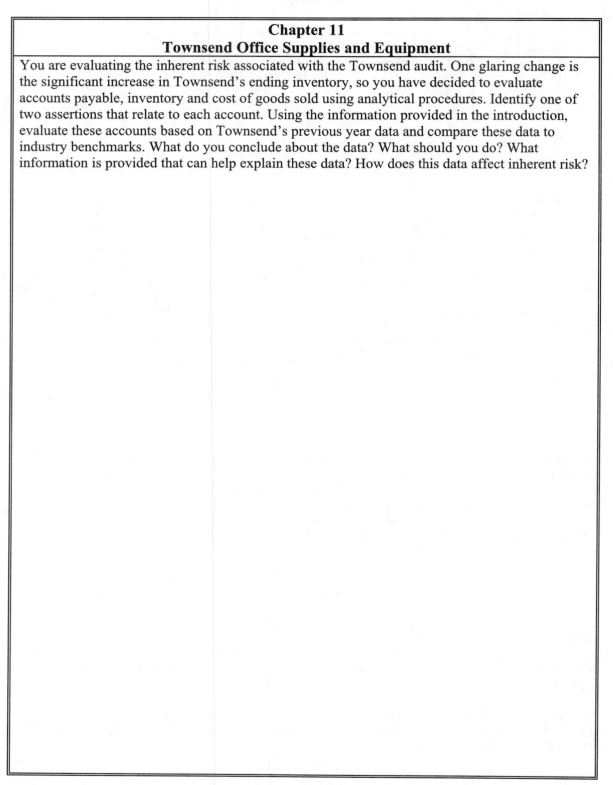

**Chapter 11**
**Townsend Office Supplies and Equipment**

You are evaluating the inherent risk associated with the Townsend audit. One glaring change is the significant increase in Townsend's ending inventory, so you have decided to evaluate accounts payable, inventory and cost of goods sold using analytical procedures. Identify one of two assertions that relate to each account. Using the information provided in the introduction, evaluate these accounts based on Townsend's previous year data and compare these data to industry benchmarks. What do you conclude about the data? What should you do? What information is provided that can help explain these data? How does this data affect inherent risk?

# CHAPTER 11: SELF-ASSESSMENT SOLUTIONS

## Part I: True or False Questions

[LO1] **True** 1. Expenses should be matched directly with specific transactions and are recognized upon recognition of revenue.

[LO4] **False** 2. A purchase transaction usually begins with the preparation of a purchase order.

[LO4] **False** 3. A receiving report is used to document the ordering of goods.

[LO4] **False** 4. The purchase journal is referred to as a check register.

[LO5] **True** 5. The principal business objectives of the purchasing process are acquiring goods and services and paying for those goods and services.

[LO5] **True** 6. The accounts payable department is responsible for ensuring that all vendor invoices, cash disbursements and adjustments are recorded in the accounts payable records.

[LO8] **True** 7. After the controls are tested, the auditor sets the level of control risk.

[LO9] **True** 8. Because of the low volume of purchase return transactions, the auditor normally does not test the controls associated with these transactions.

[LO11] **True** 9. Analytical procedures can be used to examine the reasonableness of accounts payable and accrued expenses.

[LO14] **True** 10. Account payable confirmations are used less frequently by auditors than accounts receivable confirmations.

## Part II: Multiple Choice Questions

[LO9] 1. When comparing the dates on receiving reports with the dates on the relevant vouchers, the auditor is testing the _____ assertion:
   a. Authorization.
   b. Occurrence.
   **c. Cutoff.**
   d. None of the above.

[LO9] 2. When examining paid vouchers and supporting documents for indication of cancellation, the auditor is testing the _____ assertion:
   **a. Occurrence.**
   b. Existence.
   c. Rights and obligations.
   d. None of the above.

[LO9] 3. When reviewing the client's dollar limits authorization for acquisitions, the auditor is testing the _____ assertion:
   a. Cutoff.
   b. Occurrence.

    c. **Authorization.**
    d. None of the above.

[LO9] 4. When reviewing client's procedures for reconciling vendor statements, the auditor is testing the _____ assertion:
    a. **Occurrence.**
    b. Existence.
    c. Cutoff.
    d. Both a and b.

[LO9] 5. When reviewing daily cash reconciliations, the auditor is testing the _____ assertion:
    a. **Cutoff.**
    b. Completeness.
    c. Rights and obligations.
    d. None of the above.

[LO9] 6. When reviewing cash disbursements journal for reasonableness of account distribution, the auditor is testing the _____ assertion:
    a. Completeness.
    b. Accuracy and valuation.
    c. **Classification.**
    d. Both a and c.

[LO10] 7. Assertions about classes of transactions and events for the period under audit include:
    a. Existence, completeness, and accuracy.
    b. Existence, completeness, and classification.
    c. **Occurrence, completeness, and cutoff.**
    d. Occurrence, completeness, and valuation and allocation.

[LO10] 8. Assertions about account balances at the period end include:
    a. Existence, completeness, and accuracy.
    b. Existence, completeness, and classification.
    c. **Existence, rights and obligations, and completeness.**
    d. Existence, rights and obligations, and classification.

[LO12] 9. The following test(s) of details of transactions can be used as a dual-purpose test in conjunction with tests of controls:
    a. **Test a sample of purchase requisitions for proper authorization.**
    b. Obtain selected vendors' statements and reconcile to vendor accounts.
    c. Obtain listing of accounts payable and compare total to general ledger.
    d. Review results of confirmations of selected accounts payable.

[LO12]10. The cutoff assertion can be tested by:
    a. Obtaining a listing of accounts payable and compare total to general ledger.
    b. Comparing voucher date with date transaction recorded in purchases journal.
    c. Testing transactions around year-end to determine if recorded in the proper period.
    d. **Both b and c.**

## Part III: Short Essay Questions

[LO5] Identify the primary functions in the purchases cycle and describe each function.

**Functions in the purchasing process include:**

**Requisitioning: Initiation and approval of request for goods and services by authorized individuals consistent with management criteria.**

**Purchasing: Approval of purchase orders and proper execution as to price, quantity, quality and vendor.**

**Receiving: Receipt of properly authorized goods or services.**

**Invoice Processing: Processing of vendor invoices for goods and services received; also, processing of adjustments for allowances, discounts and returns.**

**Disbursements: Processing of payment to vendors.**

**Accounts Payable: Recording of all vendor invoices, cash disbursements, and adjustments in individual vendor accounts.**

**General Ledger: Proper accumulation, classification and summarization of purchases, cash disbursements and payables in the general ledger.**

---

[LO6] Discuss the key segregation of duties in the purchases process and possible errors or fraud.

**Proper segregation of duties is one of the most important control procedures in any accounting system. Duties should be assigned so that no one individual can control all phases of processing a transaction in a way that permits errors or fraud to go undetected. Because of the potential for theft and fraud in the purchasing process, individuals responsible for requisitioning, purchasing and receiving should be segregated from the invoice-processing, accounts payable and general ledger functions. Some of the key segregation of duties for the purchasing process, as well as examples of possible errors or fraud that can result from conflicts in duties include:**

**Purchasing function should be segregated from requisition and receiving functions**
**If one individual is responsible for the requisition, purchasing and receiving functions, fictitious or unauthorized purchases can be made. This can result in the theft of goods and possibly payment for unauthorized purchases.**

**Invoice processing function should be segregated from accounts payable function**
**If one individual is responsible for invoice processing and the accounts payable functions, purchase transactions can be processed at the wrong price or terms, or a cash disbursement can be processed for goods or services not received. This can result in overpayment for goods and services or the theft of cash.**

**Disbursement function should be segregated from accounts payable function**
**If one individual is responsible for the disbursement function and also has access to the accounts payable records, unauthorized checks supported by fictitious documents can be issued, and unauthorized transactions can be recorded. This can result in theft of the entity's cash.**

**Accounts payable function should be segregated from general ledger function**
**If one individual is responsible for the accounts payable records and also for the general ledger, that individual can conceal any defalcation that would normally be detected by reconciling subsidiary records with the general ledger control account.**

[LO10] Identify the types of substantive procedures used by the auditor to test accounts payable and accrued expenses. Provide an example of how the auditor may use each substantive procedure. Identify if any of the substantive procedures can be used as a test of controls or a dual-purpose test.

**The auditor uses substantive procedures to detect material misstatements in accounts payable and related accounts. There are two categories of substantive procedures: (1) substantive analytical procedures and (2) tests of details of classes of transactions, account balances and disclosures.**

1. **Substantive analytical procedures are used to examine plausible relationships among accounts payable and related accounts.**
   **Example: The auditor might compare payables turnover and days outstanding in accounts payable to previous years' and industry data or purchase returns or amounts owed to individual vendors in the current year's accounts payable listing to amounts owed in prior years.**

2. **Tests of details focus on transactions, account balances or disclosures.**

   **In the purchasing cycle, tests of details of transactions (also called substantive tests of transactions) focus mainly on the purchases and cash disbursement transactions. Examples: To test the occurrence assertion about a purchase, the auditor can test a sample of vouchers for the presence of an authorized purchase order and receiving report. To test the completeness assertion, the auditor can trace a sample of vouchers to the purchases journal.**

   **Tests of details of account balances concentrate on the detailed amounts or estimates that make up the ending balance for accounts payable and accrued expenses. Example: To test the existence assertion about purchases, the auditor can vouch selected amounts from the accounts payable listing and schedules for accruals to voucher packets or other supporting documentation.**

   **Tests of details of disclosures are concerned with the presentation and disclosures related to accounts payable and accrued expenses. Example: To test the completeness assertions about accounts payable and accrued expenses, the auditor can complete a financial reporting checklist to ensure that all financial statement disclosures related to accounts payable and accrued expenses have been appropriately disclosed.**

**Tests of details of transactions (substantive tests of transactions) can be used as a test of controls or a dual-purpose test. However, if the tests of controls indicate that the controls are not operating effectively, the auditor may need to test transactions at the date the account balance is tested.**

## Part IV: Crossword Puzzle – Chapter 11 Solution [LO ALL]

```
                  ¹A  C  C  U  R  ²A  C  Y
                                  C
      ³A  ⁴P                      C        ⁵Z        ⁶M
          U                      R        E        A
          R                      U        R        A
      ⁷R  E  C  E  I  V  I  N  G  R  E  P  O  R  T
          H                      D                 ⁸C  D
      ⁹C  A  A  T  S                   ¹⁰C        H
          S                            C          I
          I           ¹¹P              H          N
      ¹²V  E  N  D  O  R  I  N  V  O  I  C  E     G
          G                            K
```

**Across**

1  This assertion means that amounts and other data relating to recorded transactions and events have been recorded appropriately.
3  A two-letter abbreviation used for short-term liabilities resulting from trade obligations.
7  This document is used to record the receipt of goods (two words).
8  A two-letter abbreviation for the journal used to record the outflow of cash.
9  An abbreviation for auditing technology used to test client data.
12  This document is the bill from a supplier (two words).

**Down**

2  _____ transactions represent expenses which have been incurred during the period, but that have not been paid.
4  The _____ cycle includes purchases, cash disbursements, and purchase returns and allowances.
5  A ____ balance confirmation requests that the recipient fill in the amount or furnish the information requested.
6  The _____ principle requires that expenses be accrued as incurred.
10  A negotiable document that is signed by an authorized individual to pay for goods or services.
11  A two-letter abbreviation used for a document that includes a description, quality, and quantity of, and other information on goods/services purchased.

## Part V: Townsend Office Supplies and Equipment [LO ALL]

---

### Chapter 11
### Townsend Office Supplies and Equipment

You are evaluating the inherent risk associated with the Townsend audit. One glaring change is the significant increase in Townsend's ending inventory, so you have decided to evaluate accounts payable, inventory and cost of goods sold using analytical procedures. Identify one of two assertions that relate to each account. Using the information provided in the introduction, evaluate these accounts based on Townsend's previous year data and compare these data to industry benchmarks. What do you conclude about the data? What should you do? What information is provided that can help explain these data? How does this data affect inherent risk?

**Assertions that may apply to these accounts include: Accounts payable – completeness and cutoff; Inventory – existence and valuation and allocation; and Cost of goods sold – completeness and valuation and allocation.**

| | Industry | 2007 | 2006 |
|---|---|---|---|
| COGS | 45% | 48% | 45% |
| Gross Profit | 55% | 2% | 5% |
| Inventory turnover days [$2,511/($672 +124/2)] | 45 | 8 | 2 |
| Inventory to total assets | 2% | 6% | % |

**Accounts payable has risen from $279 to $483, a 71 percent increase (483-282/282). Inventory has risen from $124 to $672, a 442 percent increase. Townsend's costs of goods sold have risen by 3 percent from 2006 and 2007, thereby driving gross profit down by the same amount. The inventory turnover in days has risen from 42 days in 2006 to 58 days in 2007, which is significantly higher than the industry benchmark of 45 days. Townsend's inventory to total assets has increased from 3 percent in 2006 to 16 percent in 2007, but both years are below the industry average of 22 percent. These data point to a higher inherent risk than would otherwise be assessed if Townsend's statistics were stable and comparable to industry averages. You are considering an initial assessment of inherent risk at 0.90, but you want to understand these data better before making a final conclusion about inherent risk. You decide to make inquires to management.**

**Management provided you the following information and documentation:**

**Increase in inventory and accounts payable. Management has provided you with a copy of a new three-year government contract that starts on February 1, 2008. Annual sales from this contract are estimated at $1.25 million. The $420 increase in inventory and resulting accounts payable is the result of this contract. Management elected to purchase the inventory needed for the first order on February 5 due to significant cost savings from the vendor. Management provided a copy of the customer's purchase order for this order, so you were able to evaluate and confirm selling price, costs and profit margin.**

**Increase in cost of goods sold and decrease in gross profit. Cost of goods sold increased. Special pricing was provided to three new customers for initial sales at prices less than the normal markup. In addition, Townsend's management and legal counsel is in the final stages of an agreement for a brand name trademark partnership with four of Townsend's primary vendors. The brand name trademark will cover 50 of Townsend's most popular products, which will allow the company to significantly reduce the selling price of these products. The trademark product project will be completed by June 2008 in time to update the 2009 product catalog pricing.**

**Based on this information and documentation provided by management, you recomputed the data (using the average inventory less the special purchase of $420 made on December 15 to meet the new contract sales).**

| | Industry | 2007 | 2006 |
|---|---|---|---|
| Inventory turnover days [$2,511/($252 + 124)/2] | 45 | 27 | 42 |

**Based in the on the information and documentation provided by management, you have decided to reduce inherent risk from 0.90 to 0.60.**

# Auditing the Human Resource Management Process

## KEY THOUGHT

Expenses are defined as "outflows or other using up of assets or incurrences of liabilities (or a combination of both) from delivering or producing goods, rendering services, or carrying out other activities that constitute the entity's ongoing major or central operations" [FASB Statement of Financial Account Concepts No. 5, paragraph 85]. Liabilities are defined as "probable future sacrifices of economic benefits arising from present obligations of a particular entity to transfer assets or provide services to other entities in the future as a result of past transactions or events [FASB Statement of Financial Accounting Concepts No. 5, paragraph 35].

## CHAPTER SUMMARY

**[LO1] Develop an understanding of the human resource management process.**

    A. This chapter introduces the basic concepts related to the human resource management process. The process starts with the establishment of sound policies for hiring, training, evaluating, counseling, promoting, compensating and taking remedial actions for employees. Figure 12-1 presents a flowchart of EarthWear's payroll system that serves as a framework for discussing control procedures and tests of controls.

**[LO2] Identify the types of transactions in the human resource management process and the financial statement accounts affected.**

    A. Two main types of transactions are processed through the human resource management cycle:

        1. Payments to employees for services rendered.

        2. Accrual and payment of payroll-related liabilities arising from employees' services, including liabilities for Social Security and unemployment taxes.

B.  The types of transactions and accounts affected in the human resource management process include:

---

### The Human Resource Management Process

| Type of Transaction | Account Affected |
|---|---|
| Payroll transactions | Cash<br>Inventory<br>Direct and indirect labor expense accounts<br>Various payroll-related liability and expense accounts |
| Accrued payroll liability transactions | Cash<br>Various accruals (such as payroll taxes and pension costs) |

---

**[LO3] Identify and describe the types of documents and records used in the payroll application.**

A.  Table 12-1 lists the important documents and records that are normally involved in the payroll application. The textbook provides a brief discussion on each of the more important documents and records that are normally contained in the human resource management cycle. They include (Table 12-1):

1.  Personnel records, including wage-rate or salary authorizations.
2.  W-4 and other deduction authorization forms.
3.  Time card.
4.  Payroll check/direct deposit records.
5.  Payroll register.
6.  Payroll master file.
7.  Payroll master file changes report.
8.  Periodic payroll reports.
9.  Various tax reports and forms.

The reader should keep in mind that in advanced IT systems some of these documents and records may exist for only a short period of time or may be maintained only in machine-readable form.

**[LO4] Understand the functions in the human resource management process.**

A.  The principal objectives of the human resource management process are to:

1.  Record production and other types of payroll costs in the accounts.

2.  Ensure that payroll costs are for legitimate entity activities.

3.  Accrue liabilities for salaries and wages, payroll taxes, and various employee benefit programs.

B.  The functions that normally take place in a typical payroll application include (Table 12-2):

### Functions in the Payroll Application

| Function | Description of Function |
|---|---|
| Personnel | Authorization of hiring, firing, wage-rate and salary adjustments, salaries, and payroll deductions. |
| Supervision | Review and approval of employees' attendance and time information; monitoring of employee scheduling, productivity, and payroll cost variances. |
| Timekeeping | Processing of employees' attendance and time information and coding of account distribution. |
| Payroll processing | Computation of gross pay, deduction, and net pay; recording and summarization of payments and verification of account distribution. |
| Disbursement | Payment of employees' compensation and benefits. |
| General ledger | Proper accumulation, classification, and summarization of payroll in the general ledger. |

**[LO5] Know the appropriate segregation of duties for the human resource management process.**

A.  As discussed in prior chapters, proper segregation of duties is one of the most important control procedures in any accounting system. Duties should be assigned so that no one individual can control all phases of processing a transaction in a way that permits errors or fraud to go undetected. Individuals responsible for supervision and timekeeping should be segregated from the personnel, payroll-processing, and general ledger functions. Table 12-3 contains some of the key segregation of duties for the human resource management process and examples of possible errors or fraud that can result from conflicts in duties.

### Key Segregation of Duties in the Human Resource Management Process and Possible Errors or Fraud

| Segregation of Duties | Possible Errors/Fraud Resulting from Conflicts of Duties |
|---|---|
| Supervision function should be segregated from personnel records and payroll-processing functions | If one individual is responsible for the supervision, personnel records, and payroll-processing functions, fictitious employees can appear on the payroll records or unauthorized payments can be made. This can result in unauthorized payments to existing employees or payments to fictitious employees. |
| Disbursement function should be segregated from personnel records, supervision and payroll-processing functions | If one individual is responsible for the disbursement function and also has the authority to hire and fire employees, approve time reports, or prepare payroll checks, unauthorized payroll checks can be issued. |
| Payroll-processing function should be segregated from general ledger function | If one individual is responsible for processing payroll transactions and also for the general ledger, that individual can conceal any defalcation that would normally be detected by independent review of accounting entries made to the general ledger. |

B.  Table 12-4 in the textbook shows the proper segregation of duties for individual payroll functions across the various departments that process payroll transactions.

**[LO6] Identify and evaluate inherent risks relevant to the human resource management process.**

A.  Generally, few inherent risk factors directly affect the human resource management process and its related accounts for non-officers. Some factors that the auditor might consider are the effect of economic conditions on payroll costs, the supply of skilled workers and the frequency of employee turnover. Additionally, the presence of labor contracts and legislation such as the Occupational Safety and Health Act may also affect the auditor's assessment of inherent risk. Because the payroll system and its related accounts generally contain few inherent risks, the auditor is normally able to set the inherent risk as low.

B.  Inherent risk associated with officer compensation is frequently not set at low because, as illustrated in Exhibit 12-1 (Tyco) officers may have motive and opportunity to take advantage of their high-ranking offices in the form of excessive compensation.

**[LO7] Assess control risk for a human resource management process.**

A.  The level of understanding of the five internal control components should be similar to that obtained for other processes. The auditor's understanding of the human resources management process is normally gained by conducting a walkthrough of the system to gather evidence about the various functions that are involved in processing the transactions through the system.

B.  The concepts involved in control risk assessment were discussed in Chapter 6. This approach is applied to the human resource management process. For discussion purposes, it is assumed that the auditor has decided to follow a reliance strategy. Three major steps in setting control risk for the human resource management process must be followed when a reliance strategy is being followed (Figure 12-2):

   1.  Understand and document the human resource management process based on a reliance approach.

   2.  Plan and perform tests of controls on payroll transactions.

   3.  Set and document the control risk for the human resource management process.

   **Step 1**. In order to assess the control risk for the human resource management process, the auditor must understand the five components of an entity's internal control including:

   1.  Control environment.
   2.  The entity's risk assessment process.
   3.  Control procedures.
   4.  Information systems and communication.
   5.  Monitoring of controls.

   Two factors are of particular importance: First, the entity's organizational structure, its personnel practices, and its methods of assigning authority and responsibility must be examined. Second, the entity should have sound policies for hiring, training, promoting and compensating employees. These policies should include specific authority and responsibility for hiring and firing employees, for setting wage rates and making salary changes, and for establishing benefits.

   Note that the auditor's understanding of internal control for the payroll system should be documented in the working papers using flowcharts, internal control questionnaires, and memoranda.

**Step 2.** When a reliance strategy is followed, the auditor must identify the control procedures that ensure that material misstatements are either prevented or detected and corrected. For example, the client may have formal procedures for classifying payroll costs in appropriate accounts. The auditor may decide to rely on this control procedure to reduce the control risk for the classification assertion. In this case, the client's procedures for classifying payroll transactions by types of payroll costs should be examined by the auditor.

**Step 3.** After the controls are tested, the auditor sets the level of control risk and documents that assessment. The documentation supporting the achieved level of control risk for the payroll system might include a flowchart, the results of tests of controls, and a memorandum indicating the overall conclusion about control risk.

**[LO8] Identify key internal controls and develop relevant tests of controls for payroll transactions.**

A. Table 12-5 summarizes the assertions and possible misstatements for payroll transactions. The table also includes key control procedures for each assertion and examples of tests of controls that can test the effectiveness of the control procedures. The assertions for the payroll transactions include (Table 12-5):

   1. **Occurrence**. Transactions and events that have been recorded have occurred and pertain to the entity.

   2. **Completeness**. All transactions and events that should have been recorded have been recorded.

   3. **Authorization**. All transactions and events are properly authorized.

   4. **Accuracy**. Amounts and other data relating to recorded transactions and events have been recorded appropriately.

   5. **Cutoff**. Transactions and events have been recorded in the correct accounting period.

   6. **Classification**. Transactions and events have been recorded in the proper accounts.

B. The auditor's decision process on planning and performing tests of controls involves considering the assertions and the possible misstatements that can occur if internal control does not operate effectively. The auditor evaluates the client's accounting system to determine the controls that will prevent or detect such misstatements. When controls are present and the auditor decides to rely on them, they must be tested to evaluate their effectiveness. The choice of which type of test of controls is appropriate for a particular assertion will be a function of the following:

   1. The volume of transactions or data.

   2. The nature and complexity of the systems by which the entity processes and controls information.

   3. The nature of the available evidential mater, including audit evidence that is available only in electronic form.

**[LO9] Relate the assessment of control risk to substantive procedures.**

A.  If the results of the tests of controls for the payroll system support the planned level of control risk, the auditor conducts substantive procedures of payroll-related accounts at the assessed level. If the results of the control tests do not support the planned level of control risk, the detection risk will have to be set lower, which will increase the nature and extent of substantive testing of payroll-related accounts.

B.  The auditor uses substantive procedures to detect material misstatements in payroll expense and payroll-related liabilities. There are two categories of substantive procedures: (1) substantive analytical procedures and (2) tests of details of classes of transactions, account balances and disclosures.

1.  **Substantive analytical procedures** are used to examine plausible relationships and the reasonableness of payroll expenses and payroll-related accrual accounts.

2.  **Tests of details** focus on transactions, account balances or disclosures.

    **Tests of details of transactions** (also called substantive tests of transactions) in the payroll process focus mainly on payroll expense and payroll-related accrued accounts.

    **Tests of details of account balances** concentrate on the detailed amounts or estimates that make up the ending balance for payroll expense and payroll-related accrued accounts.

    **Tests of details of disclosures** are concerned with the presentation and disclosures related to payroll expense and payroll-related accrued accounts.

C.  Assertions about classes of transactions and events for the period under audit include (Table 12-6):

1.  **Occurrence**. Payroll transactions and events are valid.
2.  **Completeness**. All payroll transactions and events have been recorded.
3.  **Authorization**. All payroll transactions and events are properly authorized.
4.  **Accuracy**. Payroll transactions have been properly computed and payroll expense has been properly accumulated from journals and ledgers.
5.  **Cutoff**. Payroll expense and related accruals are recorded in the correct accounting period.
6.  **Classification**. Payroll expense and related accruals have been recorded in the proper accounts.

Assertions about account balances at the period end include (Table 12-6):

1.  **Existence**. Payroll expense is a valid expense and related accruals are valid liabilities.
2.  **Rights and obligations**. The payroll-related accruals are the obligations of the entity.
3.  **Completeness**. All payroll expense and related accruals have been recorded.
4.  **Valuation and allocation**. Payroll expense and related accruals are included in the financial statements at appropriate amounts and any resulting valuation or allocation adjustments are appropriately recorded.

Assertions about presentation and disclosure include (Table 12-6):

1. **Occurrence and rights and obligations**. All disclosed events, transactions, and other matters relating to payroll expense and related accruals have occurred and pertain to the entity.

2. **Completeness**. All disclosures relating to payroll expense and related accruals that should have been included in the financial statements have been included.

3. **Classification and understandability**. Financial information relating to payroll expense and related accruals is appropriately presented and described, and disclosures are clearly expressed.

4. **Accuracy and valuation**. Financial and other information relating to payroll expense and related accruals are disclosed fairly and at appropriate amounts.

Note that the auditor may test assertions related to transactions (substantive tests of transactions) in conjunction with testing the account balance. If the tests of controls indicate that the controls are not operating effectively, the auditor may need to test transactions at the date the account balance is tested.

**[LO10] Identify substantive analytical procedures used to audit payroll expense and payroll-related accrued expenses.**

A. **Analytical procedures** are useful audit tests for examining the reasonableness of payroll expenses and payroll-related accrual accounts. When utilized as part of planning, analytical procedures can effectively identify payroll expense and accrual accounts that may be missstated. Table 12-7 lists analytical procedures that are useful in auditing payroll expenses and payroll-related accrual accounts.

**[LO11] Identify tests of details of transactions used to audit payroll expense and payroll-related accrued expenses.**

A. **Substantive tests of transactions**. The intended purpose of tests of details of transactions is to detect monetary misstatements in the individual transactions processed through the payroll application. Tests of details of transactions are often conducted in conjunction with tests of controls. Table 12-8 presents the assertions for classes of transactions (substantive tests of transactions) and examples of the procedures used to test the assertions for the tests of details of transactions. They include: (1) occurrence, (2) completeness, (3) authorization, (4) accuracy, (5) cutoff and (6) classification.

Note that tests of details of transactions are commonly conducted as dual-purpose tests in conjunction with tests of controls.

**[LO12] Identify tests of details of account balances and disclosures used to audit payroll expense and payroll-related accrued expenses.**

A. **Tests of details of account balances and tests of details of disclosures**. Table 12-8 presents the assertions for account balances and examples of the procedures used to test the assertions for account balances (details of account balances). Assertions for account balances for payroll expense and payroll-related liabilities include: (1) existence, (2) rights and obligations, (3) completeness, and (4) valuation and allocation. Table 12-8 presents the assertions for presentation and disclosure and examples of the procedures used to test the assertions for presentation and disclosure. Assertions for presentation and disclosure (details of disclosures) include: (1) occurrence, (2) rights and obligations, (3) completeness, (4) classification and understandability and (5) accuracy and valuation.

B. In addition to payroll expense accounts, organizations incur a number of other payroll-related liabilities. For example, the entity withholds various amounts from an employee's pay. These withholdings include payroll taxes (federal and state income taxes and FICA), medical and life insurance premiums, pension, and other miscellaneous deductions. Some examples of accrued payroll liabilities include:

1. Accrued wages and salaries.
2. Accrued payroll taxes.
3. Accrued commissions.
4. Accrued bonuses.
5. Accrued benefits such as vacation and sick pay.

C. In auditing accrued payroll liabilities, the auditor is concerned mainly with five audit assertions: (1) existence, (2) completeness, (3) valuation, (4) cutoff and (5) presentation and disclosure. When control risk is low or the amounts in the accounts are relatively small, the auditor can verify accrued payroll liabilities using substantive analytical procedures. For example, the auditor can compare the prior year's balance in each accrual with the current year's balance after considering changing conditions. When control risk is high or the accounts are material, the auditor can obtain a detailed account analysis schedule. Expenses can be traced to the various payroll tax returns or other documentation filed by the entity and should agree with the amount of payroll tax expense included in the income statement. Payments can be verified by tracing the amounts to the cash disbursements journal.

**[LO13] Evaluate the audit findings and reach a final conclusion on payroll expense and payroll-related accrued expenses.**

A. When the auditor has completed the planned substantive procedures of the payroll accounts, all of the identified misstatements should be aggregated. The likely misstatement is compared to the tolerable misstatement allocated to the payroll accounts. If the likely misstatement is less than the tolerable misstatement, the auditor may accept the accounts as fairly presented. Conversely, if the likely misstatement exceeds the tolerable misstatement, the auditor should conclude that the accounts are not fairly presented. In this case, the auditor would have two choices: adjust the accounts to reduce the misstatement to an amount less than the tolerable level or qualify the audit report.

B. As with other cycles, the auditor should again analyze the misstatements discovered through the application of substantive procedures because these misstatements may provide additional evidence on the control risk for the payroll system. If the auditor concludes that the audit risk is unacceptably high, additional audit procedures should be performed, or the auditor must be satisfied that the client has adjusted the payroll-related financial statement accounts to an acceptable level. For example, suppose the auditor's substantive analytical procedures indicate that commission expense is overstated. The auditor might perform detailed computations of commission expense or request the client adjust the account by the amount of the estimated misstatement.

# CHAPTER 12: SELF-ASSESSMENT

## Part I: True or False Questions

[LO1] _____ 1. Payroll-related expenses normally are not a material cost to the organization.

[LO3] _____ 2. Employees must complete a W-4 form to authorize insurance deductions from his or her pay.

[LO4] _____ 3. The personnel function is responsible for managing the human resource needs of the organization.

[LO4] _____ 4. The payroll-processing function is responsible for paying employees for services and benefits.

[LO5] _____ 5. Proper segregation of duties is critical for the human resource management process.

[LO6] _____ 6. An example of executive compensation abuses is Tyco.

[LO6] _____ 7. There are few inherent risk factors that directly affect the human resource management process and its related accounts for non-officers.

[LO6] _____ 8. Inherent risk associated with officer compensation is frequently set high because officers have motive and opportunity to take advantage of their high-ranking offices in the form of excessive compensation.

[LO9] _____ 9. If the results of the control tests do not support the planned level of control risk, the detection risk will have to be set higher.

[LO11] _____ 10. Tests of details of transactions are often conducted in conjunction with tests of controls.

## Part II: Multiple Choice Questions

[LO11] 1. Tracing a sample of payroll checks to the master employee list is an example of which assertion(s):
   a. Classification.
   b. Occurrence.
   c. Cutoff.
   d. Both b and c.

[LO11] 2. Assertions about account balances at the period end may include:
   a. Rights and obligations.
   b. Authorization.
   c. Cutoff.
   d. both b and c.

[LO11] 3. Assertions about presentation and disclosure may include:
   a. Rights and obligations.
   b. Existence.
   c. Completeness.
   d. None of the above.

[LO11] 4. Assertions about classes of transactions and events may include:
   a. Rights and obligations.
   b. Authorization.
   c. Cutoff.
   d. Both b and c.

[LO12] 5. Reviewing benefit contracts for proper disclosure of pension and postretirement benefits is an example of which assertion(s):
   a. Completeness.
   b. Rights and obligations.
   c. Accuracy and valuation.
   d. Occurrence, completeness, and valuation and allocation.

[LO12] 6. Examples of accrued payroll liabilities may include:
   a. Accrued bonuses.
   b. Accrued vacation and sick pay.
   c. Accrued interest.
   d. Both a and b.

[LO12] 7. FAS No. 87 relates to:
   a. Wages and salaries costs.
   b. Health insurance costs.
   c. Pension costs.
   d. None of the above.

[LO12] 8. FAS No. 106 relates to:
   a. Wages and salaries costs.
   b. Postretirement costs.
   c. Pension costs.
   d. None of the above.

[LO12] 9. Tracing a sample of time cards before and after period end to the weekly payroll report and tracing the weekly payroll report to the general ledger to verify payroll transactions are recorded in the proper period is an example of which assertion(s):
   a. Classification.
   b. Occurrence.
   c. Cutoff.
   d. Both b and c.

[LO12] 10. Vouching selected amounts from the account analysis schedules for the accruals to supporting documentation is an example of which assertion(s):
   a. Completeness.
   b. Existence.
   c. Classification.
   d. Both a and c.

## Part III: Short Essay Questions

[LO4] Identify the primary functions in the human resource management process and describe each function.

[LO5] Discuss the key segregation of duties in the human resources management process and possible errors or fraud.

[LO11] Identify the types of substantive procedures used by the auditor to test payroll expense and payroll-related accounts. Provide an example of how the auditor may use each substantive procedure. Identify if any of the substantive procedures can be used as a test of controls or a dual-purpose test.

# Part IV: Crossword Puzzle – Chapter 12 [LO ALL]

## Across

5    Payroll records and data for active and inactive employees are maintained in the _____ _____ (two words).

7    The accounting standard for pension costs.

8    All employers are required to prepare these forms for both federal and statement governments (two words).

10    This is often paid to executives at the end of the year as a special form of compensation for achieving specific goals.

11    The Human Resource Management process is sometimes referred to as the _____ cycle.

12    Individuals who work for an organization are called _____ .

## Down

1    Profit-sharing plans and _____ compensation arrangements must be disclosed in the footnotes.

2    The accounting statement for postretirement benefits.

3    A two-letter abbreviation used for the process which includes payments to employees for services rendered.

4    Advanced IT is used to process payroll, so _____ and application controls must be tested.

6    A W4 form is filled out by an employee for the purpose of authorizing ____ deductions from the employee's gross pay.

9    This assertion ensures that payroll transactions have been properly computed and accumulated from journals and ledgers.

3    A two-letter abbreviation used for short-term liabilities resulting from trade obligations.

7    This document is used to record the receipt of goods (two words).

8    A two-letter abbreviation for the journal used to record the outflow of cash.

9    An abbreviation for auditing technology used to test client data.

12    This document is the bill from a supplier (two words).

## Part V: Townsend Office Supplies and Equipment [LO ALL]

---

### Chapter 12
### Townsend Office Supplies and Equipment

Payroll-related expense is considered material for 2007. Payroll-related expense for Townsend's 40 employees is $1,135,000 (22%): Selling payroll-related expense equals $610,000 (12%) and G&A payroll-related expense is $525,000 (10%). A reliance strategy was chosen to test payroll-related transactions. Vouching and tracing will be used to test payroll transactions. The population of transactions is composed of the following strata:

| Number of Size of Accounts | Book Value of Stratum |
|---|---|
| Stratum 1: Officers Compensation (3) | $425,000 |
| Stratum 2: Nonofficers Compensation (32) | 675,000 |
| Stratum 3: Part-time employees Compensation (5) | 35,000 |
| 40 Employees | $1,135,000 |

Payroll-related expenses include salaries, wages, commissions and fringe benefits for 35 full-time employees. Part-time employees are not eligible to receive the benefits package. The tests of control for the payroll system support the planned level of control risk; hence a reliance strategy is appropriate and no adjustment to detection risk is necessary. Sample size will be computed separately for officer/nonofficer compensation because risk is higher for officer compensation.

Non-officers Compensation: A low assessment is made for IR and CR. The tolerable misstatement allocated collectively to payroll-related expense accounts is $12,000 and the expected misstatement is $6,000. There is a moderate risk that other auditing procedures will fail to detect material misstatements.

Officers Compensation: Because Townsend is a closely-held corporation, a slightly below maximum assessment is made for IR and CR. Tolerable misstatement allocated collectively to payroll-related expense accounts is $17,000 and the expected misstatement is $8,000. There is a moderate risk that other auditing procedures will fail to detect material misstatements. Payroll-related expenses were understated due to three misstatements (errors) that were detected. The first misstatement to compensation was not computed for employees receiving group insurance benefits over $50,000 provided by the employer (Stratum 1 $900, Stratum 2 $600 and Stratum 3 None). The second misstatement related to officer compensation for personal use of company vehicles (Stratum 1 $600 and Stratum 2 and 3 None). The third misstatement related to commissions earned for the last week of 2004, which were not accrued (Stratum 1 $2,000, Stratum 2 $1,400 and Stratum 3 None). Townsend's management has agreed to adjust the payroll-related accounts for these errors. You have concluded that the amount of misstatements in the population were likely to correlate to the total dollar amount of the items in the population and not to the number of items in the population; hence, the ratio estimation method should be used to compute misstatement in the sampling strata. Remember that sample size = (Population book value/Tolerable misstatement)(Assurance factor from Table 9-4). (1) Compute the sample size for the two sub-populations; (2) Compute the projected misstatement; and (3) Assuming no material qualitative factors need to be considered, conclude whether the payroll-related expense is fairly presented.

# CHAPTER 12: SELF-ASSESSMENT SOLUTIONS

## Part I: True or False Questions

[LO1] **False** 1. Payroll-related expenses normally are not a material cost to the organization.

[LO3] **False** 2. Employees must complete a W-4 form to authorize insurance deductions from his or her pay.

[LO4] **True** 3. The personnel function is responsible for managing the human resource needs of the organization.

[LO4] **False** 4. The payroll-processing function is responsible for paying employees for services and benefits.

[LO5] **True** 5. Proper segregation of duties is critical for the human resource management process.

[LO6] **True** 6. An example of executive compensation abuses is Tyco.

[LO6] **True** 7. There are few inherent risk factors that directly affect the human resource management process and its related accounts for non-officers.

[LO6] **True** 8. Inherent risk associated with officer compensation is frequently set high because officers have motive and opportunity to take advantage of their high-ranking offices in the form of excessive compensation.

[LO9] **False** 9. If the results of the control tests do not support the planned level of control risk, the detection risk will have to be set higher.

[LO11] **True** 10. Tests of details of transactions are often conducted in conjunction with tests of controls.

## Part II: Multiple Choice Questions

[LO11] 1. Tracing a sample of payroll checks to the master employee list is an example of which assertion(s):
   a. Classification.
   **b. Occurrence.**
   c. Cutoff.
   d. Both b and c.

[LO11] 2. Assertions about account balances at the period end may include:
   **a. Rights and obligations.**
   b. Authorization.
   c. Cutoff.
   d. both b and c.

[LO11] 3. Assertions about presentation and disclosure may include:
   a. Rights and obligations.
   b. Existence.
   **c. Completeness.**
   d. None of the above.

[LO11] 4. Assertions about classes of transactions and events may include:
   a. Rights and obligations.
   b. Authorization.
   c. Cutoff.
   **d. Both b and c.**

[LO12] 5. Reviewing benefit contracts for proper disclosure of pension and postretirement benefits is an example of which assertion(s):
   a. Completeness.
   b. Rights and obligations.
   **c. Accuracy and valuation.**
   d. Occurrence, completeness, and valuation and allocation.

[LO12] 6. Examples of accrued payroll liabilities may include:
   a. Accrued bonuses.
   b. Accrued vacation and sick pay.
   c. Accrued interest.
   **d. Both a and b.**

[LO12] 7. FAS No. 87 relates to:
   a. Wages and salaries costs.
   b. Health insurance costs.
   **c. Pension costs.**
   d. None of the above.

[LO12] 8. FAS No. 106 relates to:
   a. Wages and salaries costs.
   **b. Postretirement costs.**
   c. Pension costs.
   d. None of the above.

[LO12] 9. Tracing a sample of time cards before and after period end to the weekly payroll report and tracing the weekly payroll report to the general ledger to verify payroll transactions are recorded in the proper period is an example of which assertion(s):
   a. Classification.
   b. Occurrence.
   **c. Cutoff.**
   d. Both b and c.

[LO12]10. Vouching selected amounts from the account analysis schedules for the accruals to supporting documentation is an example of which assertion(s):
   a. Completeness.
   **b. Existence.**
   c. Classification.
   d. Both a and c.

# Part III: Short Essay Questions

[LO4] Identify the primary functions in the human resource management process and describe each function.

**The functions of the human resource management process include:**

**Personnel: Authorization of hiring, firing, wage-rate and salary adjustments, salaries and payroll deductions.**

**Supervision: Review and approval of employees' attendance and time information; monitoring of employee scheduling, productivity, and payroll cost variances.**

**Timekeeping: Processing of employees' attendance and time information and coding of account distribution.**

**Payroll Processing: Computation of gross pay, deductions, and net pay; recording and summarization of payments and verification of account distribution.**

**Disbursement: Payment of employees' compensation and benefits.**

**General Ledger: Proper accumulation, classification and summarization of payroll in the general ledger.**

---

[LO5] Discuss the key segregation of duties in the human resources management process and possible errors or fraud.

**As discussed in prior chapters, proper segregation of duties is one of the most important control procedures in any accounting system. Shown below are some of the key segregation of duties for the human resources management process and examples of possible errors or fraud that can result from conflicts of duties.**

**Supervision function should be segregated from the personnel records and payroll-processing functions: If one individual is responsible for the supervision, personnel records, and payroll-processing functions, fictitious employees can appear on the payroll records or unauthorized payments can be made. This can result in unauthorized payments to existing employees or payments to fictitious employees.**

**Disbursement function should be segregated from the personnel records, supervision, and payroll-processing functions: If one individual is responsible for the disbursement function and also has the authority to hire and fire employees, approve time reports, and prepare payroll checks, unauthorized payroll checks can be issued.**

**Payroll-processing function should be segregated from the general ledger function: If one individual is responsible for processing payroll transactions and also for the general ledger, that individual can conceal any defalcation that would normally be detected by independent review of accounting entries made to the general ledger.**

[LO11] Identify the types of substantive procedures used by the auditor to test payroll expense and payroll-related accounts. Provide an example of how the auditor may use each substantive procedure. Identify if any of the substantive procedures can be used as a test of controls or a dual-purpose test.

**The auditor uses substantive procedures to detect material misstatements in payroll expense and payroll-related liabilities. There are two categories of substantive procedures: (1) substantive analytical procedures and (2) tests of details of classes of transactions, account balances and disclosures.**

1. **Substantive analytical procedures are used to examine plausible relationships and the reasonableness of payroll expenses and payroll-related accrual accounts. Example: The auditor might compare the budgeted payroll expenses with actual payroll expenses.**

2. **Tests of details focus on transactions, account balances or disclosures.**

   **Tests of details of transactions (also called substantive tests of transactions) in the payroll process focus mainly on payroll expense and payroll-related accrued accounts.**
   **Example: To test the authorization assertion, the auditor can test a sample of payroll checks for the presence of an authorized time card.**

   **Tests of details of account balances concentrate on the detailed amounts or estimates that make up the ending balance for payroll expense and payroll-related accrued accounts.**
   **Example: To test the existence assertion, the auditor can vouch selected amounts from the account analysis schedules for the accruals to supporting documentation.**

   **Tests of details of disclosures are concerned with the presentation and disclosures related to payroll expense and payroll-related accrued accounts.**
   **Example: To test the accuracy and valuation assertions, the auditor can read footnotes and other information to ensure that the information is accurate and properly presented at the appropriate amounts.**

# Part IV: Crossword Puzzle – Chapter 12 Solution [LO ALL]

```
                                                    ¹D
         ²F              ³H              ⁴G          E
    ⁵M  A  S  T  E  R  F  I  L  E  S      ⁷F  A  S  8  7
         S     A              N          E
         1     X        ⁸T ⁹A  X  R  E  P  O  R  T  S
         0           C        R        R
         6           C        A        R
              ¹⁰B  O  N  U  S     L        E
                    R                  D
              ¹¹P  A  Y  R  O  L  L
                    C
         ¹²E  M  P  L  O  Y  E  E  S
```

## Across

5   Payroll records and data for active and inactive employees are maintained in the _____ _____ (two words).
7   The accounting standard for pension costs.
8   All employers are required to prepare these forms for both federal and statement governments (two words).
10  This is often paid to executives at the end of the year as a special form of compensation for achieving specific goals.
11  The Human Resource Management process is sometimes referred to as the _____ cycle.
12  Individuals who work for an organization are called _____ .

## Down

1   Profit-sharing plans and _____ compensation arrangements must be disclosed in the footnotes.
2   The accounting statement for postretirement benefits.
3   A two-letter abbreviation used for the process which includes payments to employees for services rendered.
4   Advanced IT is used to process payroll, so _____ and application controls must be tested.
6   A W4 form is filled out by an employee for the purpose of authorizing ___ deductions from the employee's gross pay.
9   This assertion ensures that payroll transactions have been properly computed and accumulated from journals and ledgers.
3   A two-letter abbreviation used for short-term liabilities resulting from trade obligations.
7   This document is used to record the receipt of goods (two words).
8   A two-letter abbreviation for the journal used to record the outflow of cash.
9   An abbreviation for auditing technology used to test client data.
12  This document is the bill from a supplier (two words).

# Part V: Townsend Office Supplies and Equipment [LO ALL]

## Chapter 12
## Townsend Office Supplies and Equipment

Payroll-related expense is considered material for 2007. Payroll-related expense for Townsend's 40 employees is $1,135,000 (22%): Selling payroll-related expense equals $610,000 (12%) and G&A payroll-related expenses is $525,000 (10%). A reliance strategy was chosen to test payroll-related transactions. Vouching and tracing will be used to test payroll transactions. The population of transactions is composed of the following strata:

| Number of Size of Accounts | Book Value of Stratum |
|---|---|
| Stratum 1: Officers Compensation (3) | $425,000 |
| Stratum 2: Nonofficers Compensation (32) | 675,000 |
| Stratum 3: Part-time employees Compensation (5) | 35,000 |
| 40 Employees | $1,135,000 |

Payroll-related expenses include salaries, wages, commissions and fringe benefits for 35 full-time employees. Part-time employees are not eligible to receive the benefits package. The tests of control for the payroll system support the planned level of control risk; hence a reliance strategy is appropriate and no adjustment to detection risk is necessary. Sample size will be computed separately for officer/nonofficer compensation because risk is higher for officer compensation.

Non-officers Compensation: A low assessment is made for IR and CR. The tolerable misstatement allocated collectively to payroll-related expense accounts is $12,000 and the expected misstatement is $6,000. There is a moderate risk that other auditing procedures will fail to detect material misstatements. Officers Compensation: Because Townsend is a closely-held corporation, a slightly below maximum assessment is made for IR and CR. Tolerable misstatement allocated collectively to payroll-related expense accounts is $17,000 and the expected misstatement is $8,000. There is a moderate risk that other auditing procedures will fail to detect material misstatements. Payroll-related expenses were understated due to three misstatements (errors) that were detected. The first misstatement to compensation was not computed for employees receiving group insurance benefits over $50,000 provided by the employer (Stratum 1 $900, Stratum 2 $600 and Stratum 3 None). The second misstatement related to officer compensation for personal use of company vehicles (Stratum 1 $600 and Stratum 2 and 3 None). The third misstatement related to commissions earned for the last week of 2007, which were not accrued (Stratum 1 $2,000, Stratum 2 $1,400 and Stratum 3 None). Townsend's management has agreed to adjust the payroll-related accounts for these errors. You have concluded that the amount of misstatements in the population were likely to correlate to the total dollar amount of the items in the population and not to the number of items in the population; hence, the ratio estimation method should be used to compute misstatement in the sampling strata. Remember that sample size = (Population book value/Tolerable misstatement)(Assurance factor from Table 9-4). (1) Compute the sample size for the two sub-populations; (2) Compute the projected misstatement; and (3) Assuming no material qualitative factors need to be considered, conclude whether the payroll-related expense is fairly presented.

**(1) Sample Size**
**Stratum 1 Officer Compensation**
Sample size = $425,000/$17,000(2.0) = __50__
Table 9-4: Slightly lower than maximum IR/CR and moderate risk of other substantive procedures
**Stratum 2 Nonofficer Compensation and Stratum 3 Part-time Employee Compensation**
Payroll-related expenses = $1,135,000 − 425,000 = 710,000.
Sample size = ($710,000/$11,000)(1.2) = __78__.
Table 9-4: Low IR/CR and moderate risk of other substantive procedures
The 78 sample items will be divided between Stratum 2 and Stratum 3.
Stratum 2: Sample = __74__ = [78($675,000/$710,000)] + Stratum 3: Sample size = __4__ [78 − 74]
Total payroll transactions will be tested = 128 [50 + 78]

**(2)**

| Stratum | Book Value of Stratum | Book Value of Sample | Audit Value of Sample | Amount of Overstatement |
|---|---|---|---|---|
| 1 | $425,000 | $125,000 | $128,500 | $3,500 |
| 2 | $675,000 | $152,000 | $154,000 | $2,000 |
| 3 | $ 35,000 | $ 9,200 | $ 9,200 | $ 0 |

| Stratum | Amount of Misstatement | Ratio of Misstatement Tested | Projected Misstatement |
|---|---|---|---|
| 1 | $3,500 | $3,500/($125,000 × 425,000) | $11,900 |
| 2 | $2,000 | $2,000/($152,000 × 675,000) | $ 8,882 |
| 3 | $ 0 | $200/($13,000 × $62,000) | $ 0 |
| Total projected misstatement | | | $ 20,782 |

**(3) Management has agreed to adjust the financial statements for the payroll-related accounts misstatements. No other adjustments are necessary and the auditor can conclude that the payroll-related accounts are fairly presented. Officer Compensation: You can conclude that there is an acceptably low risk that the true misstatement exceeds the tolerable misstatement because the officer compensation projected misstatement of $11,900 is less than the expected misstatement of $17,000. Non-officer Compensation: You can conclude that there is an acceptably low risk that the true misstatement exceeds the tolerable misstatement because the nonofficer compensation projected misstatement of $8,882 is less than the expected misstatement of $11,000.**

# Chapter 13

# Auditing the Inventory Management Process

**KEY THOUGHT**

Observation of inventories is a generally accepted auditing procedure. The independent auditor who issues an opinion when he has not employed them must bear in mind that he has the burden of justifying the opinion expressed [Auditing Standards Board (AU 331.01)].

## CHAPTER SUMMARY

**[LO1] Develop an understanding of the inventory management process.**

A.  For most manufacturing, wholesale, and merchandising (retail) entities, inventory is a major component of the balance sheet. Inventory also represents one of the most complex parts of the audit. The inventory management process is affected by the procedures discussed for the revenue, purchasing, and payroll processes. Figure 13-1 shows how each of these processes interacts with the inventory management process. The acquisition of and payment for inventory are controlled via the purchasing process. The cost of both direct and indirect labor assigned to inventory is controlled through the payroll process. Finished goods are sold and accounted for as part of the revenue process. Exhibit 13-1 describes EarthWear's inventory system, while Figure 13-2 flowcharts the inventory system.

**[LO2] Identify and describe the types of documents and records used in the inventory management process.**

A.  The more important documents and records that are normally involved in the inventory system include (Table 13-1):

1.  Production schedule.
2.  Receiving report.
3.  Materials requisition.
4.  Inventory master file.
5.  Production data information.
6.  Cost accumulation and variance report.
7.  Inventory status report.
8.  Shipping order.

**[LO3] Understand the functions in the inventory management process.**

A. The functions that normally take place in a typical inventory management process include (Table 13-2):

---

### Functions in the Inventory Management Process

| Function | Description of Function |
|---|---|
| Inventory management | Authorization of production activity and maintenance of inventory at appropriate levels; issuance of purchase requisitions to the purchasing department (see Chapter 11 on the purchasing process). |
| Raw materials stores | Custody of raw materials and issuance of raw materials to manufacturing departments. |
| Manufacturing | Production of goods. |
| Finished goods stores | Custody of finished goods and issuance of goods to the shipping department (see Chapter 10 on the revenue process). |
| Cost accounting | Maintenance of the costs of manufacturing and inventory in cost records. |
| General ledger | Proper accumulation, classification, and summarization of inventory and related costs in the general ledger. |

---

**[LO4] Know the appropriate segregation of duties for the inventory management process.**

A.  Segregation of duties is an important control in the inventory management process because of the potential for theft and fraud. Individuals involved in the inventory management and inventory stores functions should not have access to the inventory records, the cost-accounting records, or the general ledger. When the inventory is highly computerized, there should be proper segregation of duties within the IT department. Table 13-3 contains some of the key segregation of duties for the inventory management process and examples of possible errors or fraud that can result from conflicts in duties:

---

**Key Segregation of Duties in the Inventory Management Process and Possible Errors or Fraud**

| Segregation of Duties | Possible Errors/Fraud Resulting from Conflicts of Duties |
|---|---|
| Inventory management function should be segregated from the cost-accounting function | If the individual responsible for inventory management also has access to the cost-accounting records, production and inventory costs can be manipulated. This may lead to an over-or-understatement of inventory and net income. |
| Inventory stores function should be segregated from the cost-accounting function | If one individual is responsible for both controlling and accounting for inventory, unauthorized shipments can be made or theft of goods can be covered up. |
| Cost-accounting function should be segregated from the general ledger function | If one individual is responsible for the inventory records and also for the general ledger, it is possible for that individual to conceal unauthorized shipments. This can result in the theft of goods, leading to an overstatement of inventory. |
| Responsibility for supervising physical inventory should be separated from the inventory management and inventory stores functions | If the individual responsible for production management or inventory stores functions is also responsible for the physical inventory, it is possible that inventory shortages can be covered up through the adjustment of the inventory records to the physical inventory, resulting in an overstatement of inventory. |

---

B.  Table 13-4 in the textbook shows the proper segregation of duties for individual inventory functions across the various departments that control inventory processing.

**[LO5] Identify and evaluate inherent risks relevant to the inventory management process.**

A.  In examining the inventory management process, the auditor needs to consider the inherent risks factors that may affect the transactions processed by the system and the financial statement accounts affected by those transactions. The auditor should consider industry-related factors and operating and engagement characteristics when assessing the possibility of a material misstatement.

   1.  **Industry-related factors**. A number of industry factors may indicate the presence of material misstatements in inventory. For example, if industry competition is intense, there may be problems with the proper valuation of inventory in terms of lower-of-cost-or-market values. Technology changes in certain industries may also promote material misstatements due to obsolescence.

2. **Engagement and operating characteristics**. A number of engagement and operating characteristics are important to the assessment of inherent risk for inventory. First, the type of product sold by the client can increase the potential for defalcation. For example, products that are small and of high value (such as jewelry) are more susceptible to theft than large products are. Second, inventory is often difficult to audit, and its valuation may result in disagreements with the client. Finally, the auditor must be alert to possible related-party transactions for acquiring raw materials and selling finished products. For example, the client may purchase raw materials from a company controlled by the chief executive officer at prices in excess of market value. In such a case, the value of inventory will be overstated, and cash will have been misappropriated from the entity.

B. Audit research has shown that there is a high risk that inventory contains material misstatements. In fact, some of the most notorious accounting frauds in history have involved inventory manipulations (i.e., Phar-Mor, Centennial Technologies, Inc.).

C. Prior year misstatements are good indicators of potential misstatements in the current year, so auditors should carefully consider if misstatements found in the prior years' audit may be present in the current inventory and plan the audit accordingly.

**[LO6] Assess control risk for the inventory system.**

A. The auditor may follow a substantive strategy when auditing inventory and cost of goods sold. When a substantive strategy is used, the auditor places no reliance on the control procedures in the inventory management process and sets the level of control risk at the maximum. The auditor then relies on substantive procedures to determine the fairness of inventory. Such a strategy may be appropriate when internal control is not adequate. In many cases, however, the auditor can rely on internal control for inventory. This normally occurs when the client has an integrated cost-accounting and inventory management system.

B. The concepts involved in control risk assessment were discussed in Chapter 6. This approach is applied to the inventory management process. For discussion purposes, it is assumed that the auditor has decided to follow a reliance strategy. Three major steps in setting control risk for the inventory management process must be followed when a reliance strategy is being used (Figure 13-3):

1. Understand and document the inventory management process based on a reliance approach.

2. Plan and perform tests of controls on inventory transactions.

3. Set and document the control risk for the inventory management process.

**Step 1**. In order to assess the control risk for the inventory management process, the auditor must understand the five components of an entity's internal control including:

1. Control environment.
2. The entity's risk assessment process.
3. Control procedures.
4. Information systems and communication.
5. Monitoring of controls.

Two factors are of particular importance: First, if the client uses sophisticated IT techniques for monitoring the flow of goods and accumulating costs, the auditor will need to evaluate both the general IT controls and the inventory application controls. Second, the auditor will need a thorough understanding of the process used by the client to value inventory.

**Step 2**. The auditor must identify the relevant control procedures within the client's inventory system that ensure that material misstatements are either prevented or detected and corrected.

**Step 3**. After the controls are tested, the auditor sets the level of control risk and documents that assessment. The documentation supporting the achieved level of control risk for the inventory management process might include a flowchart, the results of tests of controls, and a memorandum indicating the overall conclusion about control risk.

**[LO7] Identify key internal controls and develop relevant tests of controls for inventory transactions.**

A. Table 13-5 summarizes the assertions and possible misstatement for inventory transactions. The table also includes key control procedures for each assertion and examples of tests of controls that can test the effectiveness of the control procedures. The assertions for the payroll transactions include (Table 13-5):

1. **Occurrence**. Transactions and events that have been recorded have occurred and pertain to the entity.

2. **Completeness**. All transactions and events that should have been recorded have been recorded.

3. **Authorization**. All transactions and events are properly authorized.

4. **Accuracy**. Amounts and other data relating to recorded transactions and events have been recorded appropriately.

5. **Cutoff**. Transactions and events have been recorded in the correct accounting period.

6. **Classification**. Transactions and events have been recorded in the proper accounts.

**[LO8] Relate the assessment of control risk to substantive procedures.**

A. The same judgment process is followed in setting control risk in the inventory management process that was used with other processes. The auditor can rely on controls if tests of controls indicate that the controls are operating effectively. If the results of the tests of controls for the inventory system do not support the planned level of control risk, the auditor would set control risk higher and set detection risk lower. This would lead to increased substantive procedures.

B. The auditor uses substantive procedures to detect material misstatements in inventory. There are two categories of substantive procedures: (1) substantive analytical procedures and (2) tests of details of classes of transactions, account balances and disclosures.

1. **Substantive analytical procedures** are used to examine plausible relationships and the reasonableness of inventory and related accounts.

2.  **Tests of details** focus on transactions, account balances or disclosures.

    **Tests of details of transactions** (also called substantive tests of transactions) in the inventory process focus mainly on inventory and cost of goods sold.

    **Tests of details of account balances** concentrate on the detailed amounts or estimates that make up the ending balance for inventory and related accounts.

    **Tests of details of disclosures** are concerned with the presentation and disclosures related to inventory and related accounts.

C.  Assertions about classes of transactions and events for inventory include (Table 13-6):

    1.  **Occurrence**. Inventory transactions and events are valid.

    2.  **Completeness**. All inventory transactions and events have been recorded.

    3.  **Authorization**. All inventory transactions and events are properly authorized.

    4.  **Accuracy**. Inventory transactions have been properly computed and ending inventory and related revenue and cost of goods sold have been properly accumulated from journals and ledgers.

    5.  **Cutoff**. Inventory receipts and shipments are recorded in the correct accounting period.

    6.  **Classification**. Inventory purchases, production and sales are recorded in the proper accounts (e.g., raw materials, work in process or finished goods).

    Assertions about account balances at the period end for inventory include (Table 13-6):

    1.  **Existence**. Inventory recorded on the books and record actually exists.

    2.  **Rights and obligations**. The entity has the legal right (i.e., ownership of the recorded inventory.

    3.  **Completeness**. All inventories are recorded.

    4.  **Valuation and allocation**. Inventory is properly recorded in accordance with GAAP (e.g., lower of cost or market).

    Assertions about presentation and disclosure for inventory include (Table 13-6):

    1.  **Occurrence and rights and obligations**. All disclosed events, transactions, and other matters relating to inventory have occurred and pertain to the entity.

    2.  **Completeness**. All disclosures relating to inventory that should have been included in the financial statements have been included.

    3.  **Classification and understandability**. Financial information relating to inventory is appropriately presented and described, and disclosures are clearly expressed.

4. **Accuracy and valuation**. Financial and other information relating to inventory are disclosed fairly and at appropriate amounts.

Note that the auditor may test assertions related to transactions (substantive tests of transactions) in conjunction with testing the account balance. If the tests of controls indicate that the controls are not operating effectively, the auditor may need to test transactions at the date the account balance is tested.

## [LO9] Identify substantive analytical procedures used to audit inventory and related accounts.

A. **Analytical procedures** are useful audit tests for examining the reasonableness of inventory and cost of goods sold. When performed as part of audit planning, preliminary analytical procedures can effectively identify whether the inventory and cost of goods sold accounts contain material misstatements. Final analytical procedures are useful as an overall review for inventory and related accounts to identify obsolete, slow-moving, and excess inventory. Substantive analytical procedures are useful for testing the valuation assertion for inventory. Such tests can also identify problems with improper inclusion or exclusion of costs in overhead.

B. Table 13-7 lists substantive analytical procedures that are useful in auditing inventory and related accounts at either the planning stage or as an overall review.

## [LO10] Know how to audit standard costs.

A. Many manufacturing entities use a standard cost system to measure performance and to value inventory. If a standard cost system is integrated with the general accounting records, cost accumulation and variance reports are direct outputs of the client's inventory-accounting system.

B. For accuracy and proper valuation, standard costs should approximate actual costs. To test the standard costs, the auditor should first review the client's policies and procedures for constructing standard costs. Once the policies and procedures are understood, the auditor normally tests the component cost buildup for a representative sample of standard product costs. Three components make up the cost of producing a product: materials, labor and overhead.

1. **Materials**. Determining the materials costs requires testing the quantity and type of materials included in the product and the price of the materials. The quantity and type of materials are tested by reviewing the engineering specifications for the product. The auditor can compare the list of materials with the standard cost card or other documentation used to support the cost accumulation. The prices used on the standard cost card can be traced to vendors' invoices as a test of actual costs.

2. **Labor**. The determination of direct labor requires evidence about the type and amount of labor needed for production and the labor rate. The amount of labor necessary can be tested by reviewing engineering estimates, which may be based on time-and-motion studies or on historical information. The labor rates for each type of labor necessary can be tested by examining a schedule of authorized wages. Labor costs included in inventory are often tested in conjunction with payroll expense.

3. **Overhead**. The auditor tests overhead costs by reviewing the client's method of overhead allocation for reasonableness, compliance with GAAP, and consistency. The auditor can examine the costs included in overhead to be sure that such costs can appropriately be assigned to the product. The inclusion or exclusion of such costs should be consistent from

one period to the next. The auditor can compare the actual costs for the period to the budgeted costs. The auditor can also compare the costs included in the current year's listing with those in the prior year's listing.

**[LO11] Know how to observe physical inventory.**

A. The auditor's observation of inventory is a generally accepted auditing procedure (AU 331). However, the auditor is not required to observe all inventories, but only inventory that is material. The primary reason for observing the client's physical inventory is to establish the existence of the inventory. The observation of the physical inventory also provides evidence on the rights and obligations and valuation assertions. Based on the physical inventory count, the client compiles the physical inventory.

B. While the form of compilation may differ among entities, it normally contains a list of the items by type and quantity, the assigned cost for each item, the inventory value for each item, and a total for the inventory. Prior to the physical count of inventory, the auditor should be familiar with the inventory locations, the major items in inventory, and the client's instructions for counting inventory. During the observation of the physical inventory count, the auditor should do the following:

1. Ensure that no production is scheduled. If production is scheduled, ensure that proper controls are established for movement between departments in order to prevent double counting.

2. Ensure that there is no movement of goods during the inventory count. If movement is necessary, the auditor and client personnel must ensure that the goods are not double counted and that all goods are counted.

3. Make sure that the client's count teams are following the inventory count instructions. If the count teams are not following the instructions, the auditor should notify the client representative in charge of the area.

4. Ensure that inventory tags are issued sequentially to individual departments. For many inventory counts, the goods are marked with multicopy inventory tags. The count teams record the type and quantity of inventory on each tag, and one copy of each tag is then used to compile the inventory. If the client uses another method of counting inventory, such as detailed inventory listings or handheld computers, the auditor should obtain copies of the listings or files prior to the start of the inventory count.

5. Perform test counts and record a sample of counts in the working papers. This information will be used to test the accuracy and completeness of the client's inventory compilation.

6. Obtain tag control information for testing the client's inventory compilation. Tag control information includes documentation of the numerical sequence of all inventory tags and accounting for all used and unused inventory tags. If inventory listings are used by the client, copies of the listing will accomplish the objective of documenting the entire inventory count.

7. Obtain cutoff information, including the number of the last shipping and receiving documents issued on the date of the physical inventory count.

8. Observe the condition of the inventory for items that may be obsolete, slow moving, or carried in excess quantities.

9. Inquire about goods held on consignment for others or held on a "bill-and-hold" basis. Such items should not be included in the client's inventory. The auditor must also inquire about goods held on consignment for the client. These goods should be included in the inventory count.

When these audit procedures are followed, the auditor has reasonable assurance that a proper inventory count has been taken.

**[LO12] Identify tests of details of transactions used to audit inventory and related accounts.**

A. The intended purpose of tests of details of transactions is to detect monetary misstatements in the inventory account. The auditor may conduct tests of details of transactions specifically for inventory. However, because the inventory management process interacts with the revenue, purchasing, and human resource management processes, transactions involving the receipt of goods, shipment of goods and assignment of labor costs are normally tested as part of those processes. As previously mentioned, tests of details of transactions are commonly conducted as dual-purpose tests in conjunction with tests of controls.

B. **Substantive tests of transactions**. Table 13-8 presents the assertions for classes of transactions (substantive tests of transactions) and examples of the procedures used to test the assertions for the tests of details of account balances of inventory. They include: (1) occurrence, (2) completeness, (3) authorization, (4) accuracy, (5) cutoff and (6) classification.

**[LO13] Identify tests of details of account balances used to audit inventory and related accounts.**

A. **Tests of details of account balances and tests of details of disclosures**. Table 13-8 summarizes the tests of the inventory account balance for each assertion and examples of the procedures used to test the assertions for account balances (tests of details of account balances). Assertions for account balances for inventory include: (1) existence, (2) rights and obligations, (3) completeness, and (4) valuation and allocation. The assertions for presentation and disclosure and examples of the procedures used to test the assertions for inventory presentation and disclosure. Assertions for presentation and disclosure (tests of details of disclosures) include: (1) occurrence, (2) rights and obligations, (3) completeness, (4) classification and understandability and (5) accuracy and valuation.

**[LO14] Evaluate the audit findings and reach a final conclusion on inventory and related accounts.**

A. When the auditor has completed the planned substantive tests of the inventory account, all of the identified misstatements should be aggregated. The likely misstatement is compared to the tolerable misstatement allocated to the inventory account. If the likely misstatement is less than the tolerable misstatement, the auditor may accept the inventory account as fairly presented. Conversely, if the likely misstatement exceeds the tolerable misstatement, the auditor should conclude that the inventory account is not fairly presented. In this case, the auditor would have two choices: adjust the accounts to reduce the misstatement to an amount less than the tolerable misstatement or qualify the audit report.

B. The auditor should again analyze the misstatements discovered through the application of substantive procedures because these misstatements may provide additional evidence on the control risk for the inventory management process. If the auditor concludes that the audit risk is unacceptably high, additional audit procedures should be performed, or the auditor must be satisfied that the client has adjusted the related financial statement accounts to an acceptable level.

# CHAPTER 13: SELF-ASSESSMENT

## Part I: True or False Questions

[LO1] _____ 1. The "cradle-to-grave" cycle for inventory begins when goods are purchased and stored and ends when the finished goods are shipped to customers.

[LO2] _____ 2. A receiving report records the shipment of goods to customers.

[LO3] _____ 3. Custody of finished goods is a part of the inventory management function.

[LO6] _____ 4. Once the controls in the inventory system have been tested, the auditor sets the level of control risk.

[LO7] _____ 5. The major control procedure for preventing fictitious inventory transactions from being recorded is proper segregation of duties.

[LO7] _____ 6. Inventory should be valued using the lower-of-cost-or-market rule.

[LO9] _____ 7. A high inventory turnover ratio normally indicates inefficient inventory policies.

[LO11] _____ 8. The three components that make up the cost of producing a product include materials, direct labor and indirect.

[LO12] _____ 9. The auditor's observation of inventory is a generally accepted auditing procedure.

[LO13] _____ 10. Obsolete inventory should be written down to its current market value.

## Part II: Multiple Choice Questions

[LO1]   1.   The inventory management process is affected by the control procedures for:
    a.   Revenue.
    b.   Purchasing.
    c.   Payroll.
    d.   All of the above.

[LO3]   2.   Production of goods is a:
    a.   Raw materials stores function.
    b.   General ledger function.
    c.   Inventory management function.
    d.   None of the above.

[LO7]   3.   Observation of the physical safeguards over inventory is a test of control for:
    a.   Accuracy.
    b.   Authorization.
    c.   Occurrence.
    d.   Classification.

[LO7] 4. Inventory obsolescence relates to:
   a. Completeness.
   b. Accuracy.
   c. Authorization.
   d. Cutoff.

[LO7] 5. The most effective control procedure for preventing fictitious inventory is:
   a. Preparing perpetual records.
   b. Review of inventory levels by design department.
   c. Segregation of duties.
   d. Both b and c.

[LO8] 6. Assertions about classes of transactions and events may include:
   a. Rights and obligations.
   b. Authorization.
   c. Existence.
   d. Both b and c.

[LO12] 7. During the observation of the physical inventory count, the auditor should:
   a. Ensure that no production is scheduled.
   b. Perform test counts and record a sample of counts in the working papers.
   c. Include "bill-and-hold" goods in the inventory.
   d. Both a and b.

[LO13] 8. Examining a sample of inventory checks for proper classification into expense accounts is used to test:
   a. Cutoff.
   b. Completeness.
   c. Classification.
   d. None of the above.

[LO13] 9. Obtaining a copy of the inventory compilation and confirming totals to general ledger is used to test:
   a. Valuation and allocation.
   b. Cutoff.
   c. Existence.
   d. Completeness.

[LO13] 10. Vouching a sample of inventory purchases to receiving reports and purchase requisitions is used to test:
   a. Valuation and allocation.
   b. Completeness.
   c. Occurrence.
   d. Existence.

## Part III: Short Essay Questions

[LO1] Discuss the relationship of the inventory management process to other accounting processes.

[LO4] Why is segregation of duties important in the inventory management process? Discuss the key segregation of duties in the inventory management process and possible errors or fraud.

[LO5] Discuss the inherent risk factors that the auditor needs to consider for the inventory management process.

# Part IV: Crossword Puzzle – Chapter 13 [LO ALL]

## Across

1     AU 331 requires the auditor to _____ all material inventories in order to establish the existence of the client's inventory.

4     An abbreviation for the valuation rule which applies to ending inventory.

7     These goods are available for sale.

9     For most manufacturing entities, this is a major component of their balance sheet.

11    A transaction where goods are treated as a sale, but the seller holds the goods until the customer needs them (three words).

12    Managers do not want to have ____ moving inventory.

## Down

2     This condition may result in obsolete inventory.

3     A conversion cost that is not direct labor.

5     A prime cost that is not direct labor.

6     An abbreviation for the inventory flow assumption where the cost of goods sold is based on the most recent inventory purchased.

8     An abbreviation for the inventory flow assumption where the cost of goods sold is based on the oldest inventory purchased.

10    An abbreviation for the account that is debited when inventory is sold.

**Chapter 13**
**Townsend Office Supplies and Equipment**

A prior year adjustment was made during the 2005 financial statement audit (the first year ABC audited Townsend) to apply the LCM rule to inventory. Gross profit has decreased in 2007 (from 55% in 2006 to 52% in 2007) and ending inventory has increased significantly in 2007. What inventory assertions are relevant to these issues and what type of substantive procedures should be used to test these assertions based on the information you know about Townsend?

# CHAPTER 13: SELF-ASSESSMENT SOLUTIONS

## Part I: True or False Questions

[LO1]  **True** 1.  The "cradle-to-grave" cycle for inventory begins when goods are purchased and stored and ends when the finished goods are shipped to customers.

[LO2]  **False** 2.  A receiving report records the shipment of goods to customers.

[LO3]  **False** 3.  Custody of finished goods is a part of the inventory management function.

[LO6]  **True** 4.  Once the controls in the inventory system have been tested, the auditor sets the level of control risk.

[LO7]  **True** 5.  The major control procedure for preventing fictitious inventory transactions from being recorded is proper segregation of duties.

[LO7]  **True** 6.  Inventory should be valued using the lower-of-cost-or-market rule.

[LO9]  **False** 7.  A high inventory turnover ratio normally indicates inefficient inventory policies.

[LO11] **False** 8.  The three components that make up the cost of producing a product include materials, direct labor and indirect.

[LO12] **True** 9.  The auditor's observation of inventory is a generally accepted auditing procedure.

[LO13] **True** 10. Obsolete inventory should be written down to its current market value.


## Part II: Multiple Choice Questions

[LO1]  1.  The inventory management process is affected by the control procedures for:
   a.  Revenue.
   b.  Purchasing.
   c.  Payroll.
   **d.  All of the above.**

[LO3]  2.  Production of goods is a:
   a.  Raw materials stores function.
   b.  General ledger function.
   c.  Inventory management function.
   **d.  None of the above.**

[LO7]  3.  Observation of the physical safeguards over inventory is a test of control for:
   a.  Accuracy.
   b.  Authorization.
   **c.  Occurrence.**
   d.  Classification.

[LO7]  4.  Inventory obsolescence relates to:
   a.  Completeness.
   **b.  Accuracy.**
   c.  Authorization.
   d.  Cutoff.

[LO7]  5.  The most effective control procedure for preventing fictitious inventory is:
   a.  Preparing perpetual records.
   b.  Review of inventory levels by design department.
   **c.  Segregation of duties.**
   d.  Both b and c.

[LO8]  6.  Assertions about classes of transactions and events may include:
   a.  Rights and obligations.
   **b.  Authorization.**
   c.  Existence.
   d.  Both b and c.

[LO12]  7.  During the observation of the physical inventory count, the auditor should:
   a.  Ensure that no production is scheduled.
   b.  Perform test counts and record a sample of counts in the working papers.
   c.  Include "bill-and-hold" goods in the inventory.
   **d.  Both a and b.**

[LO13]  8.  Examining a sample of inventory checks for proper classification into expense accounts is used to test:
   a.  Cutoff.
   b.  Completeness.
   **c.  Classification.**
   d.  None of the above.

[LO13]  9.  Obtaining a copy of the inventory compilation and confirming totals to general ledger is used to test:
   **a.  Valuation and allocation.**
   b.  Cutoff.
   c.  Existence.
   d.  Completeness.

[LO13]  10.  Vouching a sample of inventory purchases to receiving reports and purchase requisitions is used to test:
   a.  Valuation and allocation.
   b.  Completeness.
   **c.  Occurrence.**
   d.  Existence.

## Part III: Short Essay Questions

[LO1] Discuss the relationship of the inventory management process to other accounting processes.

**The inventory management process is affected by the procedures discussed for the revenue, purchasing, and payroll processes. The acquisition of and payment for inventory are controlled via the purchasing process. The cost of both direct and indirect labor assigned to inventory is controlled through the human resources management process. Finished goods are sold and accounted for as part of the revenue process.**

[LO4] Why is segregation of duties important in the inventory management process? Discuss the key segregation of duties in the inventory management process and possible errors or fraud.

**Segregation of duties is a particularly important control in the inventory management process because of the potential for theft and fraud. Therefore, individuals involved in the inventory management and inventory stores functions should not have access to the inventory records, the cost-accounting records, or the general ledger. When the inventory is highly computerized, there should be proper segregation of duties within the IT department.**

**Inventory management function should be segregated from the cost-accounting function. If the individual responsible for inventory management also has access to the cost-accounting records, production and inventory costs can be manipulated. This may lead to an over-or-understatement of inventory and net income.**

**Inventory stores function should be segregated from the cost-accounting function. If one individual is responsible for both controlling and accounting for inventory, unauthorized shipments can be made or theft of goods can be covered up.**

**Cost-accounting function should be segregated from the general ledger function. If one individual is responsible for the inventory records and also for the general ledger, it is possible for that individual to conceal unauthorized shipments. This can result in the theft of goods, leading to an overstatement of inventory.**

**Responsibility for supervising physical inventory should be separated from inventory management and inventory stores function. If the individual responsible for production management or inventory stores functions is also responsible for the physical inventory, it is possible that inventory shortages can be covered up through the adjustment of the inventory records to the physical inventory, resulting in an overstatement of inventory.**

[LO5] Discuss the inherent risk factors that the auditor needs to consider for the inventory management process.

In examining the inventory management process, the auditor needs to consider the inherent risks factors that may affect the transactions processed by the system and the financial statement accounts affected by those transactions. The auditor should consider industry-related factors and operating and engagement characteristics when assessing the possibility of a material misstatement.

Industry-related factors. A number of industry factors may indicate the presence of material misstatements in inventory. For example, if industry competition is intense, there may be problems with the proper valuation of inventory in terns of lower-of-cost-or-market values. Technology changes in certain industries may also promote material misstatements due to obsolescence.

Engagement and operating characteristics. A number of engagement and operating characteristics are important to the assessment of inherent risk for inventory. First, the type of product sold by the client can increase the potential for defalcation. For example, products that are small and of high value (such as jewelry) are more susceptible to theft than large products are. Second, inventory is often difficult to audit, and its valuation may result in disagreements with the client. Finally, the auditor must be alert to possible related-party transactions for acquiring raw materials and selling finished products. For example, the client may purchase raw materials from a company controlled by the chief executive officer at prices in excess of market value. In such a case, the value of inventory will be overstated, and cash will have been misappropriated from the entity.

Audit research has shown that there is a high risk that inventory contains material misstatements. In fact, some of the most notorious accounting frauds in history have involved inventory manipulations (i.e., Phar-Mor, Centennial Technologies, Inc.).

Prior year misstatements are good indicators of potential misstatements in the current year, thus auditors should carefully consider if misstatements found in the prior years' audit may be present in the current inventory and plan the audit accordingly.

# Part IV: Crossword Puzzle – Chapter 13 Solution [LO ALL]

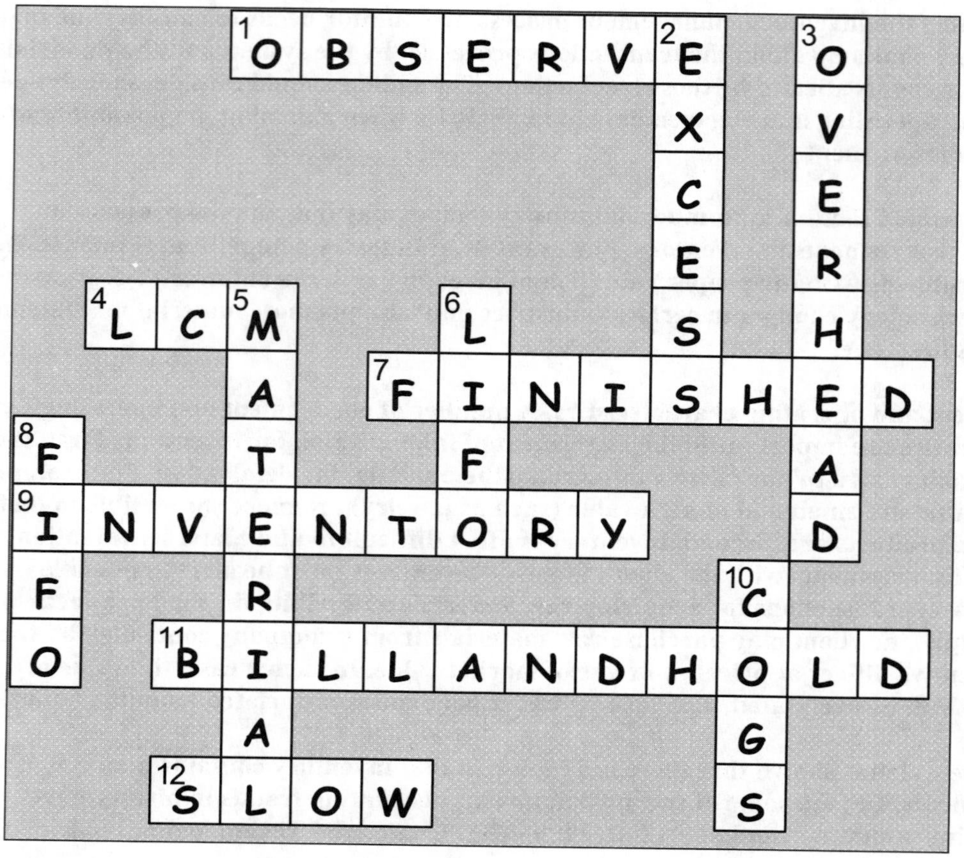

The crossword grid solution:

Across:
1. OBSERVE
4. LCM
7. FINISHED
9. INVENTORY
11. BILLANDHOLD
12. SLOW

Down:
2. EXCESS
3. OVERHEAD
5. MATERR (MATERIAL)
6. LIFO
8. FIFO
10. COGS

**Across**

1   AU 331 requires the auditor to _____ all material inventories in order to establish the existence of the client's inventory.

4   An abbreviation for the valuation rule which applies to ending inventory.

7   These goods are available for sale.

9   For most manufacturing entities, this is a major component of their balance sheet.

11   A transaction where goods are treated as a sale, but the seller holds the goods until the customer needs them (three words).

12   Managers do not want to have ____ moving inventory.

**Down**

2   This condition may result in obsolete inventory.

3   A conversion cost that is not direct labor.

5   A prime cost that is not direct labor.

6   An abbreviation for the inventory flow assumption where the cost of goods sold is based on the most recent inventory purchased.

8   An abbreviation for the inventory flow assumption where the cost of goods sold is based on the oldest inventory purchased.

10   An abbreviation for the account that is debited when inventory is sold.

---

**Chapter 13**
**Townsend Office Supplies and Equipment**

A prior year adjustment was made during the 2005 financial statement audit (the first year ABC audited Townsend) to apply the LCM rule to inventory. Gross profit has decreased in 2007 (from 55% in 2006 to 52% in 2007) and ending inventory has increased significantly in 2007. What inventory assertions are relevant to these issues and what type of substantive procedures should be used to test these assertions based on the information you know about Townsend?

**Substantive tests of transactions should be conducted as dual-purpose tests in conjunction with tests of controls to test the following assertions: (1) occurrence, (2) completeness, (3) authorization, (4) accuracy, (5) cutoff and (6) classification.**

**Accuracy should be established that the detailed records that support the inventory account agree with the general ledger account. Testing of inventory requires obtaining a copy of the compilation of the physical inventory that shows inventory quantities and prices. Additionally, test counts made by the auditor during the physical inventory and tag control information should be traced into the compilation. The auditor should determine if the totals from the compilation for inventory agrees with the general ledger. In addition, any book-to-physical adjustment made by Townsend should be evaluated. Because of the significant increase in ending inventory and the decrease in gross profit, special attention should be given to inventory valuation.**

**To test the occurrence assertion, a sample of inventory purchases should be vouched to receiving report and purchase requisitions. To test the cutoff assertion, the auditor should trace a sample of purchases to the general ledger and the inventory compilation to verify inventory transactions are recorded in the proper period.**

**Tests of details of accounts balances should be conducted to test the following assertions that relate to inventory: (1) existence, (2) rights and obligations, (3) completeness, and (4) valuation and allocation.**

**The inventory is a material account, so the auditor should observe the physical inventory to test the existence assertion. To test valuation and allocation, the auditor should obtain a copy of the inventory compilation and confirm the totals to the general ledger. In addition, trace test counts and tag control information to the inventory compilation should be tested. The mathematical accuracy of extensions and foot the inventory compilation should be checked. Inquiries should be made to management about the possibility of obsolete, slow-moving and excess inventory.**

**Tests of details of disclosures should be conducted to test the following assertions that relate to inventory: (1) occurrence, (2) rights and obligations, (3) completeness, (4) classification and understandability and (5) accuracy and valuation.**

**Accuracy and valuation are important disclosure assertions for inventory. The auditor should read the footnotes and other information to ensure that the information is accurate and properly presented at the appropriate amounts.**

# Auditing Financing/Investing Process: Prepaid Expenses, Intangible Assets, and Property, Plant, and Equipment

## KEY THOUGHT

Knowledge of the entity's business helps the auditor in: Evaluating the reasonableness of estimates, such as valuation of inventories, depreciation, allowances for doubtful accounts, and percentage of completion of long-term contracts [Auditing Standards Board (AU 311.06 (c)].

## CHAPTER SUMMARY

**[LO1] Identify the various types of prepaid expenses, deferred charges, and intangible assets.**

A.  For many entities, accounts receivable and inventory represent the major current assets included in the financial statements. Also included in most financial statements are accounts that are referred to as "other assets." Assets that provide economic benefit for less than a year are classified as current assets and are called prepaid expenses. Examples of prepaid expenses include: (1) prepaid insurance, (2) prepaid rent, and (3) prepaid interest.

B.  Assets providing economic benefit for longer than a year are classified as deferred charges or intangible assets. Examples of deferred charges and intangible assets include: (1) organization costs, (2) debt issuance costs, (3) copyrights, (4) trademarks, (5) trade names, (6) licenses, (7) patents, (8) franchises, (9) goodwill, and (10) computer software development costs.

C.  One major difference between asset accounts such as accounts receivable or inventory and prepaid expenses is the materiality of the account balances. On many engagements, prepaid expenses, deferred charges, and intangible assets are not highly material. As a result, substantive analytical procedures may be used extensively to verify these account balances.

D.  Inherent risk for prepaid expenses would generally be assessed as low because these accounts generally do not involve complex or contentious accounting issues. However, deferred charges and intangible assets may present serious inherent risk considerations. For example, the valuation and estimation of lives of patents, franchises, and goodwill involve considerable judgment and may lead to disagreements between the auditor and client. In such a situation, the auditor may assess the inherent risk as high.

301

E. Prepaid expenses, deferred charges, and intangible asset transactions are typically processed through the purchasing process. As such, the auditor's assessment of control risk for prepaid transactions is based on the effectiveness of the control procedures in the purchasing process. In addition, control procedures for prepaid transactions and estimation and allocation procedures must be evaluated.

**[LO2] Understand the auditor's approach to auditing prepaid insurance and intangible assets.**

### Prepaid Insurance

A. Using prepaid insurance as an example, the auditor can gather sufficient, competent evidence on prepaid insurance by performing substantive analytical procedures. Tests of details of transactions, if performed, are conducted as part of testing the purchasing process. Detailed tests of balances for prepaid insurance accounts are necessary only when misstatements are expected.

B. Because there are generally few transactions in the prepaid insurance account and because the amount reported in the financial statements for prepaid insurance is usually immaterial, substantive analytical procedures are effective for verifying the account balance. The following substantive analytical procedures are commonly used to test prepaid insurance:

1. Comparing the current-year balance in prepaid insurance and insurance expense with the prior year's balances after considering any changes in operations.

2. Computing the ratio of insurance expense to assets or sales and comparing it with the prior year's ratio.

C. Tests of details of balances for prepaid insurance and insurance expense may be necessary when the auditor suspects misstatements based on prior years' audits or when substantive analytical procedures indicate that the account balance may be misstated.
The auditor begins testing the prepaid insurance account balance by obtaining a schedule from the client that contains a detailed analysis of the policies included in the prepaid insurance account. An example of a prepaid insurance schedule for EarthWear is provided in Exhibit 14-1. The accuracy and completeness of this schedule is tested by footing it and tracing the ending balance to the prepaid insurance account in the general ledger. The auditor's work then focuses on testing the existence, completeness, rights and obligations, valuation, and disclosure-classification assertions. The cutoff assertion for prepaid insurance is normally tested as part of the search for unrecorded liabilities, and footnote disclosures are not generally required for prepaid insurance.

### Intangible Assets

A. Intangible assts are assets that provide economic benefit for longer than a year, but lack physical substance. The following list includes examples of five general categories of intangible assets:

1. Marketing – trademark, brand name, and Internet domain names.
2. Customer – customer lists, order backlogs, and customer relationships.
3. Artistic – item protected by copyright.
4. Contract – licenses, franchises and broadcast rights.
5. Technology – patented and unpatented technology.

Accounting standards do not allow companies to record internally generated intangibles as assets on the balance sheet. Instead, intangibles are recorded when the assets are acquired through a purchase or acquisition. Goodwill, another common intangible asset, represents the difference between the acquisition price for a company and the fair values of the identifiable tangible and intangible assets. Some intangible assets are amortized over time, while others like broadcast licenses, trademarks, and goodwill are considered to have indefinite lives and are not amortized. However, all intangibles must be tested for impairment at least annually, as well as on an interim basis if events or changes in circumstances indicate that the asset might be impaired.

B.  **Inherent Risk Assessment – Intangible Assets**. The nature of the judgments involved in accounting for intangible assets raises serious inherent risk considerations. The accounting rules are complex and the transactions are difficult to audit. Both the client and the auditor often use valuation specialist to assist in determining fair values. Asset impairment tests and determining the amount of any impairment loss are complex procedures that involve estimation. Accounting standards require different asset impairment test for different classes of intangible assets (FAS 142). With the judgment and complexity associated with valuation and estimation of intangible assets, the auditor would likely assess the inherent risk as high.

C.  **Control Risk Assessment – Intangible Assets**. Management is responsible for making the fair value measurements and disclosures and therefore must establish an accounting and reporting process for determining the fair value measures, selecting the appropriate valuation methods, identifying and supporting significant assumptions used, and preparing the valuation and disclosures in accordance with GAAP.

Intangible asset transactions and initial valuation are typically processed through the client's business acquisition processes. To rely on control in this process, the auditor needs to understand, document, and test thee operating effectiveness of key controls.

For public companies that are actively acquiring other companies or that engage in large-scale acquisitions, the business acquisition process would be considered a significant process for the audit of internal controls over financial reporting. Additional control activities are required for impairment testing. For example, the client's policies and procedures should properly consider potential events that may trigger impairment
(e.g., significant change in market price or in the way the asset is being used), ensure that all intangible assets are tested for impairment at least annually, and verify that the impairment-testing policies and procedures are in compliance with GAAP.

In assessing control risk, the auditor considers factors such as:

1.  The expertise and experience of those determining the fair value of the asset.

2.  Controls over the process used to determine fair value measurements, including controls over data and segregation of duties between those committing the client to the purchase and those undertaking the valuation.

3.  The extent to which the entity engages or employs valuation specialists.

4.  The significant management assumptions used in determining fair value.

5.  The integrity of change controls and security procedures for valuation models and relevant information systems, including approval processes (AU 328).

D. **Substantive Procedures – Intangible Assets**. While analytical procedures help direct the auditor's attention to situations needing additional investigation (e.g., potential asset impairment), the principal substantive evidence regarding intangible evidence is obtained via tests of details. Substantive analytical procedures generally are not useful in gathering sufficient, appropriate evidence regarding the assertions of primary interest for intangibles (valuation, existence, completeness, rights and obligations, and classification).

Test of details association with valuation and impairment of intangible assets are often necessary because the complexity and degree of judgment increase the risk of material misstatement. Further, some substantive evidence is required for all significant accounts, and, as noted above, substantive analytical procedures are not likely to provide sufficient, appropriate evidence for significant transactions involving intangible assets.

## [LO3] Develop an understanding of the property management process.

A. For most entities, property, plant, and equipment represent a material amount in the financial statements. When the audit is an ongoing engagement, the auditor is able to focus his or her efforts on the current year's activity because the assets acquired in earlier years were subjected to audit procedures at the time of acquisition. For a new engagement, the auditor has to verify the assets that make up the beginning balances in the client's property, plant, and equipment accounts.

B. The size of the entity may affect the auditor's approach for testing property, plant, and equipment. If the client is relatively small with few asset acquisitions during the period, it is generally more cost-effective for the auditor to follow a substantive strategy. Large entities are likely to have formal procedures for budgeting and purchasing capital assets. While routine purchases might be processed through the purchasing process, acquisition or construction of specialized assets may be subject to different requisition and authorization procedures. When the entity has a formal control system over the property management process, the auditor may follow a reliance strategy and test controls.

## [LO4] Identify the types of transactions in the property management process.

A. Four types of property, plant and equipment transactions may occur:

1. Acquisition of capital assets for cash or other nonmonetary considerations.
2. Disposition of capital assets through sale, exchange, retirement, or abandonment.
3. Depreciation of capital assets over their useful economic life.
4. Leasing of capital assets.

B. Figure 14-1 presents a flowchart of EarthWear's accounting system for the property management process.

## [LO5] Identify and evaluate inherent risks for property, plant, and equipment.

A. The assessment of inherent risk for the purchasing process provides a starting point for assessing inherent risk for property, plant and equipment. Three inherent risk factors classified as operating characteristics require consideration by the auditor:

1. Complex accounting issues.
2. Difficult-to-audit transactions.
3. Misstatements detected in prior audits.

**[LO6] Assess control risk for property, plant, and equipment.**

A.  While the auditor generally follows a substantive strategy when auditing the property management process, an understanding of internal control is still required. Major assertions (occurrence and authorization, and completeness), key control procedures and tests of controls that relate directly to the property management process must be considered. Other control procedures related to the property management process were discussed as part of the purchasing process.

**[LO7] Know the appropriate segregation of duties for property, plant, and equipment.**

A.  The existence of adequate segregation of duties for the property management process depends on the volume and significance of the transactions processed. When the number of transactions is limited or efficiency is a consideration, auditors often follow a substantive strategy when auditing property, plant, and equipment.

B.  The key segregation of duties for the property management process and examples of possible errors or fraud that can result from conflicts in duties are summarized below (Table 14-1):

Key Segregation of Duties in the Property Management Process
and Possible Errors or Fraud

| Segregation of Duties | Possible Errors/Fraud Resulting from Conflicts of Duties |
| --- | --- |
| Initiation function should be segregated from the final approval function | If one individual is responsible for initiating a capital asset transaction and also has final approval, fictitious or unauthorized purchases of assets can occur. This can result in purchases of unnecessary assets, assets that do not meet the company's quality control standards, or illegal payments to suppliers or contractors. |
| Property, plant and equipment records function should be segregated from the general ledger function | If one individual is responsible for the property, plant, and equipment records and also for the general ledger functions, that individual can conceal any defalcation that would normally be detected by reconciling subsidiary records with the general ledger control account. |
| Property, plant, and equipment records function should be segregated from the custodial function | If one individual is responsible for the property, plant, and equipment records and also has custodial responsibility for the related assets, tools and equipment can be stolen, and the theft can be concealed by adjustment of the accounting records. |
| If a periodic physical inventory of property, plant and equipment is taken, the individual responsible for the inventory should be independent of the custodial and record-keeping functions | If the individual who is responsible for the periodic physical inventory of property, plant, and equipment is also responsible for the custodial and record-keeping functions, theft of the entity's capital assets can be concealed. |

**[LO8] Identify substantive analytical procedures used to audit property, plant, and equipment.**

A. **Analytical procedures**. The following substantive analytical procedures can be used in the audit of property, plant, and equipment.

1. Compare prior-year balances in property, plant, and equipment and depreciation expense with current-year balances after consideration of any changes in conditions or asset composition.

2. Compute the ratio of depreciation expense to the related property, plant, and equipment accounts and compare to prior years' ratios.

3. Compute the ratio of repairs and maintenance expense to the related property, plant, and equipment accounts and compare to prior years' ratios.

4. Compute the ratio of insurance expense to the related property, plant, and equipment accounts and compare to prior years' ratios.

5. Review capital budgets and compare the amounts spent with amounts budgeted.

**[LO9] Identify tests of details of account balances and disclosures used to audit property, plant, and equipment.**

A. **Tests of details of account balances**. Table 14-2 summarizes the substantive tests for property, plant, and equipment accounts for each assertion relating to transactions and balances. Assertions relating to classes of transactions include: (1) occurrence, (2) completeness, (3) authorization, (4) accuracy, (5) cutoff, and (6) classification. Note that tests of details of transactions are commonly conducted in conjunction with tests of controls as dual-purpose tests. Assertions relating to account balances at period end include: (1) existence, (2) rights and obligations, (3) completeness, and (4) valuation and allocation.

B. **Disclosure issues**. Some important items that may require disclosure as part of the audit of property, plant, and equipment include (Table 14-3):

1. Classes of capital assets and valuation bases.
2. Depreciation methods and useful lives for financial reporting and tax purposes.
3. Nonoperating assets.
4. Construction or purchase commitments.
5. Liens and mortgages.
6. Acquisition or disposal of major operating facilities.
7. Capitalized and other lease arrangements.

Exhibit 14-4 provides an example of an issue that would require disclosure.

**[LO10] Evaluate the audit findings and reach a final conclusion on property, plant, and equipment.**

A. The process for evaluating the audit findings for property, plant, and equipment is the same as was discussed in previous chapters. The auditor aggregates the likely misstatements and compares this amount to the tolerable misstatement. If the likely misstatement is less than the tolerable misstatement, the evidence indicates that the property, plant, and equipment accounts are not materially misstated. However, if the likely misstatement is greater than the tolerable misstatement, the auditor would either require adjustment of the accounts or issue a qualified audit report.

# CHAPTER 14: SELF-ASSESSMENT

## Part I: True or False Questions

[LO1] _____ 1.  Prepaid expenses provide economic benefit for longer than a year.

[LO1] _____ 2.  An example of a prepaid account is prepaid interest.

[LO2] _____ 3.  Inherent risk for prepaid expenses would generally be assessed as low because these accounts do not usually include complex transactions.

[LO3] _____ 4.  Substantive analytical procedures are commonly used to test prepaid accounts.

[LO4] _____ 5.  Disposition of capital assets through sale, exchange, retirement, or abandonment are transactions that occur in the property management process.

[LO6] _____ 6.  If the auditor has detected misstatements in prior audits, the assessment of inherent risk for the property management process will be set higher.

[LO7] _____ 7.  The property, plant, and equipment records function should be segregated from the custodial function.

[LO8] _____ 8.  Substantive analytical procedures should not be used in the audit of property, plant, and equipment.

[LO8] _____ 9.  Reviewing capital budgets and comparing the amounts spent with amounts budgeted is an example of a substantive analytical procedure for auditing prepaid accounts.

[LO9] _____ 10.  Inquiry of client personnel and a review of lease transactions for the same period can provide evidence on proper cutoff for capital leases.

## Part II: Multiple Choice Questions

[LO1]  1.  An example of a deferred charge is:
   a.  Prepaid interest.
   b.  Prepaid insurance.
   c.  Trademarks.
   d.  All of the above.

[LO1]  2.  Prepaid insurance will be amortized over:
   a.  The period of coverage.
   b.  The fiscal period.
   c.  The calendar period.
   d.  None of the above.

[LO2] 3. Substantive procedures are used to test which prepaid assertion(s):
   a. Existence.
   b. Completeness.
   c. Classification.
   d. All of the above.

[LO4] 4. The following transactions may occur in the property, plant and equipment process:
   a. Depreciation of capital assets.
   b. Operating leases.
   c. Retirement of capital assets.
   d. Both a and c.

[LO5] 5. Factors that may increase inherent risk for the property management process include:
   a. Misstatements detected in prior audits.
   b. Complex accounting issues.
   c. Difficult-to-audit transactions.
   d. All of the above.

[LO7] 6. The following transactions may occur in the property, plant and equipment process:
   a. Abandonment of capital assets.
   b. Operating leases.
   c. Capital leases.
   d. Both a and c.

[LO9] 7. Vouching significant additions and dispositions to vendor invoices or other supporting documentation is used to test:
   a. Classification.
   b. Cutoff.
   c. Completeness.
   d. Occurrence.

[LO9] 8. Tracing a sample of purchase requisitions to leading dock reports and to the PP&E records is used to test:
   a. Classification.
   b. Cutoff.
   c. Completeness.
   d. Occurrence.

[LO9] 9. Vouching transactions included in repairs and maintenance for items that should be capitalized is used to test:
   a. Classification.
   b. Cutoff.
   c. Completeness.
   d. Occurrence.

[LO9] 10. Testing depreciation calculations for a sample of capital assets is used to test:
   a. Valuation and allocation.
   b. Completeness.
   c. Occurrence.
   d. Existence.

**Part III: Short Essay Questions**

[LO4] Identify the types of transactions that occur in the property management process.

[LO8] Identify several substantive analytical procedures that can be used in the audit of property, plant and equipment.

[LO9] Identify the type of audit strategy that is routinely used to audit the property management process and the major assertions tested.

# Part IV: Crossword Puzzle – Chapter 14 [LO ALL]

## Across

3. _____ accounting issues associated with some intangible assets may increase inherent risk.
4. This value represents the difference between the acquisition price paid for a company and the fair values of the identifiable tangible and intangible assets.
8. The accounting standard for the impairment or disposal of a long-lived asset.
10. All intangibles must be tested annually for this condition.
11. The process or cycle that includes prepaid expenses and property, plant and equipment transactions.
12. The disposition of a capital asset.

## Down

1. The systematic allocation of the cost of a tangible asset over its estimated useful life.
2. The systematic allocation of the cost of an intangible asset over its estimated useful life.
5. The auditor may examine or confirm property deeds or title documents for proof of _____ .
6. The largest accounting fraud in U.S. history involved improper capitalization of operation expenses as capital assets.
7. This assertion is tested to ensure that major additions of capital assets are physically examined.
9. The abbreviation for property, plant and equipment.

| |
|---|
| **Chapter 14** <br> **Townsend Office Supplies and Equipment** |
| Evaluate Townsend's property, plant, and equipment accounts. Compute the value of the capital assets retired. Using the background and financial information provided for the company, compute several substantive analytical procedures. Discuss the types of tests of transactions and account balances that should be used to audit Townsend's property management process. |

# CHAPTER 14: SELF-ASSESSMENT SOLUTIONS

## Part I: True or False Questions

[LO1] **False** 1.    Prepaid expenses provide economic benefit for longer than a year.

[LO1] **True** 2.    An example of a prepaid account is prepaid interest.

[LO2] **True** 3.    Inherent risk for prepaid expenses would generally be assessed as low because these accounts do not usually include complex transactions.

[LO3] **True** 4.    Substantive analytical procedures are commonly used to test prepaid accounts.

[LO4] **True** 5.    Disposition of capital assets through sale, exchange, retirement, or abandonment are transactions that occur in the property management process.

[LO6] **True** 6.    If the auditor has detected misstatements in prior audits, the assessment of inherent risk for the property management process will be set higher.

[LO7] **True** 7.    The property, plant, and equipment records function should be segregated from the custodial function.

[LO8] **False** 8.    Substantive analytical procedures should not be used in the audit of property, plant, and equipment.

[LO8] **False** 9.    Reviewing capital budgets and comparing the amounts spent with amounts budgeted is an example of a substantive analytical procedure for auditing prepaid accounts.

[LO9] **True** 10.    Inquiry of client personnel and a review of lease transactions for the same period can provide evidence on proper cutoff for capital leases.

## Part II: Multiple Choice Questions

[LO1]  1.  An example of a deferred charge is:
- a.  Prepaid interest.
- b.  Prepaid insurance.
- **c.  Trademarks.**
- d.  All of the above.

[LO1]  2.  Prepaid insurance will be amortized over:
- **a.  The period of coverage.**
- b.  The fiscal period.
- c.  The calendar period.
- d.  None of the above.

[LO2]  3.  Substantive procedures are used to test which prepaid assertion(s):
- a.  Existence.
- b.  Completeness.
- c.  Classification.
- **d.  All of the above.**

[LO4]  4. The following transactions may occur in the property, plant and equipment process:
    a.  Depreciation of capital assets.
    b.  Operating leases.
    c.  Retirement of capital assets.
    **d.  Both a and c.**

[LO5]  5. Factors that may increase inherent risk for the property management process include:
    a.  Misstatements detected in prior audits.
    b.  Complex accounting issues.
    c.  Difficult-to-audit transactions.
    **d.  All of the above.**

[LO7]  6. The following transactions may occur in the property, plant and equipment process:
    a.  Abandonment of capital assets.
    b.  Operating leases.
    c.  Capital leases.
    **d.  Both a and c.**

[LO9]  7. Vouching significant additions and dispositions to vendor invoices or other supporting documentation is used to test:
    a.  Classification.
    b.  Cutoff.
    c.  Completeness.
    **d.  Occurrence.**

[LO9]  8. Tracing a sample of purchase requisitions to leading dock reports and to the PP&E records is used to test:
    a.  Classification.
    b.  Cutoff.
    **c.  Completeness.**
    d.  Occurrence.

[LO9]  9. Vouching transactions included in repairs and maintenance for items that should be capitalized is used to test:
    **a.  Classification.**
    b.  Cutoff.
    c.  Completeness.
    d.  Occurrence.

[LO9] 10. Testing depreciation calculations for a sample of capital assets is used to test:
    **a.  Valuation and allocation.**
    b.  Completeness.
    c.  Occurrence.
    d.  Existence.

**Part III: Short Essay Questions**

---

[LO4] Identify the types of transactions that occur in the property management process.

**There are four types of property, plant, and equipment transaction that may occur. They include:**

1.  **Acquisition of capital assets for cash or other nonmonetary considerations.**

2.  **Disposition of capital assets through sale, exchange, retirement, or abandonment.**

3.  **Depreciation of capital assets over their useful economic life.**

4.  **Leasing of capital assets.**

---

[LO8] Identify several substantive analytical procedures that can be used in the audit of property, plant and equipment.

**The following substantive analytical procedures can be used in the audit of property, plant and equipment:**

1.  **Compare prior-year balances in property, plant, and equipment and depreciation expense with current-year balances after consideration of any changes in conditions or asset composition.**

2.  **Compute the ratio of depreciation expense to the related property, plant, and equipment accounts and compare to prior years' ratios.**

3.  **Compute the ratio of repairs and maintenance expense to the related property, plant, and equipment accounts and compare to prior years' ratios.**

4.  **Compute the ratio of insurance expense to the related property, plant, and equipment accounts and compare to prior years ratios.**

5.  **Review capital budgets and compare the amounts spent with amounts budgeted.**

---

[LO9] Identify the type of audit strategy that is routinely used to audit the property management process and the major assertions tested.

**The auditor routinely follows a substantive strategy when auditing the property management process. Assertions about classes of transactions (substantive tests of transactions) include: (1) occurrence, (2) completeness, (3) authorization, (4) accuracy, (5) cutoff and (6) classification. Assertions about account balances at period end (tests of details of account balances) include: (1) existence, (2) rights and obligations, (3) completeness, and (4) valuation and allocation.**

## Part IV: Crossword Puzzle – Chapter 14 Solution [LO ALL]

```
 1                                        2
 D                                        A
 E                                    3
 P                                    C O M P L E X
 P          4       5       6          O
 R          G O O D W I L L            R
 R              W       O              T
 E              N       R              I
 C              E       L      7       Z
 I              R       D      E       A
 A              S       C      X    8
 A              S       C      X    F A S 1 4 4
 T          9   H       O      I       I
 T          P   H       O      S       I
10                                      O
 I M P A I R M E N T                    O
 O   &   P              E              N
 N   E   P      11      T
 N   E          F I N A N C I N G
                        C
            12
            R E T I R E M E N T
```

### Across

3  _____ accounting issues associated with some intangible assets may increase inherent risk.
4  This value represents the difference between the acquisition price paid for a company and the fair values of the identifiable tangible and intangible assets.
8  The accounting standard for the impairment or disposal of a long-lived asset.
10 All intangibles must be tested annually for this condition.
11 The process or cycle that includes prepaid expenses and property, plant and equipment transactions.
12 The disposition of a capital asset.

### Down

1  The systematic allocation of the cost of a tangible asset over its estimated useful life.
2  The systematic allocation of the cost of an intangible asset over its estimated useful life.
5  The auditor may examine or confirm property deeds or title documents for proof of _____ .
6  The largest accounting fraud in U.S. history involved improper capitalization of operation expenses as capital assets.
7  This assertion is tested to ensure that major additions of capital assets are physically examined.
9  The abbreviation for property, plant and equipment.

**Part V: Townsend Office Supplies and Equipment [LO ALL]**

| Chapter 14 |
| :---: |
| **Townsend Office Supplies and Equipment** |

Evaluate Townsend's property, plant, and equipment accounts. Compute the value of the capital assets retired. Using the background and financial information provided for the company, compute several substantive analytical procedures. Discuss the types of tests of transactions and account balances that should be used to audit Townsend's property management process.

**Substantive Analytical Procedures**
**Net Book Value of Assets**
$3,719 – 1,210 = $2,509 (2007)
$3,547 – 1,120 = $2,427 (2006)

**Capital assets purchased (15 vehicles) $254,000**
Purchases $438 + 254 – X = $610 X = $82

**Capital assets retired (15 vehicles) $82,000**
Retirements $1120 + 172 – 82 = $1210 X = $82

**The return on assets is 13%, which is significantly higher than the industry return on assets of 9%. The computation of ROA is shown below:**
Net income + [Interest expense x (1 – Tax rate)]/average capital assets
{$241 + [117(1 – 0.30)]}/(2509 + 2427)/2 =
241 + 82/(2509 + 2427)/2 =
323/2468 = 13%

**Depreciation expense has increased from 2.99% ($146/4891) in 2006 to 3.29% ($172/5231) in 2007. The new vehicles were purchased on June 30, 2007 and no depreciation was taken on the old vehicles (net zero book value).**
**Estimated increase in 2007 depreciation = $254,000/5 = $50,800/2 = $25,400**
**Actual increase in 2007 depreciation = $172 – 146 = $26,000**

**Depreciation expense/related PP&E**
$172/2509 = 6.86% (2007) and $146/2427 = 6.02% (2007)

**Substantive procedures for tests of transactions and account balances**
**Accuracy of property, plant and equipment should be verified. The auditor should obtain a lead schedule and detailed schedules for additions and dispositions of assets. To test existence, the auditor obtains a listing of all major additions and vouches them to supporting documents such as vendors' invoices. The disposition of the old vehicles should be verified by examining the cash receipt for the sale of the assets. The auditor may examine or confirm the title documents of the vehicles for proof of ownership. In addition, inquiry should be made to management to verify that the company has no capital leases. Because of the limited number of transactions, the auditor will probably test 100 percent of the property, plant, and equipment accounts and transactions.**

# Auditing the Financing/Investing Process: Long-Term Liabilities, Stockholders' Equity, and Income Statement Accounts

## KEY THOUGHT

Equity is defined as "the residual interest in the assets of an entity that remains after deducting its liabilities." Characteristics of equity of business enterprises are briefly discussed under two headings: residual interest, and invested and earned equity [FASB Statement of Financial Account Concepts No. 6, paragraph 212].

## CHAPTER SUMMARY

**[LO1] Understand the types and features of long-term debt.**

A. This chapter introduces the audit of long-term liabilities, stockholders' equity, and income statement accounts. Long-term debt and equity are the major sources of financing for most entities. A substantive audit strategy is normally followed when these financial statement accounts are audited, because although the number of transactions is few, each transaction is usually material.

B. Common types of long-term debt financing include notes, bonds, and mortgages. Long-term debt may have a number of features that can affect the audit procedures used. For example, debt may be convertible into stock, or it may be combined with warrants, options, or rights that can be exchanged for equity. Debt may be callable under certain conditions, or it may require the establishment of a sinking fund to ensure that the debt can be repaid. Debt may be either unsecured or secured by assets of the entity.

C. The approach to the audit of long-term debt varies depending on the frequency of the entity's financing activities. For entities that engage in frequent financing activities, the auditor may follow a reliance strategy under which internal control is formally evaluated and tests of controls are performed in order to set control risk. However, for the vast majority of entities, it is more efficient for the auditor to follow a substantive strategy and perform a detailed audit of long-term debt and the related interest accounts.

**[LO2] Assess control risk for long-term debt.**

A. When a substantive strategy is followed, the auditor needs a sufficient understanding of the entity's internal control system over debt to be able to anticipate the types of misstatements that may occur and thus plan the substantive procedures. Proper segregation of duties is important for ensuring the propriety of long-term debt.

**[LO3] Identify key control activities for long-term debt.**

A. A number of common controls relating to long-term debt should be present. For example, the client should have adequate custodial procedures for any unissued notes or bonds to safeguard against loss from theft. In addition, procedures should provide for periodic inspections by an individual independent of both the custodial and accounting responsibilities for long-term debt.

B. The most common assertions associated with long-term debt include: (1) occurrence and authorization, (2) completeness, (3) valuation, and (4) disclosure classification.

**Occurrence and authorization**. The entity should have controls to ensure that any long-term borrowing is properly initiated by authorized individuals. Entities that engage in recurring borrowing activities should have both general and specific controls. If the client has proper controls for issuing debt, it is generally easy for the auditor to test those transactions for occurrence (validity) and authorization at the end of the period.

**Completeness**. The client should maintain adequate detailed records of long-term debt transactions to ensure that all borrowing and repayments of principal and interest are recorded.

**Valuation**. Note and bond transactions are recorded in the accounting records at their face value plus or minus any premium or discount. Premium or discount should be amortized using the effective interest method to calculate interest expense. Underwriter's fees, legal fees, and accounting fees associated with issuing long-term debt should be recorded as deferred charges and amortized over the life of the debt. The client should have control procedures to ensure that long-term debt is properly valued.

**Disclosure and Classification**. Controls should ensure that notes and bonds are properly classified in the financial statements. The major issue is to properly classify as a short-term liability the portion of long-term debt that is due in the next year.

**[LO4] Know how to conduct substantive audit procedures for long-term debt.**

A. A substantive strategy for auditing long-term debt involves examining any new debt agreements, determining the status of prior debt agreements and confirming balances and other relevant information with outside parties.

B. Substantive analytical procedures are useful in auditing interest expense because of the direct relationship between the stated interest rate and the amount of long-term debt. The auditor can estimate interest expense. The reasonableness of interest expense can be assessed by comparing the estimate to interest expense amount recorded in the general ledger. If the two amounts are not materially different, the auditor can conclude that interest expense is fairly stated. If the estimated amount of interest expense is materially higher than the recorded amount, the auditor might conclude that the client has failed to record a portion of interest expense. If the recorded amount of interest expense is materially higher than the estimated amount, the client may have failed to record debt.

C. Table 15-1 provides examples of tests of transactions and account balances for key long-term debt assertions. The auditor generally begins the audit of long-term debt by obtaining an analysis schedule for notes payable, bonds payable, and accrued interest payable. Exhibit 15-2 presents an example of such a schedule. The most important assertions are tested as follows: Each debt instrument is confirmed with the debtholders and includes a request to verify the amount owed and last date on which interest has been paid. Confirmation of the debt and accrued interest provides evidence on the existence, completeness, and valuation assertions. If the client's debt is guaranteed by another party, a confirmation should be sent to the guarantor to confirm the guarantee. The auditor also examines the due dates for the debt to ensure proper classification between current and long-term liabilities. The auditor examines the debt agreements for any restrictive covenants that require disclosure in the footnotes. Examples of such covenants include restrictions on the payment of dividends or the issuance of additional debt or equity, and the maintenance of certain financial ratios. Below is an example of the disclosure of restrictive covenants (Exhibit 15-3):

> The 7 percent bond agreement contains provisions (1) limiting funded debt, security interests, and other indebtedness, (2) requiring the maintenance of defined working capital and tangible net worth, and (3) imposing restrictions on the payment of cash dividends. The company was in compliance with, or received a waiver regarding, each of the agreements during the year ended 2007. Under the terms of these agreements, $825,000 of retained earnings was available for payment of cash dividends at December 31, 2007.

## [LO5] Understand the types of stockholders' equity transactions.

A. For most entities, stockholders' equity includes common stock, preferred stock, paid-in capital, and retained earnings. The three major types of transactions that occur in stockholders' equity include:

1. **Issuance of stock** includes transactions such as: sale of stock for cash; the exchange of stock for assets, services, or convertible debt; and issuance of stock for stock splits.

2. **Repurchase of stock** includes the reacquisition of stock (treasury stock) and the retirement of stock.

3. **Payment of dividends** includes the payment of cash dividends or issuance of stock dividends.

## [LO6] Assess control risk for stockholders' equity.

A. A substantive strategy is most often used to audit stockholders' equity because the number of transactions is usually small. Although control risk can then be set at the maximum, the auditor must still understand the types of controls that are in place to prevent the misstatement of equity transactions.

B. Many large entities, such as publicly traded companies, use an independent registrar, transfer agent, and dividend-disbursing agent to process and record equity transactions. The registrar is responsible for ensuring that all stock issued complies with the corporate charter and for maintaining the control totals for total shares outstanding. The transfer agent is responsible for preparing stock certificates and maintaining adequate stockholders' records. The dividend-disbursing agent prepares and mails dividend checks to the stockholders of record. When an entity uses an independent registrar, transfer agent, and dividend-disbursing agent, the auditor may be able to obtain sufficient evidence by confirming the relevant information with those parties.

C. If an entity uses its own employees to perform the stock transfer and dividend disbursement functions, the auditor needs to perform more detailed testing of the stock-related records and transactions that occurred during the period. The following assertions, control procedures, and segregation of duties are relevant when client personnel transfer stock and disburse dividends (LO7 and LO8).

### [LO7] Identify key control procedures for stockholders' equity.

A.  The major assertions for stockholders' equity include:

1.  **Occurrence**. Verify that stock and dividend transactions comply with the corporate charter.

2.  **Accuracy**. Verify that all stock and dividend transactions have been properly posted and summarized in the accounting records.

3.  **Authorization**. Verify that stock and dividend transactions have been properly approved.

4.  **Valuation**. Verify that stock and dividend transactions have been properly valued.

### [LO8] Know the appropriate segregation of duties for stockholders' equity.

A.  If the entity has enough personnel, the following segregation of duties should be maintained:

1.  The individuals responsible for issuing, transferring, and canceling stock certificates should not have any accounting responsibilities.

2.  The individual responsible for maintaining the detailed stockholders' records should be independent of the maintenance of the general ledger control accounts.

3.  The individual responsible for maintaining the detailed stockholders' records should not also process cash receipts or disbursements.

4.  Appropriate segregation of duties should be established among the preparation, recording, signing, and mailing of dividend checks.

### [LO9] Know how to conduct substantive audit procedures for capital stock.

A.  The capital-stock accounts include common stock, preferred stock, and paid-in capital. When auditing the capital-stock accounts, the auditor is normally concerned with the occurrence, completeness, valuation, and completeness of disclosures assertions. The auditor begins the audit of capital stock by obtaining a schedule of all activity in the accounts for the current period. The beginning balance is agreed to the prior year's working papers, and the ending balance is agreed to the general ledger. The majority of the auditor's work then focuses on the current-period activity in each account.

B.  Assertions for substantive audit procedures for capital stock include: (1) occurrence and completeness, (2) valuation, and (3) completeness of disclosures.

**Occurrence and completeness**. All valid capital-stock transactions are approved by the board of directors. The auditor can test the occurrence of capital-stock transactions by tracing the transactions recorded in the current year to the board of directors' minutes. When an independent registrar and transfer agent are used by the entity, the auditor confirms the total number of shares outstanding at the end of the period. If the amount of shares listed as outstanding on the confirmation reconciles to the general ledger capital-stock accounts, the auditor has evidence that the total number of shares outstanding at the end of the year is correct. If the entity does not use outside agents, the company will maintain a stock register and/or a stock certificate book. Under these circumstances, the auditor may perform the following tests:

1. Trace the transfer of shares between stockholders to the stock register and/or stock certificate book (accuracy and completeness).

2. Foot the shares outstanding in the stock register and/or stock certificate book and agree them to total shares outstanding in the general ledger capital-stock accounts (completeness).

3. Examine any canceled stock certificates (occurrence).

4. Account for and inspect any unissued stock certificates in the stock certificate book (completeness).

**Valuation**. When capital stock is issued for cash, the assessment of proper valuation is straightforward. The par, or stated, value for the shares issued is assigned to the respective capital-stock account, while the difference between the price and par, or stated, value is allocated to paid-in capital. The auditor can recompute the values assigned to each transaction. The proceeds from the sale of stock are normally traced to the cash receipts records. The valuation issue is more complex when capital stock is issued in exchange for other assets or services, for a merger or acquisition, for convertible securities, or for a stock dividend. To test valuation, the auditor can recompute the stock dividend and trace the entities into the general ledger.

**Completeness of Disclosures**. A number of important disclosures are frequently necessary for stockholders' equity. Examples of stockholders' equity disclosures are shown below (Table 15-2):

1. Number of shares authorized, issued, and outstanding for each class of stock.

2. Call privileges, prices, and dates for preferred stock.

3. Preferred-stock sinking funds.

4. Stock option or purchase plans.

5. Restrictions on retained earnings and dividends.

6. Any completed or pending transactions (such as stock dividends or splits) that may affect stockholders' equity.

The normal sources of this information include the corporate charter, minutes of the board of directors' meetings, and contractual agreements.

## [LO10] Know how to conduct substantive audit procedures for dividends.

A. Generally, all dividends that are declared and paid will be audited because of concerns with violations of corporate bylaws or debt covenants. When the entity uses an independent dividend-disbursing agent, the auditor can confirm the amount disbursed to the agent by the entity. This amount is agreed with the amount authorized by the board of directors. The auditor can recompute the dividend amount by multiplying the number of shares outstanding on the record date by the amount of the per share dividend approved by the board of directors. This amount should agree to the amount disbursed to shareholders and accrued at year-end. If the auditor is concerned about the client's controls over dividend disbursements, he or she may test the payee names and amounts on the individual canceled checks with the stock register or stock certificate book. The auditor also reviews the entity's compliance with any agreements that restrict the payments of dividends.

## [LO11] Know how to conduct substantive audit procedures for retained earnings.

A. Under normal circumstances, retained earnings are affected by the current year's income or loss, as well as dividends paid. Certain accounting standards require that some transactions be included in retained earnings. Prior-period adjustments, correction of errors, valuation accounts for marketable securities and foreign currency translation, and changes in appropriations of retained earnings are examples of such transactions.

B. The auditor begins the audit of retained earnings by obtaining a schedule of the account activity for the period. The beginning balance is agreed to the prior year's working papers and financial statements. Net income or loss can be traced to the income statement. If there are any prior-period adjustments, the auditor must be certain that the transactions satisfy the requirements of the relevant accounting standards. Any new appropriations or changes in existing appropriations should be traced to the contractual agreements that required the appropriations. The auditor must make sure that all necessary disclosures related to retained earnings are made in the footnotes. For example, many debt agreements restrict the amount of retained earnings that is available for payment as dividends.

## [LO12] Know how to assess control risk and conduct substantive audit procedures for income statement accounts.

A. In auditing income statement accounts, the auditor must be satisfied that the revenue and expense accounts are not materially misstated and that they are accounted for in accordance with GAAP. The audit of the revenue and expense accounts depends on the extent of work conducted by the auditor on the entity's control system and balance sheet accounts. For example, the likelihood of material misstatement in the various accounts is a function of the of the entity's controls. The level of control risk established for the different business processes directly affects the extent of testing that the auditor requires to audit the income statement accounts. Auditing the income statement includes consideration of the results of audit work conducted in other parts of the audit and completion of additional substantive procedures on selected income statement accountings, including the following:

1. The results of testing controls for the various business processes.

2. The results of the detailed tests of balance sheet accounts and the related income statement accounts.

3. Performance of substantive analytical procedures on income statement accounts.

4. Detailed tests of selected income statement accounts.

B. If the control risk is set at the maximum, the auditor does not rely on controls but conducts extensive substantive procedures. When a reliance strategy is followed, the auditor conducts tests of controls and substantive tests of transactions to determine if the client's controls are operating effectively. If the controls operate effectively, the auditor may reduce the control risk below the maximum. To understand the effect of a reduced control risk assessment on the audit of the revenue and expense accounts, consider the income statement accounts affected by the revenue and purchasing business processes. For example, a reduced control risk assessment for the revenue process provides evidence that the sales, accounts receivable, allowance for uncollectible accounts, and sales returns and allowances accounts are not materially misstated. Similarly, a reduced control risk assessment for the purchasing process provides evidence that financial statement accounts such as inventory, property, plant and equipment, accounts payable, and most expense accounts are not materially misstated. In other words, the auditor already has reliable evidence on the accounts included in the income statements. The findings for the purchasing process are particularly relevant, since proper controls provide evidence on most of the expense accounts. This allows the auditor to do fewer substantive procedures for these income statement accounts. Examples of income statement accounts audited in conjunction with the balance sheet accounts are shown below (Table 15-3):

| Balance Sheet Accounts Audited | Related Income Statement Accounts Audited |
| --- | --- |
| Accounts receivable<br>Allowance uncollectible accounts | Bad-debt expense |
| Notes receivable<br>Investments<br>Accrued interest receivable | Interest income |
| Property, plant and equipment<br>Accumulated depreciation | Depreciation expense<br>Gain/loss on sales or retirements of assets |
| Prepaid insurance | Insurance expense |
| Long-term debt<br>Accrued interest payable | Interest expense |

C. Substantive analytical procedures can be used extensively to test the revenue and expense accounts. One type of substantive analytical procedure involves comparing the current year's dollar amount for each revenue and expense account with prior year's balances. Any account that deviates from the prior year's by more than a predetermined amount should be investigated. An alternative to this type of substantive analytical procedure involves calculating the ratio of individual expense accounts to net sales and comparing these percentages across years. The auditor can also compare these percentages to industry averages. Individual expense accounts that are judged by the auditor to be out of line are investigated further. While these types of substantive analytical procedures are common, it is important that substantive analytical procedures designed to provide evidence regarding the fairness of revenue or other income statement accounts be conducted at a sufficiently disaggregated level to detect potential misstatements. Even small percentage misstatements in large income statement accounts are often material, thus the need for precise substantive analytical procedures.

D. The auditor may want to examine some income statement accounts further (i.e., sensitive information or unusual transactions). For these accounts, the auditor typically analyzes in detail the transactions included in each account. The auditor verifies the transactions by examining (vouching) the supporting documentation (i.e., legal and audit expense, travel and entertainment, charity expense and accounts containing related-party transactions).

# CHAPTER 15: SELF-ASSESSMENT

## Part I: True or False Questions

[LO1] _____ 1. Notes receivable is a common type of long-term financing.

[LO3] _____ 2. Long-term borrowing should be properly authorized.

[LO3] _____ 3. One major issue associated with long-term debt is the classification of the short-term portion of long-term debt that is due in the next year.

[LO5] _____ 4. For most companies, stockholders' equity includes three accounts: preferred stock, paid-in capital and retained earnings.

[LO5] _____ 5. Three types of transactions usually occur in stockholders' equity: issuance of stock, repurchase of stock and payment of dividends.

[LO5] _____ 6. The repurchase of stock includes the reacquisition of stock (treasury stock), but not the retirement of stock.

[LO6] _____ 7. The registrar is responsible for preparing stock certificates and maintaining adequate stockholders' records.

[LO6] _____ 8. The dividend-disbursing agent prepares and mails dividends checks to the stockholders as of the date of declaration.

[LO11] _____ 9. Substantive analytical procedures can be used extensively to test revenue and expense accounts.

[LO12] ____ 10. Income statement accounts must be accounted for in accordance with GAAP.

## Part II: Multiple Choice Questions

[LO1] 1. Common types of long-term debt financing include:
    a. Notes payable.
    b. Accounts payable.
    c. Bonds payable.
    d. Both a and c.

[LO3] 2. The major assertions related to control procedures over long-term debt include:
    a. Classification.
    b. Occurrence.
    c. Cutoff.
    d. Both a and b.

[LO4] 3. Examining copies of new notes or bond agreements can be used to test:
    a. Rights and obligations.
    b. Authorization.
    c. Occurrence.
    d. Both a and c.

[LO4]  4.  Confirmation of notes or bonds directly with creditors or trustees can be used to test:
    a.  Rights and obligations.
    b.  Existence.
    c.  Completeness.
    d.  Both b and c.

[LO6]  5.  A transfer agent is responsible for:
    a.  Ensuring that all stock issued complies with the corporate charter.
    b.  Preparing stock certificates and maintaining adequate stockholders' records.
    c.  Prepares and mails dividends checks to the stockholders of record.
    d.  None of the above.

[LO9]  6.  An example of a disclosure item for stockholders' equity may include:
    a.  Number of shares authorized, issued and outstanding for each class of stock.
    b.  Stock option or purchase plans.
    c.  Any restrictions on retained earnings and dividends.
    d.  All of the above.

[LO9]  7.  If the entity does not use outside agents, the auditor may perform the following tests:
    a.  Trace the transfers of shares between stockholders to the stock register and/or stock certification book.
    b.  Examine any canceled stock certificates.
    c.  Examine any unissued bonds.
    d.  Both a and b.

[LO9]  8.  Examining canceled stock certificates can be used to test:
    a.  Accuracy.
    b.  Completeness.
    c.  Occurrence.
    d.  Both a and b.

[LO9]  9.  Tracing the transfers of shares between stockholders to the stock register and/or stock certificate book can be used to test:
    a.  Accuracy.
    b.  Completeness.
    c.  Occurrence.
    d.  Both a and b.

[LO9]  10.  To test accuracy and completeness, the auditor should trace the transfers of shares between stockholders to the:
    a.  General ledger capital-stock accounts.
    b.  Unissued stock certificates.
    c.  Stock register and/or stock certificate book.
    d.  None of the above.

# Part III: Short Essay Questions

[LO4] Discuss how an auditor might use substantive analytical procedures to test interest expense.

[LO5 & 8] Discuss the major types of transactions and the appropriate segregation of duties for stockholders' equity.

[LO12] Identify examples of income statement accounts audited in conjunction with the balance sheet accounts.

# Part IV: Crossword Puzzle – Chapter 15 [LO ALL]

## Across

3    A common type of long-term debt.
5    Distributed net income.
7    Net income which has not been distributed (two words).
10   For the vast majority of entities, it is more efficient for the auditor to follow a _____ strategy when auditing long-term debt.
11   The transfer agent is responsible for preparing _____ certificates and maintaining adequate stockholders' records.
12   These types of lease obligations represent a form of long-term debt (not an operating lease).

## Down

1    A liability that is due in five years (two words).
2    Process of obtaining and evaluating direct communication from a third party.
4    Another title for stock registrar (two words).
6    Procedures used to evaluate plausible relationships among financial and nonfinancial data.
8    Assets – Liabilities = _____.
9    Any restrictions for debt agreements (i.e., restrictions on payment of dividends or issuance of additional debt or equity).

**Part V: Townsend Office Supplies and Equipment [LO ALL]**

| Chapter 15 |
| :---: |
| **Townsend Office Supplies and Equipment** |
| Based on the information provided about Townsend, evaluate the covenant restrictions associated with the company's line of credit. Perform substantive analytical procedures to evaluate the restrictions and discuss the implications of the results. Provide an example of the disclosure that would be required for these issues. |

# CHAPTER 15: SELF-ASSESSMENT SOLUTIONS

## Part I: True or False Questions

[LO1] **False** 1. Notes receivable is a common type of long-term financing.

[LO3] **True** 2. Long-term borrowing should be properly authorized.

[LO3] **True** 3. One major issue associated with long-term debt is the classification of the short-term portion of long-term debt that is due in the next year.

[LO5] **False** 4. For most companies, stockholders' equity includes three accounts: preferred stock, paid-in capital and retained earnings.

[LO5] **True** 5. Three types of transactions usually occur in stockholders' equity: issuance of stock, repurchase of stock and payment of dividends.

[LO5] **False** 6. The repurchase of stock includes the reacquisition of stock (treasury stock), but not the retirement of stock.

[LO6] **False** 7. The registrar is responsible for preparing stock certificates and maintaining adequate stockholders' records.

[LO6] **False** 8. The dividend-disbursing agent prepares and mails dividends checks to the stockholders as of the date of declaration.

[LO11] **True** 9. Substantive analytical procedures can be used extensively to test revenue and expense accounts.

[LO12] **True** 10. Income statement accounts must be accounted for in accordance with GAAP.

## Part II: Multiple Choice Questions

[LO1]   1. Common types of long-term debt financing include:
   a. Notes payable.
   b. Accounts payable.
   c. Bonds payable.
   **d. Both a and c.**

[LO3]   2. The major assertions related to control procedures over long-term debt include:
   a. Classification.
   b. Occurrence.
   c. Cutoff.
   **d. Both a and b.**

[LO4]   3. Examining copies of new notes or bond agreements can be used to test:
   a. Rights and obligations.
   b. Authorization.
   c. Occurrence.
   **d. Both a and c.**

[LO4] 4. Confirmation of notes or bonds directly with creditors or trustees can be used to test:
   a. Rights and obligations.
   b. Existence.
   c. Completeness.
   **d. Both b and c.**

[LO6] 5. A transfer agent is responsible for:
   a. Ensuring that all stock issued complies with the corporate charter.
   **b. Preparing stock certificates and maintaining adequate stockholders' records.**
   c. Prepares and mails dividends checks to the stockholders of record.
   d. None of the above.

[LO9] 6. An example of a disclosure item for stockholders' equity may include:
   a. Number of shares authorized, issued and outstanding for each class of stock.
   b. Stock option or purchase plans.
   c. Any restrictions on retained earnings and dividends.
   **d. All of the above.**

[LO9] 7. If the entity does not use outside agents, the auditor may perform the following tests:
   a. Trace the transfers of shares between stockholders to the stock register and/or stock certification book.
   b. Examine any canceled stock certificates.
   c. Examine any unissued bonds.
   **d. Both a and b.**

[LO9] 8. Examining canceled stock certificates can be used to test:
   a. Accuracy.
   b. Completeness.
   **c. Occurrence.**
   d. Both a and b.

[LO9] 9. Tracing the transfers of shares between stockholders to the stock register and/or stock certificate book can be used to test:
   a. Accuracy.
   b. Completeness.
   c. Occurrence.
   **d. Both a and b.**

[LO9] 10. To test accuracy and completeness, the auditor should trace the transfers of shares between stockholders to the:
   a. General ledger capital-stock accounts.
   b. Unissued stock certificates.
   **c. Stock register and/or stock certificate book.**
   d. None of the above.

**Part III: Short Essay Questions**

[LO4] Discuss how an auditor might use substantive analytical procedures to test interest expense.

**Substantive analytical procedures are useful in auditing interest expense because of the direct relationship between the stated interest rate and the amount of long-term debt. The auditor can estimate interest expense. The reasonableness of interest expense can be assessed by comparing the estimate to interest expense amount recorded in the general ledger. If the two amounts are not materially different, the auditor can conclude that interest expense is fairly stated. If the estimated amount of interest expense is materially higher than the recorded amount, the auditor might conclude that the client has failed to record a portion of interest expense. If the recorded amount of interest expense is materially higher than the estimated amount, the client may have failed to record debt.**

[LO5 & 8] Discuss the major types of transactions and the appropriate segregation of duties for stockholders' equity.

**[LO5] For most entities, stockholders' equity includes common stock, preferred stock, paid-in capital, and retained earnings. The three major types of transactions that occur in stockholders' equity include:**

**Issuance of stock. This includes transactions such as sale of stock for cash; the exchange of stock for assets, services, or convertible debt; and issuance of stock for stock splits.**

**Repurchase of stock. This includes the reacquisition of stock (treasury stock) and the retirement of stock.**

**Payment of dividends. This includes the payment of cash dividends or issuance of stock dividends.**

**[LO8] If the entity has enough personnel, the following segregation of duties should be maintained:**

**The individuals responsible for issuing, transferring, and canceling stock certificates should not have any accounting responsibilities.**

**The individual responsible for maintaining the detailed stockholders' records should be independent of the maintenance of the general ledger control accounts.**

**The individual responsible for maintaining the detailed stockholders' records should not also process cash receipts or disbursements.**

**Appropriate segregation of duties should be established among the preparation, recording, signing, and mailing of dividend checks.**

[LO12] Identify examples of income statement accounts audited in conjunction with the balance sheet accounts.

**Income statement accounts are normally audited in the course of auditing the related balance sheet accounts. Examples of income statement accounts audited in conjunction with the balance sheet accounts are shown below [balance sheet accounts (income statement accounts)]:**

**Accounts receivable and allowance for uncollectible accounts (bad-debt expense)**

**Notes receivable, investments and accrued interest receivable (interest income).**

**Property, plant and equipment and accumulated depreciation (depreciation expense and gains/losses on sales or retirements of assets).**

**Prepaid insurance (insurance expense).**

**Long-term debt and accrued interest payable (interest expense).**

The crossword grid:

|   |   |   | ¹L |   |   |   |   |   |   |   |   | ²C |   |   |   | ⁴T |
|---|---|---|---|---|---|---|---|---|---|---|---|---|---|---|---|---|
|   | ³N | O | T | E |   |   |   |   |   |   |   | O |   |   |   | R |
|   |   | N |   |   | ⁵D | I | V | I | D | E | N | D | S |   |   | A |
|   |   | G |   | ⁶A |   |   |   |   |   |   |   | F |   |   |   | N |
|   |   | T |   | N |   |   |   |   |   |   |   | I |   |   |   | S |
|   | ⁷R | E | T | A | I | N | E | ⁸D | E | A | R | N | I | N | G | S |
| ⁹C |   | R |   | L |   |   |   | Q |   |   | M |   |   |   |   | F |
| O |   | M |   | Y | ¹⁰S | U | B | S | T | A | N | T | I | V | E | E |
| V |   |   |   | T |   |   |   | I |   |   | A |   |   |   |   | R |
| E |   |   |   | I |   |   |   | T |   |   | I |   |   |   |   | A |
| N |   |   |   | C |   |   | ¹¹S | Y | T | O | C | K |   |   |   | G |
| ¹²C | A | P | I | T | A | L |   |   |   |   | N |   |   |   |   | E |
| N |   |   |   | L |   |   |   |   |   |   |   |   |   |   |   | N |
| T |   |   |   |   |   |   |   |   |   |   |   |   |   |   |   | T |
| S |   |   |   |   |   |   |   |   |   |   |   |   |   |   |   |   |

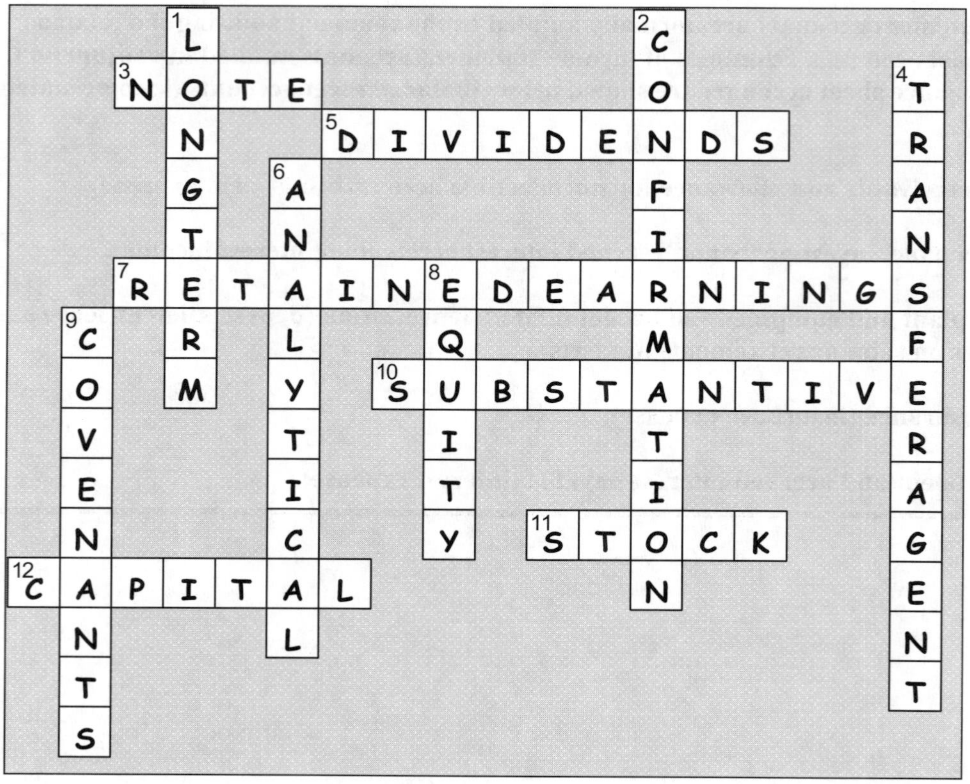

## Across

3    A common type of long-term debt.
5    Distributed net income.
7    Net income which has not been distributed (two words).
10   For the vast majority of entities, it is more efficient for the auditor to follow a _____ strategy when auditing long-term debt.
11   The transfer agent is responsible for preparing _____ certificates and maintaining adequate stockholders' records.
12   These types of lease obligations represent a form of long-term debt (not an operating lease).

## Down

1    A liability that is due in five years (two words).
2    Process of obtaining and evaluating direct communication from a third party.
4    Another title for stock registrar (two words).
6    Procedures used to evaluate plausible relationships among financial and nonfinancial data.
8    Assets – Liabilities = _____ .
9    Any restrictions for debt agreements (i.e., restrictions on payment of dividends or issuance of additional debt or equity).

**Part V: Townsend Office Supplies and Equipment [LO ALL]**

---

**Chapter 15**
**Townsend Office Supplies and Equipment**

Based on the information provided about Townsend, evaluate the covenant restrictions associated with the company's line of credit. Perform substantive analytical procedures to evaluate the restrictions and discuss the implications of the results. Provide an example of the disclosure that would be required for these issues.

**Substantive analytical procedures**
**Industry = 1.57:1 & Current ratio restriction ( ≥ 1.75:1)**
**Actual ratio (CA/CL) = 1592/898 = 1.77:1**

**Industry = 0.98:1 & Current acid ratio restriction ( ≥ 1:1)**
**Actual ratio [(Cash + A/R + MS)/CL] = (210 + 310 + 274)/898 = 0.88:1**

**Industry = 1.15:1 & Current total debt/equity ratio restriction ( ≤ 1.10:1)**
**Actual ratio (TD/Equity) = 2100/1989 = 1.06:1**

**Industry = 0.51:1 & Current short-term debt/equity ratio restriction ( ≤ 0.55:1)**
**Actual ratio (STD/Equity) = 898/1989 = 0.45:1**

**Dividend restriction total debt to equity ( ≤ 1.10:1)**

**Evaluation and implications of substantive analytical procedures. Townsend's current ratio, total debt to equity ratio, and short-term debt to equity ratio are better than the industry averages for 2007, but the company's acid ratio is below the industry average. Inherent risk is increased because of two reasons. First, the acid ratio exceeds the restrictive guideline. The covenant guidelines require that any unpaid balance on the line of credit will be callable and due if two or more of the ratios do not meet the restrictive guidelines. While the acid ratio is the only ratio that exceeds the restrictive guidelines, this increases the inherent risk and potential for material misstatements. Second, the current ratio and the total debt to equity ratio are nearing the ratio restrictions. Again, this increases inherent risk and the potential for material misstatements. Dividends are not restricted because the total debt to equity ratio does not exceed 1.10:1. The company is closely-held; hence, detection risk should be increased and a substantive strategy should be used to conduct tests of transactions and account balances for the related accounts.**

**An example of the required disclosure should include: The company maintained an open line of credit with Eastern Fidelity Bank. The average interest rate for 2007 was 5 percent. The line of credit agreement contains provisions (1) limiting funded debt, security interests, and other indebtedness, (2) requiring the maintenance of defined working capital and tangible net worth, and (3) imposing restrictions on the payment of cash dividends. The company was in compliance with, or received a waiver regarding, each of the provisions during the year ended 2007. Under the terms of these agreements, $1,869 of retained earnings was available for payment of cash dividends at December 31, 2007.**

# Auditing the Financing/Investing Process: Cash and Investments

## KEY THOUGHT

At acquisition, an enterprise shall classify debt and equity securities into one of three categories: held-to-maturity, available-for-sale, or trading. At each reporting date, the appropriateness of the classification shall be reassessed [FASB Statement of Accounting Standards No. 115, paragraph 6].

## CHAPTER SUMMARY

**[LO1] Understand the relationship of the various business processes to cash.**

A.  This chapter covers the audit of cash and investments. These are the last two accounts studied because each of the other business processes interacts with cash. Additionally, the evidence gathered during the audit of other business processes affects the type and amount of evidence required to audit cash.

B.  The line item "cash" reported in the financial statements represents cash and cash equivalents. FASB defines "cash equivalents" as short-term, highly liquid investments that are readily convertible to cash or so near their maturity that there is little risk of change in their value (FAS 95, paragraph 8). Examples of such financial instruments include Treasury bills, commercial paper, and money market funds.

C.  Because virtually all accounting transactions pass through the cash account as part of their "cradle-to-grave" cycle, cash is affected in one way or another by all of the entity's business processes. Figure 16-1 shows the effect each major business process has on the cash account.

D.  Although the main source of cash receipts is the revenue process, other sources of cash include: (1) the sale of property, plant, and equipment and (2) the proceeds from issuing long-term debt or capital stock.

E.  The main sources of disbursements from cash are the purchasing and human resource management processes. Generally, large payments from the purchasing process are for acquisitions of inventory and property, plant and equipment. Payments on long-term debt and repurchase of stock are other types of cash disbursements.

**[LO2] Know the different types of bank accounts.**

A.  Cash management is an important function in all organizations. In order to maximize its cash position, an entity implements procedures for accelerating the collection of cash receipts and properly delaying the payment of cash disbursements. Such procedures allow the entity to earn interest on excess cash or to reduce the cost of cash borrowings.

B.  Management must be concerned with the control and safekeeping of cash. Using different types of bank accounts aids in controlling the entity's cash. The following types of bank accounts are typically used:

1.  **General cash account.** The general cash account is the principal cash account for most entities. For many small entities, the general account may be the only cash account maintained.

2.  **Imprest cash account.** An imprest bank account contains a stipulated amount of money, and the account is used for limited purposes. Imprest accounts are frequently used for disbursing payroll and dividend checks. In the case of payroll, a separate bank account containing a minimum balance is established for disbursing payroll. Disbursements may be by check or direct deposit. Prior to the disbursement of payroll, a check is drawn or a cash transfer is made from the general cash account to the payroll account for the amount of the net payroll. The payroll is then drawn on the imprest account. In other words, the payroll account serves as a clearing account for payments and facilitates the disbursement of cash, while also maintaining adequate control over cash. Use of imprest accounts also minimizes the time required to reconcile the general cash account.

3.  **Branch accounts.** Companies that operate branches in multiple locations may maintain separate accounts at local banks. This allows each branch to pay local expenses and to maintain a banking relationship in the local community. Branch cash accounts can be operated in a number of ways. In some cases, the branch accounts are nothing more than imprest accounts for branch payments in which a minimum balance is maintained. The branch submits periodic cash reports to headquarters, and the branch account receives a check or transfer from the general cash account. In other cases, the branch account functions as a general cash account by recording both cash receipts and cash disbursements. For proper control, the branch should be required to submit periodic cash reports to headquarters, and the entity's management should carefully monitor the cash balances in the branch accounts.

## [LO3] Identify tests of details of transactions used to audit cash.

A.  Because of its residual nature, cash does not have a predictable relationship with other financial statement accounts. As a result, the auditor's use of substantive analytical procedures for auditing cash is limited to comparisons with prior years' cash balances and to budgeted amounts. This limited use of substantive analytical procedures is normally offset by (1) extensive tests of controls and/or substantive tests of transactions for cash receipts and cash disbursements or (2) extensive tests of the entity's bank reconciliations.

B.  Table 16-1 contains examples of substantive tests of transactions for both cash receipts and cash disbursements. By testing both cash receipts and disbursements, the auditor obtains important evidence about the relevant assertions for the cash account. On most audits, the substantive tests of transactions for cash receipts and cash disbursements are conducted together with the tests of controls for the revenue and purchasing processes, respectively.

**[LO4] Identify tests of details of account balances used to audit cash.**

A. The reliability of the client's controls over cash receipts and cash disbursements affects the nature and extent of the auditor's tests of details. A major control that directly affects the audit of cash is the completion of a monthly bank reconciliation by client personnel who are independent of the handling and recording of cash receipts and cash disbursements. Such bank reconciliations ensure that the client's books reflect the same balance as the bank's after reconciling items have been considered. Control can be improved further if an independent party, such as the internal auditor, reviews the bank reconciliation. If the client has good bank reconciliation procedures that are promptly performed, the auditor may be able to reduce the audit work on the ending cash balance.

**[LO5] Know how to audit a bank reconciliation.**

A. Table 16-2 shows that the main source of evidence for the existence, completeness, and valuation assertions is the audit work completed on the bank reconciliation. To audit a cash account, the auditor should obtain the following documents: (1) a copy of the bank reconciliation, (2) a standard form to confirm account balance information with financial institutions (referred to as a standard bank confirmation), and (3) a cutoff bank statement.

　　1. **Bank Reconciliation Working Paper**. Exhibit 16-1 provides an example of a bank reconciliation working paper for EarthWear's general cash account.

　　2. **Standard Bank Confirmation Form**. The auditor generally confirms the account balance information with every bank or financial institution that maintains an account for the client. Exhibit 16-2 contains a completed copy of the confirmation form. Note that this form is also used to obtain information about any loans the client may have with the bank.

　　3. **Cutoff Bank Statement**. A major step in auditing a bank reconciliation is verifying the propriety of the reconciling items such as deposits in transit and outstanding checks. The auditor obtains a cutoff bank statement to test the reconciling items included in the bank reconciliation. The statement normally covers the 7-to-10-day period after the date on which the bank account is reconciled. The auditor obtains this cutoff bank statement by having the client request that the bank send the statement, including canceled checks, directly to the auditor.

B. The auditor uses the following audit procedures to test the bank reconciliation:

　　1. Test the mathematical accuracy of the bank reconciliation working paper and agree the balance per the books to the general ledger.

　　2. Agree the bank balance on the bank reconciliation with the balance shown on the standard bank confirmation.

　　3. Trace the deposits in transit on the bank reconciliation to the cutoff bank statement.

　　4. Compare the outstanding checks on the bank reconciliation working paper with the canceled checks contained in the cutoff bank statement for proper payee, amount, and endorsement.

　　5. Agree any charges included on the bank statement to the bank reconciliation.

　　6. Agree the adjusted book balance to the cash account lead schedule.

**[LO6] Understand fraud-related audit procedures for cash.**

A. If the client does not have adequate control procedures over cash or the auditor suspects that some type of fraud or defalcation involving cash has occurred, it may be necessary to extend the normal cash audit procedures. Although many types of fraud, such as forgery or collusion, are difficult to detect, auditing standards (AU 316) indicate that the auditor has a responsibility to plan and perform the audit to obtain reasonable assurance about whether the financial statements are free of material misstatement, whether caused by error or fraud. Three audit procedures that auditors typically use to detect fraudulent activities in the cash accounts include (1) extended bank reconciliation procedures, (2) proof of cash, and (3) tests for kiting.

   1. **Extended bank reconciliation procedures.** In some instances, the year-end bank reconciliation can be used to cover cash defalcations. This is usually accomplished by manipulating the reconciling items in the bank reconciliation. Thus, the typical approach to searching for possible fraud is to extend the bank reconciliation procedures to examine the disposition of the reconciling items included on the prior months' reconciliations and the reconciling items included in the current bank reconciliation.

   2. **Proof of cash.** A proof of cash is used to reconcile the cash receipts and disbursements recorded on the client's books with the cash deposited into and disbursed from the client's bank account for a specific time period. The primary purposes of the proof of cash are (a) to ensure that all cash receipts recorded in the client's cash receipts journal were deposited in the client's bank account, (b) to ensure that all cash disbursements recorded in the client's cash disbursements journal have cleared the client's bank account, and (c) to ensure that no bank transactions have been omitted from the client's accounting records. Note that a proof of cash will not detect a theft of cash when the cash was stolen before being recorded in the client's books. If the auditor suspects that cash was stolen before being recorded in the client's books, the audit procedures discussed under the completeness assertion for cash receipt transactions in the revenue process should be performed. Exhibit 16-4 provides an example of the proof of cash.

   3. **Tests for kiting.** When cash has been stolen by an employee, it is possible to cover the cash shortage by following a practice known as kiting. This involves an employee covering the cash shortage by transferring money from one bank account to another and recording the transactions improperly on the client's books. Concealing the cash shortage can be accomplished by preparing a check on one account before year-end but not recording it as a cash disbursement in the account until the next period. The check is deposited in a second account before year-end and recorded as a cash receipt in the current period. The deposit must occur close enough to year-end that it will not clear the first bank account before the end of the year. One approach that auditors commonly use to test for kiting is the preparation of an interbank transfer schedule (see Exhibit 16-5). In some instances, such a schedule is used even though control procedures are adequate and no fraud is suspected. When a client maintains many cash accounts, cash transfers may be inadvertently mishandled. The use of an interbank transfer schedule provides the auditor with evidence on the proper cutoff for cash transactions.

B. **Imprest Accounts.** The audit of any imprest cash account such as payroll or a branch account follows the same basic audit steps discussed under the audit of the general cash account. The auditor obtains a bank reconciliation, along with a standard bank confirmation and a cutoff bank statement. However, the audit testing is less extensive for two reasons. First, the imprest balance in the account is generally not material. Second, the types of disbursements from the account are homogeneous. The checks are for similar types of transactions and for relatively small amounts.

C. **Petty Cash Funds**. Most entities maintain a petty cash fund for paying certain types of expenses or transactions. Although the balance in the fund is not material, there is a potential for defalcation because a client's employee may be able to process numerous fraudulent transactions through the fund over the course of a year. Auditors seldom perform substantive procedures on the petty cash fund, except when fraud is suspected. The auditor may document the controls over the petty cash fund, especially for smaller clients. A petty cash fund should be maintained on an imprest basis by an independent custodian. It is preferable for the custodian not to be involved in any other cash functions. When the petty cash custodian does have other cash-related functions to perform, another supervisory person, such as the controller, should review the petty cash activity. Prenumbered petty cash vouchers should be used for withdrawing cash from the fund, and a limit should be placed on the size of reimbursements made from petty cash. The auditor may select a sample of petty cash reimbursements and examine the propriety of the items paid for by the fund. The auditor tests the balance in the petty cash fund by counting it. When the count is conducted, the total of cash in the fund plus the vouchers should equal the imprest balance. This count may be done at an interim date or at year-end.

D. The auditor must consider a number of important financial statement disclosures when auditing cash. Some of the more common disclosure issues for cash are shown below (Table 16-3):

1. Accounting policy for defining cash and cash equivalents.

2. Any restrictions on cash such as a sinking fund requirement for funds allocated by the entity's board of directors for special purposes.

3. Contractual obligations to maintain compensating balances.

4. Cash balances restricted by foreign exchange controls.

5. Letters of credit.

The auditor's review of the minutes of board of directors' meetings, line-of-credit arrangements, loan agreements, and similar documents is the primary source of the information for the financial statement disclosures. In addition, the auditor typically confirms items such as compensating balances required under a bank line of credit. Exhibit 16-6 illustrates a letter for confirmation of compensating balances, while Exhibit 16-7 presents an example of footnote disclosures for compensating balances.

## [LO7] Understand why clients invest in securities of other entities.

A. Entities frequently invest in securities of other entities. Such investments might include equity securities such as common and preferred stock, debt securities such as notes and bonds, and hybrid securities such as convertible bonds and stocks. The accounting for such instruments is affected by factors such as the percentage of the other entity owned, the degree of influence exercised over the entity, the classification of the investment as a current or noncurrent asset, and myriad other factors (FAS No. 115).

B. The auditor approach to the audit of investments varies depending on the size of the investment and the amount of investment activity. For an entity that has a large investment portfolio, the auditor is likely to follow a reliance strategy in which internal control is formally evaluated and tests of controls are performed in order to set the control risk below the maximum. For the vast majority of entities, it is more efficient for the auditor to follow a substantive strategy and perform a detailed audit of the investment securities at year-end.

**[LO8] Identify key controls for investments.**

A. General types of control procedures should be present to minimize the likelihood of a material misstatement. Even when a substantive strategy is followed, the auditor must reasonably understand control over investments in order to anticipate the types of misstatements that may occur and plan the substantive procedures. The main assertions that concern the auditor are occurrence, authorization, completeness, accuracy, and classification.

B. Some important accuracy and classification issues are related to investment securities. FAS No. 115 addresses accounting and reporting for investments in equity securities that have readily determinable fair values and for all investments in debt securities. The standard requires that those investments be classified in three categories and accounted for as held-to-maturity securities, trading securities, and available-for-sale securities.

**Held to maturity securities**. Debt securities that the entity has the positive intent and ability to hold to maturity are classified as held-to-maturity securities and reported at amortized cost.

**Trading securities**. Debt and equity securities that are bought and held principally for the purpose of selling them in the near term are classified as trading securities and reported at fair value, with unrealized gains and losses included in earnings.

**Available-for-sale securities.** Debt or equity securities not classified as either held-to-maturity or trading securities are classified as available-for-sale securities and are reported at fair value, with unrealized gains and losses excluded from earnings and reported in a separate component of shareholders' equity.

The client's control should ensure that securities are properly classified and that appropriate prices are used to value investments for financial statements.

C. One final issue related to the control risk for investments is that the client should have adequate custodial procedures to safeguard against theft. When securities are held by the client, they should be stored in a safe or safe-deposit box. Procedures should provide for periodic inspections by an individual independent of both the custodial and accounting responsibilities for securities. If an independent custodian such as a broker maintains securities, the client needs to establish procedures for authorizing the transfer of securities. One approach would require dual authorization by appropriate management personnel.

**[LO9] Know the appropriate segregation of duties for investments.**

A. Only entities that engage in a significant number of investment activities are likely to have adequate segregation of duties. Some key segregation of duties for investments and examples of possible errors or fraud that can result from conflicts in duties are shown below (Table 16-4):

Key Segregation of Duties for Investments and Possible Errors or Fraud

| Segregation of Duties | Possible Errors/Fraud Resulting from Conflicts of Duties |
| --- | --- |
| Initiation function should be segregated from the final approval function | If one individual is responsible for both the initiating and approving of securities transactions, fictitious transactions can be made or securities can be stolen. |
| Valuation-monitoring function should be segregated from the acquisition function | If one individual is responsible for both acquiring and monitoring the investments, securities values can be improperly recorded or not reported to management. |
| Responsibility for maintaining the securities ledger should be separate from that of making entries in the general ledger | If one individual is responsible for both the securities ledger and the general ledger entries, that individual can conceal any defalcation that would normally be detected by reconciliation of subsidiary records with general ledger control accounts. |
| Responsibility for custody of the securities should be separate from that of accounting for the securities | If one individual has access both to securities and to the supporting accounting records, a theft of the securities can be concealed. |

**[LO10] Identify tests of details of account balances used to audit investments.**

A. It is generally more efficient to follow a substantive strategy for auditing investments. When the control risk is set at the maximum, the auditor conducts extensive substantive procedures to reach the planned level of detection risk. Substantive analytical procedures such as the following can be used to test the overall reasonableness of investment:

1. Comparison of the balances in the current year's investment accounts with prior years' balances after consideration of the effects of current-year operating and financing activities on cash and investments.

2. Comparison of current-year interest and dividend income with the reported income for prior years and with the expected return on investments.

B. Auditing standards (AU 332) provide guidance concerning substantive auditing procedures the auditor can perform when gathering evidential matter related to assertions for investments. Table 16-5 summarizes the tests of the investment account balance and presentation and disclosure. Assertions about account balances at the period end for investments include: (1) existence, (2) rights and obligations, (3) completeness, and (4) valuation and allocation. Assertions about presentation and disclosure for investments include: (1) occurrence, rights and obligations, (2) completeness, (3) classification and understandability, (4) accuracy and valuation.

**Existence.** Auditing standards state that the auditor should perform one or more of the following audit procedures when gathering evidence for existence:

1. Physical examination.
2. Confirmation with the issuer.
3. Confirmation with the custodian.
4. Confirmation of unsettled transactions with the broker-dealer.
5. Confirmation with the counterparty.
6. Reading executed partnership or similar agreements.

If the client maintains custody of the securities, the auditor normally examines the securities. When the securities are held by an issuer or a custodian, such as a broker or investment adviser, the auditor gathers sufficient, competent evidence for the existence assertion by confirming the existence of the securities. The information contained in the confirmation needs to be reconciled with the client's investment records.

**Valuation and allocation.** The auditor should verify the purchase price of the debt and the effective interest rate should be used to recognize the interest income, which the auditor can recompute. The fair value of most equity securities is available from securities exchanges registered with the SEC or on the over-the-counter market. The auditor must determine if there has been any permanent decline in the value of an investment security. The following factors are cited as indicating other-than-temporary impairment of the investment:

1. Fair value is significantly below cost.

2. The decline in fair value is attributable to specific adverse conditions affecting a particular investment.

3. The decline in fair value is attributable to specific conditions, such as conditions in an industry or in a geographic area.

4. Management does not possess both the intent and the ability to hold the investment long enough to allow for any anticipated recovery in fair value.

5. The decline in fair value has existed for an extended period.

6. A debt security has been downgraded by a rating agency.

7. The financial condition of the issuer has deteriorated.

8. Dividends have been reduced or eliminated, or scheduled interest payments on debt securities have not been made.

If the investment value is determined to be permanently impaired, the security should be written down and a new carrying amount established. The auditor should examine the sale of any security to ensure that proper values were used to record the sale and any realized gain or loss.

C. The auditor must also consider disclosure issues for investments. Two issues are important when the auditor examines the proper classification of investments. First, marketable securities need to be properly classified as held-to-maturity, trading, and available-for-sale because both the balance sheet and income statement are affected by misclassification. Second, the financial statement classification requires that all trading securities be reported as current assets. Held-to-maturity securities and individual available-for-sale securities should be classified as current or noncurrent assets based on whether management expects to convert them to cash within the next 12 months. If the security is expected to be converted to cash within 12 months, it should be classified as a current asset. The auditor should ask management about its plans for disposing of securities.

D. Auditing standards also guide auditors in evaluating management's intent and the entity's ability to hold a debt security to maturity. The auditor should examine evidence such as written and approved records of investment strategies, records of investment activities, instructions to portfolio managers, and minutes of meetings of the board of directors or the investment committee. In evaluating an entity's ability to hold a debt security to maturity, the auditor should consider factors such as the entity's financial position, working capital needs, operating results, debt agreements, guarantees, and other relevant contractual obligations, as well as laws and regulations. The auditor should also consider operating and cash flow projections or forecasts when considering the entity's ability to hold the debt security to maturity.

E. FAS No. 115 requires specific disclosures for securities. For example, the aggregate fair value and gross unrealized holding gains or losses on securities should be presented for securities classified as available-for-sale. Most of the information necessary for such disclosures is developed as the other assertions are being tested. In addition, the amount of any securities pledged as collateral should be disclosed. Asking management and reviewing board of directors' minutes, loan agreements, and other documents would be the auditor's sources of such information.

# CHAPTER 16: SELF-ASSESSMENT

## Part I: True or False Questions

[LO1] _____ 1. The cash account is affected by all of the entity's business processes.

[LO2] _____ 2. The general cash account is the principal account used to disburse payroll.

[LO2] _____ 3. An imprest cash account is used for specific purposes.

[LO3] _____ 4. The auditor's use of analytical procedures for auditing cash is limited.

[LO4] _____ 5. A major control that directly affects the audit of cash is the bank reconciliation prepared by the auditor.

[LO5] _____ 6. A cutoff bank statement is used to verify the propriety of the reconciling items shown on the bank reconciliation.

[LO6] _____ 7. Kiting is an audit procedure used to test the accuracy of the cash receipts.

[LO8] _____ 8. FAS 115 provides detailed guidance on how to account for cash and cash equivalents.

[LO9] _____ 9. It is generally more efficient to follow a substantive strategy for auditing investments.

[LO10] _____ 10. If the client maintains custody of its investments, the auditor normally examines the securities.

## Part II: Multiple Choice Questions

[LO1] 1. FAS 95 defines:
    a. Held-to-maturity investments.
    b. Available-for-sale investments.
    c. Cash equivalents.
    d. None of the above.

[LO1] 2. The cash account is affected by the:
    a. Revenue cycle.
    b. Financing cycle.
    c. Purchasing cycle.
    d. All of the above.

[LO3] 3. The auditor can use the following substantive analytical procedures to audit cash:
    a. Comparing the entity's cash balances to industry standards.
    b. Extensive tests of the entity's bank reconciliations.
    c. Comparing the ratio of cash to inventory.
    d. All of the above.

[LO3]　4.　Tracing a sample of canceled checks to the cash disbursements journal is used to test:
a. Accuracy.
b. Existence.
c. Completeness.
d. Both b and c.

[LO3]　5.　Comparing the dates for a sample of checks with the dates the checks cleared the bank is used to test:
a. Existence.
b. Cutoff.
c. Accuracy.
d. None of the above.

[LO6]　6.　The auditor typically uses the following procedures to detect fraud in the cash accounts:
a. Extended bank reconciliation procedures.
b. Tests for kiting.
c. Inquiries of management.
d. Both a and b.

[LO8]　7.　Investments should be classified in the following three categories:
a. Held-to-maturity, high-risk, and available-for-sale securities.
b. Held-to-maturity, high-risk, and stock securities.
c. Held-to-maturity, trading securities, and available-for-sale securities.
d. Held-to-maturity, trading securities, and stock securities.

[LO10]　8.　Auditing standards state that the auditor should perform one or more of the following audit procedures when gathering evidence for existence of investments:
a. Confirmation with the issuer.
b. Confirmation with the counterparty.
c. Confirmation with the custodian.
d. All of the above.

[LO10]　9.　Examining brokers' advices for a sample of securities purchased during the year is used to test:
a. Accuracy.
b. Rights and obligations.
c. Valuation and allocation.
d. Both a and b.

[LO10] 10.　Determining that all disclosures required by FAS 115 have been made for investments is used to test:
a. Completeness.
b. Valuation and allocation.
c. Accuracy and valuation.
d. None of the above.

## Part III: Short Essay Questions

[LO6] Identify and discuss the audit procedures typically used to detect fraudulent activities in the cash accounts.

[LO8] Identify and discuss the criteria that should be used to classify investment securities.

[LO10] Discuss the factors that must be considered to determine if a permanent decline in the value of an investment security has occurred.

## Part IV: Crossword Puzzle – Chapter 16 [LO ALL]

### Across

3   A major control that directly affects the audit of cash is the completion of a monthly _____ reconciliation.
5   An account used for paying minor expenses (two words)
6   This fraudulent act occurs when an employee covers a cash shortage by transferring money from one bank account to another.
10  A three-word phrase that means start to finish for transactions passing through the cash account.
11  The accounting standard for "Accounting for Certain Investments in Debt and Equity Securities."
12  Debt and equity trading securities are reported at _____ _____ and unrealized gains and losses are included in earnings (two words).

### Down

1   This fraudulent act occurs when an employee who has access to both the cash receipts and the accounts receivable records steals cash and manipulates the accounting records to hide the misstatement.
2   The most liquid asset on the balance sheet.
4   The accounting standard for the "Statement of Cash Flows."
7   A bank account that contains a stipulated amount of money used for limited purposes.
8   Reliability of the client's _____ controls over cash is important because of the high volume activity in the account.
9   A _____ bank statement is used to test the reconciling items included in the bank reconciliation.

| **Chapter 16** |
|:---:|
| **Townsend Office Supplies and Equipment** |
| Discuss the audit procedures that should be used to test Townsend's bank reconciliation. |

# CHAPTER 16: SELF-ASSESSMENT SOLUTIONS

## Part I: True or False Questions

[LO1] **True** 1.  The cash account is affected by all of the entity's business processes.

[LO2] **False** 2.  The general cash account is the principal account used to disburse payroll.

[LO2] **True** 3.  An imprest cash account is used for specific purposes.

[LO3] **True** 4.  The auditor's use of analytical procedures for auditing cash is limited.

[LO4] **False** 5.  A major control that directly affects the audit of cash is the bank reconciliation prepared by the auditor.

[LO5] **True** 6.  A cutoff bank statement is used to verify the propriety of the reconciling items shown on the bank reconciliation.

[LO6] **False** 7.  Kiting is an audit procedure used to test the accuracy of the cash receipts.

[LO8] **False** 8.  FAS No. 115 provides detailed guidance on how to account for cash and cash equivalents.

[LO9] **True** 9.  It is generally more efficient to follow a substantive strategy for auditing investments.

[LO10] **True** 10.  If the client maintains custody of its investments, the auditor normally examines the securities.

## Part II: Multiple Choice Questions

[LO1]  1.  FAS 95 defines:
    a.  Held-to-maturity investments.
    b.  Available-for-sale investments.
    **c.  Cash equivalents.**
    d.  None of the above.

[LO1]  2.  The cash account is affected by the:
    a.  Revenue cycle.
    b.  Financing cycle.
    c.  Purchasing cycle.
    **d.  All of the above.**

[LO3]  3.  The auditor can use the following substantive analytical procedures to audit cash:
    a.  Comparing the entity's cash balances to industry standards.
    **b.  Extensive tests of the entity's bank reconciliations.**
    c.  Comparing the ratio of cash to inventory.
    d.  All of the above.

[LO3] 4. Tracing a sample of canceled checks to the cash disbursements journal is used to test:
   a. Accuracy.
   b. Existence.
   **c. Completeness.**
   d. Both b and c.

[LO3] 5. Comparing the dates for a sample of checks with the dates the checks cleared the bank is used to test:
   a. Existence.
   **b. Cutoff.**
   c. Accuracy.
   d. None of the above.

[LO6] 6. The auditor typically uses the following procedures to detect fraud in the cash accounts:
   a. Extended bank reconciliation procedures.
   b. Tests for kiting.
   c. Inquiries of management.
   **d. Both a and b.**

[LO8] 7. Investments should be classified in the following three categories:
   a. Held-to-maturity, high-risk, and available-for-sale securities.
   b. Held-to-maturity, high-risk, and stock securities.
   **c. Held-to-maturity, trading securities, and available-for-sale securities.**
   d. Held-to-maturity, trading securities, and stock securities.

[LO10] 8. Auditing standards state that the auditor should perform one or more of the following audit procedures when gathering evidence for existence of investments:
   a. Confirmation with the issuer.
   b. Confirmation with the counterparty.
   c. Confirmation with the custodian.
   **d. All of the above.**

[LO10] 9. Examining brokers' advices for a sample of securities purchased during the year is used to test:
   a. Accuracy.
   **b. Rights and obligations.**
   c. Valuation and allocation.
   d. Both a and b.

[LO10] 10. Determining that all disclosures required by FAS 115 have been made for investments is used to test:
   **a. Completeness.**
   b. Valuation and allocation.
   c. Accuracy and valuation.
   d. None of the above.

## Part III: Short Essay Questions

[LO6] Identify and discuss the audit procedures typically used to detect fraudulent activities in the cash accounts.

**The auditor typically uses three audit procedures to detect fraudulent activities in the cash accounts including (1) extended bank reconciliation procedures, (2) proof of cash, and (3) tests for kiting.**

**Extended bank reconciliation procedures. In some instances, the year-end bank reconciliation can be used to cover cash defalcations. This is usually accomplished by manipulating the reconciling items in the bank reconciliation. Thus, the typical approach to searching for possible fraud is to extend the bank reconciliation procedures to examine the disposition of the reconciling items included on the prior months' reconciliations and the reconciling items included in the current bank reconciliation.**

**Proof of cash. A proof of cash is used to reconcile the cash receipts and disbursements recorded on the client's books with the cash deposited into and disbursed from the client's bank account for a specific time period. The primary purposes of the proof of cash are (1) to ensure that all cash receipts recorded in the client's cash receipts journal were deposited in the client's bank account, (2) to ensure that all cash disbursements recorded in the client's cash disbursements journal have cleared the client's bank account, and (3) to ensure that no bank transactions have been omitted from the client's accounting records. Note that a proof of cash will not detect a theft of cash when the cash was stolen before being recorded in the client's books. If the auditor suspects that cash was stolen before being recorded in the client's books, the audit procedures discussed under the completeness assertion for cash receipt transactions in the revenue process should be performed.**

**Tests for kiting. When cash has been stolen by an employee, it is possible to cover the cash shortage by following a practice known as kiting. This involves an employee covering the cash shortage by transferring money from one bank account to another and recording the transactions improperly on the client's books. Concealing the cash shortage can be accomplished by preparing a check on one account before year-end but not recording it as a cash disbursement in the account until the next period. The check is deposited in a second account before year-end and recorded as a cash receipt in the current period. The deposit must occur close enough to year-end that it will not clear the first bank account before the end of the year. One approach that auditors commonly use to test for kiting is the preparation of an interbank transfer schedule (see Exhibit 16-4). In some instances, such a schedule is used even though control procedures are adequate and no fraud is suspected. When a client maintains many cash accounts, cash transfers may be inadvertently mishandled. The use of an interbank transfer schedule provides the auditor with evidence on the proper cutoff for cash transactions.**

[LO8] Identify and discuss the criteria that should be used to classify investment securities.

Some important accuracy and classification issues are related to investment securities. FAS No. 115 addresses accounting and reporting for investments in equity securities that have readily determinable fair values and for all investments in debt securities. The standard requires that those investments be classified in three categories and accounted for as (1) held-to-maturity securities, (2) trading securities, and (3) available-for-sale securities.

Held to maturity securities. Debt securities that the entity has the positive intent and ability to hold to maturity are classified as held-to-maturity securities and reported at amortized cost.

Trading securities. Debt and equity securities that are bought and held principally for the purpose of selling them in the near term are classified as trading securities and reported at fair value, with unrealized gains and losses included in earnings.

Available-for-sale securities. Debt or equity securities not classified as either held-to-maturity or trading securities are classified as available-for-sale securities and are reported at fair value, with unrealized gains and losses excluded from earnings and reported in a separate component of shareholders' equity.

The client's control should ensure that securities are properly classified and that appropriate prices are used to value investments for financial statements.

---

[LO10] Discuss the factors that must be considered to determine if a permanent decline in the value of an investment security has occurred.

The auditor must determine if there has been any permanent decline in the value of an investment security. Auditing standards provide guidance for determining whether a decline in value below amortized cost is other than temporary. The following factors are citied as indicating other-than-temporary impairments:
1. Fair value is significantly below cost.
2. The decline in fair value is attributable to specific adverse conditions affecting a particular investment.
3. The decline in fair value is attributable to specific conditions, such as conditions in an industry or in a geographic areas.
4. Management does not possess both the intent and the ability to hold the investment long enough to allow for any anticipated recovery in fair value.
5. The decline in fair value has existed for an extended period.
6. A debt security has been downgraded by a rating agency.
7. The financial condition of the issuer has deteriorated.
8. Dividends have been reduced or eliminated, or scheduled interest payments on debt securities have not been made.

If the investment value is determined to be permanently impaired, the security should be written down and a new carrying amount established. In addition, the auditor should examine the sale of any security to ensure that proper values were used to record the sale and any realized gain or loss.

# Part IV: Crossword Puzzle – Chapter 16 Solution [LO ALL]

```
                    ¹L                          ²C
               ³B  A  N  K                       A
                    P               ⁴F           S
                   ⁵P  E  T  T  Y  C  A  S  H
                    I               S           ⁸G
           ⁶K  ⁷I  T  I  N  G       9           E
               M        G       ⁹C  5           E
               P                 U               N
              ¹⁰C  R  A  D  L  E  T  O  G  R  A  V  E
               E                 O               R
             ¹¹F  A  S  1  1  5  F               A
               T              ¹²F  A  I  R  V  A  L  U  E
```

## Across

3  A major control that directly affects the audit of cash is the completion of a monthly ____ reconciliation.
5  An account used for paying minor expenses (two words)
6  This fraudulent act occurs when an employee covers a cash shortage by transferring money from one bank account to another.
10  A three-word phrase that means start to finish for transactions passing through the cash account.
11  The accounting standard for "Accounting for Certain Investments in Debt and Equity Securities."
12  Debt and equity trading securities are reported at ____ _____ and unrealized gains and losses are included in earnings (two words).

## Down

1  This fraudulent act occurs when an employee who has access to both the cash receipts and the accounts receivable records steals cash and manipulates the accounting records to hide the misstatement.
2  The most liquid asset on the balance sheet.
4  The accounting standard for the "Statement of Cash Flows."
7  A bank account that contains a stipulated amount of money used for limited purposes.
8  Reliability of the client's _____ controls over cash is important because of the high volume activity in the account.
9  A _____ bank statement is used to test the reconciling items included in the bank reconciliation.

### Chapter 16
### Townsend Office Supplies and Equipment

Discuss the audit procedures that should be used to test Townsend's bank reconciliation.

A major control that directly affects the audit of cash is the completion of a monthly bank reconciliation by client personnel who are independent of the handling and recording of cash receipts and cash disbursements. Control can be improved further if an independent party, such as the internal auditor, reviews the bank reconciliation. If the client has good bank reconciliation procedures that are promptly performed, the auditor may be able to reduce the auditor work on the ending cash balance. The auditor uses the following procedures to test the bank reconciliation:

1. Test the mathematical accuracy of the bank reconciliation working paper and agree the balance per the books to the general ledger. The working paper should be footed and the balance per the books should be agreed to the general ledger.

2. Agree the bank balance on the bank reconciliation with the balance shown on the standard bank confirmation.

3. Trace the deposits in transit on the bank reconciliation to the cutoff bank statement. Any deposit in transit shown on the bank reconciliation should be listed as a deposit shortly after the end of the period and deposits in transit should be traced to the cutoff bank statement.

4. Compare the outstanding checks on the bank reconciliation working paper with the canceled checks contained in the cutoff bank statement for proper payee, amount, and endorsement. The auditor should ensure that no checks dated prior to the end of the year are included with the cutoff bank statement that are not included as outstanding checks on the bank reconciliation. The checks should be traced to the cutoff bank statement and canceled checks should be examined for propriety.

5. Agree any charges included on the bank statement to the bank reconciliation. For example, bank service charges should be adjusted in the clients' records.

6. Agree the adjusted book balance to the cash account lead schedule. The adjusted book balance would be part of the amount included in the financial statements for cash.

# Completing the Engagement

## KEY THOUGHT

Written representations from management should be obtained for all financial statements and periods covered by the auditor's report. For example, if comparative financial statements are reported on, the written representations obtained at the completion of the most recent audit should address all periods being reported on. The specific written representations obtained by the auditor will depend on the circumstances of the engagement and the nature and basis of presentation of the financial statements [Auditing Standards Board (AU 333.05)].

## CHAPTER SUMMARY

**[LO1] Understand the audit issues related to contingent liabilities.**

A. Once the auditor has completed auditing the various business processes and their related financial statement accounts, the evidence is summarized and evaluated. In addition, before choosing the appropriate audit report the auditor considers a number of additional issues that may impact the financial statements.

B. A **contingent liability** is defined as an existing condition, situation, or set of circumstances involving uncertainty as to the possible loss to an entity that will ultimately be resolved when some future event occurs or fails to occur. FAS 5 states that when a contingent liability exists, the likelihood that the future event will result in a loss or impairment of an asset or the incurrence of a liability can be classified into three categories:

1. **Probable**. The future event is likely to occur. If the event is probable and the amount of the loss can be reasonably estimated, the loss is accrued by a charge to income.

2. **Reasonably possible**. The chance of the future event occurring is more than remote but less than likely. When the outcome of the event is judged to be reasonably possible or the amount cannot be estimated, a disclosure of the contingency is made in the footnotes to the financial statements.

3. **Remote**. The chance of the future event occurring is slight. In general, loss contingencies that are judged to be remote are not disclosed in the footnotes.

C. Examples of contingent liabilities include: pending or threatened litigation, actual or possible claims and assessments, income tax disputes, product warranties or defects, guarantees of obligations to others, and agreements to repurchase receivables that have been sold.

**[LO2] Know the audit procedures used to identify contingent liabilities.**

A. The auditor may identify contingent liabilities while conducting audit procedures directed at assertions related to specific business processes or financial statement accounts. Examples of such audit procedures include:

1. Reading the minutes of meetings of the board of directors, committees of the board, and stockholders.

2. Reviewing contracts, loan agreements, leases, and correspondence from government agencies.

3. Reviewing income tax liability, tax returns, and IRS agents' reports.

4. Confirming or otherwise documenting guarantees and letters of credit obtained from financial institutions or other lending agencies.

5. Inspecting other documents for possible guarantees.

B. Near the completion of the engagement, the auditor conducts specific audit procedures to identify contingent liabilities. Such procedures include:

1. Inquiry of and discussion with management about its policies and procedures for identifying, evaluating, and accounting for contingent liabilities. Management has the responsibility for establishing polices and procedures to identify, evaluate, and account for contingencies. Large entities may implement such policies and procedures within their risk assessment process. The management of smaller entities may rely on legal counsel and auditors to identify and account for contingencies.

2. Examining documents in the entity's records such as correspondence and invoices from attorneys for pending or threatened lawsuits. Even if the amount of legal expense is immaterial, the auditor normally examines the legal expense account to identify actual or potential litigation against the client. The account analysis can also be used to develop a list of attorneys who have been consulted by the entity.

3. Obtaining a legal letter that describes and evaluates any litigation, claims, or assessments.

4. Obtaining written representation from management that all litigation, asserted and unasserted claims, and assessments have been disclosed in accordance with FAS 5. This information is obtained in a representation letter furnished by the client.

**[LO3] Understand the audit issues related to a legal letter.**

A. A letter of inquiry (referred to as a legal letter) sent to the client's attorneys is the primary means of obtaining or corroborating information about litigation, claims, and assessments. Auditors typically analyze legal expense for the entire period and send a legal letter to each attorney who has been consulted by management. Examples of types of litigation that the auditor may encounter (Table 17-1):

1. Breach of contract.
2. Patent infringement.

3. Product liability.
4. Violations of government legislation, including
    a. Securities laws.
    b. Antidiscrimination statutes (race, sex, age and other characteristics).
    c. Antitrust laws.
    d. Income tax regulations.
    e. Environmental protection laws.
    f. Foreign Corrupt Practices Act.
    g. Racketeer Influenced and Corrupt Organizations Act (RICO).

B. The auditor should ask management to send a legal letter to the attorneys, requesting that they provide the following information:

1. A list and evaluation of any pending or threatened litigation to which the attorney has devoted substantial attention. The list may be provided by the client.

2. A list of unasserted claims and assessments considered by management to be probable of assertion and reasonably possible of unfavorable outcome.

3. A request that the attorney describe and evaluate the outcome of each pending or threatened litigation. This should include the progress of the case, the action the entity plans to take, the likelihood of an unfavorable outcome, and the amount or range of potential loss.

4. A request for additions to the list provided by management or a statement that the list is complete.

5. A request that the attorney comment on unasserted claims where his or her views differ from management's evaluation.

6. A statement by management acknowledging an understanding of the attorney's professional responsibility involving unasserted claims and assessments.

7. A request that the attorney indicate if his or her response is limited and the reasons for such limitations.

8. A description of any materiality levels agreed upon for the purposes of the inquiry and response (AU 337).

C. Exhibit 17-2 presents an example of a legal letter. Attorneys are generally willing to provide evidence on actual or pending litigation. However, they are sometimes reluctant to provide information on unasserted claims or assessments. An unasserted claim or assessment is one in which the injured party or potential claimant has not yet notified the entity of a possible claim or assessment. In general, disclosing an unasserted claim is not required unless it is probable that the claim will be asserted and there is a reasonable possibility that the outcome will prove to be unfavorable. Attorneys may limit their responses to items to which they have given substantial attention. Attorneys may also be unable to respond to the outcome of a matter because the factors in the case do not allow them to reasonably estimate the likelihood of the outcome or to estimate the possible loss. Finally, refusal to furnish information in a legal letter is a limitation on the scope of the audit sufficient to preclude an unqualified opinion.

**[LO4] Understand why the auditor must be concerned with commitments.**

A. Companies often enter long-term commitments to purchase raw materials or to sell their products at a fixed price. Long-term commitments are usually identified through inquiry of client personnel during the audit of the revenue and purchasing processes. In most cases, such commitments are disclosed in a footnote to the financial statements. In certain instances, the entity may have to recognize a loss on a long-term commitment even though there has been no exchange of goods.

**[LO5] Know the types of subsequent events.**

A. Sometimes events or transactions that occur after the balance sheet date but before the issuance of the financial statements materially affect the financial statements. These events or transactions are referred to as **subsequent events** and require adjustment or disclosure in the financial statements (AU 560 and 561).

B. Two types of subsequent events require consideration by management and evaluation by the auditor:

1. **Type I**. Events that provide additional evidence about conditions that existed at the date of the balance sheet date and affect the estimates that are part of the financial statement preparation process. Such an event is a Type I event, which requires adjustment of the financial statements. Examples of Type I subsequent events include:

   a. An uncollectible account receivable resulting from continued deterioration of a customer's financial condition leading to bankruptcy after the balance sheet date.

   b. The settlement of a lawsuit after the balance sheet date for an amount different from the amount recorded in the year-end financial statements.

2. **Type II**. Events that provide evidence about conditions that did not exist at the date of the balance sheet but arose subsequent to that date. Such an event is a Type II event, which usually require financial statement disclosure. In some instances, where the effect of the event or transaction is so significant, pro forma financial statements may be required in order to prevent the financial statements from being misleading. Examples of Type II events include:

   a. Purchase or disposal of a business by the entity.

   b. Sale of a capital stock or bond issue by the entity.

   c. Loss of the entity's manufacturing facility or assets resulting from a casualty such as a fire or flood.

   d. Losses on receivables caused by conditions such as a casualty arising subsequent to the balance sheet date.

   In some instances, a Type II subsequent event may result in the auditor's adding an explanatory paragraph to the auditor's report to emphasize the event or transaction.

Note that in both of the above examples, additional evidence became available before the financial statements were issued that shed light on estimates previously made in the financial statements. Subsequent events affecting the realization of assets or the settlement of estimated liabilities normally requires adjustment of the financial statements.

C. Figure 17-1 presents a diagram of the subsequent-events period for EarthWear. The period from the date of the financial statements to the date of the auditor's report is sometimes referred to as the formal subsequent-events period. During this time frame, the auditor actively conducts audit procedures related to the current-year audit. The period from the date of the auditor's report to the issuance of the financial statements is also part of the subsequent-events period, but the auditor is not responsible for making any inquires or conducting any audit procedures after the date of the audit report. However, subsequent events may come to the auditor's attention during this period. If the subsequent event is Type I, the financial statements should be adjusted. Depending on the event and its circumstances, additional disclosure may be made in the footnotes. When the subsequent event is Type II, a footnote describing the event should be included with the financial statements.

**[LO6] Understand the effect of subsequent events on the dating of the audit report.**

A. When a subsequent event is recorded or disclosed in the financial statements after completion of the fieldwork but before the issuance of the financial statements, the auditor must consider the dating of the auditor's report. Two methods are available for dating the audit report: the auditor may dual date the report or use the date of the subsequent event. Dual dating is intended to limit the auditor's responsibility for events occurring subsequent to the completion of fieldwork to the specific subsequent event referred to in the footnote. If the audit report is dated using the date of the subsequent event, the auditor's responsibility extends to that date.

**[LO7] Know the audit procedures used to identify subsequent events.**

A. Some audit procedures for business processes and their related financial statement accounts are conducted before year-end, while others may be conducted during the subsequent-events period. Some of these procedures are applied to transactions after the balance sheet date. Such audit procedures may detect subsequent events. In addition, the auditor should conduct specific audit procedures for the period from the balance sheet date to the audit report date. Examples of these audit procedures include:

1. Asking management about the following matters: (a) whether there were or are any substantial contingent liabilities or commitments existing at the balance sheet date or at the date of inquiry; (b) whether there have been any significant changes in capital stock, long-term debt, or working capital; (c) the current status of any items in the financial statements that were accounted for based on preliminary or inconclusive date; and (d) whether any unusual adjustments have been made during the subsequent-events period.

2. Reading any interim financial statements that are available for the period after year-end; they should be compared to the prior-period statements, and any unusual fluctuations should be investigated.

3. Examining the books of original entry (such as sales journal, purchases journal, cash receipts and cash disbursements journals, and general ledger) for the subsequent-events period and investigating any unusual transactions.

4. Reading the available minutes of meetings of stockholders, directors, or other committees for the subsequent-events period.

5. Asking legal counsel about any litigation, claims, or assessments against the company.

6. Obtaining a representation letter from management.

B. Auditors of public companies are responsible to report on any changes in internal control that might affect financial reporting between the end of the reporting period and the date of the auditor's report (AS5). The auditor's treatment of subsequent events relating to internal control is similar to the Type I and Type II treatments discussed above. In other words, the treatment depends on whether the change in control reveals information about a material weakness that existed as of the end of the reporting period or whether the event creates or reveals information about a new condition that did not exist as of the end of the reporting period. If the event reveals information about a material weakness that existed as of the end of the reporting period, the auditor should issue an adverse opinion on the effectiveness of internal control over financial reporting (and issue an adverse opinion on management's assessment of internal control over financial reporting if management's report does not appropriately assess the effect of the subsequent event). If the auditor is unable to determine the effect of the subsequent event on the effectiveness of the company's internal control, the auditor should disclaim any opinion. If the event creates or reveals information about an internal control condition that did not exist as of the end of the reporting period and the information has a material effect on the company, the auditor should include an explanatory paragraph describing the event and its effects or directing the reader's attention to the event and its effects as disclosed in management's report. Auditors of public companies are required to inquire of management whether there were any changes in internal control that might affect financial reporting between the end of the reporting period and the date of the auditor's report, and should obtain written representations regarding such changes. The public company auditor should also inquire about and examine, for this subsequent period, the following:

1. Relevant internal audit reports (or similar functions, such as loan review in a financial institution) issued during the subsequent period.

2. Independent auditor reports (if other than the primary auditor's) of significant deficiencies or material weaknesses.

3. Regulatory agency reports on the company's internal control over financial reporting.

4. Information about the effectiveness of the company's internal control over financial reporting obtained through other engagements (AS5).

**[LO8] Know the audit steps included in the auditor's final evidential evaluation process.**

A. In addition to the search for unrecorded liabilities and the review for subsequent events, the auditor conducts a number of audit steps before deciding on the appropriate audit report to issue for the entity. These include the following:

1. Performance of final analytical procedures.

2. Evaluation of the entity's ability to continue as a going-concern.

3. Obtaining a representative letter.

4. Review of working papers.

5. Final assessment of the audit results.

6. Evaluation of financial statement presentation and disclosure.

7. Obtaining an independent review of the engagement.

B. **Final Analytical Procedures**. Auditing standards (AU 329) require that the auditor perform analytical procedures at the final review stage of the audit. The objective of conducting analytical procedures near the end of the engagement is to help the auditor assess the conclusions reached on the financial statement components and evaluate the overall financial statement presentation. This may include recalculating some of the ratios for planning the audit. However, more frequently, they involve reviewing the adequacy of the evidence gathered in response to unexpected fluctuations in the account balances identified during the planning of the audit and identifying any unusual or unexpected balances not previously considered. These final analytical procedures may indicate that more evidence is needed for certain account balances.

The auditor performs final analytical procedures to consider the overall reasonableness of the financial statement amounts. In doing this analysis, the auditor reexamines the client's business risks. For example, the auditor considers the critical issues and significant industry business risks and whether such risks might impact the financial statements. The auditor also assesses the structure and profitability of the industry and how the client fits within the industry in terms of its profitability and solvency. In other words, the auditor considers whether the financial statement amounts make sense given the auditor's knowledge of the client's business risks.

A. **Representative Letter**. During the course of the financial statement and internal control audits, management makes a number of representations to the auditor as part of the inquires made to obtain sufficient competent evidence. Auditing standards (AU 333, AS5) require that the auditor obtain a representation letter from management. The purpose of this letter is to corroborate oral representations made to the auditor and to document the continued appropriateness of such representations. The representation letter also reduces the possibility of misunderstanding concerning the responses provided by management to the auditor's inquiries. Exhibit 17-3 presents an example of a representation letter. The representation letter should be addressed to the auditor and is dated using the same date as the auditor's report. Normally, the chief executive officer and chief financial officer sign the representation letter. Management's refusal to provide a representation letter results in a scope limitation that is sufficient to preclude an unqualified opinion and is ordinarily sufficient to cause an auditor to disclaim an opinion or withdraw from the engagement. In such cases, the auditor should also consider management's refusal when assessing whether he or she can rely on other management representations.

B. **Working Paper Review**. All audit work should be reviewed by an audit team member senior to the person preparing the working papers. Thus, the senior-in-charge should conduct a detailed review of the working papers prepared by the staff and follow up on any unresolved problems or issues. In turn, the manager should review all working papers, although the extent of the manager's review may vary with how much the manager relies on the senior-in-charge. The engagement partner normally reviews working papers related to critical audit areas as well as working papers prepared by the manager. In reviewing the working papers, the reviewers must ensure that the working papers document that the audit was properly planned and supervised, that the evidence supports the assertions tested, and that the evidence is sufficient for the type of audit report issued.

C. **Evaluating Financial Audit Results**. The auditor must evaluate the results of the audit tests. The evaluation is concerned with two issues. First, the auditor must determine if the audit evidence is sufficient to support each relevant assertion. If the evidence is not sufficient to meet the planned level of audit risk, the auditor may need to gather additional evidence. Second, the auditor must evaluate the effects of detected misstatements in the financial statements. This involves performing the third step in applying materiality. The auditor must estimate the likely misstatements and compare the amount arrived at to the amount of materiality allocated to the relevant component of the financial statement. Note that likely misstatements include both known and projected misstatements. The auditor should also consider the effects of unadjusted misstatements on aggregated components of the financial statements such as assets, liabilities, equity, revenue, and expenses. In addition, the overall effect of the misstatements in terms of aggregated components of the financial statements must be considered.

D. **Evaluating Financial Statement Presentation and Disclosure**. Either the client or the auditor normally prepares a draft of the financial statements, including footnotes. The auditor reviews the financial statements to ensure compliance with GAAP, proper presentation of accounts, and inclusion of all necessary disclosures.

E. **Independent Engagement Quality Review**. Most firms have a policy requiring an engagement quality review for publicly traded companies and for privately held companies whose financial statements are expected to be widely distributed. The engagement quality reviewer is a partner who is not associated with the details of the engagement and is expected to provide an independent, objective review. The reviewer should understand the audit approach, findings, and conclusions for critical audit areas and should review the audit report, financial statements, and footnotes for consistency.

F. **Archiving and Retention**. The events leading up to the Sarbanes-Oxley Act of 2002 focused the spotlight on the practice of archiving and retaining audit files. The Act imposed new guidelines for audit files archiving and retention. The PCAOB's auditing standard complies with the guidance under the Act (AS3). This standard requires that accounting firms archive their public-company audit files (workpapers and other documentation) for retention within 45 days following the time the auditor grants permission to use the auditor's report in connection with the issuance of the company's financial statements. The documentation requires that audit documentation be retained for seven years from the date of completion of the engagements, as indicated by the date of the auditor's report.

**[LO9] Understand how to identify and assess entities with going-concern problems.**

A. **Going Concern**. Auditing standards (AU 341) indicate that the auditor has a responsibility to evaluate whether there is substantial doubt about an entity's ability to continue as a going concern for a reasonable period of time (defined as one year beyond the date of the financial statements being audited). The auditor should follow three overall steps in making the going-concern evaluation:

1. Consider whether the results of audit procedures performed during the planning, performance, and completion of the audit indicate whether there is substantial doubt about the entity's ability to continue as a going concern for a reasonable period of time (one year).

2. If there is substantial doubt, the auditor should obtain information about management's plan to mitigate the going-concern problem and assess the likelihood that such plans can be implemented.

3. If the auditor concludes, after evaluating management's plans, that there is substantial doubt about the ability of the entity to continue as a going concern, he or she should consider the adequacy of the disclosures about the entity's ability to continue and include an explanatory paragraph in the audit report.

Auditing standards identify four major categories of conditions or events: negative financial trends, other financial difficulties, internal problem and external matters. Normal audit procedures that may identify conditions and events indicating going-concern problems include (Table 17-2):

1. Analytical procedures.
2. Review of subsequent events.
3. Tests for compliance with debt agreements.
4. Reading of board of directors and other committee minutes.
5. Inquiry of legal counsel.
6. Confirmations with parties providing or maintaining financial support.

**Financial conditions** that indicate financial distress are shown below (Table 17-3):

1. Recurring operating losses.
2. Current-year deficit.
3. Accumulated deficits.
4. Negative net worth.
5. Negative working capital.
6. Negative cash flow.
7. Negative income from operations.
8. Inability to meet interest payments.

**Ratios** that indicate financial distress are shown below (Table 17-3):

1. Net worth/total liabilities.
2. Working capital from operations/total liabilities.
3. Current assets/current liabilities.
4. Total long-term liabilities/total assets.
5. Total liabilities/total assets.
6. Net income before taxes/net sales.

See Table 17-4 for examples of other conditions and events indicating a problem with the going-concept assumption.

B. **Consideration of Management's Plans**. Once conditions have been identified that indicate substantial doubt about the ability of the entity to continue, the auditor should consider management's plans for dealing with the adverse effects of the conditions or events. The auditor should consider the following actions by management:

1. Plans to dispose of assets.
2. Plans to borrow money or restructure debt.
3. Plans to reduce or delay expenditures.
4. Plans to increase ownership equity.

Note that if the auditor concludes that there is substantial doubt about the entity's ability to continue as a going concern, the auditor will normally issue a modified audit report similar to the one shown in Chapter 18 (Exhibit 18-3).

**[LO10] Understand the auditor's communication with management and those charged with governance and the matters that should be addressed.**

A.  Auditing standards (AU 380) require the auditor communicate certain matters related to the conduct of the audit to those individuals responsible for oversight of the financial reporting process. The communication should address the following matters:

1.  The auditor's responsibility under GAAS.

2.  Significant accounting policies.

3.  Management judgments and accounting estimates.

4.  Significant audit adjustments.

5.  The auditor's judgments about the quality of the entity's accounting principles.

6.  Disagreements with management.

7.  Consultation with other accountants.

8.  Major issues discussed with management before the auditor was retained.

9.  Difficulties encountered during the audit.

10. Fraud involving senior management and fraud that causes material misstatement of the financial statements.

This communication should be in writing, and the report should indicate that it is intended solely for the use of those charged with governance and, if applicable, management.

B.  The auditor has a number of communication responsibilities with respect to the audit of internal control over financial reporting (AS5). The auditor must communicate in writing to management and the audit committee all significant deficiencies and material weaknesses identified during the audit. The written communication should be made prior to the issuance of the auditor's report on internal control over financial reporting. If a significant deficiency or material weakness exists because the oversight of the company's external financial reporting and internal control over financial reporting by the company's audit committee is ineffective, the auditor must communicate that specific significant deficiency or material weakness in writing to the board of directors. The auditor must communicate, in writing, all control deficiencies identified (deficiencies that are of a lesser magnitude than significant deficiencies).

C.  In addition to the communications discussed above, the auditor normally prepares a management letter. The general intent of a management letter is to make recommendations to the client based on observations during the audit; the letter may include suggested improvements in various areas, such as organizational structure and efficiency issues.

**[LO11] Know the auditor's responsibility for subsequent discovery of facts existing at the date of the auditor's report.**

A.  An auditor has no obligation to make any inquires or conduct any audit procedures after the financial statements and audit report have been issued. However, facts may come to the auditor's attention after the issuance of the financial statements that might have affected the report had he or she known about them. The most common situation is where the previously issued financial statements contain material misstatements due to either unintentional or intentional actions by management. Events that occur after the issuance of the auditor's report, such as financial settlements of litigation or additional information on accounting estimates becoming available, do not apply to this auditing standard. The auditor should consult with his or her attorney because legal implication may be involved and actions taken by the auditor may involve confidential client-auditor communications. The auditor should determine whether the facts are reliable and whether they existed at the date of the audit report. The auditor should discuss the matter with an appropriate level of management and request cooperation in investigating the potential misstatement.

B.  If the auditor determines that the previously issued financial statements are in error and the audit report is affected, he or she should request that the client issue an immediate revision to the financial statements and auditor's report. The reasons for the revisions should be described in the footnotes to the revised financial statements. If the effect on the financial statements cannot immediately be determined, the client should notify persons known to be relying on the financial statements and auditor's report. If the stock is publicly traded or subject to regulatory jurisdiction, the client should contact the SEC, stock exchanges, and other regulatory agencies. If the client refuses to cooperate and make the necessary disclosures, the auditor should notify the board of directors and take the following steps, if possible:

1.  Notify the client that the auditor's report must no longer be associated with the financial statements.

2.  Notify any regulatory agencies having jurisdiction over the client that the auditor's report can no longer be relied upon.

3.  Notify each person known to the auditor to be relying on the financial statements. Usually, notifying a regulatory agency such as the SEC is the only practical way of providing appropriate disclosure.

The practical outcome of these procedures is that the auditor has withdrawn his or her report on the previously issued financial statements. In notifying the client, regulatory agencies, and other persons relying on the auditor's report, the auditor should disclose the effect the information would have had on the auditor's report had it been known to the auditor.

# CHAPTER 17: SELF-ASSESSMENT

## Part I: True or False Questions

[LO1] _____ 1. A contingent liability must be recorded.

[LO1] _____ 2. An example of a contingent liability is an income tax dispute.

[LO2] _____ 3. Reading contracts and loan agreements is one way to identify unrecorded contingent liabilities.

[LO3] _____ 4. A letter of audit inquiry is referred to as a legal letter.

[LO5] _____ 5. Type II subsequent events are conditions that require an adjustment to the account balance shown on the financial statements.

[LO5] _____ 6. An example of a Type I event or condition is the settlement of a lawsuit after the balance sheet date for an amount different from the amount recorded in the year-end financial statements.

[LO5] _____ 7. An example of a Type II event or condition is an uncollectible account receivable resulting from continued deterioration of a customer's financial condition leading to bankruptcy after the balance sheet date.

[LO6] _____ 8. Dual date is used to identify unrecorded contingent liabilities.

[LO8] _____ 9. The auditor must perform final analytical procedures before deciding on the appropriate audit report to issue for the entity.

[LO9] _____ 10. If there is substantial doubt about the entity's ability to continue as a going concern, the auditor should obtain information about management's plans to mitigate the problem and assess the likelihood that such plans can be implemented.

## Part II: Multiple Choice Questions

[LO1] 1. A disclosure of a contingent liability must be included in the footnotes to the financial statements when:
   a. The outcome of the event is judged to be reasonably possible.
   b. The loss can be reasonably estimated.
   c. The loss cannot be reasonably estimated.
   d. Both a and c.

[LO1] 2. A contingent liability is considered probable when:
   a. The chance of the future event occurring is more than remote but less than likely.
   b. The future event is likely to occur.
   c. The chance of the future event occurring is slight.
   d. None of the above.

[LO1] 3. Generally, loss contingencies that are judged to be remote:
   a. Should be disclosed in the footnotes.
   b. Should be recorded in the financial statements.
   c. Should not be disclosed in the footnotes.
   d. Should be recorded in the financial statements and the footnotes.

[LO5] 4. A Type I subsequent event usually requires:
   a. An adjustment to the financial statements.
   b. No adjustment to the financial statements.
   c. An adjustment to the footnotes.
   d. None of the above.

[LO5] 5. A Type II subsequent event usually requires:
   a. An adjustment to the financial statements.
   b. No adjustment to the financial statements.
   c. An adjustment to the footnotes.
   d. None of the above.

[LO9] 6. The following conditions or events are used to assess going-concern problems:
   a. Positive financial treads.
   b. Internal problems but not external matters.
   c. Negative financial treads but not external matters.
   d. Negative financial treads and external matters.

[LO9] 7. Ratios that indicate financial distress include:
   a. Long long-term liabilities/current assets.
   b. Total liabilities/total equity.
   c. Net income before taxes/net sales.
   d. Short-term liabilities/total assets.

[LO10] 8. Auditing standards require communication that addresses the following matters:
   a. Significant audit adjustments.
   b. Disagreements with management.
   c. Profitability of the engagement.
   d. Both a and b.

[LO10] 9. Auditing standards require communication that address the following matters:
   a. Difficulties encountered during the audit.
   b. Profitability of the engagement.
   c. The auditor's responsibility under GAAP.
   d. Both a and c.

[LO10] 10. Auditing standards (AU 380) requires that the auditor communicate certain matters to those individual responsible for oversight of the financial reporting process if:
   a. The entity has an audit committee or similar group.
   b. The entity is a public company and subject to the SEC regulations.
   c. All audit engagements.
   d. Both a and b.

## Part III: Short Essay Questions

[LO1] Define the term "contingent liabilities" and discuss the criteria used to classify these events or conditions. Provide some example of contingent liabilities.

[LO5] Discuss the types of subsequent events that the auditor will search for during a financial statement audit and provide some examples of these events.

[LO9] Discuss the steps used to evaluate an entity's ability to continue as a going-concern.

# Part IV: Crossword Puzzle – Chapter 17 [LO ALL]

**Across**

2  Substantial doubt about an entity's ability to continue for a reasonable period of time (two words).
6  Abbreviation for the agency that issues auditing standards for public companies.
7  Integrated framework of internal control.
9  PCAOB auditing standard for "Audit Documentation."
10  An example of a common contingent liability (two words).
12  When subsequent events are present, the auditor must consider the _____ of the auditor's report.

**Down**

1  A letter that corroborates oral communication made by management and documents appropriateness of communication.
3  An event or transaction that occurs after the balance sheet date, but prior to the issuance of the financial statements.
4  Audit report when a subsequent event occurs after the completion of field work, but before the financial statements are issued.
5  An existing condition or situation involving uncertainty as to possible loss that will be resolved when some future event occurs.
8  AS2 requires the auditor communicate all significant deficiencies and material control weaknesses to this committee.
11  PCAOB standard for issues related to internal control.

| |
|---|
| **Chapter 17** <br> **Townsend Office Supplies and Equipment** |
| Discuss the "representation letter" that should be provided to ABC. Discuss any specific issues that should be included in the representation letter for an organization such as Townsend Office Supplies and Equipment. |

# CHAPTER 17: SELF-ASSESSMENT SOLUTIONS

## Part I: True or False Questions

[LO1] **False** 1. A contingent liability must be recorded.

[LO1] **True** 2. An example of a contingent liability is an income tax dispute.

[LO2] **True** 3. Reading contracts and loan agreements is one way to identify unrecorded contingent liabilities.

[LO3] **True** 4. A letter of audit inquiry is referred to as a legal letter.

[LO5] **False** 5. Type II subsequent events are conditions that require an adjustment to the account balance shown on the financial statements.

[LO5] **True** 6. An example of a Type I event or condition is the settlement of a lawsuit after the balance sheet date for an amount different from the amount recorded in the year-end financial statements.

[LO5] **False** 7. An example of a Type II event or condition is an uncollectible account receivable resulting from continued deterioration of a customer's financial condition leading to bankruptcy after the balance sheet date.

[LO6] **False** 8. Dual date is used to identify unrecorded contingent liabilities.

[LO8] **True** 9. The auditor must perform final analytical procedures before deciding on the appropriate audit report to issue for the entity.

[LO9] **True** 10. If there is substantial doubt about the entity's ability to continue as a going concern, the auditor should obtain information about management's plans to mitigate the problem and assess the likelihood that such plans can be implemented.

## Part II: Multiple Choice Questions

[LO1]   1. A disclosure of a contingent liability must be included in the footnotes to the financial statements when:
   a. The outcome of the event is judged to be reasonably possible.
   b. The loss can be reasonably estimated.
   c. The loss cannot be reasonably estimated.
   **d. Both a and c.**

[LO1]   2. A contingent liability is considered probable when:
   a. The chance of the future event occurring is more than remote but less than likely.
   **b. The future event is likely to occur.**
   c. The chance of the future event occurring is slight.
   d. None of the above.

[LO1]  3.  Generally, loss contingencies that are judged to be remote:
    a.  Should be disclosed in the footnotes.
    b.  Should be recorded in the financial statements.
    **c.  Should not be disclosed in the footnotes.**
    d.  Should be recorded in the financial statements and the footnotes.

[LO5]  4.  A Type I subsequent event usually requires:
    **a.  An adjustment to the financial statements.**
    b.  No adjustment to the financial statements.
    c.  An adjustment to the footnotes.
    d.  None of the above.

[LO5]  5.  A Type II subsequent event usually requires:
    a.  An adjustment to the financial statements.
    b.  No adjustment to the financial statements.
    **c.  An adjustment to the footnotes.**
    d.  None of the above.

[LO9]  6.  The following conditions or events are used to assess going-concern problems:
    a.  Positive financial treads.
    b.  Internal problems but not external matters.
    c.  Negative financial treads but not external matters.
    **d.  Negative financial treads and external matters.**

[LO9]  7.  Ratios that indicate financial distress include:
    a.  Long long-term liabilities/current assets.
    b.  Total liabilities/total equity.
    **c.  Net income before taxes/net sales.**
    d.  Short-term liabilities/total assets.

[LO10]  8.  Auditing standards require communication that addresses the following matters:
    a.  Significant audit adjustments.
    b.  Disagreements with management.
    c.  Profitability of the engagement.
    **d.  Both a and b.**

[LO10]  9.  Auditing standards require communication that address the following matters:
    **a.  Difficulties encountered during the audit.**
    b.  Profitability of the engagement.
    c.  The auditor's responsibility under GAAP.
    d.  Both a and c.

[LO10]10.  Auditing standards (AU 380) requires that the auditor communicate certain matters to those individual responsible for oversight of the financial reporting process if:
    a.  The entity has an audit committee or similar group.
    b.  The entity is a public company and subject to the SEC regulations.
    c.  All audit engagements.
    **d.  Both a and b.**

## Part III: Short Essay Questions

[LO1] Define the term "contingent liabilities" and discuss the criteria used to classify these events or conditions. Provide some example of contingent liabilities.

**A contingent liability is defined as an existing condition, situation, or set of circumstances involving uncertainty as the possible loss to an entity that will ultimately be resolved when some future event occurs or fails to occur. FAS No. 5 states that when a contingent liability exists, the likelihood that the future event will result in a loss or impairment of an asset or the incurrence of a liability can be classified into three categories:**

**Probable. The future event is likely to occur. If the event is probable and the amount of the loss can be reasonably estimated, the loss is accrued by a charge to income.**

**Reasonably possible. The chance of the future event occurring is more than remote but less than likely. When the outcome of the event is judged to be reasonably possible or the amount cannot be estimated, a disclosure of the contingency is made in the footnotes to the financial statements.**

**Remote. The chance of the future event occurring is slight. In general, loss contingencies that are judged to be remote are not disclosed in the footnotes.**

**Examples of contingent liabilities include: pending or threatened litigation, actual or possible claims and assessments, income tax disputes, product warranties or defects, guarantees of obligations to others, and agreements to repurchase receivables that have been sold.**

[LO5] Discuss the types of subsequent events that the auditor will search for during a financial statement audit and provide some examples of these events.

Sometimes events or transactions that occur after the balance sheet date but before the issuance of the financial statements materially affect the financial statements. These events or transactions are referred to as subsequent events and require adjustment or disclosure in the financial statements (AU 560 and 561). Two types of subsequent events require consideration by management and evaluation by the auditor:

Type I. Events that provide additional evidence about conditions that existed at the date of the balance sheet date and affect the estimates that are part of the financial statement preparation process. Such an event is a Type I event, which requires adjustment of the financial statements. Examples of Type I subsequent events include:

An uncollectible account receivable resulting from continued deterioration of a customer's financial condition leading to bankruptcy after the balance sheet date.

The settlement of a lawsuit after the balance sheet date for an amount different from the amount recorded in the year-end financial statements.

Type II. Events that provide evidence about conditions that did not exist at the date of the balance sheet but arose subsequent to that date. Such an event is a Type II event, which usually require financial statement disclosure. In some instances, where the effect of the event or transaction is so significant, pro forma financial statements may be required in order to prevent the financial statements from being misleading. Examples of Type II events include:

Purchase or disposal of a business by the entity.

Sale of a capital stock or bond issue by the entity.

Loss of the entity's manufacturing facility or assets resulting from a casualty such as a fire or flood.

Losses on receivables caused by conditions such as a casualty arising subsequent to the balance sheet date.

In some instances, a Type II subsequent event may result in the auditor's adding an explanatory paragraph to the auditor's report to emphasize the event or transaction.

Note that in both of the above examples, additional evidence became available before the financial statements were issued that shed light on estimates previously made in the financial statements. Subsequent events affecting the realization of assets or the settlement of estimated liabilities normally requires adjustment of the financial statements.

[LO9] Discuss the steps used to evaluate an entity's ability to continue as a going-concern.

**Auditing standards (AU 341) indicate that the auditor has a responsibility to evaluate whether there is substantial doubt about an entity's ability to continue as a going concern for a reasonable period of time (defined as one year beyond the date of the financial statements being audited). The auditor should follow three overall steps in making the going-concern evaluation:**

**Step 1. Consider whether the results of audit procedures performed during the planning, performance, and completion of the audit indicate whether there is substantial doubt about the entity's ability to continue as a going concern for a reasonable period of time (one year).**

**Step 2. If there is substantial doubt, the auditor should obtain information about management's plan to mitigate the going-concern problem and assess the likelihood that such plans can be implemented.**

**Step 3. If the auditor concludes, after evaluating management's plans, that there is substantial doubt about the ability of the entity to continue as a going concern, he or she should consider the adequacy of the disclosures about the entity's ability to continue and include an explanatory paragraph in the audit report.**

**Auditing standards identify four major categories of conditions or events: negative financial trends, other financial difficulties, internal problem and external matters.**

**Part IV: Crossword Puzzle – Chapter 17 Solution [LO ALL]**

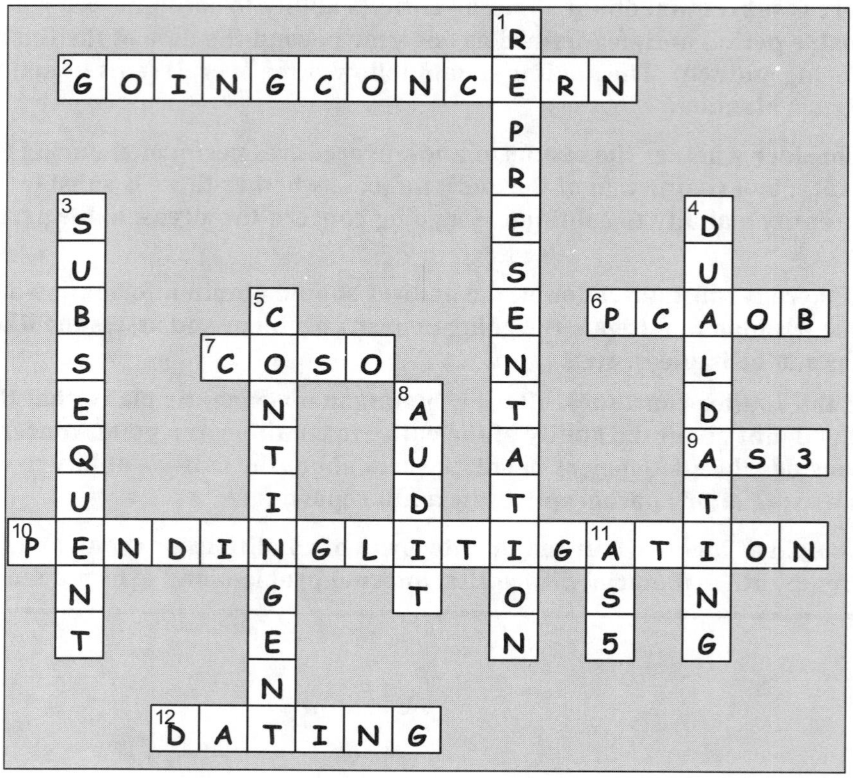

```
                                    ¹R
      ²G O I N G C O N C E R N
                                     P
                                     R
    ³S                                E                        ⁴D
     U                                S                         U
     B                   ⁵C            E         ⁶P C A O B
     S              ⁷C O S O          N                         L
     E                  N         ⁸A  T                         D
     Q                  T          U  A            ⁹A S 3
     U                  I          D  T                         T
  ¹⁰P E N D I N G L I T I G A T I O N      ¹¹A T I O N
     N                  G          T  O                         N
     T                  E          N  N      5                  G
                        N
                     ¹²D A T I N G
```

### Across

2  Substantial doubt about an entity's ability to continue for a reasonable period of time (two words).
6  Abbreviation for the agency that issues auditing standards for public companies.
7  Integrated framework of internal control.
9  PCAOB auditing standard for "Audit Documentation."
10  An example of a common contingent liability (two words).
12  When subsequent events are present, the auditor must consider the _____ of the auditor's report.

### Down

1  A letter that corroborates oral communication made by management and documents appropriateness of communication.
3  An event or transaction that occurs after the balance sheet date, but prior to the issuance of the financial statements.
4  Audit report when a subsequent event occurs after the completion of field work, but before the financial statements are issued.
5  An existing condition or situation involving uncertainty as to possible loss that will be resolved when some future event occurs.
8  AS2 requires the auditor communicate all significant deficiencies and material control weaknesses to this committee.
11  PCAOB standard for issues related to internal control.

---

**Chapter 17**
**Townsend Office Supplies and Equipment**

Discuss the "representation letter" that should be provided to ABC. Discuss any specific issues that should be included in the representation letter for an organization such as Townsend Office Supplies and Equipment.

**During the course of the financial statement and internal control audits, management makes a number of representations to the auditor as part of the inquires made to obtain sufficient competent evidence. Auditing standards (AU 333, AS5) require that the auditor obtain a representation letter from management. The purpose of this letter is to corroborate oral representations made to the auditor and to document the continued appropriateness of such representations. The representation letter also reduces the possibility of misunderstanding concerning the responses provided by management to the auditor's inquiries.**

**The representation letter should be addressed to the auditor and generally given the same date as the auditor's report. Normally, the chief executive officer and chief financial officer sign the representation letter. Management's refusal to provide a representation letter results in a scope limitation that is sufficient to preclude an unqualified opinion and is ordinarily sufficient to cause an auditor to disclaim an opinion or withdraw from the engagement. In such cases, the auditor should also consider management's refusal when assessing whether he or she can rely on other management representations.**

**The representation letter for an engagement such as the audit of Townsend Office Supplies and Equipment is important for two specific reasons. First, the company is a closely-held corporation; thus the auditor is relying on assertions which are being made by individuals who have a direct interest in the results of the audit. These relationships increase the overall risk of the engagement. Second, Eastern Fidelity Bank is an identified third party that will rely on the audit report. Again, this issue increases audit risk. These two issues should be discussed in the representation letter. In addition, information as illustrated in Exhibit 17-3, as applicable, should be included in the representation letter provided to ABC.**

---

# Reports on Audited Financial Statements

## KEY THOUGHT

The fourth standard of reporting is: The report shall either contain an expression of opinion regarding the financial statements, taken as a whole, or an assertion to the effect that an opinion cannot be expressed. When an overall opinion cannot be expressed, the reasons therefore should be stated. In all cases where an auditor's name is associated with financial statements, the report should contain a clear-cut indication of the character of the auditor's work, if any, and the degree of responsibility the auditor is taking [Auditing Standards Board (AU 504.01)].

## CHAPTER SUMMARY

**[LO1] Understand the standard unqualified financial statement audit report.**

A. A **standard unqualified** financial statement audit report is issued when:

1. The auditor has gathered sufficient evidence.
2. The audit was performed in accordance with GAAS.
3. The financial statements conform to GAAP.

B. The report contains eight elements: (1) the report title, (2) the addressee, (3) the introductory paragraph, (4) the scope paragraph, (5) the opinion paragraph, (6) an explanatory paragraph referring to the audit of internal control over financial reporting, (7) the name of the auditor, and (8) the audit report date.

C. Exhibit 18-1 contains the auditor's standard unqualified audit report, which was introduced in Chapter 2. The report is a separate report on the financial statement audit. Note that the report refers to the auditor's opinions relating to the audit of internal control over financial reporting. When separate audit reports are presented, the reports must be dated the same and each must include an explanatory paragraph referring to the opinion(s) expressed in the other report.

**[LO2] Know the situations that result in the addition of explanatory language to the standard unqualified audit report.**

A.   Five situations may require the auditor to modify the wording or add an explanatory paragraph to the standard unqualified audit report:

1.   **Opinion based in part on the report of another auditor**. On some engagements, part of the audit may be completed by another public accounting firm (i.e., reporting on consolidated financial statements, one of the subsidiaries may be audited by other auditors). In such cases, the auditor for the parent company must be satisfied that he or she is the principal auditor. This is normally determined by the portion of the financial statements audited by the parent-company auditor in relation to the portion of the consolidated financial statements audited by the other independent auditors. The principal auditor must decide whether to refer to the other auditors in the report. Exhibit 18-2 presents an example of an opinion based in part on the report of another auditor.

2.   **Going concern**. When there is substantial doubt about the entity's ability to continue as a going concern, the auditor should consider the possible effects on the financial statements and the related disclosures. The audit report should include an explanatory paragraph such as the one shown in Exhibit 18-3. The auditor may disclaim an opinion on the entity. If the entity's disclosures with respect to the entity's ability to continue as a going concern are inadequate, a departure from GAAP exists. If a client received a going-concern report in the prior period and the doubt regarding going concern is removed in the current period, the explanatory paragraph included with the prior year's audit report is not included with the auditor's report covering the comparative financial statements. Exhibit 18-3 presents an example of an unqualified audit report with an explanatory paragraph for going-concern problems.

3.   **Agreement with a departure from promulgated accounting principles**. In unusual circumstances, financial statements may be misleading if a given promulgated accounting principle was followed. Rule 203 of the Code of Professional Conduct allows the auditor, in such circumstances, to issue an unqualified opinion. However, an explanatory paragraph should be added to the report, which should describe the departure, the approximate effects of the departure, if practicable, and the reasons that compliance with the accounting principle results in misleading financial statements.

4.   **Lack of consistency**. A standard unqualified audit report implies that the comparability of the financial statements is not affected by changes in accounting principles or that any change is immaterial. From the auditor's perspective, accounting changes can be categorized into changes that affect consistency and those that do not affect consistency:

   a.   Change in accounting principles.
   b.   Change in reporting entity.
   c.   Correction of an error in principles.

Exhibit 18-4 is an example of an unqualified opinion with an explanatory paragraph for an accounting change that results in a lack of consistency. Other changes may affect comparability but do not affect consistency. These include:

   1.   Change in accounting estimate.
   2.   Correction of an error that does not involve an accounting principle.

3. Change in classification and reclassification.
4. Change expected to have a material future effect.

5. **Emphasis of a matter**. Under certain circumstances an auditor may want to emphasize a specific matter regarding the financial statements even though he or she intends to express an unqualified opinion. This information should be presented in an explanatory paragraph. Some examples of situations that might cause the auditor to add an explanatory paragraph are significant related-party transactions and important events occurring after the balance sheet date. However, when a client has an FAS No. 5 contingency that is properly disclosed in the client's financial statements or footnotes, auditing standards explicitly instruct the auditor not to emphasize the matter through explanatory language.

**[LO3] Know the conditions that lead to a departure from the standard unqualified audit report.**

A. The auditor can issue three types of audit reports that depart from the unqualified audit report including:

1. **Scope limitation**. A scope limitation results from an inability to collect sufficient competent evidence, such as when management prevents the auditor from conducting an audit procedure considered necessary.

2. **Departure from GAAP**. The financial statements are affected by a departure from GAAP.

3. **Lack of auditor independence.** The auditor must comply with the second general standard and the Code of Professional Conduct in order to issue an unqualified opinion.

**[LO4] Know the types of financial statement audit reports other than unqualified.**

A. The three types of reports other than unqualified are:

1. **Qualified**. The auditor's opinion is qualified because of either a scope limitation or a departure from a GAAP, but overall the financial statements present fairly.

2. **Disclaimer**. The auditor disclaims an opinion on the financial statements either because there is insufficient competent evidence to form an opinion on the overall financial statements or because there is a lack of independence.

3. **Adverse**. The auditor's opinion states that the financial statements do not present fairly in conformity with GAAP because the departure materially affects the overall financial statements.

The choice of audit report depends on both the nature and the materiality of the condition giving rise to the departure from the unqualified report. Figure 18-1 presents an overview of the auditor's reporting options, including the type of report to be issued under various conditions and the effect of materiality.

**[LO5] Understand the effect of materiality on the auditor's choice of audit reports.**

A. The concept of **materiality** plays a major role in the auditor's choice of audit reports. If the condition that might lead to the departure is judged by the auditor to be immaterial, a standard unqualified audit report can be issued. As the materiality of the condition increases, the auditor must judge the effect of the item on the overall financial statements.

1. **Scope limitation**. When the auditor is faced with a scope limitation, the assessment of the omitted procedure(s) should consider the nature and magnitude of the potential effects of the items and its significance to the overall financial statements. If the effects relate to many items in the financial statements or if the effect of the item is so significant that the overall financial statements are affected, the auditor is more likely to issue a disclaimer than a qualified report (Exhibit 18-5). If a material effect relates to a specific item in the financial statements but the overall financial statements still present fairly, the auditor should issue a qualified opinion (Exhibit 18-6). In other words, the pervasiveness of the item on the financial statements determines whether the auditor should issue a qualified opinion or disclaim an opinion.

2. **Statements not in conformity with GAAP**. If the departure from GAAP is immaterial, the auditor should issue an unqualified opinion. If the departure from GAAP is material and the overall financial statements still present fairly, the auditor should issue a qualified opinion (Exhibit 18-7). If the departure is so pervasive that its effects are highly material, the auditor should issue an adverse opinion (Exhibit 18-8). If the client fails to disclose information in the financial statements or footnotes that is required by GAAP, the auditor should issue a qualified (material but not pervasive) or adverse report (pervasive), depending on the materiality of the omission (Exhibit 18-9).

3. **Auditor not independent**. Materiality is not a factor that determines an auditor's independence. When an auditor is not independent, a disclaimer should be issued (Exhibit 18-10).

**[LO6] Understand the situations that may cause different types of reports on comparative financial statements.**

A. When a client presents financial statements for the current period and one or more prior periods, the auditor must update the audit report on the financial statements presented on a comparative basis. Normally, the date of the auditor's report on the comparative statements is the date of the most recently completed audit. The auditor should be alert for events that may affect prior-period financial statements including:

1. Different reports on comparative financial statements (Exhibit 18-11 and Exhibit 18-12).

2. A change in report on the prior-period financial statements (Exhibit 18-13).

3. A report issued by a predecessor auditor.

**[LO7] Know the auditor's responsibility for other information in documents containing audited financial statements.**

A. A client may publish documents such as annual reports and registration statements that contain other information in addition to the audited financial statements and the audit report. Auditing standards (AU 550) provide guidance for the auditor's consideration of other information in (1) annual reports of entities and (2) other documents to which the auditor devotes attention at the client's request. The auditor has no responsibility beyond the financial information contained in the report, and he or she has no obligation to perform any audit procedures to corroborate the other information. However, the auditor is required to read the other information and consider whether such information is consistent with the information contained in the audited financial statements.

B. Auditors are sometimes engaged to report on financial statements not prepared on the basis of GAAP. Auditors may also be engaged to report on parts of the financial statements or on a client's compliance with contractual agreements or regulatory requirements. Auditing standards (AU 623) provide the auditor with specific guidance for such engagements and cover the auditor's reporting responsibilities for the following situations:

1. Financial statements prepared on a comprehensive basis of accounting other than GAAP (e.g., the cash basis of accounting).

2. Specified elements, accounts, or items of a financial statement.

3. Compliance with aspects of contractual agreements or regulatory requirements related to audited financial statements.

**[LO8] Understand the auditor's reporting responsibility for financial statements prepared on a comprehensive basis other than GAAP.**

A. A widely used type of special report is employed when an entity has prepared its financial statements on a comprehensive basis other than GAAP ("other comprehensive basis of accounting," or OCBOA). Auditing standards define OCBOA financial statements as including those prepared under the following bases:

1. **Regulatory basis.** The basis used to comply with the requirements or financial reporting provisions of a governmental regulatory agency. An example would be when an insurance company reports in compliance with the rules of a state insurance commission.

2. **Tax basis.** The basis the entity uses to file its income tax return. Real estate partnerships frequently use this basis for reporting to partners. Exhibit 18-14 is an example of a report on a set of financial statements prepared on a tax basis.

3. **Cash (or modified cash) basis.** When the entity reports on revenue received and expenses paid. This may be modified to record depreciation or to accrue income taxes.

4. **A definite set of criteria having substantial support**. Financial statements prepared on a price-level-adjusted basis are an example of such a set of criteria.

**[LO9] Understand the auditor's responsibility for reporting on specified elements, accounts, or items of a financial statement.**

A. **Specified elements, accounts or items of a financial statement.** In some situations an auditor may be engaged to audit only part of the financial statements. Examples include a report on rentals, royalties, or profit participation or on the provision for income taxes. The basis of accounting for the elements, accounts, or items may be GAAP, OCBOA, or a basis of accounting prescribed by a contract or agreement. This type of engagement is generally more extensive than if the same information were considered as part of an auditing of the overall financial statements. Thus, materiality needs to be set in relation to the individual element, account, or item, and the auditor should consider how the item relates to other parts of the financial statements. In the case when the specified element, account or item is audited in compliance with the provisions of a contract or agreement, the auditor includes a paragraph limiting distribution of the report to the parties who are part of the contract.

B. **Agreed-upon procedures.** The auditor may be engaged to apply only agreed-upon procedures. Attestation standards (AT 201) provide the auditor with the necessary guidance for such engagements. An engagement to apply agreed-upon procedures is one in which the auditor is engaged by a client to issue a report of findings based on specific procedures performed on the specific subject matter of specified elements, accounts, or items of a financial statement. On such engagements, standards require that the specified users take responsibility for the sufficiency of the agreed-upon procedures. The report does not express an opinion. The auditor can satisfy this requirement by performing one of the following or similar procedures:

   1. Compare the procedures to be applied to the written requirements of the specified users.

   2. Discuss the procedures to be applied with appropriate representatives of the users involved.

   3. Review relevant contracts or correspondence from the specified users.

Exhibit 18-15 is an example of an agreed-upon procedures report. The report (1) identifies the specified users, (2) references the specified elements, accounts, or items of a financial statement and the character of the engagement, (3) lists the procedures performed and related findings, (4) disclaims an opinion, and (5) states restrictions on the use of the report.

**[LO10] Understand the auditor's reporting responsibility for compliance with contractual agreements or regulatory requirements related to financial statements.**

A. An auditor may be asked to report on an entity's compliance with certain contractual agreements or regulatory requirements related to audited financial statements. For example, loan agreements may include covenants such as restrictions on dividends or maintenance of certain levels for selected financial ratios. Exhibit 18-16 is an example of a special report related to compliance with contractual provisions. Note that the auditor provides negative assurance as to compliance with the provisions of the loan agreement. Negative assurance consists of a statement that, as a result of specified procedures, nothing came to the auditor's attention that indicates that the provisions of the loan agreement had not been complied with.

# CHAPTER 18: SELF-ASSESSMENT

## Part I: True or False Questions

[LO2] _____ 1. A going concern issue requires a modification of the wording for the three paragraphs included in the standard unqualified audit report.

[LO2] _____ 2. An opinion based in part on the report of another auditor requires a modification of the wording for the three paragraphs included in the standard unqualified audit report.

[LO2] _____ 3. A basic assumption that underlies financial reporting is that an entity will continue as a going concern.

[LO2] _____ 4. A change in accounting estimate is an example of an accounting change that affects comparability and requires an explanatory paragraph in the audit report.

[LO2] _____ 5. A change in reporting entity is an example of an accounting change that affects comparability and requires an explanatory paragraph in the audit report.

[LO2] _____ 6. Changes that do not affect consistency are normally disclosed in the footnotes but do not require an explanatory paragraph in the audit report.

[LO3] _____ 7. An auditor may be unable to express an unqualified opinion if an immaterial departure from GAAP is present in the financial statements.

[LO3] _____ 8. An auditor must disclaim an opinion when the auditor lacks independence.

[LO4] _____ 9. The choice of which audit report to issue depends on the condition and the materiality of the departure.

[LO4] _____ 10. A scope limitation results from an inability to obtain sufficient competent evidence about some component of the financial statements.


## Part II: Multiple Choice Questions

[LO6] 1. Special reporting issues that affect the financial statement audit report include:
    a. Reports on comparative financial statements.
    b. Other information in documents containing audited financial statements.
    c. The going concern assumption.
    d. Both a and b.

[LO6] 2. A predecessor auditor should do the following before reissuing a report on statements presented on a comparative basis:
    a. Read the financial statements of the current period.
    b. Read the financial statements of the past five years.
    c. Obtain a letter of representations from the current-year, successor auditor.
    d. Both a and c.

[LO8] 3. Auditing standards define OCBOA financial statements as including those prepared under the following base:
   a. Tax basis.
   b. Cash basis but not modified cash basis.
   c. A definite set of criteria having substantial support.
   d. Both a and c.

[LO8] 4. Auditing standards define OCBOA financial statements as including those prepared under the following base:
   a. Regulatory basis.
   b. Tax basis.
   c. A definite set of criteria having substantial support.
   d. All of the above.

[LO9] 5. An auditor may be engaged to audit only part of the financial statements including:
   a. Specified elements or accounts.
   b. The entity's net income.
   c. The entity's stockholders' equity.
   d. Both a and b.

[LO9] 6. An auditor can satisfy the requirements that specified users take responsibility for the sufficiency of an agreed-upon procedure by:
   a. Comparing the procedures to be used to the written requirements of the users.
   b. Discussing the procedures to be used with appropriate user representatives.
   c. Reviewing relevant contracts or correspondence from the specified users.
   d. All of the above.

[LO9] 7. In some situations an auditor may be engaged to audit only part of the financial statements. Examples include:
   a. a report on rentals.
   b. a report on royalties.
   c. a report on profit participation.
   d. All of the above.

[LO9] 8. An engagement to apply agreed-upon procedures is one in which the auditor:
   a. Issues an unqualified opinion.
   b. Issues a qualified opinion.
   c. Does not express an opinion.
   d. Both a or b.

[LO9] 9. A report for an agreed-upon procedures engagement includes:
   a. Identifies the specified users.
   b. Includes references relating to the character of the engagement.
   c. Disclaims an opinion.
   d. All of the above.

[LO10] 10. A special report related to compliance with contractual provisions provides:
   a. Positive assurance.
   b. Negative assurance.
   c. No assurance.
   d. None of the above.

**Part III: Short Essay Questions**

[LO2] Discuss the accounting changes that affect consistency and the accounting changes that would not affect consistency.

[LO3 & 4] Discuss the conditions that prohibit the auditor from issuing an unqualified opinion and the types of reports that the auditor may issue for a financial statement audit.

[LO8] Identify and define the four bases used to prepare financial statements on a comprehensive basis other than GAAP.

# Part IV: Crossword Puzzle – Chapter 18 [LO ALL]

## Across

1. Financial statements prepared under regulatory, tax, cash basis, or other definitive criteria have substantial support.
6. This is the end product from a financial statement engagement (two words).
8. A lack of evidence, such as an inability to conduct an audit procedure considered necessary (two words).
10. A "clean" opinion.
11. The auditor should issue this when he or she lacks independence.
12. The choice of which audit report to issue depends on the condition and the _____ of the departure.

## Down

2. The "kiss of death" opinion.
3. Integrated framework for internal control.
4. When a scope limitation is material, but not pervasive.
5. An assumption that an entity has the ability to continue operations for a reasonable period of time (two words).
7. The abbreviation for accounting and reporting standards.
9. A level of which materiality which affects the overall financial statements.

| |
|---|
| **Chapter 18** |
| **Townsend Office Supplies and Equipment** |
| ABC has been asked to report on the entity's compliance with the contractual agreements related to its line of credit with Eastern Fidelity Bank. Discuss the contractual terms associated with the line of credit and evaluate the company's compliance. Discuss the type of assurance that ABC will provide to Townsend and Eastern Fidelity and provide an example of the report on compliance with the contractual provisions of the line of credit that ABC with issue. |

# CHAPTER 18: SELF-ASSESSMENT SOLUTIONS

## Part I: True or False Questions

[LO2] **False** 1.   A going concern issue requires a modification of the wording for the three paragraphs included in the standard unqualified audit report.

[LO2] **True** 2.   An opinion based in part on the report of another auditor requires a modification of the wording for the three paragraphs included in the standard unqualified audit report.

[LO2] **True** 3.   A basic assumption that underlies financial reporting is that an entity will continue as a going concern.

[LO2] **False** 4.   A change in accounting estimate is an example of an accounting change that affects comparability and requires an explanatory paragraph in the audit report.

[LO2] **True** 5.   A change in reporting entity is an example of an accounting change that affects comparability and requires an explanatory paragraph in the audit report.

[LO2] **True** 6.   Changes that do not affect consistency are normally disclosed in the footnotes but do not require an explanatory paragraph in the audit report.

[LO3] **False** 7.   An auditor may be unable to express an unqualified opinion if an immaterial departure from GAAP is present in the financial statements.

[LO3] **True** 8.   An auditor must disclaim an opinion when the auditor lacks independence.

[LO4] **True** 9.   The choice of which audit report to issue depends on the condition and the materiality of the departure.

[LO4] **True** 10.   A scope limitation results from an inability to obtain sufficient competent evidence about some component of the financial statements.

## Part II: Multiple Choice Questions

[LO6]   1.  Special reporting issues that affect the financial statement audit report include:
    a.  Reports on comparative financial statements.
    b.  Other information in documents containing audited financial statements.
    c.  The going concern assumption.
    **d.  Both a and b.**

[LO6]   2.  A predecessor auditor should do the following before reissuing a report on statements presented on a comparative basis:
    a.  Read the financial statements of the current period.
    b.  Read the financial statements of the past five years.
    c.  Obtain a letter of representations from the current-year, successor auditor.
    **d. Both a and c.**

[LO8]  3.  Auditing standards define OCBOA financial statements as including those prepared under the following base:
  a.  Tax basis.
  b.  Cash basis but not modified cash basis.
  c.  A definite set of criteria having substantial support.
  **d.  Both a and c.**

[LO8]  4.  Auditing standards define OCBOA financial statements as including those prepared under the following base:
  a.  Regulatory basis.
  b.  Tax basis.
  c.  A definite set of criteria having substantial support.
  **d.  All of the above.**

[LO9]  5.  An auditor may be engaged to audit only part of the financial statements including:
  **a.  Specified elements or accounts.**
  b.  The entity's net income.
  c.  The entity's stockholders' equity.
  d.  Both a and b.

[LO9]  6.  An auditor can satisfy the requirements that specified users take responsibility for the sufficiency of an agreed-upon procedure by:
  a.  Comparing the procedures to be used to the written requirements of the users.
  b.  Discussing the procedures to be used with appropriate user representatives.
  c.  Reviewing relevant contracts or correspondence from the specified users.
  **d.  All of the above.**

[LO9]  7.  In some situations an auditor may be engaged to audit only part of the financial statements. Examples include:
  a.  a report on rentals.
  b.  a report on royalties.
  c.  a report on profit participation.
  **d.  All of the above.**

[LO9]  8.  An engagement to apply agreed-upon procedures is one in which the auditor:
  a.  Issues an unqualified opinion.
  b.  Issues a qualified opinion.
  **c.  Does not express an opinion.**
  d.  Both a or b.

[LO9]  9.  A report for an agreed-upon procedures engagement includes:
  a.  Identifies the specified users.
  b.  Includes references relating to the character of the engagement.
  c.  Disclaims an opinion.
  **d.  All of the above.**

[LO10]10.  A special report related to compliance with contractual provisions provides:
  a.  Positive assurance.
  **b.  Negative assurance.**
  c.  No assurance.
  d.  None of the above.

## Part III: Short Essay Questions

---

[LO2] Discuss the accounting changes that affect consistency and the accounting changes that would not affect consistency.

**A standard unqualified audit report implies that the comparability of the financial statements is not affected by changes in accounting principles or that any change is immaterial. From the auditor's perspective, accounting changes can be categorized into changes that affect consistency and those that do not affect consistency:**

1. **Change in accounting principles.**
2. **Change in reporting entity.**
3. **Correction of an error in principles.**

**Other changes may affect comparability but not consistency. These include:**

1. **Change in accounting estimate.**
2. **Correction of an error that does not involve an accounting principle.**
3. **Change in classification and reclassification.**
4. **Change expected to have a material future effect.**

---

[LO3 & 4] Discuss the conditions that prohibit the auditor from issuing an unqualified opinion and the types of reports that the auditor may issue for a financial statement audit.

**The auditor can issue three types of audit reports that depart from the unqualified audit report (see Figure 18-1) including:**

1. **Scope limitation. A scope limitation results from an inability to collect sufficient competent evidence, such as when management prevents the auditor from conducting an audit procedure considered necessary.**

2. **Departure from GAAP. The financial statements are affected by a departure from GAAP.**

3. **Lack of auditor independence. The auditor must comply with the second general standard and the Code of Professional Conduct in order to issue an unqualified opinion.**

**The three types of reports other than unqualified are:**

1. **Qualified. The auditor's opinion is qualified because of either a scope limitation or a departure from a GAAP, but overall the financial statements present fairly.**

2. **Disclaimer. The auditor disclaims an opinion on the financial statements either because there is insufficient competent evidence to form an opinion on the overall financial statements or because there is a lack of independence.**

3. **Adverse. The auditor's opinion states that the financial statements do not present fairly in conformity with GAAP because the departure materially affects the overall financial statements.**

[LO8] Identify and define the four bases used to prepare financial statements on a comprehensive basis other than GAAP.

**Auditing standards define OCBOA financial statements as including those prepared under the following bases:**

1. **Regulatory basis. The basis used to comply with the requirements or financial reporting provisions of a governmental regulatory agency. An example would be when an insurance company reports in compliance with the rules of a state insurance commission.**

2. **Tax basis. The basis the entity uses to file its income tax return. Real estate partnerships frequently use this basis for reporting to partners.**

3. **Cash (or modified cash) basis. When the entity reports on revenues when received and expenses when paid. The cash basis may be modified to record depreciation or to accrue income taxes.**

4. **A definite set of criteria having substantial support. Financial statements prepared on a price level-adjusted basis are an example of such a set of criteria.**

**Part IV: Crossword Puzzle – Chapter 18 Solution [LO ALL]**

| | | | | | | | | | | | | | | |
|---|---|---|---|---|---|---|---|---|---|---|---|---|---|---|
| ¹O | C | B | O | ²A | | | | | | | | | | |
| | | | | D | | ³C | | | | | ⁴Q | | | |
| | | | | V | | O | | | | | U | | ⁵G | |
| | | | | E | | S | | | | | A | | O | |
| ⁶A | U | D | I | T | R | E | P | O | R | T | L | | I | |
| | | | | S | | | | | ⁷G | | I | | N | |
| ⁸S | C | O | ⁹P | E | L | I | M | I | T | A | T | I | O | N |
| | | | E | | | | | | A | | F | | G | |
| | | | R | | | | | | P | | I | | C | |
| | | | V | | | | | | | | E | | O | |
| ¹⁰U | N | Q | U | A | L | I | F | I | E | D | | | N | |
| | | | S | | | | | | | | | | C | |
| | | | ¹¹D | I | S | C | L | A | I | M | E | R | E | |
| | | | V | | | | | | | | | | R | |
| ¹²M | A | T | E | R | I | A | L | I | T | Y | | | N | |

**Across**

1    Financial statements prepared under regulatory, tax, cash basis, or other definitive criteria have substantial support.
6    This is the end product from a financial statement engagement (two words).
8    A lack of evidence, such as an inability to conduct an audit procedure considered necessary (two words).
10   A "clean" opinion.
11   The auditor should issue this when he or she lacks independence.
12   The choice of which audit report to issue depends on the condition and the _____ of the departure.

**Down**

2    The "kiss of death" opinion.
3    Integrated framework for internal control.
4    When a scope limitation is material, but not pervasive.
5    An assumption that an entity has the ability to continue operations for a reasonable period of time (two words).
7    The abbreviation for accounting and reporting standards.
9    A level of which materiality which affects the overall financial statements.

**Part V: Townsend Office Supplies and Equipment [LO ALL]**

---

### Chapter 18
### Townsend Office Supplies and Equipment

ABC has been asked to report on the entity's compliance with the contractual agreements related to its line of credit with Eastern Fidelity Bank. Discuss the contractual terms associated with the line of credit and evaluate the company's compliance. Discuss the type of assurance that ABC will provide to Townsend and Eastern Fidelity and provide an example of the report on compliance with the contractual provisions of the line of credit that ABC with issue.

**Contractual terms of line of credit: According to contract, Townsend must have an annual audit completed by March 1 of each year in order to maintain its line of credit with Eastern. In addition, the company must maintain a current ratio of 1.75:1, an acid ratio of 1:1, a total debt to equity ratio that cannot exceed 1.1:1 and a short-term debt to equity ratio that cannot exceed 0.55:1. Should any two or more of the ratio restrictions not be maintained, any unpaid balance will be callable and the account will be closed for a period not less than a year. No dividends can be distributed if the total debt to equity ratio exceeds 1.10:1.**

**Analysis of Townsend's contractual compliance**
**Current ratio restriction ( $\geq$ 1.75:1)**
**Actual ratio (CA/CL) = 1592/898 = <u>1.77:1</u>**

**Current acid ratio restriction ( $\geq$ 1:1)**
**Actual ratio [(Cash + A/R + MS)/CL] = (210 + 310 + 274)/898 = <u>0.88:1</u>**

**Current total debt/equity ratio restriction ( $\leq$ 1.10:1)**
**Actual ratio (TD/Equity) = 2100/1989 = <u>1.06:1</u>**

**Current short-term debt/equity ratio restriction ( $\leq$ 0.55:1)**
**Actual ratio (STD/Equity) = 898/1989 = <u>0.45:1</u>**

**Dividend restriction total debt to equity ( $\leq$ 1.10:1)**

**Type of assurance: ABC will provide negative assurance as to its compliance with the provisions of the line of credit. Negative assurance consists of a statement that, as a result of specified procedures, nothing came to the auditor's attention which indicated that the provisions had not been complied with.**

**Example of report on compliance issued by ABC**

**Independent Auditor's Report**

**We have audited, in accordance with auditing standards generally accepted in the United States of America, the balance sheet of Townsend Office Supplies and Equipment as of December 31, 2007, and the related statement of income, retained earnings, and cash flows for the year then ended, and have issued our report thereon dated February 20, 2008.**
**In connection with our audit, nothing came to our attention that caused us to believe that the Company failed to comply with the terms, covenants, provisions, or conditions of sections 5 and 6, inclusive, of the line of credit dated April 1, 2007, with Eastern Fidelity Bank insofar as they relate to accounting matters. However, our audit was not directed primarily toward obtaining knowledge of such noncompliance.**
**This report is intended solely for the information and use of the board of directors and management of Townsend Office Supplies and Equipment and Eastern Fidelity Bank and is not intended to be and should not be used by anyone other than these specified parties.**

# Professional Conduct, Independence, and Quality Control

## KEY THOUGHT

Auditors have been characterized as "gatekeepers" to the public securities markets that are crucial for capital formation. The independent public accountant performing this special function owes ultimate allegiance to the corporation's creditors and stockholders, as well as the investing public. This "public watchdog" function demands that the accountant maintain total independence from the client at all times and requires complete fidelity to the public trust [Initial Decision Release No. 249, Administrative Proceeding, File No. 3-10933, United States of American before the Securities and Exchange Commission in the Matter of Ernst & Young LLP].

## CHAPTER SUMMARY

**[LO1] Know the definitions and general importance of ethics and professionalism.**

A.  Ethics refers to a system or code of conduct based on moral duties and obligations that indicate how an individual should behave in society. Ethical conduct is the bedrock of modern professionalism. Professionalism, broadly defined, refers to the conduct, aims, or qualities that characterize or mark a profession or professional person. All professions establish rules or codes of conduct that define ethical (professional) behavior for members of the profession.

B.  Competence, objectivity, and integrity are critical to the accounting profession. Auditors, as information inspectors, play a role in reducing information risk through independent verification of management assertions. To be a credible source of objective, independent assurance, the professional must have a solid reputation not only for competence, but also for unquestioned character and integrity. The concepts of ethical behavior and professional conduct are central to the success of the accounting profession. The most important concept you will read in this chapter is that of personal responsibility and integrity. As an accountant, auditor, manager, or businessperson you will face numerous difficult ethical issues, and you will experience pressures and temptations. Given the importance of reputation, ethical behavior, and professionalism, the accounting profession has developed a **Code of Professional Conduct** (AICPA) that guides the behavior of accounting professionals.

**[LO2] Understand three basic theories of ethical behavior.**

A. Mintz (1997) has suggested that there are three methods or theories of ethical behavior that can guide the analysis of ethical issues in accounting: (1) utilitarianism, (2) a rights-based approach, and (3) a justice-based approach. While none of these theories by itself can provide a perfect ethical framework, each can be useful in helping an auditor to solve dilemmas by providing an ethical perspective. These theories are:

1. The **utilitarianism theory** (also called consequentialist theory) recognizes that decision making involves trade-offs between the benefits and burdens of alternative actions, and it focuses on the consequences of an action on the individuals affected. The theory proposes that the interests of all parties affected, not just one's self-interest, should be considered. It other words, the "rightness" of an action depends only on the value of the consequences of the action.

2. The **theory of rights** assumes that individuals have certain rights and other individuals have a duty to respect those rights. Under this approach, an individual should undertake an action only if it does not violate the rights of any individual. The theory of rights is important to auditors because of their public-interest responsibility. According to the concept known as the "moral point of view" auditors must be willing, at least sometimes, to put the interests of other stakeholders, such as investors and creditors, ahead of their own self-interests and those of the CPA firm. Thus, if a difference of opinion with top management exists over an accounting or reporting issue, the auditor should emphasize the interests of the investors and creditors in deciding what action to take, even if it means losing the client.

3. The **theory of justice** is concerned with issues such as equity, fairness, and impartiality. The theory of justice involves two basic principles. The first principle posits that each person has a right to have the maximum degree of personal freedom that is still compatible with the liberty of others. The second principle asserts that social and economic actions should be to everyone's advantage and available to all. In other words, decisions made within this theory should fairly and equitably distribute resources among those individual or groups affected.

**[LO3] Begin to understand how to deal with ethical challenges through an example situation.**

A. See Sun City Savings and Loan Company to consider how an auditor might reason through an ethical situation.

**[LO4] Understand the stages through which moral judgment develops in an individual.**

A. Substantial research indicates that moral judgment develops over time and is a function of age, education, and complexity of experience. Kohlberg (1976) proposed that moral development has six stages that can be divided into three levels of moral reasoning, which includes preconventional, conventional, and postconventional. A stage refers to a mode or pattern of behaviors that characterizes some definable point in an individual's life. See Table 19-1 for definitions of the six stages of ethical development.

**[LO5] Be familiar with how professional ethics standards for auditors have developed over time and the entities involved.**

A. Early in the history of the public accounting profession in the United States, nongovernmental associations took charge of setting standards and establishing codes of conduct for practicing accounts. In particular, the AICPA (and its predecessor, the American Association of Public Accountants) established auditing standards and a Code of Professional Conduct, mapping out the primary areas in which ethical conduct is expected of public accountants. The AICPA, being a private, nongovernmental association, only has the authority to require its members to comply with the code. However, state and federal courts have consistently held that all practicing CPAs, whether in public or private practice and whether or not a member of the AICPA, must follow professional ethical standards as laid out in the Code of Professional Conduct.

B. The SEC has legal authority to oversee the public accounting profession. Through much of its history, the SEC has allowed such private-sector entities as the FASB and the ASB to set accounting and auditing standards, respectively. The SEC has not hesitated to exercise its influence in the standard-setting process and has established standards of its own from time to time, some of which differ from those established by private-sector bodies.

C. The PCAOB adopted the professional standards established by the AICPA on an interim basis in 2003, including the Code of Professional Conduct. However, the PCAOB and the SEC have additional, more stringent standards of professional conduct, mostly in the key area of auditor independence, which must be followed by auditors of public companies. Because the Code of Professional Conduct provides the broadest map of the areas in which professionalism is expected from auditors, the code serves as the organizing framework for the following discussion of standards of professional conduct. The chapter highlights the important ways in which SEC and PCAOB rules governing the conduct and independence of public-company auditors differ from AICPA rules and standards.

D. Figure 19-1 summarizes the auditor's responsibilities with respect to auditing standards and standards of professional conduct for the audits of private and public companies.

P. 649

Relevant Professional Standards for Audits of Private versus Public Companies

| **Auditing Standards** | **Auditing Standards** |
|---|---|
| ASB (AICPA) – GAAS | PCAOB – currently similar to ASB standards, with notable exceptions |
| **Standards of Professional Conduct** | **Standards of Professional Conduct** |
| AICPA – Code of Professional Conduct | PCAOB – Code of Professional Conduct (adopted from AICPA) |
| ISB – standards apply unless AICPA expressly disagrees | SEC – more stringent independence rules for public company audits |
| | ISB – a cooperative effort between the AICPA and SEC; now defunct but standards apply |
| **Private company audit** | **Public company audit** |

**CPA**
**(auditor)**

**[LO6] Understand the framework for the Code of Professional Conduct.**

A. The **Code of Professional Conduct** (AICPA) defines both ideal principles and minimum acceptable behavior for auditors. The code deals mainly with the behavior and actions of individual auditors, though firms are also responsible for the conduct of their employees and partners. The AICPA bylaws provide a means by which the Institute can discipline individual members and member firms that do not comply with professional standards.

B. The Code of Professional Conduct consists of two sections:

1. **Principles of Professional Conduct**. The principles set forth ideal attitudes and behaviors.

2. **Rules of Conduct**. The rules define the minimum standards.

The Principles of Professional Conduct provide the framework for the Rules of Conduct. Additional guidance for applying the Rules of Conduct is provided by:

1. **Interpretations of Rules of Conduct**. The interpretations are promulgated by the Professional Ethics Executive Committee to provide guidelines as to the scope and application of the Rules of Conduct.

2. **Rulings** by the Professional Ethics Executive Committee.

Note that the interpretations and ethics rulings are enforceable, and an auditor who departs from such standards has the burden of justifying such departures.

P.658 Figure 19-2 provides a pictorial representation of the four parts of the Code of Professional Conduct.

**[LO7] Know the principles of professional conduct.**

A. Six ethical principles provide a framework for the Code of Professional Conduct. Table 19-2 presents the definition of each principle. Note that the principles are stated at a conceptual level. Because they are conceptual ideals, these principles of ethical behavior are not specifically enforceable. The six ethical principles are:

1. **Responsibilities**. In carrying out their responsibilities as professionals, members should exercise sensitive professional and moral judgments in all their activities.

2. **The public interest**. Members should accept the obligation to act in a way that will serve the public interest, honor the public trust, and demonstrate commitment to professionalism.

3. **Integrity**. To maintain and broaden public confidence, members should perform all professional responsibilities with the highest sense of integrity.

4. **Objectivity and independence**. A member should maintain objectivity and be free of conflicts of interest in discharging professional responsibilities. A member in public practice should be independent in fact and appearance when providing auditing and other attestation services.

406

5. **Due care.** A member should observe the profession's technical and ethical standards, strive continually to improve competence and the quality of services, and discharge professional responsibility to the best of the member's ability.

6. **Scope and nature of services.** A member in public practice should observe the Principles of the Code of Professional Conduct in determining the scope and nature of services to be provided.

## [LO8] Understand the framework for the Rules of Conduct.

A. The Bylaws of the AICPA require that members adhere to the **Rules of Conduct** of the Code of Professional Conduct and that members must be prepared to justify any departures from the rules. The rules are more specific that the Rules of Conduct. Table 19-3 provides an overview of the AICPA Rules of Conduct. The rules are grouped and numbered in five categories:

*Similar with Principle of Professional conduct, but more specific.*

1. **Section 100.** Independence, Integrity and Objectivity.

   a. 101 Independence.
   b. 102 Integrity and objectivity.

2. **Section 200.** General Standards and Accounting Principles.

   a. 201 General standards.
   b. 202 Compliance with standards.
   c. 203 Accounting principles.

3. **Section 300.** Responsibilities to Client.

   a. 301 Confidential client information.
   b. 302 Contingent fees.

4. **Section 400.** Responsibilities to Colleagues (no rules currently exist).

5. **Section 500.** Other Responsibilities and Practices.

   a. 501 Acts discreditable.
   b. 502 Advertising and other forms of solicitation.
   c. 503 Commissions and referral fees.
   d. 505 Form of organization and name.

See Table 19-4 for a summary of the Rules of Conduct and related Interpretations.

Table 19-5 provides the definitions for a number of key terms and definitions relating to the AICPA rules of Conduct. These terms and definitions should be understood in order to understand the rules and interpretations.

## [LO9] Be familiar with the rules of conduct that apply to independence, integrity, and objectivity.

A. **Section 100.** This section of the AICPA Rules of Conduct currently contains two rules related to independence, integrity, and objectivity. SEC and ISB rules and standards relating to auditor independence are also discussed in this section to the extent that they differ in important ways.

**Rule 101.** If an auditor is not independent of his or her client, it is unlikely that a user of financial statements will place much reliance on the CPA's work. Rule 101 is a very general statement concerning auditor independence and relates only to attestation-related services. Rule 101 states:

> **A member in public practice shall be independent in the performance of professional services as required by standards promulgated by bodies designated by Council.**

AICPA professional standards require a public accounting firm, including the firm's partners and professional employees, to be independent in accordance with AICPA Rule 101 whenever the firm performs an attest service for a client. Attest services include:

1. Financial statement audits.
2. Financial statement reviews.
3. Other attest services as defined in the SSAEs.

Note that performing a compilation of a client's financial statements does not require independence, but an accountant or firm that lacks independence must explicitly indicate this fact in the compilation report. Likewise, independence is not required to perform other nonattest services (e.g., tax preparation, financial planning or consulting services) if those services are the only services provided to a particular client.

Because of the difficulty that sometimes arises in defining independent relationships, numerous interpretations of Rule 101 have been issued. Table 19-4 lists the interpretations of Rule 101 that are currently in effect. Table 19-6 presents Interpretation 101-1, a major interpretation related to independence. It is important to consider the definition of a "covered member." The AICPA uses an engagement team approach to determine independence. Thus, a covered member includes:

1. An individual on the attest engagement team.

2. An individual in a position to influence the attest engagement.

3. A partner or manager who provides nonattest services to the attest client beginning once he or she provides 10 hours of nonattest services to the client within any fiscal year and ending on the later of the date (1) the firm signs the report on the financial statements for the fiscal year during which those services were provided or (2) he or she non longer expects to provide 10 or more hours of nonattest services to the attest client on a recurring basis.

4. A partner in the office in which the lead attest engagement partner primarily practices in connection with the attest engagement.

5. The firm, including the firm's employee benefit plans.

6. An entity whose operating, financial, or accounting policies can be controlled (as defined by generally accepted accounting principles for consolidation purposes) by any of the individuals or entities described above or by two or more such individuals or entities if they act together.

Note that the independence rules apply to more than just the partner on the attest engagement. Every individual on the engagement team and others who may be in a position to influence the engagement must be independent with respect to the attest client. Other partners or managers of the CPA firm who are not on the attest engagement team must also generally be independent of the client if they provide nonattest services to that client (such as tax or consulting services), or even if a partner simply works in the same office as the attest engagement's lead partner.

The CPA firm itself must also be independent with respect to the client. Note that with a few exceptions, the independence requirements under Rule 101 extend to the CPA's immediate family members (spouse, spousal equivalent, or dependents) and, in a few cases, to the CPA's close relatives (nondependent children, siblings, parents, etc.).

Interpretation 101-1 examines independence along two dimensions (financial relationships and business relationships) and considers the effects of family relationships on independence. A number of other interpretations of Rule 101 provide further explanations on such financial and business relationships.

1. **Financial Relationships**. Interpretation 101-1 prohibits members from any financial relationship with a client that may impair or give the appearance of impairing independence. This includes any direct or materially indirect financial interest in the client. A direct financial interest results when a covered member (sometimes hereafter referred to as a CPA) has a financial interest in an attest client, such as ownership of stock (more than 5 percent) or a loan to or from the client. With few exceptions (see below), direct financial interests by CPAs in attest clients impair independence. An indirect financial interest results when a CPA has a financial interest in an entity that is associated with an attest client. For example, an indirect financial interest is created if a CPA invests in a mutual fund that owns a client's shares. Indirect financial interests are generally permissible only if the amount involved is immaterial with respect to the covered member's income and wealth. Additional interpretations have been issued to clarify or provide exceptions to such financial interests. Generally a loan to or from a client is considered to impair the member's independence. However, there are situations in which a CPA is permitted to obtain loans from a financial institution that is a client. Interpretation 101-5 permits the following types of personal loans from a client that is a financial institution:

    1. Automobile loans and leases collateralized by the automobile.

    2. Loans fully collateralized by the surrender value of an insurance policy.

    3. Loans fully collateralized by cash deposits at the same financial institution.

    4. Credit cards and cash advances where the aggregate outstanding balance is reduced to $10,000 or less by the payment due date.

       Such loans must be made in accordance with the financial institution's normal lending procedures, terms, and requirements and must, at all times, be kept current as to all terms.

2. **Business Relationships**. Rule 101 (including relevant interpretations) essentially indicates that the independence of a CPA is impaired if the CPA performs a managerial or other significant role for a client's organization during the time period covered by an attest engagement. Such situations often arise when a former employee of the client becomes employed by the CPA firm or, more commonly, when a CPA takes a job with a former audit client. Interpretations of this rule, however, provide for certain exceptions.

Interpretation 101-2 indicates that a firm's independence will be considered to be impaired with respect to a client if a partner or professional employee leaves the firm and is subsequently employed by or associated with that client in a key position unless a number of conditions are met (Table 19-5 and Table 19-7).

3. **Provisions of Nonaudit Services.** The AICPA Code of Professional conduct restricts the types of nonaudit services that can be provided to attest clients. Interpretation 101-3 outlines these requirements and also binds member CPAs to follow the relevant requirements of other regulatory bodies where applicable. Thus, failure to comply with more restrictive provisions of other regulatory bodies also violates the Code of Professional Conduct. The Code permits CPAs to provide bookkeeping, systems implementation, internal audit outsourcing, and other service to attest clients subject to certain conditions and limits. Interpretation 101-3 of the Code outlines general requirements for performing other professional services for attest clients:

   a. The CPA should not perform management functions or make management decisions for the attest client. However, the CPA may provide advice, research materials, and recommendations to assist the client's management in performing its functions and making decisions.

   b. The client must agree to perform the following functions in connection with the nonattest engagement:

      1. Make all management decisions and perform all management functions.
      2. Designate a competent employee, preferably within senior management, to oversee the services.
      3. Evaluate the adequacy and results of the services performed.
      4. Accept responsibility for the results of the services.

Establish and maintain internal control, including monitoring ongoing activities.

   a. Before performing nonattest services, the CPA should establish and document in writing his or her understanding with the client (board of directors, audit committee, or management, as appropriate in the circumstances) regarding the following:

      1. Objectives of the engagement.
      2. Services to be performed.
      3. Client's acceptance of its responsibilities.
      4. Member's responsibilities.
      5. Any limitations of the engagement.

Interpretation 101-3 offers the following examples of general activities that would be considered to impair a CPA's independence:

1. Authorizing, executing, or consummating a transaction or otherwise exercising authority on behalf of a client.

2. Preparing source documents, in electronic or other form, evidencing the occurrence of a transaction.

3. Having custody of client assets.

410

4. Supervising the client's employees in the performance of their normal recurring activities.

5. Determining which recommendations of the member should be implemented.

6. Reporting to the board of directors on behalf of management.

7. Serving as a client's stock transfer or escrow agent, registrar, general counsel, or its equivalent.

The central issue is that the CPA is prohibited from assuming a management or decision-making role when providing nonaudit services to attest clients. For example, Interpretation 101-3 allows a CPA firm to provide outsourced internal audit services for a client for which the member also performs a professional service that requires independence (i.e., an audit or other attest service). Performing these extended audit services would not be considered to impair independence provided the member or his or her firm does not act or appear to act as either employee or management of the client. Thus, if a member provides assistance in the performance of an audit client's internal audit function, the member and client must understand that the client is responsible for:

1. Designating a competent individual or individuals, preferably within senior management, to be responsible for the internal audit function.

2. Determining the scope, risk, and frequency of internal audit activities, including those to be performed by the member providing the extended audit services.

3. Evaluating the findings and results arising from the internal audit activities, including those performed by the member providing the extended audit services.

4. Evaluating the adequacy of the audit procedures performed and the findings resulting from the performance of those procedures by, among other things, obtaining from the member.

While the AICPA Code of Professional Ethics permits internal audit outsourcing, the SEC prohibits providing this and several other types of nonaudit professional services to a public-company audit client.

**[LO10] Know the basic differences between the SEC's independence rules for public company auditors and AICPA standards for audits of nonpublic entities.**

A. The SEC's mission is to protect investors and maintain the integrity of the capital markets in which the securities of publicly traded companies are bought and sold. As part of its mission, the SEC has authority to establish standards relating to financial accounting, auditing, and the professional conduct of public accountants in the context of public-company accounting and auditing. The SEC has established standards that differ from those established by the AICPA, particularly in the area of auditor independence. The SEC's standards must be followed by auditors of public companies.

B. The SEC implemented more stringent independence rules for auditors of public companies in November 2000, which were further revised in January 2003, after Title II of the Sarbanes-Oxley Act required additional independence restrictions. While most of the SEC's independence rules are similar to the AICPA's, the recent changes resulted in some important differences relating to three important areas. They include (1) provision of other professional services, (2) handling of human resource and compensation-related issues, and (3) certain required communications:

1. **Provision of Other Professional Services**. The SEC's rules with respect to services provided by auditors are predicated on three basic principles of auditor objectivity and independence:

   a. An auditor should not audit his or her own work.
   b. An auditor should not function in the role of management.
   c. An auditor should not serve in an advocacy role for the client.

   Consistent with these principles, the SEC prohibits the provision of several types of professional services by accounting firms to public-company audit clients, sometimes with the qualifier "unless it is reasonable to conclude that the results of these services will not be subject to audit procedures during an audit of the client's financial statements." Note that the rules do not limit the scope of nonaudit services provided by accounting firms to nonpublic companies or to public companies that are not audit clients. The SEC specifies nine categories of nonaudit services that, with few exceptions, are considered to impair independence if provided to a public-company audit client:

   a. Bookkeeping or other services related to the accounting records or financial statements of the audit client.

   b. Financial information systems design and implementation.

   c. Appraisal or valuation services, fairness opinions, or contribution-in-kind reports.

   d. Actuarial services.

   e. Internal audit outsourcing services.

   f. Management functions or human resources.

   g. Broker or dealer, investment adviser, or investment banking services.

   h. Legal services.

   i. Expert services.

   Consistent with the Sarbanes-Oxley Act, SEC regulations also prohibit any other service that the PCAOB determines impermissible. At this point, the PCAOB has not added any prohibited services to the list. While the first eight categories of services listed above were prohibited under pre-Sarbanes SEC independence rules (expert services is a newly added category), a number of exceptions to these prohibitions have been eliminated.

   All audit and nonaudit services provided by a public company's auditor must be approved by the company's audit committee, either on a case-by-case basis or pursuant to preestablished policies and procedures. A company's audit committee is charged with overseeing the effectiveness of the company's internal and external audits. This rule essentially requires the audit committee to consider the possible effects of nonaudit services on the auditor's objectivity and on investors' perceptions of the auditor's independence from the company.

2. **Human Resource and Compensation-Related Issues**. SEC rules in this area are primarily concerned with the potential for audit partners to become "too close" to an engagement or a client over time and with potential threats to an auditor's objectively resulting from employment and compensation arrangements that can create conflicts of interest.

   a. SEC rules prohibit the lead and concurring partners on the engagement team for a public-company audit from providing audit services to the company for more than five consecutive years. Once the partners "roll off" a client, a five-year "time-out" period is required before they can return to their former duties with that client. Audit partners other than the lead and concurring partners are prohibited from performing audit services for a particular client for more than seven consecutive years, with a two-year "time-out" period.

   b. If any individual with a "financial reporting oversight role" at a public company (subject to specified exceptions) was a member of the accounting firm's audit engagement team within a one-year "cooling off" period (defined as the one-year period preceding the commencement of audit procedures for the period that included the date the engagement team member was first employed by the client company), the accounting firm is prohibited from auditing the company's financial statements.

   c. The SEC does not consider an accounting firm to be independent from a public-company audit client if an audit partner receives compensation based on selling engagements to that client for services other than audit, review and attest services. This applies not only to audits of domestic issuers but also to audits of foreign subsidiaries and affiliates of U.S. issuers, as well as of foreign private issuers, by U.S. and foreign accounting firms.

3. **Required Communications**. SEC rules also differ from those of the AICPA in requiring additional communication between auditors and their clients' audit committees and in requiring public-company audit clients to publicly report information regarding the fees paid to their auditors.

   a. The auditor of a public company must report to the company's audit committee all "critical accounting policies" used by the company, all alternative treatments within GAAP for policies and procedures related to material items discussed with management, and other material written communications between the auditor and the company's management. In addition, the audit committee must be responsible for the appointment, compensation, and oversight of the external auditor's work. This is important, because it establishes the audit committee as the auditor's client, rather than management itself. Remember that management is ultimately responsible for a company's financial statements. Because the audit committee of a public company must be independent of management, setting up the audit committee as the point of contact for the auditor creates a healthier environment in which the auditor does not answer directly to or receive compensation from management.

b. Proxy statements and annual reports issued by public companies must contain disclosures regarding (1) audit fees, (2) audit-related fees, (3) tax fees, and (4) all other fees billed during the prior two fiscal years by the principal auditor of the company's financial statements. Details must also be provided on the nature of services provided in earning "other fees." The pre-approval policies of the company's audit committee must also be disclosed. A purpose of this requirement is to make companies more sensitive to public perceptions of auditor independence and objectivity.

C. **Effects of Family Relationships**. The issues related to a CPA's financial or managerial interest in a client may extend to members of the CPA's family. Certain relationships between members of a CPA's family and a client are considered to affect the CPA's independence. A distinction is made in Interpretation 101-1 between a covered member's immediate family (spouse, spousal equivalent, or dependent) and close relatives (parent, sibling, or nondependent child). A covered member's immediate family is subject to Rule 101 and its interpretations and rulings. Table 19-6 contains two exceptions. For example, a covered member's spouse employed by a client would not impair independence if he or she were not employed in a key position. Financial or business interests by close relatives such as nondependent children, brothers, sisters, parents, grandparents, parents-in-law, and their respective spouse do not normally impair independence. Interpretation 101-1 (Table 19-6) lists the situations where independence would be impaired by a close relative. The two major situations that can impair independence are:

1. A close relative has a financial interest in the client that is material to the close relative, and the CPA participating in the engagement is aware of the interest.

2. An individual participating in the engagement has a close relative who could exercise significant influence over the financial or accounting policies of the client (key position).

D. **Effect of Actual or Threatened Litigation**. Sometimes threatened or actual litigation between the client and the auditor can impair the auditor's independence. Interpretation 101-6 cites three categories of litigation: (1) litigation between the client and the CPA, (2) litigation by shareholders, and (3) other third-party litigation where the CPA's independence may be impaired. The following criteria are offered as guidelines for assessing independence when actual or threatened litigation exists between the client and the CPA:

1. The commencement of litigation by the present management alleging deficiencies in audit work for the client would be considered to impair independence.

2. The commencement of litigation by the CPA against the present management alleging management fraud or deceit would be considered to impair independence.

3. An expressed intention by the present management to commence litigation against the CPA alleging deficiencies in audit work would impair independence if the auditor concluded that it is probable that such a claim will be filed.

Litigation by client security holders or other third parties also may impair the auditor's independence under certain circumstances. For example, litigation may arise from a class action lawsuit by stockholders alleging that the client, its management, its officers, its directors, it underwriters, and its auditors were involved in the issuance of "false or misleading financial statements." Generally, such lawsuits do not alter the fundamental relationship between the CPA and the client. However, independence may be impaired if material client-auditor cross-claims are filed. In such a situation, an adversarial relationship would exist and the CPA would no longer be independent. When this occurs, the CPA should either (1) withdraw from the engagement or (2) disclaim an opinion because of a lack of independence. Other third-party litigation against the CPA may be commenced by lending institutions or by other creditors who rely on the client's financial statements that were opined on by the CPA. Normally, such lawsuits do not impair the CPA's independence unless the relationship between the CPA and the client is affected.

E. **Rule 102.** This rule expands slightly on the principle from which it was developed and requires that a member maintain integrity and objectivity. It reads:

> **In the performance of any professional service, a member shall maintain objectivity and integrity, shall be free of conflicts of interest, and shall not knowingly misrepresent facts or subordinate his or her judgment to others.**

There are a number of important interpretations of Rule 102 including:

1.  Interpretation 102-1 indicates that a member who knowingly asks or permits false and misleading entries in financial statements or records violates Rule 102.

2.  Interpretation 102-2 states that a conflict of interest may occur if a member performs a professional service for a client or employer and the member of his or her firm has a relationship with another person, entity, product, or service that could be viewed as impairing the CPA's objectivity.

3.  Interpretation 102-3 states that, in dealing with his or her employer's external accountants, a member must be candid and not knowingly misrepresent facts or knowingly fail to disclose material facts.

4.  Interpretation 102-4 states that if a member and his or her supervisor have a disagreement or dispute relating to the preparation of financial statements or the recording of transactions, the member must take steps to ensure that the situation does not result in a subordination of judgment. If the member concludes that the financial statements or record could be materially misstated, he or she should communicate those concerns to a higher level of management within the organization. If appropriate action is not taken, the member should consider whether to continue the relationship with the employer. The member should also consider whether any responsibility exists to communicate the problem to third parties, such as regulatory agencies, or the employer's external accountants.

5.  Interpretation 102-5 states that education services are professional services and subject to Rule 102. Thus a member must maintain objectivity and integrity when performing such services.

6.  Interpretation 102-6 states that when a member is asked by a client to act as an advocate in performing tax or consulting services or in support of a client's position on an accounting or auditing issue, the member may accept such an engagement, but he or she must be sure that the requested services does not go beyond the bounds of sound professional practice and impair independence, integrity and objectivity.

**[LO11] Be familiar with the rules of conduct that apply to general standards and accounting principles.**

A. **Section 200.** The Rules of Conduct contain two rules related to general standards and one rule related to accounting principles.

B. **Rule 201** captures much of what is contained in the 10 generally accepted auditing standards and codifies it as part of the Code. It reads:

> **A member shall comply with the following standards and with any interpretations thereof by bodies designated by Council.**
>
> **A. Professional Competence. Undertake only those professional services that the member of the member's firm can reasonably expect to be completed with professional competence.**
>
> **B. Due Professional Care. Exercise due professional care in the performance of professional services.**
>
> **C. Planning and Supervision. Adequately plan and supervise the performance of professional services.**
>
> **D. Sufficient Relevant Data. Obtain sufficient relevant data to afford a reasonable basis for conclusions or recommendations in relation to any professional services performed.**

C. **Rule 202** addresses compliance with standards for professional services. It reads:

> **A member who performs auditing, review, compilation, management consulting, tax, other professional services shall comply with standards promulgated by bodies designated by Council.**

D. **Rule 203** relates to compliance with accounting principles. Rule 203 reads:

> **A member shall not (1) express an opinion or state affirmatively that the financial statements or other financial data of any entity are presented in conformity with generally accepted accounting principles or (2) state that he or she is not aware of any material modifications that should be made to such statements or data in order for them to be in conformity with generally accepted accounting principles, if such statements or data contain any departure from an accounting principle promulgated by bodies designated by Council to establish such principles that has a material effect on the statements or data taken as a whole. If, however, the statements or data contain such a departure and the member can demonstrate that due to unusual circumstances the financial statements or data would otherwise have been misleading, the member can comply with the rule by describing the departure, its approximate effects, if practicable, and the reasons why compliance with the principle would result in a misleading statement.**

**[LO12] Be familiar with the rules of conduct that apply to responsibilities to clients.**

A. **Section 300.** The Rules of Conduct contains two rules related to a CPA's responsibilities to his or her clients.

B. **Rule 301** specifies four situations in which a CPA can disclose confidential information without the client's consent: (1) to meet disclosure requirements for GAAP and GAAS, (2) to comply with a valid and enforceable subpoena, (3) as required by an authorized peer review board or body, and (4) as part of an investigative or disciplinary proceeding. It reads:

> **A member in public practice shall not disclose any confidential client information without the specific consent of the client.**
>
> **This rule shall not be construed (1) to relieve a member of his or her professional obligations under rules 202 and 203, (2) to affect in any way the members' obligation to comply with a validly issued and enforceable subpoena or summons, or to prohibit a member's compliance with applicable laws and governmental regulations, (3) to prohibit review of a member's professional practice under AICPA or state CPA society or Board of Accountancy authorization, or (4) to preclude a member from initiating a complaint with, or responding to any inquiry made by, the professional ethics division or trial board of the Institute or a duly constituted investigative or disciplinary body of a state CPA society or Board of Accountancy.**
>
> **Members of any of the bodies identified in (4) above and members involved with professional practice reviews identified in (3) above shall not use to their own advantage or disclose any member's confidential client information that comes to their attention in carrying out those activities. This prohibition shall not restrict members' exchange of information in connection with the investigative or disciplinary proceedings described in (4) above or the professional practice reviews described in (3) above.**

Interpretation 301-3 specifically allows a review of a CPA's professional practice in conjunction with the purchase, sale, or merger of the practice. The CPA should take precautions that the prospective buyer does not disclose any confidential client information. This can generally be accomplished through the use of a confidentiality agreement. Members who review a CPA's practice in connection with a prospective purchase or merger should not use the information to their advantage, nor should they disclose any confidential client information that comes to their attention.

C. **Rule 302** relates to contingent fees. It reads:

> **A member in public practice shall not**
>
> (1) **Perform for a contingent fee any professional services for, or receive such a fee from a client for whom the member or the member's firm performs**
>    (a) **an audit or review of financial statements; or**
>    (b) **a compilation of a financial statement when the member expects, or reasonably might expect, that a third party will**

417

use the financial statement and the member's compilation report does not disclose a lack of independence; or

(c)  an examination of prospective financial information; or

(2)  Prepare an original or amended tax return or claim for a tax refund for a contingent fee for any client.

The prohibition in (1) above applies during the period in which the member or member's firm is engaged to perform any of the services listed above and the period covered by any historical financial statements involved in any such listed services.

Except as stated in the next sentence, a contingent fee is a fee established for the performance of any service pursuant to an arrangement in which no fee will be charged unless a specific finding or result is attained, or in which the amount of the fee is otherwise dependent upon the finding or result of such service. Solely for purposes of this rule, fees are not regarded as being contingent if fixed by courts or other public authorities, or, in tax matters, if determined based on the results of judicial proceedings or the findings of governmental agencies.

A member's fee may vary depending, for example, on the complexity of the services rendered.

Note that if contingent fees were allowed for attestation-related services, users of those services might question the CPA's independence.

**[LO13] Be familiar with the rules of conduct that apply to other responsibilities and practices.**

A.  **Section 500**. The Rules of Conduct includes four rules that relate to other aspects of the profession.

B.  **Rule 501** relates to acts discreditable. It reads:

**A member shall not commit an act discreditable to the profession.**

Seven interpretations have been issued that identify acts considered discreditable under Rule 501:

1.  Interpretation 501-1. Retention of client records.

2.  Interpretation 501-2. Discrimination and harassment in employment practices.

3.  Interpretation 501-3. Failure to follow standards and/or procedures or other requirements in government audits.

4.  Interpretation 501-4. Negligence in the preparation of financial statements or records.

5.  Interpretation 501-5. Failure to follow requirements of government bodies, commissions, or other regulatory agencies in performing attest or similar services.

6.  Interpretation 501-6. Solicitation/disclosure of CPA examination questions/answers.

7.  Interpretation 501-7. Failure to file tax return or pay tax liability.

C. **Rule 502** relates to advertising and other forms of solicitation. It reads:

> **A member in public practice shall not seek to obtain clients by advertising or other forms of solicitation in a manner that is false, misleading, or deceptive. Solicitation by the use of coercion, over-reaching, or harassing conduct is prohibited.**

Interpretation 502-2 provides specific examples of activities that are prohibited by this rule. These include:

1. Creating false or unjustifiable expectations of favorable results.

2. Implying an ability to influence any court, tribunal, regulatory agency, or similar body or official.

3. Claiming that specific professional services in current or future periods will be performed for a stated fee, estimated fee, or fee range when it is likely at the time of representation that such fees will be substantially increased and the prospective client is not advised of that likelihood.

4. Making any other representations that would be likely to cause a reasonable person to misunderstand or be deceived.

D. **Rule 503** relates to commissions and referral fees. It reads:

> A. **Prohibited commissions**
> **A member in public practice shall not for a commission recommend or refer to a client any product or service, or for a commission recommend or refer any product or service to be supplied by a client, or receive a commission, when a member or the member's firm also performs for that client**
> - **An audit or review of financial statements; or**
> - **A compilation of a financial statement when the member expects, or reasonably might expect, that a third party will use the financial statement and the member's compilation report does not disclose a lack of independence; or**
> - **An examination of prospective financial information.**
> **This prohibition applies during the period in which the member is engaged to perform any of the services listed above and the period covered by any historical financial statements involved in the listed services.**
>
> B. **Disclosure of permitted commissions**
> **A member in public practice who is not prohibited by this rule form performing services for or receiving a commission and who is paid or expects to be paid a commission shall disclose that fact to any person or entity to whom the member recommends or refers a product or service to which the commission relates.**

C. **Referral fees**

Any member who accepts a referral fee for recommending or referring any service of a CPA to any person or entity or who pays a referral fee to obtain a client shall disclose such acceptance or payment to the client.

Note that the current rule does not allow commissions or referral fees in situations where the CPAs independence and objectivity are a focal point of attestation-related services.

E. **Rule 505** relates to the form of organization and name. It reads:

A member may practice public accounting only as a form of organization permitted by law or regulation whose characteristics conform to resolutions of Council.

A member shall not practice public accounting under a firm name that is misleading. Names of one or more past partners may be included in the firm name of a successor organization.

A firm may not designate itself as "Members of the American Institute of Certified Public Accountants" unless all of its CPA owners are members of the Institute.

F. The AICPA has a number of avenues by which members can be disciplined for violating the Code of Professional Conduct. For violations that are not sufficient to warrant formal actions, the Professional Ethics Executive Committee can direct a member to take remedial or corrective actions. If the member rejects the committee's recommendation, the committee can refer the case to a hearing panel of the Trial Board. Membership in the AICPA can be suspended or terminated without a hearing if the member has been convicted of certain criminal offenses (such as a crime punishable by imprisonment for more than one year or filing a false income tax return on a client's behalf) or if the member's CPA certificate is suspended or revoked by a government agency. A member may also be expelled or suspended for up to two years by the Trial Board for violating any rule of the Code of Professional Conduct.

Note that the SEC and the PCAOB also have several options for pursuing disciplinary actions against auditors.

**[LO14] Understand the definition of a system of quality control and the AICPA's two-tiered quality peer review program.**

A. CPA firms are required to implement policies and procedures to monitor the firms' practices and ensure that professional standards are being followed. In 1977 the AICPA started a voluntary peer review program, and by January 1988 had approved mandatory quality peer reviews. The program is structured in two tiers: one for firms that have public-company audit clients and one for (usually smaller) firms that audit only private companies. The purpose of the quality peer review program is to ensure that firms comply with relevant quality control standards.

B. In 2004, the PCAOB assumed the AICPA's responsibilities relating to firms that audit public clients and instituted a mandatory quality inspection program for those firms. The AICPA continues to administer a two-tiered quality review system in order to enable firms to meet their state licensing, federal regulatory, and AICPA membership requirements and to serve firms that audit only privately held clients. The two tiers of quality reviews are offered through (1) the AICPA Center for Public Company Audit Firms Peer Review Program and (2) the AICPA

Peer Review Program (designed for firms that audit only private companies). All AICPA member firms subject to PCAOB inspections are required to join the Center, whose peer review program is designed to review and evaluate those portions of a firm's accounting and auditing practice that are not subject to inspection by the PCAOB. The Center's program is nationally administered by a Center peer review committee made up of firms that are also subject to PCAOB inspection. Firms that are not subject to PCAOB inspection may choose to join the Center or may opt for the AICPA Peer Review Program.

C. **Statement on Quality Control Standards (SQCS) No. 2**, "System of Quality Control for a CPA Firm's Accounting and Auditing Practice" (QC10), provides CPA firms professional guidance in establishing a system of quality control SQCS No. 2 applies only to auditing and accounting practice (audit, attest, and review services). While not required, it is recommended that the guidance in this statement be applied to other services such as tax services and consulting services.

## [LO15] Know the elements of quality control and how a firm monitors its quality control system.

A. A firm's system of quality control encompasses its organizational structure and the policies and procedures established to provide the firm with reasonable assurance of conforming with professional standards (QC 10.03). A firm's system of quality control has to be tailored to its size, the nature of its practice, its organization, and cost-benefit considerations.

B. **SQCS No. 2** identifies the following five elements of quality control:

1. Independence, integrity and objectivity.
2. Personnel management.
3. Acceptance and continuance of clients and engagements.
4. Engagement performance.
5. Monitoring.

Table 19-8 defines each the elements. Note that the elements are interrelated.

Table 19-9 provides some examples of the types of policies or procedures a firm can implement to comply with a sound system of quality control.

C. Quality control standards require consistent monitoring of (1) the relevance of and compliance with the firm's policies and procedures, (2) the adequacy of the firm's guidance materials and practice aids, and (3) the effectiveness of professional development programs (QC 20). Firms should implement monitoring procedures to identify and communicate circumstances that may necessitate changes and improvements to the firm's system of quality control. Procedures for monitoring include:

1. Inspection procedures.

2. Pre- and postcompletion review of selected engagements.

3. Analysis and assessment of:

    a. New professional pronouncements.

    b. Results of independence confirmations.

c. Continuing professional education and other professional development activities undertaken by firm personnel.

d. Decision related to acceptance and continuance of client relationships and engagements.

e. Interviews of firm personnel.

4. Determination of any corrective actions to be taken and improvements to be made in the quality control system.

5. Communication to appropriate firm personnel of any weaknesses identified in the quality control system or in the level of understanding or compliance therewith.

6. Follow-up by appropriate firm personnel to ensure that any necessary modifications are promptly made to the quality control policies and procedures.

The AICPA requires member firms to have their practices reviewed by peer firms every three years.

## [LO16] Be familiar with the PCAOB inspection program for accounting firms that audit public companies.

A. In addition to the AICPA peer review programs, the PCAOB conducts regular inspections of public accounting firms that are required to register with the board. These inspections review selected audit and quarterly review engagements and evaluate the sufficiency of the quality control system of registered firms. The purpose of these inspections is to ensure that registered firms, in connection with their audits of public companies, comply with the Sarbanes-Oxley Act, PCAOB rules, and professional standards.

B. The PCAOB conducts special inspections on an ad hoc basis when it has specific cause, but the frequency with which regulation inspections are conducted is established by law. Registered firms that issue more than 100 audit reports for public companies per year are subject to an annual inspection, while those firms that regularly issues more than 1 but less than 100 audit reports in a year must be inspected at least once every three years.

C. Should a PCAOB inspection find that a firm, or anyone associated with it, may be in violation of legislation, accounting regulations, any professional standard, or even the firm's own quality control policies, then the PCAOB can conduct a special investigation into the possible violation. Following an investigation, the board will issue a draft report at which time the firm has 30 days to respond to any accusations. At the end of this period, the board then issues a final report outlining the violations; however, assuming such violations do not involve fraud, the firm is granted a 12-month period in which to take necessary corrective action. If sufficient action is taken, the PCAOB does not publicly reveal the firm's violations – otherwise, public disciplinary action ensures against responsible parties.

D. Mandatory inspections apply to all firms that audit public U.S. companies. However, if the accounting firm is not based in the United States, there may be some exceptions to the inspection requirements. For instance, at the PCAOB's discretion, the board may rely (at least in part) on foreign authorities to conduct inspections.

# CHAPTER 19: SELF-ASSESSMENT

## Part I: True or False Questions

[LO1] _____ 1.  The term "ethics" refers to a person's model view of the world.

[LO1] _____ 2.  Professionalism refers to the conduct of a given profession.

[LO5] _____ 3.  When auditing a public company, a CPA must follow the auditing standards of the PCAOB.

[LO6] _____ 4.  The AICPA Code of Professional Conduct deals mainly with behavior and actions of individual auditors.

[LO6] _____ 5.  The principles of conduct set forth the minimum standards.

[LO6] _____ 6.  Interpretations of rules are enforceable.

[LO6] _____ 7.  Ethical rulings are not enforceable.

[LO7] _____ 8.  Principles are stated at a conceptual level.

[LO8] _____ 9.  The rules contained in Section 100 cover issues relating to independence, integrity and auditing standards.

[LO9] _____ 10.  If an auditor is not independent of the client, it is unlikely that a user of financial statements will place much reliance on the CPA's work.

## Part II: Multiple Choice Questions

[LO9]  1.  The statement concerning auditor independence for attestation services is:
   a.  Rule 102.
   b.  Rule 101.
   c.  Rule 301.
   d.  None of the above.

[LO9]  2.  Examples of general activities that would be considered to impair a CPA's independence under Interpretation 101-3 include:
   a.  Reporting to the board of directors on behalf of management.
   b.  Having custody of client assets.
   c.  Communicating with the auditor committee about audit related issues.
   d.  Both a and b.

[LO10] 3.  For private companies, accounting firms are prohibited from providing:
   a.  Actuarial services.
   b.  Audit services.
   c.  Review services.
   d.  None of the above.

[LO10] 4. Accounting firms cannot provide legal services to:
   a. Private companies.
   b. Public companies.
   c. Private or public companies.
   d. All of the above.

[LO10] 5. During its brief tenure, the IBS issued:
   a. Three standards.
   b. Three interpretations.
   c. Three standards and three interpretations.
   d. None of the above.

[LO10] 6. The standard that provides guidance about an accountant's integrity and objectivity is:
   a. Rule 101.
   b. Rule 301.
   c. Rule 102.
   d. None of the above.

[LO11] 7. The standard that provides guidance about general standards and compliance with the standards is:
   a. Rule 101.
   b. Rule 201.
   c. Rule 102.
   d. Rule 202.

[LO12] 8. The standard that provides guidance about client confidentiality is:
   a. Rule 101.
   b. Rule 301.
   c. Rule 201.
   d. None of the above.

[LO12] 9. The standard that provides guidance about contingent fees is:
   a. Rule 301.
   b. Rule 201.
   c. Rule 302.
   d. Rule 202.

[LO13] 10. The standard that provides guidance about an accounting firm's form of organization and name is:
   a. Rule 501.
   b. Rule 503.
   c. Rule 504.
   d. Rule 505.

## Part III: Short Essay Questions

[LO10] Discuss the SEC's rules with respect to services provided by accounting firms to public companies. Identify the services that an accounting firm is prohibited from providing to public companies.

[LO12] Discuss the AICPA's rule on confidential client information and why the concept of confidentially is so important to the accounting profession.

[LO16] Discuss the PCAOB's inspection process for peer reviews of registered public accounting firms.

# Part IV: Crossword Puzzle – Chapter 19 [LO ALL]

## Across

1     A system or code of conduct based on moral duties and obligations that indicates how an individual should behave.
3     AICPA rule on integrity and objectivity.
5     The third general auditing standard requires this level of performance of the audit and preparation of the report (three words).
9     AICPA rule on general standards.
10    AICPA rule on contingent fees.
11    The \_\_\_\_\_ \_\_ _____ define the minimum acceptable standards that are enforceable (three words).

## Down

2     The topics of AICPA Rule No. 101.
3     AICPA rule on client confidentiality.
4     The measures of the quality of the auditor's performance developed by the ASB.
6     AICPA rule on discreditable acts.
7     An abbreviation for the federal law that mandated the establishment of the PCAOB.
8     AICPA rule on advertising and solicitation.

**Part V: Townsend Office Supplies and Equipment [LO ALL]**

| |
|---|
| **Chapter 19**<br>**Townsend Office Supplies and Equipment** |
| Discuss the guidelines that ABC should follow to meet its peer review responsibilities. Visit the AICPA's website to learn more about the most current peer review standards. |

# CHAPTER 19: SELF-ASSESSMENT SOLUTIONS

## Part I: True or False Questions

[LO1] **False** 1.   The term "ethics" refers to a person's moral view of the world.

[LO1] **True** 2.   Professionalism refers to the conduct of a given profession.

[LO5] **True** 3.   When auditing a public company, a CPA must follow the auditing standards of the PCAOB.

[LO6] **True** 4.   The AICPA Code of Professional Conduct deals mainly with behavior and actions of individual auditors.

[LO6] **False** 5.   The principles of conduct set forth the minimum standards.

[LO6] **True** 6.   Interpretations of rules are enforceable.

[LO6] **False** 7.   Ethical rulings are not enforceable.

[LO7] **True** 8.   Principles are stated at a conceptual level.

[LO8] **False** 9.   The rules contained in Section 100 cover issues relating to independence, integrity and auditing standards.

[LO9] **True** 10.   If an auditor is not independent of the client, it is unlikely that a user of financial statements will place much reliance on the CPA's work.

## Part II: Multiple Choice Questions

[LO9]  1.  The statement concerning auditor independence for attestation services is:
- a.  Rule 102.
- **b.  Rule 101.**
- c.  Rule 301.
- d.  None of the above.

[LO9]  2.  Examples of general activities that would be considered to impair a CPA's independence under Interpretation 101-3 include:
- a.  Reporting to the board of directors on behalf of management.
- b.  Having custody of client assets.
- c.  Communicating with the auditor committee about audit related issues.
- **d.  Both a and b.**

[LO10]  3.  For private companies, accounting firms are prohibited from providing:
- a.  Actuarial services.
- b.  Audit services.
- c.  Review services.
- **d.  None of the above.**

[LO10] 4. Accounting firms cannot provide legal services to:
   a. Private companies.
   **b. Public companies.**
   c. Private or public companies.
   d. All of the above.

[LO10] 5. During its brief tenure, the IBS issued:
   a. Three standards.
   b. Three interpretations.
   **c. Three standards and three interpretations.**
   d. None of the above.

[LO10] 6. The standard that provides guidance about an accountant's integrity and objectivity is:
   a. Rule 101.
   b. Rule 301.
   **c. Rule 102.**
   d. None of the above.

[LO11] 7. The standard that provides guidance about general standards and compliance with the standards is:
   a. Rule 101.
   **b. Rule 201.**
   c. Rule 102.
   d. Rule 202.

[LO12] 8. The standard that provides guidance about client confidentiality is:
   a. Rule 101.
   **b. Rule 301.**
   c. Rule 201.
   d. None of the above.

[LO12] 9. The standard that provides guidance about contingent fees is:
   a. Rule 301.
   b. Rule 201.
   **c. Rule 302.**
   d. Rule 202.

[LO13]10. The standard that provides guidance about an accounting firm's form of organization and name is:
   a. Rule 501.
   b. Rule 503.
   c. Rule 504.
   **d. Rule 505.**

## Part III: Short Essay Questions

[LO10] Discuss the SEC's rules with respect to services provided by accounting firms to public companies. Identify the services that an accounting firm is prohibited from providing to public companies.

**As part of its mission, the SEC has authority to establish standards relating to financial accounting, auditing, and the professional conduct of public accountants in the context of public-company accounting and auditing. The SEC has established standards that differ from those established by the AICPA, particularly in the area of auditor independence. The SEC's standards must be followed by auditors of public companies. The SEC implemented more stringent independence rules for auditors of public companies in November 2000, which were further revised in January 2003, after Title II of the Sarbanes-Oxley Act required additional independence restrictions. While most of the SEC's independence rules are similar to the AICPA's, the recent changes resulted in some important differences relating to three important areas. The SEC's rules with respect to services provided by auditors are predicated on three basic principles of auditor objectivity and independence:**

1. **An auditor should not audit his or her own work.**
2. **An auditor should not function in the role of management.**
3. **An auditor should not serve in an advocacy role for the client.**

**Consistent with these principles, the SEC prohibits the provision of several types of professional services by accounting firms to public-company audit clients, sometimes with the qualifier "unless it is reasonable to conclude that the results of these services will not be subject to audit procedures during an audit of the client's financial statements." Note that the rules do not limit the scope of nonaudit services provided by accounting firms to nonpublic companies or to public companies that are not audit clients. The SEC specifies nine categories of nonaudit services that, with few exceptions, are considered to impair independence if provided to a public-company audit client:**

1. **Bookkeeping or other services related to the accounting records or financial statements of the audit client.**

2. **Financial information systems design and implementation.**

3. **Appraisal or valuation services, fairness opinions, or contribution-in-kind reports.**

4. **Actuarial services.**

5. **Internal audit outsourcing services.**

6. **Management functions or human resources.**

7. **Broker or dealer, investment adviser, or investment banking services.**

8. **Legal services.**

9. **Expert services.**

[LO12] Discuss the AICPA's rule on confidential client information and why the concept of confidentially is so important to the accounting profession.

**The Rules of Conduct contains two rules related to a CPA's responsibilities to his or her clients. Rule 301 specifies four situations in which a CPA can disclose confidential information without the client's consent: (1) to meet disclosure requirements for GAAP and GAAS, (2) to comply with a valid and enforceable subpoena, (3) as required by an authorized peer review board or body, and (4) as part of an investigative or disciplinary proceeding.**

**Interpretation 301-3 specifically allows a review of a CPA's professional practice in conjunction with the purchase, sale, or merger of the practice. The CPA should take precautions that the prospective buyer does not disclose any confidential client information. This can generally be accomplished through the use of a confidentiality agreement. Members who review a CPA's practice in connection with a prospective purchase or merger should not use the information to their advantage, nor should they disclose any confidential client information that comes to their attention.**

[LO16] Discuss the PCAOB's inspection process for peer reviews of registered public accounting firms.

**The PCAOB conducts regular inspections of public accounting firms that are required to register with the board. These inspections review selected audit and quarterly review engagements and evaluate the sufficiency of the quality control system of registered firms. The purpose of these inspections is to ensure that registered firms, in connection with their audits of public companies, comply with the Sarbanes-Oxley Act, PCAOB rules, and professional standards. The PCAOB conducts special inspections on an ad hoc basis when it has specific cause, but the frequency with which regulation inspections are conducted is established by law. Registered firms that issue more than 100 audit reports for public companies per year are subject to an annual inspection, while those firms that regularly issue more than 1 but less than 100 audit reports in a year must be inspected at least once every three years.**

**Should a PCAOB inspection find that a firm, or anyone associated with it, may be in violation of legislation, accounting regulations, any professional standard, or even the firm's own quality control policies, then the PCAOB can conduct a special investigation into the possible violation. Following an investigation, the board will issue a draft report at which time the firm has 30 days to respond to any accusations. At the end of this period, the board then issues a final report outlining the violations; however, assuming such violations do not involve fraud, the firm is granted a 12-month period in which to take necessary corrective action. If sufficient action is taken, the PCAOB does not publicly reveal the firm's violations, otherwise, public disciplinary action ensures against responsible parties. Mandatory inspections apply to all firms that audit public U.S. companies. However, if the accounting firm is not based in the United States, there may be some exceptions to the inspection requirements.**

**Part IV: Crossword Puzzle – Chapter 19 Solution [LO ALL]**

```
 1E  T  H  2I  C  S        3R  U  L  E  1  0  2
        N        U                    4G
        D        L                    G
     5D  U  E  P  6R  O  F  E  7S  I  O  N  A  L  C  A  8R  E
        P        U        3  O        A              U
        E        L        0  X        S              L
        N        E        1                          E
        D        5                                   5
     9R  U  L  E  2  0  1              10R  U  L  E  3  0  2
        N        1                                2
        C
    11R  U  L  E  S  O  F  C  O  N  D  U  C  T
```

**Across**

1    A system or code of conduct based on moral duties and obligations that indicates how an individual should behave.

3    AICPA rule on integrity and objectivity.

5    The third general auditing standard requires this level of performance of the audit and preparation of the report (three words).

9    AICPA rule on general standards.

10   AICPA rule on contingent fees.

11   The _____ __ _____ define the minimum acceptable standards that are enforceable (three words).

**Down**

2    The topics of AICPA Rule No. 101.

3    AICPA rule on client confidentiality.

4    The measures of the quality of the auditor's performance developed by the ASB.

6    AICPA rule on discreditable acts.

7    An abbreviation for the federal law that mandated the establishment of the PCAOB.

8    AICPA rule on advertising and solicitation.

> ## Chapter 19
> ## Townsend Office Supplies and Equipment
>
> Discuss the guidelines that ABC should follow to meet its peer review responsibilities. Visit the AICPA's website to learn more about the most current peer review standards.
>
> **As a firm member of the AICPA, ABC should follow the AICPA Standards for Performing and Reporting on Peer Reviews (Peer Review Program). In October 2003, the AICPA Peer Review Board (Board) revised the standards for system reviews. The Board also revised some of the existing interpretations and approved new interpretations that will assist individuals in understanding the revised standards. The new standards and interpretations are effective for peer reviews commencing on or after January 1, 2005. Some of the most salient issues are summarized below.**
>
> **Firms and individuals enrolled in the AICPA Peer Review Program have the responsibility to (paragraph 2): (a) Establish and maintain appropriate quality control policies and procedures and comply with them to ensure the quality of their practices consistent with SQCS Statement No. 2 (System of Quality Control for a CPA Firm's Accounting and Auditing Practice). This standard requires every CPA firm, regardless of its size, to have a system of quality control for its accounting and auditing practice; (b) Perform accounting and auditing engagements in accordance with professional standards by competent professionals; (c) Engage a peer reviewer to perform a peer review in accordance with these Standards, in a timely manner; (d) Have independent peer reviews of their accounting and auditing practices. All firms that an AICPA member is associated with should undergo a peer review if the services performed and reports issued by the firm require a peer review; (e) Take such measures, if any, as may be necessary to satisfy its obligations concerning client confidentially any time state statues or ethics rules promulgated by state boards of accountancy do no clearly provide an exemption from confidentiality requirements when peer reviews are undertaken; (f) Provide such written representations to the peer reviewer indicating that the firm has complied with the standards; (g) Take remedial, corrective actions as needed; (h) Understand the AICPA Peer Review Boards guidance on resignations form the Program issued by Interpretation(s).**
>
> **Firms and individuals enrolled or seeking enrollment in the Program should comply with Council resolutions. In addition, for firm's enrolled, at least one of its partners must be a member of the AICPA (paragraph 6). A firm's due date for its initial peer review is 18 months from the date it enrolled in the Program or should have enrolled, whichever date is earlier (paragraph 8). A firm's subsequent peer review ordinarily has a due date of three years and six months from the year-end of the previous review (paragraph 10). Peer reviews must cover a current period of one year to be mutually agreed upon by the reviewed firm and the reviewing firm. Ordinarily, the review should be conducted with three to five months following the end of the year to be reviewed (paragraph 13). If a firm resigns from the Program and subsequently rejoins the Program, the firm's due date is the later of the due date originally assigned or ninety days after rejoining the Program (paragraph 16). Effective January 1, 2005, there are 13 Interpretations of the Standards for Performing and Reporting on Peer Reviews. These Interpretations are applicable to firms enrolled in the Program, individuals and firms who perform and report on peer reviews, entities that participate in the administration of the Program, associations of CPA firms that assist their members in arranging and carrying out peer reviews, and the AICPA Program staff. Interpretations are effective upon issuance unless otherwise issued.**

# Legal Liability

## KEY THOUGHT

Cooley on Torts, a legal treatise, describes the obligation for due care as follows. "Every man who offers his services to another and is employed assumes the duty to exercise in the employment such skill as he possesses with reasonable care and diligence. In all these employments where peculiar skill is requisite, if one offers his services, he is understood as holding himself out to the public as possessing the degree of skill commonly possessed by others in the same employment, and if his pretentions are unfounded, he commits a species of fraud upon every man who employs him in reliance on his public profession. But no man, whether skilled or unskilled, undertakes that the task he assumes shall be performed successfully, and without fault or error; he undertakes for good faith and integrity, but not for infallibility, and he is liable to his employer for negligence, bad faith, or dishonesty, but not for losses consequent upon purse errors of judgment" [Auditing Standards Board (AU 230.03)].

## CHAPTER SUMMARY

### [LO1] Understand the four general stages in the audit-related dispute process.

A.  Palmrose discusses the four general stages in the initiation and disposition of audit-related disputes:

   1.  The occurrence of events that result in losses for users of the financial statements (i.e., client bankruptcy, financial distress, fraudulent financial report, misappropriation of assets).

   2.  The investigation by plaintiff attorneys before filing suit to link the user losses with allegations of material omissions or misstatements of financial statements (i.e., a board of directors may hire a public accounting firm other than the external auditor to investigate potential fraud).

   3.  The legal process that commences with the filing of the suit (i.e., filing of complaints, discovery, trial preparation and trial).

   4.  The final resolution of the dispute (i.e., summary judgment, settlement to avoid or discontinue litigation, or court decision on appeal after a trial).

**[LO2] Know the definitions of key legal terms.**

A. Auditors can be sued by clients, investors, creditors and the government for failure to perform professional services adequately. Auditors can be held liable under two classes of law:

    1. **Common law**. Case law developed over time by judges who issue legal opinions when deciding a case. Note that the legal principles announced in these cases become precedent for judges deciding similar cases in the future.

    2. **Statutory law**. Written law enacted by the legislative branch of federal and state governments that establishes certain courses of conduct that must be adhered to by covered parties.

B. Definition of key legal terms include (Table 20-1):

    1. **Privity**. Absent a contractual or fiduciary relationship, the accountant does not owe a duty of care to an injured party.

    2. **Breach of contract**. Occurs when the client or auditor fails to meet the terms and obligations established in a contract, which is normally finalized in the engagement letter. Third parties may have privity or near privity of contract.

    3. **Tort**. A wrongful act other than a breach of contract for which civil action may be taken.

    4. **Ordinary negligence**. An absence of reasonable or due care in the conduct of an engagement. Due care is evaluated in terms of what other professional accountants would have done, under similar circumstances.

    5. **Gross negligence**. An extreme, flagrant, or reckless departure from professional standards of due care. This is also referred to as constructive fraud.

    6. **Fraud**. Actions taken with the knowledge and intent to deceive.

    7. **Criminal law**. Statutory law which defines the duties citizens owe to society and prescribes penalties for violations.

    8. **Civil law**. All law which is not criminal.

    9. **Class action**. Lawsuit filed by one or more individuals on behalf of all persons who may have invested on the basis of the same false and misleading information.

C. The types of liability and auditors' actions resulting in liability can include (Table 20-2):

    1. **Common law-clients**. Includes breach of contract, negligence, gross negligence (constructive fraud) and fraud.

    2. **Common law-third parties**. Includes negligence, gross negligence (constructive fraud) and fraud.

    3. **Federal statutory law-civil liability**. Includes negligence, gross negligence (constructive fraud) and fraud.

    4. **Federal statutory law-criminal liability**. Includes the willful violation of federal statutes.

D. Typical civil actions under common law allege that the auditor did not properly perform the audit. The auditor's liability to third parties (e.g., investors and creditors) under common law is complicated by the fact that legal precedent differs by jurisdictions. Most common-law cases are decided in state courts, but there are circumstances where common-law cases can be decided in federal court. The outcome of a common-law case depends on the location where the case is tried. Some jurisdictions follow a common-law doctrine that provides a very narrow interpretation of auditors' liability to third parties, while others follow a more liberal interpretation.

E. Under statutory law an auditor can be held civilly or criminally liable. A civil claim can result in fines and sanctions but not incarceration. Auditors are liable mainly for gross negligence and fraud under federal and state statutes; however, some parts of the federal acts have been used to hold auditors liable for ordinary negligence. Under certain circumstances an auditor can be held criminally liable under statutory law.

**[LO3] Know the auditor's liability to clients under common law.**

A. **Common law** does not require that the CPA guarantee his or her work product. It does, however, require that the auditor perform professional services with due care. This requires that the auditor perform all professional services with the same degree of skill, knowledge and judgment possessed by other members of the profession. When an auditor fails to carry out contractual arrangements with the client, he or she may be held liable for breach of contract or negligence. Under common law, the auditor is also liable to the client for gross negligence and fraud.

B. **Breach of contract**. A breach of contract liability is based on the auditor's failing to complete the services agreed to in the contract with the client. An engagement letter should establish the responsibilities for both the CPA and the client. If the client breaches its obligations under the engagement letter, the auditor is excused from his or her contractual obligations. If the CPA discontinues an audit without adequate cause, he or she may be liable for economic injury suffered by the client. Other issues (timely delivery of audit report or failure to detect a material defalcation) can lead to litigation by the client against the auditor.

C. **Negligence**. A tort is a wrongful act other than a breach of contract for which civil action may be taken. If an engagement is performed without due care, the CPA may be held liable for an actionable tort in negligence. Liability for negligence represents a deviation from a standard of behavior that is consistent with that of a "reasonable person." When an individual such as a CPA possesses special skills and knowledge, ordinary reasonable care is not sufficient (see Cooley's Torts). A CPA has the duty to conduct an engagement using the same degree of care that would be used by an ordinary, prudent member of the public accounting profession. To recover against an auditor in a negligence case, the client must prove the following:

1. A duty owed to the client to conform to a required standard of care.
2. Failure to act in accordance with that duty.
3. A causal connection between the auditor's negligence and the client's damage.
4. Actual loss or damage to the client.

Suits by clients against auditors often allege that the auditors did not detect some type of fraud or defalcation. Auditors' defense against client negligence claims includes the following:

1. No duty was owed.

2. The client was negligent (contributory negligence, comparative negligence, or management fraud).

3.  The auditor's work was performed in accordance with professional standards.

4.  The client suffered no loss.

5.  Any loss was caused by other events.

6.  The claim is invalid because the statute of limitations has expired (statute limitations vary from jurisdiction to jurisdiction).

The client can generally prove the existence of a duty of care based on the engagement contract. However, the auditor may be able to argue successfully that the client's loss was due to the client's negligence.

D.  **Fraud**. An auditor can be held liable to clients for fraud when he or she acted with knowledge and intent to deceive. Generally, actions alleging fraud result from lawsuits by third parties.

**[LO4] Understand the auditor's liability to third parties under common law.**

A.  Under **common law**, auditors can be held liable to third parties for negligence, gross negligence and fraud. This area of liability is very complex, and court rulings are not always consistent across federal and state judicial jurisdictions.

B.  **Negligence**. When an auditor fails to conduct an engagement with due care, he or she can be held liable for ordinary negligence to third parties (plaintiffs) under common law. To prevail in a suit alleging negligence, the third party must prove all of the following.

1.  The auditor had a duty to the plaintiff to exercise due care.

2.  The auditor breached that duty and was negligent in not following professional standards.

3.  The auditor's breach of due care was the direct cause of the third party's injury (e.g., the financial statements were misleading and the third party relied on the financial statements).

4.  The third party suffered an actual loss as a result.

The main difficulty faced by third parties in proving negligence against an auditor is showing that the auditor's duty to exercise due care extended to them. Over time, four common-law standards have evolved for determining the types of third parties that can successfully sue auditors for ordinary negligence. The four legal standards are:

1.  Privity (see Ultramares v. Touche, et al.).
2.  Near privity (see Credit Alliance v. Arthur Andersen & Co.).
3.  Foreseen third parties (see Rusch Factors, Inc. V. Levin).
4.  Reasonably foreseeable third parties (see H. Rosenblum, Inc. v. Adler).

C.  **Fraud**. If an auditor has acted with knowledge and intent to deceive a third party, he or she can be held liable for fraud. Common-law liability for fraud is not limited to persons in privity of contact with the auditor. The plaintiff must prove:

1.  A false representation by the accountant.

2.  Knowledge or belief by the accountant that the presentation was false.

3. The accountant intended to induce the third party to rely on the false representation.

4. The third party relied on the false representation.

5. The third party suffered damages.

Liability is not limited only to cases where the auditor was knowingly deceitful. Some courts have interpreted gross negligence as an instance of fraud (constructive fraud). Gross negligence is defined to be an extreme, flagrant, or reckless deviation from professional standards of due care (see State Street Trust Co. v. Ernst 1938).

D. **Damages under common law**. Plaintiffs who are awarded damages for a negligence or gross negligence claim against an auditor are eligible for compensatory damages, which means they are awarded damages to return them to a position equivalent to where they would have been in the absence of the auditor's negligence. Punitive damages are awarded to punish outrageous conduct and may be awarded when the auditor is found guilty of fraud or constructive fraud. Punitive damages are not permitted under federal statutory law, which provides plaintiffs incentive to file fraud charges under common law (in addition to statutory fraud charges). However, the Securities Litigation Uniform Standards Act of 1998 forces certain fraud charges to be brought in federal court under statutory law. Where the damages to the plaintiff can be apportioned between contributing parties, the auditor is only liable for his or her share of the total damages. If apportionment is not possible, some states follow the principle of joint and several liability, which means that the auditor can be responsible for the entire loss even if other parties contributed to the loss. Some courts have ruled that joint and several liability is inconsistent with the comparative fault concept, and some state legislatures have abolished joint and several liability in favor of a proportionate fault approach (i.e., if the auditor is found to be 30 percent at fault, he or she is only liable for 30 percent of the damages awarded).

**[LO5] Understand the auditor's legal liability under the Securities Act of 1933.**

A. **The Securities Act of 1933** generally regulates the disclosure of information in a registration statement for a new public offering of securities (Securities Exchange Act of 1934 regulates trading of securities after they are issued). Section 11 of the Securities Act of 1933 imposes a liability on issuers and others, including auditors, for losses suffered by third parties when false or misleading information is included in a registration statement. The plaintiff does not have to prove negligence or fraud, reliance on the auditor's opinion, a causal relationship, or a contractual relationship; the plaintiff need only prove that a loss was suffered by investing in the registered security and that the audited financial statements contained a material omission or misstatement. The misstatement can be the result of mere ordinary negligence. Section 11 is more favorable for plaintiffs than is common law because the burden of proof is shifted to the auditor to prove that he or she was not negligent. In other words, the auditor is presumed to have been negligent unless he or she can prove otherwise. The extremely plaintiff-friendly legal standards under the 1933 act reflects the fact that audited financial statements are typically more crucial for purchase decisions for new public offerings because few other credible sources of information are typically available for new issues. One defense available to the auditor sued under Section 11 is that of due diligence. The auditor must have made a reasonable investigation of the facts supporting or contradicting the information included in the registration statement.

**[LO6] Understand the auditor's legal liability under the Securities Exchange Act of 1934.**

A. **The Securities Exchange Act of 1934** is concerned primarily with ongoing reporting by companies whose securities are listed and traded on a stock exchange or that meet certain other statutory requirements. Two sections are important: Section 18 and Section 10(b), including Rule 10b-5.

B. **Section 18** imposes liability on any person who makes a material false or misleading statement in documents filed with the SEC. The auditor's liability can be limited if the auditor can show that he or she "acted in good faith and had no knowledge that such statement was false or misleading." A number of cases have limited the auditor's good-faith defense when the auditor's action has been judged to be grossly negligent.

C. Perhaps the greatest source of liability for auditors under the 1934 act is **Section 10(b)** and the related **Rule 10b-5**. Section 10(b) provides for a wide scope of liability. To sue under Rule 10b-5, the following elements must be proved:

1. A material, factual misrepresentation or omission.
2. Reliance by the plaintiff on the financial statements.
3. Damages suffered as a result of reliance on the financial statements.
4. Scienter.

The first element can include materially misleading information or the omission of material information. The term "scienter" is defined as intent to deceive, manipulate, or defraud. Some courts have ruled the gross negligence or reckless behavior is sufficient to satisfy the fourth element.

D. Prior to 1994, courts frequently held that an auditor who was not liable as a primary violator of Section 10(b) and Rule 10b-5 could still be held liable aiding and abetting if the auditor had knowledge and had substantially assisted in the primary violation. In 1994 the Supreme Court held that there is no aiding and abetting liability under Section 10(b). However, as a result of the numerous accounting frauds disclosed in the last few years, bills have been introduced in Congress to restore aiding and abetting liability in private damage actions.

E. The issue of what is necessary to establish primary liability under Section 10(b) can be significant in determining when an individual accountant may be held liable. This is an issue in the litigation arising out the Enron-Andersen collapse. While Andersen as a firm clearly made statements that permit Section 10(b) claims, stating primary liability claims against most of the individual Andersen defendants has proved difficult for plaintiffs (see Exhibit 20-9).

F. Measure of damages in most Section 10(b) and Rule 10b-5 cases is the out-of-pocket loss suffered by the plaintiff. The out-of-pocket loss is the difference between what the plaintiff paid or received for the securities and what he or she would have paid or received had there been no wrongful conduct by the auditor. Punitive damages are not permitted in a Section 10(b) or Rule 10b-5, although, such damages can sometimes be recovered in a concurrent common-law fraud action.

G. The Sarbanes-Oxley Act lengthened the statute of limitations for actions under Section 10(b) and Rule 10b-5 based on claims of "fraud, deceit, manipulation, or contrivance in contravention of a regulatory requirement concerning the securities laws." The Sarbanes-Oxley Act provides that any action shall be brought no later than two years from discovery and within five years from when the fraudulent conduct occurred. This provision was the only portion of Sarbanes-Oxley that specifically affected private securities fraud actions. The prior statute of limitations was one and three years, respectively.

**[LO7] Know how the Private Securities Litigation Reform Act of 1995 and the Securities Litigation Uniform Standards Act of 1998 relieve some of the auditor's legal liability.**

A. Prior to the passage of the **Private Securities Litigation Reform Act of 1995**, auditors sued under federal statutory law were held to the legal doctrine of joint and several liability, which holds each defendant fully liable for all assessed damages, regardless of the extent to which he or she contributed to the injury. This legislation provides, in general, for proportionate liability, where each defendant is liable solely for the portion of the damages that corresponds to the percentage of responsibility of that defendant. The act also raises the pleading requirement at the beginning of a case. The act requires that misrepresentation claims state the time, place and contents of the allegedly false representations, the identity of the person making them, and what he or she obtained as a result of the fraud. This may discourage "deep-pockets" lawsuits where plaintiffs hope to pressure defendants to settle out of court because the legal costs to fight the lawsuit may be greater than the costs to settle.

B. As a result of concerns that plaintiff lawyers would attempt to circumvent the Private Securities Litigation Reform Act of 1995 by bringing class action suits involving nationally traded securities to state court, Congress passed the **Securities Litigation Uniform Standards Act of 1998**. The purpose of the Uniform Standards Act was to "prevent plaintiffs from seeking to evade the protections that Federal law provides against abusive litigation by filing suit in State, rather than Federal Court." The primary federal protections to which the act refers are proportionate liability, disallowed punitive damages, and higher filing standards. As a result of the Uniform Standards Act, most large class actions against auditors alleging securities fraud must now be brought in federal court. The Uniform Standards Act defines a "covered class action" to include any lawsuit or group of lawsuits where damages are sought on behalf of more than 50 persons. Thus, smaller class actions lawsuits can still be pursued in state court.

**[LO8] Understand the auditor's legal liability under the Sarbanes-Oxley Act of 2002.**

A. The **Sarbanes-Oxley Act of 2002** is considered the most sweeping securities law since the 1933 and 1934 acts. Its main objectives are to restore investor confidence in the securities markets and to deter future corporate frauds. The act does include sections directly addressing legal liability, but the other aspects of the act (e.g., the creation of the PCAOB, stricter independence rules, audits of internal controls, and increased reporting responsibilities) are more important to auditors' performance and create new federal laws that the auditor must comply with. The creation of the PCAOB is the single most significant aspect of the legislation, ending decades of self-regulation by the accounting profession. While the Sarbanes-Oxley Act and PCAOB standards and enforcement actions only relate to public company auditors, state boards of accountancy may very well adopt or refer to the PCAOB rules in carrying out their regulatory functions for all public accountants.

B. Some of the most important provisions of the Sarbanes-Oxley Act are aimed at increasing the responsibility of corporate officers and directors for the reliability of their company's financial statements. Congress understood that the primary culprits in corporate fraud are dishonest officers and directors. Section 302 and 906 of the act requires the chief executive and chief financial officers of each public company to certify personally, among other things, the fairness of the financial information and the company's compliance with the 1934 act in each annual or quarterly report filed with the SEC (see LO12 for criminal liability).

**[LO9] Know how the SEC and PCAOB can sanction an auditor or audit firm.**

A. **Rule 102(e)** of the Rules of Practice empowers the SEC to suspend for any person the privilege of appearing and practicing before it if that person if found:

1. To not possess the necessary qualifications to represent others before the SEC; including, but not limited to persons whose license to practice as an accountant has been revoked or suspended by any state, territory, district, etc.;

2. To be lacking in character or integrity;

3. To have engaged in unethical or improper professional conduct; including, but not limited to felony conviction or misdemeanor conviction involving moral turpitude; or

4. To have willfully violated or willfully aided and abetted any violations of the federal securities laws or any rules or regulations promulgated pursuant to those laws.

This sanction can be applied not only to an individual auditor but also to an entire accounting firm. If a firm is suspended or barred from practice before the SEC, the impact on the firm's clients can be severe.

B. The SEC can also impose fines. A study of SEC sanctions imposed on auditors for their association with fraudulently misstated financial statements found that the most common problems cited were the auditor's failure to gather sufficient audit evidence, properly apply GAAP, exercise due professional care and an appropriate level of professional skepticism, and properly tailor audit procedures to address inherent risk.

C. The Sarbanes-Oxley Act grants the PCAOB broad investigative and disciplinary authority over registered public accounting firms and persons associated with such firms. As directed by the act, the board adopted rules relating to investigations and adjudications in September 2003. Under the adopted rules, the PCAOB may conduct investigations concerning any acts or practices involving auditors of publicly traded firms that may "violate any provision of the Act, the rules of the Board, the provisions of the securities laws relating to the preparation and issuance of audit reports and the obligations and liabilities of accountants with respect thereto, including the rules of the SEC issued under the Act, or professional standards."

D. When violations are detected, the board has the authority to impose sanctions. The sanctions can include revoking a firm's registration, barring a person from participating in audits of public companies, monetary penalties (up to $750,000 per individual or $15 million per firm) and requirements for remedial measures, such as training, new quality control procedures, and the appointment of an independent monitor. The PCAOB's rules, disciplinary decisions, and sanctions are subject to the approval of the SEC.

**[LO10] Understand how the Foreign Corrupt Practices Act can result in legal liability for auditors.**

A. The **Foreign Corrupt Practices Act** (FCPA) was passed by Congress in 1977 in response to the discovery of bribery and other misconduct on the part of more than 300 American companies. The act was codified in 1988 as an amendment to the Securities Exchange Act of

1934. As a result, an auditor may be subject to administrative proceedings, civil liability, and civil penalties under the FCPA. This legislation prohibits corporate officers from knowingly participating in bribing foreign officials to obtain or retain business. It imposes record-keeping and internal control requirements on public companies. To comply with the provisions of the FCPA, many corporations have established codes of conduct that prohibit bribery. Compliance with corporate codes of conduct should be checked by the audit committee and the internal auditors. If the external auditor detects activities that violate the FCPA, such violations should be communicated to management immediately.

**[LO11] Understand how the Racketeer Influenced and Corrupt Organizations Act can affect the auditor's legal liability.**

A.  While the **Racketeer Influenced and Corrupt Organizations Act** (RICO) was enacted by Congress in 1970 to combat the infiltration of legitimate businesses by organized crime, it has been used against auditors. RICO provides civil and criminal sanctions for certain types of illegal acts. A major factor in bringing an action under RICO is that the law provides for treble damages in civil RICO cases.

B.  Racketeering activity includes federal and state crimes, with mail fraud and wire fraud the most common acts alleged against auditors. A single instance of racketeering activity is not sufficient to establish a pattern of racketeering (see Reves v. Ernst & Young 1993).

C.  Prior to the Private Securities Litigation Reform Act of 1995, securities fraud was an offense under RICO. The reform act eliminated securities fraud as an offense in civil suits under RICO unless the auditor is criminally convicted of the fraud. Experts believe that after the reform act, Section 10(b) and Rule 10b-5 violations will almost never be grounds for a civil damage claim against an auditor under RICO. As a result of the wave of massive accounting frauds disclosed in 2000-2002, a bill was introduced in Congress to restore securities fraud as a basis for a civil RICO damage claim. However, this bill was not passed, and the Sarbanes-Oxley Act of 2002 did not restore securities fraud as a basis for a civil RICO damage claim.

**[LO12] Know how an auditor can be held criminally liable for various federal and state laws.**

A.  Auditors can be held criminally liable under the laws discussed in the previous sections. Auditors can be held criminally liable for various federal and state laws, such as banking and insurance regulations. Criminal prosecutions require that some form of criminal intent be present. Many of the laws contain provisions for criminal penalties to be levied if an auditor's actions reflect gross negligence. A number of significant cases against auditors have resulted in criminal prosecution, with auditors being given large fines and serving time in prison (United States v. Simon, United States v. Natelli, United States v. Weiner, In re Alexander Grant & Co. Litigation). In addition to criminal prosecution of the auditors, the auditors' firms were civilly liable for violating various statutes and paid large sums to settle the cases.

B.  Numerous sections of the Sarbanes-Oxley Act include criminal provisions. It enhances prosecutorial tools available in major fraud cases by expanding statutory prohibitions against fraud and obstruction of justice, increasing criminal penalties for traditional fraud and cover-up crimes, and strengthening sentencing guidelines applicable to large-scale financial frauds. The act adds a new securities fraud offense and increases authorized penalties for securities and financial reporting fraud (e.g., up to 25 years in prison). It is expected that the act's increased penalties will result in longer prison terms because of the corresponding changes in the federal sentencing guidelines.

C.  The Sarbanes-Oxley Act increases penalties for impeding official investigations, and because most frauds are discovered by employees rather than external auditors, the act strengthens the legal protections accorded whistleblowers. It is common for employers to retaliate against informants by demoting or firing them. The act makes it s felony punishable by 10-year imprisonment to retaliate against anyone who voluntarily comes forward to report suspected violations of any federal laws.

D.  Individual ethics and integrity cannot be legislated; hence, the Sarbanes-Oxley Act will not be a cure-all for corporate reform. Greed, mismanagement, conflicts of interest, and professional failures will never completely disappear, but most observers in the legal and accounting professions generally believe that the reforms imposed by the Sarbanes-Oxley Act were needed, will contribute to improved governance, and will send a signal that society does not tolerate widespread deceit in financial reporting.

**See the Advanced Module in the textbook for an example of an accounting fraud and litigation against an auditing firm (Phar-Mor case and Coopers & Lybrand).**

# CHAPTER 20: SELF-ASSESSMENT

## Part I: True or False Questions

[LO2] _____ 1. Common law is written law enacted by the legislative branches of governments.

[LO2] _____ 2. An auditor can be sued by a client for negligence under common law.

[LO2] _____ 3. An auditor can be sued by a third party for willful violation of statutes.

[LO2] _____ 4. An auditor can be sued for constructive fraud under federal statutory law.

[LO3] _____ 5. Common law requires the auditor perform professional services with due care.

[LO3] _____ 6. Breach-of-contract liability is based on the auditor failing to complete the services agreed to in the contract with the client.

[LO3] _____ 7. A tort is a breach of contract for which civil action may be taken.

[LO3] _____ 8. To recover against an auditor in a negligence case, the client must prove that the client sustained an actual loss or damage.

[LO4] _____ 9. To prevail in a suit alleging negligence, a third party must prove that the auditor had a duty to the auditor's client to exercise due care.

[LO4] _____ 10. Privity of contract is the most restrictive view under common law.

## Part II: Multiple Choice Questions

[LO2] 1. Auditors can be sued under third party common law for:
   a. Breach of contract.
   b. Negligence.
   c. Willful violation of federal statutes.
   d. All of the above.

[LO2] 2. To prevail in a suit alleging negligence, the third party must prove the following:
   a. The auditor had a duty to the plaintiff to exercise due care.
   b. The auditor had a duty to the client to exercise due care.
   c. The auditor's breach of due care was the direct cause of the client's injury.
   d. Both a and c.

[LO3] 3. To recover against an auditor in a negligence case, the client must prove the following:
   a. Actual loss or damage to the client.
   b. A duty owed to the client to conform to a required standard of care.
   c. Any loss was caused by other events.
   d. Both a and b.

[LO4] 4. To prevail in a suit alleging negligence, the third party must prove the following:
   a. The auditor had a duty to the plaintiff to exercise due care.
   b. The auditor breached that duty and was negligent in not following professional standards.
   c. The third party suffered an actual loss as a result.
   d. All of the above.

[LO4] 5. Joint and several liability means that the auditor can be responsible for:
   a. Punitive damages.
   b. Apportionment of the liability.
   c. For the entire loss.
   d. None of the above.

[LO5] 6. The Securities Act of 1933 regulates the disclosure of:
   a. Securities traded on a stock exchange.
   b. Securities for a new public offering.
   c. Securities for a new public offering and securities traded on a stock exchange.
   d. None of the above.

[LO5] 7. The Securities Exchange Act of 1934 regulates the disclosure of:
   a. Securities traded on a stock exchange.
   b. Securities for a new public offering.
   c. Securities for a new public offering and securities traded on a stock exchange.
   d. None of the above.

[LO6] 8. Section 10(b) relates to:
   a. The Securities Act of 1933.
   b. The Securities Exchange Act of 1934.
   c. The Sarbanes-Oxley Act of 2002.
   d. None of the above.

[LO6] 9. Rule 10b-5 relates to:
   a. The Securities Act of 1933.
   b. The Securities Exchange Act of 1934.
   c. The Sarbanes-Oxley Act of 2002.
   d. None of the above.

[LO6] 10. Under Rule 10b-5, a plaintiff must prove:
   a. Reliance by the plaintiff on the financial statement.
   b. Damages were suffered as a result of reliance on the financial statements.
   c. A material, factual misrepresentation or omission.
   d. All of the above.

## Part III: Short Essay Questions

[LO7] Discuss the difference between joint and several liability and proportionate liability under the Private Securities Litigation Reform Act of 1995.

[LO8] Discuss the Sarbanes-Oxley Act of 2002.

[LO9] Discuss Rule 102(e) of the Rules of Practice.

# Part IV: Crossword Puzzle – Chapter 20 [LO ALL]

## Across

1     A professional attitude that includes a questioning mind and a critical assessment of audit evidence.
5     A level of negligence where reasonable due care is absent in the conduct of an engagement.
9     The ___ ___ of ____ is the federal law which regulates the disclosure of information in a registration statement for initial public offerings (IPOs) (three words).
10     Breach of contract and negligence are examples of this type of law.
11     Measures of the quality of the auditor's performance (AICPA and PCAOB).
12     This occurs when the auditor fails to meet the terms or obligations, which are normally established in the engagement letter (three words).

## Down

2     A party's contractual or fiduciary relationship with the auditor or audit firm.
3     The ___ ___ of ____ is the federal law which regulates the trading of securities after they are initially issued (three words).
4     A level of negligence where extreme, flagrant or reckless departure from professional standards of due care is present.
6     Level of assurance that implies some risk that material misstatement could be present in the financial statements without detection.
7     The SEC is empowered to apply _____ to individual auditors as well as to an entire accounting firm.
8     Various laws that have been passed at both the federal and state levels, which are intended to protect the general public.

**Part V: Townsend Office Supplies and Equipment [LO ALL]**

| Chapter 20 |
| --- |
| **Townsend Office Supplies and Equipment** |
| Discuss some of the steps that ABC can take to minimize and avoid litigation. |

# CHAPTER 20: SELF-ASSESSMENT SOLUTIONS

## Part I: True or False Questions

[LO2] **False** 1.   Common law is written law enacted by the legislative branches of governments.

[LO2] **True** 2.   An auditor can be sued by a client for negligence under common law.

[LO2] **False** 3.   An auditor can be sued by a third party for willful violation of statutes.

[LO2] **True** 4.   An auditor can be sued for constructive fraud under federal statutory law.

[LO3] **True** 5.   Common law requires the auditor perform professional services with due care.

[LO3] **True** 6.   Breach-of-contract liability is based on the auditor failing to complete the services agreed to in the contract with the client.

[LO3] **False** 7.   A tort is a breach of contract for which civil action may be taken.

[LO3] **True** 8.   To recover against an auditor in a negligence case, the client must prove that the client sustained an actual loss or damage.

[LO4] **False** 9.   To prevail in a suit alleging negligence, a third party must prove that the auditor had a duty to the auditor's client to exercise due care.

[LO4] **True** 10.   Privity of contract is the most restrictive view under common law.

## Part II: Multiple Choice Questions

[LO2]   1.   Auditors can be sued under third party common law for:
   a.   Breach of contract.
   **b.   Negligence.**
   c.   Willful violation of federal statutes.
   d.   All of the above.

[LO2]   2.   To prevail in a suit alleging negligence, the third party must prove the following:
   **a.   The auditor had a duty to the plaintiff to exercise due care.**
   b.   The auditor had a duty to the client to exercise due care.
   c.   The auditor's breach of due care was the direct cause of the client's injury.
   d.   Both a and c.

[LO3]   3.   To recover against an auditor in a negligence case, the client must prove the following:
   a.   Actual loss or damage to the client.
   b.   A duty owed to the client to conform to a required standard of care.
   c.   Any loss was caused by other events.
   **d.   Both a and b.**

451

[LO4]  4.  To prevail in a suit alleging negligence, the third party must prove the following:
  a.  The auditor had a duty to the plaintiff to exercise due care.
  b.  The auditor breached that duty and was negligent in not following professional standards.
  c.  The third party suffered an actual loss as a result.
  **d.  All of the above.**

[LO4]  5.  Joint and several liability means that the auditor can be responsible for:
  a.  Punitive damages.
  b.  Apportionment of the liability.
  **c.  For the entire loss.**
  d.  None of the above.

[LO5]  6.  The Securities Act of 1933 regulates the disclosure of:
  a.  Securities traded on a stock exchange.
  **b.  Securities for a new public offering.**
  c.  Securities for a new public offering and securities traded on a stock exchange.
  d.  None of the above.

[LO5]  7.  The Securities Exchange Act of 1934 regulates the disclosure of:
  **a.  Securities traded on a stock exchange.**
  b.  Securities for a new public offering.
  c.  Securities for a new public offering and securities traded on a stock exchange.
  d.  None of the above.

[LO6]  8.  Section 10(b) relates to:
  a.  The Securities Act of 1933.
  **b.  The Securities Exchange Act of 1934.**
  c.  The Sarbanes-Oxley Act of 2002.
  d.  None of the above.

[LO6]  9.  Rule 10b-5 relates to:
  a.  The Securities Act of 1933.
  **b.  The Securities Exchange Act of 1934.**
  c.  The Sarbanes-Oxley Act of 2002.
  d.  None of the above.

[LO6]  10.  Under Rule 10b-5, a plaintiff must prove:
  a.  Reliance by the plaintiff on the financial statement.
  b.  Damages were suffered as a result of reliance on the financial statements.
  c.  A material, factual misrepresentation or omission.
  **d.  All of the above.**

## Part III: Short Essay Questions

[LO7] Discuss the difference between joint and several liability and proportionate liability under the Private Securities Litigation Reform Act of 1995 and the subsequent enactment of the Securities Litigation Uniform Standards Act of 1998.

**Prior to the passage of the Private Securities Litigation Reform Act of 1995 (PSLR), auditors sued under federal law were held to the legal doctrine of joint and several liability, which holds each defendant fully liable for all assessed damages, regardless of the extent to which he or she contributed to the injury. This legislation provides for proportionate liability, where each defendant is liable solely for the portion of the damages that corresponds to the percentage of responsibility of that defendant. The act also raises pleading requirements and requires that claims state the time, place and contents of the allegedly false representations, the identity of the person making them, and what he or she obtained as a result of the fraud. This may discourage "deep-pockets" lawsuits where plaintiffs hope to pressure defendants to settle out of court because the legal costs to fight the lawsuit may be greater than the costs to settle. As a result of concerns that plaintiff lawyers would attempt to circumvent the PSLR act by bringing class action suits involving nationally traded securities to state court, Congress passed the Securities Litigation Uniform Standards Act of 1998. The purpose of the act was to "prevent plaintiffs from seeking to evade the protections that Federal law provides against abusive litigation by filing suit in State, rather than Federal Court." The primary federal protections include proportionate liability, disallowed punitive damages, and higher filing standards. As a result, most large class actions against auditors alleging securities fraud must now be brought in federal court. The act defines a "covered class action" to include any lawsuit or group of lawsuits where damages are sought on behalf of more than 50 persons. Thus, smaller class actions lawsuits can still be pursued in state court.**

[LO8] Discuss the Sarbanes-Oxley Act of 2002.

**The Sarbanes-Oxley Act of 2002 is considered the most sweeping securities law since the 1933 and 1934 acts. Its main objectives are to restore investor confidence in the securities markets and to deter future corporate frauds. The act includes sections which address legal liability, but other aspects of the act (creation of the PCAOB, stricter independence rules, audits of internal controls, and increased reporting responsibilities) are more important to auditors' performance and create new federal laws that the auditor must comply with. The creation of the PCAOB is the single most significant aspect of the legislation, ending decades of self-regulation by the accounting profession. While the Sarbanes-Oxley Act and PCAOB standards and enforcement actions only relate to public company auditors, state boards of accountancy may adopt or refer to the PCAOB rules in carrying out their regulatory functions for all public accountants. Some of the most important provisions of the Sarbanes-Oxley Act are aimed at increasing the responsibility of corporate officers and directors for the reliability of their company's financial statements. Congress understood that the primary culprits in corporate fraud are dishonest officers and directors. Section 302 and 906 of the act requires a public company's CEO and CFO to certify personally, among other things, the fairness of the financial information and the company's compliance with the 1934 act in each annual or quarterly report filed with the SEC.**

[LO9] Discuss Rule 102(e) of the Rules of Practice.

**Rule 102(e) of the Rules of Practice empowers the SEC to suspend for any person the privilege of appearing and practicing before it if that person:**

1. **To not possess the necessary qualifications to represent others before the SEC; including, but not limited to persons whose license to practice as an accountant has been revoked or suspended by any state, territory, district, etc.;**

2. **To be lacking in character or integrity;**

3. **To have engaged in unethical or improper professional conduct; including, but not limited to felony conviction or misdemeanor conviction involving moral turpitude; or**

4. **To have willfully violated or willfully aided and abetted any violations of the federal securities laws or any rules or regulations promulgated pursuant to those laws.**

This sanction can be applied not only to an individual auditor but also to an entire accounting firm. If a firm is suspended or barred from practice before the SEC, the impact on the firm's clients can be severe.

The SEC can also impose fines. A study of SEC sanctions imposed on auditors for their association with fraudulently misstated financial statements found that the most common problems cited were the auditor's failure to gather sufficient audit evidence, properly apply GAAP, exercise due professional care and an appropriate level of professional skepticism, and properly tailor audit procedures to address inherent risk.

The Sarbanes-Oxley Act grants the PCAOB broad investigative and disciplinary authority over registered public accounting firms and persons associated with such firms. As directed by the act, the board adopted rules relating to investigations and adjudications in September 2003. Under the adopted rules, the PCAOB may conduct investigations concerning any acts or practices involving auditors of publicly traded firms that may "violate any provision of the Act, the rules of the Board, the provisions of the securities laws relating to the preparation and issuance of audit reports and the obligations and liabilities of accountants with respect thereto, including the rules of the SEC issued under the Act, or professional standards."

When violations are detected, the board has the authority to impose sanctions. The sanctions can include revoking a firm's registration, barring a person from participating in audits of public companies, monetary penalties and requirements for remedial measures, such as training, new quality control procedures, and the appointment of an independent monitor. The PCAOB's rules, disciplinary decisions, and sanctions are subject to the approval of the SEC.

**Part IV: Crossword Puzzle – Chapter 20 Solution [LO ALL]**

```
  1S  K  E  2P  T  I  C  I  S  M                    3S
               R                                    E
               I                                    C
               V              4G                     A
  5O  6R  D  I  N  A  R  Y                           C
      E      T               O                       T
      A      Y               S          7S      8S   1
      S                               9S  E  C  A  C  T  1  9  3  3
      S                               N       A       3
 10C  O  M  M  O  N                    C       T       4
      N                               T       U
 11G  A  A  S                          I       T
      B                               O       O
      L                                        
 12B  R  E  A  C  H  O  F  C  O  N  T  R  A  C  T
      S                               Y
```

## Across

1. A professional attitude that includes a questioning mind and a critical assessment of audit evidence.
5. A level of negligence where reasonable due care is absent in the conduct of an engagement.
9. The ___ ___ of ___ is the federal law which regulates the disclosure of information in a registration statement for initial public offerings (IPOs) (three words).
10. Breach of contract and negligence are examples of this type of law.
11. Measures of the quality of the auditor's performance (AICPA and PCAOB).
12. This occurs when the auditor fails to meet the terms or obligations, which are normally established in the engagement letter (three words).

## Down

2. A party's contractual or fiduciary relationship with the auditor or audit firm.
3. The ___ ___ of ___ is the federal law which regulates the trading of securities after they are initially issued (three words).
4. A level of negligence where extreme, flagrant or reckless departure from professional standards of due care is present.
6. Level of assurance that implies some risk that material misstatement could be present in the financial statements without detection.
7. The SEC is empowered to apply _____ to individual auditors as well as to an entire accounting firm.
8. Various laws that have been passed at both the federal and state levels, which are intended to protect the general public.

| **Chapter 20** |
| **Townsend Office Supplies and Equipment** |

Discuss some of the steps that ABC can take to minimize and avoid litigation.

**ABC should take a number of important steps to avoid litigation including:**

**Institute sound quality control and review procedures.**
A system of quality control and review can give the firm reasonable assurance of conforming to professional standards.

**Ensure that members of the firm are independent.**
Members of the firm must be independent in both fact and appearance. A review of legal cases indicates that on numerous occasions auditors did not maintain a sufficiently high level of "professional skepticism" and accepted a clients' responses without investigating the facts adequately.

**Follow sound client acceptance and retention procedures.**
Auditors need to be very careful in accepting new clients. If a client is known to lack integrity, the likelihood increases that its management will take actions that are detrimental to user groups, including management fraud.

**Be alert to risk factors that may result in lawsuits.**
A number of important risk factors seem to lead to litigation. These include: (1) the presence of management fraud, (2) the commission of illegal acts, (3) insolvency, (4) disagreements between auditors and management, (5) first-year audits, and (6) acquisition audits.
For example, when management fraud occurs, auditors are usually subject to litigation, and such cases are more costly to resolve. Some audit deficiencies have also been noted in the litigation against public accounting firms. These include incomplete client acceptance or retention procedures, unrealistic risk assessments given the client's circumstances, staff that is inadequately trained to audit specialized industries, inadequate documentation of difficult decisions, insufficient partner and manager participation in resolving key issues, and excessive reliance on management representations.

**Perform and document work diligently.**
A quality audit involves following relevant professional standards and includes:
(1) planning properly, (2) understanding the client's internal control adequately,
(3) obtaining sufficient competent evidence as to financial assertions, (4) having experienced personnel review the work done, and (5) issuing an appropriate audit report.

The threat of legal liability serves to prevent or limit inappropriate behavior on the part of auditors. However, auditors cannot be expected to ensure the accuracy of either financial statements or the financial health of a business entity. The auditor's responsibility is to provide reasonable assurance that there are no material misstatements in the financial statements.

# Assurance, Attestation, and Internal Auditing Services

## KEY THOUGHT

Two principal conceptual differences exist between the attestation standards and the ten existing GAAS. First, the attestation standards provide a framework for the attest function beyond historical financial statements. Accordingly, references to "financial statements" and "generally accepted accounting principles," which exist in GAAS, are omitted from the attestation standards. Second, as is apparent in the standards of fieldwork and reporting, the attestation standards accommodate the growing number of attest services in which the practitioner expresses assurances below the level that is expressed for the traditional audit ("positive opinion") [Auditing Standards Board (AT 100.89.1)].

## CHAPTER SUMMARY

**[LO1] Know the definition of assurance services.**

A. The AICPA Special Committee on Assurance Services has defined assurance services as follows:

> **Assurance services are independent professional services that improve the quality of information, or its context, for decision makers.**

B. The above definition captures a number of important concepts. First, the definition focuses on decision making. Making good decisions requires quality information, which can be financial or nonfinancial. Figure 21-1 presents the relationship of assurance services to attest and auditing. Adapted from the Elliott Committee's report, Figure 21-2 presents a model for decision making and the role of information in decision-making activities. Information is critical in this decision model. An assurance service engagement can help the decision maker search through this information in order to identify which pieces of information are relevant for the required decision. The second concept relates to improving the quality of information or its context. In the decision model shown in Figure 21-2, an assurance service engagement can improve quality through increasing confidence in the information's reliability and relevance. Context can be improved by the format in which information is presented. The third important concept in the definition of assurance services is independence. As discussed, independence is the hallmark of the profession. The last concept is professional services, which encompasses the application of professional judgment. The practitioner applies professional judgment to the information that is the subject of the assurance service. In summary, assurance services can capture information, improve its quality, and enhance its usefulness for decision makers.

**[LO2] Be familiar with the types of assurance services.**

A. The AICPA, through its Assurance Services Executive Committee, identified and developed six general categories of assurance services.

    1. **Risk assessment**. Assurance that an entity's profile of business risks is comprehensive and evaluation of whether the entity has appropriate systems in place to effectively manage those risk.

    2. **Business performance measurement**. Assurance that an entity's performance measurement system contains relevant and reliable measures for assessing the degree to which the entity's goals and objectives are achieved or how its performance compares to competitors.

    3. **Information system reliability**. Assurance that an entity's internal information systems provide reliable information for operating and financial decisions.

    4. **Electronic commerce**. Assurance that systems and tools used in electronic commerce provide appropriate data integrity, security, privacy, and reliability.

    5. **Health care performance measurement**. Assurance about the effectiveness of health care services provided by HMOs, hospitals, doctors, and other providers.

    6. **PrimePlus**. Assurance that specified goals regarding the elderly are being met by various caregivers.

B. Seven other areas where assurance services might be appropriate include:

    1. Corporate policy compliance.

    2. Outsourced internal auditing.

    3. Trading partner accountability.

    4. Mergers and acquisitions.

    5. ISO 9000 certification.

    6. Investment managers' compliance with Association of Investment Management and Research Performance Presentation Standards.

    7. World Wide Web assertions.

**[LO3] Know the definition of an attestation engagement.**

A. An attest engagement is defined as (SSAE No. 10):

> **Attest services occur when a practitioner is engaged to issue or does issue a report on subject matter, or an assertion about subject matter, that is the responsibility of another party.**

In this definition, practitioner refers to a certified public accountant in the practice of public accounting. Because attestation engagements are attest engagements other than audits, the attestation standards use practitioner instead of auditor. Subject matter of an attest engagement may take many forms, including historical or prospective performance information, analyses, systems and processes, and behavior. The term assertion refers to any declaration, or set of related declarations, about whether the subject matter is based on or in conformity with the criteria selected.

B. Typically, an attestation engagement involves three parties: a user or users; a party responsible for the subject matter or the assertion, such as management; and a CPA (Figure 21-3). Note that the responsible party is responsible for the subject matter or assertion to the user and acknowledges that responsibility to the CPA. The CPA expresses a conclusion to the user on the subject matter or assertion. In some cases, the engagement may involve only two parties because the user and the responsible party are the same.

C. The practitioner should use an attestation risk model to meet the standards of fieldwork in an attestation engagement. Attestation risk is defined in a manner similar to audit risk and is composed of the same three components (inherent risk, control risk, and detection risk) as the audit risk model. The attestation risk should be set consistent with the type of engagement being performed.

**[LO4] Know the types of attestation engagements.**

A. Attestation standards generally provide three types of engagements: examination, review, and agreed-upon procedures. Table 21-1 provides an overview of the types of attestation engagements. The AICPA's Statements on Standards for Attestation Engagements (SSEA) provide additional guidance on these types of engagements. The PCAOB adopted the SSEAs on an interim basis in April 2003.

   1. **Examination.** In an examination, the practitioner expresses an opinion that (a) the subject matter is based on (or in conformity with) the criteria in all material respects or (b) the assertion is presented (or fairly stated), in all material respects, based on the criteria. Such an opinion may be for general or limited distribution. If distribution is limited, the opinion must state the limitations on the use of the report. Because an examination engagement provides the highest level of assurance on an assurance on an assertion, the practitioner must gather sufficient evidence to limit the attestation risk to a low level, and expresses positive assurance.

   2. **Review.** In a review engagement, the practitioner expresses negative assurance. That is, the accountant indicates that no information came to his or her attention indicating that (a) the subject matter is not based on (or in conformity with) the criteria in all material respects or (b) the assertion is not presented (or fairly stated), in all material respects, based on the criteria. Distribution of a review report can also be either general or limited. A review engagement should provide sufficient evidence to limit the attestation risk to a moderate level.

   3. **Agreed-Upon Services.** An agreed-upon procedures engagement is one in which a practitioner is engaged by a client to issue a report of findings based on specific procedures performed on the subject matter. The level of assurance provided by such an engagement depends on the nature and scope of the procedures agreed upon with the specified parties. Thus, the attestation risk is a function of the intended level of assurance.

Distribution of the report based on such an engagement is limited to the specified users. The report on an agreed-upon procedures engagement summarizes findings resulting from the application of the agreed-upon procedures.

**[LO5] Be familiar with the 11 attestation standards and how they compare to the 10 generally accepted auditing standards.**

A. **General standards**. There are five general standards for attestation engagements. They are:

1. The engagement shall be performed by a practitioner having adequate technical training and proficiency in the attest function.

2. The engagement shall be performed by a practitioner having adequate knowledge in the subject matter.

3. The practitioner shall perform an engagement only if he or she has reason to believe that the subject matter is capable of evaluation against criteria that are suitable and available to users.

4. In all matters relating to the engagement, an independence in mental attitude shall be maintained by the practitioner.

5. Due professional care shall be exercised in the planning and performance of the engagement.

B. **Standards of Fieldwork**. There are two standards of fieldwork for attestation engagements. They are:

1. The work shall be adequately planned and assistants, if any, shall be properly supervised.

2. Sufficient evidence shall be obtained to provide a reasonable basis for the conclusion that is expressed in the report.

C. **Standards of Reporting**. There are four standards of reporting for attestation engagements. They are:

1. The report shall identify the subject matter or the assertion being reported on and state the character of the engagement.

2. The report shall state the practitioner's conclusion about the subject matter or the assertion in relation to the criteria against which the subject matter was evaluated.

3. The report shall state all of the practitioner's significant reservations about the engagements, the subject matter, and, if applicable, the assertion related thereto.

4. The report shall state that the use of the report is restricted to specified parties under the following circumstances:

   a. When the criteria used to evaluate the subject matter are determined by the practitioner to be appropriate only for a limited number of parties who either participated in their establishment or can be presumed to have an adequate understanding of the criteria.

460

b. When the criteria used to evaluate the subject matter are available only to specified parties.

c. When reporting on subject matter and a written assertion has not been provided by the responsible party.

d. When the report is on an attest engagement to apply agreed-upon procedures to the subject matter.

Table 21-2 lists the 11 attestation standards and the 10 generally accepted auditing standards for comparative purposes.

## [LO6] Understand an attestation engagement that reports on an entity's internal control over financial reporting.

A. In recent years, accountants have increasingly been asked to provide reports on the effectiveness of an entity's internal control. Impetus was given for such reporting when Congress passed the Federal Deposit Insurance Corporation Act of 1991, which requires that the management of large financial institutions issue a report on the effectiveness of the institution's internal control. The act also requires that these institutions engage accountants to attest to management's report. As discussed in Chapter 7, the Sarbanes-Oxley Act of 2002 imposed similar requirements on all publicly held companies. While an audit of internal control is not required of privately held companies, some such companies may engage an accounting firm to provide attestation services relating to internal control.

B. In order for the practitioner to examine management's assertions about the effectiveness of internal control in an attestation engagement, the following conditions are necessary:

1. Management of the entity accepts responsibility for the effectiveness of the entity's internal control.

2. The responsible party evaluates the effectiveness of the entity's internal control using suitable criteria (referred to as control criteria).

3. Sufficient competent evidence exists or could be developed to support the responsible party's evaluation.

4. Management provides to the practitioner its written assertion based on control criteria referred to in its report.

Note that criteria issued by the AICPA, regulatory agencies, and other bodies of experts that follow due process qualify as control criteria. For example, management may use the criteria provided in AU 319 (Consideration of Internal Control in a Financial Statement Audit), which is based on the control criteria included in the COSO Report.

C. A practitioner is allowed to perform either of two types of attestation engagements for reporting on internal control: examinations and agreed-upon procedures. The standard specifically prohibits the practitioner from accepting an engagement to review and report on management's assertion relating to internal control.

**[LO7] Understand an attestation engagement that reports on an entity's financial forecasts and projections.**

A.  Auditors have been asked to provide assurance with respect to prospective financial statements. Attestation standards provide guidance for practitioners providing such services. The practitioner's involvement may include (1) assembling or assisting the client in assembling prospective financial statements or (2) reporting on prospective financial statements. In either of these situations, the practitioner can examine, apply agreed-upon procedures, or compile the prospective financial statements if such statements are expected to be used by a third party.

B.  **Prospective financial statements** contain financial information made up of either financial forecasts or financial projections.

  1.  **Financial forecasts** are prospective financial statements that present an entity's expected financial position, results of operations, and cash flows. They are based on assumptions reflecting conditions the responsible party expects to exist and the course of action it expects to take.

  2.  **Financial projections** are prospective financial statements that present, given one or more hypothetical assumptions, an entity's expected financial position, results of operations, and cash flows. These assumptions may not reflect the most likely or expected conditions.

Prospective financial statements are for either general use or limited use. **General use** of prospective financial statements refers to the use of the statements by persons with whom the responsible party is not negotiating directly. Because the intended users cannot question the responsible party, the only appropriate basis of presentation is the expected results. Therefore, only a financial forecast is appropriate for general use. **Limited use** of prospective financial statements refers to use of the statements by the responsible party alone or by the responsible party and third parties with whom the responsible party is directly negotiating. In such cases, third parties can question the responsible party about the prospective financial information and can agree on the assumed conditions on which it is based. Thus, any type of prospective financial statement is appropriate for limited use. While the responsible party is responsible for presentation of prospective financial statements, other parties, such as accountants, may assist in meeting the presentation guidelines specified in the attestation standards. Prospective financial statements should preferably be in the same format as the historical statements; however, they may be limited to the items shown in Table 21-3. A presentation that omits any item in Table 21-3 is referred to as a partial presentation.

C.  **Examination of prospective financial statements**. An examination of prospective financial statements involves the following steps:

  1.  Evaluating the preparation of the prospective financial statements.

  2.  Evaluating the support underlying the assumptions.

  3.  Evaluating the presentation of the prospective financial statements for conformity with SSAE No. 10.

  4.  Issuing an examination report.

The accountant should be independent, have adequate technical training and proficiency to examine prospective financial statements, and obtain sufficient evidence to issue an examination report. Exhibits 21-1 and 21-2 present examples of the standard examination report for a forecast and projection, respectively. The following circumstances may require a departure from the standard examination report:

1. Departure from SSAE No. 10 presentation guidelines.
2. Unreasonable assumptions.
3. Scope limitation.

The presence of such events can result in a report that is either qualified or adverse. A disclaimer may also be issued.

D. **Agreed-upon procedures for prospective financial statements**. An agreed-upon procedures engagement is significantly more limited in scope than an examination. An accountant may perform an agreed-upon procedures attestation engagement for prospective financial statements provided that attestation standards are complied with and:

1. The practitioner and the specified users agree upon the procedures performed or to be performed by the practitioner.

2. The specified users take responsibility for the sufficiency of the agreed-upon procedures for their purposes.

3. The prospective financial statements include a summary of significant assumptions.

4. The prospective financial statements to which the procedures are to be applied are subject to reasonably consistent evaluation against criteria that are suitable and available to the specified parties.

5. Criteria to be used in determining findings are agreed upon between the practitioner and the specified users.

Exhibit 21-3 presents an example of a report on the use of agreed-upon procedures. Use of an agreed-upon procedures report is always explicitly restricted to the users specified in the report.

E. **Compilation of prospective financial statements**. A practitioner can perform a compilation of prospective financial information. A compilation of prospective financial statements involves:

1. Assembling, to the extent necessary, the prospective financial statements based on the responsible party's assumptions.

2. Performing the required compilation procedures, which include reading the prospective financial statements with their summaries of significant assumptions and accounting policies, and considering whether they appear to be (1) presented in conformity with the attestation standards shown in Table 21-2 and (2) not obviously inappropriate.

3. Issuing a compilation report.

A practitioner should not issue a compilation report on prospective financial statements that exclude disclosure of the summary of significant assumptions. Exhibit 21-4 provides an example of a compilation report for a forecast. Note that the report explicitly indicates that the accountant does not offer assurance in providing a compilation service.

**[LO8] Be familiar with accounting and review services.**

A. Many nonpublic businesses do not need an audit for their financial statements. This typically occurs because the entity is small and the owner is involved in the day-to-day operations, there are no debts or regulations requiring an audit, or an audit may be too costly for the entity. However, these same entities may employ a CPA to assist with preparing their financial statements, tax returns or other financial documents. SSARS provide two types of services: compilation of financial statements and review of financial statements. Compilations and reviews specifically apply to engagements for which the output of the service is a set of financial statements.

B. A **compilation** is defined as presenting, in the form of financial statements, information that is the representation of management or owners without undertaking to express any assurance on the statements. In conducting a compilation, the accountant must have the following knowledge about the entity:

1. The accounting principles and practices of the industry in which the entity operates.

2. A general understanding of the nature of the entity's business transactions, the form of its accounting records, the stated qualifications of its accounting personnel.

3. The accounting basis on which the financial statements are to be presented and the form and content of the financial statements.

Note that the accountant is not required to conduct any inquires or to perform any procedures to verify or corroborate any information supplied by the client. However, the accountant should read the complied financial statements to determine whether they are presented in an appropriate form and free from obvious errors (i.e., mathematical or clerical mistakes or mistakes in the application of accounting principles). There are three forms of compilation reports:

1. **Compilation with full disclosure**. Financial statements contain all necessary financial disclosures required by GAAP or another comprehensive basis of accounting. Exhibit 21-5 is an example of a standard compilation report.

2. **Compilation that omits substantially all disclosures**. The financial statements are prepared without the necessary disclosures. The accountant can compile such financial statements as long as the omission is clearly indicated in the report and the client's intent is not to mislead the user. Exhibit 21-6 is an example of a compilation report in which financial disclosures have been omitted.

3. **Compilation when the accountant is not independent**. An accountant can perform a compilation engagement even though he or she is not independent of the entity. If the accountant is not independent, the lack of independence must be disclosed in the report. The reasons for the lack of independence should not be described.

C. A **review** is defined as the performance of inquiry and analytical procedures to provide the accountant with a reasonable basis for expressing limited assurance that no material modifications should be made to the statements in order for them to conform to GAAP or another comprehensive basis of accounting. In conducting a review, the accountant's work involves the following:

1. Obtaining knowledge of the accounting principles and practices of the industry in which the entity operates and an understanding of the entity's business.

2. Obtaining a general understanding of the entity's organization, its operating characteristics, and the nature of its assets, liabilities, revenues, and expenses (this would include general knowledge of the entity's production, distribution and compensation methods, types of products and services, operating locations, and material transactions with related parties).

3. Asking the entity's personnel about some of the items noted in Table 21-4.

4. Performing analytical procedures to identify relationships and individual items that appear to be unusual (the process followed for conducting analytical procedures is similar to the one described for audits).

5. Reading the financial statements to determine if they conform to GAAP.

6. Obtaining reports from other accountants, if any, who have audited or reviewed the financial statements or significant components thereof.

7. Obtaining a representation letter from management (generally, the chief executive officer and chief financial officer should sign the representation letter).

Note that a review engagement does not require the accountant to obtain an understanding of internal controls, test accounting records, by performing detailed tests, or corroborate inquires, as would normally be done on an audit. However, if while conducting the review the accountant becomes aware of information that is incorrect, incomplete, or misleading, he or she should perform any additional procedures necessary to provide limited assurance that no material modifications to the financial statements are required. A standard review report assumes that the financial statements are in accordance with GAAP or another comprehensive basis of accounting. This includes all necessary disclosures. The review report should be dated as of the completion of the accountant's inquiry and analytical procedures. Exhibit 21-7 is an example of the standard review report.

When the accountant conducts a compilation or review, he or she may become aware of situations that require modification to the standard report. Two particular situations are:

1. **A departure from GAAP**. If there is a departure from GAAP, the departure should be disclosed in a separate paragraph of the report. Exhibit 21-8 is an example of a review report modified for a departure from GAAP.

2. **A going-concern uncertainty**. The process the accountant follows in determining whether the entity is a going concern is similar to the process used for assessing going-concern issues during an audit.

D.  The level of assurance for a compilation, a review, and an audit is shown below (Figure 21-4):

**Assurance Levels for a Compilation, a Review, and an Audit**

**Level of Assurance**

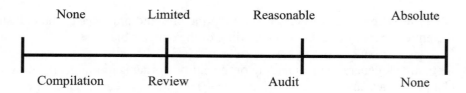

**Type of Professional Engagement**

**[LO9] Understand the role of standards pertaining to and services provided by internal auditors.**

A.  The **Institute of Internal Auditors** (IIA) oversees and sets standards for internal auditing internally. The Institute defines internal auditing as follows:

> **Internal auditing is an independent, objective assurance and consulting activity designed to add value and improve an organization's operations. It helps an organization accomplish its objectives by bringing a systematic, disciplined approach to evaluate and improve the effectiveness of risk management control, and governance processes.**

B.  Established in 1941, the IIA is an international professional association with 93,000 members in internal auditing, risk management, governance, internal control, IT audit, education, and security. The IIA is the recognized authority, principal educator, and acknowledged leader in certification, research and technological guidance for the internal auditing profession worldwide. It offers not only the general Certified Internal Auditor (CIA) certification but also specialty certifications in areas including government accounting and financial services. The standards for the professional practice of internal auditing are presented in Table 21-5.

C.  The IIA developed a Professional Practices Framework. This framework consists of three broad categories of guidance:

1.  Standards and Ethics (consisting of the Code of Ethics and the International Standards for the Professional Practice of Internal Auditing).

2.  Practice advisories.

3.  Practice aids.

D.  Members of the IIA must follow guidelines (AICPA and PCAOB) promoting ethical conduct. Members must follow the IIA Code of Ethics. The Code of Ethics specifies four main principles of ethical conduct and some associated rules that underpin the expected conduct of IIA members including: (1) integrity, (2) objectivity, (3) confidentiality, and (4) competency.

See Tables 21-6 and 21-7 for a summary of the Code of Ethics Principles and the Rules of Conduct, respectively.

E.  Internal auditors are called "internal" because they work within an individual entity and report the results of their work to management or ideally to the entity's audit committee or board of directors. They are not typically expected to report to the public or to parties outside the entity. Internal audit functions differ widely in how they are managed and staffed. Some entities have internal audit functions that are staffed entirely "in-house," while others are "co-sourced" to a public accounting firm. Ideally an entity will have a chief audit executive (CAE), whose role is to oversee the internal audit function (whether in-house or co-sourced) and to help coordinate the work of the internal and external auditors.

F.  The roles played by internal auditors fall into two primary categories – assurance services and consulting services:

1.  **Assurance services** involve the internal auditor's objective assessment of evidence to provide an independent opinion or conclusion regarding a process, system or other subject matter. The nature and scope of the assurance engagement are determined by the internal auditor. There are generally three parties involved in assurance services: (1) the person or group directly involved with the process, system or other subject matter – the process owner, (2) the person or group making the assessment – the internal auditor, and (3) the person or group using the assessment – the user.

2.  **Consulting services** are advisory in nature, and are generally performed in the specific request of an engagement client. The nature and scope of the consulting engagement are subject to agreement with the engagement client. Consulting services generally involve two parties: (1) the person or group offering the advice – the internal auditor, and (2) the person or group seeking and receiving the advice – the engagement client. When performing consulting services the internal auditor should maintain objectivity and not assume management responsibility.

In general terms, an organization's internal audit function is most often used by management and the board of directors in the broad areas of evaluating risk, evaluating compliance, and performing financial and operational auditing. Through these activities, internal auditors contribute to effective corporate governance within an organization, which entails all management-administered policies and procedures to control risk and oversee operations within a company. The IIA and other influential organizations, such as the NYSE, identify the internal audit function as one of the cornerstones of effective corporate governance.

G.  **Evaluating risks and controls.** As outlined by IIA Standard 2110, internal auditors should be directly involved in an entity's risk management process. The internal auditor's specific experience within the organization enables him or her to accurately gauge risks relating to the integrity of financial and operational information, the safeguarding of asserts, and compliance with laws and regulations. Section 404 of the Sarbanes-Oxley Act requires public companies to implement and annually assess internal control over financial reporting. Internal auditors have long been involved in evaluating and enhancing their organizations' system of internal control over financial reporting and over other areas of the organization, and internal auditors often play a substantial role in ensuring compliance with these new requirements.

H. **Reviewing Compliance**. In many industries, compliance with relevant laws and regulations is an extremely complicated and important endeavor. For example, if a company fails to comply with the many requirements of the Occupational Safety and Health Act of 1970 (OSHA), the government can levy significant fines and penalties against the offending company. Many other governmental agencies have also issued rules and regulations that must be followed by businesses and other organizations. Such agencies include the Environmental Protection Agency (EPA) and the Food & Drug Administration (FDS), among many others. Internal auditors play an important role in helping management ensure that the organization complies with the laws, rules, and regulations that apply to the entity, as well as in ensuring that employees comply with organizational guidelines and rules.

I. **Financial Auditing**. Although the financial auditing performed by internal auditors involves many of the same concepts you have already studied in this text, it differs from the audits conducted by external auditors in several ways. For example, internal auditors do not generally audit periodic financial statements, but tend to focus on specific financial issues as directed by management. The nature of their audit report is also different. Because the intention of the audit may relate to either very general or very specific factors, it is impossible to require a standardized internal audit report. Consequently, internal audit reports are normally uniquely composed to fulfill the requirements of the particular assignment, as opposed to external audit reports which are standardized. Exhibit 21-9 describes a real-life situation where an organization's internal auditor uncovered a fraud while evaluating a specific financial area at the request of the organization's management.

J. **Operational Auditing**. Due to their unique position in an organization, internal auditors typically achieve a thorough understanding of how the organization operates, and internal auditors are thus able to provide various types of services to improve the entities in which they work. An auditor should be prepared to recognize when enhancements could be made to align current operations with the entity's objectives. Operational audits serve a wide variety of purposes. They are primarily conducted to identify the causes of problems or to enhance the efficiency or effectiveness of operations. In many organizations, internal auditors spend most of their time performing operational audits. In fact, because they often spend relatively little of their time performing financial audits, the term internal auditing is often (incorrectly) used interchangeably with operational auditing.

K. See the example using **DuPont** for an illustration of the diversity of services offered by internal auditors (see Figure 21-5 and Exhibit 21-10).

L. **Interactions between internal and external auditors**. The objectives and type of work performed by internal and external auditors are often quite different, but as you may imagine, there is some overlap. External auditors do their work with the purpose of expressing an opinion as to whether the entity's financial statements are free of material misstatements. Because external auditors rely on the concept of materiality, they typically are not concerned with auditing a particular area in a great deal of depth – they gather evidence until they obtain reasonable assurance that no misstatements are present that would be considered significant in the context of the financial statements taken as a whole. They then report externally to the organization being audited.

Internal auditors, on the other hand, assist management and the board of directors in evaluating and managing risk, assessing compliance with laws and regulation, assessing operational efficiency, and performing detailed financial audits of areas requiring particular attention. Because their objectives are often different from those of external auditors, the concept of materiality is usually quite different as well. For example, in auditing for employee fraud, the amounts involved are usually far from material in terms of the financial statements taken as a whole. However, internal auditors can reduce the incidence of employee fraud, save money and improve controls in the process.

Some of the work performed by internal auditors is directly relevant to the work of the independent auditors. For example, the external auditor can sometimes make use of controls-testing work performed by the internal auditor. Before relying on the work of internal auditors, the external auditor must evaluate the internal auditors' objectivity and competence. If the external auditor decides that some reliance is justified, the cost savings in terms of the reduction in the external audit fee can be significant.

# ADVANCED MODULE
## EXAMPLES OF ASSURANCE SERVICES
## TRUST SERVICES AND PRIMEPLUS SERVICES

**[LO10] Understand CPA *Trust Services* and know the *Trust Services* Principles and Criteria.**

A. Electronic commerce involves individuals and organizations conducting business transactions, without paper documents, using computer and telecommunications networks. This includes transactions under electronic date interchange (EDI), where formal contracts exist between the parties, and business over the Internet (World Wide Web), where the parties do not have a preexisting contractual relationship. Electronic commerce over the Internet has grown tremendously, as have the system requirements necessary to support this technology.

B. This growth in technology has also increased concerns by businesses and individuals. Businesses are concerned with such things as maintaining reliable, effective systems, while individuals worry about such things as the confidentiality of their information. To respond to these concerns, the AICPA and the Canadian Institute of Chartered Accountants (CICA) developed SysTrust and WebTrust – two unique sets of principles by which CPAs could evaluate business systems and controls.

C. Trust Services are built on five principles. These principles are nontechnical and easy to understand. Using these principles, CPAs can offer a wide variety of advisory and assurance services to their clients. They are (Table 21-8):

1. **Security**. The system is protected against unauthorized access (both physical and logical).

2. **Availability**. The system is available for operation and use as committed or agreed.

3. **Processing integrity**. System processing is complete, accurate, timely and authorized.

4. **Online privacy**. Personal information obtained as a result of e-commerce is collected, used, disclosed, and retained as committed or agreed.

5. **Confidentiality**. Information designated as confidential is protected as committed or agreed.

**[LO11] Understand the assurance process for *WebTrust*.**

A. Three broad risk are associated with electronic commerce (Table 21-9 and Exhibit 21-11):

1. Business practices.
2. Transaction integrity.
3. Information protection.

**[LO12] Understand the assurance process for SysTrust.**

A. As more organizations become dependent on information technology to run their businesses and to interact with customers, suppliers, and business partners, it is critical that an entity's information systems operate effectively. The AICPA and CICA have identified this as an opportunity for CPAs and CAs to provide assurance on the information system by offering a service called SysTrust. The system components include its infrastructure, software, personnel, procedures and data. SysTrust follows the Trust Services Principles and Criteria.

B. A SysTrust engagement is conducted under attestation standards. The CPA evaluates a system against the Trust Services Principles and Criteria and determines whether controls over the system exist. The CPA then performs tests to determine whether those controls were operating effectively during the specified period. In order for the entity to receive an unqualified opinion, the system must meet all of the Trust Service Principles and Criteria (see Exhibit 21-12).

**[LO13] Understand CPA PrimePlus (formerly ElderCare) assurance service.**

A. The population in the United States and Canada is aging, and many of these people have accumulated significant wealth. The CPA can bring another level of assurance or comfort to the elderly person and his or her family members. PrimePlus Services are defined as:

> **a unique, customizable package of services offered by Certified Public Accounts to assist the elderly in maintaining – for as long as possible – their lifestyle and financial independence. Practitioners who provide ElderCare/PrimePlus Services draw upon their strengths and competencies in a variety of areas, including cash flow planning and budgeting, pre- and post-retirement planning, insurance reviews and tax planning ... the services included in each individual ElderCare/PrimePlus engagement will be based upon the needs and wants to each ElderCare/PrimePlus client as well as the skill set of the ElderCare/PrimePlus practitioner.**

B. Practitioners can offer three types of PrimePlus services:

1. Consulting and facilitating services.
2. Direct services.
3. Assurance services.

# CHAPTER 21: SELF-ASSESSMENT

## Part I: True or False Questions

[LO1] _____ 1. Assurance services are independent professional services that improve the quality of information specifically for internal decision makers.

[LO2] _____ 2. Electronic commerce is an example of an assurance service.

[LO3] _____ 3. An attest service occurs when a practitioner is engaged to issue a report on a subject matter that is the responsibility of another party.

[LO4] _____ 4. Examples of attest engagements include examination, review and agreed-upon procedures.

[LO4] _____ 5. Negative assurance is provided for a review engagement.

[LO5] _____ 6. There are six general standards for attestation engagements.

[LO5] _____ 7. There are two standards of fieldwork for attestation engagements.

[LO6] _____ 8. Management is responsible for the effectiveness of the entity's internal control.

[LO6] _____ 9. A practitioner is allowed to perform either of two types of attestation engagements for reporting on internal control: (1) examination or (2) review.

[LO7] _____ 10. Attestation standards provide guidance for performing assurance services with respect to prospective financial statements.

## Part II: Multiple Choice Questions

[LO7] 1. Prospective financial statements may be prepared for:
    a. General use.
    b. Limited use.
    c. Internal use.
    d. Both a and b.

[LO7] 2. A departure from the standard examination report is required under the following circumstances:
    a. Departure from SSEA No. 10 presentation guidelines.
    b. Assumptions made are reasonable.
    c. No scope limitations are present.
    d. None of the above.

[LO7] 3. An accountant may perform the following activities during an agreed-upon engagement for prospective financial statements:
    a. Verify that the statements conform with SSEA No. 10 guidelines.
    b. Verify that all assumptions are valid.
    c. Verify agreed-upon criteria between practitioner and specified users.
    d. Verify practitioner's criteria are valid.

[LO8] 4. Limited assurance is provided for:
    a. An audit engagement.
    b. A compilation engagement.
    c. A review engagement.
    d. None of the above.

[LO8] 5. Absolute assurance is provided for:
    a. An audit engagement.
    b. A compilation engagement.
    c. A review engagement.
    d. None of the above.

[LO8] 6. Reasonable assurance is provided for:
    a. An audit engagement.
    b. A compilation engagement.
    c. A review engagement.
    d. None of the above.

[LO8] 7. Compilation reports may include:
    a. Compilation when the accountant is not independent.
    b. Compilation with full disclosure.
    c. Compilation that omits substantially all disclosures.
    d. All of the above.

[LO9] 8. IIA Standards include:
    a. Practice advisories.
    b. Code of Ethics.
    c. Interpretations.
    d. Both a and b.

[LO10] 9. Internal auditors may perform:
    a. Compliance audits.
    b. Financial audits.
    c. Operational audits.
    d. All of the above.

[LO10] 10. Trust service principles cover:
    a. Hardware design.
    b. Confidentiality.
    c. Software design.
    d. Both b and c.

## Part III: Short Essay Questions

[LO4] Identify and discuss the different types of attestation engagements.

[LO5] Identify the 11 attestation standards.

[LO8] Discuss the type or level of assurance provided by the CPA for a compilation engagement, a review engagement, and an audit engagement.

# Part IV: Crossword Puzzle – Chapter 21 [LO ALL]

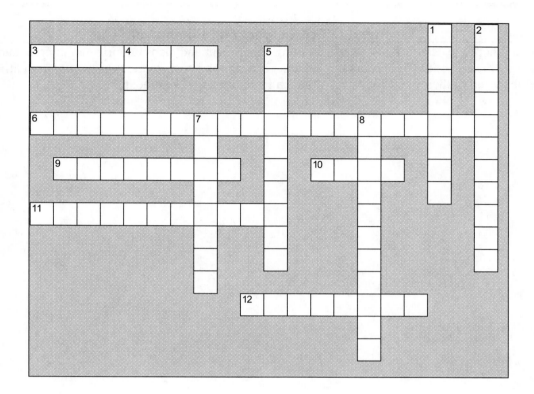

## Across

3    This type of auditor investigates fraud.

6    Specific services performed on the subject matter of an assertion, where the practitioner will issue a reporting of findings (three words).

9    Criteria used to evaluate privacy, security, availability, and the confidential of electronic commerce.

10   The abbreviation for ten broad guidelines used to conduct an audit.

11   A presentation, in the form of financial statements, of information that is the representation of management, where the practitioner provides no assurance.

12   The level of assurance provided at the completion of a review engagement.

## Down

1    Criteria used to evaluate system components including infrastructure, software, personnel, procedures, and data.

2    A service to issue a report on subject matter or assertions made by another party.

4    The level of assurance for a compilation engagement.

5    A service to evaluate relevant laws and regulations.

7    The level of assurance provided at the completion of an audit.

8    The practitioner expresses an opinion that the subject matter conforms to specific criteria in all material respects.

**Chapter 21**
**Townsend Office Supplies and Equipment**

Townsend hopes to establish an internal auditing department and plans on hiring an internal audit director by the end of 2009. Discuss the potential benefits and costs to the organization for earlier implementation of their plans for establishing an internal audit department.

# CHAPTER 21: SELF-ASSESSMENT SOLUTIONS

## Part I: True or False Questions

[LO1] **False** 1.  Assurance services are independent professional services that improve the quality of information specifically for internal decision makers.

[LO2] **True** 2.  Electronic commerce is an example of an assurance service.

[LO3] **True** 3.  An attest service occurs when a practitioner is engaged to issue a report on a subject matter that is the responsibility of another party.

[LO4] **True** 4.  Examples of attest engagements include examination, review and agreed-upon procedures.

[LO4] **True** 5.  Negative assurance is provided for a review engagement.

[LO5] **False** 6.  There are six general standards for attestation engagements.

[LO5] **True** 7.  There are two standards of fieldwork for attestation engagements.

[LO6] **True** 8.  Management is responsible for the effectiveness of the entity's internal control.

[LO6] **False** 9.  A practitioner is allowed to perform either of two types of attestation engagements for reporting on internal control: (1) examination or (2) review.

[LO7] **True** 10.  Attestation standards provide guidance for performing assurance services with respect to prospective financial statements.

## Part II: Multiple Choice Questions

[LO7]  1.  Prospective financial statements may be prepared for:
   a.  General use.
   b.  Limited use.
   c.  Internal use.
   **d.  Both a and b.**

[LO7]  2.  A departure from the standard examination report is required under the following circumstances:
   **a.  Departure from SSEA No. 10 presentation guidelines.**
   b.  Assumptions made are reasonable.
   c.  No scope limitations are present.
   d.  None of the above.

[LO7]  3.  An accountant may perform the following activities during an agreed-upon engagement for prospective financial statements:
   a.  Verify that the statements conform with SSEA No. 10 guidelines.
   b.  Verify that all assumptions are valid.
   **c.  Verify agreed-upon criteria between practitioner and specified users.**
   d.  Verify practitioner's criteria are valid.

[LO8]  4. Limited assurance is provided for:
- a. An audit engagement.
- b. A compilation engagement.
- **c. A review engagement.**
- d. None of the above.

[LO8]  5. Absolute assurance is provided for:
- a. An audit engagement.
- b. A compilation engagement.
- c. A review engagement.
- **d. None of the above.**

[LO8]  6. Reasonable assurance is provided for:
- **a. An audit engagement.**
- b. A compilation engagement.
- c. A review engagement.
- d. None of the above.

[LO8]  7. Compilation reports may include:
- a. Compilation when the accountant is not independent.
- b. Compilation with full disclosure.
- c. Compilation that omits substantially all disclosures.
- **d. All of the above.**

[LO9]  8. IIA Standards include:
- a. Practice advisories.
- b. Code of Ethics.
- c. Interpretations.
- **d. Both a and b.**

[LO10] 9. Internal auditors may perform:
- a. Compliance audits.
- b. Financial audits.
- c. Operational audits.
- **d. All of the above.**

[LO10]10. Trust service principles cover:
- a. Hardware design.
- **b. Confidentiality.**
- c. Software design.
- d. Both b and c.

## Part III: Short Essay Questions

[LO4] Identify and discuss the different types of attestation engagements.

Attestation standards generally provide three types of engagements: examination, review, and agreed-upon procedures. Table 21-1 provides an overview of the types of attestation engagements. The AICPA's Statements on Standards for Attestation Engagements (SSEA) provide additional guidance on these types of engagements. The PCAOB adopted the SSEAs on an interim basis in April 2003.

1. Examination. In an examination, the practitioner expresses an opinion that (a) the subject matter is based on (or in conformity with) the criteria in all material respects or (b) the assertion is presented (or fairly stated), in all material respects, based on the criteria. Such an opinion may be for general or limited distribution. If distribution is limited, the opinion must state the limitations on the use of the report. Because an examination engagement provides the highest level of assurance on an assertion, the practitioner must gather sufficient evidence to limit the attestation risk to a low level, and expresses positive assurance.

2. Review. In a review engagement, the practitioner expresses negative assurance. That is, the accountant indicates that no information came to his or her attention indicating that (a) the subject matter is not based on (or in conformity with) the criteria in all material respects or (b) the assertion is not presented (or fairly stated), in all material respects, based on the criteria. Distribution of a review report can also be either general or limited. A review engagement should provide sufficient evidence to limit the attestation risk to a moderate level.

3. Agreed-Upon Services. An agreed-upon procedures engagement is one in which a practitioner is engaged by a client to issue a report of findings based on specific procedures performed on the subject matter. The level of assurance provided by such an engagement depends on the nature and scope of the procedures agreed upon with the specified parties. Thus, the attestation risk is a function of the intended level of assurance. Distribution of the report based on such an engagement is limited to the specified users. The report on an agreed-upon procedures engagement summarizes findings resulting from the application of the agreed-upon procedures.

[LO5] Identify the 11 attestation standards.

**There are 11 standards for attestation engagements, including 5 general standards, 2 standards of fieldwork, and 4 standards of reporting.**

**General standards. There are 5 general standards. They are:**

1. **The engagement shall be performed by a practitioner having adequate technical training and proficiency in the attest function.**

2. **The engagement shall be performed by a practitioner having adequate knowledge in the subject matter.**

3. **The practitioner shall perform an engagement only if he or she has reason to believe that the subject matter is capable of evaluation against criteria that are suitable and available to users.**

4. **In all matters relating to the engagement, an independence in mental attitude shall be maintained by the practitioner.**

5. **Due professional care shall be exercised in the planning and performance of the engagement.**

**Standards of Fieldwork. There are 2 standards of fieldwork. They are:**

1. **The work shall be adequately planned and assistants, if any, shall be properly supervised.**

2. **Sufficient evidence shall be obtained to provide a reasonable basis for the conclusion that is expressed in the report.**

**Standards of Reporting. There are four standards of reporting. They are:**

1. **The report shall identify the subject matter or the assertion being reported on and state the character of the engagement.**

2. **The report shall state the practitioner's conclusion about the subject matter or the assertion in relation to the criteria against which the subject matter was evaluated.**

3. **The report shall state all of the practitioner's significant reservations about the engagements, the subject matter, and, if applicable, the assertion related thereto.**

4. **The report shall state that the use of the report is restricted to specified parties under the following circumstances:**

   a. **When the criteria used to evaluate the subject matter are determined by the practitioner to be appropriate only for a limited number of parties who either participated in their establishment or can be presumed to have an adequate understanding of the criteria.**

   b. **When the criteria used to evaluate the subject matter are available only to specified parties.**

   c. **When reporting on subject matter and a written assertion has not been provided by the responsible party.**

   d. **When the report is on an attest engagement to apply agreed-upon procedures to the subject matter.**

[LO8] Discuss the type or level of assurance provided by the CPA for a compilation engagement, a review engagement, and an audit engagement.

**Compilation Engagement. No assurance is provided in the compilation report.**

**Review Engagement. Limited (also referred to as negative) assurance is provided in the review report.**

**Audit Engagement. Reasonable (also referred to as positive) assurance is provided in the audit report.**

## Part IV: Crossword Puzzle – Chapter 21 Solution [LO ALL]

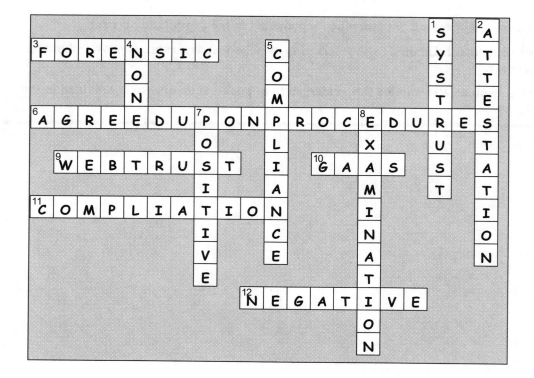

### Across

3    This type of auditor investigates fraud.

6    Specific services performed on the subject matter of an assertion, where the practitioner will issue a reporting of findings (three words).

9    Criteria used to evaluate privacy, security, availability, and the confidential of electronic commerce.

10    The abbreviation for ten broad guidelines used to conduct an audit.

11    A presentation, in the form of financial statements, of information that is the representation of management, where the practitioner provides no assurance.

12    The level of assurance provided at the completion of a review engagement.

### Down

1    Criteria used to evaluate system components including infrastructure, software, personnel, procedures, and data.

2    A service to issue a report on subject matter or assertions made by another party.

4    The level of assurance for a compilation engagement.

5    A service to evaluate relevant laws and regulations.

7    The level of assurance provided at the completion of an audit.

8    The practitioner expresses an opinion that the subject matter conforms to specific criteria in all material respects.

---

**Chapter 21**
**Townsend Office Supplies and Equipment**

Townsend hopes to establish an internal auditing department and plans on hiring an internal audit director by the end of 2009. Discuss the potential benefits and costs to the organization for earlier implementation of their plans for establishing an internal audit department.

**Townsend can achieve a number of benefits from establishing an internal control function earlier than 2009. Internal auditors work within an organization and report the results of their work to management or to the entity's audit committee or board of directors. They are not typically expected to report to the public or to parties outside the entity. Internal auditors may provide assurance services and consulting services. In general terms, an organization's internal audit function is most often used by management and the board of directors in the broad areas of evaluating risks, evaluating compliance, and performing financial and operational auditing. Through these activities, internal auditors contribute to effective corporate governance within an organization, which entails all management-administered policies and procedures to control risk and oversee operations within the company.**

**Townsend is planning on becoming a public company in 2010. To that end, Section 404 of the Sarbanes-Oxley Act requires public companies to implement and annually assess internal control over financial reporting. Internal auditors are trained to evaluate the system of internal control over financial reporting and over other areas of the organization. Internal audits often play a substantial role in ensuring compliance with these new requirements for public companies.**

**As the organization continues to grow, compliance issues may be of particular importance to an company like Townsend. Internal auditors are trained to conduct operational audits. Due to the unique position in an organization, the internal auditor understands how the organization operates and he or she is able to provide various types of services to improve the organization's efficiency and effectiveness. Such improvements are particularly important for a smaller organization, such as Townsend, as the company continues to compete against larger competitors. Internal auditors can identify the causes of and solutions to problems that can lead to significant organizational improvements.**

**Townsend may benefit if the company establishes the internal auditing function prior to the end of 2009. For example, the company plans on selling its stock to the public by 2010, and obviously, management will want its stock valued at the highest possible price. The internal auditor can identify significant inefficiencies and make recommendations for operational improvements. Early implementation will require the company to fund the additional costs associated with establishing the internal auditing department and the human resources needed to achieve the company's strategic and operational goals and objectives of the internal auditing function. ABC should recommend, and upon approval, complete a cost-benefit analysis to determine the exact financial and nonfinancial benefits and costs associated with establishing the entity's internal control function. If the analysis does not support early implementation, as a privately-held company, some of the internal audit functions could be outsourced to ABC.**

# Extra Crossword Puzzles and Solutions

# Index of Puzzles

| | | |
|---|---|---|
| Chapter 1 | Major Phases of an Audit | 491 |
| Chapter 2 | Accounting Process and Management Assertions | 493 |
| Chapter 2 | Consideration of Fraud in a Financial Statement Audit | 495 |
| Chapter 2 | Generally Accepted Auditing Standards | 497 |
| Chapter 3 | Audit Risk and Materiality | 499 |
| Chapter 4 | Audit Evidence and Documentation | 501 |
| Chapter 4 | Audit Procedures | 503 |
| Chapter 4 | Confirmation Process | 505 |
| Chapter 5 | Analytical Procedures | 507 |
| Chapter 5 | Planning the Engagement | 509 |
| Chapter 6 | Internal Control in a Financial Audit | 511 |
| Chapter 7 | Sarbanes-Oxley Act Section 404 Internal Control | 513 |
| Chapters 8–9 | Audit Sampling | 515 |
| Chapter 10 | Revenue Process | 517 |
| Chapter 11 | Purchasing Process | 519 |
| Chapter 12 | Human Resource Management Process | 521 |
| Chapter 13 | Inventory Management Process | 523 |
| Chapters 14–16 | Financing Process | 525 |
| Chapter 17 | Contingent Liabilities and Subsequent Events | 527 |
| Chapter 18 | Reports on Audited Financial Statements | 529 |
| Chapter 19 | Professional Conduct | 531 |
| Chapter 20 | Legal Liability | 533 |
| Chapter 21 | Review and Compilation Services | 535 |

# Major Phases of an Audit – Puzzle 1
## Chapter 1

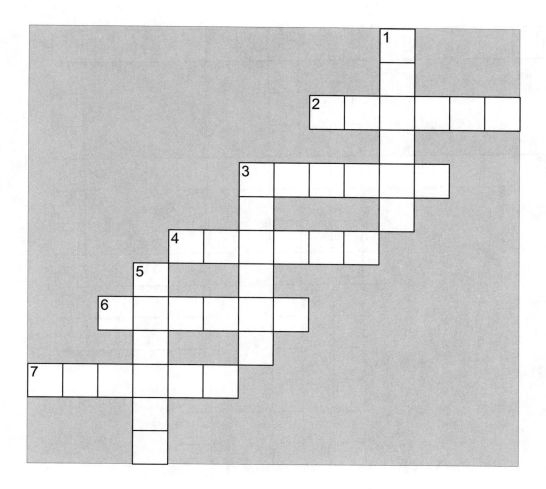

## Across

2    The auditor accepts the client and establishes the terms of the engagement.
3    The auditor audits the business processes and related accounts (cycles).
4    The auditor preplans the engagement.
6    The auditor plans the audit.
7    The auditor considers and audits internal controls.

## Down

1    The auditor completes the audit.
3    The auditor establishes materiality and assesses risks.
5    The auditor evaluates the results and issues the audit report.

# Major Phases of an Audit – Puzzle 2
## Chapter 1

## Across

1    This activity occurs during the fifth phase of the audit (two words).
5    This activity occurs during the first phase of the audit (two words).
7    This activity occurs during the third phase of the audit (two words).
8    This activity occurs during the fourth phase of the audit.

## Down

2    This activity occurs during the seventh phase of the audit (two words).
3    This activity occurs during the eighth phase of the audit (two words).
4    This activity occurs during the sixth phase of the audit.
6    This activity occurs during the second phase of the audit.

# Accounting Processes and Management Assertions – Puzzle 1
## Chapter 2

## Across

2    This cycle includes capital transactions generated through borrowing or stock investments.
6    This cycle includes the delivery of goods and services to the company's customers.
9    An assertion that all transactions and events that should have been recorded have been recorded.
10   An assertion that transactions and events have been recorded in the correct accounting period.
11   An assertion that the entity holds or controls the rights to its assets.
12   An assertion that the entity is responsible for its liabilities.
13   An assertion that all transactions and events are properly authorized.
14   An assertion that the recorded transactions and events actually occurred and pertain to the entity.

## Down

1    An assertion that transactions and events that have been recorded actually exist.
3    Manufacturers and retailers typically have a significant number of transactions in this cycle.
4    An assertion that transactions and events recorded are included in the financial statements at the appropriate amounts.
5    The cycle that includes acquisition of goods and services.
7    An assertion that transactions and events are appropriately presented in the financial statements.
8    The cycle that includes hiring of personnel to perform functions in the organization (two words).

# Accounting Processes and Management Assertions – Puzzle 2
## Chapter 2

## Across

3    An assertion that transactions and events have been recorded in the correct accounting period.

6    A transaction in this cycle may include a debit to accounts receivable and a credit to sales.

7    An assertion that all transactions and events are properly authorized.

9    An assertion that transactions and events that have been recorded actually exist.

10    An assertion that transactions and events recorded are included in the financial statements at the appropriate amounts.

11    A transaction in this cycle may include a debit to office supplies and a credit to accounts payable.

12    Explicit and implicit representations made by management.

## Down

1    An assertion that all transactions and events that should have been recorded have been recorded.

2    An assertion that recorded transactions and events actually occurred and pertain to the entity.

4    A transaction in this cycle may include a debit to depreciation expense and a credit to accumulated depreciation.

5    A transaction in this cycle may include a debit to salaries expense and a credit to accrued payroll (two words).

7    An assertion that the disclosure of financial and other information is fairly presented.

8    A transaction in this cycle may include a debit to finished goods and a credit to work in process.

# Consideration of Fraud in a Financial Statement Audit – Puzzle 1
## Chapter 2

## Across

2   A type of intentional misstatement (three words).
4   The risk that management may override the controls is an example of this fraud factor.
6   SAS 99 requires the auditor perform these procedures related to revenues when considering fraudulent reporting.
9   A type of intentional misstatement (two words).
12  This type of management behavior reduces the risk of fraud.

## Down

1   An intentional act that results in a material misstatement in the financial statements.
3   The existence of an organizational culture that will encourage fraud.
5   A factor that should be considered when evaluating the possibility of fraud.
7   Management has the opportunity to _____ the internal controls.
8   This pronouncement requires that the client make certain written representations concerning fraud.
10  The difference between an error and fraud.
11  The pronouncement entitled "Consideration of Fraud in a Financial Statement Audit."

# Consideration of Fraud in a Financial Statement Audit –Puzzle 2
## Chapter 2

## Across

2     Management has the opportunity to _____ the internal controls.

5     The auditor should communicate with this group when he or she believes that fraud has been committed by senior management (two words).

7     The auditor may consider this action when he or she believes that fraud has been committed by senior management.

10    Revenue is generally recognized when _____.

11    This pronouncement provides guidance about obtaining written representations from a client.

## Down

1     These types of transactions can be the basis for the recording of fraudulent transactions (two words).

3     This type of management behavior reduces the risk of fraud.

4     The difference between an error and fraud.

6     An intentional act that results in a material misstatement in the financial statements.

8     The pronouncement entitled "Consideration of Fraud in a Financial Statement Audit."

9     This pronouncement requires that the client make certain written representations concerning fraud.

# Generally Accepted Auditing Standards – Puzzle 1
## Chapter 2

## Across

3    Generally Accepted Auditing Standards must be followed by these companies.
5    Sufficient competent evidence must be obtained to form an opinion about the financial statements.
8    The report shall identify circumstances that GAAP has not been observed.
9    An audit must be conducted using due professional care.
10   The report shall state whether financial statements are presented in accordance with GAAP.
11   The auditor must possess independence in mental attitude.

## Down

1    Disclosures must be adequate unless otherwise stated.
2    The auditor must obtain a sufficient understanding of the internal control to plan the audit.
4    Abbreviation for the group that issues Generally Accepted Auditing Standards.
6    The audit must be adequately planned and assistants must be properly supervised.
7    The audit report shall contain an opinion regarding the statements or an assertion that an opinion cannot be expressed.
9    The auditor must be adequately trained.

# Generally Accepted Auditing Standards – Puzzle 2
## Chapter 2

## Across

2    Four standards that relate to the auditor's communication of his or her opinion.
4    The first general standard.
5    The second reporting standard.
7    The third general standard (three words).
8    Three standards that relate to the auditor's professional qualifications.
9    The third field standard.
10   The second general standard.
11   The third reporting standard.
12   Three standards that must be followed during the engagement.

## Down

1    The first field standard.
3    The second field standard (two words).
6    The fourth reporting standard.
8    The first reporting standard.

# Audit Risk & Materiality – Puzzle 1
## Chapter 3

## Across

1    The risk that a material misstatement that could occur will not be prevented or detected on a timely basis by the internal controls.
4    Unintentional misstatements or omissions of amounts or disclosures in financial statements.
6    The auditor's exposure to loss or injury to professional practice from litigation, adverse publicity, or other events arising in connection with financial statements audited and reported on.
7    The susceptibility of an assertion to material misstatements, assuming no related controls.
8    Another term for inherent risk and control risk.
9    The auditor should perform this function during planning (two words).
10   The auditor uses professional judgment when considering this concept.
12   AR = IR × CR × DR (three words).
13   Factors of this concept include incentive, opportunity and rationalization.

## Down

2    Level of assurance provided by auditor that financial statements are free from material misstatement.
3    An attitude that includes a questioning mind and a critical assessment of audit evidence (two words).
5    The risk that the auditor will not detect a material misstatement that exists in an assertion.
11   Intentional misstatements arising from fraudulent reporting or misappropriation of assets.
14   The risk that the auditor may fail to modify the opinion on financial statements that are materially misstated.

# Audit Risk & Materiality – Puzzle 2
## Chapter 3

## Across

2 Unintentional misstatements or omissions of amounts or disclosures in financial statements.
3 AR = IR × CR × DR (three words).
7 Specific acts performed as the auditor gathers evidence to determine if specific audit assertions are being met (two words).
9 Pronouncement that explains how the auditor should integrate the concepts of materiality and audit risk into the audit engagement.
10 Pronouncement entitled "Audit Risk and Materiality in Conducting an Audit."
11 Professional attitude that includes a questioning mind and a critical assessment of audit evidence.
12 This term includes quantitative and qualitative misstatement factors.

## Down

1. A maximum amount the auditor believes that the financial statements could be misstated and still not affect the decisions of reasonable users (two words).
4 The risk that the auditor will not detect a material misstatement that exists in the statements.
5 Preliminary judgment about materiality that is allocated to a financial statement account.
6 Intentional misstatements arising from incorrect reporting or misappropriation of assets.
8 Pronouncement entitled "Consideration of Fraud in a Financial Statement Audit."

# Audit Evidence and Documentation – Puzzle 1
## Chapter 4

## Across

1    A set of audit procedures to test assertions about the financial statements (two words).
3    Authoritative pronouncement entitled "Audit Documentation."
8    Confidentiality of audit documentation does not apply under this condition.
9    Demonstrates procedures employed, evidence collected and conclusions drawn (two words).
10    Rule 301 of the Rules of Professional Conduct.
11    Direction of testing is from source documents to the journals or ledgers.
12    Another name for audit documentation (two words).
13    Tracing normally is used to test this assertion.

## Down

2    This individual owns the workpapers.
3    The measure of the quantity of audit evidence.
4    Direction of testing is from journals or ledgers to source documents.
5    A term which means that the audit evidence is both relevant and reliable.
6    An assertion being tested when vouching is used.
7    All information used by the auditor in arriving at the conclusions on which the audit opinion is based (two words).

# Audit Evidence and Documentation – Puzzle 2
## Chapter 4

## Across

2     Documentation considered more reliable than that generated within the organization.
4     Expressed or implied representations by management that are reflected in the financial statement components.
5     The chart of accounts and organizational chart are examples of this audit documentation (two words).
7     Demonstrates procedures employed, evidence collected and conclusions drawn (two words).
8     Reperformance is an example of this level of evidence reliability.
9     Another name for audit documentation (two words).
10    Inquiry is an example of this level of evidence reliability.
11    Audit plan and audit programs are examples of this audit documentation (two words).

## Down

1     Scanning is an example of this level of evidence reliability.
3     All information used by the auditor in arriving at the conclusions on which the audit opinion is based (two words).
6     This individual owns the workpapers.

# Audit Procedures – Puzzle 1
## Chapter 4

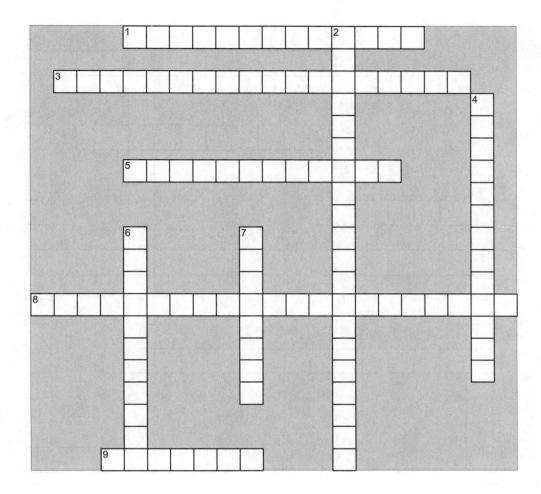

## Across

1    The auditor executes procedures or controls.
3    Examination of resources owned by the client (three words).
5    Obtaining and evaluating direct communication from a third party.
8    Examination of internal and external records (three words).
9    Seeking information of knowledge persons from within and outside of the entity.

## Down

2    Studying plausible relationships (two words).
4    Determination of mathematical accuracy.
6    Watching a process or procedure being performed by others.
7    Reviewing accounting data to identify significant or unusual items.

# Audit Procedures – Puzzle 2
## Chapter 4

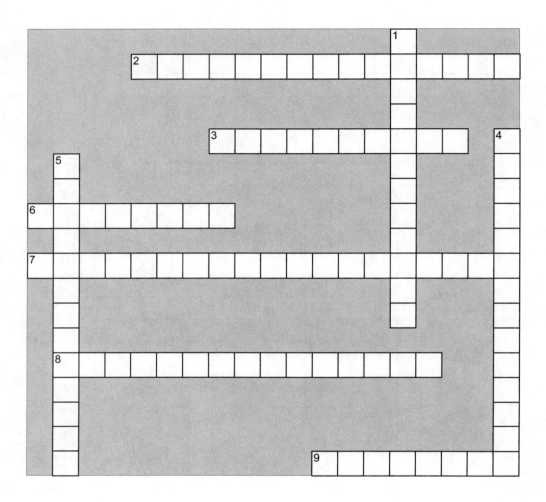

## Across

2     Analytical Procedures (two words).
3     Scanning (two words).
6     Observation.
7     Confirmation (two words).
8     Inquiry (two words).
9     Reperformance.

## Down

1     Recalculation (two words).
4     Inspection of documents (two words).
5     Inspection of assets (two words).

# Confirmation Process – Puzzle 1
## Chapter 4

## Across

6    The respondent should always return the confirmation directly to the auditor.

7    Respondents return the confirmation directly to the auditor only when they disagree with the confirmation.

8    Exceptions noted may result from these differences.

10   The auditor uses confirmations less frequently when testing this account (two words).

11   Authoritative pronouncement that addresses the confirmation of accounts receivable.

12   Differences between the recorded balance and the balance confirmed by the respondent.

## Down

1    This individual must maintain control over the accounts receivable confirmations.

2    This form of positive confirmation generally is used for accounts payable (two words).

3    Accounts payable confirmations are mailed at this time because of the risk associated with unrecorded liabilities (two words).

4    The audit term that means at an interim date or at year-end.

5    A process of obtaining and evaluating a direct communication provided by a third party in response to an auditor's request for information.

9    The authoritative pronouncement entitled "The Confirmation Process."

# Confirmation Process – Puzzle 2
## Chapter 4

## Across

4    The source of confirmation for accounts payable.
10   A source of confirmation for common stock outstanding (two words).
11   A source of confirmation for bonds payable.
12   A source of confirmation for common stock outstanding.
13   Confirmations may be used to test the completeness assertion for this account (two words).

## Down

1    Confirmations may be used to test the existence assertion for this account (two words).
2    A source of confirmation for bonds payable (two words).
3    A source of confirmation for insurance coverage (two words).
5    A specific type of inquiry.
6    A source of confirmation for collateral for loan.
7    A source of confirmation for accounts receivable.
8    A source of confirmation for inventory on consignment.
9    The source of confirmation for the cash account.

# Analytical Procedures – Puzzle 1
## Chapter 5

## Across

1   This form of test utilizes financial and nonfinancial data to determine the acceptability of an account balance or a change in an account balance.
4   Analytical procedures are part of this phase of the engagement.
6   This form of analysis is a more sophisticated procedure based on a model to predict the relationship between the account balance and various other factors.
7   Analytical procedures are part of this phase of the engagement (two words).

## Down

1   This form of analysis can be used to compare the relationship between the client's accounts over time and the client's accounts to data from the client's industry.
2   Authoritative pronouncement entitled "Analytical Procedures."
3   These procedures are used to determine whether information is consistent with the auditor's expectations.
5   This form of analysis is based on changes in a balance over a period of time that can vary from year to year.

# Analytical Procedures – Puzzle 2
## Chapter 5

## Across

2     Net Income/Net Sales (two words).
4     These expectations result from the use of analytical procedures and should be documented.
6     Net Credit Sales/Average Accounts Receivable (two words).
7     Interest Expense/Average Interest-Bearing Debt (two words).
8     Cost of Goods Sold/Average Inventory (two words).
9     Net Sales/Average Total Assets (two words).
10    Income taxes/Income before Taxes (three words).

## Down

1     Depreciation Expense/Depreciable Property (two words).
3     Current Assets/Current Liabilities (two words).
5     Analytical procedures applied early in the engagement are used by auditor to establish this type of risk.

# Planning the Engagement – Puzzle 1
## Chapter 5

## Across

3    This letter formalizes the arrangement reached between the auditor and the client.
4    This professional should make certain inquiries of the predecessor before accepting engagement.
5    Section 301 of the Sarbanes-Oxley Act requires each member of the audit committee be this.
6    The auditor must assess the client's business risks in order to establish this.
8    When planning the engagement, the auditor must assess the possibility of these acts.
9    The first standard of fieldwork requires the auditor do this.
10   The external auditor may request assistance from this auditor when conducting the audit.
12   The title of the previous auditor.
13   When planning the engagement, the auditor must identify these parties.

## Down

1    This person ensures that all members of the audit team are independent of the client (three words).
2    Ensuring the independence of the audit team and the firm must be completed during this phase.
4    A person or firm possessing knowledge in a field other than accounting or auditing.
7    Audit procedures used to evaluate plausible relationships among financial and nonfinancial data.
11   This committee should meet with the external auditor before the engagement is formally started.

# Planning the Engagement – Puzzle 2
## Chapter 5

## Across

1     The auditor must assess the client's business risks in order to establish this.
5     The external auditor may request assistance from this auditor when conducting the audit.
11    The auditor assesses the preliminary level of control risk during this phase.
12    The auditor will conduct these procedures to understand the client's business and transactions.
13    AR = IR × CR × DR (three words).
14    A characteristic that the auditor should consider when relying on the work of the internal auditor.

## Down

2     Failure to file tax returns or pay government duties are examples of these acts.
3     This letter formalizes the arrangement reached between the auditor and the client.
4     This assessment of control risk is necessary for the auditor to plan testing.
6     The risk of a misstatement would be material assuming there were no related controls.
7     Ensuring the independence of the audit team and firm must be completed during this phase.
8     The risk that misstatements will not be prevented or detected by the internal controls.
9     A characteristic that the auditor should consider when relying on the work of the internal auditor.
10    A person or firm possessing knowledge in a field other than accounting or auditing.

# Internal Control in a Financial Audit – Puzzle 1
## Chapter 6

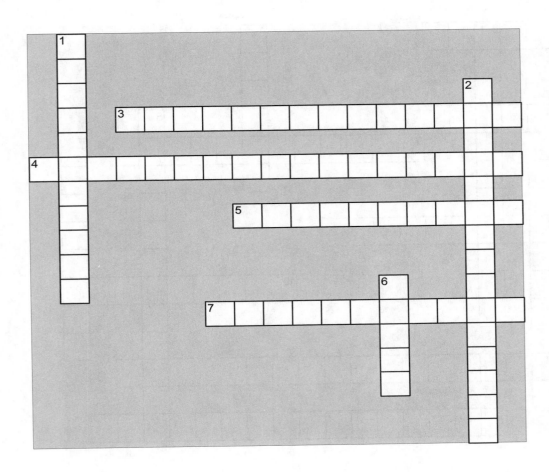

## Across

3   This component of internal control is a process that the organization uses to identify and assess threats to its objectives (two words).

4   This component of internal control includes policies and procedures which help ensure that management's directives are carried out (two words).

5   This component of internal control is a process that an entity uses to assess the quality of its control performance over time.

7   This component of internal control includes elements that help management carry out its responsibilities.

## Down

1   This component of the internal control sets the tone of an organization.

2   A process designed to provide reasonable assurance regarding the achievement of an organization's objectives (two words).

6.  Pronouncement entitled "Consideration of Internal Control in a Financial Statement Audit."

# Internal Control in a Financial Audit – Puzzle 2
## Chapter 6

## Across

1    A pronouncement that classifies control activities as (1) performance reviews, (2) information processing, (3) physical controls, and (4) segregation of duties.

4    Pronouncement entitled "The Effect of Information Technology on the Auditor's Consideration of Internal Control in a Financial Statement Audit."

6    Assertion that components of the financial statements are properly classified.

9    Management must exhibit this behavior to support an appropriate control environment.

10    Assertion that elements have been included in the financial statements at appropriate amounts.

11    Infrastructure, software, people, procedures and data are examples of this component of internal control (two words).

12    Tests of details and analytical procedures performed to detect misstatements (two words).

## Down

2    An audit strategy is used when control risk is assessed at a high level and controls are not tested.

3    An assertion that assets are owned by the entity.

5    An assertion that all transactions and accounts that should be presented in the financial statements are included.

7    An audit strategy is used when control risk is assessed at a low level and controls are tested.

8    An assertion that assets or liabilities exist at a given date and recorded during a given period.

# Sarbanes-Oxley Act Section 404 Internal Control – Puzzle 1
## Chapter 7

## Across

1    This group must assess the effectiveness of its internal control over financial reporting.

4    An abbreviation for Sarbanes-Oxley Act of 2002.

6    Assertions that have a meaningful bearing on whether an account is fairly stated.

7    A control deficiency that adversely affects the entity's ability to initiate, authorize, record, process, or report external financial data reliability in accordance with GAAP.

9    A control that does not prevent or detect misstatements on a timely basis.

## Down

1    A significant deficiency that results in more than a remote likelihood that a misstatement will not be prevented or detected.

2    Management must develop this to support its assessment of the effectiveness of internal control.

3    The auditor must plan and perform the audit to obtain this level of assurance regarding the effectiveness of the internal control over financial reporting.

5    Sarbanes-Oxley Act requires the management of a public company to issue a report that states its responsibility for and effectiveness of the internal control over financial reporting.

8    A recognized control framework established by a body of experts.

# Sarbanes-Oxley Act Section 404 Internal Control – Puzzle 2
## Chapter 7

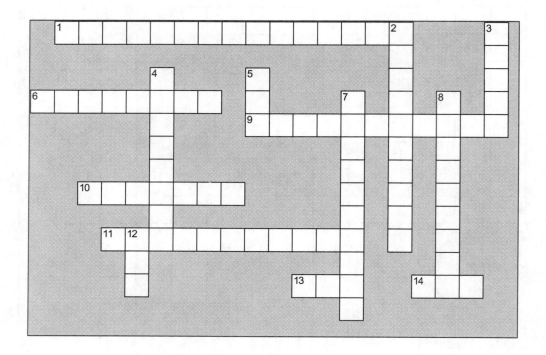

## Across

1 Auditing standards require the auditor to obtain these in writing.
6 Assertions that have a meaningful bearing on whether an account is fairly stated.
9 A control deficiency that adversely affects the entity's ability to initiate, authorize record, process or report external financial data reliably in accordance with GAAP.
10 This professional must evaluate the design effectiveness of internal control and form an opinion on the effectiveness of internal control.
11 AS5 requires the auditor to perform this procedure for all major class of transactions each year that an audit of internal control is performed.
13 Management's representations must be signed by this executive.
14 Management's representations must be signed by this executive.

## Down

2 Sarbanes-Oxley Act requires the management of a public company to issue a report that states its responsibility for and effectiveness of the internal control over financial reporting.
3 This committee plays an important role within the control environment and monitoring components of the internal control framework.
4 A significant deficiency that results in more than a remote likelihood that a misstatement will not be prevented or detected.
5 The auditor must evaluate this (abbreviation).
7 One of the two dimensions of control deficiency that management and the auditor must consider when evaluating the effectiveness of internal control.
8 One of the two dimensions of control deficiency that management and the auditor must consider when evaluating the effectiveness of internal control.
12 The PCAOB pronouncement which requires the auditor to conduct an "integrated audit" of a public company's internal and its financial statements.

514

## Audit Sampling – Puzzle 1
## Chapters 8 – 9

### Across

6    The symbol for this term is "N."

7    The risk of underreliance or the risk of assessing control risk too high (two words).

9    SAS 39 defines this term as any information that has an effect on determining whether the financial statements are presented in accordance with GAAP.

10   The application of an audit procedure to less than 100 percent of the items being tested.

### Down

1    Divide the number of deviations by the number of units in the sample (two words).

2    The symbol for this term is "n" (two words).

3    The complement of sampling risk (two words).

4    The historical defect rate (two words).

5    SAS 39 defines this concept as the maximum percentage of deviations (errors) in a population that an auditor will accept without changing the planned level of control risk (two words).

8.   The risk of overreliance or the risk of assessing control risk too low (two words).

# Audit Sampling – Puzzle 2
## Chapters 8 – 9

## Across

1     The risk of incorrect acceptance relates to the _____ of the audit.
4     This sampling technique is used to estimate the proportion of a population that possesses a specified characteristic.
5     Abbreviation for a sampling technique that is based on the normal distribution theory.
6     An audit sampling technique that relies on the auditor's judgment to determine issues such as sample size and selection of the sample.
7     The individual member of the population being sampled (two words).

## Down

1     The risk of incorrect rejection relates to the _____ of the audit.
2     Abbreviation for a sampling technique used to estimate the dollar amount of misstatement.
3     This term relates to how close a sample estimate is to the population characteristic being estimated, given a specified sampling risk.

# Revenue Process – Puzzle 1
## Chapter 10

## Across

1  This document is used to investigate the creditworthiness of a customer (three words).
3  This document must be prepared when goods are shipped to a customer (two words).
4  This document contains the details of the products and services ordered by a customer (three words).
5  This document is used to record information for each sales transaction (two words).
7  This type of transaction includes a credit to accounts receivable (two words).
8  This document is mailed to a customer monthly (two words).

## Down

2  This document shows all customer orders for which processing has not been completed (three words).
3  This document is used to bill the customer (two words).
6  This type of transaction includes a debit to accounts receivable.

# Revenue Process – Puzzle 2
## Chapter 10

## Across

1   This document is used to record information for each sales transaction (two words).
3   This document is normally prepared weekly or monthly based on a summary of the customer balances in accounts receivable based on the date of the invoices (two words).
4   This document is used to record the entity's cash (three words).
7   Acceptance of customer orders into the system (two words).
9   This function is to ensure that all goods shipped and all services provided are invoiced at authorized prices and terms.
10  This document is usually mailed with the customer's bill and returned with customer's payment (two words).

## Down

2   This function should be segregated from the billing function.
5   This type of transaction includes a credit to a sales account.
6   This type of transaction includes a debit to cash (two words).
8   This function should be segregated from the billing function.

# Purchasing Process – Puzzle 1
## Chapter 11

## Across

3    This type of transaction includes a credit to cash.
5    This document, signed by an authorized individual, pays for goods or services.
6    This document is used to record the receipt of goods (two words).
7    This statement is sent monthly by the supplier to indicate the account activity (two words).
9    This document is the bill from the supplier (two words).
10   This journal is used to record payments made by check (two words).
11   This document includes the description, quality and quantity of goods or services being purchased (two words).

## Down

1    The department that is responsible for ensuring that all vendor invoices, cash disbursements, and adjustments are recorded (two words).
2    This type of transaction includes a debit to inventory.
4    This document requests goods or services for a department within the entity (two words).
8    This document is used by entities to control payment for acquired goods and services.

# Purchasing Process – Puzzle 2
## Chapter 11

## Across

4　The department that is responsible for ensuring that all vendor invoices, cash disbursements, and adjustments are recorded (two words).

6　This type of transaction includes a debt to accounts payable.

8　Costs that include selling and administrative expenses.

9　This function should be segregated from the accounts payable function.

10　This function should be segregated from the purchasing function.

## Down

1　This function should be segregated from the general ledger function (two words).

2　This type of transaction includes a credit to accounts payable.

3　This function should be segregated from the receiving function.

5　Direct costs that are matched to sales.

7　Outflows or other using up of assets or incurrence of liabilities from delivering or producing goods, rendering services or carrying out other activities.

# Human Resource Management Process – Puzzle 1
## Chapter 12

## Across

2 This document is used to record the hours worked by an employee.

3 These summary reports are used to monitor payroll data.

4 This journal is used to summarize all payroll payments issued to employees (two words).

5 This function is used to prepare employees' time information for payroll processing.

6 These records contain information on each employee's work history, rate or salary, deductions, adjustments and performance evaluations.

7 This function includes the authorization of hiring, firing, wage-rate and salary adjustments, and employee deductions.

## Down

1 This computer file maintains all the entity's records related to payroll (two words).

2 Various reports prepared for both federal and state governments.

# Human Resource Management Process – Puzzle 2
## Chapter 12

## Across

2    These records contain information on each employee's work history, rate or salary, deductions and other adjustments, and employee performance evaluations.

8    This function includes the authorization of hiring, firing, wage-rate and salary adjustments, and employee deductions.

9    Various reports prepared for both federal and state governments.

10    This function should be segregated from the supervision function (two words).

11    This function should be segregated from the personnel function.

## Down

1    This function should be segregated from the supervision function.

3    This computer file maintains all the entity's records related to payroll (two words).

4    This journal is used to summarize all payroll payments issued to employees (two words).

5    This function is used to prepare employees' time information for payroll processing.

6    This function should be segregated from the payroll-processing function (two words).

7    This function should be segregated from the personnel records.

# Inventory Management Process – Puzzle 1
## Chapter 13

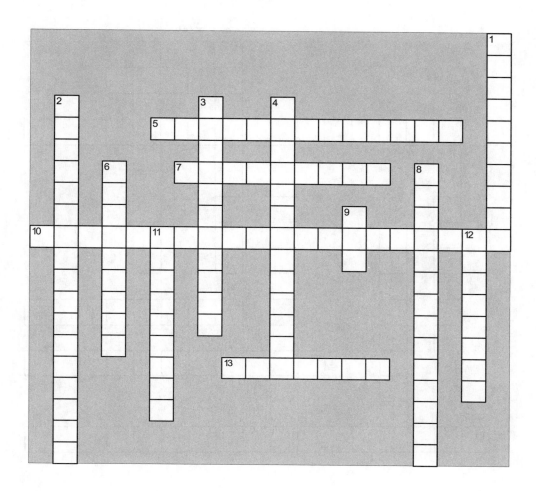

## Across

5      This document is used to remove goods from the inventory (two words).
7      A report used to record the receipt of goods from vendors.
10     This document is used to track materials during the production process (two words).
13     This function should be segregated from the inventory management and stores functions.

## Down

1      This schedule is prepared periodically based on the expected demand for the entity's products.
2      Based on GAAS, the auditor should observe this activity (two words).
3      One of the two prime manufacturing costs (two words).
4      This function is responsible for the storage of goods available for sale (two words).
6      One of the two prime manufacturing costs.
8      This function maintains the manufacturing and cost records (two words).
9      An inventory-planning system used by a manufacturing entity (abbreviation).
11     This function should be segregated from the cost-accounting function.
12     One of the conversion manufacturing costs.

# Inventory Management Process – Puzzle 2
## Chapter 13

## Across

3    An inventory-planning system used by a manufacturing entity (abbreviation).
6    This document is prepared periodically based on the expected demand for the entity's products (two words).
8    One of the conversion manufacturing costs.
9    These goods should not be included in the client's inventory (three words).
10   Based on GAAS, the auditor should observe this activity (two words).

## Down

1    The primary reason for observing the client's physical inventory is to evaluate this assertion.
2    One of the two prime manufacturing costs (two words).
4    An example of a disclosure item for inventory (two words).
5    These differences include inventory cutoff errors, unreported scrap or spoilage, and pilferage or theft (three words).
7    One of the two prime manufacturing costs.

# Financing Process – Puzzle 1
## Chapters 14 – 16

## Across

1   Examples of this type of element include common stock and paid-in-capital (two words).
5   The auditor generally uses this audit procedure to verify the account balance information with every bank or financial institution that maintains an account for the client.
7   Assets which provide economic benefit for less than a year (two words).
9   This document is used to verify the propriety of the reconciling items on the bank reconciliation such as deposits in transit and outstanding checks (three words).
10   This document shows that the balance per the bank and the balance per the books are equal (two words).

## Down

2   Custody of the property, plant and equipment should be segregated from this function.
3   The term that means distribution of corporate earnings.
4   Examples of this type of element include notes, bonds and mortgages (three words).
6   The most liquid balance sheet account.
7   Abbreviation for managing an entity's property, plant and equipment.
8   A technique used to conceal an employee's theft of cash.

## Across

1   One of the two major sources of financing (three words).
4   Examples of this asset account include equity and debt securities.
5   This document is used to verify the propriety of the reconciling items on the bank reconciliation such as deposits in transit and outstanding checks (three words).
6   One of the two major sources of financing (two words).
7   The pronouncement for accounting standards relating to investments.
8   A substantive audit strategy normally is followed when these accounts are audited (two words).
9   Most of these accounts are audited when related balance sheet accounts are audited (three words).
12  These accounts are normally classified as current assets (two words).

## Down

2   This document shows that the balance per the bank and the balance per the books are equal      (two words).
3   Custody of the assets should be segregated from this function.
10  The most liquid balance sheet account.
11  These accounts are classified as noncurrent assets (abbreviation).

# Contingent Liabilities and Subsequent Events – Puzzle 1
## Chapter 17

## Across

1  The chance of the future event occurring is more than remote but less than likely (two words).
3  An accrual will be made when both of these contingent conditions exist (three words).
5  Authoritative pronouncement entitled "Accounting for Contingencies."
8  A future event is likely to occur.
9  An existing condition, situation, or set of circumstances involving uncertainty as the possible loss to an entity that will be resolved in the future (two words).
10  An example of a contingent liability.

## Down

2  An event or transaction that occurs after the balance sheet date but before the issuance of the financial statements.
4  This is required when a contingency is probable but the amount cannot be estimated.
6  When a subsequent event is recorded after the completion of the fieldwork but before the issuance of the financial statements (two words).
7  Use this audit procedure to obtain evidence on litigation, claims and assessments.

# Contingent Liabilities and Subsequent Events – Puzzle 2
## Chapter 17

## Across

7     An accrual will be made when both of these contingent conditions exist (three words).

8     The chance of the future event occurring is more than remote but less than likely (two words).

10    Obtain this letter from management.

## Down

1     The auditor should search for these events (two words).

2     When a subsequent event is recorded after the completion of the fieldwork but before the issuance of the financial statements (two words).

3     An event or transaction that occurs after the balance sheet date but before the issuance of the financial statements.

4     This is required when a contingency is probable but the amount cannot be estimated.

5     A future event is likely to occur.

6     Authoritative pronouncement entitled "Accounting for Contingencies."

9     An audit procedure that includes asking management about whether any unusual adjustments have been made during the subsequent-event period.

# Reports on Audited Financial Statements – Puzzle 1
## Chapter 18

## Across

1     Abbreviation for the criteria used when auditing a public company.
3     The audit of a public entity must be conducted using criteria established by this body (abbreviation).
5     The auditor will issue a standard unqualified opinion for a GAAP departure at this level.
8     The fourth standard of reporting states that the audit report must express this.
9     The "materiality" of this condition is not a factor in determining the opinion (three words).
10    The audit for a private entity is to be conducted using these criteria.
11    When a scope limitation is at this level the auditor is more likely to issue a disclaimer.

## Down

2     A standard unqualified report cannot be issued when this condition is material (two words).
4     When this condition is pervasive the auditor will issue an adverse opinion (two words).
6     The audit report must include this term.
7     The auditor must take this action when he or she lacks independence.

# Reports on Audited Financial Statements – Puzzle 2
## Chapter 18

## Across

2    The choice of which report to issue depends on both the condition and materiality of any departures (two words).

6    This pronouncement requires the auditor to evaluate the implications of the financial statement audit for the effectiveness of internal control over financial reporting.

7    When reporting for the audit of internal control over financial reporting, a material weakness control deficiency will result in this opinion.

8    When auditing internal control, management imposed a major scope limitation.

10   The auditor will modify the standard report on the effectiveness of internal control when this event is significant.

11   When auditing internal control, this level of control deficiency will not require a modified opinion.

## Down

1    This phrase means that the client's internal control is free of any material weakness (four words).

3    A condition that requires modification of the opinion on the effectiveness of internal control (two words).

4    PCAOB auditing standards require that the audit of internal control over financial reporting and of a financial statement audit be evaluated using an iterative process (two words).

5    A condition that requires modification of the report on the effectiveness of internal control (two words).

9.   This action will be taken when a serious scope limitation is present when auditing internal control over financial reporting.

# Professional Conduct – Puzzle 1
## Chapter 19

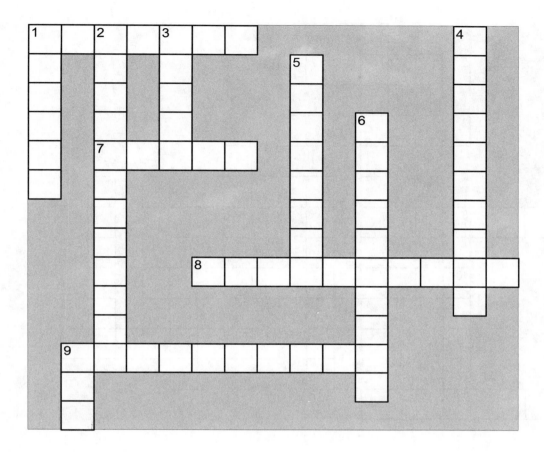

## Across

1    The auditor must follow GAAS when auditing these entities.

7    These standards of conduct are more stringent than the AICPA Code of Professional Conduct.

8    The category of the professional conduct that includes the guidelines for the other responsibilities and practices.

9    The category of the professional conduct that includes the general standards and accounting principles.

## Down

1    The auditor must follow PCAOB auditing standards when auditing these entities.

2    A professional standard that must be present for all members of the audit engagement.

3    Author of the Code of Professional Conduct.

4    The category of the professional conduct that includes the guidelines for the responsibilities to the client.

5    The SEC prohibits the auditor from performed these nine types of services to audit clients.

6    The category of the professional conduct that includes independence, integrity and objectivity.

9    This agency's mission is to protect investors and maintain the integrity of the capital markets.

## Professional Conduct – Puzzle 2
## Chapter 19

## Across

2     The SEC prohibits the auditor from performing these nine types of services to audit clients.
3     The Code of Professional Conduct guideline for client confidentiality.
5     The Code of Professional Conduct guideline for integrity and objectivity.
7     Author of the Code of Professional Conduct.
10     A professional standard that must be present for all members of the audit engagement.
11     The SEC prohibits the auditor from assuming this role for the client.
12     The Code of Professional Conduct guideline for independence.

## Down

1     Auditors assume this role to protect users of financial statements in a capital market economy.
4     This agency's mission is to protect investors and maintain the integrity of the capital markets.
5     The Code of Professional Conduct guideline for advertising and other forms of solicitation.
6     The auditor must follow PCAOB auditing standards when auditing these entities.
8     The auditor must follow GAAS when auditing these entities.
9     These standards of conduct are more stringent than the AICPA Code of Professional Conduct.

# Legal Liability – Puzzle 1
## Chapter 20

## Across

1    The law regulates the disclosure of information in a registration statement for a new public offering of securities (four words).

3    Under common law, auditors can be held liable to these individuals for negligence, gross negligence and fraud (two words).

4    This liability is based on the auditor's failing to complete the services agreed to in the contract with the client (three words).

6    An absence of reasonable or due care in the conduct of an engagement (two words).

8    Case law developed over time (two words).

9    Passed in 2002, this law is considered the most sweeping securities law since the 1933 and 1934 acts (two words).

## Down

2    Written law enacted by federal and state governments (two words).

5    A tort is a wrongful act other than a breach of contract for which civil action may be taken.

7    A party's contractual or fiduciary relationship with the accountant.

# Legal Liability – Puzzle 2
## Chapter 20

## Across

2    Auditors can be held _____ liable under federal securities laws.

4    The SEC is empowered to apply _____ against an accountant or auditing firm for professional wrong doing.

5    An absence of reasonable or due care in the conduct of an engagement (two words).

6    The level of assurance that implies some risk that a material misstatement could be present in the financial statements without the auditor detecting it.

8    A wrongful act other than a breach of contract for which civil action may be taken.

## Down

1    This letter formalizes the contract between the auditor and the client and outlines the responsibilities of both parties.

3    A landmark case that held the auditor was not liable to third parties who rely on a negligently prepared audit report because of a lack of privity.

7    Passed in 2002, this law is considered the most sweeping securities law since the 1933 and 1934 acts (abbreviation).

# Review and Compilation Services – Puzzle 1
## Chapter 21

## Across

4  The number of general standards for attestation engagements.
5  The number of reporting standards for attestation engagements.
6  The number of fieldwork standards for attestation engagements.
10  An engagement in which a practitioner issues a report based on specific procedures (three words).

## Down

1  The practitioner expresses this type of assurance in a review engagement.
2  The report shall state all of the practitioner's significant reservations about the engagement.
3  During this engagement, the practitioner prepares the client's financial statements but expresses no assurance about the financial statements.
7  The engagement shall be performed by a practitioner having adequate knowledge in the subject matter.
8  This engagement includes the performance of inquiry and analytical procedures to provide the basis for expressing limited assurance about the financial statements.
9  Sufficient evidence shall be obtained to provide a reasonable basis for the conclusion that is expressed in the report.

# Review and Compilation Services – Puzzle 2
## Chapter 21

## Across

2    Prospective financial statements that present expected financial information, given one or more hypothetical assumptions.

3    This engagement includes the performance of inquiry and analytical procedures to provide the basis for expressing limited assurance about the financial statements.

9    These types of statements include financial forecasts and financial projections.

10    These pronouncements include general, field and reporting standards.

11    During this engagement, the practitioner issues a report based on specific procedures (three words).

12    This standard requires that work shall be adequately planned and assistants, if any, shall be properly supervised.

## Down

1    During this engagement, the practitioner prepares the client's financial statements but expresses no assurance about the statements.

4    This level of assurance is provided for a review engagement.

5    Prospective financial statements that present expected financial information.

6    This standard requires that the report shall identify the subject matter or the assertion being reported on and state the charter of the engagement.

7    The practitioner must possess knowledge about the client's type of business.

8    This standard requires that an engagement shall be performed by a practitioner having adequate technical training and proficiency in the attest function.

# Index of Solutions

Chapter 1        Major Phases of an Audit..............................................................539

Chapter 2        Accounting Process and Management Assertions ........................540
Chapter 2        Consideration of Fraud in a Financial Statement Audit...............541
Chapter 2        Generally Accepted Auditing Standards......................................542

Chapter 3        Audit Risk and Materiality.........................................................543

Chapter 4        Audit Evidence and Documentation .............................................544
Chapter 4        Audit Procedures.......................................................................545
Chapter 4        Confirmation Process.................................................................546

Chapter 5        Analytical Procedures ...............................................................547
Chapter 5        Planning the Engagement ..........................................................548

Chapter 6        Internal Control in a Financial Audit.........................................549

Chapter 7        Sarbanes-Oxley Act Section 404 Internal Control........................550

Chapters 8–9     Audit Sampling..........................................................................551

Chapter 10       Revenue Process .......................................................................552

Chapter 11       Purchasing Process....................................................................553

Chapter 12       Human Resource Management Process..........................................554

Chapter 13       Inventory Management Process....................................................555

Chapters 14–16   Financing Process .....................................................................556

Chapter 17       Contingent Liabilities and Subsequent Events .............................557

Chapter 18       Reports on Audited Financial Statements.....................................558

Chapter 19       Professional Conduct ................................................................559

Chapter 20       Legal Liability..........................................................................560

Chapter 21       Review and Compilation Services................................................561

# Major Phases of an Audit – Puzzle 1
## Chapter 1

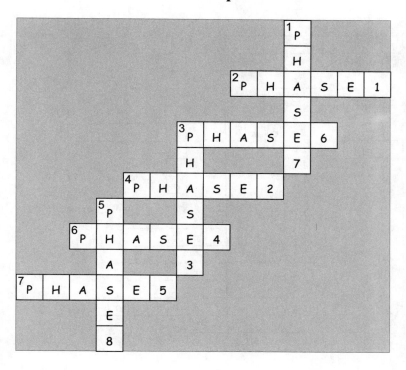

# Major Phases of an Audit – Puzzle 2
## Chapter 1

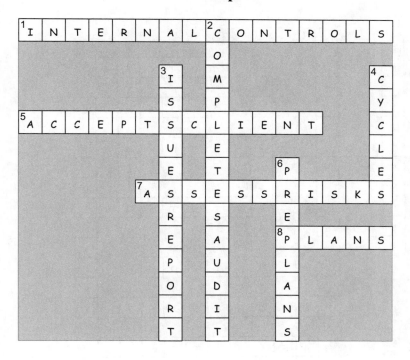

# Accounting Processes and Management Assertions – Puzzle 1
## Chapter 2

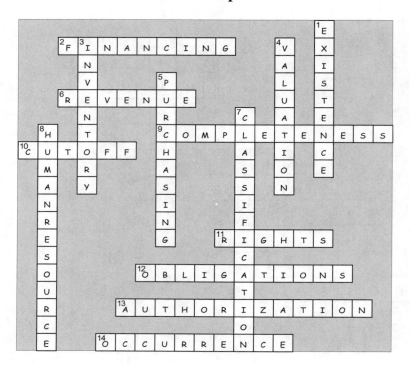

# Accounting Processes and Management Assertions – Puzzle 2
## Chapter 2

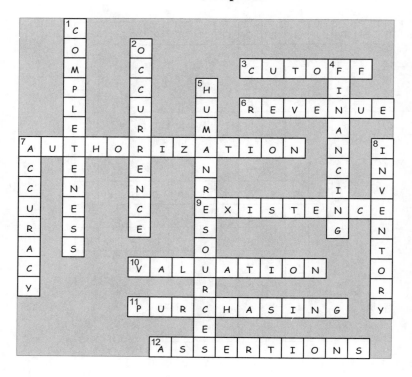

# Consideration of Fraud in a Financial Statement Audit – Puzzle 1
## Chapter 2

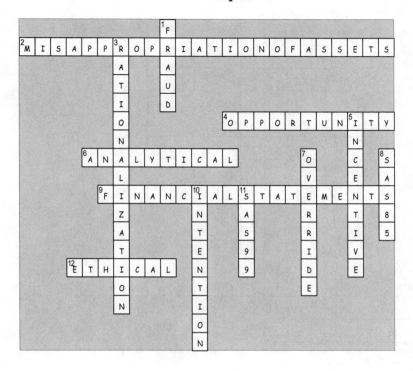

# Consideration of Fraud in a Financial Statement Audit – Puzzle 2
## Chapter 2

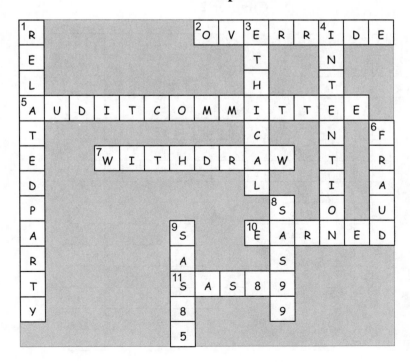

## Generally Accepted Auditing Standards – Puzzle 1
### Chapter 2

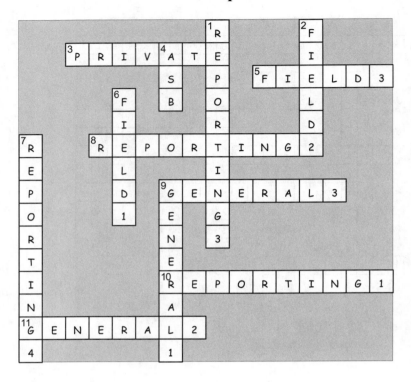

## Generally Accepted Auditing Standards – Puzzle 2
### Chapter 2

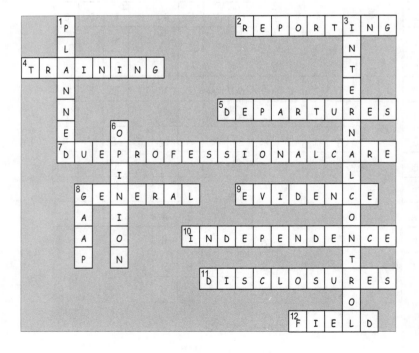

# Audit Risk and Materiality – Puzzle 1
## Chapter 3

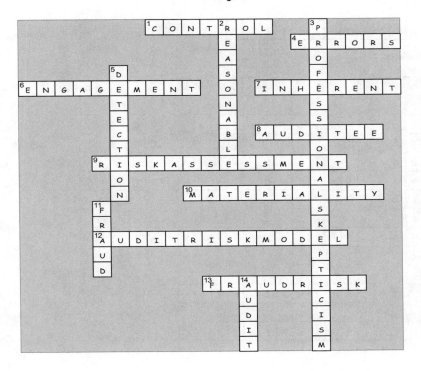

# Audit Risk and Materiality – Puzzle 2
## Chapter 3

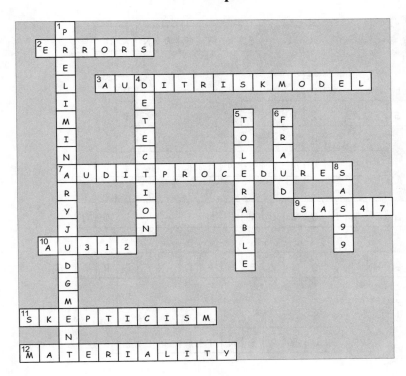

## Audit Evidence and Documentation – Puzzle 1
### Chapter 4

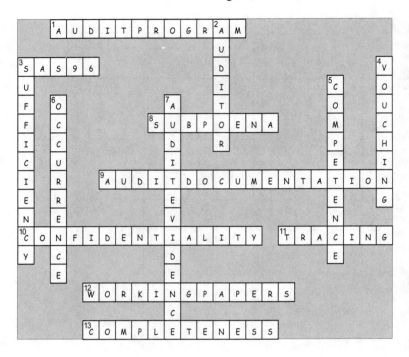

## Audit Evidence and Documentation – Puzzle 2
### Chapter 4

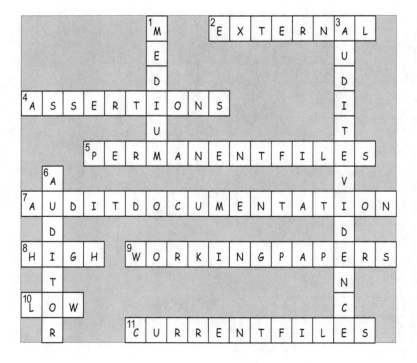

# Audit Procedures – Puzzle 1
## Chapter 4

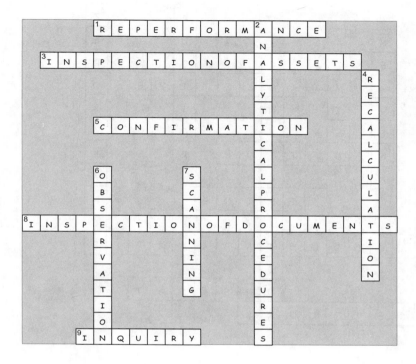

# Audit Procedures – Puzzle 2
## Chapter 4

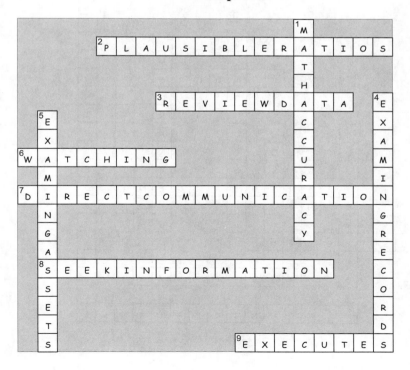

# Confirmation Process – Puzzle 1
## Chapter 4

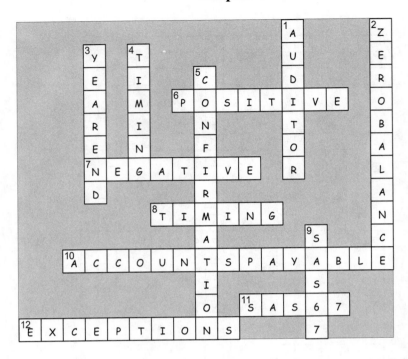

# Confirmation Process – Puzzle 2
## Chapter 4

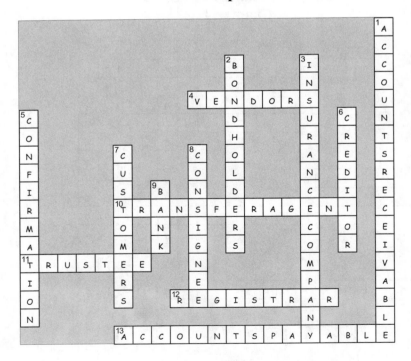

## Analytical Procedures – Puzzle 1
### Chapter 5

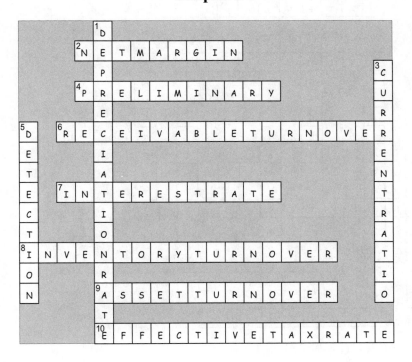

## Analytical Procedures – Puzzle 2
### Chapter 5

## Planning the Engagement – Puzzle 1
## Chapter 5

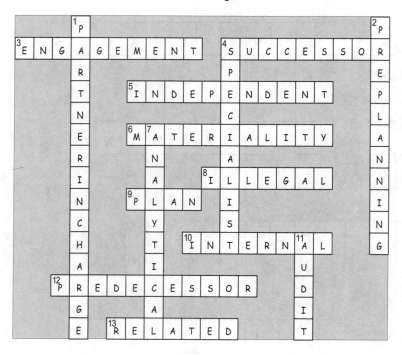

## Planning the Engagement – Puzzle 2
## Chapter 5

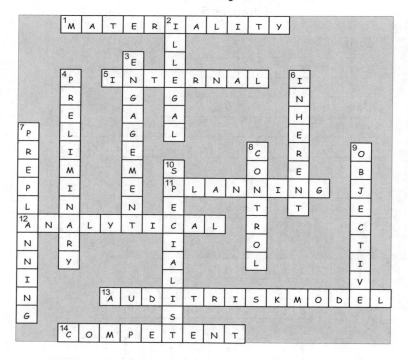

# Internal Control in a Financial Audit – Puzzle 1
## Chapter 6

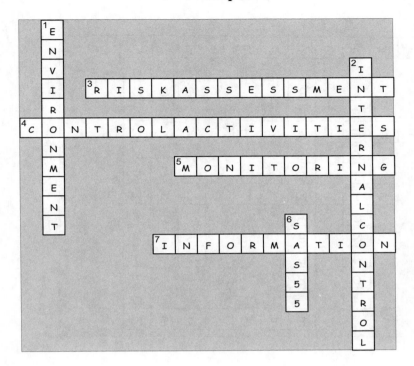

# Internal Control in a Financial Audit – Puzzle 2
## Chapter 6

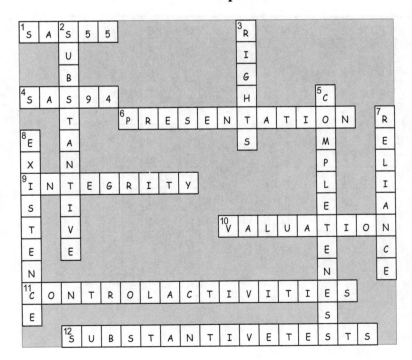

## Sarbanes-Oxley Act Section 404 Internal Control – Puzzle 1
### Chapter 7

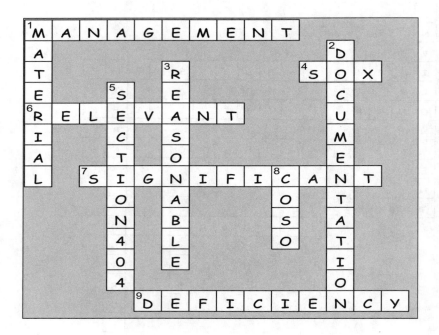

## Sarbanes-Oxley Act Section 404 Internal Control – Puzzle 2
### Chapter 7

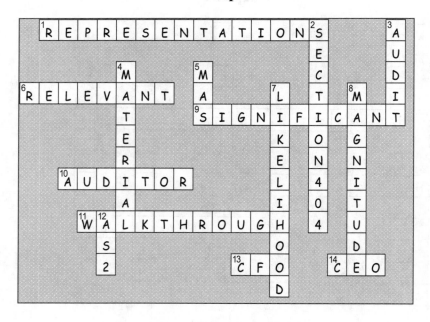

# Audit Sampling – Puzzle 1
## Chapters 8 – 9

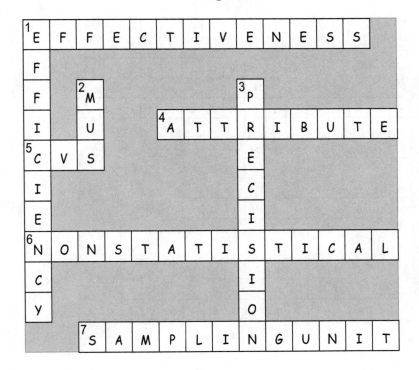

# Audit Sampling – Puzzle 2
## Chapters 8 – 9

## Revenue Process – Puzzle 1
## Chapter 10

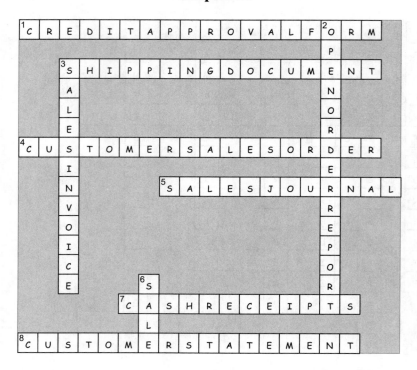

## Revenue Process – Puzzle 2
## Chapter 10

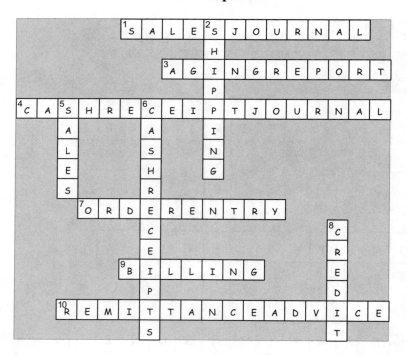

# Purchasing Process – Puzzle 1
## Chapter 11

**Across:**
3. DISBURSEMENTS
5. CHECK
6. RECEIVINGREPORT
7. VENDORSTATEMENT
9. VENDORINVOICE
10. CASHDISBURSEMENTS
11. PURCHASEORDER

**Down (visible letters):**
1. ACCOUNTSPAYABLE
2. PURCHASING
4. REQUISITION
8. VOUCHER

# Purchasing Process – Puzzle 2
## Chapter 11

**Across:**
4. ACCOUNTSPAYABLE
6. DISBURSEMENTS
8. PERIOD
9. DISBURSEMENT
10. RECEIVING

**Down (visible letters):**
1. ACCOUNTSPAYABLE
2. PURCHASING
3. REQUISITION
5. PRODUCT
7. EXPENSES
8. PENDING

## Human Resource Management Process – Puzzle 1
## Chapter 12

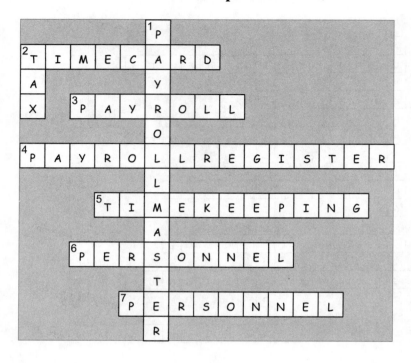

## Human Resource Management Process – Puzzle 2
## Chapter 12

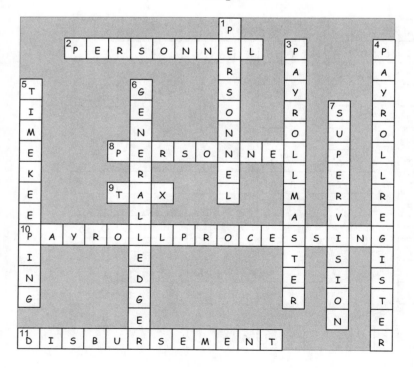

## Inventory Management Process – Puzzle 1
## Chapter 13

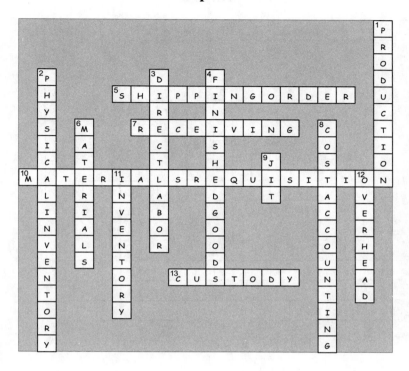

## Inventory Management Process – Puzzle 2
## Chapter 13

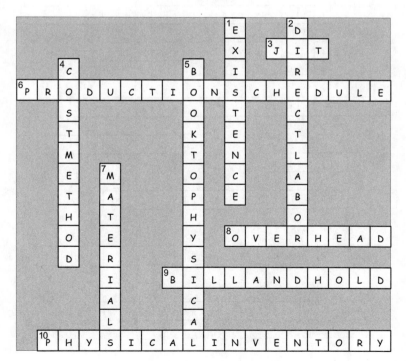

## Financing Process – Puzzle 1
## Chapters 14 – 16

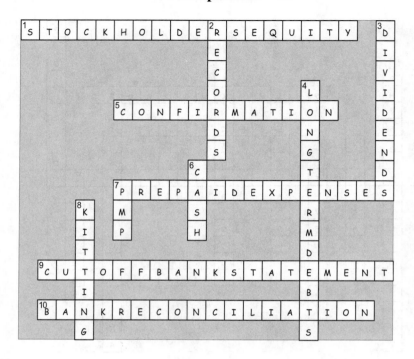

## Financing Process – Puzzle 2
## Chapters 14 – 16

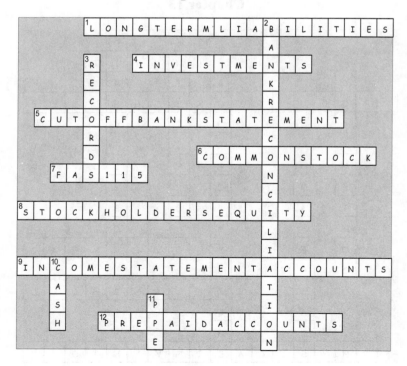

## Contingent Liabilities and Subsequent Events – Puzzle 1
## Chapter 17

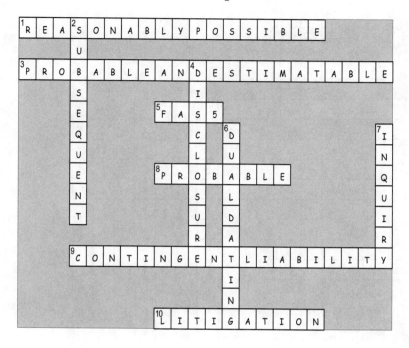

## Contingent Liabilities and Subsequent Events – Puzzle 2
## Chapter 17

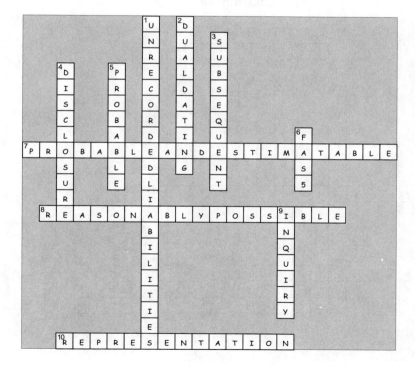

# Reports on Audited Financial Statements – Puzzle 1
## Chapter 18

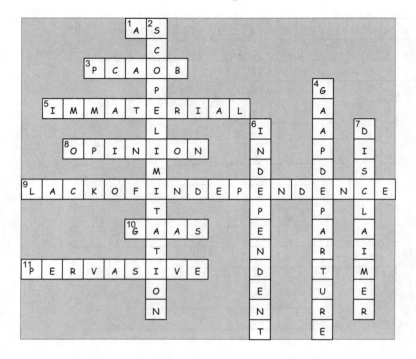

# Reports on Audited Financial Statements – Puzzle 2
## Chapter 18

## Professional Conduct – Puzzle 1
### Chapter 19

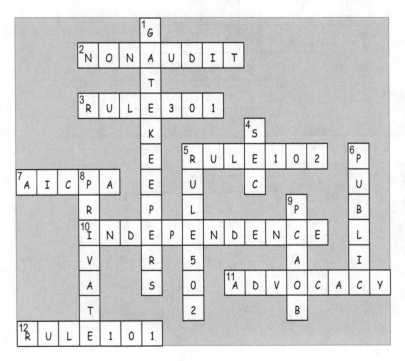

## Professional Conduct – Puzzle 2
### Chapter 19

# Legal Liability – Puzzle 1
## Chapter 20

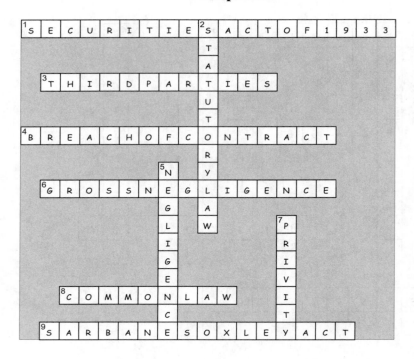

# Legal Liability – Puzzle 2
## Chapter 20

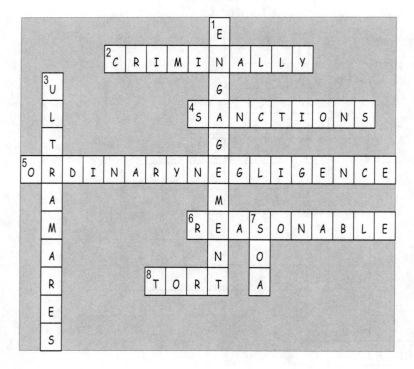

## Review and Compilation Services – Puzzle 1
## Chapter 21

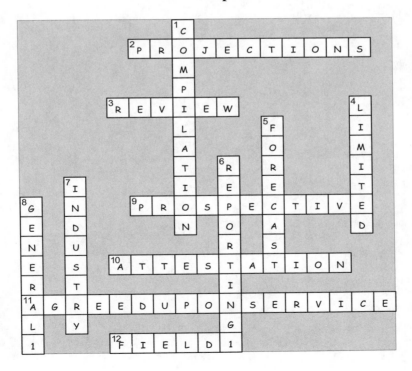

## Review and Compilation Services – Puzzle 2
## Chapter 21